Handbook of Research on Urban Politics and Policy in the United States

Edited by
RONALD K. VOGEL

GREENWOOD PRESS
Westport, Connecticut • London

HT
110
.H36
1997
2 an.1999

Library of Congress Cataloging-in-Publication Data

Handbook of research on urban politics and policy in the United States
  / edited by Ronald K. Vogel.
     p.   cm.
   Includes bibliographical references and index.
   ISBN 0–313–29166–7 (alk. paper)
    1. Cities and towns—Research—United States.   2. Metropolitan
government—United States.   3. Urban policy—United States.
   I. Vogel, Ronald K.
   HT110.H36   1997
   307.76'0973—dc20   96–5786

British Library Cataloguing in Publication Data is available.

Library of Congress Catalog Card Number: 96–5786
ISBN: 0–313–29166–7

First published in 1997

Greenwood Press, 88 Post Road West, Westport, CT 06881
An imprint of Greenwood Publishing Group, Inc.

Printed in the United States of America

The paper used in this book complies with the
Permanent Paper Standard issued by the National
Information Standards Organization (Z39.48–1984).

10 9 8 7 6 5 4 3 2 1

In memory of my mother,
Maxine S. Vogel

Contents

PART II: GOVERNANCE AND POLITICS

PART III: DEVELOPMENT

PART IV: PROBLEMS AND POLICY

Preface

The aim of this handbook is to provide a way to access research on urban politics and policy in the United States. Experts were solicited to write review chapters guiding readers through major controversies and evaluating and assessing the subfields of urban politics and policy. Each chapter more or less follows the same basic pattern: First, an overview of the field and how it has evolved is presented. Then the major methodological issues and/or theoretical issues of concern to researchers are considered. This is followed by the current state of the field and directions for future research.

The book is targeted toward three main audiences: the undergraduate and graduate student in urban studies—sociology, political science, or urban and public affairs; the urban scholar—faculty or researchers in academic settings; and urban administrators or practitioners—policy analysts, public officials, or staff attempting to solve local problems.

Undergraduate and graduate students enrolled in urban studies programs or courses in urban politics or urban sociology are confronted with a multidisciplinary field. When they undertake research for term papers or prepare for comprehensive exams, there are few reference sources to guide their search for relevant materials. This handbook provides a starting place to guide students to the most important works in a particular subfield of urban studies and a context to place their work in a larger body of knowledge.

Urban scholars also need a reference work that can immediately familiarize them with major subfields of the discipline. Urban studies is by definition an interdisciplinary field. For example, inner-city revitalization involves economic development, urban development, neighborhood organization, government, crime, transportation, and so on. Urbanists are hard-pressed to stay on top of all aspects of other fields with which they may have little experience. Frequently, a researcher must quickly learn what the classic studies or major research questions are that have been addressed in a related subfield. This volume provides a starting point.

Urban practitioners (e.g., city managers, council persons, interest group representatives, news reporters) are confronted daily with a host of urban problems requiring solutions. Although no single chapter can anticipate or cover every issue or problem facing a policy maker, the chapters individually and collectively provide a wealth of information and should help urban policy makers identify existing knowledge and research relevant to the problem at hand.

I would like to thank Mim Vasan of Greenwood Press, now retired, for help in planning and editing this volume. I am grateful to the contributing authors who made editing this volume an easier task by their own high standards. At the University of Louisville, a President's Project Completion grant provided me with a course reduction that facilitated the completion of this book. I thank Bert Swanson for his early mentorship and interdisciplinary training that prepared me to undertake this task. David Imbroscio offered advice on my own chapters that was much appreciated. I also thank my research assistant Geetha Suresh, who provided invaluable assistance during the editorial process and Moshen Mani, who did an excellent job preparing the index.

Finally, I thank my wife Jeanie for her love, friendship, and support throughout this endeavor.

Part I

Theories, Methods, and Concepts

Chapter 1

Theoretical Models in Urban Politics

Peter Eisinger

Seeking to understand the underlying nature of cities of the past, archaeologists and social historians often turn to the physical vestiges of these early population concentrations. For Lewis Mumford (1961), the essential clues to the urban character in antiquity lay in the ancient hearths, marketplaces, and sacred tombs that dot the Middle East. For Max Weber (1958) it was the ring wall that explained the European medieval city, while for Henry Adams (1936) the keys to understanding were the great cathedrals built to the Virgin Mary. Through such urban artifacts, interpreters of the past have been able to extrapolate the social processes—family, war, trade, administration, religion—that accounted for the character of these first cities.

Though modern social scientists may also be interested in the physical aspects of the urban environment, their need to rely on material clues to understand the nature of contemporary urban life is lessened by their ability to observe the key social processes directly. But if the method for observing the modern city is different, the questions are still the same as those that drive the archaeological enterprise: What accounts for the city? How do we explain its physical shape, its distribution of people and functions in space, its array of amenities and infrastructure, its economic base and opportunity structure, and its civic life and political character? To what extent may we attribute these urban outcomes to collective human agency?

Approaches to answering these questions are numerous and varied and rarely fall neatly into disciplinary cubbyholes. The boundaries that divide the historians, geographers, planners, sociologists, economists, and political scientists who study the modern city are often difficult to discern. Urbanists are by training intellectually larcenous, borrowing freely from neighboring disciplines. Nevertheless, it is possible to say that most urbanists tend to sort themselves into one of two broad camps: One group focuses on the social processes of politics as a means of accounting for the city; the other focuses on the social processes of the market.

To assume that the processes of politics shape the city is to begin with the classic questions, Who governs? and To what effect? Scholars once believed that the way to answer these questions lay in a close examination of the legal rules that define the capacity and limits of government and the formal structures that apportion responsibility and authority. But social scientists long ago came to understand that although these formal elements, such as mayoral powers, city charters, and councilmanic electoral arrangements, may create advantages or disadvantages for certain interests, they are finally like the lines on a playing field on which the struggle for influence takes place (Banfield and Wilson 1963). The clash of interests and ideas may be constrained by legal and constitutional structures, but it is seldom determined by them.

Thus, instead of the formal elements of law and administration, it was the nature of competition and conflict that became the central focus of inquiry. Competition and conflict raise questions first about the distribution and use of political resources in the city and second about the resultant patterns of domination, subordination, and coalition. These patterns may be described in terms of the *structure of political power*.

This simple phrase—the structure of power—implies a lifetime's research agenda for explaining the city. To understand how the structure of power shapes the city, one must know not only the resource endowments of the participants in the competition to promote interests and ideas but also their strategies and goals. One can then begin to account for the contours of civic and associational life of the city; the role of government in allocating collective goods; the nature of the built environment of neighborhoods, commercial centers, and industrial space; the array of public amenities; and the economic activities that generate jobs, tax revenues, and opportunities. In this paradigm, power, purposefully exercised through, in league with, or against government, ultimately influences the nature of the city.

If this political process model assumes that urban outcomes are for the most part volitional, the paradigm that draws on market processes has a certain deterministic bent. Whereas in the former, the nature of the city is the product of compromises by competitors or the imposition of will by the powerful, in the market model outcomes are often, from a collective point of view, unplanned or perhaps even unintended. Outcomes are largely the by-products of the efforts of individual or collective actors intent on pursuing their own economic ends. Utility-maximizing behavior, rather than competition and conflict, is the key social process in the market model. When government acts, either it does so to maximize some unitary "city interest" (Peterson 1983: 17) or it does so as the handmaiden of private capital.

The quest by individuals, firms, and even city governments for maximal economic well-being may be observed, for example, in their choices of housing location, investment decisions, and tax policy. These choices ultimately shape the physical layout of the city and its economic life and public policies. Since all these actors may pursue their quest in response to national and even global economic factors, an obvious advantage of the market process model for understanding the city is that it calls our attention to these larger forces at work at the local level. By contrast, the political process model, though it may be attentive to the impact of federalism on the city, is nevertheless relatively hermetic in its focus (Peterson 1981: 5).

THE POLITICAL PROCESS MODEL

The genealogy of the political process model begins with the community power studies that absorbed the efforts of urbanists from the 1950s to the 1970s. The exhausting and exhaustive debate over who governed at the local level was never satisfactorily resolved (Polsby 1980: ix). Nevertheless, though we rarely speak in the language of the community power debate anymore, this literature taught us to be attentive to the ways in which political power and influence were distributed and exercised in cities. We learned that by observing urban politics we could construct a map of the sociometry of power. The questions posed by the community power scholars still animate a good deal of research on race, neighborhood power, the relative influence of public officials and private actors, and the nature of urban governing coalitions. Thus, though it is well-trod ground that we traverse, it is worth briefly reviewing the key poles of the debate as a way of seeing how these alternative perspectives on the structure of power posed issues of contemporary importance.

The antecedents of community power research lie in the sociological investigations of local stratification systems that began in the late 1920s. Helen and Robert Lynd's portrayal (1937) of the social landscape of "Middletown" (Muncie, Indiana) as dominated by the business class was typical. The apparent convergence of social, economic, and political status and the resulting pyramidal shape of the distribution of power in local settings clearly troubled Floyd Hunter, whose book *Community Power Structure* (1953) marks the real beginning of the debate over who governed American communities. "This situation," Hunter wrote, "does not square with the concepts of democracy that we have been taught to revere" (1). If the structure of power was not democratic, then who really ruled? Hunter set out to explore this question in Atlanta. By asking knowledgeable insiders the question, "Who are the top leaders around here?" Hunter inevitably compiled a roster of people whom he claimed occupied the apex of Atlanta's pyramidal power structure.

Robert Dahl's response to this notion of how American cities were run, *Who Governs?* (1963), offered a quite different proposition. Dahl, like Hunter, was interested in the larger issue of the paradox of democratic beliefs and forms and the inequality of resources. He believed that he had found in New Haven not a single pyramid of power but rather many centers of power and influence, each with its own set of key actors. Everything depended on the issue at stake. Dahl's notion of pluralism, with its emphasis on diffused power and the high penetrability of the political system by mobilized citizens, quickly achieved wide currency as the ruling (and reassuring) description of the American political process at every level.

In the wake of *Who Governs?* scholars fanned out into American communities to test and refine the competing methods and assumptions of the elitists and pluralists. In the end, they did not settle the debate over the nature of the structure of power in cities. Politics in some places, it seemed, conformed to the model of dispersed power; in others, to the model of concentrated power. But what is of enduring interest from a contemporary point of view is that the community power studies trained us to be alert to the changing roster and roles of participants in the struggle to govern the city. Scholars began to ask first about the political influence of minorities, particularly black Americans. Others have been concerned with the manner in which business interests have adapted to the growing strength of new participants in local politics, particularly minority and grassroots groups. A third issue is the extent to which neighborhood and other forms of citizen organization are a force in urban politics. In effect, the classic question that originally animated the political process model—namely, Who governs?—has been restated in the following terms: To what extent and under what circumstances is governance shared among groups in the city?

When Hunter and Dahl set the terms of the debate over the structure of community power, African Americans were minor players in local politics. Hunter notes that no black leader in Atlanta was ever "called upon to contribute to top policy-making in the larger community" (Hunter 1953: 148). In New Haven a decade later, black voters found no impediment to participating in politics (and in fact did so at a high rate), but if their interests and problems were of concern in the halls of city government, one could not discern this fact from reading *Who Governs?* In Sayre and Kaufman's massive study of pluralist politics in New York City (1960), blacks and black organizations are mentioned only half a dozen times or so (and even then mostly in passing). But, of course, it is hardly surprising that the community power investigators spent so little time on black politics: The black political awakening lay just out of sight around the corner. As James Q. Wilson observed in the introduction to his book on black leadership, *Negro Politics* (1960: 3), "This is a study of a phenomenon which many people believe does not exist."

Matters changed very quickly. Summers of rioting, the Community Action Program, the passage of the Voting Rights Act, the dissolution of the civil rights movement and the rise of black power, white suburban flight and black urban in-migration, and the election in 1967 of black mayors in Cleveland and Gary all converged to announce the arrival in force of black interests in urban politics. But where, once having arrived, did African Americans fit in the structures of power of American cities? To what extent did they share in local governance? Scholarly energies that earlier might have been devoted to waging the community power war now turned to documenting the black penetration of urban electoral politics (e.g., Masotti, Hadden, and Theissen 1969; Pettigrew 1972; MacManus 1978; Robinson and Dye 1978; Kleppner 1985).

But it quickly became evident to observers that getting to city hall was only the first modest step for blacks in their quest to occupy a significant place in the local structure of power. Investigators began to explore the extent to which achieving formal positions of authority bestowed on black politicians the power to produce visible policy effects, particularly with respect to budget decisions and municipal employment (Karnig and Welch 1980; Eisinger 1982).

Several important syntheses emerged from these efforts. In their study of 10 northern California cities, Browning, Marshall, and Tabb (1984) suggest that simple representation—the achievement of office—offers an inadequate gauge of a minority group's place in the structure of power. What is needed, they argue, is to focus on "incorporation," a concept that implies not simply formal representation but an influential position in the dominant governing coalition. In a later edited volume of case studies of minority incorporation in 11 major cities, Browning, Marshall, and Tabb conclude not only that blacks and Latinos have been able to achieve strong political incorporation in many places but also that membership at the heart of the local governing coalition has produced genuine, if limited, gains for those minority groups (1990: 212).

While the incorporation studies focused primarily on the role of minority representatives in relation to other actors within government, Clarence Stone's *Regime Politics* (1989) confronts the issue of the relationship between a minority-dominated government and a white-dominated local business sector (see also Eisinger 1980). In Hunter's Atlanta the white business elite had ruled unchallenged through handpicked white mayors. By the time Stone was writing, however, the mayor and many of the city's public officials were black and had come to office with the support of an electoral base independent of business domination. Yet Stone discovers that the two groups managed to work across the racial divide, constituting what he calls a governing "regime," an informal but ongoing cooperative working arrangement between private interests and government for the purpose of making and implementing authoritative decisions. The regime is held together by a mutual interest in merging resources to accomplish certain ends. Unlike the view of power in the elitist and pluralist debate as an instrument of dominance or social control, power in regime theory is harnessed for the purposes of "social production," that is, to pursue common purposes and to realize collective benefits.

Like the elitists, Stone believes that business is the most important of the private interests that government actors might seek as regime partners, for business controls crucial resources, particularly the ability to invest in economic undertakings (Stone 1980). As one black mayor of Atlanta comments to downtown business leaders, encapsulating the essence of the regime idea, "I didn't get elected with your help . . . [but] I can't govern without you" (Stone 1989: 110).

The structures of local power observed in the community power debate—monolithic business domination or plural competition—had clearly altered with the rise of black mayors backed by united black electorates. Business was neither dominant nor a competitor with government, yet it was hardly displaced: It remained a key player in an informal "regime."

Other interests perform roles in Stone's regime too, not the least of which are grassroots organizations of poor, working-class, and middle-class citizens, intent on preserving the integrity of their neighborhoods. Active neighborhood organizations proliferated in the cities in the 1960s and 1970s, stimulated at first by the threat of development that threatened to destroy residential communities (Thomas 1986). In some cities, neighborhood groups fought highway plans that promised to slash through areas of low- and middle-income housing. In other places, grassroots organizations galvanized to fight commercial development and the incursion of multifamily housing. Federal programs that required citizen participation, from the Community Action Program to the Community Development Block Grant program, were also responsible for much local organizing. Somewhat later, citizen groups in poor areas began to form community development corporations to pursue economic development.

The flowering of these local organizations naturally raised the question of their role in city policy making. Where did neighborhood groups fit into the local structure of power? Were the pluralists right when they argued that local political systems are essentially open to all mobilized groups? Though some scholars suggest that neighborhood organizations are not very durable participants in local politics (Crenson 1983), one recent study offers a different conclusion (Berry, Portney, and Thomson 1993). In the five cities chosen for study, neighborhood associations are not only well-institutionalized but formidable participants in processes of "cooperation and negotiation" with business interests in the politics of development (158).

If some descendants of the elitist-pluralist debate appear to have identified stable and ordered structures of urban power, where the various old and new groups contending for influence in the city have managed to find a role in a productive dance of conflict and cooperation, other scholars suggest that in modern urban America there is no discernible power structure at all. Beginning with Yates's *The Ungovernable City* (1977), some observers believe that the once-ordered relationships of domination or competition and compromise have given way to extreme fragmentation or "hyperpluralism" (Thomas and Savitch 1991). The old political machines have disappeared, and the political parties have disintegrated. Business has dispersed to the suburbs or moved offshore, while a new politics of identity has generated unbridgeable divisions among those who were once partners in electoral coalitions. Under such conditions, a sort of paralysis sets in. No interest—not business or minorities or neighborhoods—can impose its will on government. Nor can government act in the ensuing din: As Carolyn Adams writes of Philadelphia, under such chaotic circumstances, "the city's chief administrator finds it difficult to move the machinery of government in rational, purposive ways'' (Adams et al. 1991: 152).

How well can we account for the city by focusing on its structure of power? How powerful is this paradigm that assumes that urban outcomes are the product of the play of competition and cooperation among the interests in the city? Some have argued that a focus on political power offers a quite-limited view. In a well-known critique of the community power literature, Paul Peterson suggests that to concentrate exclusively on local political conflict is to miss the often overwhelming influence of external forces (1981: 5). Local policy choices, particularly those having to do with development and taxation, are finally determined by imperatives to which local actors, no matter who they are, are more or less compelled to respond.

Certainly it is true that every sort of structure of power—elitist, pluralist, regime—seems to produce quite similar development outcomes, regardless of the race or electoral base of the elected officials. Yet this is not to say that to seek an understanding of the sociometric map of the power and influence relations among various interests and actors in the city is a fruitless undertaking. To focus on the structure of power is at the very least to bring a democratic standard to bear on the city. Thus, to understand that structure is to gauge the penetrability of urban politics by various participants and the openness of the community to different ideas and agendas. It is in addition to open a window for exploring the dimensions or limits of a city's powers of adaptation and culture of tolerance. Thus, the question, Who governs? may be read in both normative and empirical terms. An investigation of the structure of local power permits us to measure the degree of congruence between American political ideals and urban reality.

THE MARKET PROCESS MODEL

The view that cities are best understood as the product of some conjunction of economic forces is embedded in the writings of a number of influential urban historians (Warner 1968; Teaford 1975; Cronon 1991). A good example is Sam Bass Warner's important study of Philadelphia, where the author argues that the prosperity, physical shape, and governing traditions of the American city are the product of a culture of privatism, whose essence lies in the individual's determined search for wealth.

Just as the field of economics has built a rich theoretical superstructure on the basis of the assumption of individual utility-maximizing behavior, so have varieties of urban scholars taken the same imperative and crafted accounts of the city. Three versions of the market-based explanation are notable: the neo-Marxist model and its progeny; the economic restructuring thesis; and economic individualism. Each begins from the premise that individuals seek to maximize their economic well-being, but each constructs a different theoretical edifice on this base.

The Neo-Marxist Model

For the neo-Marxist analysts of the city, the key utility-maximizing individual is the corporate capitalist, whose profit seeking "articulates" with space to generate "sociospatial patterns of production, distribution, and consumption" (Feagin 1988: 23). Upper-income groups enlist government to foster capital accumulation, manage the social costs of growth (such as housing displacement or structural unemployment), and divide and allocate space in some economically optimal way. Conflicts arise between those classes who would exploit land for profit and those classes who simply seek to live on it. Space is clearly a central concept in this framework (Gottdiener 1985). Since the regulation of space is one of the few exclusive municipal powers, capitalist interests enlist the "local state" to bring its land use planning powers to bear in the service of development and investment.

One of the most important works to build on neo-Marxist ideas is Logan and Molotch's *Urban Fortunes* (1987). Urban conflict is portrayed by these sociologists as a contest between those who would use land for profit (its *exchange* value) and those who seek to build or preserve communities on it (its *use* value). Urban processes are driven by utility maximizers, namely, "[p]eople dreaming, planning, and organizing themselves to make money from property," and those who oppose those dreams that threaten neighborhood and community (12). The archetypal struggles, therefore, are not between owners of capital and labor, as in orthodox Marxism, but between developers and residents, landlords and tenants.

Growth is such an overriding imperative that it succeeds in uniting elites who stand to profit against anyone who poses an obstacle to development. The consensus on the desirability of growth between "place entrepreneurs" and government generates efforts to intensify the economic functions of land use. Logan and Molotch refer to this concerted action as a "growth machine." Seeking to promote the exchange value of land, the growth machine is a powerful engine: It "closely determines the shape of the city, the distribution of people, and the way they live together" (2). Many of the city's basic forms of social organization—downtown business groups, corporations, neighborhood associations, social clubs, parent-teacher organizations—are in fact created to pursue use or exchange values (43), and government itself, through its zoning, planning, and economic development functions, is enlisted in the struggle, usually on the side of the growth machine. As the authors conclude, "[T]he most durable feature in U.S. urban planning is the manipulation of government resources to serve the exchange interests of local elites" (178).

The emphasis on the importance of development entrepreneurs in shaping the city seems to parallel work by political scientists on the postwar "progrowth coalitions" that emerged to transform downtowns (Mollenkopf 1983; see also Salisbury 1964; and Savitch 1988). These analyses, however, offer a different perspective on the development process from the sociological model. Whereas

Logan and Molotch view the individual rent-seeking entrepreneur as the driving force in the "growth machine," political scientists tend to see a political, rather than entrepreneurial, logic to the construction of "progrowth coalitions" (Dahl 1963).

Economic Restructuring

Conflict between use and exchange values provides a useful framework for understanding what Logan and Molotch call the sociology of urban property relations, a process, mainly internal to the city, of entrepreneurial initiative, competition, and resistance surrounding the issue of land use and the purposes of local government. Although at the end of their book they seek to link the city to the larger world by pointing out that place entrepreneurs compete with growth machines of other cities for investment and that cities play different economic roles in the new international marketplace, it is the economic restructuring literature, another variant of the market paradigm, that makes external market forces and their impact on the city its principal focus.

Some of those who investigate economic restructuring and its urban consequences draw from the neo-Marxist tradition, but others do not. All, however, begin from the same premise, namely, that restructuring is a function of the increased national and international mobility of capital in search of maximum profit (Soja 1991: 361; Beauregard 1989: 211). The shift in the geography of investment has changed social and economic patterns in American cities. Specifically, the increasing dispersion of capital from historic urban manufacturing locales, some of it to low-wage countries overseas, some of it to domestic suburban locations or low-wage states in the Sunbelt, has diminished the traditional role of the city as a place of economic opportunity, particularly for the unskilled. The sectoral shift in investment from heavy manufacturing to broadly defined service and high-tech industries has also contributed to the disappearance of well-paid work in the cities. In the face of disappearing working-class opportunities, the distribution of earnings is increasingly bifurcated.

Income and social polarization is one of the most striking urban consequences of economic restructuring (Soja 1991: 363). The gulf between the social classes, created by an ever-diminishing lower middle class, conveys the tensions and contingent social order of cities in the late stages of capitalism. A somewhat different perspective on the polarization that results from this postindustrial transformation is associated with the underclass thesis. Seeking to account for the high levels of social disorganization and pathology in the inner cities, particularly among minorities, William J. Wilson explores a variety of converging causes. Among the most important is the restructuring process, which has generated increasing demands for an educated workforce to run the information-processing and business service industries of the central city. The lack of schooling to compete for such jobs, Wilson argues, has been particularly costly to urban blacks (1987: 39), producing a "mismatch" between the low skills of inner-city workers and the white-collar job opportunities in the service sector (Kasarda 1989). As prospects erode for unskilled workers, minority unemployment rises, and poverty rates in ghetto neighborhoods increase in intensity (Massey and Denton 1993). The results of this hopelessness are the high rates of drug use, street crime, illegitimacy, and welfare dependency that define the underclass (W. Wilson 1987).

Economic Individualism

Both the neo-Marxist and the restructuring literatures see the city and its poorer classes as the helpless victims of economic forces. Utility-maximizing behavior has largely negative consequences for *community:* The quest for profit by owners of capital threatens neighborhoods and creates deep polarities among people. The flight of manufacturing jobs from the central city destroys the structure of opportunities that once sustained strong working-class communities among both blacks and whites. But a quite different view of the impact of economic forces is offered by the economic individualists, who believe that market behavior achieves an efficient allocation of resources and results in matching demand for consumption of public goods with ability to pay.

This tributary of the market model has been used first to explain the pattern of metropolitan settlement and political fragmentation as a product of individual preferences and migration behavior. Utility-maximizing behavior produces a logical sorting of tastes, lifestyles, and individual tax capacity across metropolitan areas, resulting in a proliferation of suburban municipalities. But this variant of the model is also the foundation for the argument that *cities* themselves may engage in utility maximizing, seeking some unitary corporate city interest. Thus, on the one hand, individual behavior may explain the distribution of social classes, racial groups, and suburban governments in metropolitan space; on the other hand, a city's attempt to maximize its corporate well-being explains how it crafts taxing and spending policies in order to attract productive residents and firms and discourage in-migrants who might pose a burden on the public treasury.

The pure form of economic individualism, or public choice, may be traced to Charles Tiebout, who posited that individuals in metropolitan areas seek out the jurisdiction that best matches their preferences for public services with their willingness or ability to pay for them through taxes (Tiebout 1956; Ostrom, Tiebout, and Warren 1961). Communities compete for residents by offering different packages of services at different tax prices. Competition among communities generates pressures for the efficient administration of public services. This public choice perspective is thus said to explain the origin of political fragmentation in metropolitan areas and resistance to single government reforms, differing tax rates and service packages, and relatively homogeneous communities of consumers of public goods.

Paul Peterson has adapted the individualist framework but replaced the individual utility maximizer, voting with his or her feet in quest of the optimal community, with the city as a corporate actor. Utility maximizing for cities means that they constantly "seek to improve their market position, their attractiveness as a locale for economic activity" (Peterson 1981: 22). For Peterson this insight provides a powerful means for understanding municipal policy choices. In response to this economic imperative, cities tend to eschew redistributive programs, fearing to drive away those whose incomes would be redistributed, and favor developmental policies, designed to encourage investment. Intercommunity tax competition and the proferring of business incentives are among the clearest consequences of this strategic calculus (Schneider 1989).

The variants of the market model provide vehicles for understanding what Norton Long once called "the unwalled city" (Long 1972), a concept meant to stand in contrast to the comparatively self-contained city of the political structure model. In the latter, local interests struggle for dominance, search for voice, and craft coalitions in the effort to make the institution of government act in certain ways. The results are seen in policy, projects, and programs. But in the unwalled city, all this institution-focused activity takes a distant second place among the factors that account for the city. The unwalled city is a porous city, the product of forces of global dimensions whose penetration it cannot bar. It is a place located literally in the larger world. Entrepreneurs, capitalists, business firms, and residents in the city respond to incentives that lie beyond the city's control. Migrants, still attracted by dreams of opportunity, arrive from all corners of the globe, passing across the city's boundaries as easily as one crosses the street. The results of all this individual striving in response to great economic incentives are seen in the city's land use patterns, tax and development policies, and social climate. The institutional power of government is a product more of market than of internal political forces. In the terms of the market model, then, we can only account for the city if we see it as a neighborhood in the global village.

CONCLUSIONS

Neither model provides a complete account of the American city, yet each provides a useful perspective. To focus on the nature of the structure of power is to assess the city's democratic possibilities. Democracy is measured by the permeability of the structure of power, the breadth of political participation, and the degree of dispersion of influence on public policy. Thus, an account of the structure of power is best understood as a snapshot of a city's political opportunity structure. By understanding this structure, we may gauge the relative influence of different groups and actors in the city. This in turn provides a perspective on local patterns of conflict and coalition. In addition, by observing the concerns of those situated at different places in the structure of power, we may also understand the creation of the political agenda. Finally, to understand the *politics* of the city is to measure patterns of commitment, loyalty, apathy, and alienation among citizens as they go about the task of local self-government. The political structure model tells us much, then, about the texture of civic life.

The market model provides a different window on the city. One important product of economic thinking is that it helps us to assess the array of economic opportunities in the city. In addition, the market model helps mightily to account for the physical city. The convergence in space of individuals and firms in search of well-being, which we observe in the patterns of clustering by race and class and in the efforts of entrepreneurs to pursue development and investment, literally shapes the city's housing, its neighborhoods, its infrastructure, and its downtown. Moreover, utility-maximizing behavior by firms and individuals explains the rise of metropolitan or suburban America in a way that eludes the capacity of the political structure model.

In the end, if the political structure model informs us about the democratic possibilities inherent in the political opportunity structure, the market model offers us a view of the possibilities of utility maximization through the economic opportunity structure. Just as some cities are more democratic than others, so do some places offer greater potential for the satisfaction of economic aims. No theory or paradigm in urban politics research adequately accounts for both the structure of economic and democratic possibilities at once. The task that looms is to draw the connection between the two worlds of human striving as it is played out in the urban setting.

ACKNOWLEDGMENT

I am grateful to Richard Merelman and Dan Smith for reading an earlier draft of this chapter.

REFERENCES

Adams, Carolyn, David Bartelt, David Elesh, Ira Goldstein, Nancy Kleniewski, and William Yancey. 1991. *Philadelphia: Neighborhoods, Division, and Conflict in a Postindustrial City.* Philadelphia: Temple University Press.

Adams, Henry. 1936. *Mont-St.-Michel and Chartres.* Boston: Houghton Mifflin.

Banfield, Edward, and James Q. Wilson. 1963. *City Politics.* New York: Vintage Books.

Beauregard, Robert. 1989. "Space, Time, and Economic Restructuring." In Robert Beauregard, ed., *Economic Restructuring and Political Response.* Beverly Hills, CA: Sage.

Berry, Jeffrey, Kent Portney, and Ken Thomson. 1993. *The Rebirth of Urban Democracy.* Washington, D.C.: Brookings.

Browning, Rufus, Dale Rogers Marshall, and David Tabb. 1984. *Protest Is Not Enough.* Berkeley: University of California Press.

Browning, Rufus, Dale Rogers Marshall, and David Tabb, eds. 1990. *Racial Politics in America.* New York: Longman.

Crenson, Matthew. 1983. *Neighborhood Politics.* Cambridge, MA: Harvard University Press.

Cronon, William. 1991. *Nature's Metropolis: Chicago and the Great West.* New York: Norton.

Dahl, Robert. 1963. *Who Governs?* New Haven, CT: Yale University Press.

Eisinger, Peter. 1980. *The Politics of Displacement.* New York: Academic Press.

Eisinger, Peter. 1982. "Black Employment in Municipal Jobs: The Impact of Black Political Power." *American Political Science Review* 76 (November): 754–771.

Feagin, Joe. 1988. *Free Enterprise City.* New Brunswick, NJ: Rutgers University Press.

Gottdiener, Mark. 1985. *The Social Production of Space.* Austin: University of Texas Press.

Hunter, Floyd. 1953. *Community Power Structure.* Chapel Hill: University of North Carolina Press.

Karnig, Albert, and Susan Welch. 1980. *Black Representation and Urban Politics.* Chicago: University of Chicago Press.

Kasarda, John. 1989. "Urban Industrial Transition and the Underclass." *Annals of the American Academy of Political and Social Science* 501 (January): 26–47.

Kleppner, Paul. 1985. *Chicago Divided: The Making of a Black Mayor.* DeKalb: Northern Illinois University Press.

Logan, John, and Harvey Molotch. 1987. *Urban Fortunes.* Berkeley: University of California Press.

Long, Norton. 1972. *The Unwalled City.* New York: Basic Books.

Lynd, Robert, and Helen Lynd. 1937. *Middletown in Transition.* New York: Harcourt, Brace.

MacManus, Susan. 1978. "City Council Election Procedures and Minority Representation: Are They Related?" *Social Science Quarterly* 59 (June): 153–161.

Masotti, Louis, Jeffrey Hadden, and Victor Theissen. 1969. "The Making of the Negro Mayors." In L. Ruchelman, ed., *Big City Mayors.* Bloomington: Indiana University Press.

Massey, Douglas, and Nancy Denton. 1993. *American Apartheid.* Cambridge, MA: Harvard University Press.

Mollenkopf, John. 1983. *The Contested City.* Princeton, NJ: Princeton University Press.

Mumford, Lewis. 1961. *The City in History: Its Origins, Its Transformations, and Its Prospects.* New York: Harcourt Brace Jovanovich.

Ostrom, Vincent, Charles Tiebout, and Robert Warren. 1961. "The Organization of Government in Metropolitan Areas." *American Political Science Review* 55 (December): 831–842.

Peterson, Paul. 1981. *City Limits.* Chicago: University of Chicago Press.

Pettigrew, Thomas. 1972. "When a Black Candidate Runs for Mayor: Race and Voting Behavior." In Harlan Hahn, ed., *People and Politics in Urban Society.* Beverly Hills, CA: Sage.

Polsby, Nelson. 1980. *Community Power and Political Theory.* 2nd ed. New Haven, CT: Yale University Press.

Robinson, Theodore, and Thomas Dye. 1978. "Reformism and Black Representation on City Councils." *Social Science Quarterly* 59 (June): 133–141.

Salisbury, Robert. 1964. "Urban Politics: The New Convergence of Power." *Journal of Politics* 26 (November): 775–797.

Savitch, H. V. 1988. *Post-Industrial Cities.* Princeton, NJ: Princeton University Press.

Sayre, Wallace, and Herbert Kaufman. 1960. *Governing New York City.* New York: Russell Sage.

Schneider, Mark. 1989. *The Competitive City.* Pittsburgh: University of Pittsburgh Press.

Soja, Edward. 1991. "Poles Apart: Urban Restructuring in New York and Los Angeles." In J. Mollenkopf and M. Castells, eds., *Dual City: Restructuring New York.* New York: Russell Sage.

Stone, Clarence. 1980. "Systemic Power in Community Decision Making." *American Political Science Review* 74 (December): 978–990.

Stone, Clarence. 1989. *Regime Politics.* Lawrence: University of Kansas Press.

Teaford, Jon. 1975. *The Municipal Revolution in America.* Chicago: University of Chicago Press.

Thomas, John Clayton. 1986. *Between Citizen and City.* Lawrence: University of Kansas Press.

Thomas, John Clayton, and H. V. Savitch. 1991. "Introduction: Big City Politics, Then and Now." In H. V. Savitch and John Clayton Thomas, eds., *Big City Politics in Transition.* Beverly Hills, CA: Sage.

Tiebout, Charles. 1956. "A Pure Theory of Local Expenditures." *Journal of Political Economy* 64: 416–424.

Warner, Sam Bass. 1968. *The Private City.* Philadelphia: University of Pennsylvania Press.

Weber, Max. 1958. *The City.* Translated and edited by Don Martindale and Gertrud Neuwirth. Glencoe, IL: Free Press.

Wilson, James Q. 1960. *Negro Politics.* Glencoe, IL: Free Press.

Wilson, William Julius. 1987. *The Truly Disadvantaged.* Chicago: University of Chicago Press.

Yates, Douglas. 1977. *The Ungovernable City.* Cambridge, MA: MIT Press.

Chapter 2

Research Methods in Urban Politics and Policy

Richard E. DeLeon

OVERVIEW OF THE FIELD

Methodology is the study of how we know things rather than what we know. The value of what we know or think we know depends critically on how we came to know it. Here we are concerned with knowledge about urban politics and policy based upon scientific research. As defined here, *scientific research* is any inquiry, qualitative or quantitative, that (1) describes or explains phenomena based on empirical data about the world; (2) uses explicit, public methods of data collection and analysis—methods that can be assessed and replicated by others; (3) provides estimates of the uncertainty associated with any descriptions or explanations arrived at; and (4) adheres to standard rules of descriptive and causal inference (cf. King, Keohane, and Verba 1994: 7–9).

Within this framework, methodological issues can be engaged at three different levels: philosophy of social science, research design, and research methods. The main emphasis here will be on research design, with selective attention to certain methods used widely in the urban politics and policy field, particularly case studies.

Philosophy of Social Science

Regarding philosophy, it should be noted that this conception of scientific knowledge and research is controversial to some. Critics include those who view all knowledge as subjective, interpretive, and profoundly biased by one's class, race, and gender; those who challenge the assumption of an objective reality existing apart from our socially and politically constructed images of it; those who view society as a patchwork of human artifice and historical accidents incapable of deep-structure comprehension; and those who object to the perceived imposition of a master narrative of concepts, methods, and rules on those who practice other, equally valid, ways of knowing. To all such critics one may reply that these are points well taken. (The literature is vast. Cogent discussions are found in Rorty [1989], Edelson [1985], Unger [1987], and Harvey [1992].) Several chapters in this volume discuss advances in urban research methodology that respond to these challenges.

Research Design

The design of research has four main parts. As suggested by King, Keohane, and Verba, these are the research question, the theory, the data, and the use of the data (King, Keohane, and Verba 1994: 13). As outlined and slightly modified below, the principles and rules they recommend for improving research designs are heartily endorsed.

Research Questions. Pose questions for research that (1) are important in the real world, (2) make a specific contribution to the scholarly literature, and (3) increase our ability to learn more about the world based on the results (King, Keohane, and Verba 1994: 14–19). Although the focus here will be on the scholarly literature, many important studies of urban politics and policy take the form of applied research in the areas of planning analysis, program evaluation, impact assessment, community advocacy, and political action (Hedrick, Bickman, and Rog 1993; Rossi and Freeman 1993). (For a concise and lucid treatment of applied urban research, see Andranovich and Riposa [1993].)

Theory. A theory is "a reasoned and precise speculation about the answer to a research question, including a statement about why the proposed answer is correct" (King, Keohane, and Verba 1994: 19). Choose a theory that (1) could be wrong, (2) can be falsified by the data, (3) has as many observable implications as possible, (4) is concrete and precise in its predictions, and (5) is plausible. Further, if a theory is amended based on the findings, (6) test the amended theory on new data (19–23).

Data. Data "are systematically collected elements of information about the world" (23). The data can be quantitative (e.g., budget figures, precinct voting tallies, counts of participants at rallies) or qualitative (e.g., field notes, interview transcripts, newspaper editorials). Recommendations: (1) Record and report data sources and data collection procedures to enhance replicability. (2) Collect data on as many observable implications of a theory as possible and for all contexts and units of analysis for which implications can be drawn. (3) Maximize the validity of measurements to ensure that what one thinks is being measured is being measured; where there is doubt, abandon higher-level concepts and stick closer to the data. And (4) maximize the reliability of measurements to ensure (a) that different researchers get the same results using the same measurement procedures and (b) that the same researcher gets the same results at different times if the object or phenomenon being measured has not changed (King, Keohane, and Verba 1994: 24–27).

Use of the Data. Given a set of data, (1) check sources for possible selection biases that can produce cases and observations that misrepresent the study population; (2) guard against omitted variable bias by considering rival hypotheses and including variables that might influence hypothesized causal relationships; and (3) maximize efficiency by using all data at their most fine-grained level in making inferences (King, Keohane, and Verba 1994: 27–28).

Research Methods

Research methods are the planned operational procedures used to collect and analyze data in implementing a research design. Methods may be classified by whether or not they allow the investigator to control and manipulate variables (Campbell and Stanley 1966); are qualitative or quantitative in style (Ragin 1987; Marshall and Rossman 1989); are obtrusive (reactive) or unobtrusive (nonreactive) in their impact on the subjects studied (Webb et al. 1966); involve original or secondary analysis (Jacob 1984; Kiecolt and Nathan 1985); and cover many cases or only one or a few. No one type of method or combination of methods is intrinsically more "scientific" than the others. A single qualitative case study can be more scientific in its conception, design, and execution than a large-sample statistical study employing the most advanced quantitative techniques. (Useful general surveys of research methods include Babbie [1989], Black [1993], Johnson and Joslyn [1994], Miller [1991], Vogt [1993], Denzin and Lincoln [1994], and Ragin [1994].)

CURRENT STATE OF THE FIELD

The state of research methods in urban politics and policy is something of a stew. The wide range of methods used reflects the diversity of theoretical perspectives and research interests among scholars and also the variety, complexity, multilayeredness, and tumult of the people, places, and phenomena being studied. Methodological differences abound, and it is hard to generalize about differences. As evidenced by publication of this volume, however, researchers in the field are now motivated to increase their methodological self-awareness, set clearer and higher standards, synchronize conceptual vocabularies, and report research in ways that facilitate replication and cumulative results. Obviously, there is no "one best way" to conduct inquiry. Yet clearly some ways are better than others for certain purposes, and the goal here will be to identify useful theory and exemplary practice that might guide future methodological advances.

Typically lacking any control over the research environment or the ability to assign subjects and manipulate treatment variables, investigators in the urban politics field engage almost entirely in some form of nonexperimental research. (There are a few exceptions—for example, innovations in computer-assisted telephone interviewing [CATI] allow experimentation in the context of sample surveys.) That means nearly all urban research is at risk of omitted variable bias and that researchers must find ways to minimize potentially confounding influences through statistical controls, "most similar" sampling designs (see below), matching cases, and other means.

Although sample survey research and secondary analysis of sample survey data continue to dominate mainstream political science methodology (Dillman 1978; Fowler 1989), the case study is most favored in urban political research. Most case studies focus on a single city (or neighborhoods and population groups within cities) and tend to be mainly qualitative in style. However, there has been an increase in recent years in the number of collaborative and comparative projects involving two or more cities. There are also a number of excellent examples of large-scale sample surveys (e.g., Welch and Bledsoe 1988) and cross-sectional and longitudinal studies (e.g., Rich 1993) that employ sophisticated statistical models and techniques, but these are relatively rare. Some of the most impressive comparative case studies incorporate sample surveys, structured elite interviews, extensive fieldwork, and other methods (e.g., Browning, Marshall, and Tabb 1984; Berry, Portney, and Thomson 1993). Indeed, most urban political studies employ hybrid or mixed designs and are difficult to classify methodologically. Main emphasis below will be given to case studies and their variants in the urban politics field.

Case Studies

Given limited resources, many case studies are conducted as a second-best alternative to more expensive large-scale research. Case studies have a pedigree in the methodological literature, however, and even those that involve purely qualitative "shoe leather" research and "street ethnography" often contribute more to a real understanding of urban politics than the best multivariate statistical research (Eckstein 1975; Yin 1984; Freedman 1991; Feagin, Orum, and Sjoberg 1991; Collier 1993). Case studies excel at description, and descriptions are primary in all research; they inspire explanatory theory and furnish its grist. Many of the conceptual frameworks that guide and focus current studies have roots in earlier descriptive case research: "urban regime" (Elkin 1987; Stone 1989); "governing" versus "electoral" coalitions (Ferman 1985); "progrowth coalition" (Mollenkopf 1983); "political incorporation" (Browning, Marshall, and Tabb 1984); and "solution sets" (Jones and Bachelor 1993).

Individual Case Studies. An earlier tradition of single case studies focused mainly on community power structures and often had the aim of testing general theories in a local setting (e.g., Dahl 1961). As the field has broadened in scope and become multidisciplinary, case studies of individual cities have had to encompass more complexity, describe things more thickly, and adopt a more exploratory thrust. Theories are typically the products rather than the motivators of such research (cf. Glaser and Strauss 1967). Illustrative case studies of this sort include books on Cleveland (Swanstrom 1985), Atlanta (Stone 1989), Houston (Thomas and Murray 1991), Chicago (Grimshaw 1992), New York (Mollenkopf 1992), San Francisco (DeLeon 1992), and Los Angeles (Sonenshein 1993). With much variation, data sources usually include some mixture of direct observation, soaking and poking, elite interviews, newspaper accounts, census statistics, and local government documents and reports—all typically marinated in a narrative of the city's history told from a point of view.

Critics might object that a "sample" of one case offers slim basis for generalizing results to other cities. If statistical inference were the goal, that would indeed be a real limitation. Case studies have a different aim, however, which is to gain insight into the conjunctural patterns linking many variables in one city and to describe them accurately in terms that might apply to other cities (cf. Stone 1989: 255–256). Conducted in the spirit of "good description is better than bad explanation" (King, Keohane, and Verba 1994: 45), well-designed single case studies put explanatory theory and statistical inference on the right track. Many good descriptions of growth politics in U.S. cities, for example, undermined the long-held assumption that developmental policy is "consensual" and moved theory in a new direction.

Yet at some point broader inference and generalization must be attempted in the form of statistical model building. That requires dissection of wholes into parts and the abstraction of real cities into sets of variables and relationships. Stripped of their proper names and reduced to data points in large sample studies, real cities die in our models. In building such models, it is important to know where to cut and what to pull out. Case studies show the way.

Another response to the "sample of one" criticism is to point out that there are many opportunities within a single case study to "expand the number of observations" available for testing theory (King, Keohane, and Verba 1994: 221; Lieberson 1991). Typically, numerous variables are measured over many units and levels of analysis—wards, neighborhoods, precincts, interest groups, business firms, government organizations, individuals, and so on. King and coauthors write:

Although case-study research rarely uses more than a handful of cases, the total number of observations is generally immense. It is therefore essential to distinguish between the number of cases and the number of observations. The former may be of some interest for some purposes, but only the latter is of importance in judging the amount of information a study brings to bear on a theoretical question. (King, Keohane, and Verba 1994: 52)

For example, preliminary fieldwork in a study of San Francisco politics (DeLeon 1992) suggested that the social base of the city's slow-growth movement was predominantly middle class. Analysis of aggregate voting data for 710 precincts confirmed this, and analysis of sample survey data for 406 registered voters confirmed it also. Thus, one "case" (San Francisco) generated a total of

1,116 "observations" made on two different units of analysis (precincts and voters) to back up theoretical claims. The best case studies are fertile in this sense; if numbers count, then the number of observations made should be counted.

Comparative Case Studies. In one form or another, explicitly or implicitly, comparison is at the heart of scientific inquiry (Collier 1993; Keating 1990; Przeworski and Teune 1970; Ragin 1987). Small N comparative case studies occupy a methodological middle ground in the trade-offs between thick and thin description, qualitative and quantitative analysis, and depth of understanding and statistical generalizability. Qualitative comparative analysis, according to Ragin, achieves the goal of "comparing wholes as configurations of parts. This is the *via media* between complexity and generality, between the radically analytic variable-oriented strategy and the highly personalized case-oriented strategy" (Ragin 1987: 84). Comparative case studies allow use of "pattern matching" (Campbell 1975) and "process tracing" (George and McKeown 1985) to identify similarities and differences in the causal mechanisms that shape political systems.

Much of the recent and current research in the urban politics field falls under the heading of comparative case studies. These projects range from loose collaborations of scholars conducting case studies of individual cities within a common framework of research questions (e.g., Squires 1989; Browning, Marshall, and Tabb 1990; Savitch and Thomas 1991) to methodologically sophisticated and sharply focused comparative studies designed to test theories and produce generalizable results (e.g., Browning, Marshall, and Tabb 1984; Stone, Henig, and Jones 1992; Berry, Portney, and Thomson 1993). Studies comparing two cities or three cities at a time are quite common, typically with the choice of cities guided by a "most similar systems" approach to case selection (see below). Examples include comparative studies of growth politics and mayoral leadership in Boston and San Francisco (Mollenkopf 1983; Ferman 1985); of black political incorporation in Baltimore and Detroit (Orr 1993); and of politics and planning in the postindustrial global cities of New York, London, and Paris (Savitch 1988; Fainstein 1994).

Case selection is a critical issue in the design of comparative studies. In large N studies, random selection of cases minimizes sample bias and statistically controls for potential confounding factors. In small N research, however, random selection is usually unwise. It can actually increase sample bias as well as risk omitting important cases (King, Keohane, and Verba 1994: 124–125). Also to be avoided are selection rules that restrict or eliminate variation on the dependent variable—for example, selecting for study only those cities that have experienced riots in research on urban violence. Such rules produce biased samples that attenuate estimates of causal effects and that at best confirm hypothesized causal factors as necessary but not sufficient conditions (King, Keohane, and Verba 1994: 128–132; Most and Starr 1982; Olzak 1992: 50–53).

As a guide to purposive sampling in small N research, several rules are recommended for selecting cases on the independent variable(s). One is the "most similar systems" design (Przeworski and Teune 1970: 32–33), which selects cases that are as similar as possible in as many ways as possible to minimize the set of remaining differences that might be theorized as causes of the dependent variable. The logic of this strategy is clear in the design of Browning, Marshall, and Tabb's comparative, longitudinal study of 10 northern California cities:

By selecting cities in the same region and state, we control for some structural and political variables. . . . Intensive study of this purposive sample designed to reduce variation on some factors has enhanced our ability to penetrate behind the gross variables used in large sample studies. We are thus able to analyze political phenomena that are causally much closer to the changes under study, and in this way to develop a fuller understanding of the political processes at work. (Browning, Marshall, and Tabb 1984: 10–11)

The "most different systems" rule of case selection, in contrast, seeks to maximize differences among sampled cities, but only if units such as neighborhoods, legislative councils, and individuals are included at a lower level of analysis within each city. If only one level of analysis exists, according to Przeworski and Teune, a study is not truly comparative (Przeworski and Teune 1970: 36–39).

Still a third approach to case selection is Ragin's suggestion to maximize causal complexity, that is, to select cases that represent all logically possible combinations of relevant causal conditions that are hypothesized to explain some phenomenon. More than one combination of factors might produce the same output value, so it is important to include them all, if possible (Ragin 1987: 105). The number of cases selected to represent each type is not of great concern. "More important than relative frequency," Ragin argues, "is the *variety* of meaningful patterns of causes and effects that exist" (52). For example, one might hypothesize that the combination of three factors is necessary and sufficient to produce growth control policies in large U.S. cities: (A) a large middle class, (B) high population density, *and* (C) a politically divided downtown business community. Let A, B, and C symbolize the presence of each condition and a, b, and c its absence. The theory asserts not only that the combination ABC leads to growth controls but also that the combinations ABc, AbC, aBC, abC, aBc, Abc, and abc do not. Applying Ragin's case selection rule, at least one city of each type should be included in the study to allow a meaningful test of the hypothesis. (See Clarke [1993] for what may be the first application of Ragin's Boolean algebraic methods in the urban politics field.)

One can debate the relative merits of these case selection rules, but each has a certain logic and all are aimed at minimizing sample bias, reducing (or controlling for) the effects of potentially confounding factors, and maximizing the amount of generalizable knowledge that can be gained from studying just a few cases. Given the continuing strong need in the field for basic descriptive studies, the limitations on resources, and the still-formative state of urban political theory, concerns about sample bias and case selection might not seem urgent. Catch as catch can is still acceptable, and all new studies are welcome. However, as more scholars move beyond the stage of exploration and description and into the stage of explanation and verification, these methodological issues become important to address.

DIRECTIONS FOR FUTURE RESEARCH

The field of urban politics is ripe for the application of new research and analytical methods, especially those that help to consolidate and generalize the findings of past work, that increase the rigor of structural analyses and comparisons of whole systems, and that integrate qualitative and quantitative approaches. These methods include (1) meta-analysis and meta-ethnographic analysis, (2) political cultural analysis, (3) contextual analysis, and (4) network analysis.

Meta-Analysis and Meta-Ethnographic Analysis

Meta-analysis uses quantitative procedures to summarize, integrate, or synthesize the statistical findings obtained from a systematic literature review of many different studies of the same phenomenon (Wolf 1986; Hunger, Schmidt, and Jackson 1984). Meta-ethnographic analysis uses interpretive procedures involving metaphors, analogies, and reciprocal translations of meanings to compare and synthesize the texts of qualitative or ethnographic studies (Silverman 1993; Noblit and Hare 1988). Both types of "meta"-analysis will help to develop cumulative findings and well-grounded generalizations in the urban politics field. Given the growing number of case studies, meta-ethnographic analyses are especially needed to bridge linguistic gaps between seemingly disparate texts and to inspire consistent use of a common theoretical vocabulary. Jezierski and Vogel's pioneering meta-ethnographic comparison of four urban political economy case studies illustrates both the meticulous close reading required by such an approach and the critical insights it can offer (Jezierski and Vogel 1992).

Political Cultural Analysis

Cultural studies have intellectual roots and diverse applications in many social science disciplines. In urban research, the concept of political culture is often used interpretively to characterize a city's communal life-world as understood and experienced by inhabitants: its civic traditions, formative institutions, value hierarchies, and patterns of citizen engagement and political participation. Case studies are particularly effective in providing the thick descriptions and contextual narratives required to convey these holistic images of a city's political life. With few exceptions (e.g., Rosdil 1991; Tarrow 1992; Clark and Quillian 1994), however, the concept of urban political culture itself is rarely theorized or explicated in ways that facilitate systematic comparison and cumulative research. Recent comparative case studies of urban democracy (Berry, Portney, and Thomson 1993) and the ongoing 11-city "civic capacity in education" project (Pedescleaux et al. 1994) have moved the field in this general direction. In addition, Putnam's recent comparative study of civic traditions and institutional performance in 20 Italian regional planning districts has considerable theoretical and methodological relevance to urban politics scholars. This exemplary work demonstrates not only the explanatory power of political culture but also the feasibility of operationalizing important aspects of it (e.g., social capital stocks, horizontal versus vertical networks of citizen engagement) for purposes of research (Putnam 1993).

Contextual Analysis

Quantitative methods of contextual analysis offer new ways to study the effects of social and cultural environments on individual political behavior, particularly at the level of neighborhoods but also at higher levels of spatial inclusiveness (Huckfeldt and Sprague 1993). Contextual analysis enhances the use of other urban research methods, especially sample surveys of individuals that, until recently, have ignored the social context of behavior or randomized it out of existence. For example, the social class composition of a neighborhood might well be a better predictor of a resident's choice of political party than his or her own social class. It is now becoming routine in survey research to collect information on a respondent's census tract or zipcode, thus allowing the merging of individual-level and contextual data. These multilayered data sets are made to order for quantitative methods of contextual analysis. Illustrating the power and scope of such methods is Huckfeldt's contextual analysis of friendship choice, partisan attachment, ethnic conflict, white flight, and racial tipping in Buffalo and Detroit (Huckfeldt 1986). Urban scholars of all methodological persuasions will find much of value in the contextual analysis literature. It should be noted, however, that most applications require knowledge of appropriate statistical models and procedures (Iversen 1991; Aiken and West 1991; Hosmer and Lemeshow 1989).

Network Analysis

The concept of networks is central to studies of political cultures (e.g., Putnam 1993) and urban regimes (e.g., Stone 1989). Emerging as stable patterned linkages from the countless interactions among individuals, groups, and organizations, networks are important structural features of whole systems. Such "global network structures," write Laumann and Knoke, "can affect the perceptions, orientations, and actions of its organizational components. Relationships between actors, not simply the attributes of these individuals, hold the key to modeling social structures'' (Laumann and Knoke 1987: 226). Network analysis provides an array of formal tools for studying and comparing networks of communication, resource exchange, political influence, informal cooperation, and citizen engagement in urban communities (Wasserman and Galaskiewicz 1994; Knoke 1990; Laumann and Pappi 1976). As an approach to ''comparing wholes as configurations of parts'' (Ragin 1987: 84), network analysis offers another *via media* between qualitative and quantitative methods.

A FINAL COMMENT ON QUANTITATIVE AND QUALITATIVE RESEARCH METHODS

One theme of this brief review has been that there is an underlying unity in the practice of qualitative and quantitative research methods. As viewed here, these are merely different styles of scientific inquiry, each with its own traditions of methodological discourse and standards of excellence. Despite growing recognition of a common objective and logic of inquiry beneath the surface of differences (cf. Kirk and Miller 1986; Creswell 1994; Ragin 1987; King, Keohane, and Verba 1994), urban researchers continue to be divided into these two main camps. This unfortunate specialization breeds trained incapacities, and learning opportunities on both sides are lost. Shoe leather and statistics are both necessary to achieve a more complete and general understanding of urban phenomena. The methodology curriculum should make room for both, and all scholars should convey more exactly how they know what they know in presenting their results.

REFERENCES

Aiken, Leona S., and Stephen G. West. 1991. *Multiple Regression: Testing and Interpreting Interactions*. Newbury Park, CA: Sage.

Andranovich, Gregory D., and Gerry Riposa. 1993. *Doing Urban Research*. Newbury Park, CA: Sage.

Babbie, Earl. 1989. *The Practice of Social Research*. 5th ed. Belmont, CA: Wadsworth.

Berry, Jeffrey M., Kent E. Portney, and Ken Thomson. 1993. *The Rebirth of Urban Democracy*. Washington, D.C.: Brookings Institution.

Black, Thomas R. 1993. *Evaluating Social Science Research: An Introduction*. Thousand Oaks, CA: Sage.

Browning, Rufus B., Dale Rogers Marshall, and David H. Tabb. 1984. *Protest Is Not Enough: The Struggle of Blacks and Hispanics for Equality in Urban Politics*. Berkeley and Los Angeles: University of California Press.

Browning, Rufus B., Dale Rogers Marshall, and David H. Tabb, eds. 1990. *Racial Politics in American Cities*. New York. Longman.

Campbell, Donald T. 1975. '' 'Degrees of Freedom' and the Case Study.'' *Comparative Political Studies* 8: 178–193.

Campbell, Donald T., and J. C. Stanley. 1966. *Experimental and Quasi-Experimental Designs for Research*. Chicago: Rand McNally.

Clark, Terry Nicholas, and Lincoln Quillian. 1994. "The New Political Culture Emerges: Sources and Dynamics among Citizens and Others." Paper presented at the annual meeting of the American Political Science Association, September 1–4, New York City.

Clarke, Susan E. 1993. "Changing Patterns of Local Interest Representation: A Contextualized Analysis of Political Change in Eight Cities." Paper presented at the annual meeting of the Western Political Science Association, March 18–20, Pasadena, California.

Collier, David. 1993. "The Comparative Method." In Ada W. Finifter, ed., *Political Science: The State of the Discipline*. Washington, D.C.: American Political Science Association.

Creswell, John. 1994. *Research Design: Qualitative and Quantitative Approaches*. Newbury Park, CA: Sage.

Dahl, Robert. 1961. *Who Governs: Democracy and Power in an American City*. New Haven, CT: Yale University Press.

DeLeon, Richard E. 1992. *Left Coast City: Progressive Politics in San Francisco, 1975–1991*. Lawrence: University Press of Kansas.

Denzin, Norman, and Yvonna Lincoln, eds. 1994. *Handbook of Qualitative Research*. Newbury Park, CA: Sage.

Dillman, Don A. 1978. *Mail and Telephone Surveys: The Total Design Method*. New York. John Wiley.

Eckstein, Harry. 1975. "Case Study and Theory in Political Science." In Fred Greenstein and Nelson Polsby, eds., *Handbook of Political Science*. Vol. 7. Reading, MA: Addison-Wesley.

Edelson, Marshall. 1985. "The Hermeneutic Turn and the Single Case Study in Psychoanalysis." In David N. Berg and Kenwyn K. Smith, eds., *Exploring Clinical Methods for Social Research*. Beverly Hills, CA: Sage.

Elkin, Stephen. 1987. *City and Regime in the American Republic*. Chicago: University of Chicago Press.

Fainstein, Susan. 1994. *The City Builders: Property, Politics, and Planning in London and New York*. New York: Blackwell.

Feagin, Joe, Anthony Orum, and Gideon Sjoberg. 1991. *A Case for the Case Study*. Chapel Hill: University of North Carolina Press.

Ferman, Barbara. 1985. *Governing the Ungovernable City: Political Skill, Leadership, and the Modern Mayor*. Philadelphia: Temple University Press.

Fowler, Floyd J., Jr. 1989. *Survey Research Methods*. Newbury Park, CA: Sage.

Freedman, David A. 1991. "Statistical Models and Shoe Leather." In Peter Marsden, ed., *Sociological Methodology 1991*. San Francisco: Jossey-Bass.

George, Alexander L., and Timothy J. McKeown. 1985. "Case Studies and Theories of Organizational Decision Making." In *Advances in Information Processing in Organizations*. Vol. 2. Santa Barbara, CA: JAI Press.

Glaser, Barney G., and Anselm L. Strauss. 1967. *The Discovery of Grounded Theory: Strategies for Qualitative Research*. Chicago: Aldine.

Grimshaw, William J. 1992. *Bitter Fruit: Black Politics and the Chicago Machine, 1931–1991*. Chicago: University of Chicago Press.

Harvey, David. 1992. "Social Justice, Postmodernism and the City." *International Journal of Urban and Regional Research* 16, no. 4: 588–601.

Hedrick, Terry, Leonard Bickman, and Debra Rog. 1993. *Applied Research Design: A Practical Guide.* Newbury Park, CA: Sage.

Hosmer, David W., and Stanley Lemeshow. 1989. *Applied Logistic Regression.* New York: John Wiley & Sons.

Huckfeldt, Robert. 1986. *Politics in Context: Assimilation and Conflict in Urban Neighborhoods.* New York: Agathon.

Huckfeldt, Robert, and John Sprague. 1993. "Citizens, Contexts, and Politics." In Ada W. Finifter, ed., *Political Science: The State of the Discipline.* Washington, D.C.: American Political Science Association.

Hunger, John E., Frank C. Schmidt, and Gregg B. Jackson. 1984. *Meta-Analysis: Cumulating Research Findings across Studies.* Beverly Hills, CA: Sage.

Iversen, Gudmund R. 1991. *Contextual Analysis.* Newbury Park, CA: Sage.

Jacob, Herbert. 1984. *Using Published Data: Errors and Remedies.* Beverly Hills, CA: Sage.

Jezierski, Louise, and Ronald K. Vogel. 1992. "Translating Urban Political Economy Case Studies: A Meta-Ethnographic Approach." Unpublished manuscript.

Johnson, Janet B., and Richard A. Joslin. 1994. *Political Science Research Methods.* 3rd ed. Washington, D.C.: CQ Press.

Jones, Bryan D., and Lynn W. Bachelor. 1993. *The Sustaining Hand: Community Leadership and Corporate Power.* 2nd ed. Lawrence: University Press of Kansas.

Keating, Michael. 1990. *Comparative Urban Politics.* Brookfield, VT: Edward Elgar.

Kiecolt, K. Jill, and Laura Nathan. 1985. *Secondary Analysis of Survey Data.* Beverly Hills, CA: Sage.

King, Gary, Robert O. Keohane, and Sidney Verba. 1994. *Designing Social Inquiry: Scientific Inference in Qualitative Research.* Princeton, NJ: Princeton University Press.

Kirk, Jerome, and Marc Miller. 1986. *Reliability and Validity in Qualitative Research.* Newbury Park, CA: Sage.

Knoke, David. 1990. *Political Networks: The Structural Perspective.* New York: Cambridge University Press.

Laumann, Edward O., and David Knoke. 1987. *The Organizational State: Social Choice in National Policy Domains.* Madison: University of Wisconsin Press.

Laumann, Edward O., and Franz U. Pappi. 1976. *Networks of Collective Action: A Perspective on Community Influence Systems.* New York: Academic.

Lieberson, Stanley. 1991. "Small N's and Big Conclusions: An Examination of the Reasoning in Comparative Studies Based on a Small Number of Cases." *Social Forces* 70: 307–320.

Marshall, Catherine, and Gretchen Rossman. 1989. *Designing Qualitative Research.* Newbury Park, CA: Sage.

Miller, Delbert C. 1991. *Handbook of Research Design and Social Measurement.* 5th ed. Newbury Park, CA: Sage.

Mollenkopf, John H. 1983. *The Contested City.* Princeton, NJ: Princeton University Press.

Mollenkopf, John H. 1992. *A Phoenix in the Ashes: The Rise and Fall of the Koch Coalition in New York City Politics.* Princeton, NJ: Princeton University Press.

Most, Benjamin, and Harvey Starr. 1982. "Case Selection, Conceptualizations and Basic Logic in the Study of War." *American Journal of Political Science* 26, no. 4: 834–855.

Noblit, George W., and R. Dwight Hare. 1988. *Meta-Ethnography: Synthesizing Qualitative Studies.* Beverly Hills, CA: Sage.

Olzak, Susan. 1992. *The Dynamics of Ethnic Competition and Conflict.* Stanford, CA: Stanford University Press.

Orr, Marion. 1993. "Black Political Incorporation—Phase Two: The Cases of Baltimore and Detroit." Paper presented at the annual meeting of the Western Political Science Association, March 18–20, Pasadena, California.

Pedescleaux, Desiree, Jorge Ruiz-de-Velasco, Lana Stein, and Clarence Stone. 1994. "Urban Education as an Arena of Reform." Paper presented at the annual meeting of the American Political Science Association, September 1–4, New York City.

Przeworski, Adam, and Henry Tenue. 1970. *The Logic of Comparative Social Inquiry.* New York: Wiley Inter Science.

Putnam, Robert D., with Robert Leonardi and Raffaella Y. Nanetti. 1993. *Making Democracy Work: Civic Traditions in Modern Italy.* Princeton, NJ: Princeton University Press.

Ragin, Charles. 1987. *The Comparative Method: Moving Beyond Qualitative and Quantitative Strategies.* Berkeley and Los Angeles: University of California Press.

Ragin, Charles. 1994. *Constructing Social Research: The Unity and Diversity of Method.* Thousand Oaks, CA: Pine Forge Press.

Rich, Michael J. 1993. *Federal Policymaking and the Poor. National Goals, Local Choices, and Distributional Outcomes.* Princeton, NJ: Princeton University Press.

Rorty, Richard. 1989. *Contingency, Irony, and Solidarity.* New York: Cambridge University Press.

Rosdil, Donald L. 1991. "The Context of Radical Populism in U.S. Cities: A Comparative Analysis." *Journal of Urban Affairs* 13, no. 1: 77–96.

Rossi, Peter, and Howard Freeman. 1993. *Evaluation.* Newbury Park, CA: Sage.

Savitch, H. V. 1988. *Post-Industrial Cities: Politics and Planning in New York, Paris, and London.* Princeton, NJ: Princeton University Press.

Savitch, H. V., and John Clayton Thomas, eds. 1991. *Big City Politics in Transition.* Newbury Park, CA: Sage.

Silverman, David. 1993. *Interpreting Qualitative Data: Methods for Analyzing Talk, Text, and Interaction.* Newbury Park, CA: Sage.

Sonenshein, Raphael J. 1993. *Politics in Black and White: Race and Power in Los Angeles.* Princeton, NJ: Princeton University Press.

Squires, Gregory D., ed. 1989. *Unequal Partnerships: The Political Economy of Urban Redevelopment in Postwar America.* New Brunswick, NJ: Rutgers University Press.

Stone, Clarence N. 1989. *Regime Politics: Governing Atlanta 1946–1988.* Lawrence: University Press of Kansas.

Stone, Clarence N., Jeffrey R. Henig, and Bryan D. Jones. 1992. "Civic Capacity and Urban Education: A Draft Proposal." Mimeographed.

Swanstrom, Todd. 1985. *The Crisis of Growth Politics: Cleveland, Kucinich, and the Challenge of Urban Populism.* Philadelphia: Temple University Press.

Tarrow, Sidney. 1992. "Mentalities, Political Cultures, and Collective Action Frames:

Constructing Meanings through Action.'' In Aldon D. Morris and Carol M. Mueller, eds., *Frontiers in Social Movement Theory*. New Haven: Yale University Press.

Thomas, Robert D., and Richard W. Murray. 1991. *Progrowth Politics: Change and Governance in Houston*. Berkeley, CA: IGS Press.

Unger, Roberto M. 1987. *False Necessity*. New York: Cambridge University Press.

Vogt, W. Paul. 1993. *Dictionary of Statistics and Methodology: A Nontechnical Guide for the Social Sciences*. Newbury Park, CA: Sage.

Wasserman, Stanley, and Joseph Galaskiewicz, eds. 1994. *Advances in Social Network Analysis: Research in the Social and Behavioral Sciences*. Newbury Park, CA: Sage.

Webb, Eugene J., Donald T. Campbell, Richard D. Schwartz, and Lee Sechrest. 1966. *Unobtrusive Measures: Nonreactive Research in the Social Sciences*. Chicago: Rand McNally.

Welch, Susan, and Timothy Bledsoe. 1988. *Urban Reform and Its Consequences: A Study in Representation*. Chicago: University of Chicago Press.

Wolf, Frederic M. 1986. *Meta-Analysis: Quantitative Methods for Research Synthesis*. Beverly Hills, CA: Sage.

Yin, Robert K. 1984. *Case Study Research: Design and Methods*. Beverly Hills, CA: Sage.

Chapter 3

Urbanization

J. John Palen

OVERVIEW OF URBANIZATION

Urbanization is a process having both demographic and organizational components. Demographically, urbanization refers to the proportion of the population of a unit (usually a nation-state) living in defined urban places. The term *urbanization* is also used to refer to the changes that occur in social organization as a consequence of population concentration. Urbanization thus is the process by which rural areas become transformed into urban places. (The term *urbanization* comes from the Latin *urbs*, which refers to the built form of the city. This is to be distinguished from *civilization*, which comes from *civitas* and refers to the moral and political community in urban places.) Thus, urbanization as a demographic process has beginning and end points. It is assumed that the practical upper limit of urbanization for large nation-states is roughly 85 percent.

Historically, urbanization is a new phenomenon, with urban places having existed for less than 9,000 years. Thus, the vast bulk of the millions of years the human species has existed, and the 40,000 or so years *Homo sapiens* have existed, has been an existence without cities. Nonetheless, what we label as civilization refers to the few centuries of economic, political, and social domination of cities. The history of cities, whether Babylon, Beijing, or Rome, composes much of the history of the world. However, even the most powerful of these cities were small urban islands awash in rural seas. Until roughly two centuries ago, limited food surpluses and the difficulty of transportation meant that no more than a few percentage points of any nation's population could reside in densely settled urban places. Few of even the largest preindustrial cities ever exceeded 200,000 population (Hawley 1981: 30–33). At the opening of the nineteenth century the world's population was only 3 percent urban, and at the beginning of the twentieth century, the globe was only 14 percent urban. Today, three quarters of the U.S. population is urban, with the world range varying from only 5 percent urban in Burundi and Rwanda to 100 percent urban in the city-state of Singapore. Currently, the world as a whole is 45 percent urban, and around the year 2005, the globe for the first time in history will have a majority of its people in urban places. Historically, we have no experience as a species living in a predominantly urban world.

Urban growth has never been spread uniformly around the globe. During the nineteenth and first half of the twentieth century, the fastest rates of urbanization were found in European nations and those countries settled by Europeans. These were places where agricultural and transportation technologies were most developed. At the opening of the twentieth century, England was the only urban nation on earth. Not until 1920 did the United States have half its population residing in urban places. Currently, Western nations are experiencing little, if any, urban growth. Over 90 percent of urban growth now is occurring in less developed countries (LDCs). This growth amounts to a million new urban persons every week. As the twenty-first century begins, there will be worldwide some 391 cities of over 1 million residents, and 284 of these places will be located in less developed countries. There also will be 26 megacities of over 10 million inhabitants, and 21 of these megacities will be in LDCs. Virtually all urban increases for the next 25 years will occur in Third World cities. The much-discussed population explosion is in fact a Third World urban explosion.

THEORETICAL APPROACHES TO URBANIZATION

The first systematic study of urbanization, and of urbanism (which is defined as the social psychological and behavioral consequences of urbanization), is associated with the so-called Chicago School of scholars working at the University of Chicago in the 1920s. Theirs was the first systematic collection of data done with an explicitly scientific rather than social welfare orientation. Members of the Chicago School were concerned with documenting both the patterns of urban change and the consequences of these changes for social institutions such as the family. Scholars such as Robert Park, Ernest Burgess, and Roderick McKenzie used the city of Chicago as a social laboratory to examine urbanization and to document its consequences on the conditions of social life for urban residents (Park, Burgess, and McKenzie 1925). The Chicago School studied the city from three perspectives: first, as a physical-social structure having a population base, technology, and ecological order; second, as a system of social organization having patterned institutions and social relationships; and third, as a constellation of personalities, attitudes, and ideas (Wirth 1938: 18–19).

Ecological Paradigm

Urban Ecology. From the first two of the above perspectives developed classical urban ecology (also known as human ecology). Classical ecology focused on the spatial-social organization of the city. Urban ecology with its evolutionary focus, and environmental terminology, borrowed heavily from plant and animal ecology. Thus, in urban ecology competition played a central explanatory role. The focus was on examining the independence and interdependence of specialized urban roles and functions (defined as recurrent patterns of behavior) within the society. According to ecologists, the spatial pattern of the metropolitan area developed not through planning or government actions but rather through competition for space influenced by the ecological patterns of invasion, succession, and segregation of new land usages and social groups.

Urbanism Perspective. The third perspective of the Chicago School was that of "urbanism." Urbanism, with its social psychological and behavioral emphasis on social problems, focused on the way urban life disrupted traditional ties to family and community. Urbanism examined the consequences of increasing levels of urbanization on the customs, mores, values, and behaviors of those residing in urban places. Conceptually, urbanism was seen as the behavioral response to urbanization. (Some of the classic works describing the effects of urbanization are Thomas and Znaniecki [1918–1920], Wirth [1928], Shaw [1928], and Zorbaugh [1929].) The focus on the consequences of urbanization for urban dwellers was heavily influenced by Georg Simmel's turn-of-the-century writings on how the mental stimulus of the size and density of city life results in the replacement of close, meaningful relationships with an anonymous, calculated sophistication (Simmel 1950).

The classic formulation of how the urbanization factors of size, density, and heterogeneity produce a unique way of life known as urbanism is Louis Wirth's influential essay "Urbanism as a Way of Life" (Wirth 1938). Although much challenged, Wirth's essay has remained influential for over half a century. The urbanism perspective is also sometimes refered to as the Wirthian perspective. Urbanism as a way of life was viewed as being economically successful but socially disruptive. Wirth suggested that urbanization and its components—size, density, and heterogeneity—are the independent variables that determine urbanism, that is, urban lifestyles and behaviors. Moreover, Wirth saw the relationship as being linear, with the larger, the denser, and the more heterogeneous the urban place, the more definite the consequences of urbanism as a way of life. The effects of urbanism were expected to apply in all urban contexts.

Burgess Hypothesis. The best-known product of the aggregate spatial-organizational focus was Ernest Burgess's well-known concentric-zone growth hypotheses. Burgess suggested that city growth is not random or haphazard but rather the consequence of ecological patterns. He sought to explain the evolution of urban land use patterns from simpler preindustrial forms to more complex patterns of segregated land usage for particular purposes (e.g., central business district [CBD], manufacturing, and residential zones) based on the evolutionary concept of competition for prime space. The Burgess hypothesis suggested that urban industrial cities grow radially through a series of concentric zones: from the valuable land of the CBD through the zone of transition, the zone of working men's homes, and the zone of better residences to the commuter's zone (Burgess

1924: 85–97). As a consequence of economic competition, land values are highest in the center of the city and decrease as one moves toward the periphery. Consequently, the city had an inverse relationship between the value of land and the economic status of those occupying it. That all of this seems commonsense to us today is a reflection of the degree to which somewhat bastardized versions of the hypothesis have become "general" knowledge. The growth hypothesis, by implying that change came from outside the neighborhood, and was more or less inevitable, also has affected real estate practices for 70 years. Few realtors are aware of it, but the "filter down" model of housing usage in which it was assumed that once change began in a neighborhood, it was virtually impossible to reverse the pattern would have negative effects for much of the twentieth century. Thus, for example, it was assumed by realtors and lending institutions that recycling older neighborhoods through gentrification was impossible.

Contemporary Theoretical Paradigms

The complementary ecological and Wirthian perspectives remained dominant in urban studies until the 1970s when the ecological model was challenged by the emergence of critical political-economy paradigms. These new paradigms, often identified during the 1980s as the "new urban sociology," discarded ecological models for theories based on neo-Marxist and conflict models (Smith and Timberlake 1992: 340). Political-economic perspectives differ in specifics, but all stress that urban growth is a consequence of capitalist modes of capital accumulation, conflictual class relations, and exploitation of the powerless (Gottdiener and Feagan 1988). Those espousing conflict models criticize the ecological model as being ahistorical and mechanistic and suggest that social conflict is an inevitable consequence of capitalist political economies. Thus, the ecological model is discounted for its reliance on transportation and communication technologies as major factors in the development of suburbs. Political-economic perspectives put greater emphasis on the deliberate and conscious conspiracy and manipulation of real estate and government interests to promote growth and profits. Thus, suburbanization, which the ecological paradigm explains in terms of land usage patterns and technological factors such as access to outer land through streetcar and automobile, is viewed as a consequence not of individual homeowner choices but of deliberate decisions of economic elites to disinvest in central cities and to manipulate real estate usage and markets for capital gain (Feagan and Parker 1990). Social inequality and social conflict within the city are seen as direct and inevitable consequences of capitalistic real estate and land usage patterns (Harvey 1973). Rather than the ecological focus on economic processes and technology, the political-economic theorists stress class conflict and deliberate action by economic and political elites.

Assumptions common to those adopting the political-economic paradigm are: "(1) Societal interaction is dominated by antagonistic social relationships. . . .

(2) Social development is unstable in societies with antagonistic owner relationships. Contradictions of development and inequalities of growth fuel antagonism and define the nature of political activities. (3) Power inequality is a basic element in societal relationships, and the exercise of power can be a factor in societal development. (4) No society can be adequately analyzed without reference to either its long-term history or its global context'' (Gottdiener and Feagan 1988: 174). The underlying assumption is that urban space in capitalistic cities "is developed according to a logic that is internal to capital itself" (Smith and LeFaivre 1984: 53).

Most, but not all, political-economy models are Marxist or neo-Marxist. A non-Marxian political-economy examination of how corporate and governmental elites manage property markets to sustain the urban growth machine at the expense of the use value of land to homeowners and communities is made by Logan and Molotch (1987). They suggest that land is valued both as an object of exchange to be bought and sold and as a place where one does business or lives. In the second usage, spatial places achieve a symbolic or sentimental value associated with hometown, jobs, neighborhood, and community. Urban growth machines of corporate political elites, on the other hand, are interested in land simply as an investment to be bought and sold. Thus, they want to create "a good business environment" and increase the market value of the land, regardless of the consequences for local communities and residences. "Use values of the majority are sacrificed for the exchange values of the few" (96). Community groups that value slow growth and local needs are thus in opposition to economic elites who profit from maintaining the growth machine.

Changing Spatial Patterns

Historical Patterns. For the nineteenth and the first half of the twentieth century, American industrial cities were relatively compact places with dense population concentration. Industrialization was built upon steam power, and steam power cannot easily be transported, accentuating centralization and concentration. Factories were concentrated in the zone of transition near the CBD and abutting the railroad lines that both brought the fuel (coal) to run the factories and provided the means to ship the goods that were produced. This in turn concentrated wholesale, storage, and distributing activities, and also population, near the factories. Low-quality crowded tenement residences for workers were built cheek by jowl with manufacturing plants. Low pay, long hours, and limited transportation technology meant that workers had to live within walking distance of the factories. Slum neighborhoods of densely packed tenements provided immigrant workers access to the factories, but at an excessive price in terms of family health and quality of life.

During the last quarter of the nineteenth century, inventions such as Otis's elevator and Jenny's steel frame building further increased central business district densities. Buildings for the first time in history were not supported by their thick outer walls (and could as a result go more than 10 stories high), and thus officeworkers could be stacked layer upon layer. Both the CBD offices, and the new department stores, could be reached by the new electric streetcars and, in the largest cities, electrified subways. All this led to concentration and competition for prime central space. The Burgess growth hypothesis reflected this era of industrial city concentration prior to the full centrifugal effect of the internal combustion engine.

Suburban Decentralization. Since World War II the overarching urbanization pattern has been one of decentralization and dispersion to the metropolitan periphery. Population, commercial, and industrial dispersion have reworked the metropolitan landscape. A monumental suburban housing boom followed the war, fueled by generous federal government housing and highway subsidies. Middle- and working-class ex-GIs and their new families rushed to take advantage of the new no-money-down 25-year mortgages. That virtually all open land was suburban, that suburban housing costs were often cheaper than urban rents, and that the postwar marriage and baby booms resulted in some 10 million new families further ensured that there would be a major suburban exodus (Palen 1995). The decades of the 1950s and 1960s saw the population of suburbs more than double from 35 to 84 million. By 1970 the suburbs had become demographically dominant, with the suburbs of metropolitan areas having more residents than the central cities.

In the United States the study of urbanization increasingly has a suburban focus. The 1990 census indicated that within metropolitan areas half again as many Americans now live in suburbs as central cities. The census recorded that overall some 115 million Americans lived in suburbs, while 78 million lived in central cities and 56 million in nonmetropolitan places. Suburban outer or edge cities also have come to dominate the economic landscape. Employment increasingly has a suburban zip code. Two times as many manufacturing jobs now are located in suburbs as in central cities. The industrial park has supplanted the central city factory. White-collar jobs have also suburbanized, with two thirds of America's office space now located in suburbia. Atlanta, the site of the 1996 Olympic Games, has an impressive downtown skyline, but only a quarter of Atlanta's office space is located in the CBD. Similarly, outer Dallas has three times the office space of the center city, while in the New York metropolitan area, northern New Jersey now has more offices than Manhattan.

Since 1980 the major commute has not been from suburb to city but from suburb to suburb. Places that once were bedroom suburbs now attract commuters. Plano, Texas, north of Dallas, for example, is now the national headquarters for five national corporations: Frito-Lay, Electronic Data Systems, Murata Business Systems, Southland Life Insurance, and J. C. Penny. The last moved its headquarters to Plano from New York City. Similarly, Sears in 1992 moved its 5,000 merchandise group employees from the world's tallest building, the 110-story Sears Tower in downtown Chicago, to suburban Hoffman Estates 35 miles to the northwest. The new headquarters, named Prairie Stone, occupies a former soybean field and includes 200 acres of reconstructed prairie and wetlands. The tallest building is 6 stories high. Metaphorically, Sears has gone from having its head in the urban clouds to planting itself in the suburban landscape. An examination of what has occurred in Washington, D.C. is illustrative of the national pattern. As of 1970 the District held half (46 percent) of the metropolitan area's jobs, while suburban Virginia and suburban Maryland each held a quarter (27 percent each). By 1990 the pattern had reversed. In spite of adding 78,000 jobs during the decade, the District's share of Washington metropolitan area jobs had shrunk to 29 percent. Suburban Maryland increased to 33 percent, and northern Virginia had the highest share, at 36 percent. Even with all its government jobs, 7 out of 10 Washington area workers are employed in the suburbs, and of those working in the city, 7 out of 10 live in the suburbs.

Outer Cities

In contrast to the Burgess model emphasizing the urban area growing outward in rings from a dominant central core, Harris and Ullman, following World War II, proposed a model that had growth occurring around discrete nuclei (Harris and Ullman 1945: 7–17). Known as the multiple nuclei theory, this polycentric model of functionally integrated nodes of economic activity, with access to communications and transportation technology, has come to best represent the spatial form of edge cities. Rather than being dominated by people and goods flows, the various economic nuclei serve as information and administration nodes.

Outer or edge cities differ from the old CBDs in a number of ways (Garreau 1991). First, they are difficult to define spatially since, unlike central cities, they commonly lack any clearly defined borders. They are not legal entities having clearly demarcated borders. Legally, they are nonplace places—having names but not legal status. Tysons Corner, located on the beltway in the Washington, D.C. metropolitan area, may be the largest shopping center in the region, and have more office space than Tucson, but it doesn't appear on Virginia state maps. Legally, Tysons Corner is just another part of Fairfax County, Virginia.

Second, outer cities differ from the old center cores, not because they are planned or because they are newer or because they have more glass and marble, but because the outer cities are private places. The old downtowns, whether planned or unplanned, were public spaces open to all. The regulations governing dress and behavior were the laws and ordinances passed by public officials elected by citizens of the jurisdiction. By contrast the outer retail and business cities are private property governed by rules promulgated by executives appointed by corporate boards. Thus, fundamental questions such as who can be in an edge city, and what they can and cannot do while there, are determined by corporate policy rather than elected representatives. Public looking, but privately owned, malls can exclude those soliciting funds for the Salvation Army, those proselytizing for a religious belief or political party, or those not meeting the required dress code (e.g., not wearing shoes, or street people having dirty or torn clothing). Even the mall or office park police aren't trained legal officers, but rather they are privately hired security guards dressed to look like police.

These outer cities administered by decree may be safe, but they are not democratic. While an attraction of the central downtowns is their variety and spontaneity, the outer cities promise predictability. For example, there are no street musicians but preselected music designed to be inoffensive. In many ways the privatization of public space, and public activities, represents nothing so modern as a shift back to the medieval and Renaissance concept of a city-state as a privately managed place controlled by an oligarchy. Remarkably, this shift from public to private control has occurred almost completely without public notice. It certainly has occurred without public discussion or debate. The once public city has been replaced by a privatized edge city.

Race and Ethnicity

One of the critical issues facing urban places is that of residential segregation. Historically, metropolitan area blacks and whites have resided in segregated neighborhoods (Farley and Allen 1987; Massey and Mullan 1984; Taeuber and Taeuber 1965). Research done through the 1970s indicated that for both cities and suburbs the in-movement of nonwhites commonly resulted in the out-movement of whites. With integration being only the period between the in-movement of the first blacks and the out-movement of the last whites, little long-term racial integration occurred (HUD 1978). Black suburbanization represented not integration so much as invasion-succession, with black suburbanization being substantially the expansion of ghettos across city lines.

This pattern has now changed. One still hears suburbs described as being lily white, but it less and less is a reliable generalization. One third of all metropolitan area blacks are now suburbanites. Residential segregation clearly still exists, but the contemporary model is more one of parallel growth rather than invasion-succession. The old idea of the racial tipping point has less empirical validity (Denton and Massey 1991). The succession model has less validity than commonly believed (Lee and Wood 1991). The rate of African-American suburbanization has exceeded that of whites for a quarter of a century, and three quarters of all African-American population growth is now in the suburbs (Palen 1995). However, old beliefs die hard. Some of those brought up to view black suburbanization as middle-class spillover don't seem really comfortable with the reality of substantial black middle-class suburbanization. In spite of the 1990 census counting over 620,000 black suburbanites in Washington, D.C., 500,000 in Atlanta, and over 400,000 in Los Angeles, black suburbanization is still sometimes spoken of as if it is an exception to the pattern. It isn't.

Hispanics, who will be the nation's largest minority population by the year 2010, have been rapidly suburbanizing. Some 43 percent of all Latinos live in suburbs, and Hispanics accounted for a quarter of all the suburban population gain from 1980 to 1990 (Frey and O'Hare 1993: 32). As with the Anglo population, poorer Latinos live in central city neighborhoods, while the more affluent have outlying residences.

Asians, the nation's fastest growing minority group, are often thought of as residing primarily in central city Chinatowns, Little Tokyos, or Koreatowns. However, as a group, Asians are more suburban than the white population, with half of all Asians (50.6 percent) being suburban residents. In Washington, D.C., for example, most Koreans live in suburban Fairfax and Montgomery counties. Only 800 of the 44,000 Koreans in the Washington area actually live in the District (Palen 1995). While poorer immigrants still gravitate toward the city, better-educated Asian immigrants now settle directly in the suburbs where employment opportunities are greatest, bypassing the traditional American pattern of settling first in the central cities.

DIRECTIONS FOR FURTHER RESEARCH

Urbanization, historically a relatively new phenomenon, has become a worldwide process. Within a decade the world will for the first time have over half its population in urban places. In the United States the ecological model of urban spatial-social growth, with its economic emphasis and weight given to communication and transportation technologies, was dominant from the 1920s to the 1970s. More recently, political-economic paradigms, stressing conflict between the economic elites pushing the urban growth machine and the needs of communities, have had theoretical dominance. Spatially, American urban areas have been undergoing decentralization and dispersion. The bulk of the nation's population, retail trade, manufacturing, and office space is now located in the suburbs. Privately governed edge cities with vague boundaries increasingly displace the role of the public and legally defined central city. Racially and ethnically, suburbs are now heterogeneous, housing a third of all metropolitan area blacks, over 4 out of 10 Hispanics, and over half of all Asians. As first suggested by Park in the 1920s, in urban places there remains a close relationship between spatial processes and social relationships.

As we enter the new century, studies of American urbanization need to be done on the consequences of being a predominantly suburban nation. For example, are inner-ring suburbs replicating central city patterns of decline? If so, can these patterns be reversed? More studies also are needed on the characteristics and consequences for metropolitan areas of edge cities. Can we spatially define such areas? What are their dominant economic activities? Who lives there? Are there regional differences?

Also badly needed is case study research on minorities in suburbs. There are many case studies of central city communities but few discussing what it means to be a black (Hispanic, Asian) suburbanite. Do patterns differ by region or economic activities of central cities? Does the region of the country make a difference, or are all patterns now national? The most pressing research questions of the early twenty-first century concern what is occurring on the outer urban frontier.

REFERENCES

Burgess, Ernest. 1924. "The Growth of the City: An Introduction to a Research Project." *Publications of the American Sociological Society* 18: 85–97.

Denton, Nancy, and Douglass S. Massey. 1991. "Patterns of Neighborhood Transition in a Multiethnic World: U.S. Metropolitan Areas 1970–1980." *Demography* 28: 41–63.

Farley, Reynolds, and Walter R. Allen. 1987. *The Color Line and the Quality of American Life.* New York: Russell Sage Foundation.

Feagan, Joe, and Robert Parker. 1990. *Building American Cities: The Real Estate Game.* Englewood Cliffs, NJ: Prentice-Hall.

Frey, William H., and William P. O'Hare. 1993. "Vivano los Suburbios!" *American Demographics* (April): 30–37.

Garreau, Joel. 1991. *Edge City: Life on the New Frontier.* New York: Doubleday.

Gottdiener, Mark, and Joe Feagan. 1988. "The Paradigm Shift in Urban Sociology." *Urban Affairs Quarterly* 24 (December): 171–174.

Harris, Chauncy, and Edward Ullman. 1945. "The Nature of Cities." *Annals of the Academy of Political and Social Sciences* 242: 7–17.

Harvey, David. 1973. *Social Justice and the City.* London: Edward Arnold.

Hawley, Amos H. 1981. *Urban Society: An Ecological Approach.* New York: John Wiley.

HUD. 1978. *1978 HUD Survey on the Quality of Community Life: A Data Book.* Washington, D.C.: U.S. Department of Housing and Human Development.

Lee, Barrett A., and Peter B. Wood. 1991. "Is Neighborhood Racial Succession Place Specific?" *Demography* 28: 21–40.

Logan, John, and Harvey Molotch. 1987. *Urban Fortunes: The Political Economy of Place.* Berkeley: University of California Press.

Massey, Douglas S., and Brendan P. Mullan. 1984. "Processes of Hispanic and Black Spatial Assimilation." *American Journal of Sociology* 89: 836–879.

Palen, J. John. 1995. *The Suburbs.* New York: McGraw-Hill.

Park, Robert E., Ernest W. Burgess, and Roderick D. McKenzie. 1925. *The City.* Chicago: University of Chicago Press.

Shaw, Clifford R. 1928. *The Jack Roller.* Chicago: University of Chicago Press.

Simmel, Georg. 1950. "The Metropolis and Mental Life." In *The Sociology of Georg Simmel.* Translated by Kurt H. Wolff. Glencoe, IL: Free Press.

Smith, David A., and Michael F. Timberlake. 1992. "The New Urban Sociology." In J. John Palen, ed., *The Urban World.* New York: McGraw-Hill.

Smith, Neil, and Michele LeFaivre. 1984. "A Class Analysis of Gentrification." In J. John Palen and Bruce London, eds., *Gentrification, Displacement and Neighborhood Revitalization.* Albany: State University of New York.

Taeuber, Karl E., and Alma F. Taeuber. 1965. *Negroes in Cities: Residential Segregation and Neighborhood Change.* Chicago: Aldine.

Thomas, W. I., and Florian Znaniecki. 1918–1920. *The Polish Peasant in Europe and America.* 5 vols. Chicago: University of Chicago Press.

Wirth, Louis. 1925. *The Ghetto*. Chicago: University of Chicago Press.
Wirth, Louis. 1938. "Urbanism as a Way of Life." *American Journal of Sociology* 44 (July): 1–24.
Zorbaugh, Harvey W. 1929. *The Gold Coast and the Slum*. Chicago: University of Chicago Press.

Chapter 4

Community

Larry Lyon and Jason Miller

"Community" is a unique concept that no other idea in urban theory and research approaches in philosophical import, romantic nostalgia, or breadth of meaning. Janet Abu-Lughod (1991: 269) notes that "the concept of community occupies a privileged place in the romantic symbolic lexicon of America, as significant as mother, apple pie, and democracy." Roland Warren (1978: 156) compares community to St. Augustine's definition of God: "an infinite circle whose center is everywhere and whose periphery is nowhere." Robert Nisbet (1966: 2) defines community as "a fusion of feeling and thought, of identity and commitment, of membership and volition." Obviously, community is something considerably different than a census tract, urbanized area, or some other precise, neutral term. We are considering a concept as much in the domain of poets and politicians as urban researchers and city planners. While this chapter will focus on how community is understood in urban research and theory, it is important to remember that we share this remarkable concept with audiences far beyond our traditional urban purview.

DEFINING COMMUNITY

One of the first American social scientists to define community was Robert Park. Park and his colleagues at the University of Chicago established community as a central concept in their ecological method of urban research: "The essential characteristics of a community, so conceived, are those of: (1) a population territorially organized, (2) more or less completely rooted in the soil it occupies, (3) its individual units living in a relationship of mutual interdependence" (Park 1936: 3).

Less than 20 years after Park's initial effort, George Hillery, Jr. (1955) found

94 separate published definitions of community. Hillery encountered definitions of community as a group process, social system, geographic place, consciousness of kind, totality of attitudes, common lifestyle, the possession of common ends, local self-sufficiency, and on and on. The only area of complete agreement was the rather obvious point that communities are made up of people. Fortunately, some areas of partial agreement emerged. Hillery found that 69 of his 94 community definitions contained the common elements of area, common ties, and social interaction. Thus, if we defined a community as people living within a specific *area*, sharing common *ties*, and *interacting* with one another, we would have a definition that largely agrees with most of the definitions Hillery analyzed and a definition very much like Park's initial concept. Still, the type and degree of these three elements remain nebulous. The area of the community might be a politically defined municipal boundary, an economically defined zone of metropolitan dominance, or a psychologically defined neighborhood. Likewise, the basis of the common ties or bonds (family, ethnicity, propinquity, social class, religion), as well as the amount and quality of social interaction, can vary. So, we are still left with a definition broad enough to include a sprawling, multicounty metropolis, an ethnic neighborhood, or a largely rural village.

Although many analysts view the broad and sometimes competing definitions of community as a problem requiring more specific definitions (Hillery 1963; Rossi 1972; Bernard 1973), another and perhaps more accepted view is that the multiple definitions of community indicate the importance and richness of the term (Day and Murdoch 1993). As Albert Hunter (1975: 538) argues, "[T]he very looseness of the concept [community] is valuable in providing a common whetstone on which to sharpen the cutting edge of competing ideas." We will examine a number of "competing ideas" about community in this chapter, but most can be traced from the same original source—Ferdinand Tönnies.

THE ORIGINS OF COMMUNITY THEORY: TÖNNIES'S *GEMEINSCHAFT UND GESELLSCHAFT*

If it is possible to mark the beginning of community theory, it is probably 1887, with the publication of Tönnies's book *Gemeinschaft und Gesellschaft* (usually translated as *Community and Society* [1963]). Tönnies contrasted the types of human relationships appearing in extended families or rural villages (*Gemeinschaft*) with those found in emerging modern, capitalist states (*Gesellschaft*).

Gemeinschaft-like relationships are based on a natural will (*Wesenwille*) that includes sentiment, tradition, and common bonds. This natural will is based on either the family or the "soil" (i.e., living and working in a common place). *Gemeinschaft* is characterized by a strong identification with the community, emotionalism, traditionalism, and holistic conceptions of other members of the community (i.e., viewing another as a total person rather than only as a segment of his status or viewing a person as significant in her own right rather than as a means to an end). In contrast, *Gesellschaft*-like relationships are based on a rational will (*Kurwille*) that includes rationality, individualism, and emotional disengagement. The basis for this rational will is urban, industrial capitalism. *Gesellschaft* is characterized by little identification with the community, affective neutrality, legalism, and segmental relations. In short, *Gesellschaft* is the opposite of *Gemeinschaft*.

Tönnies, in common with many of his contemporaries (e.g., Durkheim's movement from mechanical to organic solidarity, Weber's focus on increasing rationalization, and Simmel's blasé attitude), held that European social relationships were becoming more *Gesellschaft*-like. Thus, concern with the quality and quantity of *Gemeinschaft*-like relationships in an increasingly *Gesellschaft*-dominated society (i.e., the community question) became one of the basic and continuing themes in community research. One of the most important applications illustrating this concern with the potential loss of *Gemeinschaft* is the typological approach.

THE TYPOLOGICAL APPROACH: COMMUNITY ON A RURAL/URBAN CONTINUUM

Although Max Weber pioneered the methodology of ideal types, Tönnies's use of contrasting, opposite ideal types to create a rural/urban continuum became one of the most common and useful analytic tools for community research. We can find this concept reflected in many of the most important American theoretical efforts including Becker's (1957) sacred/secular continuum and Parsons's pattern variables (Parson and Shils 1951). Although the causes, speed, and degree of movement from *Gemeinschaft* to *Gesellschaft* differ by theorist, all insist that Western society has evolved into a culture fundamentally different from earlier *Gemeinschaft*-like societies. However, two major issues and potential applications remain for the rural/urban continuum.

First is the degree to which rural and urban lifestyles still differ in a mobile, modern, postindustrial, mass society such as ours. Many analysts conclude significant rural/urban lifestyle differences no longer exist (Dewey 1960; Palen 1979; Abu-Lughod 1991), but the evidence is largely anecdotal. In fact, recent empirical research (such as the surveys by Claude Fischer considered later in this chapter) confirms what would seem to be obvious: The lifestyles of residents in cities like New York (population 7,322,546) still differ significantly from those in small towns such as New London, Texas (population 916). The rural/urban continuum remains a potentially powerful tool to explain these differences.

Second, the social disorganization plaguing the traditionally rural, *Gemeinschaft*-based, developing societies as they become increasingly urban and *Gesellschaft*-like desperately needs greater insight. Over 20 years ago, Robert Nisbet (1966) and Jessie Bernard (1973) suggested this European-based continuum may aid our understanding of these Asian and African societies. Since that time, the threats of civil war, AIDS (acquired immunodeficiency syndrome), and famine have all grown along with our need to understand and ameliorate the social disorganization of lost *Gemeinschaft*.

THE CHICAGO SCHOOL AND THE ECOLOGICAL APPROACH

Community became a significant term in the urban research vocabulary largely through the efforts of Robert Park and his colleagues at the University of Chicago. Employing ecological terms such as *competition*, *symbiosis*, *evolution*, and *dominance*, they suggested that the scientific concepts developed in biology could successfully explain the structure and dynamics of American cities. Community was the most important component in their ecological complex since it represented the basic, biotic, Darwinian part of urban existence.

Tönnies's theory of increasingly *Gesellschaft*-like relationships can be seen throughout the human ecology emphasis of the Chicago School. The most famous example is in Louis Wirth's "Urbanism as a Way of Life" (1938), which explains how three ecological variables—population size, density, and heterogeneity—combine to produce a more *Gesellschaft*-like lifestyle. Wirth, however, was not the only Chicago sociologist to deal with movement toward *Gesellschaft*-like relationships. Some of the best-known portraits of the weakened social integration and accompanying disorganization that beset Chicago during the rapid urbanization of the 1920s can be found in Nels Anderson's *The Hobo* (1923), Thrasher's *The Gang* (1927), Zorbaugh's *Gold Coast and Slum* (1929), Wirth's *The Ghetto* (1928), Shaw's *The Jack-roller, a Delinquent Boy's Own Story* (1930), and Cressey's *The Taxi Dance Hall* (1932).

The most influential of the Chicago School's contributions came from their work on spatial patterning, with Burgess's (1925) concentric zone model of urban growth and Zorbaugh's (1926) analysis of natural areas, leading to more sophisticated research in urban economics (Hoyt 1939) and geography (Bell 1955). This ecological approach (Hawley 1950; Duncan 1959; Berry and Kasarda 1977) moved away from traditional community concerns since its emphasis on precise measures of precise places did not lend itself to the more subjective, more qualitative issues traditionally associated with the community. Thus, the ecological approach, while becoming the dominant paradigm for urban analysis in the 1950s and 1960s, lost its original concern with community. Yet the potential for ecological explanation of the *Gesellschaft/Gemeinschaft* mix originally posited by Wirth remains, and important research continues in this area (Tittle 1989; Wilson 1993).

HOLISTIC COMMUNITY STUDIES

While the ecological approach was flourishing at Chicago, Robert and Helen Lynd (1929) were popularizing another form of community research: holistic studies that described all the interrelated parts of community. Their book, *Middletown*, became a bestseller and a classic community study. It is the best-known, the most widely cited, and probably the most influential community study ever published. A primary reason for *Middletown*'s significance and acceptance lay in the rich, relatively objective description of small-town life. Muncie is described in very much the same way as an anthropologist would detail the activities of a preindustrial village. The research methods were decidedly eclectic, including participant observation, content analysis of historical records, and surveys. *Middletown* describes the various activities and beliefs of Muncie residents in copious detail; but, of equal importance, the Lynds also attempted to explain why Muncie is the way it is. For example, they explained how religious and political values supported business interests and why residents could claim that there were no class differences in Muncie when their own research revealed class difference so pervasive as to affect virtually every aspect of life.

The publication of *Middletown* began a long series of holistic community studies. In fact, the holistic approach has provided some of the most significant applications of community theory and research—from the Chicago studies mentioned earlier and the "Yankee City" studies of W. Lloyd Warner during the 1940s to the more recent works on urban, typically ethnic, neighborhoods (e.g., Suttles 1968; Stack 1974; Horowitz 1983; E. Anderson 1990). These studies typically employ ethnographic techniques focusing on the quality of social interactions within a particular locality and, as such, closely follow the community tradition of concern for *Gemeinschaft*. Some debate exists over how much we have learned from these holistic studies (Stein 1960; Bell and Newby 1972; Warren and Lyon 1988; Abu-Lughod 1991), but this approach certainly documents and popularizes the decline and tenacity of *Gemeinschaft* in vivid ways beyond the realm of other methods.

THE RISE AND FALL OF COMMUNITY POWER

Serious, extended study of community power began with the publication of Floyd Hunter's *Community Power Structure* in 1953. Hunter, who was frustrated with Atlanta's inability to experience meaningful social change, wanted to discover the "real" leaders and pressure them for significant local improvement. Using a variety of methods, most of which were based on face-to-face interviews with strategically placed people in Atlanta, Hunter uncovered a group of businessmen who met frequently to determine the future of Atlanta. In short, Hunter concluded, democracy was not operating as it should. The elected officials of the community had relatively little influence on important, supposedly public, decisions.

Naturally, Hunter's findings were controversial. Political scientists were especially skeptical, not only of Hunter's findings but of his research methods as well. Robert Dahl's *Who Governs?* (1961), a study of decision making in New Haven, set the tone for the polemic that followed. Dahl avoided the interview techniques used by Hunter that asked for the names of powerful people. Rather, he focused on actual decisions, identified conflicting positions and their supporters, and determined whose views prevailed. Dahl's findings were in many ways the exact opposite of Hunter's. Dahl found a pluralistic democracy in New Haven with an elected official, the mayor, playing the pivotal role in most major community decisions.

A remarkable quantity of research and debate followed these two books. During the 1960s and early 1970s, hundreds of articles and books describing local power distribution and voluminous exchanges between pluralists and elitists were published. Equally remarkable is how this vein of research has disappeared. Exactly why this concern with local politics rose and fell so rapidly is open to debate (Walton 1976; Warren 1977; Waste 1986), but the outpouring of research that characterized the 1960s has clearly ended (Schmandt and Wendel 1988). Still, as a result of that research and debate, it is now possible to measure the local distribution of power (even though these distributions are seldom determined anymore). Also, we now know that power structures are complex, multidimensional phenomena (Schumaker 1993) that can vary considerably among communities (Grimes et al. 1976). Finally, these studies have discovered three determinants of local power distribution: (1) The larger the community's population, (2) the more diversified its economy, and (3) the less "reformed" its formal political structure, the more pluralistic the community's decision making (Lyon 1989).

It is doubtful that we will again witness the concern with community power that occurred in the 1960s. Since the statistical relationships between who governed locally and what happened locally proved to be disappointingly small, it is difficult now to justify community power research of such magnitude. The one area where local elites appear to matter significantly is community growth (Lyon, Felice, and Perryman 1981), but that field has emerged with little reference to the community power literature. Instead, community growth emerged from the political economy approach.

THE NEO-MARXIST, POLITICAL ECONOMY APPROACH TO COMMUNITY

Karl Marx explained the movement toward *Gesellschaft* in terms of a change in the "means of production," in this case, a change from agricultural production based on the land to industrial production based on the factory. Marx's macroanalysis viewed the city as relatively unimportant. However, his colleague Friedrich Engels devoted much of his writings to describing urban capitalism in ways reflecting the traditional community emphasis on social interaction. In *The Condition of the Working Class in England in 1844*, Engels describes the *Gesellschaft*-like conditions of the city in terms of unnatural alienation:

The very turmoil of the streets has something repulsive, something against which human nature rebels. . . . The brutal indifference, the unfeeling isolation of each in his private interest becomes the more repellent and offensive, the more these individuals are crowded together, within a limited space. (Engels 1973: 64)

Still, the city represented more than simply an extreme example of capitalist exploitation. In 1848, Marx and Engels, in the *Communist Manifesto* (1959), argued that the bourgeoisie had actually rendered a service to the proletariat by creating cities that have "rescued a considerable part of the population from the idiocy of rural life." Classical Marxism, then, holds an ambivalent view of the city. While the city manifested the most extreme evils of capitalism, it also provided the necessary conditions for the proletarian class consciousness. In either case, however, it remained only a reflection of the larger, capitalistic society. The city is not the major focus of classic Marxist analysis. Still, a neo-Marxist approach finally did make it to the city, but its timing left something to be desired.

Based on the pioneering, paradigm-shifting work of British geographer David Harvey (*Social Justice and the City*, 1973) and Spanish/French sociologist Manuel Castells (*The Urban Question*, 1977), an urban analysis with a distinctly Marxist heritage began to emerge and quickly grow. This neo-Marxist, or conflict, or political economy approach found very little in the urban environment that reflected urban ecology's concern with functional integration, economic competition of a free market, and the common good. Rather, the city is viewed as the product of an unequal distribution of power (Walton 1981; Gottdiener and Feagin 1988). Those who own the means of production use political power to guarantee that class conflicts will be resolved in ways that benefit the ruling class (Zukin 1980). The urban environment, then, reflects class struggles—struggles, to date, won by the capitalist class. However, an initial goal of this new approach was not to merely document the urban class struggle but to change the outcome. By the late 1970s, economists William Tabb and Larry Sawers (1978: 19) argue for the relevance of a neo-Marxist approach by noting that "the popular forces for change are building even as the crisis of capitalism deepens. We do not await this 'inevitable' occurrence. We put our scholarship at the service of the class forces which will bring about this transition."

Unfortunately, by the late 1980s and the early 1990s, the "transition" was going the other way. Just as the neo-Marxist approach to urban analysis was becoming the dominant urban paradigm, the European societies nominally based on Marxist precepts began moving abruptly and quickly toward capitalism. In the preface to his excellent book *supporting* neo-Marxist urban analysis, Ira Katznelson (1992: vii) acknowledges this recent development.

Defeated in the East and discredited in the West, and lacking in knowledgeable or popular support, Marxism has broken down as an ideology and as a guide to governance. . . . And even if Marxism remains an important analytical tool and critical resource in countries that are capitalist and democratic, why treat Marxism and the *city*? Over the timespan of its development . . . Marxism has had relatively little to say about cities.

Since he continued to write his book, Katznelson obviously and correctly concludes that the approach still has merit, but the point remains that it is now harder to argue for a neo-Marxist urban analysis than it was 10 years ago.

One new avenue for neo-Marxist research is focusing on change in Eastern European cities after the fall of communism (Harloe, Szelenyi, and Andruz 1992). A more popular response is to ignore the local focus and Marxist underpinnings and use the broader, less ideological concept of "political economy" that emerged during the 1980s. For example, John Walton (1993: 301) discusses neither the lack of traditional theoretical concern with the city (because the globalization of labor markets by international capitalism makes the city an effect rather than cause) nor the fall of communism (because political economy has moved beyond its Marxist origins) in declaring that the political economy approach "became the predominant, if not the exclusive orientation in the 1980s," while admitting that "some of its former enthusiasts [now] look to new sources of inspiration." Walton, among others (see also Pahl 1989), has argued for supplementing political economy's traditional emphasis on "structure" with "culture" and "agency." The degree to which "new sources of inspiration" can be incorporated may hold the key to the continuing predominance of the political economy paradigm. Ironically, these new sources may also move the paradigm back to local concerns more traditionally associated with the community (Flanagan 1993).

THE COMMUNITY AS A GROWTH MACHINE

One of the most enduring contributions of the neo-Marxist approach comes from the view of the community as a "growth machine." Harvey Molotch (1976: 313), in one of the most widely cited urban articles in the last quarter of this century, developed the growth machine thesis by noting that "this organized effort to affect the outcome of growth distribution is the essence of local government as a dynamic political force. It is not the only function of government, but it is the key one and, ironically, the one most ignored." After Molotch's article, local growth was no longer ignored. An explosion of related research followed.

While the thrust of Molotch's original article was on the cause of urban growth, much of the subsequent research has been directed toward the negative effects of growth and ways in which "grassroots" local groups can fight and defeat the growth machine (Trounstine and Christensen 1982; Swanstrom 1985; Fainstein et al. 1986; Logan and Molotch 1987). In fact, fighting the local growth machine may be the 1990s equivalent of the 1970s fight against capitalism referred to in the earlier Tabb and Sawers quotation. If so, the fight is not an easy one. Other research has documented the failures of antigrowth crusaders (Molotch 1988; Logan and Zhou 1989; Vogel and Swanson 1989; Schneider and Teske 1993). Many of the failures are explained by the ability of the growth machine to convince local residents of the necessity of a "good business climate'' to create jobs and expand the tax base. However, the broad community support for local growth seems to exceed even the considerable manipulative powers of the growth machine coalition. Paul Peterson argues that cities will seek growth not simply because elites support it but because cities that do not grow will stagnate and decline. Peterson's analysis is similar to Molotch's but does not question the local value of growth. According to Peterson (1981: 143), local elites who seek growth ''will not be in sharp conflict with the interests of the community as a whole'' and those who oppose growth are really advocates of ''residential exclusivity.''

It appears that most communities desire growth because most people believe the local effects will be positive. Is growth positive? Remarkably, what remains to be done in this field is a thorough examination of the effects of growth (Vogel and Swanson 1989). In spite of all the research on why communities grow, and if they should grow, and how to stop them from growing or making them grow faster, definitive analysis on the effects of growth is scarce. Mark Schneider's (1992) recent study of the fiscal effects of growth in suburban communities suggests that while local economic growth does indeed lead to lower taxes and a stronger tax base, the payoff is less today than it was in the 1970s and may no longer justify the increases in congestion and pollution. However, the increase in congestion and pollution is never demonstrated beyond the case study level (e.g., Feagin 1988). The causal specifications between different kinds of growth (population, economic, geographic) and different community characteristics (unemployment, wage levels, crime rate, housing costs) are unknown. Most growth machine theorists posit growth advantages for large property owners, but the new jobs ideology is targeted to the working class. Class and race differences in the payoff for local growth are clearly important but also unknown.

NETWORK ANALYSIS AND THE COMMUNITY QUESTION

The nature of social interaction within an increasingly *Gesellschaft*-dominated society has been a topic of theoretical and analytical interest since the writings of Tönnies. Until recently, most of the research in the area was composed of ethnographies on suburbs or urban neighborhoods (Whyte 1955; Berger 1960; Suttles 1968) that typically found higher levels of local interaction than one would predict from the writings of Tönnies, Simmel, Wirth, and Durkheim. Additional evidence for *Gemeinschaft* relationships soon emerged from a more objective type of community research. With the advances in survey research and the development of powerful, computer-supported tools for the statistical analysis of social networks, the quantity and quality of social interactions could be empirically assessed.

Barry Wellman (1979) was among the first to demonstrate the applications of network analysis by positing three possible answers to the community question: (1) community *lost*, with socially isolated, blasé, alienated local residents predicted by Wirth et al.; (2) community *saved*, with socially integrated neighborhoods replete with close personal relationships such as those found in the ethnographies of ethnic neighborhoods; and (3) community *liberated*, with most important social interactions taking place outside the local community (e.g., at work or via kinship and friendship groups spread over large geographic areas). Based on the networks of social interaction reported in his surveys in East York (a working-class neighborhood in Toronto), Wellman concluded that community is definitely not lost, partially saved, and clearly liberated. Significant social interaction occurs; some of it is within the neighborhood, but much of it is outside East York.

Claude Fischer (1982) extended Wellman's analysis by surveying a larger and broader sample that included residents with substantial variations in social class, family status, and residence (urban San Francisco, suburban, small-town, and rural north California). Fischer found social class to be extremely important in defining the nature of social interactions, with what Wellman called the "community liberated" arrangement being especially common among higher-class respondents. They have the means and inclination to move beyond their neighborhoods and establish broad, metropolitan social networks.

Of special relevance for this chapter is Fischer's finding that significant rural/urban differences in social interaction exist beyond those associated with social class and family status. Urban residents, for example, are much less likely to have relatives in their social networks than their rural and small-town counterparts. Other rural/urban differences include subculture participation, the types of exchanges between associates and friends, the organizational basis of friendship, and the geographical dispersion of friends. A major conclusion, then, from Fischer's analysis relates to the rural/urban continuum approach discussed earlier—the rural/urban distinction is a real one in U.S. lifestyles that has yet to disappear.

Network analysis is especially well suited to address the community question. Yet after the promising beginnings by Wellman and Fischer, it seems to have lost its way. Much of the newer research is concerned with methods more than substance, and even when the nature of human relationships is the primary focus, the community question is seldom addressed. For example, in Wellman's second survey of East York (Wellman and Wortley 1990), the community "lost," "saved," and "liberated" positions are only tangentially and briefly considered.

THE FUTURE ROLE OF COMMUNITY IN URBAN RESEARCH

This survey of how the community has fared in urban research does not give much encouragement for its future relevance in the field.

- Not much has been done to expand on Tönnies's theory of *Gemeinschaft/Gesellschaft* since Talcott Parsons's work of over 30 years ago. The typologies it inspired may have relevance to developing societies, but little has been done along those lines.

- The ecological approach long ago lost its interest in community, and while holistic community studies continue the *Middletown* tradition, they are somewhat removed from the lines of research that predominate the urban journals. They often resemble journalistic descriptions of troubled neighborhoods rather than the more theoretical, methodologically eclectic, holistic approach pioneered by the Lynds.

- The community rose to an extremely high level of research prominence during the community power debates of the 1960s, but the genre is almost nonexistent today.

- The neo-Marxist, or more correctly, the political economy paradigm, dominates most urban research, and the role of community is limited. While Engels was clearly concerned with how people lived, today's analysis, with its global, structural focus, seems far removed from most community-type questions. The growth machine approach is probably the branch of political economy research most tied to traditional community concerns, especially those that emphasize elite actions.

- The type of current urban research most closely associated with typical community concerns is network analysis. However, most of the research published in this area has little or nothing to do with community.

Thus, the conclusion of this review may seem obvious—the community once mattered a lot, but changes in society and social science have made it irrelevant for most of the major urban approaches today—but the actual importance of community may be greater than this review would indicate, for two reasons.

First, too much can be made of paradigms and approaches to urban research. While they are handy ways to categorize a complex field, most of us do not think and work within a single paradigm. Roland Warren (1983: 85) argues for "a multiplicity of paradigms. Those which endure, despite their shortcomings, will find supporters and utilizers only because they can do some things—though not all things—better than can their alternatives." We would go beyond Warren and posit that many of us do not work within *any* paradigm. In a review of every article published in the *Urban Affairs Quarterly* between 1965 and 1987, Schmandt and Wendel (1988: 15) conclude that while two "upper-range" theoretical approaches predominate—public choice (similar to what is referred to in our review as ecological) and neo-Marxist—"neither of the two models enjoys wide acceptance among urban scholars. . . . The reality is that the direction and limits of the field have been determined not by reference to theoretical constructs or paradigms but by what urban analysts have chosen to research." Since most urban researchers are not tied to paradigms, community's lack of significance in the major paradigms is not necessarily an indication of its lack of relevance.

Second, because community is different from most other urban concepts—more subjective, more qualitative, more humanistic—it will not typically flourish in a field that Schmandt and Wendel (1988: 24) characterized by its "conceptualization of the city as a legal-political unit" and "obscur[ing] . . . the classical notion of the city as a social collectivity designed to aid its members in their quest for the good life." Thus, it is often outside the urban mainstream where the greatest contributions of community research and analysis can be found. *Habits of the Heart* (Bellah et al. 1985) contrasted community with individualism in ways that not only influenced social scientists but initiated a national conversation about American values. Rupert Wilkinson makes similar use of community in his book *The Pursuit of American Character* (1988). David Hummon, in *Commonplaces* (1990), shows that what we believe about where we live and how it differs from beliefs about where others live is a key to understanding how we "make sense" of our world. These important books on community do not neatly fit into any of the categories discussed in this review, and their subject matter seldom appears in our urban research journals.

Now it may be argued that the kind of community discussed in works such as *Habits of the Heart* has little to do with the locality-specific issues associated with urban research. Yet this type of analysis is certainly tied to how we live and interact with one another, which was, of course, the original intent of the term as conceived by Tönnies. It may also be argued that *how* we live has less and less to do with *where* we live in our modern, mass society, but the opposite may actually be true. Claude Fischer (1991) notes that due to rising levels of (1) residential stability, (2) suburban government, (3) local homogeneity, and (4) home ownership, "Americans are more 'rooted,' practically and sentimentally, to their communities than ever before." If this is true, urban research based on the concept of community could contribute more to understanding how we interact with one another and how we make sense out of our lives than much of what is done in the more traditional urban approaches.

REFERENCES

Abu-Lughod, Janet L. 1991. *Changing Cities: Urban Sociology.* New York: Harper-Collins.

Anderson, Elijah. 1990. *Streetwise: Race, Class, and Change in an Urban Community.* Chicago: University of Chicago Press.

Anderson, Nels. 1923. *The Hobo.* Chicago: University of Chicago Press.

Becker, Howard P. 1957. "Current Sacred-Secular Theory and Its Development." In Howard Becker and Alvin Boskoff, eds., *Modern Sociological Theory in Continuity and Change.* New York: Dryden Press.

Bell, Colin, and Howard Newby. 1972. *Community Studies: An Introduction to the Sociology of Local Community.* New York: Praeger Publishers.

Bell, Wendell. 1955. *Social Area Analysis.* Stanford, CA: Stanford University Press.

Bellah, Robert N., Richard Madsen, William M. Sullivan, Ann Swidler, and Steven M. Tipton. 1985. *Habits of the Heart: Individualism and Commitment in American Life.* New York: Harper & Row.

Berger, Bennett M. 1960. *Working Class Suburb.* Berkeley: University of California Press.

Bernard, Jessie. 1973. *The Sociology of Community*. Glenview, IL: Scott, Foresman.

Berry, Brian J. L., and John D. Kasarda. 1977. *Contemporary Urban Ecology*. New York: Macmillan.

Burgess, Ernest. 1925. "The Growth of the City." In Robert Park, Ernest Burgess, and R. D. McKenzie, eds., *The City*. Chicago: University of Chicago Press.

Castells, Manuel. 1977. *The Urban Question*. Translated by Alan Sheridan. London: Edward Arnold Publishers.

Cressey, Paul Goalby. 1932. *The Taxi Dance Hall*. Chicago: University of Chicago Press.

Dahl, Robert. 1961. *Who Governs?* New Haven: Yale University Press.

Day, Graham, and Jonathan Murdoch. 1993. "Locality and Community: Coming to Terms with Place." *Sociological Review* 41:82–112.

Dewey, Richard. 1960. "The Rural-Urban Continuum." *American Journal of Sociology* 66:60–66.

Duncan, Otis Dudley. 1959. "Human Ecology and Population Studies." In Philip M. Hauser and Otis Dudley Duncan, eds., *The Study of Population*. Chicago: University of Chicago Press.

Engels, Friedrich. 1973. *The Condition of the Working Class in England in 1844*. Moscow: Progress Publishers.

Fainstein, Susan, N. I. Fainstein, R. C. Hill, D. R. Judd, and M. P. Smith. 1986. *Restructuring the City*. New York: Longman.

Feagin, Joe R. 1988. "Tallying the Social Costs of Urban Growth Under Capitalism: The Case of Houston." In Scott Cummings, ed., *Business Elites and Urban Development: Case Studies and Critical Perspectives*. Albany: State University of New York Press.

Fischer, Claude S. 1982. *To Dwell Among Friends: Personal Networks in Town and City*. Chicago: University of Chicago Press.

Fischer, Claude S. 1991. "Ambivalent Communities: How Americans Understand Their Localities." In Alan Wolfe, ed., *America at Century's End*. Los Angeles: University of California Press.

Flanagan, William G. 1993. *Contemporary Urban Sociology*. New York: Cambridge University Press.

Gottdiener, Mark, and Joe R. Feagin. 1988. "The Paradigm Shift in Urban Sociology." *Urban Affairs Quarterly* 24, no. 2: 163–187.

Grimes, Michael D., Charles M. Bonjean, J. Larry Lyon, and Robert Lineberry. 1976. "Community Structure and Leadership Arrangements." *American Sociological Review* 14, no. 4: 706–725.

Harloe, M., I. Szelenyi, and G. Andruz. 1992. *Cities after Socialism*. Oxford: Basil Blackwell.

Harvey, David. 1973. *Social Justice and the City*. Baltimore: Johns Hopkins University Press.

Hawley, Amos. 1950. *Human Ecology*. New York: Ronald Press.

Hillery, George A., Jr. 1955. "Definitions of Community: Areas of Agreement." *Rural Sociology* 20:779–791.

Hillery, George A., Jr. 1963. "Villages, Cities, and Total Institutions." *American Sociological Review* 28:779–791.

Horowitz, Ruth. 1983. *Honor and the American Dream*. New Brunswick, NJ: Rutgers University Press.

Hoyt, Homer. 1939. *The Structure and Growth of Residential Neighborhoods in American Cities.* Washington, D.C.: Federal Housing Administration.

Hummon, David M. 1990. *Commonplaces: Community Ideology and Identity in American Culture.* Albany: State University of New York Press.

Hunter, Albert. 1975. "The Loss of Community." *American Sociological Review* 40: 537–552.

Hunter, Floyd. 1953. *Community Power Structure.* Chapel Hill: University of North Carolina Press.

Katznelson, Ira. 1992. *Marxism and the City.* New York: Oxford University Press.

Logan, John R., and Harvey L. Molotch. 1987. *Urban Fortunes: The Political Economy of Place.* Berkeley: University of California Press.

Logan, John R., and Min Zhou. 1989. "Do Suburban Growth Controls Control Growth?" *American Sociological Review* 54:461–471.

Lynd, Robert S., and Helen M. Lynd. 1929. *Middletown.* New York: Harcourt Brace and Co.

Lyon, Larry. 1989. *The Community in Urban Society.* Lexington, MA: Lexington Books.

Lyon, Larry, Lawrence G. Felice, and M. Ray Perryman. 1981. "Community Power and Population Increase: An Empirical Test of the Growth Machine Model." *American Journal of Sociology* 86, no. 6: 1387–1399.

Marx, Karl, and Friedrich Engels. 1959. *Manifesto of the Communist Party.* In Lewis S. Feuer, ed., *Marx and Engels: Basic Writings on Politics and Philosophy.* Garden City, NY: Doubleday Anchor Books. (Originally published 1848)

Molotch, Harvey. 1976. "The City as a Growth Machine: Toward a Political Economy of Place." *American Journal of Sociology* 82:309–332.

Molotch, Harvey. 1988. "Strategies and Constraints of Growth Elites." In Scott Cummings, ed., *Business Elites and Urban Development: Case Studies and Critical Perspectives.* Albany: State University of New York Press.

Nisbet, Robert. 1966. *The Sociological Tradition.* New York: Basic Books.

Pahl, R. E. 1989. "Is the Emperor Naked? Some Questions on the Adequacy of Sociological Theory in Urban Research." *International Journal of Urban Regional Research* 13:709–720.

Palen, John J. 1979. "The Urban Nexus: Toward the Year 2000." In Amos Hawley, ed., *Societal Growth.* New York: Free Press.

Park, Robert E. 1936. "Human Ecology." *American Journal of Sociology* 42, no. 1: 1–15.

Parsons, Talcott, and Edward Shils, eds. 1951. *Toward a General Theory of Action.* Cambridge, MA: Harvard University Press.

Peterson, Paul E. 1981. *City Limits.* Chicago: University of Chicago Press.

Rossi, Peter H. 1972. "Community Social Indicators." In Angus Campbell and Phillip E. Converse, eds., *The Human Meaning of Social Change.* New York: Russell Sage Foundation.

Schmandt, Henry J., and George D. Wendel. 1988. "Urban Research 1965–1987: A Content Analysis of *Urban Affairs Quarterly.*" *Urban Affairs Quarterly* 24: 3–32.

Schneider, Mark. 1992. "Undermining the Growth Machine: The Missing Link between Local Economic Development and Fiscal Payoffs." *Journal of Politics* 54, no. 1: 214–231.

Schneider, Mark, and Paul Teske. 1993. "The Antigrowth Entrepreneur: Challenging the 'Equilibrium' of the Growth Machine." *Journal of Politics* 55, no. 3: 720–736.

Schumaker, Paul. 1993. "Estimating the First and (Some of the) Third Faces of Community Power." *Urban Affairs Quarterly* 28, no. 3: 441–461.

Shaw, Clifford. 1930. *The Jack-roller, a Delinquent Boy's Own Story*. Chicago: University of Chicago Press.

Stack, Carol B. 1974. *All Our Kin: Strategies for Survival in a Black Community*. New York: Harper & Row.

Stein, Maurice R. 1960. *The Eclipse of Community: An Interpretation of American Studies*. Princeton, NJ: Princeton University Press.

Suttles, Gerald D. 1968. *The Social Order of the Slum*. Chicago: University of Chicago Press.

Swanstrom, Todd. 1985. *The Crisis of Growth Politics: Cleveland, Kucinich, and the Challenge of Urban Population*. Philadelphia: Temple University Press.

Tabb, William K., and Larry Sawers, eds. 1978. *Marxism and the Metropolis*. New York: Oxford University Press.

Thrasher, Frederick M. 1927. *The Gang*. Chicago: University of Chicago Press.

Tittle, Charles R. 1989. "Influences on Urbanism: A Test of Predictions from Three Perspectives." *Social Problems* 36, no. 3 (July): 270–288.

Tönnies, Ferdinand. 1963. *Community and Society*. Edited by Charles P. Loomis. New York: Harper & Row. (Originally published 1887)

Trounstine, Philip J., and Terry Christensen. 1982. *Movers and Shakers*. New York: St. Martin's Press.

Vogel, Ronald K., and Bert E. Swanson. 1989. "The Growth Machine versus the Antigrowth Coalition: The Battle for Our Communities." *Urban Affairs Quarterly* 25, no. 1: 63–85.

Walton, John. 1976. "Community Power and the Retreat from Politics." *Social Problems* 23, no. 3: 292–303.

Walton, John. 1981. "The New Urban Sociology." *International Social Science Journal* 33: 374–390.

Walton, John. 1993. "Urban Sociology: The Contributions and Limits of Political Economy." In Judith Black and John Hagen, eds., *Annual Review of Sociology* 19. Palo Alto, CA: Annual Reviews Inc.

Warren, Roland. 1978. *The Community in America*. Chicago: Rand McNally and Company.

Warren, Roland. 1983. "Observations on the State of Community Theory." In Roland Warren and Larry Lyon, eds., *New Perspectives on the American Community*. Homewood, IL: Dorsey Press.

Warren, Roland, ed. 1977. *New Perspectives on the American Community*. 3rd ed. Chicago: Rand McNally and Company.

Warren, Roland, and Larry Lyon, eds. 1988. *New Perspectives on the American Community*. Homewood, IL: Dorsey Press.

Waste, Robert J., ed. 1986. *Community Power: Directions for Future Research*. Beverly Hills, CA: Sage.

Wellman, Barry. 1979. "The Community Question: The Intimate Network of East Yorkers." *American Journal of Sociology* 84, no. 5 (March): 1201–1231.

Wellman, Barry, and Scot Wortley. 1990. "Different Strokes from Different Folks: Communities and Social Support.'' *American Journal of Sociology* 96, no. 3: 558–588.

Whyte, William Foote. 1955. *Street Corner Society.* Chicago: University of Chicago Press.

Wilkinson, Rupert. 1988. *The Pursuit of American Character.* New York: Harper & Row.

Wilson, Thomas C. 1993. ''Urbanism and Kinship Bonds: A Test of Four Generalizations.'' *Social Forces* 71, no. 3 (March): 703–712.

Wirth, Louis. 1928. *The Ghetto.* Chicago: University of Chicago Press.

Wirth, Louis. 1938. ''Urbanism as a Way of Life.'' *American Journal of Sociology* 44: 1–24.

Zorbaugh, Harvey. 1926. ''The Natural Areas of the City.'' *Publications of the American Sociological Society* 20: 188–197

Zorbaugh, Harvey. 1929. *Gold Coast and Slum.* Chicago: University of Chicago Press.

Zukin, Sharon. 1980. ''A Decade of the New Urban Research.'' *Theory and Society* 9: 575–601.

Chapter 5

Power in Urban America

Bert E. Swanson

OVERVIEW—THE SCOPE OF COMMUNITY POWER STUDIES

The study of power moves with the ebb and flow of human events, from conflicts between princes, nation-states, and ideologies to the clash of civilizations (Huntington 1993). Power has been and continues to be a significant concept, whether the topic be war and peace, perquisites to democracy, or ''who gets what, when, and how?'' Power analysts have included virtually every formal decision-making setting from international to community policy making, as well as such informal centers of power as the Trilateral Commission, military-industrial complex, organizations, and small groups and committees.

Philosophers Plato, Aristotle, Machiavelli, Hobbes, Locke, Mill, Marx, and many others have long mused about power as they advanced many normative ideas about who should govern, to what end, and how. A blend of normative and empirical analysis of power has focused upon: What kind of political structures exist and which seems best? Who is best qualified to govern and who should rule? What is the role of power and influence in the political system and how should it be used? and What kinds of policies are adopted and which are the best policies for government to prescribe and implement? Answers to these questions appear to be very different, depending on which polity is studied, the era examined, and who conducted the analysis.

This discussion will focus primarily upon empirically based theories, concepts, methods, findings, and interpretations of power systems and dynamics. While most power studies have been conducted on American communities, there has been an ongoing exchange of ideas about national power, as well as political systems around the world. Rather than attempt to reconcile the apparent differences between competing schools of thought, this discussion will use them to clarify the variety of concepts, operational definitions, methods, and classification schemes and report on the correlates of power—contributing factors and consequences. It will also comment on the assessments by observers and identify some of the lessons learned from four decades of intensive power analysis.

Many of our first impressions about a self-governing society, modern democracy, and urban power were offered by travelogues, essayists, and journalists— de Tocqueville, Bryce, and Steffens. Early community studies of small towns used social class analysis where notions of power were secondary. The Lynds (1937) found wealth and income to be highly concentrated among the upper class, and power to be held in the hands of a single family in Muncie, Indiana. Warner and Lunt (1941) discovered six strata of socioeconomic status that distinguished the importance of residential location, religious affiliation, property ownership, symbolic behavior, and political participation in Newburyport, Massachusetts. Again, power was found to be concentrated in a handful of a few upper-class members who used it to promote their class interests.

Post–World War II sociologists, less wedded to social class analysis, discerned structural patterns of power that dominated big cities and the nation. Hunter (1953: 96), a former social worker who became aware that his professional advice was overruled by businessmen in Atlanta, used reputational and sociometric techniques to document the existence of a set of a half dozen stratified institutional pyramids. He identified some 40 leaders, essentially economic elites holding general influence and dominating community development. Incidentally, he also identified a black power structure that seemed to parallel the white-dominated general power structure. At the national level, Mills (1956) specifically dismissed the Marxian analysis of a ruling capitalist class pitted in a constant struggle against the working class and proposed the power elite thesis, which was made up of the "war lords," corporate chieftains, and "political directorate" challenge to the very essence of a democratic America.

Political scientists, primarily interested in public policy and decision making made by government, were quick to attack the power elite concept in the United States, which they believed was one of the most democratic nations in the world. Kaufman and Jones (1954: 209) declared of Hunter's version of power in Atlanta that he had "not given us a study of the power structure of Atlanta at all! Rather, he has set forth a portrait of one of the groups having some power over some things at some time." Dahl (1958) also rejected the "ruling elite model" of Mills and Hunter because their findings had not met his proposed strict test to determine if such a hypothetical ruling elite existed: (1) it be a well-defined group; (2) they be involved in those political decisions where their preferences run counter to others; and (3) the elite regularly prevailed.

A replacement of elite rule was empirically elaborated by Dahl's (1961) classic pluralistic view of urban power, one wherein power was effectively disaggregated and noncumulative. He found little overlap between social, economic, and political notables, as politicians shaped community issues, and their influence was specialized to policy arenas in New Haven. He enuciated the importance of the democratic creed whereby the electorate had significant indirect influence upon politicians. The demand for change would and could be handled through political competition that served as a fundamental constraint upon politicians, a crucial obstacle to powerful factions, and a stimulant to governments to ensure political liberties.

Students of community power were prolific in producing dozens of book-length studies and hundreds of articles of commentary and critiques on community power in America (for a bibliographic review, see Hawley and Svara 1972; Lief and Clark 1973). This outburst of research stimulated a number of symposia to find some common ground to this growing field of research. One group urged a common language of power and a focus upon the ideological predispositions of leaders and citizens (Swanson 1962), another endorsed the proposal to establish a permanent sample of 200 American cities (Dye 1966), while a third called for cross-cultural comparative power studies (Wirt 1971).

The reliance of case studies of community power has been supplemented by a few comparative studies that have facilitated the refinements of concepts, methods, and interpretations. Agger, Goldrich, and Swanson (1964) not only found differences in the distribution of power and prevailing ideologies of leaders in four American communities in the South and West, but they discovered changes of power patterns. Presthus (1964) found public support for local hospitals depended upon the nature of power in two communities in upstate New York. D'Antonio and Form (1965) found El Paso, Texas, to be more democratic than Ciudad Juarez, Mexico. Miller (1970) compared communities in North and South America and Britain and found the pattern of social stratification to be more important than any other social factor associated with community power.

By the 1960s the importance of community power had become a part of various training programs of urban professionals. Schools of education used the concept of power to train top administrators to recognize how those with informal power could affect their formal authority to operate the school system (Kimbrough 1964). Similarly, Bollens and Ries (1969) proposed that city managers examine their power environment, which may very well impact upon their administrative effectiveness and tenure. Those in public health had long understood the usefulness of knowing more about the power dynamics surrounding their operations. Urban planners were encouraged to discern who were the ''powers that be'' when engaged in long-range planning. Journalists conducted their own studies of leadership to better understand the underlying interconnections between key influentials who make the decisions they report on daily (Trounstine and Christensen 1982). Business journals and other periodicals have compiled specific lists of city, state, and national leaders. Consultants are hired to discover the nature of the power systems for specific clients and conduct risk analysis for business firms prepared to invest in some distant community or abroad (Coplin and O'Leary 1983).

So, too, has the rhetoric of power been used to mobilize a variety of relatively powerless or latent political forces that challenged the well-established power holders, using such slogans as "power to the people," "black power," and "gray power." Leaders of the civil rights movement during the 1960s used Hunter's model of community power to advocate empowerment of minorities. Antiwar advocates during the 1970s used Mills's model of the power elite and the "military-industrial complex" to protest the war in Vietnam. In fact, it is likely that effective politicians have a fairly good sense about who the most influential persons in the polity are, what decisional outputs and outcomes they prefer, and what means they will use to achieve their ends.

CONCEPTUAL, METHODOLOGICAL, AND INTERPRETIVE ISSUES

By 1960, the classic power systems of Hunter and Dahl posed significant theoretical and methodological issues in the social sciences. A long and vigorous exchange ensued among power analysts over concepts and definitions, methods, and interpretations of their findings. Polsby (1980: ix) characterized the community power literature as a debate that had become "more dense with misunderstandings of all kinds, while burgeoning in nearly every direction—every direction, that is, except toward the resolution of empirical problems and the shape and scope of power in American communities." At times, the exchange between the two schools became acrimonious. For example, Scoble (1971: 110) was disturbed with the "unprofessional and unbecoming personal vendetta" by his fellow political scientist Polsby against Hunter. Polsby (1980: x) scoffed at Scoble's comments as "pious."

The notion of a debate implied winners and losers. The perspective here is to explore the intellectual exchanges, seldom face to face, that produced a very rich paper trail from which one can clarify the dynamics of power in urban America. Power analysts should codify their agreements on what they seek (questions), how to find it (methods), and how to interpret what they find (analytic scheme). These will be discussed as (1) orienting questions, (2) operational definitions, (3) selected methods, (4) correlates of power, and (5) classification of power systems.

Orienting Questions

Many power researchers appear to be asking similar orienting questions: Who has power? How did they acquire it? How do they use it? What constraints are there upon power holders? Do they share their power with others; if so, with whom and under what circumstances? How accessible and responsive are power holders to others? and What do those with relatively little or no power do to promote their interests? Agger, Goldrich, and Swanson (1964), who were interested in the political ideological and culture, shifted the question to record the understandings and preferences of leaders as to "Who should rule?" Those who focus more on socioeconomic and political structures than individuals raise such questions as, Does it matter who governs? (Domhoff 1990) and, What does the ruling class do when it rules? (Therborn 1980). The urban political economy approach of Vogel (1992: 30–31) addressed four questions: What factors shape a political regime structure? Are the relations between business and government within a regime marked by conflict, cooperation, or indifference? How does the regime structure affect policy outputs? and What can a local regime accomplish, in light of economic dependence on businesses and political dependence on higher levels of government?

Pluralist Schumaker (1991: 17) addressed three main questions: What principles guide the resolution of community issues, and do these reflect the dominant values of the citizens (Elkin [1987] suggested they should) or reflect the economic imperatives (Peterson [1981] suggests they must)? To what extent are political communities dominated by private elite (suggested by elite model), by governmental bureaucrats (suggested by managerial model), or by special-interest groups (suggested by hyperpluralist model), and under what circumstances are issues resolved through democratic processes that instead empower citizens and elected representatives (Dahl [1961] claimed by orthodox pluralist model)? And to what extent do political communities exhibit systematic biases that result in political subordination of the lower class, minorities, and women (suggested by regime theorists), and do inequalities in power have legitimate explanations (implied by orthodox pluralists)?

Operational Definitions

The language of power has come to mean many things to different people. Agger, Goldrich, and Swanson (1964) carefully defined key concepts in operational terms for use in their multifaceted research approach: (1) political-influence index, (2) latent leaders, (3) manifest leaders, (4) leadership's ideology, (5) power distribution among citizens, (6) sense of electoral potency, and (7) permeability of the power structure. The level of discomfort over power definitions has stimulated some analysts to use the concept of "faces" of power. Bachrach and Baratz (1970) added agenda setting as a second face. Galbraith (1983) proffered three more abstract faces of power—threats, economic, and integrative. Schumaker (1991: 223) distinguished three faces of power as he measured democratic performance: (1) is exercised by participating to achieve one's goal in resolving issues already on the agenda; (2) is exercised in setting the agenda; and (3) involves influencing preferences of other participants. Issac (1987) contends that there is little distinction between the three faces.

Selective Methods

Power analysts have used a variety of methods to collect their data (for major distinctions between several methods, see Miller 1970: 8). The positional method identifies those who hold formal (structural) leadership positions and assumes these individuals can and do use their authority of the office to affect decision making (Mills 1956). The reputational technique specifies the sociometric choices of potential influentials by collecting information from knowledgeables and influentials who are most likely to have insights about who has general influence or on a specific issue in a community (Hunter 1953). The decisional approach follows the course of events and issues that contribute to a particular decision, identifying the individuals, groups, and organizations that initiate and ultimately resolve the final decision (Dahl 1961). Network analysis collects detailed information on the interconnections between individuals and groups in a given decisional setting such as a community (Laumann and Pappi 1976) and corporate interlocked directorates (Mintz and Schwartz 1985; Swanson 1987).

There is no generally accepted methodology nor decision rules guiding power analysis. The choice of methods and the discipline of the investigator are believed to be significant in the findings of power studies. Some power analysts use a combination of methods. Journalists prefer the reputational method, as it takes less time and resources to identify local leaders.

Correlates of Power—Causes and Consequences

Power analysts have identified a number of socioeconomic and political factors associated with types of power patterns. The study of correlates of power has involved both contributing factors as well as associated consequences.

Secondary analysis of existing studies was used to identify the major determinants of the power systems. Walton (1970) systematically reviewed the results of 33 studies and found valid, significant relationships existed with regard to research method, academic discipline, community issues, number of leaders, population growth, absentee ownership of business firms, political party competition, and change in the power structure. Aiken (1970) added that southern communities were more likely to be pyramidal and pluralism to be located in the older cities of the North, with a high degree of absentee-owned industry and nonreformed local governments. Gilbert (1972), reviewing the studies of 166 cities, found the more concentrated power systems had leadership coming from the economic sector. However, the larger the polity, the more likely political leaders were key participants and the greater the number of issues and policy discussions and less likely controversial issues were controlled.

Of equal importance is to determine what consequences, if any, may be associated with one power system or another. That is, who receives benefits or bears the burden of costs of community policies in certain power systems? Aiken's (1970) analysis of some 90 cities found that "decentralized" power systems were more effective in taking advantage of several federal programs—public housing, urban renewal, war on poverty, and model cities. Clark (1971) used an "ersatz decisional method" to provide an index of centralized decision-making structures and found reformed local government—adoption of a city manager, nonpartisan ballot, and at-large elections of representatives—was highly correlated with "centralized" (pyramidal power systems) and found decentralized (pluralism) to be positively associated with economic diversification, population size, and (very slightly) active civic voluntary associations and negatively associated with the index of reform government. He also found centralized power systems encouraged nonseparable public goods, while decentralized systems generate separable goods. Williams (1980) found that decentralized influence structures used their federal general revenue sharing to expand the scope of local governmental services.

Lineberry's (1977: 159) study of equality in the distribution of municipal services in San Antonio specifically rejected the potential of the power explanation, as he found no evidence that political power clustering in sociospatial areas was related to service advantages; in fact, he believed there was a slight tendency in the opposite direction. However, he and his colleagues found power configurations to help explain local police expenditures in 10 cities (Beecher, Lineberry, and Rich 1981).

Classification of Power Systems

It is disconcerting to read the variety of power studies that use many terms interchangeably, using synonyms to depict a power system, especially when classifications are provided without some common agreement on their meaning and application. For example, Gilbert (1971: 221) highlighted the synonyms associated with elite power systems: monolithic, integrated, stable, highly structured, coordinated, rational, and clustered potential. Pluralistic systems were described as unconcentrated, unintegrated, unstable, uncoordinated, no structure, amorphous, and diffused.

Agger, Goldrich, and Swanson (1964: 73) offered a typology of political power, distinguishing between consensual and competitive elite and mass power systems. They also classify four types of political regimes: developed democracy—wherein citizens expect and actually stand a good chance of obtaining their decisional preferences through elections; guided democracy—wherein the optimistic expectations of the developed democracy are mistaken as political leaders cancel the results of elections; oligarchy—wherein the sense of electoral potency is low in part because they sense leaders will illegitimately block their efforts; and underdeveloped democracy—wherein citizens have an unrealistic, lower expectation of electoral efficacy, as the use of illegitimate sanctions are low.

Vogel (1992: 118) created a classification scheme that dichotomized centralization and decentralization of both economic and political structures. This produced four types of community decision-making systems: hyperpluralism—both economic and political structures are highly decentralized; neither subsystem is able to act or shape an agenda and gives the appearance that it is "ungovernable," as there is no overall policy coordination; economic elite—leaders in the private sector are centralized (organized and cohesive), and public leaders are decentralized, thereby creating a "vacuum" to be filled by economic elites; political elite—government is highly structured with the capacity to govern and the private sector is fragmented; and cooperative—both economic and political sectors are centralized, stimulating cooperation and collaboration.

Stone (1993: 18–21) discerned four types of political regimes: maintenance—make no effort to introduce significant change, as small businesses and home-owners prefer marketplace approaches to sort out and calculate the transactional costs and benefits of growth; development—is mainly concerned with promoting the development interests of major downtown corporations, as they provoke opposition and contain risks to political leaders who are a part of the development elite; middle-class progressive—focus upon environmental protection, historic preservation, affordable housing, quality design, affirmative action and linkage funds for various social purposes; lower-class opportunity expansion—which would expand opportunities and public services, and residential options for diverse income levels.

Turner (1992) elaborated on two distinctive types of leadership patterns involved in downtown development: facilatator and satisficer. Waste (1986) distinguished four types of modern pluralist theory and their associated theorists: classical, comprising multiple groups, with government engaged in brokerage; hyperpluralism, comprising strong political groups and a weak government; stratified activist groups, with a government engaged in brokerage; and privatized, a limited number of participants usurp the authority and resources of public policy making for private ends. Elite theorists have been less inclined to differentiate types of elite power systems, as they believe most all communities are dominated by elites. Domhoff (1978: 174), for example, indicated that the shape and size of the power structure may vary from city to city due to its economic base, size, function, strength of working-class organizations: "But it is likely, except in very small towns and dying cities, that the local power structure will be related to or part of the national ruling class."

While the concept of power is difficult to see, touch, taste, hear, or smell directly, power analysts have constructed a number of indirect indicators of power such as memberships in community and corporate organizations, a reputation of influence, and participation impact upon decision making. Table 5.1 summarizes the key differences between the pluralistic and power elite heuristic models (for alternatives, see Whitt 1982: 10; Alford and Friedman 1987: 16; Schumaker 1991: 10). Pluralism indicates potentially many power holders operating openly and competitively in specific substantive policy arenas. They acknowledge that political resources are unequally distributed, but given the generally slack utilization, there are opportunities for those with fewer resources to use them as constraints upon politicians to ensure the neutrality of government. While pluralists believe structural and public policy changes are needed, these are most likely to be achieved incrementally through mutual adjustments.

The characteristics of the power elite tend to be presented as almost the op-

Table 5.1
Distinguishing Contrasts between Pluralism and Elitism

Items	Pluralism	Elitism
Number of power holders	Potentially many	Few
Visibility	Overt	Covert integration
Scope of influence	Highly specialized	Very general
Political resources	Slack, unequal, noncumulative resources can be used, if interests at stake	Very difficult for average citizen to acquire; numerous obstacles to mobilize
Beliefs on issues	Competitive	Consensual
Role of government	Neutral but more responsive to mobilized interests/electorate	Agents of privileged place of business
Probabilities of changing	Social class structure weak; those with merit gain access to power, incremental changes	Elites protect/promote strong ruling elite interests; thereby face and resist dramatic changes

posite of those of the pyramidal power systems. Power is held by a few covert, economic elites with overwhelming political resources. They hold general power, act consensually, and use government to protect and promote their interests. They resist drastic changes, especially by those who may attempt to reduce their domination or influence over community issues, policies, and decisions they consider significant to their interests. These elite, more than most, believe government should facilitate their interests because they are at the heart of the local economy. Therefore, they are politically attentive to what happens at city hall, especially over the agenda-setting community goals and directions. Politicians, in turn, have learned to accommodate this ''privileged place of the marketplace'' (Lindbloom 1982).

CONTINUING EFFORTS TO RESOLVE AND REFINE POWER PATTERNS

The stark contrasts in Table 5.1 persist as the variety of power analysts have multiplied into other academic disciplines. They continue to improve upon our understandings and applications of political power and influence. For the most part, they continue to utilize past research reports, perhaps not as sympathically as they should, given the tremendous efforts that have been made to compile the existing body of knowledge. That knowledge can be found in reviews of power studies, occasional revisits to field sites by the same or other analysts, secondary analysis of the hundred or so reports, quantitative analysis of a permanent sample of cities, and commentaries by those who critique empirical efforts.

Waste (1986: 200) suggested that his symposium reflected a general climate of peace as the protagonists talked with—and not at—each other. However, it is difficult to discern very much congruence among power analysts. Dye (1986: 37–39) distinguished types of public policies and allowed that "allocational policy making" supports the pluralist model, while elite theory accounts for developmental policy, whereas federalism has taken most redistributive policies out of local politics. He suggested that neither pluralist nor elite models have studied the struggle over governmental reorganization, where the propertied elites have prospered under machine and reformed administrations. Domhoff (1986: 70) did not change his views toward pluralism; instead, he approved recent essentially elite approaches—the City as Growth Machine (Logan and Molotch 1987) and political regimes dealing with neighborhood discontent and challenges to the development elite (Stone 1976). Furthermore, Stone (1989b) contended that neither pluralists nor elitists have reconciled fragmented control with the conditions of highly unequal influence, especially in the "ecological-power game" of forming partnerships with government.

While many researchers and commentators have emphasized their differences, some have contributed ideas and behavioral data that can and have been used by researchers and those who may wish to apply knowledge of power to practical affairs of urban America. Vogel (1992: 11) attempted to explain such contradictory findings: The two theories—pluralism and elitism—are fairly similar but result in different labels being applied; different methods are used by different social science disciplines; there are real differences among power systems, and conflicting evidence reflects, in fact, reality of power in different places at different times; there is an ideological predisposition of the researchers toward one result and to discount evidence to their original views; researchers formulate different operational definitions in particular ways.

The Search for New Directions

The power exchange stimulated additional empirical research on the local level by those who continue to treat power as a core variable, as well as those who introduced robust new approaches, concepts, methods, and analytic schemes. While some continue to advance the knowledge of the two primary schools of thought—pluralism versus power elite—others have introduced classificatory schemes using such dependent variables as the convergence or divergence of the ideologies of leaders, the sense of electoral efficacy, and the perceived use of illegitimate sanctions (Agger, Goldrich, and Swanson 1964).

To move beyond what some consider a "sterile" debate over no discernible difference between the two schools of thought, Garson (1978: 207) advanced political economy as an alternative approach. Political economy treats the political culture and economy as interdependent, resolving conflicts over economic programs, with pluralists' means and elitists' ends being compatible. Lineberry (1980: 305) indicated that the study of power was being transformed from political sociology to political economy. The central question was shifting from Who governs? to With what effects? He distinguished the ideological "Right" from the "Left" among political economists. The former prefer the public choice model of individuals voting with their feet and advocating "contracting out" for smaller governments that may not desire to produce all of their own services (Bish and Ostrom 1973: 99). The Left, on the other hand, focused on distributive inequalities (Rawls 1971), the concentration of surplus (Harvey 1973), and the twofold function of the state as socially legitimating and unprofitable by socially essential public investment in infrastructure (Friedland, Piven, and Alford 1978). Walton (1992) pointed to the success of the political economy of the Left in explaining such social and political movements as labor, civil rights, and welfare rights; however, its very success suggests its limitations based on "prefigured" answers to new questions. Vogel (1992: 14) contends that the political economy approach is evolutionary rather than a replacement of community power. Several variants of this approach have produced the concept of the growth machine (Molotch 1976) and political regimes (Stone 1989b). While some growth machines, according to Logan and Molotch (1987: 67), are conservative and suspicious of overt governmental intervention, others are liberal and use government programs to "pacify, co-opt, and placate oppositions." Vogel and Swanson (1989) found antigrowth coalitions to briefly challenge these machines (see also Bowman 1987; Turner 1990).

A quantitative approach became feasible with the creation of a permanent sample of 50 American cities at the National Opinion Research Center. This sample has been used to study school desegregation (Crain 1968), fluoridation of water supplies (Crain, Katz, and Rosenthal 1969), urban renewal (Clark 1971), urban civil disorder (Rossi, Berk, and Edison 1974), and fiscal strain (Clark and Ferguson 1983). However, it should be noted that quantitative studies tended to depend "little, if at all, on first-hand research . . . to sacrifice depth and measurement validity as regards the local political process in favor of comparative breath."

Many empirical power studies have run ahead of their theoretical base of inquiry. Much remains to be done to go beyond the study of a single community formulating developmental policy. Emphasis should be given to the operational definitions of governing regimes, the decision rules used to explain comparative trends, and incentives and disincentives of those pursuing self-interest while affecting the public interest. Special attention should be given to the comparative trends of converging and diverging behavior of governing regimes of complex urban political systems that may have many similarities or differences, depending on their stage of development and particular mix of ideologies associated with pattern of influentials. Greater efforts should be given to formulating middle-range theory about the distribution and exercise of power, as well as the normative implications of power sharing in a democratic society. Greater care should be given to the building theory and a body of knowledge that can more effectively be transferred into practice.

AN ASSESSMENT OF POWER RESEARCH

The assessment of power analysis has been mixed. Some considered the intellectual exchange had reached an impasse and "gradually faded" (Ricci 1971), was dead and in need of a "decent burial" (Wolfinger 1964), and was strewn with "conceptual and theoretical debris" (Polsby 1980: x). In fact, the field continues, as power analysts have produced as many, if not more, studies since the proclamation of these pessimistic views. These critics have persuaded some social scientists that the debate has been fruitless and that if to continue, a paradigm shift is essential. But power analysis, as with much of social science, has been evolutionary rather than experiencing the often-cited paradigm shifts that some have contended have occurred (Walton 1981; Ricci 1984; Stone 1989a) or that some have called for to account for the anomalies experienced during the 1960s (Bernard 1973).

Power analysts have used power as both a dependent and independent variable, as well as contrasted the significance of power with other factors to explain the adoption of public policy and socioeconomic change. The vigor of the power debate has stimulated the development and refinement of the elite more than the pluralistic approach. Urban researchers have shifted some of their attention to the cohesive, inclusive capacity of power holders and how they leverage benefits to cope with such constraints as fragmentation, capital flight, political talent, and urban social movements.

While the power debate has not been settled, its contributions to the social sciences have been as notable as those from any other field of inquiry, perhaps more than most. Alford and Scoble (1969: 194) believe there is "remarkable" agreement between and among power analysts in that the public decision-making agenda occurs within a relatively narrow range of alternatives determined by political, economic, and cultural constraints; middle and upper classes provide most of the leadership; when working-class groups are organized, they form a base of opposition that allows a variety of issues to be raised; a variety of groups are active, but the same individuals, except public leaders such as the mayor, are not active in all issues; distinctions of the proper boundaries between private and public actions establish the legitimacy of government and public leaders; and many major decisions are made autonomously by private economic leaders who are not subject to public control.

Much remains to be done as researchers to go beyond the case study of a particular community, formulating developmental policies or making specific decisions. Future empirical power studies should continue efforts to appreciate past research and use it to build a body of knowledge with warrantable concepts, methods, and findings of power patterns.

Given impending current and future turbulence, power analysts should explore the conditions for changing power systems and the importance of political ideologies and culture, as well as analyze who bears the burden and who receives the benefits of community policies and decisions and social or distributive justice (Bowie 1971). They should also pay more attention to normative questions concerning political viability (Lehman 1992), sustainable communities (Milbrath 1989), the role of the state (Alford and Friedman 1987), democracy and political inequality (Dahl 1989), and urban social movements and social and racial disparities (Boggs 1986). Future empirical research should pursue the relationship between the nature of political power and policy outputs such as nonroutine *leadership* and routine *administration* (Lyon and Bonjean 1981), as well as Dye's (1986) distinctions between allocative (pluralism), developmental (elite), governmental reorganization and minority and black power (Hunter 1953, 1980). Greater efforts should be given to conducting "natural experiments" (Agger, Goldrich, and Swanson 1964) and engaging predictive studies about power and issue outcomes as reported in Miller (1970). While basic research should continue, it is imperative that applications of our existing base of knowledge concerning power should be intensified and nourished; in addition, efforts should be undertaken to provide strategic futures and engage in political prototyping (Lasswell 1963). More care should be taken to define the terms of discourse: for example, to distinguish *authority* using coercion or constrained by the judicial system, *power* over or with, from relative weights of *influence* to negotiate and bargain to get things done. This is what was intended in this review of the power literature for those who continue the quest to understand power, who wields it, and to what end, which remains for political scientists a core variable (suggested by Apter 1977: 17).

REFERENCES

Agger, Robert E., Daniel Goldrich, and Bert E. Swanson. 1964. *The Rulers and the Ruled.* New York: John Wiley & Sons.

Aiken, Michael. 1970. "The Distribution of Community Power." In Michael Aiken and Paul E. Mott, eds., *The Structure of Community Power.* New York: Random House.

Alford, Robert R., and Roger Friedman. 1987. *Power of Theory.* Cambridge: Cambridge University Press.

Alford, Robert R., and Harry Scoble. 1969. *Bureaucracy and Participation.* Chicago: Rand McNally & Co.

Apter, David E. 1977. *Introduction to Political Analysis.* Cambridge, MA: Winthrop.

Bachrach, Peter, and Morton S. Baratz. 1970. *Power and Poverty.* New York: Oxford University Press.

Banfield, Edward C. 1965. *Big City Politics.* New York: Random House.

Banfield, Edward C., and James Q. Wilson. 1963. *City Politics.* New York: Vintage Books.

Beecher, Janice, Robert L. Lineberry, and Michael J. Rich. 1981. "Community Power, the Urban Agenda, and Crime Policy." *Social Science Quarterly* 62, no. 4 (December): 630–643.

Bernard, Jessie. 1973. *The Sociology of Community*. Glenview: Scott, Foresman and Co.

Bish, Robert A., and Vincent Ostrom. 1973. *Understanding Urban Government*. Washington, D.C.: American Enterprise Institute.

Boggs, Carl. 1986. *Social Movements and Political Power*. Philadelphia: Temple University Press.

Bollens, John C., and John C. Ries. 1969. *The City Manager Profession*. Chicago: Public Administration Service.

Bowie, Norman E. 1971. *Towards a New Theory of Distributive Justice*. Amherst: University of Massachusetts Press.

Bowman, Ann O'M. 1987. "Elite Organization and the Growth Machine." In G. William Domhoff and Thomas R. Dye, eds., *Power Elites and Organizations*. Beverly Hills: Sage Publishing.

Clark, Terry N. 1971. "Community Structure, Decision-Making, Budget Expenditures and Urban Renewal in 51 American Communities." In Charles M. Bonjeans, Terry N. Clark, and Robert L. Lineberry, eds., *Community Politics*. New York: Free Press.

Clark, Terry N. 1973. *Community Power and Policy Outputs*. Beverly Hills: Sage Publishing.

Clark, Terry N., and Lorna C. Ferguson. 1983. *City Money*. New York: Columbia University Press.

Coplin, William D., and Michael K. O'Leary. 1983. *Political Analysis through the Prince System*. Syracuse: Syracuse University Public Affairs.

Crain, Robert L. 1968. *The Politics of School Desegregation*. Chicago: Aldine Publishing Co.

Crain, Robert, L., Elihu Katz, and Donald B. Rosenthal. 1969. *The Politics of Community Conflict*. Indianapolis, IN: The Bobbs-Merrill Company Inc.

Dahl, Robert A. 1958. "A Critique of the Ruling Elite Model." *American Political Science Review* 52: 463–469.

Dahl, Robert A. 1961. *Who Governs?* New Haven: Yale University Press.

Dahl, Robert A. 1979. "Who Really Rules." *Social Science Quarterly* 60, no. 1 (June): 141–151.

Dahl, Robert A. 1989. *Democracy and Its Critics*. New Haven: Yale University Press.

D'Antonio, William V., and William H. Form. 1965. *Influentials in Two Border Cities*. Notre Dame: University of Notre Dame Press.

Domhoff, G. William. 1978. *Who Really Rules?* New Brunswick: Transaction Books.

Domhoff, G. William. 1986. "The Growth Machine and the Power Elite." In Robert J. Waste, ed., *Community Power*. Beverly Hills: Sage Publications.

Domhoff, G. William. 1990. *The Power Elite and the State*. New York: Aldine De Gruyer.

Dye, Thomas. 1986. "Community Power and Public Policy." In Robert J. Waste, ed., *Community Power*. Beverly Hills: Sage Publications.

Dye, Thomas R., ed. 1966. *Comparative Research in Community Politics*. Athens: University of Georgia Press.

Elkin, Stephen. 1987. *City and Regime in the American Republic*. Chicago: Chicago University Press.

Friedland, Roger, Frances Piven, and Robert Alford. 1978. "Political Conflict, Urban Structure and Fiscal Crisis." In Douglas Ashford, ed. *Comparing Urban Policies*. Beverly Hills: Sage Publications.

Galbraith, John K. 1983. *The Anatomy of Power.* Boston: Houghton Mifflin Co.

Garson, G. David. 1978. *Group Theories of Politics.* Beverly Hills: Sage Publications.

Gilbert, Clair W. 1971. "Community, Power Structures & Research Bias." *Polity* 4: 218–235.

Gilbert, Clair W. 1972. *Community Power Structure.* Gainesville: University of Florida Press.

Harvey, David. 1973. *Social Justice in the City.* Baltimore: Johns Hopkins University Press.

Hawley, Amos H. 1963. "Community Power and Urban Renewal Success." *American Journal of Sociology* 68: 422–431.

Hawley, Willis D., and James H. Svara. 1972. *The Study of Community Power.* Santa Barbara: A.B.C.–Clio, Inc.

Hunter, Floyd. 1953. *Community Power Structure.* Chapel Hill: University of North Carolina Press.

Hunter, Floyd. 1961. Review of *Who Governs? Administrative Science Quarterly* 6, no. 4 (March): 517–519.

Hunter, Floyd. 1980. *Community Power Succession.* Chapel Hill: University of North Carolina Press.

Huntington, Samuel P. 1993. "The Clash of Civilizations?" *Foreign Affairs* (summer): 22–49.

Issac, Jeffry C. 1987. *Power and Marxist Theory.* Ithaca: Cornell University Press.

Jennings, Kent. 1964. *Community Influentials.* New York: Free Press.

Kammerer, Gladys, Charles D. Farris, John M. DeGrove, and Alfred B. Clubok. 1963. *The Urban Political Community.* Boston: Houghton Mifflin Co.

Kaufman, Herbert, and Victor Jones. 1954. "The Mystery of Power." *Public Administration Quarterly* 14 (summer): 205–212.

Kimbrough, Ralph B. 1964. *Political Power and Educational Decision-Making.* Chicago: Rand McNally.

Lasswell, Harold D. 1963. *The Future of Political Science.* New York: Atherton Press.

Laumann, Edward O., and Franz U. Pappi. 1976. *Networks of Collective Action.* New York: Academic Press.

Lehman, Edward W. 1992. *The Viable Polity.* Philadelphia: Temple University Press.

Lief, I. P., and Terry N. Clark. 1973. *Community Power and Decision-Making.* The Hague: Mouton.

Lindbloom, Charles. 1982. "The Market as Prison." *Journal of Politics* 44: 323–336.

Lineberry, Robert L. 1977. *Equality and Urban Policy.* Beverly Hills: Sage Publications.

Lineberry, Robert L. 1980. "From Political Sociology to Political Economy." *American Behavioral Scientist* 24, no. 2 (November–December): 299–317.

Lineberry, Robert L., and Ira Sharkansky. 1971. *Urban Politics.* New York: Harper and Row, Publishers.

Logan, John R., and Harvey L. Molotch. 1987. *Urban Fortunes.* Berkeley: University of California Press.

Long, Norton E. 1958. *The Polity.* Chicago: Rand McNally.

Lynd, Robert S., and Helen M. Lynd. 1937. *Middletown in Transition.* New York: Harcourt, Brace.

Lyon, Larry, and Charles M. Bonjean. 1981. "Community Power and Policy Outputs." *Urban Affairs Quarterly* 17, no. 1. (September): 3–21.

Milbrath, Lester W. 1989. *Envisioning a Sustainable Society*. Albany: State University of New York Press.

Miller, C. Delbert. 1970. *International Community Power Structures*. Bloomington: Indiana University Press.

Miller, C. Delbert. 1975. *Leadership and Power in the BosWash Megalopolis*. New York: Wiley & Sons.

Mills, C. Wright. 1956. *The Power Elite*. New York: Oxford University Press.

Mintz, Beth, and Michael Schwartz. 1985. *The Power Structure of American Business*. Chicago: University of Chicago Press.

Molotch, Harvey. 1976. "The City as Growth Machine: Toward a Political Economy of Place." *American Journal of Sociology* 82: 309–331.

Peterson, Paul E. 1981. *City Limits*. Chicago: University of Chicago Press.

Polsby, Nelson. 1980. *Community Power and Political Theory,* 2nd edition. New Haven: Yale University Press.

Presthus, Robert Vance. 1964. *Men at the Top: A Study in Community Power*. New York: Oxford University Press.

Rawls, John. 1971. *A Theory of Social Justice*. Cambridge: Harvard University Press.

Ricci, David M. 1971. *Community Power and Democratic Theory*. New York: Random House.

Ricci, David M. 1984. *The Tragedy of Political Science*. New Haven: Yale University Press.

Rossi, Peter H., Richard A. Berk, and Bettye K. Edison. 1974. *The Roots of Urban Discontent*. New York: John Wiley & Sons.

Schumaker, Paul. 1991. *Critical Pluralism, Democratic Performance, and Community Power*. Lawrence: University Press of Kansas.

Scoble, Harry. 1971. "Where the Pluralists Went Wrong." In Frederick Wist, ed., *Future Directions in Community Power Research*. Berkeley: Institute of Governmental Studies, University of California.

Stone, Clarence N. 1976. *Economic Growth and Neighborhood Discontent*. Chapel Hill: University of North Carolina.

Stone, Clarence N. 1988. "Preemptive Power," *American Journal of Political Science* 32: 82–104.

Stone, Clarence N. 1989a. "Paradigms, Power, and Urban Leadership." In B. D. Jones, ed., *Leadership and Politics*. Lawrence: University Press of Kansas.

Stone, Clarence N. 1989b. *Regime Politics*. Lawrence: University Press of Kansas.

Stone, Clarence. 1993. "Urban Regimes and the Capacity to Govern." *Journal of Urban Affairs* 15, no. 1: 1–28.

Stone, Clarence, and Heywood T. Sanders. 1987. "Reexamining a Classic Case of Development Politics." In Clarence Stone and Heywood T. Sanders, eds., *The Politics of Urban Development*. Lawrence: University Press of Kansas.

Swanson, Bert E. 1987. "Discovering an Economic Clique in the Development and Growth of Houston." In *Essays in Economic and Business History*. Los Angeles: Economic and Business Historical Society.

Swanson, Bert E., ed. 1962. *Current Trends in Comparative Community Studies*. Kansas City: Community Studies, Inc.

Therborn, Goran. 1980. *What Does the Ruling Class Do When It Rules?* London: Verso.

Trounstine, Philip J., and Terry Christensen. 1982. *Movers and Shakers*. New York: St. Martin's Press.

Turner, Robyne S. 1990. "New Rules for the Growth Game," *Journal of Urban Affairs* 12, no. 1: 35 to 47.

Turner, Robyne S. 1992. "Growth Politics and Downtown Development." *Urban Affairs Quarterly* 28 (September): 3–21.

Vogel, Ronald K. 1992. *Urban Political Economy*. Gainesville: University Press of Florida.

Vogel, Ronald K., and Bert E. Swanson. 1989. "The Growth Machine versus the Anti Growth Coalition." *Urban Affairs Quarterly* 25, no. 1: 63–85.

Walton, John. 1970. "A Systematic Survey of Community Power Research." In Michael Aiken and Paul Mott, eds., *The Structure of Community Power*. New York: Random House.

Walton, John. 1976. "Community Power and the Retreat from Politics." *Social Problems* 23: 292–303.

Walton, John. 1981. *Labour, Class and the International System*. New York: Academic Press.

Walton, John. 1992. "Urban Sociology." *Annual Review of Sociology* 19: 301–320.

Warner, W. Lloyd, and Paul S. Lunt. 1941. *The Social Life of a Community*. New Haven: Yale University Press.

Waste, Robert J. 1986. *Community Power*. Beverly Hills: Sage Publications.

Whitt, J. Allen. 1982. *Urban Elites and Mass Transportation*. Princeton: Princeton University Press.

Williams, Ann S. 1980. "Relationships between the Structure of Local Influence and Policy Outcomes." *Rural Sociology* 45, no. 4: 621–643.

Wirt, Frederick M. 1974. *Power in the City*. Berkeley: University of California Press.

Wirt, Frederick M., ed. 1971. *Future Directions in Community Power Research*. Berkeley: Institute of Governmental Studies, University of California.

Wolfinger, Raymond E. 1964. "A Plea for a Decent Burial." *American Sociological Review* 27, no. 6 (December): 841–847.

Chapter 6

Race and Ethnicity in the City

Dianne M. Pinderhughes

This chapter reviews the major approaches and research by scholars of racial and ethnic politics over the last half century. Because of the patterns of entry, virtually all new racial and ethnic groups have entered American life through urban gateways, and thus the literature tends to intersect with studies of the politics of specific cities and with case studies of single groups, at various points in time. Immigration laws previously limited entrants almost entirely to northern Europeans until the 1965 Immigration Act, which changed the formulas and admitted much larger proportions and numbers from non-European world regions. *Race* and *ethnicity* have thus had considerably different meanings in the political science literature in recent decades. Roughly, the literature has had four main orientations. In the immediate post–World War II era, scholars addressed racial and ethnic politics in New Haven as a problem of political assimilation, primarily of European ethnic groups; they predicted the gradual political integration and cultural assimilation of racial and ethnic groups into the existing socioeconomic and political system. Others more strongly emphasized the power of group identity and its continuing impact on political activities (Banfield 1965; Dahl 1961; Wolfinger 1974).

A second theme was struck by Glazer and Moynihan (1963) in their study of racial and ethnic groups in New York City, in which, they argued, "The ethnic group in American society became not a survival from the age of mass immigration [eventually to disappear] but a new social form" (16). The groups in this study reflected the increasingly heterogeneous, that is, non-European, population groups of American cities: "Negroes, Puerto Ricans, Jews, Italians and Irish," which also incorporated class as well as racial or ethnic issues (Parenti 1970).

More recently, racial and ethnic politics has raised Rodney King's question,

"Can We All Get Along?" (Jackson and Preston 1991; McClain and Stewart 1995; Sonenshein 1993). Immigrants in larger numbers and from all corners of the globe have become a larger presence in American cities, especially those on the coastal cities such as Los Angeles. Urban politics has rapidly become more complex and more conflictual, whether in educational policy, where students speaking 50 or more languages is not unusual, or in the management of the tensions arising from competition over increasingly scarce jobs, economic development, and status. Scholars no longer puzzle over the issues of assimilation or whether the groups will survive in observable form but whether the polity can handle the tensions arising from their simultaneously powerful and distinctive presences.

Finally, the economic crisis produced by the disintegration of the industrial economy reinforces and reframes the economic and class themes addressed in the literature (Stone 1989; Squires 1994). William J. Wilson (1978, 1987) opened the question of how economic changes have bifurcated and differentiated groups, especially blacks, in an unprecedented way, and Paul Peterson addressed the economic impact of racial and ethnic groups on the capacities of cities to function (Peterson 1981; Peterson and Rom 1990).

DEFINING GROUPS

Racial and ethnic "groups" have considerably different degrees of autonomy, identity, and political cohesion. A brief review of the three most commonly identified groups reveals the distinctions among them and the ways in which these characteristics evolve.

The Hispanics: Diverse Group Identities and Politics

A contemporary example of a nongroup might be "Hispanics" whose numbers include peoples of differing histories, races, ethnicities, generations, geographic origins, and national backgrounds. Spanish-language status is a classification of sorts, one that incorporates a multitude of nationalities within it. De la Garza et al. found in the Latino National Political Survey that "Mexicans, Puerto Ricans and Cubans have a great deal in common. . . . [T]here may be a Hispanic political community, but its parameters do not fit any existing presuppositions" (1992: 13). They also found that the three major Spanish-language/heritage groups prefer a national origin identity—Mexican American, Puerto Rican, or Cuban—to pan-ethnic nomenclature.

A group with close proximity and easy access to the United States is more likely to have continuing migration than one separated by greater distance and ocean barriers. In the case of proximate groups, that "immigration" may be of several types: informal, such as illegal border crossing; political action, such as the victory of the United States over Mexico in the War of 1848; and the acquisition of land (e.g., land addition of what became the southwestern United

States introduced a population of former Mexican citizens into the United States; this occurred not by the physical migration of the population but by political migration of American boundaries to the population) (Barrera 1979: 1–13).

These first Chicanos have been succeeded by waves of immigrants drawn by work in industrial factories in the Midwest, by work in agricultural sectors in different regions of the United States, and by available work in western cities. American immigration policy not only did not encourage Mexican immigration for purposes of citizenship but implemented a deportation policy. Still immigration has continued over the last decades because of surplus agricultural population in Mexico, American agricultural policies that use Mexican farmworkers in California and other produce-growing regions, and the increased attractiveness of jobs north of the Mexican border in the industrial, service, and agricultural sectors.

Although perceived as a single group, Cubans, Puerto Ricans, Mexican Americans, Panamanians, Bolivians, Colombians, and so on, cannot be expected to have a consistently united impact upon the politics of a city or region or to approach politics with similar concepts, unless a variety of factors encourage their union into a single group. One example might be if groups begin to create a communal identity, to intermarry, and to form a coherent new group. There is some evidence that the Puerto Rican and Mexican American populations of Chicago are beginning this process and may eventually form a cohesive new group (Latino Institute 1986: ii; Flores and Attinas 1988). The larger society would also have to respond to them as a cohesive ''group'' by separately identifying them in their places of residence, in schools, and in law.

The appearance of unity created by linguistic similarities is deceptive at least at this point. Hispanics are not a political group, as was indicated above. Even Mexican Americans incorporate several distinct generations, creating the bases for political heterogeneity within a single nationality group. Long-term residents of the territory that was once part of Mexico and is now part of the United States, early twentieth-century immigrants who have become well established and interested in political and social assimilation, and mid- to late-twentieth-century immigrants have distinctive political attitudes (Barrera 1979; Marquez 1987). Even as past generations of Mexican Americans are identified and politically mobilized, successive generations of immigrants, often illegal aliens, join them, thereby continuing to complicate the politicization and mobilization process. In this case, there is political ethnicity, but it is not an especially homogeneous form of group political expression.

The African American Population: An Example of Group-Based Political Expression

The African American population consistently displays the clearest signs of group autonomy, identity, and political cohesion; their homogeneous behavior arises out of distinctive historical experiences. The continuing presence of racially discriminatory traditions has isolated blacks and has reinforced their willingness and even their ability to approach the political arena in other than a group-based orientation (Dawson 1994; Gurin, Hatchett, and Jackson 1989; Carmichael and Hamilton 1967; Katznelson 1973; Kilson 1987: 527–528; Pinderhughes 1987: 109–140). There is also great political diversity within the black population, powerful recurring divisions about political values, strategy, and beliefs and on the usefulness of electoral participation. Analysis of racial or political orientations on one dimension and economic orientations along a second, for example, revealed 31 philosophical coalitions possible for black groups (Pinderhughes 1987: 124–130).

The process by which the group entered the country shapes both the size of the group and the extent to which there are internal variations in socialization and identification within groups. Most African Americans are descendants of people exposed to slavery and its legacies and to highly conservative rural agricultural life with extremely constrained systems of racial hierarchy and collectivism (Bunche 1973; Key 1949). At present, two thirds or more live in southern, western, or northern urban areas, and 40 percent had settled in the urban North in the decades after World War II. Separation from one's home and family in Africa, mixing of the various tribal (more appropriately nationality), groupings after capture, the middle passage, sale into slavery, and the gradual development of a phenotypically and culturally distinct African American (mixed with Native American) population subject to pervasive social, economic, political, and cultural controls created an unusually homogeneous population group substantially differentiated from the larger white American society. Such a group had and has distinctive leadership institutions and leadership styles, coherent patterns of political socialization, distinct kinds and types of partisan identification, and responsiveness to political issues. This has tended almost uniformly throughout American cities and rural areas, as the limitations on black political participation have been lifted, to result in group-based political expressions.[1]

Geographic location affects the ease with which immigration occurs and the extent to which the United States is a focus for migration. African American group identity and homogeneity have also been reinforced by North America's distance from Africa combined with legislative barriers that have kept legal and illegal immigration from Africa to a minimum. Hawk (1987) shows that in every decade from 1820 through 1970 immigration from Africa into the United States has remained virtually undetectable—less than 1 percent of the total. Relatively small proportions of the ancestors of contemporary African Americans arrived after the 1860s when the last of the slave ships sailed into southern harbors, with some numbers from the Caribbean, Africa, and Central and South America. American immigration limitations created an extremely homogeneous black American population, especially when compared with the European population.[2]

Asian Americans: Old, New, and Uncertain Identity

Asian American history in American cities mixes elements of Latino and African American experience. From approximately 1882 through 1965, U.S. law barred Asian immigration to the United States, as well as Asian citizenship and political participation. Asian Pacific Americans have also been constrained by laws limiting their landownership, employment, and intermarriage. These laws continued until the mid-twentieth century so that Asian American political participation has occurred primarily after World War II, among those already in residence. Since immigration restrictions have been lifted as recently as the 1965 Immigration and Nationality Acts, and because Asians were geographically distant, Asian Americans' presence in urban areas has increased only within the last three decades. Despite this increase, only about 45 percent could vote as of 1980 (Chan 1991; Espiritu 1992: 58; Sandmeyer 1991). With increased population, the diversity of the Asian "group" has grown; Espiritu notes that "the very force that has boosted Asian American political clout—immigration—has also produced a population more divided among ethnic, class and generational lines" (1992: 60).

Legal discrimination as early as the Naturalization Act of 1790 denied the right of first-generation Asian immigrants to vote or to hold elected positions. Chun-Hoon noted that "all of these varied Asian groups, each representing a separate country and unique culture, encountered a similar or identical pattern of racial oppression and economic exploitation" (cited in Espiritu 1992: 37). Espiritu has examined the conditions under which multinational Asian groups begin to cohere into a pan-ethnic group, examining sources of new ethnic boundaries and intergroup cooperation. To the extent such developments occur, they are primarily urban phenomena.

The Asian Pacific population is much more concentrated in metropolitan urban areas inside central cities than the white population. By the early 1990s when the population had reached 7 million, 94 percent of Asian Pacifics lived in metropolitan areas, in contrast to 77 percent of the white and 86 percent of the black population. Forty-five percent of Asian Pacifics, 56.8 percent of blacks, and 26 percent of whites lived inside central cities. Asians are also much more concentrated in the West than other groups, 59 percent, where their geographic concentration in western cities is the same as in the nation (Asians: Bennett 1992: 2; blacks: Bennett 1995: 5).

Asian Americans are like Hispanics, with more than 10 national origin groups enumerated in the 1990 census.[3] Chinese and Filipinos constitute the two largest groups, 22.6 percent and 19.3 percent, respectively, followed by the Japanese, Asian Indians, and Koreans, each about 11 percent. As of 1980 the Japanese had the highest citizenship rates, at 81 percent, followed by the Chinese and Filipinos at under 60 percent; the voter registration rates for the groups followed a similar pattern in Los Angeles in 1984 with Japanese at 43 percent, the Chinese at 35 percent, and Filipinos at 27 percent (U.S. Bureau of the Census 1990; Espiritu 1992).

Asian Pacific Americans thus are highly concentrated geographically, including a complex array of groups, a substantial portion of which are not citizens, and even when they are, only a minority participate in electoral politics. Their impact on politics is more likely to occur in urban nonelectoral, group-oriented settings.

POLITICAL PARTICIPATION

The conventional political science model of political participation assumes that voting correlates positively with socioeconomic status and the type and intensity of one's political partisanship. In this chapter, two aspects of the model have significance for understanding urban racial and ethnic group political activity: the emphasis on socioeconomic status as a predictor of participation and the rather narrow definitions of political participation. Dahl assumed black and European ethnic voters passed through a transitory ethnic stage of political identification on their way to a nonethnic, socioeconomically based system of partisanship for political identification and participation (Campbell et al. 1960; Dahl 1961; Pinderhughes 1987: 69–70).

Successive literature suggests different patterns. Andersen shows that ethnicity became *increasingly* important in the early twentieth century for partisan political mobilization over time rather than of decreasing significance. The Democratic Party mobilized European ethnic voters more successfully than the Republicans (Andersen 1979: 103). Pinderhughes shows that Chicago's black voters were coverted from high levels of Republican support to Democratic Party allegiance (Pinderhughes 1987: 72). Socioeconomic status was not a singular determinant of political participation and partisan identification either for blacks or for European ethnics.

Recent work has reconsidered the socioeconomic status model of voting; controlling for socioeconomic status, black voter participation equals or exceeds that of whites (Baxter and Lansing 1981; Pinderhughes 1985: 530; Verba and Nie 1972; Wolfinger and Rosenstone 1980). Other research shows that there are *fewer* significant differences in voting among blacks by socioeconomic status than among whites (Cavanagh 1985; Gurin, Hatchett, and Jackson 1989; Tate 1993). However, Hanes Walton argues that the socioeconomic status (SES) model has not been validated for black voters because of the relatively small numbers of black respondents in the numerous surveys on which most of the SES theories have been based (Walton 1985: 79–81). Walton notes that initial voting studies and therefore the conceptualization of participation and partisanship patterns were based on an overwhelmingly white population of respondents. The numbers of blacks have been too small, geographically limited, idiosyncratic, or most important, blind to the severe structural constraints within which "black politics" existed.[4]

Defining Political Participation

The earliest models of political participation assumed political participation was expressed primarily through electoral politics and voting for public office. African American, Hispanic, and Asian American experiences vary, and it is best to be cautious in applying findings about any one group to another. Researchers may have to look to specific information such as patterns of group history, or the ways in which society responds to the group, to develop general theory and to make no prior assumptions about the character or dimensions of political participation. Political assimilation should neither be presumed nor denied on the part of the researcher. If one assumes assimilation is the process through which each group will necessarily proceed, then the researcher will miss much of what may be happening in a particular "community" because the person will key observations to only one set of expectations.

Second, racial and/or ethnic communities will have varying sets of political institutions for carrying out these functions or for the functions they may choose to address. A group may have a set of specialized institutions developed to deal with politics, or it may have some relatively to totally unspecialized bodies that handle several types of issues. Similarly, if the researcher defines politics as only including voting or party organizations, then a researcher may miss a great deal that is politically significant to the group, to its definition of politics, and to the larger society.

Aldon Morris's study of the civil rights movement, for example, opens up social science to the important role of churches and groups ordinarily seen as nonpolitical in their organization and development of infrastructures that permitted the mobilization of the black populations for political protest in cities all over the South. A search for highly specialized political organizations attached to electoral politics that governed the mobilization and leadership of the black population at the local level and communicated those interests at the national level would have produced meager results. Morris showed that such a finding need not lead to the conclusion that no institutions address these areas of concern (Morris 1984; Payne 1995; Pinderhughes 1988; Reed 1986; Robinson 1987).

Politics may include in addition to voting, campaigning, cooperative activity (which includes community organizing), and contacting public officials (Verba and Nie 1972: 162–166; Travis 1990: 9, 315). Other kinds of activity might be included under the cooperative activity category, such as infrastructure building and political mobilization. These are critical predecessors to black electoral politics and have frequently preceded recent successful black mayoral elections in Chicago and Philadelphia (Barker and Walters 1989; Cavanagh 1985; Morrison 1987; Pinderhughes 1985). Often these activities are carried out by a mix of organizations that vary in their degree of political specialization and that are not typically recognized as politically significant. Social groups, religious organizations, fraternal groups, and business associations are all mobilized to contribute to the political process (Pinderhughes 1990).

Political participation conforms to patterns but also varies by group and includes activities that support, encourage, and provide a basis for political participation, broadly defined: contacting, cooperative, and campaigning activities. The next section outlines stimuli that may precipitate group-based political behavior.

THE POLITICAL PARTICIPATION MODEL

The political participation model was developed to explore factors affecting black and European ethnic political participation and to identify a number of interactive variables that affected levels of group-based political participation. It required researchers to consider the factors external and internal to a group, and others such as demographic factors, to predict the impact of a group within a political environment (Pinderhughes 1987).

Political behavior, especially group-based electoral behavior, is the product of a complex variety of stimuli. There are no easily predictable patterns that explain what happens when a group "arrives" in the United States that leads to its involvement, individually or collectively, in politics. First, is there a cohesive group? The researcher must know a great deal about the role or place of the group in the society, how it is viewed, and what actions, if any, the larger society takes to distinguish it. Other measures external to the group rest on whether the actions of the society in response to the group are primarily informal or formal (that is, reflected in the legal system), widely reinforced throughout the society, or limited to specific geographic areas (Barnett 1976). Are whatever tendencies the group has toward self-identification (and they may be weak or strong) reinforced or discouraged by the society?

Nineteenth-century European ethnic groups such as Poles or Italians arrived in the United States prior to the creation of the Polish or Italian nation-states with culturally identifiable similarities not previously expressed in political terms in their native lands. Moreover, while Poles and Italians faced some identifiable discrimination in the United States, American society rarely invented a singular set of responses for all members of each group (Pinderhughes 1987: 16–38). Marguerite Barnett has argued that only blacks faced a consistent pattern of racial hierarchy in all locations in the United States, while European ethnics faced inconsistent patterns of discrimination or privilege (Barnett 1976; Erie 1989).

Poles and Italians did not necessarily see their groups as bases for political organization, nor was their political identity manifested in singular partisan identification with either the Democratic or Republican parties, high agreement on political issues or goals, or consolidated support for singular leaders or political institutions (Pinderhughes 1987: 57–65, 69–79). Blacks typically have strong agreement on all of these measures.

A combination of internal and external stimuli produces political expression first to generate group coherence and then to direct its expression toward the political arena. Direct access to other spheres of influence may reduce or mitigate the interest of the group in politics. In describing black politics in New York, Kilson has argued, "The racial limits on black entry into entrepreneurial and professional roles creates an oversupply of persons seeking mobility through politics" (1987: 526).

External factors therefore seek to measure a group's access to the economic marketplace and to the political arena (presumably outside the group's domain of influence) and to determine residential settlement patterns (Pinderhughes 1987: 39–65). Internal factors assess whether the group's patterns of political activity can be distinguished from those of the larger society as measured by leadership institutions and individual leaders, political socialization, partisan identification, and political issues. Where there are no distinctive group norms, or where they affect those individuals who are identifiable by national origins, but not also by institutional structures, normative standards, political values, social behavior patterns, or political beliefs, it is unlikely there will be a "group political identity" or that it will be consistently reflected in the political arena. And if their identity as a group is only lightly reinforced by the surrounding environment, it is also less likely that members of the group will express that identity politically.

RACIAL AND ETHNIC POLITICS IN AMERICA'S CITIES

In recent decades, Gary, Newark, Detroit, Atlanta, New Orleans, Chicago, Philadelphia, Baltimore, and most recently, New York City have mobilized in support of the election of black mayors. These mayors have often been elected with the support of a small proportion of white voters. But without the almost universal loyalty and turnout of nearly all black voters, they could not have won. In Cleveland in 1967, New Orleans in 1977, and Chicago in 1983, black candidates won with about 40 percent black voters in the electorate but turnout of 81 percent in Cleveland and 77 percent turnout in the latter two cities. Blacks supported Morial and Washington almost unanimously. The percentages suggest quite dramatically the fallacies in the SES model; with a black candidate, who addresses issues of substantive interest to the black population, who also mobilizes that population using the complex array of political and nonpolitical organizations available, black turnout rises well above the norm in American politics, and black voter loyalty is very high (Grimshaw 1992; Karnig and Welch 1980; Persons 1993; Rich 1989; Pinderhughes 1989: 291; Nelson 1982).

These successes were followed by considerable intragroup conflict; however, black candidates such as Harold Washington in 1977 were unable to mobilize black voters in unified fashion. His successors were also unable to monopolize black support. The consequences for political control are greatest in these cities where blacks are close to a minority or are a bare majority of the electorate; where they are significant majorities, such as in Gary, Newark, Detroit, or Washington, D.C., black mayors were elected and reelected for several terms in succession. In

Chicago, Cleveland, and New Orleans, intragroup conflict quickly transformed the first campaigns after the first black mayor had stepped down from office into a delicate, sometimes losing, balancing process. Blacks in cities such as St. Louis only recently mobilized their black populations to elect an African American candidate. New York City's black population subordinated its ethnic and borough-based differences only in 1989 to support the election of David Dinkins as mayor, although he lost his reelection effort (Browning, Marshall, and Tabb 1984, 1990; Schexnider 1982).

Asian Americans have begun to elect Asian Pacifics to political office as they have increased their size in the population, their citizenship, and political participation, but they face important constraints in electoral politics. Forty percent of Asian Pacifics reside in California, which suggests they are more likely to be elected from districts where the Asian Pacific population is most concentrated (Political Roster 1995: 1). Sixty percent of Hawaii's population is Asian, although only 11 percent of the nation's Asians reside there. Asian Pacifics are highly urban, and 45 percent are concentrated in only a few cities: Honolulu, Los Angeles–Long Beach, San Francisco–Oakland, New York, Chicago, and San Jose (Espiritu 1992: 54).

The *National Asian Pacific American Political Roster and Resource Guide* (Political Roster 1995) reports over 230 elected officials. Twenty-two Asian Pacific mayors and 66 city council members serve as of 1995. In both cases, a large majority, 72.7 percent of the mayors and 81.8 percent of city council positions, are from the West. Of these western officials, 62.5 percent of the mayors and 80 percent of the council members are from California or Hawaii. In California, only San Jose among its large cities has elected an Asian Pacific mayor, although Asian candidates have competed unsuccessfully in Los Angeles, Oakland, and San Francisco in recent years.

In recent years, their presence in the political environment has been manifested by the rise of economic-political conflict with other groups, often African Americans, about commercial operations in black neighborhoods, leading to boycotts in Brooklyn and violent attacks or the threat of violence in Los Angeles during the Rodney King riots (Kim 1992; Jackson and Preston 1991). Asian Pacifics who have focused primarily on the economic sector have begun to glean the importance of political representation as protection for their economic activities. Their small size, weak or independent partisanship, multiple nationality groups, and concentration in only a few states and locations means they have limited influence, and without aggressive use of electoral redistricting through the creation of majority minority districts, and the like, they are unlikely to be able to generate significant group political influence at the state or national levels if they rely only on Asian American voters. Coalition politics among Asian Pacific groups and with other racial and ethnic minority groups may prove an effective strategy. Greater economic resources may also earn great political influence through campaign concentrations. They also used the organizational resources of the war on poverty and the organizing strategies of the civil rights movement to build community-based organizations in the 1960s and 1970s (Greenstone and Peterson 1976; Wei 1993: 169–202; Espiritu 1992: 53–81).

Hispanics are somewhat more distributed throughout the United States than Asians, although they remain primarily in western and southwestern urban areas. They parallel Asian Pacifics in that the gap between their population and citizenry and registered voters is considerable, leaving them less influential in the political arena than their population would suggest (Pachon 1991). They have begun to win election to office, but Browning, Marshall, and Tabb's 1984 study of 10 cities in northern California showed Hispanic representation on city councils well below their proportion in the population. Their incorporation into dominant policy coalitions on minority issues was low, and there was also little policy responsiveness. In Colorado, Hero found higher Hispanic representation, incorporation, and policy responsiveness in Denver than Pueblo (1992: 144–151). He also found Mexican American forays into politics in San Antonio under Cisneros, in Los Angeles, and in New York generally unproductive on these measures. Hispanics are powerful and incorporated in Miami, but Cubans, with a strong economic base and wealth, which distinguishes them from Mexican Americans and Puerto Ricans, dominate the population. In recent years, as Hispanics have placed greater emphasis on using majority/minority electoral districts, their election to political office has increased.

Falcon (1988) found several factors reduced the possibilities of Latino and African American political coalitions in New York City. Historical differences including colonial settings versus slavery have created a distinctive set of institutions for African Americans; class and occupational patterns advantage blacks; blacks have strong national networks in contrast to Latinos, whose local networks are more developed; residential factors result in greater black than Latino political representation; cultural factors and societal responses have produced distinctions that will tend to lead to conflict rather than coalition. In general, however, the large size of the Hispanic population and its regional concentration provide a constituency on which to ground political representation, but their low citizenship, voter registration, and turnout reduce their impact.

FUTURE DIRECTIONS FOR RESEARCH

Research on racial and ethnic group politics in American urban politics offers an especially rich prospect for some time to come. Increasingly complex politics awaits urban environments as the groups described in this chapter create the institutions and develop the experiences that make participation in politics, electoral and nonelectoral, possible. Group autonomy, identity, and political cohesion are strongest among African Americans, complex among Hispanics, and uncertain among Asian Americans. Several major factors help explain some of the differences among the groups, but further research will assist scholars in understanding racial and ethnic politics in general as well as the behavior of specific groups. Access to the American continent increases the numbers of the group, as in the case of Hispanics, but simultaneously decreases group focus and orientation toward American national politics. African Americans and Asian Pacifics originated in territory quite distant from the North American mainland, which reduced the possibility of continuing migration and created conditions encouraging a distinctive identity. Racially restrictive immigration laws limited the arrival of new population cohorts among Asians and blacks, although the ceiling on Asians was established at much lower numbers than had been the case for blacks. After immigration reform, Asians have sharply increased their numbers and their heterogeneity. Asians and Hispanics have relatively low rates of citizenship, although racially discriminatory citizenship laws limited Asian access to the polity. Finally, economic forces resulted in the importation of Africans for slave labor such that their descendants, the African American population, constitute a significant portion of the population of the South, and are distributed throughout most regions of the country.

This chapter has also addressed the limitations of the socioeconomic status model of political participation used in isolation to understand the electoral behavior of racial and ethnic groups within the United States. The model evolved from social psychological theories of attachment to the political system. More recent research examines the impact of structural economic factors on racial and ethnic groups and on their political participation. The political participation model is proposed as an alternative strategy for identifying the factors that shape the likelihood that racial or ethnic groups will express their identity as a group in the political arena. Specific references to blacks, Asian Pacifics, Mexican Americans, and other groups were used to indicate the situations in which "group" might indicate cultural similarities, but not political expressions, and those extremes such as black Americans who represent both cultural similarities and political expressions of group identity. Even in this latter case, strong external and internal factors supporting group-based political expression do not guarantee continuing political unanimity. Increases within racial/ethnic group distinctions and socioeconomic differences arising from the lifting of the most extreme barriers of racial discrimination may reduce the strong group-based political expression that has characterized black political identity in the past. However, continuing economic stress among blacks and the growing economic distress of the nation that faces increased competition from abroad, the impact of the penetration of drugs into the society, and the response of the black social structure to all of these forces may also reinforce, rather than dissipate, group-based political expression.

NOTES

1. There are locations where there is genuine black political ethnicity. In Boston, for example, Toni Travis (1990) reports on the multiethnic character of the black population including American blacks of different economic and ethnic variation, such as West Indians, and Cape Verdeans (1990: 113, 316). New York has a sizable and more complex

community of black ethnics because of the large number of Caribbean immigrants, including those from the Dutch West Indies, the American Virgin Islands, Guyana, Haiti, Jamaica, and Panama who have settled in the city (Green and Wilson 1989: 117–138).

2. New York City is a recent example. Green and Wilson note, "Between 1966 and 1979, European immigration was held to 22.9 percent while Caribbean and Latin American changed from 15 percent to 46.6 percent" (1989: 117). This has significantly increased the ethnic heterogeneity of black New York, given the tendency for black immigrants from the Caribbean to settle primarily in the city, specifically in Brooklyn.

3. The Pacific Islanders as a group are only 5.1 percent of the total, while the Cambodians, Hmong, Laotians, and Thais are each only 2 percent or less.

4. Only the National Black Election Studies attempted to generate a methodologically significant sample size; a panelist at the University College of Los Angeles conference at which an earlier version of this paper was originally presented (Pinderhughes 1989), Frank Gilliam conducted an oversample (total black N = 544) of the 1987 General Social Survey, which he reported on in a 1990 article. Walton comments on this type of strategy: "The mere doubling, or tripling of the black percentage in the population would not resolve the error" (1985: 81). Bobo and Gilliam found that "blacks in high–black empowerment areas—as indicated by control of the mayor's office—are more active than either blacks living in low-empowerment areas or their white counterparts of comparable socioeconomic status" (1990: 377).

REFERENCES

Andersen, Kristi. 1979. *The Creation of a Democratic Majority, 1928–1936*. Chicago, IL: University of Chicago Press.

Banfield, Edward C. 1965. *Political Influence*. New York: Free Press.

Barker, Lucius J., and Ron Walters, eds. 1989. *Jesse Jackson's 1984 Presidential Campaign, Challenge and Change in American Politics*. Urbana: University of Illinois Press.

Barnett, Marguerite Ross. 1976. "A Theoretical Perspective on Racial Public Policy." In Marguerite Ross Barnett and James A. Hefner, eds., *Public Policy for the Black Community: Strategies and Perspectives*. New York: Alfred Publishing. 1–54.

Barrera, Mario. 1979. *Race and Class in the Southwest: A Theory of Racial Inequality*. South Bend, IN: University of Notre Dame Press.

Baxter, Sandra, and Marjorie Lansing. 1981. *Women and Politics: The Invisible Majority*. Ann Arbor: University of Michigan Press.

Bennett, Claudette E. 1992. *The Asian and Pacific Islander Population in the United States: March 1991 and 1990*. U.S. Bureau of the Census. *Current Population Reports*, P20–459. Washington, D.C.

Bennett, Claudette E. 1995. *The Black Population in the United States: March 1994 and 1993*. U.S. Bureau of the Census. *Current Population Reports*, P20–480. Washington, D.C.

Bobo, Lawrence, and Franklin D. Gilliam, Jr. 1990. "Race, Sociopolitical Participation and Black Empowerment." *American Political Science Review* 84 (June): 378–393.

Browning, Rufus, Dale Rogers Marshall, and David Tabb. 1984. *Protest Is Not Enough: The Struggle of Blacks and Hispanics for Equality in Urban Politics*. Berkeley: University of California Press.

Browning, Rufus, Dale Rogers Marshall, and David Tabb. 1990. *Racial Politics in American Cities*. New York: Longman.

Bunche, Ralph J. 1973. *The Political Status of the Negro in the Age of FDR*. Chicago: University of Chicago Press.

Campbell, Angus, William Converse, Donald Stokes, and Warren Miller. 1960. *The American Voter*. New York: John Wiley.

Carmichael, Stokely, and Charles V. Hamilton. 1967. *Black Power*. The Politics of Liberation in America. New York: Vintage.

Cavanagh, Thomas E. 1985. *Inside Black America: The Message of the Black Vote in the 1984 Elections*. Washington, D.C.: Joint Center for Political Studies.

Chan, Sucheng. 1991. *Entry Denied: Exclusion and the Chinese Community in America 1882–1943*. Philadelphia: Temple University Press.

Dahl, Robert A. 1961. *Who Governs? Democracy and Power in the American City*. New Haven, CT: Yale University Press.

Dawson, Michael C. 1994. *Behind the Mule Race and Class in African-American Politics*. Princeton, NJ: Princeton University Press.

de la Garza, Rodolfo O., Louis DeSipio, F. Chris Garcia, John Garcia, and Angelo Falcon. 1992. *Latino Voices: Mexican, Puerto Rican and Cuban Perspectives on American Politics* Boulder, CO: Westview Press.

Erie, Steven P. 1989. *Rainbow's End: Irish Americans and the Dilemmas of Urban Politics 1940–1985*. Berkeley: University of California Press.

Espiritu, Yen Le. 1992. *Asian American Panethnicity Bridging Institutions and Identities*. Philadelphia: Temple University Press.

Falcon, Angelo. 1988. "Black and Latino Politics in New York City: Race and Ethnicity in a Changing Urban Context." In F. Chris Garcia, ed., *Latinos and the Political System*. Notre Dame: University of Notre Dame Press. 152–170.

Flores, Raymundo, and John Attinas. 1988. "The Latino Experience." Paper presented at the Midwest Political Science Association, April 14–16, Chicago, Illinois.

Glazer, Nathan, and Daniel P. Moynihan. 1963. *Beyond the Melting Pot: The Negroes, Puerto Ricans, Jews, Italians and Irish of New York City*. Cambridge, MA: MIT Press.

Green, Charles, and Basil Wilson. 1989. *The Struggle for Black Empowerment in New York City: Beyond the Politics of Pigmentation*. New York: Praeger.

Greenstone, J. David, and Paul E. Peterson. 1976. *Race and Authority in Urban Politics, Community Participation and the War on Poverty*. Chicago: University of Chicago Press.

Grimshaw, William J. 1992. *Bitter Fruit: Black Politics and the Chicago Machine, 1931–1991*. Chicago: University of Chicago Press

Gurin, Patricia, Shirley Hatchett, and James S. Jackson. 1989. *Hope and Independence: Blacks' Response to Electoral and Party Politics*. New York: Russell Sage.

Hawk, Beverly. 1987. "Keeping the Africans Out: Immigration Law as Cultural Engineering." Paper presented at the American Political Science Association, September, Chicago.

Hero, Rodney E. 1992. *Latinos and the U.S. Political System: Two Tiered Pluralism*. Philadelphia: Temple University Press.

Jackson, Bryan O., and Michael B. Preston, eds. 1991. *Racial and Ethnic Politics in California*. Berkeley: IGS Press, University of California at Berkeley.

Karnig, Albert K., and Susan Welch. 1980. *Black Representation and Urban Policy*. Chicago: University of Chicago Press.

Katznelson, Ira. 1973. *Black Men, White Cities*. Chicago: University of Chicago Press.

Key, V. O. 1949. *Southern Politics in State and Nation*. New York: Random House.

Kilson, Martin. 1987. "The Weakness of Black Politics: Cursed by Factions and Feuds." *Dissent* (fall): 523–529.

Kim, Claire Jean. 1992. "The Red Apple Boycott: Black-Korean Conflict, Racial Mobilization, and Political Incorporation in New York City." Unpublished paper, Yale University, October.

Latino Institute. 1986. *Al Filol at the Cutting Edge: The Empowerment of Chicago's Latino Electorate*. Chicago: Latino Institute.

McClain, Paula D., and Joseph Stewart, Jr. 1995. *"Can We All Get Along?" Racial and Ethnic Minorities in American Politics*. Boulder, CO: Westview Press.

Marquez, Benjamin. 1987. "The Politics of Race and Class: The League of MALDER United Latin American Citizens in the Post–World War II Period." *Social Science Quarterly* 68, no. 1 (March): 84–101.

Morris, Aldon D. 1984. *The Origins of the Civil Rights Movement: Black Communities Organizing for Change*. New York: Free Press.

Morrison, Minion K. C., 1987. *Black Political Mobilization, Leadership, Power and Mass Behavior*. Albany: State University of New York Press.

Nelson, William E., Jr. 1982. "Cleveland: The Rise and Fall of the New Black Politics." In Michael B. Preston, Lenneal J. Henderson, Jr., and Paul Puryear, eds., *The New Black Politics*. New York: Longman. 187–208.

Nie, Norman H., Sidney Verba, and John R. Petrocik. 1979. *The Changing American Voter*. Cambridge, MA: Harvard University Press.

Pachon, Harry. 1991. "U.S. Citizenship and Latino Participation in California Politics." In Byran O. Jackson and Michael B. Preston, eds., *Racial and Ethnic Politics in California*. Berkeley: IGS Press, University of California at Berkeley. 71–88.

Parenti, Michael. 1970. "Ethnic Politics and the Persistence of Ethnic Identification." In Brett W. Hawkins and Robert A. Lorinskas, eds., *The Ethnic Factor in American Politics*. Columbus, OH: Charles E. Merrill. 63–78.

Payne, Charles. 1995. *I've Got the Light of Freedom*. Berkeley: University of California Press.

Persons, Georgia, ed. 1993. *Dilemmas of Black Politics: Issues of Leadership and Strategy*. New York: HarperCollins.

Peterson, Paul E. 1981. *City Limits*. Chicago: University of Chicago Press.

Peterson, Paul E., and Mark C. Rom. 1990. *Welfare Magnets*. Washington, D.C.: Brookings Institution.

Pinderhughes, Dianne M. 1985. "Legal Strategies for Voting Rights: Political Science and the Law." *Howard University Law Journal* 18: 515–540.

Pinderhughes, Dianne. 1987. *Race and Ethnicity in Chicago Politics: A Reexamination of Pluralist Theory*. Urbana: University of Illinois Press.

Pinderhughes, Dianne M. 1988. "Black Political Participation." *Polity* 20, no. 3 (spring): 552–562.

Pinderhughes, Dianne M. 1989. "Racial and Ethnic Politics in America." In James H. Johnson, Jr., and Melvin L. Oliver, eds., *Proceedings of the Conference on Comparative Ethnicity: Ethnic Dilemmas in Comparative Perspective*, June 1–3, 1988. Institute for Social Science Research, University of California, Los Angeles. 279–291.

Pinderhughes, Dianne M. 1990. "The Articulation of Black Interests by Black, Civil Rights, Professional and Religious Organizations in the Jackson Campaign." In Lorenzo Morris, Charles Jarmon, and Arnold Taylor, eds., *The Social and Political Implications of the Jesse Jackson Presidential Campaign*. New York: Praeger.

Political Roster. 1995. *National Asian Pacific American Political Roster and Resource Guide*. Los Angeles: UCLA Asian American Studies Center.

Reed, Adolph L., Jr. 1986. *The Jesse Jackson Phenomenon, The Crisis of Purpose in Afro-American Politics*. New Haven: Yale University Press.

Rich, Wilbur C. 1989. *Coleman Young and Detroit Politics*. Detroit: Wayne State University Press.

Robinson, Jo Ann Gibson. 1987. *The Montgomery Bus Boycott and the Women Who Started It: The Memoir of Jo Ann Gibson Robinson*. Knoxville: University of Tennessee Press.

Sandmeyer, Elmer Clarence. 1991. *The Anti-Chinese Movement in California*. Urbana: University of Illinois Press.

Schexnider, Alvin J. 1982. "Political Mobilization in the South: The Election of a Black Mayor in New Orleans." In Michael B. Preston, Lenneal J. Henderson, Jr., and Paul Puryear, eds., *The New Black Politics*. New York: Longman. 221–238.

Sonenshein, Ralphael J. 1993. *Politics in Black and White: Race and Power in Los Angeles*. Princeton: Princeton University Press.

Squires, Gregory D. 1994. *Capital and Communities in Black and White: The Intersections of Race, Class and Uneven Development*. Albany: State University of New York Press.

Stone, Clarence N. 1989. *Regime Politics: Governing Atlanta*. 1946–1986 Lawrence: University Press of Kansas.

Tate, Katherine. 1993. *From Protest to Politics: The New Black Voters in American Elections*. New York: Russell Sage; Cambridge, MA: Harvard University Press.

Travis, Toni-Michelle C. 1990. "Boston: The Unfinished Agenda." In Rufus Browning, Dale Rogers Marshall, and David Tabb, eds., *Racial Politics in American Cities*. New York: Longman.

U.S. Bureau of the Census. 1990. *1990 Census of Population and Housing*. Summary Tape File 1C. Washington, D.C.

Verba, Sidney, and Norman Nie. 1972. *Participation in America*. New York: Harper and Row.

Walton, Hanes. 1985. *Invisible Politics: Black Political Behavior*. Albany: State University of New York Press.

Wei, William. 1993. *The Asian American Movement*. Philadelphia: Temple University Press.

Wilson, James Q. 1960. *Negro Politics: The Search for Leadership*. New York: Free Press.

Wilson, William J. 1978. *The Declining Significance of Race: Blacks and Changing American Institutions*. Chicago: University of Chicago Press.

Wilson, William J. 1987. *The Truly Disadvantaged*. Chicago: University of Chicago Press.

Wolfinger, Raymond. 1974. *The Politics of Progress*. Englewood Cliffs, NJ: Prentice-Hall.

Wolfinger, Raymond, and Steven Rosenstone. 1980. *Who Votes*. New Haven: Yale University Press.

Chapter 7

Class and Inequality in the City

Louise Jezierski

Cities are organized through inequality. As sites of both poverty and opulence, they seem to Americans, who have faith in the mass and the middle class, both perverse and fascinating. In the United States we are ambivalent about our cities, evident in our particular patterns of social class settlements (Beauregard 1993; White and White 1962). Moreover, our choices of residences reinforce inequality. In the United States, most wealthy and middle-class Americans have abandoned the city for the suburbs in an idealized attempt to ''control'' democracy, escape difference, and reify homogeneity along lines of class and race and patriarchal gender relations. Yet cities are wonderful precisely because of the surprise and challenge that come with the extensive social differentiation and juxtaposition found there: They contain a ''mosaic of social worlds'' (Wirth 1938). Our nation's concerns over diversity and inequality seem to be concentrated on the city as a site of social problems: homelessness, ghettoization, gentrification, and the increasing gaps in income and wealth between cities and suburbs. The city is a compelling subject because there is no greater test of our democratic ideals than in the multifaceted metropolis.

Urban research is guided by widespread agreement that urban processes are constituted through uneven development. It focuses on causes and patterns of social inequality and the politics of managing it. Theories of social stratification and urban research have been developed together, since the city, to some degree, contributes to the creation and maintenance of inequalities. Moreover, uban theories reflect upon and inform social reform policies. Below, I discuss how urban research incorporates theories of social inequality. First, I review definitions of social class in urban ecology and political economy, the convergence of a conflict approach with the paradigm shift in urban research, and new debates over polarization and fragmentation in the postindustrial city.

The major intellectual debates and paths of contemporary research on urban inequality are reformulations of concepts, theories, and methodologies first introduced in classical works to explain industrial capitalism and the rise of major industrial cities such as London, Manchester, and Chicago. A persistent question shaping the debate is how class positions and relations are defined, since capitalism itself has evolved to a postindustrial form. Second, how do other forms of inequality, especially race, ethnicity, and gender, fit into these earlier formations of social class inequality?

CLASSICAL APPROACHES AND THE INDUSTRIAL CITY

The city was a central focus of social theory and stratification theory because of the key role that it played in the transformation from feudalism to mercantile and industrial capitalism (Saunders 1986). Classical works have provided us with conceptions of social inequality that have led to three important strands used in contemporary studies of urban inequality. From Emile Durkheim (1893, 1964) and Georg Simmel (1964), a theory of social differentiation influenced the urban ecology paradigm. Max Weber (1978) provides a multidimensional view of power, including economic class, social status and prestige, and political or associational power. The works of Karl Marx (1967) and Friedrich Engels (1967) suggest that urban form and class struggle are based upon oppositional and exploitative class relations, determined within a particular social formation of the prevailing mode of production. These classical theories have modern adaptations.

The explosive growth and heterogeneity of industrial cities like Chicago and New York prompted academic researchers and social commentators to examine the interrelationship among the processes of modernization, industrialization, and urbanization. The ecological approach of the Chicago School explored the social differentiation and pathologies of the city. Starting with assumptions taken from Durkheim, the large size, density, and heterogeneity of the city prompt increased competition among individuals, who, in a process of adaptation to these conditions, pursue specialized niches in the local social system (Wirth 1938; Burgess 1925). The ecology of the city proceeds through the economies of land rent and the differentiation of subcultures (McKenzie 1967). A group or function may command or dominate a particular urban space—for example, an ethnic enclave or an industrial district—but this "uneven development" is assumed to result naturally into a functional, efficient equilibrium (see Wirth's *The Ghetto* [1928] or Zorbaugh's *Gold Coast and the Slum* [1929]). (Social inequality is therefore viewed as, in Durkheim's terminology, an "abnormal form" of the social division of labor.) One consequence for the viability of urban life is that differentiation and secondary relations can contribute to social distance among people (Simmel 1964; Fischer 1975; Savage and Warde 1993).

The ecological paradigm remained the mainstream approach for researching the city through the 1960s. Urban ecology provided a coherent view of rational economic competition and settlement patterns that sorted and segregated diverse urban populations in space. Since inequality was considered adaptive, "functional," and temporary, created by waves of immigration and industrialization, this approach undertheorized the political aspects of community structure. Pluralism seemed a popular and plausible explanation for the social division of labor found in communities in the early postwar period, as a belief in "progress" prompted a rational(e) approach to urban inequality. For example, little attention was paid to the fact that so-called natural enclaves were aided, of course, by explicit housing discrimination and the deliberate policy tools of urban planning, such as zoning and restrictive covenants that were advanced at this time. These policies institutionalized segregation by class and race. Labor struggles and the class analysis that accompanied them, prominent during the 1930s and 1940s, gave way to bureaucratic bargaining in the "managerial demiurge" of the 1950s and 1960s (Mills 1956). An underlying assimilation model expected the breakdown of ethnic and class differences, nurtured by the experience of urban to suburban mobility. Social analysis turned to tracing the trajectory of individuals and households within a stratified social system. New survey techniques and statistical methodology, as well as the expansion of federal funding for the U.S. Bureau of the Census and other survey data sets, enabled quantitative examination of large populations and the mathematical measurement of social and geographic mobility. Factorial ecology mapped residential patterns by age, race, and income. Socioeconomic status could be measured with a multidimensional scale of education levels, income, and occupational status. Generational mobility among fathers and sons could provide some measure of the attainment of the American dream (Gilbert and Kahl 1993).

The ecological framework essentially succeeded by pursuing a science of classifying group differences. Yet even as urban researchers were documenting inequality by mapping subcultures or demographic indicators in space, critical judgments about its systemic creation and maintenance seemed lost in the clinical evidence. Urban social policy was based on expectations that poverty or ethnic identity could be addressed by federal welfare or urban renewal policies and that the working class, immigrants, or racial minorities would assimilate into the mainstream, middle-class institutions of the white-collar job and the suburb. Downtown renewal projects assumed a mass society model of postindustrial urban growth in services and bureaucracies. The zero-sum relations between these downtown growth poles and their surrounding enclaves were rationalized in the name of progress. Urban renewal policy was designed to "help" people along in this process by obliterating the social spaces that housed diverse ethnic and working-class subcultures, leaving them little alternative but to follow the "dream of the rational city" (Weiss 1990; Boyer 1983) and move into tract developments. Moreover, the destruction of the city was designed to remove "old order status inequalities," especially classes, and to promote a new vision of democratic, middle-class homogeneity. As Gans (1982) so movingly portrayed, "modernization" would take precedence over community ties and contribute to further inequality.

The continued poverty and racism in the midst of the hopeful 1950s and 1960s, however, begged for new perspectives. Urban rebellions in our nation's cities belied a conception of urban "functional differentiation." The civil rights movement, grassroots neighborhood movements, and the feminist movement all required rethinking the distribution of power in our cities and suburbs. Some of these movements emerged in response to urban renewal and local social welfare policies. Community power analysis remained salient, influenced by the work of C. Wright Mills (1956), who criticized the disconnection between empirical research and social reform. This critical period inspired some of the best ethnographic studies in urban research, enlarging our understandings of the variety of urban community life—of the ghetto poor, the immigrant enclave, the middle-class suburb, the working-class urban village, and local stratification systems. But it also prompted urban researchers to contextualize the community study by reconnecting locality and politics. Another debate took hold—between pluralist and elite views of community power (Walton 1970).

Political structures and status hierarchies of the urban community were addressed by Weberian contributions to urban sociology. Max Weber's classical works on the city and on stratification are probably the most influential in urban analysis today. His multidimensional view of power extended Marx's view of class relations based in production to include assets of consumption, as well as status power, or power based on social honor. He also viewed political power as relatively autonomous from economic power, with the state having its own basis of authority. "Life chances" are determined as individuals amass variable degrees of power in any of these spheres—class, status, or political power. Weberian epistemology begins with the individual who consciously interacts with society. Thus, classes are not determined a priori. Class groups are composed of those with similar positions in the market. However, social class formation is an empirical question—classes must be consciously formed by the actions of those who share material interests. The city, in his view, organizes various dimensions of power, including political-religious authority, market relations, fortification, and law, which regulate exchange. Given competition over assets and power, it is assumed that the city is shaped by conflict and uneven development.

The multidimensional view of power was effectively explored through studies of community power structures, the main form of research between 1920 and 1970. The keen observations of social life undertaken by urban researchers exposed class and status inequalities in specific communities, and these case studies greatly influenced general stratification theory (Walton 1970). A lengthy debate over elite and pluralistic views of power dominated urban research from the 1950s to the 1970s. But comparative examination of this research revealed that using different research protocols uncovered different levels of power, including decision making, non–decision making, and systemic power (Walton

1970; Bachrach and Baratz 1974; Lukes 1974). However, the emphasis on analyzing discrete localities led to a dead end. Explaining urban inequality required further contextualization and linkages to broader social processes.

PARADIGM SHIFT

A paradigm shift from a social ecological perspective to a political economy view of the city occurred in the 1970s and was advanced by two concurrent events (Zukin 1980; Saunders 1986; Gottdiener and Feagin 1988; Walton 1993). The first is the empirical experience of a global restructuring of capitalism since the 1970s and its local repercussions of deindustrialization and reconcentration of services in "global cities" (Bluestone and Harrison 1982; Smith and Feagin 1987; Sassen 1991). New forms of inequality have been introduced as global changes in the political economy transform our cities from industrial centers to fragmented, metropolitan, postindustrial economies built on personal, entertainment, and financial services. Today, the primary issues are the increasing polarization of social classes in our metropolitan areas and the fragmentation of the "quartered city," which entail hyperghettoization, gentrification, fiscal crisis, urban rebellions, and the use of mass spectacle as a substitute for community (Davis 1990; Harvey 1989).

Second, a theoretical debate over the definition of class has had a lively run since the 1980s that has engaged mostly Marxists versus Weberians. This debate is centered on the degree to which class is based upon positions in production or in a multidimensional, marketplace view. Since capitalist restructuring is a global phenomenon with specific local consequences, a profound rethinking of the nature of social class in contemporary society has developed. Those who eschew Marxism are concerned about the privileging of class analysis, arguing that industrial classes are no longer the norm. Rather, they believe modernization has brought about increased status differences determined more by lifestyles than by labor relations. From another position, postmodern challenges suggest that the nature of contemporary life is so fragmented that there is little shared experience and that class can no longer serve as a primary form of identity or solidarity.

The theoretical challenge to urban ecology came most explosively from urban scholars rooted in European theoretical traditions and the social movements of the 1960s. The new urban paradigm took into account a deeper, systemic level of power (Lukes 1974). Castells (1977) first exposed the assumptions underlying ecological theory in his contemporary classic *The Urban Question*, which questioned the too-ready acceptance of competition and land-based profit as "natural" processes in defining the city, while ignoring social conflict. A neo-Marxist critique of mainstream urban research argued that urban inequality could be explained by contexualizing urban processes historically, within capitalism. This was an important corrective to the view of the community in isolation. It argued that inequality was not caused merely by internal differentiation but that macrostructural processes such as capitalist accumulation, the role of the state in regulating capitalism, and growth ideology became important causal variables. Local decision making evolved from both local class struggles and external, global structures. Class struggle and conflict are endemic to the capitalist city and urban development, shaped by the oppositional relations of those who own and control capital assets in the city and those who do not.

The city, moreover, can influence class relations because space is a material force of production. The urban form concentrates and controls forms of capital, such as skills and technology, real estate, and dense populations of workers and owners. Social reproduction is also shaped in and through the city as unique patterns of consumption, political regimes, and cultural representations emerge. Different urban social formations emerge as capitalism changes over time. David Gordon's (1984) seminal article shows how different regimes of accumulation—the mercantilist city, the industrial city, and the corporate city—each produced specific power relations and class inequalities. He argues that spatial segregation by class has increased over time and that technology is less important than labor relations in shaping the metropolitan location of work and residences. Katznelson (1981, 1992) has written extensively on the role of the city in class formation. He argues that an urban-geographical imagination must be incorporated into the analysis of class formation. The spatial separation of workplace and residence, along with the peculiar nature of federalism and the greater local role in the distribution of urban services, has produced a place-specific politics, rather than a class-based politics in the United States.

Contemporary urban methodology incorporates both quantitative analysis and critical ethnography, that is, "reading the city" to analyze the power relations found there. Much of this work aims to show the linkages among culture and ideology, politics, and economic structure within a contested capitalist locale (Burawoy et al. 1991; Harvey 1989).

ECONOMIC RESTRUCTURING AND POSTSTRUCTURALISM: WHITHER CLASS?

The consequences of global, postindustrial restructuring in the latter half of the twentieth century have prompted new interpretations of social inequality and a recurrence of an old debate over the relevance of social class. Whether this change is viewed as a phase of postindustrialism, radical modernization, late capitalism, or postmodernism (Soja 1989; Harvey 1989; Sassen 1990) is a matter of heated argument, but there is some convergence of thought that a postindustrial approach improves upon a class analysis based on an industrial capitalism model. Realignment of class formations and class-identified political behavior has occurred due to the loss of industrial manufacturing, the emergence of new labor market distinctions, and the rise of credentialism.

How do we measure localized, fluid, postindustrial class formations? The interpretation of service-based cities, emergent suburban landscapes, and new middle-class positions requires better theoretical tools. Neo-Marxist and neo-Weberian social theories of inequality show some convergence (Burris 1986), but a substantive debate over the measurement of class has affected the analysis of urban inequality. A neo-Marxist definition of class position is determined abstractly and deductively by the commonality of class locations, including material interests, lived experiences, and capacities for collective action.[1] Erik Olin Wright defines class as ownership and control of three productive assets: capital, organizational resources, and skills and expertise (Wright 1985, 1989).[2] Thus, there are sites of multiple exploitations and contradictory class positions (1989: 305–313).[3] The definition of class in a Marxist perspective is not just that classes have *different* material interests, as in Weberian notions, but that classes have *opposed* material interests (Wright 1985: 285; 1994: 607). A Weberian analysis understands the relative accumulation of these assets in determining an individual's life chances. In a Marxist frame, class position is based not upon a cumulation of market capacities but upon a relation of exploitation and ideological domination. For Wright, while a Weberian analysis allows for mapping hierarchical class *positions*, the Marxian analysis is a more powerful analysis because it involves mapping dynamic, relational class *oppositions*.

The neo-Weberian perspective results in a conception of hierarchical stratification composed of many class positions. Beyond production relations, consumption is also included in the definition of economic class position. Mobility and the relative open or closed nature of a social class structure are key issues (Parkin 1979; Goldthorpe 1987; Goldthorpe and Marshall 1992). Cultural resources and ideologies play a causal role in creating interest groups. The state acts as a semiautonomous mediator of interests and distributor of resources and may be implicated in bias, with its ''neutrality'' compromised: either through capture by an elite or because it is bureaucratically dependent upon taxes and upon business growth in the long run (Logan and Molotch 1987; Peterson 1981). Stone (1980: 979) explains that the propensity of government officials to cooperate with upper-strata interests must be traced to a hierarchical arrangement of resources in the larger socioeconomic system. Biases in the distribution of resources can be institutionalized, and hence, no identifiable ruling elite is required to perpetuate inequality.

Other accounts suggest that actors are the fundamental thing: Logan and Molotch (1987) suggest that ''urban fortunes'' are determined by growth-minded local elites, especially those of a rentier class who own and control real estate, retailers, newspaper and television owners, and local banks (Squires 1989; Cummings 1988; Schwartz 1987; Whitt 1982). This neo-Weberian view of the distribution of resources in the urban marketplace leaves a fluid definition of class. Thus, an array of interests can coalesce around different projects for growth and the accumulation of land rents (exchange values) or antigrowth movements organized for the preservation of various use-values. These growth coalitions may work to enhance the decision-making power of some interests at the expense and exclusion of others to form a sort of local governing regime. The various configurations of interest groups organized into a decision-making elite, both inside and outside of local government, constitute an urban political ''regime'' (Elkin 1987; Stone 1980, 1989).

Neo-Marxist critics claim that this multidimensional view can go too far, losing class analysis in the interest of a wider factor analysis. What results is a more sophisticated version of pluralism and a continued reliance upon ''interest group theory'' (Manley 1983). In this view, class is insufficiently theorized, the capitalist nature of the local state needs specification, and culture and ideology must be grounded in capitalist processes (Cox and Mair 1989; Wright 1989).

However, the Weberian account of urban power structures is presently the most popular because it captures the empirical complexities of urban life and shows how multiple dimensions of inequality work in crosscutting ways. For example, Anderson (1991) argues that being ''streetwise'' requires a negotiation and consciousness of class, race, gender, and age between residents of a middle-class, mixed-race, gentrifying neighborhood and residents of a poor, black neighborhood. ''New'' cleavages subvert class divisions and are organized around political faultlines of race and racism, pro- versus antigrowth coalitions, or neighborhoods versus downtown real estate or corporate interests. Homeownership may also be considered a ''new class'' cleavage (Pahl 1989; Saunders 1990).

New considerations of local social structures and community subcultures have prompted analysis beyond class. Postmaterialist, or social value, issues and new social movements emerge that cut across class positions, such as environmentalism, ethnic and racial identity, and sexuality (Inglehart 1977). Laclau and Mouffe (1985) argue that we must get beyond class ideology and class cleavages in order to promote equality, democracy, and freedom, since power and identity are expressed in a multitude of forms. New social movements represent these bases of resistance (Scott 1990).

A poststructuralist approach emphasizes culture, space, and place. In some articulations, culture is equal to economic determinants, while in others, culture is a primary terrain of politics of representation and discourse. Castells (1983) applied a cultural-structuralist viewpoint to urban social movements. He argued that the urban experience can foster collective solidarities over issues such as collective consumption and democratic and cultural representation, as well as class formation. The roles of space and place have become an explicit object of urban theory (Soja 1989; Harvey 1989). Late capitalism succeeds globally, like never before, and standardization and commodification of lived experiences result. One consequence is the blurring of time and space (liminality), which has the contradictory result of both increased differentiation and homogeneity. Economic and cultural machinations of growth and consumption envelope both urban landscapes and inner landscapes: A new form of alienation emerges. Hometowns become expendable within global capitalism (Newman 1988). The unique familiarity of the small town is replaced with comfortable recognition of the mall. (Inter)National retail chains sell standardized hamburgers or intimate lingerie. Products and places all look alike, no matter where you are. The postmodern skyscraper and the empty steelmill are indicative of the relations of power that are exercised in late capitalism. Shifting landscapes are a modern form of alienation that extends beyond labor relations (Zukin 1991).

The postmodern dilemma not only sets up expectations of the end of ideology but also rejects the promise of "progress" and historical deliverance. Thus, empowerment and understanding must come from efforts to contextualize, historicize, and pluralize the fleeting, fragmenting, and contradictory experiences that one experiences in the present. A postmodern approach applied to cities celebrates them for their diversity and hopes that the greater independence and flourishing of localities, given an encompassing, yet fragmented world system, will provide a new base for resistance that connects localities with global power structures (Cooke 1989; Soja 1989; Harvey 1989). Given this new social formation, postmodernists argue that we can no longer privilege the concept of class since difference and multiple inequalities are so intertwined.

Though rejecting of a postmodernist view, some Weberian theorists go further and discount class analysis as no longer relevant. In a provocative statement that prompted furious debate, Pahl (1989) argued that "forms of identity and social consciousness other than social class" have become more salient, especially access to credit, housing classes, race, and gender. In a related perspective, Holton and Turner (1994) argued that class is best understood as a form of metaphor and is more rhetorical than intellectually persuasive. Finally, Clark and Lipset (1991; Clark, Lipset, and Rempel 1993) suggest that the decline of class identity in the West and the collapse of Communist states in Eastern Europe make class analysis outmoded.

Poststructuralism incorporates a multifaceted view of inequality and predicts increased fragmentation of identities and interests. Yet ample evidence requires us to see that class divisions, though complex, still exist and their effect is significant (Wright 1989; Hout, Brooks, and Manza 1993; Marshall et al. 1988; Goldthorpe and Marshall 1992).

DEBATING THE MEASUREMENT OF INEQUALITY: FRAGMENTATION OR POLARIZATION?

The shift to a postindustrial economy and the crises of capitalist restructuring are realigning social classes. Some evident trends include (1) job shifts from manufacturing to service industries; (2) increases in credentialed workers; (3) greater insecurity in job tenure; (4) declines in organized labor membership; (5) rising unemployment, income inequality, and poverty; (6) realignments by race, gender, age, and regional employment; (7) declines in welfare state provision; and (8) increases in privatism (Silver 1993: 339). The emergence of a more "flexible" accumulation regime has required a "new accommodation with 'flexible patterns of work,' legitimating pliability, insecurity, unemployment, and 'getting by' with self-employment" (Pollert 1988: 50).

Capturing these trends and their significance for the city is exceedingly difficult, as Mollenkopf and Castells illustrate in their observations of New York. "From a spatial perspective, New York is increasingly dual and increasingly plural" (Mollenkopf and Castells 1991: 414). This complex and seemingly contradictory observation is the crux of a debate over the measurement and interpretation of the uneven development processes in cities (Morris, Bernhardt, and Handcock 1994). A thesis of polarization argues that there is increasing inequality between those at the top and bottom of the power distribution (Harrison and Bluestone 1988). Castells and Mollenkopf suggest that the social structure of New York can be characterized by two opposing forces: "a coherent social network of upper professionals from the corporate sector whose interests are directly linked to the development of the corporate economy" and "the remaining social strata [who] occupy increasingly diverse positions and have plural interests and values" (1991: 402). The power of a concentrated elite is reinforced by the fragmentation of subaltern classes who are a peripheralized, heterogeneous, and politically disorganized population (402–403).

Mollenkopf and Castells defend their paradoxical approach. On the one hand, a dualistic conception of stratification has the analytic power to describe a dynamic of opposition and to predict the nature of social relations. Yet they recognize this dualistic analysis is hindered empirically because it fails to capture the complexity of urban reality. Critics of dualistic analysis suggest our theories must capture a more complex social division of labor (Sayer and Walker 1992; Marcuse 1993).

HOW MUCH INEQUALITY?

Substantial evidence suggests an increasing income gap between the richest and the poorest in the United States, a trend toward polarization that threatens a shrinking middle class (Bradbury 1986; Harrison and Bluestone 1988; Newman 1988; Goldsmith and Blakely 1992; Danzinger and Gottschalk 1993; Morris, Bernhardt, and Handcock 1994). The particular articulation of polarization in the urban setting includes greater concentration of poverty, along with some gentrification and displacement in the center city, and increasing gaps between cities and suburbs (Nathan and Adams 1989). Overall, greater geographic segregation by class and race is the result of lower incomes (Jargowsky and Bane 1991; Lorence and Nelson 1993), continued racial segregation (Massey and Denton 1993), and social isolation (Wilson 1987).

The geographical concentration of the poor can be attributed to different processes. Wilson (1987) argues that social isolation results when nonpoor blacks migrated out of central-city neighborhoods for higher-income neighborhoods and suburbs, leaving only the most disadvantaged behind. Tienda (1991) suggests that poor people are more likely to move into already poor neighborhoods. Second, as general poverty increases, poor neighborhoods will increase, including the concentration of non-Hispanic white, poor neighborhoods (Jargowsky and Bane 1991). In a third hypothesis, Massey and his colleagues argue that the increasing concentration of poor blacks stems from discrimination in the housing market against African Americans, that the black middle class is also segregated, and that class segmentation is higher for Asians and Hispanics than for African Americans (Massey and Denton 1993; Massey, Gross, and Shibuya 1994).

Polarization and fragmentation in the city have prompted profound discussion of issues of representation and "governability" in urban research and policy. Despite the ultimate optimism of the postmodern's faith in diversity, or the "moral order" sustained by interdependent differentiation, as professed by social ecology, polarizing fragmentation may render the center untenable. "Rainbow rebellions" like the Los Angeles uprisings of April 1992 signal dissatisfactions and resistances from many different quarters simultaneously (Jaret 1991; Davis 1990; Gooding-Williams 1993; Baldassare 1994). Less visible, but more consequential, the greater capacity of elites to exit the city and to express their more powerful voice deserves more public scrutiny and debate (Squires 1989). Institutional disinvestment, such as federal cutbacks to cities and local fiscal crises, exacerbate the plight of the poor, the working class, and the middle class. Without access to jobs or social services such as public libraries, basic physical infrastructure, and safety—resources that mainstream America takes for granted—urban populations risk becoming increasingly disadvantaged (Gans 1993; Rusk 1993). Increasing segregation, repression, and reliance on the "fortress city" constitute a paradoxical solution for the urban middle classes as they try to maintain homogenous "community" and property values while polarization becomes ever more threatening: They are creating autonomous spaces within which alienation grows (Davis 1990).

THE CITY AND THE FORMATION OF SOCIAL CLASS

City space works as a material force in shaping classes. As Weber suggested, the city remains provocative ground for working out social values and institutions: The city continues to define the social cleavages found in American society as a whole (Castells and Mollenkopf 1991: 412). Landscapes are infused with power, and the built environment can create profit and community (Zukin 1991; Harvey 1989). The production and control of urban space are a means of creating, managing, and resisting inequality. As the urban environment sustains subcultures (Fischer 1975; Gans 1982), it also concentrates and segregates along class, racial, or gendered lines. The peculiar spatial separation of work life and home life in American society creates unique, class-related fault lines, emphasizing consumption, more abstract political loyalties, and especially, a more complex and fluid form of social class (Katznelson 1981).

Marcuse (1993) outlines the interactive role that space plays in exacerbating the problems of the "divided" city. The following list represents facets of increasing urban inequality, especially since the 1980s:

1. The irrationality of advanced homelessness in an age of abundance.
2. Increases in both the gentrified city and the abandoned city, which are linked.

3. Displacement as a mechanism of expansion.

4. The importance of neighborhood or turf for social identification.

5. Increased barriers among people defined in space or turf.

6. The government's role in fortifying the gentrified and abandoned city without redistributive policies to mitigate these inequalities.

7. Reoriented political cleavages that make coalitions more difficult.

This clear list of symptoms allows us to see that urban policy designed to mitigate inequality will require more generous social policy targeted to cities, an effort to break down barriers among social groups, and the reorganization of democratic organizations, such as political parties, that will give a stronger means to coordinate interests. Obviously, the scope of the problem belies any quick and effective policy antidote.

Hopefully, however, a renewed research effort can help shape understanding and social policy. Wilson's (1987) pathbreaking study of the poor in Chicago broke a deafening, decade-long silence on the issue of urban poverty. And we have more kinds of inequalities that also need attention. New research on the gendering of space, life cycle and age in community, the interaction of different ethnic communities, and gay and lesbian neighborhoods have created inroads to getting at discrete and interactive aspects of multidimensional inequality. Thus, a complex task is required, one that includes consciousness of the role of space in concentrating and separating or integrating the distribution of wealth and status in the city. To capture these complexities, new statistical methods will be required to map and analyze social networks, to measure causal paths, and to weigh variables. But we will also need qualitative narratives to capture the depth and breadth of unequal relations. The challenge is to capture and measure power and domination, acquiescence, and resistance in the city.

NOTES

1. As Katznelson put it, class formation involves four levels: the structure of class based upon production; class-based patterns of life and social relations, at work and off work; the constituted cultural order of class, which sets preferences, cognitions, and possibilities; and collective action.

2. Wright provides a rationale for why a neo-Marxist class analysis is still salient and why one can pass on the "Weberian temptation": Marxism provides a coherent theory of history and social change; the concept of exploitation provides a deeper, structural analysis of power that links social macrostructure with micropatterns of conflict and social change; and Marxism provides a coherent ordering of concepts within a larger, structural analysis of society (1989: 313–322). A Marxist view of class exploitation implies antagonistic conflicts among actors, whereas life chances does not.

3. Thus, beyond capitalist and proletarian positions, the middle class may be considered exploited as wage earners but also as exploiters in their position of ownership and control of organizational or skills assets.

REFERENCES

Anderson, Elijah. 1991. *Streetwise.* Chicago: University of Chicago Press.

Bachrach, Peter, and Morton Baratz. 1974. *Power and Poverty: Theory and Practice.* New York: Oxford University Press.

Baldassare, Mark. 1994. *The Los Angeles Riots.* Boulder, CO: Westview.

Beauregard, Robert A. 1993. *Voices of Decline: The Post War Fate of U.S. Cities.* Cambridge: Blackwell.

Bell, Daniel. 1960. *The End of Ideology.* Glencoe, IL: Free Press.

Bluestone, Barry, and Bennett Harrison. 1982. *The Deindustrialization of America.* New York: Basic Books.

Boyer, Christine. 1983. *Dreaming the Rational City: The Myth of American City Planning.* Cambridge, MA: MIT Press.

Bradbury, Katherine. 1986. "The Shrinking Middle Class." *New England Economic Review* (September–October): 41–55.

Burawoy, Michael, Alice Burton, Ann Arnett Ferguson, Kathryn J. Fox, Joshua Gamson, Nadine Gartrell, Leslie Hurst, Charles Hurzman, Leslie Salzinger, Josepha Schiffman, and Shiori Ui. 1991. *Ethnography Unbound: Power and Resistance in the Modern Metropolis.* Berkeley: University of California Press.

Burgess, Ernest W. 1925. "The Growth of the City: An Introduction to a Research Project." In Robert Park and Ernest Burgess, eds., *The City.* Chicago: University of Chicago Press. 47–62.

Burris, Val. 1986. "The Discovery of the New Middle Class." *Theory and Society* 15: 317–349.

Capek, Stella, and John Gilderbloom. 1992. *Community versus Commodity.* Albany: SUNY Press.

Castells, Manuel. 1977. *The Urban Question.* London: Edward Arnold.

Castells, Manuel. 1983. *City and the Grassroots.* Berkeley: University of California Press.

Castells, Manuel, and John Mollenkopf. 1991. "Conclusion: Is New York a Dual City?" In John Mollenkopf and Manuel Castells, eds., *Dual City: Restructuring New York.* New York: Russell Sage Foundation.

Clark, Terry, and Seymour Martin Lipset. 1991. "Are Social Classes Dying?" *International Sociology* 6, no. 4: 397–410.

Clark, Terry Nichols, Seymour Martin Lipset, and Michael Rempel. 1993. "The Declining Political Significance of Social Class." *International Sociology* 8, no. 3: 293–316.

Cooke, Peter. 1989. *Localities.* London: Unwin Hyman.

Cox, Kevin, and Andrew Mair. 1989. "Urban Growth Machines and the Politics of Local Economic Development." *International Journal of Urban and Regional Research* 13, no. 1: 137–146.

Cummings, Scott, ed. 1988. *Business Elites and Urban Development.* Albany: SUNY Press.

Dahl, Robert. 1961. *Who Governs? Democracy and Power in an American City.* New Haven, CT: Yale University Press.

Danzinger, Sheldon, and Peter Gottschalk, eds. 1993. *Uneven Tides: Rising Inequality in America.* New York: Russell Sage.

Davis, Mike. 1990. *City of Quartz*. London: Verso.

Domhoff, G. William. 1978. *Who Really Rules? New Haven and Community Power Reexamined*. New Brunswick, NJ: Transaction Books.

Durkheim, Emile. 1964. *The Division of Labor in Society*. New York: Free Press. (Originally published in 1893)

Elkin, Stephen. 1987. *City and Regime in the American Republic*. Chicago: University of Chicago Press.

Fainstein, Susan, Norman I. Fainstein, Richard Child Hill, Dennis Judd, and Michael Peter Smith. 1986. *Restructuring the City*. New York: Longman.

Fischer, Claude. 1975. "Toward a Subcultural Theory of Urbanism." *American Journal of Sociology* 80: 1319–1341.

Gans, Herbert. 1982. *The Urban Villagers: Group and Class in the Life of Italian-Americans*. New York: Free Press. (Originally published in 1962)

Gans, Herbert. 1993. "From Underclass to Undercaste." *International Journal of Urban and Regional Research* 17, no. 3: 327–335.

Gilbert, Dennis, and Joseph Kahl. 1993. *The American Class Structure: A New Synthesis*. Belmont, CA: Wadsworth.

Goldsmith, William, and Edward Blakely. 1992. *Separate Societies: Poverty and Inequality in U.S. Cities*. Philadelphia: Temple University Press.

Goldthorpe, John H. 1987. *Social Mobility and Class Structure in Modern Britain*, 2nd ed. Oxford: Clavendon Press.

Goldthorpe, John H., and Gordon Marshall. 1992. "The Promising Future of Class Analysis: A Response to Recent Critiques." *Sociology* 26, no. 3: 381–400.

Gooding-Williams, Robert, ed. 1993. *Reading Rodney King, Reading Urban Uprising*. New York: Routledge.

Gordon, David. 1984. "Capitalist Development and the History of American Cities." In William K. Tabb and Larry Sawers, eds., *Marxism and the Metropolis: New Perspectives in Urban Political Economy*. New York: Oxford University Press. 21–53.

Gottdiener, Mark, and Joe Feagin. 1988. "The Paradigm Shift in Urban Sociology." *Urban Affairs Quarterly* 24, no. 2: 163–188.

Harrison, Bennett, and Barry Bluestone. 1988. *The Great U-Turn: Corporate Restructuring and the Polarizing of America*. New York: Basic Books.

Harvey, David. 1989. *The Condition of Postmodernity*. Oxford: Blackwell.

Holton, Robert, and Bryans Turner. 1994. "Debate and Psuedo Debate in Class Analysis: Some Unpromising Page of Goldthorpe and Marshall's Defence." *Sociology* 28, no. 35: 789–804.

Hout, Mike, Clem Brooks, and Jeff Manza. 1993. "The Persistence of Classes in Post-Industrial Societies." *International Sociology* 8, no. 3: 259–277.

Hunter, Floyd. 1953. *Community Power Structure: A Study of Decision Makers*. Chapel Hill: University of North Carolina Press.

Inglehart, R. 1977. *The Silent Revolution: Changing Values and Political Styles among Western Publics*. Princeton: Princeton University Press.

Jaret, Charles. 1991. "Recent Structural Change and U.S. Urban Ethnic Minorities." *Journal of Urban Affairs* 13, no. 3: 307–336.

Jargowsky, Paul, and Mary Jo Bane. 1991. "Ghetto Poverty in the United States, 1970–1980." In C. Jencks and P. E. Peterson, eds., *The Urban Underclass*. Washington, D.C.: Brookings Institution. 235–273.

Jencks, Christropher, and Paul Peterson, eds. 1991. *The Urban Underclass*. Washington, D.C.: Brookings Institution.

Katznelson, Ira. 1981. *City Trenches: Urban Politics and the Patterning of Class in the United States*. New York: Pantheon Books.

Katznelson, Ira. 1992. *Marxism and the City*. New York: Oxford University Press.

Kozol, Jonathan. 1991. *Savage Inequalities: Children in America's Schools*. New York: HarperCollins.

Laclau, Ernesto, and Chantal Mouffe. 1985. *Hegemony and Socialist Strategy: Towards a Radical Democratic Politics*. London: Verso.

Logan, John, and Harvey Molotch. 1987. *Urban Fortunes: The Political Economy of Place*. Berkeley: University of California Press.

Lorence, Jon, and Joel Nelson. 1993. "Industrial Restructuring and Metropolitan Earnings Inequality, 1970–1980." *Research in Social Stratification and Mobility* 12: 145–184.

Lukes, Steven. 1974. *Power: A Radical View*. London: Macmillan Press, Ltd.

McKenzie, Roderick. 1967. "The Ecological Approach to the Study of the Human Community." In Robert Park, Ernest W. Burgess, and Roderick D. McKenzie, eds., *The City*, Chicago: University of Chicago Press. (Originally published in 1925)

Manley, John. 1983. "Neo-Pluralism: A Class Analysis of Pluralism I and Pluralism II." *American Political Science Review* 77 (June): 368–389.

Marcuse, Peter. 1993. "What's So New about Divided Cities?" *International Journal of Urban and Regional Research* 17, no. 3: 355–365.

Marshall, Gordon. 1991. "In Defence of Class Analysis: A Comment on R. E. Pahl." *International Journal of Urban and Regional Research* 15: 114–118.

Marshall, Gordon, Howard Newby, David Rose, and Carolyn Vogler. 1988. *Social Class in Modern Britain*. London: Unwin Hyman.

Marx, Karl, and Friedrich Engels. 1967. *Capital: A Critique of Political Economy*. New York: International Publishers.

Massey, Doreen. 1984. *Spatial Divisions of Labor*. London: Macmillan.

Massey, Douglas, and Nancy Denton. 1993. *American Apartheid: Segregation and the Making of the Underclass*. Cambridge, MA: Harvard University Press.

Massey, Douglas, Andrew Gross, and Kumiki Shibuya. 1994. "Migration, Segregation and the Geographic Concentration of Poverty." *American Sociological Review* 59 (June): 425–445.

Mills, C. Wright. 1956. *The Power Elite*. New York: Oxford University Press.

Mincey, Ronald. 1988. *Is There a White Underclass?* Washington, D.C.: Urban Institute. (Cited in Jencks, C. 1992. *Rethinking Social Policy*. Cambridge, MA: Harvard University Press. 252)

Mollenkopf, John, and Manuel Castells. 1991. *Dual City: Restructuring New York*. New York: Russell Sage Foundation.

Morris, Martina, Annette Bernhardt, and Mark Handcock. 1994. "Economic Inequality: New Methods for New Trends." *American Sociological Review* 59, no. 2: 205–219.

Nathan, Richard, and Charles Adams. 1989. "Four Perspectives on Urban Hardship." *Political Science Quarterly* 104, no. 3: 483–508.

Newman, Katherine. 1988. *Falling from Grace: The Experience of Downward Mobility in the American Middle Class*. New York: Vintage.

Pahl, Ray. 1989. "Is the Emperor Naked? Some Questions on the Adequacy of Sociological Theory in Urban and Regional Research." *International Journal of Urban and Regional Research* 13: 709–720.

Park, Robert. 1915. "The City: Suggestions for the Investigation of Human Behavior in the City." *American Journal of Sociology* 20: 577–612.

Parkin, Frank. 1979. *Marxism and Class Analysis: A Bourgeois Critique.* New York: Columbia University Press.

Peterson, Paul. 1981. *City Limits.* Chicago: University of Chicago Press.

Pollert, Anna. 1988. "Dismantling Flexibility." *Capital and Class* 34: 42–75.

Rusk, David. 1993. *Cities without Suburbs.* Washington, D.C.: Woodrow Wilson Center Press.

Sassen, Saskia. 1990. "Economic Restructuring and the American City." *Annual Review of Sociology* 16: 465–490.

Sassen, Saskia. 1991. *The Global City: New York, London, Tokyo.* Princeton, NJ: Princeton University Press.

Saunders, Peter. 1986. *Social Theory and the Urban Question.* 2nd ed. London: Unwin Hyman.

Saunders, Peter. 1990. *A Nation of Home Owners.* London: Unwin Hyman.

Savage, Mike, and Alan Warde. 1993. *Urban Sociology, Capitalism and Modernity.* New York: Continuum Publishing Company.

Sayer, Andrew, and Richard Walker. 1992. *The New Social Economy: Reworking the Division of Labor.* Cambridge, MA: Blackwell.

Schwartz, Michael. 1987. *The Structure of Power in America.* New York: Holmes and Meier.

Scott, Alan. 1990. *Ideology and the New Social Movements.* London: Unwin Hyman.

Silver, Hilary. 1993. "National Conceptions of the New Urban Poverty: Social Structural Change in Britain, France, and the United States." *International Journal of Urban and Regional Research* 17, no. 3: 336–354.

Simmel, Georg. 1964. "The Metropolis and Mental Life." In Kurt Wolff, ed., *The Sociology of Georg Simmel.* New York: Free Press. 409–424. (Originally published in 1905)

Smith, Michael Peter, and Joe Feagin. 1987. *The Capitalist City: Global Restructuring and Community Politics.* Oxford: Basil Blackwell.

Soja, Edward. 1989. *Postmodern Geographies.* London: Verso.

Squires, Gregory, ed. 1989. *Unequal Partnerships: The Political Economy of Urban Redevelopment in Postwar America.* New Brunswick, NJ: Rutgers University Press.

Stone, Clarence. 1980. "Systemic Power in Community Decision Making: A Restatement of Stratification Theory." *American Political Science Review* 74: 978–990.

Stone, Clarence. 1989. *Regime Politics: Governing Atlanta, 1946–1988.* Lawrence: University Press of Kansas.

Tienda, Marta. 1991. "Poor People and Poor Places: Deciphering Neighborhood Effects on Poverty Outcomes." In Joan Huber, ed., *Macro-Micro Linkages in Sociology.* Newbury Park, CA: Sage. 212–244.

Tobin, Gary, ed. 1987. "Divided Neighborhoods: Changing Patterns of Racial Segregation." *Urban Affairs Annual Reviews,* vol. 32. Newbury Park, CA: Sage.

Walton, John. 1970. "A Systematic Survey of Community Power Research" In Michael Aiken and Paul Mott, eds., *The Structure of Community Power.* New York: Random House.

Walton, John. 1993. ''Urban Sociology: The Contributions and Limits of Political Econ-
    omy.'' *Annual Review of Sociology* 19: 301–320.
Warner, Lloyd, and Paul Lunt. 1941. *The Social Life of a Modern Community*. New
    Haven, CT: Yale University Press.
Weber, Max. 1978. *Economy and Society*. Berkeley: University of California Press.
Weiss, Mark. 1990. *The Rise of the Community Builders: The American Real Estate
    Industry and Urban Land Planning*. New York: Columbia University Press.
White, Morton, and Lucia White. 1962. *The Intellectual versus the City*. Cambridge,
    MA: Harvard University Press and MIT Press.
Whitman, David and Dorian Friedman. 1994. ''The White Underclass.'' *U.S. News and
    World Report*, October 17, 40–53.
Whitt, J. Allen. 1982. *Urban Elites and Mass Transportation*. Princeton, NJ: Princeton
    University Press.
Wilson, William Julius. 1987. *The Truly Disadvantaged: The Inner City, the Underclass,
    and Public Policy*. Chicago: University of Chicago Press.
Wirth, Louis. 1928. *The Ghetto*. Chicago: University of Chicago Press.
Wirth, Louis. 1938. ''Urbanism as a Way of Life.'' *American Journal of Sociology* 4:
    1–24.
Wright, Erik Olin. 1985. *Classes*. London: Verso.
Wright, Erik Olin. 1994. *Interrogating Inequality*. London: Verso.
Wright, Erik Olin. 1989. ''Rethinking, Once Again, the Concept of Class Structure.'' In
    E. O. Wright et al., eds., *The Debate on Classes*. London: Verso.
Zorbaugh, H. W. 1929. *The Gold Coast and the Slum*. Chicago: University of Chicago
    Press.
Zukin, Sharon. 1980. ''A Decade of the New Urban Sociology.'' *Theory and Society* 9,
    no. 4: 575–602.
Zukin, Sharon. 1991. *Landscapes of Power: From Detroit to Disney World*. Berkeley:
    University of California Press.

Chapter 8

Gender in the City

Genie N. L. Stowers

GENDER IN THE CITY: THE FORGOTTEN VARIABLE?

As in most social science and other fields, until recently the importance of
women and gender in urban research has been ignored. With the advent of
women's studies and women and feminist scholars in the 1970s and 1980s, this
began to change. Still, the consideration of gender as a variable or factor of
importance varies widely by subfield in the areas of urban research. In many
subfields, gender is still the "forgotten variable," and in some others, women
and gender issues have only experienced the "grafting of a new empirical object
of study onto existing disciplinary discourses" (MacKenzie 1988: 14–15). This
chapter focuses on the more recent research in this growing field in an attempt
to understand the entirety of the field today.[1]

WHY STUDY GENDER AND CITIES?

It is unfortunate that a chapter reviewing research on gender in the city still
needs to begin by arguing why the consideration of gender is important for
contemporary urban scholars. Stimpson suggests, "The American city has both
enhanced and constricted women's lives; the experience of men and women in
American cities is quite significantly different; and, finally, studies of such divergence and their effects are original, suggestive, and necessary" (Stimpson
1981: ix). Others (Freeman 1981; Madigan, Munro, and Smith 1990) define
some of the gender differences that make gender and the city an important and
critical topic. Not only have cities had disproportionately more women, they
have also had more single older women and disproportionately more female-
headed households. Women are located in cities due to the concentration of jobs

there and the public transportation necessary to get to these jobs. However, women (particularly female-headed households) earn less money than men in similar circumstances, so they are more dependent upon these central city resources. These and other trends have clear policy, political, and economic implications for cities.

Despite the clear implications of these trends, the degree to which women and other scholars are still struggling to have their work on gender seen and accepted suggests that many urban scholars still do not see why gender is important to the study of urban areas, much less why it should be incorporated as a matter of course into their work.

THE FIELD OF GENDER AND URBAN RESEARCH

The beginning of the field of women or gender in urban research can be traced back to the publication of a special edition of the women's studies journal *Signs*, devoted to the role of women in the city and later published in book form (Stimpson, et al. 1981). This and another early work (a special edition of the *International Journal of Urban and Regional Research* in 1978) were both interdisciplinary works, a trait that has characterized this growing field over time as largely women scholars banding together to ensure that women are considered in urban research.

Since that time, much of the field and its theoretical underpinnings have been dominated by scholars in the planning, architectural, geography, history, and sociology fields. An important source of the emerging field was the environment and behavior movement, a multidisciplinary effort stemming from scholars in the planning, architecture, and geography disciplines in both the United States and Canada (Wekerle, Peterson, and Morley 1980). These disciplinary emphases were apparent in the dominant themes of the early development of the field. Early scholarly efforts at incorporating gender into urban theory focused on the differences between the public and private spheres of society, the urban environment and how it influences behavior and urban designs, and women's equal access to urban services (Wekerle 1981). While these trends are still important, the field has clearly expanded and moved beyond these to empirical studies of new phenomena and explanations of more complex phenomena.

Another development in the field has been the movement beyond consideration of gender itself to the more complex relationships involved in the intersection of gender, race, class, ethnicity, sexual orientation, and age. Yet another critical development has been the expansion of gender considerations into other disciplines involved in the study of urban studies, such as political science, economics, and political economy. Thus, the field itself is growing in complexity at the same time it is growing in size and across disciplines.

CHANGING THEORETICAL PERSPECTIVES

Much of the work by women scholars, no matter what subdiscipline, has called for essential redefinitions of the city and of the urban studies field in order to incorporate gender into urban analysis. One of the central theoretical concepts is the separation of human lives into two dichotomous spheres—the public and the private—work and home life (MacKenzie 1988; Wekerle, Peterson, and Morley 1980). From this dichotomy arises many other theoretical insights, such as the perception of cities as masculine and suburbs as feminine (Saegert 1981). Women are still largely identified with the home and the private sphere; many of these private activities are situated in suburbs, where many would prefer to live and raise their children but where women still tend to be isolated from outside, public activities. Cities, on the other hand, are where much of the activity in the public domain takes place; research has also indicated less satisfaction with urban environments as residential sites. Spain (1992) extends this comparison. She posits that the female is associated with declining cities, and cities are now home to disproportionately more women and more female-headed households that are disproportionately poorer. These declining cities are thus seen as female, while growing, vibrant suburbs are considered male.

Writing later, Appleton also calls for a fundamental and more complex re-conceptualization of the city as the "nexus of three basic institutions that shape patriarchy: the family, the economy, and the state" (Appleton 1995: 45), arguing that discussion of economic and political systems without simultaneous discussion of the family in urban analysis is ludicrous. In this important theoretical article, Appleton also builds upon Stone's concept of urban regimes by identifying the concept of an urban gender regime, pointing out that different cities have different gender regimes. Appleton (47) defines a gender regime as "the way that gender is shaped by and shapes a particular social institution or, in the case of the city, a confluence of social institutions." According to her, every city has a gender regime that can be "characterized in terms of the prevailing ideologies of how men and women should act, think, and feel, the availability of cultural and behavioral alternatives to those ideologies, men's and women's access to social positions and control and resources, and the relationships between men and women." These are far-reaching conceptualizations of the city and urban behavior.

Part of the theoretical revisioning that scholars have engaged in is a literal reexamination of how the nonsexist city of the future would look. One major theme of urban gender theorists has been a complete revisioning of a future city without the constraints of a male-dominated and sexist society. Two classic pieces by Dolores Hayden ("What Would a Non-Sexist City Be Like? Speculations on Housing, Urban Design, and Human Work" [1981b] and *Redesigning the American Dream: The Future of Housing, Work, and Family Life* [1984]) feature a revisioning of the nonsexist city; these pieces clearly define and identify the role that gender has played in urban development and functioning. She examines the separation of the single-family home from any communal or shared spaces that could offer opportunities for sharing day care and house care responsibilities. She also notes that today's suburbs and some neighborhoods isolate women even more and create additional travel time just to get to employment and day care. The essential design of the city creates differences and disadvantages for women. The focus of these classic pieces of scholarship is not just to "add in women and mix"; instead, it is to reenvision what cities and urban spaces would look like if they were designed for women. Some of Hayden's visions for the redesign of urban areas include ways to reduce the sharp divisions between public and private spaces for women—the real sharing of home responsibilities and the development of housing facilities with common spaces allowing for centralized cooking and child care. Spain (1993a, 1993b) has also examined alternative futures by comparing feminist, utopian, and sustainable visions of cities and concluded that social and design changes such as building common spaces would be necessary to change the urban gender imbalance.

A LOST HISTORY

Some of the most important scholarly work on gender in the city is reclaiming the lost contributions of women activists and scholars from earlier periods. Even our understanding of the basis of the field of urban studies itself has been affected by sexism. While Robert Park and Donald Burgess are routinely given credit for the first systematic studies of urban phenomena, and so the creation of the "Chicago School" of urban analysis, there is evidence to suggest (Sibley 1990) that members of the University of Chicago School of Social Service Administration (mostly women) had already conducted systematic studies and made theoretical contributions earlier than the Park et al. studies. These women included Edith Abbott (the dean of the School), Sophonisba Breckinridge, Jane Addams (of Hull House), and Julia Lathrop. Earlier in this century, they published a series of studies on urban social problems that detailed issues of race, ethnicity, immigration, and housing in Chicago. These studies and the contributions of this group were later "lost," partly because of the role of male sociologists like Park who refused to acknowledge them.

Dolores Hayden is also responsible for retrieving a critically important contribution of urban women activists, thinkers, and designers from the past. In her 1981 book *The Grand Domestic Revolution* (1981a), she talked about the work and ideas of thinkers and activists such as Charlotte Perkins Gilman, Melusina Fay Pierce, and Victoria Woodhull—the "materialist feminists." During the mid-1890s, these materialist feminists were the first to "identify the economic exploitation of women's domestic labor by men as the most basic cause of women's inequality. They dared define a 'grand domestic revolution' in women's materials conditions" (1). These women theorized about and redesigned urban dwellings and spaces to optimize the collective spaces and reduce the amount of time women spent cleaning, taking care of children, and cooking. Although much of the written work and record of these early feminists was out of print or forgotten by the 1960s, many of the basic feminist theories of the 1960s had been expressed a century earlier by the material feminists.

Partly due to the very active role of women during these times, the Progressive and reform periods of American history represent a prime area for much work by historians on women and gender. Ethington (1992) argues that women have been left out of much urban history because much of the private sphere (incorporating the household) was itself left out. He and others (Locke 1990; Wolfe and Strachan 1988; Gittell and Shtob 1981; Cranz 1981; Ewen 1981) also argue that women were very active political and economic actors before they had the vote or moved fully into the workplace, particularly during the reform movements of the turn of the century. These findings counter the popular perceptions of politically passive women who worked only in the home prior to World War II and the 1960s.

SPATIAL CONSIDERATIONS AND IMPLICATIONS

Because of the importance of women planners, geographers, architects, and other environment and women scholars, much work has focused on the spatial and design dimensions of women in urban areas. Among these scholars, there is a consensus that urban space does have a gender-specific dimension (Johnston-Anumonwo, McLafferty, and Preston 1995; Turner 1995; Spain 1992, 1995; Michelson 1988; Hayden 1984).

Spain (1992) examines the continued occupational segregation by gender in the contemporary workplace; while men and women now work in the same workplace and are not spatially segregated as they once were, men are still disproportionately managers, while women are still disproportionately clerical and support staff.

Other gender differences in the spatial distribution of the urban workplace exist, particularly in the location of jobs and trip to work patterns (Johnston-Anumonwo, McLafferty, and Preston 1995; Turner 1995; Michelson 1988; Hayden 1984; Cichocki 1980). The spatial patterns of cities make these trips more difficult and time-consuming for women, as homes are separated, by zoning laws and design, from jobs, day care, and schools (Ritzdorf 1993; Spain 1992; Hayden 1981a, 1984). Women tend to work closer to home, and so have shorter commutes, but are also generally responsible for seeing their children to day care or school; therefore, their trips can become home to day care/school to work, extending commutes even further. Women, particularly women of color, are also much more likely to take public transportation; this makes what might be a short trip in geographic terms much longer in terms of time spent in transit (Johnston-Anumonwo, McLafferty, and Preston 1995). In fact, according to Johnston-Anumonwo, McLafferty, and Preston (1995), for minority women, the trip to work can equal minority men's in length.

Much of urban space has become "gendered" space. Evidence is clear that cities and downtowns, in particular, have disproportionately more female-headed households than cities in general (Turner 1995; Freeman 1981). Downtowns become gendered when women's choices are not considered and women and female-headed households are more prevalent (Turner 1995). These patterns are reinforced by continued development decisions (Turner 1995) and the lack of political power and political representation of women (MacManus and Bullock 1993, 1995) in urban areas.

Within cities, public housing has also become a gendered space (Spain 1993a, 1993b, 1995):

The effects of public housing eligibility criteria, combined with national changes in household composition trends and fiscal policies affecting housing authorities, transformed public housing from a place in which married couples predominated to a gendered space consisting of poor women. This shift has been accompanied by a decline in the proportion of public housing tenants earning wages and an increase in the proportion receiving welfare. (Spain 1995: 265)

Other gendered patterns also exist but are even less obvious to the casual observer. To date, most of the academic work on lesbian and gay behavior in cities can be found in the examination of spatial patterns of the gay community, particularly the gay male community. Ritzdorf (1993) argues that urban zoning systems reinforce heterosexual values by discouraging nonrelated unmarried persons from living in single-family areas and, in general, by reinforcing those single-family areas.

The work on lesbians and gay men also provides an interesting way to determine if gender differences exist in urban spatial orientations, by allowing an examination of gender differences in urban spatial patterns without the confounding effects of family. This and a basic description of the boundaries of gay male communities within cities have been accomplished by Castells and Murphy (1982) and Adler and Brenner (1992) in their examinations of lesbians and gay men and their spatial distributions in urban neighborhoods. According to Castells (1983), Castells and Murphy (1982), and Adler and Brenner (1992), gay men are located in more readily identifiable and publicly visible territory, while lesbians tend to be more evenly distributed across cities. This pattern is alleviated somewhat by some evidence of concentration in some communities as lesbians attempt to informally live near their friends, although in less publicly identified or visible neighborhoods than the gay male concentrations. Lesbians tend to live in older, less-affluent neighborhoods as a result of their status as women who have less disposable income than gay men.

These spatial patterns, creating definitive gendered spaces, also have repercussions for women's interactions with the urban political economy.

ECONOMICS

The restructuring of urban economies has had quite an impact upon women in urban areas over the past decades. Women attained two thirds of all new jobs created in the 56 largest cities from 1970 to 1986 (Clark 1990). This feminization of the urban workforce, begun after World War II and strengthened over the decades, has continued to the present time (Jezierski 1995; Rose and Villeneuve 1988). However, another trend found in the urban economy was the bipolarization of the workforce; more top-level and more bottom-level jobs were being created in cities than any other areas. The result of these two trends was the gendering of the urban workforce, focusing women's participation disproportionately at the lower end of the spectrum in the lower-paying service industry jobs (Jezierski 1995; Clark 1990; Rose and Villeneuve 1988).

These trends have led to the third important trend involving women in cities: the increased disproportional poverty of women and female-headed households, the so-called feminization of poverty (Pearce 1978). In 1980, 43.5 percent of all female-headed households were in the central city; 47.6 percent of female-headed households in the central city lived in poverty. This compares to the 32.8 percent of female-headed households living in poverty in the suburbs and the 41.2 percent in rural areas (Cautley and Schlesinger 1988). Clearly, the feminization of poverty can be considered an urban phenomenon. The feminization of poverty deepens for elderly and African American women, who experience significantly higher levels of poverty than white women (Worobey and Angel 1990; Franklin 1992). The percentage of female-headed households among the African American community grew from 20.6 to 43.7 from 1960 to 1985, as compared to growing from 8.4 to 12 percent for white families during the same period (Ricketts 1990).

These economic trends make it all the more difficult for women to operate successfully within the traditional political sphere of urban life, in the ''public'' sphere.

WOMEN AND URBAN POLITICS

Due to the traditional separation of the public and private spheres of politics, the focus of political science upon the public sphere, the still-limited movement of women in the public sphere, and a narrow definition of political actors, much of the work on women in urban politics has been limited to a discussion on political elites, organized groups, and ''big issues'' such as development and growth (Staeheli and Clarke 1995). This has meant that women and their role in the city have been overlooked, since women have tended to be active in neighborhoods and their schools (Rabrenovic 1995; DeSena 1994) and with developing and working within coalitions focusing on service delivery or safety issues (Kathlene 1995). In urban politics, the scholarly focus upon the public versus the private sphere (of the home) has led away from understanding the kind of political involvement in which women have participated. Staeheli and Clarke suggest a movement away from elite and ''big issue'' focus to citizenship and coalition politics as a way to incorporate gender, race, and ethnicity, place, and politics.

At the elite level, Susan MacManus (1992; MacManus and Bullock 1993, 1995) provides evidence of the still-limited election of women as mayors—14.3

percent in larger cities (MacManus and Bullock 1995). The degree to which this is true differs by region and type of local government; women tend to be more successful in the West and New England and in town meetings, representative town meetings, and district elections (MacManus and Bullock 1993, 1995). However, MacManus and Bullock (1993) report that there are more women mayors and council members than in any time in history, including as mayors of the nation's largest cities.

Although women council members are slightly more numerous than mayors (18.7 percent) and their numbers are increasing, their numbers are still limited (MacManus and Bullock 1993, 1995). MacManus and Bullock (1993) report that the proportion of female city council members across all cities, 18.7 percent, is not much better than the proportion of women mayors. The proportion of female council members increases with the size of the city, size of the council, and structure of the council. This work shows no gender differences in the proportion of council members selected from partisan versus nonpartisan elections and very few and insignificant differences from at-large versus district elections. This supports the results of earlier research (Bullock and MacManus 1991) that suggested only slight differences in proportion of councilwomen according to electoral structure, but these differences were themselves inconsistent across regions.

One of the main barriers to getting women elected to local office is getting women to run for local office (MacManus 1992). This is not always true in an urban setting, as there is some indication that more female candidates ran for and won office than male candidates in urban-based state legislative seats (Burrell 1990), and certainly school boards have been a traditional site for women candidates to get started in political life (MacManus and Bullock 1995). Other research has indicated that gender differences remain as local women officeholders see themselves differently than their male counterparts—as public servants and neighborhood and issue activists rather than as career politicians using an office as a stepping-stone (MacManus and Bullock 1995; Beck 1990). In some cases, this difference could actually be helping women get elected (MacManus and Bullock 1995). Women candidates who are also women of color have additional burdens placed upon them, as is clear from Randolph and Tate's (1995) case study examining the intersection of gender, race, and class in an African American city councilwoman's run for reelection in Richmond and the double standards placed upon her.

At the neighborhood and coalition level, there is a much different story of women's involvement because of the local association with home and families and the reduced barriers to women's involvement there (Rabrenovic 1995; Fincher and McQuillen 1989; Boles 1986). Much of women's involvement in local political activity occurred in voluntary organizations, in informal coalitions, and around local social issues because women were kept out of mainstream political involvement (DeSena 1994; Boles 1986; Gittell and Shtob 1981). In fact, women have typically been extremely active in their local communities, organizing rent strikes (Castells 1983), working on health and safety issues (Lois Gibbs in Love Canal, for instance), working on welfare issues and tenant and housing issues (Young and Christos-Rodgers 1994; Lawson, Barton, and Joselit 1980; Gittell and Schtob 1980), and even working to keep their neighborhoods segregated (DeSena 1994) or more people oriented (Stamp 1980) by serving in a neighborhood guardian role. Some of that local activism has led directly to efforts to provide services to women.

SERVING WOMEN IN URBAN AREAS

Much has changed in the way that services are provided to women in urban areas. Most important, scholars have begun to break down the assumptions that women are and behave like men in their needs and desires for services (LeVeen 1994; Santiago 1994; Schoenbaum and Webber 1993; Mansfield, Preston, and Crawford 1988, 1989; Hurst and Zambrana 1981).

Women's needs differ from men's in their need for basic health care (LeVeen 1994; Schoenbaum and Webber 1993; Worobey and Angel 1990; Markson and Hess 1981) and shelter (Beck 1995; Birch 1983a, 1983b, 1985; Anderson-Khlief 1981; Card 1981) services. Even among women, there is now a recognition that needs and behaviors differ by residence (Mansfield, Preston, and Crawford 1988, 1989), race and ethnicity (Santiago and Morash 1995; Santiago 1994; Stowers 1994; Miranne 1994; Franklin 1992), age (Miranne 1994; Worobey and Angel 1990; Markson and Hess 1981), disability (Santiago 1994), and sexual orientation (Stowers 1994) in today's urban areas.

''New'' social problems affecting women, like AIDS (acquired immunodeficiency syndrome) (Schoenbaum and Webber 1993), homelessness (Battle 1990; Kline and Saperstein 1982), domestic violence (Andrew 1995; Stowers 1994; Boles 1986; Schechter 1982; Cools 1980), sexual assault (Kathlene 1995; Gordon et al. 1981), and other crimes (Markson and Hess 1981), have developed (Schoenbaum and Webber 1993), are being reinterpreted as affecting women (Santiago and Morash 1995; Kathlene 1995; Santiago 1994; Stowers 1994; Schoenbaum and Webber 1993; Boles 1986; Schechter 1982), or have finally reached the public policy agenda through the efforts of women (Andrew 1995; Schechter 1982; Boles 1986) and their allies.

And the ''old'' problems of inadequate housing (Spain 1992, 1993a, 1995; Beck 1995; Miranne 1994; Birch 1983b, 1985; Anderson-Khlief 1981; Card 1981; Cook 1994), inadequate child care (Young and Miranne 1995; Michelson 1981), and lack of employment (Clark 1990; Dabelko and Sheak 1990; Cautley and Schlesinger 1988; Roistacher and Young 1981) still exist for women.

Due to the efforts of social movements, practitioners have been, and are still, recognizing that the traditional models for serving and providing services to women are not adequate or appropriate for many groups in urban areas (Santiago and Morash 1995; Santiago 1994; Stowers 1994). In fact, the recognition of these differences and the need to empower women rather than simply serve them has led in some cases to the use of women's networks (Thurston 1990; Boles 1986; Steinberg 1981) to develop innovative and creative models of social and health services in cities (Kathlene 1995; Santiago and Morash 1995; Stowers 1994; Boles 1986; Hurst and Zambrana 1981; Schechter 1982).

RESEARCH DIRECTIONS FOR THE FUTURE

It is clear that much more work is needed in the field of gender and the city. Although large strides have been made in the last 15 years, much still needs to be investigated and discussed (Sandercock and Forsyth 1992). First among these is the need for continued work on the differences among the wider community of women. How do urban behaviors, needs, and attitudes differ among women by race, ethnicity, age, sexual orientation, disability status, immigrant status, and nationality? Scholars are just beginning to acknowledge and examine these differences, and it is important to know more about them as the crucial basis for moving toward solutions for the urban problems that affect women.

In addition, there is much disparity between disciplines in their acknowledgement of the importance (or even reality) of gender in the city. In some disciplines, gender is still the "forgotten" variable. There is much work to do in disciplines like political science and economics to match the strides of geography, planning, and architecture. There is a need for an integration of the findings from all these fields by the scholars involved in these investigations. Most important, it is crucial that the scholars outside these investigations of gendered phenomena in the city start paying attention to gender, acknowledge that gender makes a difference in behavior, attitude, and status, and move to incorporate these findings into their own work (Sandercock and Forsyth 1992). Only then can we be sure that the assumptions of the past are clearly investigated and that women and gender are truly integrated into the urban research of today.

NOTE

1. There is much discussion about the differences between (and even the definitions of) women's studies, feminism, and gender studies. *Women's studies* is the interdisciplinary study of women, who are generally overlooked by more traditional disciplines. Women's studies emerged from and is informed by *feminist thought*, which can be defined as "a perspective that views gender as one of the most important bases of the structure and organization of the world" (Sapiro 1990: 417). Since its inception, women's studies scholars have had to fight for credibility as serious scholars and teachers, as many of their methods, findings, and analyses have been critical of the status quo in society and in academia. Because of these controversies, some programs and studies have adopted the more neutral term of *gender studies* to describe the field.

REFERENCES

Adler, Sy, and Johanna Brenner. 1992. "Gender and Space: Lesbians and Gay Men in the City." *International Journal of Urban and Regional Research* 16, no. 1: 24–36.

Anderson-Khlief, Susan. 1981. "Housing Needs of Single-Parent Mothers." In Suzanne Keller, ed., *Building for Women*. Lexington, MA: Lexington Books.

Andrew, Caroline. 1995. "Getting Women's Issues on the Municipal Agenda: Violence against Women." In Judith A. Garber and Robyne S. Turner, eds., *Gender in Urban Research*. Newbury Park, CA: Sage Publications.

Andrew, Caroline, and Beth Moore Milroy, eds. 1988. *Life Spaces: Gender, Household, Employment*. Vancouver, British Columbia: University of British Columbia Press.

Appleton, Lynn M. 1995. "The Gender Regimes of American Cities." In Judith A. Garber, and Robyne S. Turner, eds., *Gender in Urban Research*. Newbury Park, CA: Sage Publications.

Battle, Stanley F. 1990. "Homeless Women and Children: The Question of Poverty." *Child and Youth Services* 14, no. 1: 111–127.

Beck, Susan Abrams. 1990. "Rethinking Local Governance: Gender Distinctions on Municipal Councils." Presented at the 1990 meetings of the American Political Science Association, San Francisco.

Beck, Susan Abrams. 1995. "Gender and the Politics of Affordable Housing." In Judith A. Garber and Robyne S. Turner, eds., *Gender in Urban Research*. Newbury Park, CA: Sage Publications.

Berkeley, Ellen Perry. 1980. "Architecture: Toward a Feminist Critique." In Gerda R. Wekerle, Rebecca Peterson, and David Morley, eds., *New Space for Women*. Boulder, CO: Westview Press.

Birch, Ladner Eugenie. 1983a. "From Civic Worker to City Planner: Women and Planning, 1890–1980." In Donald A. Krueckberg, ed., *The American Planner: Biographies and Recollections*. New York: Methuen.

Birch, Ladner Eugenie. 1983b. "Women-Made America: The Case of Early Public Housing Policy." In Donald A. Krueckberg, ed., *The American Planner: Biographies and Recollections*. New York: Methuen.

Birch, Ladner Eugenie, ed. 1985. *The Unsheltered Woman: Women and Housing in the 80s*. New Brunswick, NJ: Center for Urban Policy Research.

Boles, Janet K. 1986. "The Women's Movement and the Redesign of Urban Services." Presented at the 1986 meeting of the American Political Science Association, Washington, D.C.

Bullock, III, Charles S., and Susan A. MacManus. 1991. "Municipal Electoral Structure and Electoral Structure and the Election of Council Women." *Journal of Politics* 53, no. 1 (February 1): 75–91.

Burns, Ruth Ann. 1981. "Breaking Down the Barriers: Women in Urban Management." In Catharine R. Stimpson, Elsa Dixler, Martha J. Nelson, and Kathryn Yatrakis, eds., *Women and the American City*. Chicago: University of Chicago Press.

Burrell, Barbara. 1990. "The Presence of Women Candidates and the Role of Gender in Campaigns for State Legislature in an Urban Setting: The Case of Massachusetts." *Women and Politics* 10, no. 3: 85–102.

Card, Emily. 1981. "Women, Housing Access, and Mortgage Credit." In Catharine R. Stimpson, Elsa Dixler, Martha J. Nelson, and Kathryn Yatrakis, eds., *Women and the American City*. Chicago: University of Chicago Press.

Castells, Manuel. 1983. *The City and the Grassroots: A Cross-Cultural Theory of Urban Social Movements*. Berkeley: University of California Press.

Castells, Manuel, and Karen Murphy. 1982. "Cultural Identity and Urban Structure: The Spatial Organization of San Francisco's Gay Community." In Norman I. Fainstein and Susan S. Fainstein, eds., *Urban Policy under Capitalism*. Beverly Hills: Sage Publications.

Cautley, Eleanor, and Doris P. Schlesinger. 1988. "Labor Force Participation and Poverty Status among Rural and Urban Women Who Head Families." *Policy Studies Review* 7, no. 4 (summer): 795–809.

Cichocki, Mary K. 1980. "Women's Travel Patterns in a Suburban Development." In Gerda R. Wekerle, Rebecca Peterson, and David Morley, eds., *New Space for Women*. Boulder, CO: Westview Press.

Clark, Thomas A. 1990. "Gender in the Emerging Urban Work Force: Educational Correlates of Industrial Shift in Large Cities." *Journal of Urban Affairs* 12, no. 4: 379–399.

Cook, Christine C. 1994. "Transitioning to Security: Alternative Housing for Single-Parent Women." Presented at the 1994 meeting of the Urban Affairs Association, New Orleans.

Cools, Anne. 1980. "Emergency Shelter: The Development of an Innovative Women's Environment." In Gerda R. Wekerle, Rebecca Peterson, and David Morley, eds., *New Space for Women*. Boulder, CO: Westview Press.

Cranz, Galen. 1981. "Women in Urban Parks." In Catharine R. Stimpson, Elsa Dixler, Martha J. Nelson, and Kathryn Yatrakis, eds. *Women and the American City*. Chicago: University of Chicago Press.

Dabelko, David D., and Robert J. Sheak. 1990. "Employment, Subemployment, and the Feminization of Poverty." Presented at the 1990 meetings of the American Political Science Association, San Francisco.

DeSena, Judith N. 1994. "Women: The Gatekeepers of Urban Neighborhoods." *Journal of Urban Affairs* 16, no. 3: 271–283.

Ethington, Philip J. 1992. "Recasting Urban Political History: Gender, the Public, the Household, and Political Participation in Boston and San Francisco during the Progressive Era." *Social Science History* 16, no. 2 (summer): 301–327.

Ewen, Elizabeth. 1981. "City Lights: Immigrant Women and the Rise of the Movies." In Catharine R. Stimpson, Elsa Dixler, Martha J. Nelson, and Kathryn Yatrakis, eds., *Women and the American City*. Chicago: University of Chicago Press.

Fincher, Ruth, and Jacinta McQuillen. 1989. "Women in Urban Social Movements." *Urban Geography* 10, no. 6: 604–613.

Flanagan, Maureen A. 1990. "Gender and Urban Political Reform: The City Club and the Woman's City Club of Chicago in the Progressive Era." *American Historical Review* 95, no. 4: 1032–1045.

Franklin, Donna L. 1992. "Feminization of Poverty and African American Families: Illusions and Realities." *Affilia* 7, no. 2 (summer): 142–155.

Freeman, Jo. 1981. "Women and Urban Policy." In Catharine R. Stimpson, Elsa Dixler, Martha J. Nelson, and Kathryn Yatrakis, eds., *Women and the American City*. Chicago: University of Chicago Press.

Gittell, Marilyn, and Teresa Shtob. 1981. "Changing Women's Roles in Political Volunteerism and Reform of the City." In Catharine R. Stimpson, Elsa Dixler, Martha J. Nelson, and Kathryn Yatrakis, eds., *Women and the American City*. Chicago: University of Chicago Press.

Gordon, Margaret T., Stephanie Riger, Robert K. LeBailly, and Linda Heath. 1981. "Crime, Women, and the Quality of Urban Life." In Catharine R. Stimpson, Elsa Dixler, Martha J. Nelson, and Kathryn Yatrakis, eds., *Women and the American City*. Chicago: University of Chicago Press.

Hayden, Dolores. 1981a. *The Grand Domestic Revolution*. Cambridge: MIT Press.

Hayden, Dolores. 1981b. "What Would a Non-Sexist City Be Like? Speculations on Housing, Urban Design, and Human Work." In Catharine R. Stimpson, Elsa Dixler, Martha J. Nelson, and Kathryn Yatrakis, eds. *Women and the American City*. Chicago: University of Chicago Press.

Hayden, Dolores. 1984. *Redesigning the American Dream: The Future of Housing, Work, and Family Life*. New York: W. W. Norton and Company.

Hurst, Marsha, and Ruth E. Zambrana. 1981. "The Health Careers of Urban Women: A Study in East Harlem." In Catharine R. Stimpson, Elsa Dixler, Martha J. Nelson, and Kathryn Yatrakis, eds., *Women and the American City*. Chicago: University of Chicago Press.

Ihlanfeldt, Keith R. 1992. "Intraurban Wage Gradients: Evidence by Race, Gender, Occupational Class, and Sector." *Journal of Urban Economics* 32: 70–91.

Jezierski, Louise. 1995. "Women Organizing Their Place in Restructuring Economies." In Judith A. Garber and Robyne S. Turner, eds. *Gender in Urban Research*. Newbury Park, CA: Sage Publications.

Johnston-Anumonwo, Sara McLafferty, and Valerie Preston. 1995. "Gender, Race, and the Spatial Context of Women's Employment." In Judith A. Garber and Robyne S. Turner, eds., *Gender in Urban Research*. Newbury Park, CA: Sage Publications.

Kathlene, Lyn. 1995. "Developing Rape Programs and Policies Based on Women's Victimization Experiences: A University/Community Model." In Judith A. Garber and Robyne S. Turner, eds., *Gender in Urban Research*. Newbury Park, CA: Sage Publications.

Kline, Elise Navratil, and Arlyne B. Saperstein. 1992. "Homeless Women: The Context of an Urban Shelter." *Nursing Clinics of North America* 27, no. 4 (December): 885–899.

Lawson, Ronald, Stephen Barton, and Jenna Weissman Joselit. 1980. "From Kitchen to Storefront: Women in the Tenant Movement." In Gerda R. Wekerle, Rebecca Peterson, and David Morley, eds., *New Space for Women*. Boulder, CO: Westview Press.

Leavitt, Jacqueline. 1980. "Women in Planning: There's More to Affirmative Action Than Gaining Access." In Gerda R. Wekerle, Rebecca Peterson, and David Morley, eds., *New Space for Women*. Boulder, CO: Westview Press.

Leavitt, Jacqueline. 1981. "The History, Status, and Concerns of Women Planners." In Catharine R. Stimpson, Elsa Dixler, Martha J. Nelson, and Kathryn Yatrakis, eds., *Women and the American City*. Chicago: University of Chicago Press.

LeVeen, Deborah. 1994. "Midwives as Providers for Inner-City Women: Critical Policy Issues for the 1990s." Presented at the 1994 meeting of the Urban Affairs Association, New Orleans.

Locke, Mary Lou. 1990. "Out of the Shadows and into the Western Sun: Working Women of the Late Nineteenth Century Urban Far West." *Journal of Urban History* 16, no. 2: 175–204.

Lopata, Helena Znaniecki. 1981. "The Chicago Woman: A Study of Patterns in Mobility and Transportation." In Catharine R. Stimpson, Elsa Dixler, Martha J. Nelson, and Kathryn Yatrakis, eds., *Women and the American City.* Chicago: University of Chicago Press.

MacKenzie, Suzanne. 1988. "Building Women, Building Cities: Toward Gender Sensitive Theory in the Environmental Disciplines." In Caroline Andrew and Beth Moore Milroy, eds., *Life Spaces: Gender, Household, Employment.* Vancouver, British Columbia: University of British Columbia Press.

MacManus, Susan A. 1992. "How to Get More Women in Office: The Perspectives of Local Elected Officials (Mayors and City Councils)." *Urban Affairs Quarterly* 28, no. 1 (September): 159–170.

MacManus, Susan A., and Charles S. Bullock, III. 1993. "Women and Racial/Ethnic Minorities in Mayoral and Council Positions." In *The Municipal Year Book 1993.* Washington, D.C.: International City Management Association.

MacManus, Susan A., and Charles S. Bullock, III. 1995. "Electing Women to Local Office." In Judith A. Garber, and Robyne S. Turner, eds., *Gender in Urban Research.* Newbury Park, CA: Sage Publications.

Madigan, Ruth, Moira Munro, and Susan J. Smith. 1990. "Gender and the Meaning of Home." *International Journal of Urban and Regional Research* 14, no. 4: 625–643.

Mansfield, Phyllis Kernoff, Deborah Bray Preston, and Charles O. Crawford. 1988. "Rural-Urban Differences in Women's Psychological Well-Being." *Health Care for Women International* 9: 289–304.

Mansfield, Phyllis Kernoff, Deborah Bray Preston, and Charles O. Crawford. 1989. "The Health Behaviors of Rural Women: Comparisons with an Urban Sample." *Health Values* 13, no. 6 (November–December): 12–20.

Markson, Elizabeth W., and Beth B. Hess. 1981. "Older Women in the City." In Catharine R. Stimpson, Elsa Dixler, Martha J. Nelson, and Kathryn Yatrakis, eds., *Women and the American City.* Chicago: University of Chicago Press.

Markusen, Ann R. 1981. "City Spatial Structure, Women's Household Work, and National Urban Policy." In Catharine R. Stimpson, Elsa, Dixler, Martha J. Nelson, and Kathryn Yatrakis, eds., *Women and the American City.* Chicago: University of Chicago Press.

Michelson, William. 1981. "Spatial and Temporal Dimensions of Child Care." In Catharine R. Stimpson, Elsa Dixler, Martha J. Nelson, and Kathryn Yatrakis, eds., *Women and the American City.* Chicago: University of Chicago Press.

Michelson, William. 1988. "Divergent Convergence: The Daily Routines of Employed Spouses as a Public Affairs Agenda." In Caroline Andrew and Beth Moore Milroy, eds., *Life Spaces: Gender, Household, Employment.* Vancouver, British Columbia: University of British Columbia Press.

Miranne, Kristine B. 1994. "The Social Organization of Sheltering and Space: Housing Independence among Older, African-American Women." Working Paper no. 27. College of Urban and Public Affairs, University of New Orleans.

Novac, Sylvia. 1986. *Women and Housing: An Annotated Bibliography.* Chicago: Council of Planning Librarians.

Nuccio, Kathleen E., and Roberta G. Sands. 1992. "Using Postmodern Feminist Theory to Deconstruct 'Phallacies' of Poverty." *Affilia* 7, no. 4 (winter): 26–48.

Pearce, Diane. 1978. "The Feminization of Poverty: Women, Work and Welfare." *Urban and Social Change Review* 11: 28–36.

Rabrenovic, Gordana. 1995. "Women and Collective Action in Urban Neighborhoods." In Judith A. Garber and Robyne S. Turner, eds., *Gender in Urban Research*. Newbury Park, CA: Sage Publications.

Randolph, Lewis A., and Gayle T. Tate. 1995. "The Rise and Decline of African American Political Power in Richmond: Race, Class, and Gender." In Judith A. Garber and Robyne S. Turner, eds., *Gender in Urban Research*. Newbury Park, CA: Sage Publications.

Ricketts, Erol. 1990. "The Origin of Black Female-Headed Families." *Focus* 12: 32.

Ritzdorf, Marsha. 1993. "Gender, Space, and the Politics of Hate." Presented at the 1993 meetings of the Urban Affairs Association, Indianapolis.

Roistacher, Elizabeth A., and Janet Spratin Young. 1981. "Working Women and City Structure: Implications of the Subtle Revolution." In Catharine R. Stimpson, Elsa Dixler, Martha J. Nelson, and Kathryn Yatrakis, eds., *Women and the American City*. Chicago: University of Chicago Press.

Rose, Damaris, and Paul Villeneuve. 1988. "Women Workers and the Inner City: Some Implications of Labour Force Restructuring in Montreal, 1971–1981." In Caroline Andrew and Beth Moore Milroy, eds., *Life Spaces: Gender, Household, Employment*. Vancouver, British Columbia: University of British Columbia Press.

Rose, Gillian. 1993. *Feminism and Geography: The Limits of Geographical Knowledge*. Minneapolis: University of Minnesota Press.

Saegert, Susan. 1981. "Masculine Cities and Feminine Suburbs: Polarized Ideas, Contradictory Realities." In Catharine R. Stimpson, Elsa Dixler, Martha J. Nelson, and Kathryn Yatrakis, eds., *Women and the American City*. Chicago: University of Chicago Press.

Sandercock, Leonie, and Ann Forsyth. 1992. "A Gender Agenda: New Directions for Planning Theory." *Journal of the American Planning Association* 58, no. 1 (winter): 49–59.

Santiago, Anna M. 1994. "Latina, Female, and Disabled: The Consequences of Multiple Minority Status." Presented at the 1994 meeting of the Urban Affairs Association, New Orleans.

Santiago, Anna M., and Merry Morash. 1995. "Strategies for Serving Latina Battered Women." In Judith A. Garber and Robyne S. Turner, eds., *Gender in Urban Research*. Newbury Park, CA: Sage Publications.

Sapiro, Virginia. 1990. *Women in American Society*. 2nd ed. Mountain View, CA: Mayfield Publishing.

Schechter, Susan. 1982. *Women and Male Violence: The Visions and Struggles of the Battered Women's Movement*. Boston: South End Press.

Schoenbaum, Ellie E., and Mayris P. Webber. 1993. "The Underrecognition of HIV Infection in Women in an Inner-City Emergency Room." *American Journal of Public Health* 83, no. 3 (March): 363–367.

Schoenberg, Sandra Perlman. 1981. "Some Trends in the Community Participation of Women in Their Neighborhoods." In Catharine R. Stimpson, Elsa Dixler, Martha J. Nelson, and Kathryn Yatrakis, eds., *Women and the American City*. Chicago: University of Chicago Press.

Sibley, D. 1990. "Invisible Women? The Contribution of the Chicago School of Social Service Administration to Urban Analysis." *Environment and Planning* 22: 733–745.

Soper, Mary. 1980. "Housing for Single Parent Families: A Women's Design." In Gerda R. Wekerle, Rebecca Peterson, and David Morley, eds., *New Space for Women.* Boulder, CO: Westview Press.

Spain, Daphne. 1992. *Gendered Spaces.* Chapel Hill: University of North Carolina Press.

Spain, Daphne. 1993a. "Built to Last: Public Housing as an Urban Gendered Space." Presented at the 1993 meetings of the Urban Affairs Association, Indianapolis.

Spain, Daphne. 1993b. "Gendered Space and Women's Status." *Sociological Focus* 11, no. 2: 137–153.

Spain, Daphne. 1994. "Sustainability, Gender Equity, and the Utopian Tradition." Presented at the 1994 meetings of the Urban Affairs Association, New Orleans.

Spain, Daphne. 1995. "Public Housing and the Beguinage." In Judith A. Garber and Robyne S. Turner, eds., *Gender in Urban Research.* Newbury Park, CA: Sage Publications.

Staeheli, Lynn A., and Susan E. Clarke. 1995. "Gender, Place, and Citizenship." In Judith A. Garber and Robyne S. Turner, eds., *Gender in Urban Research.* Newbury Park, CA: Sage Publications.

Stamp, Judy. 1980. "Toward Supportive Neighborhoods: Women's Role in Changing the Segregated City." In Gerda R. Wekerle, Rebecca Peterson, and David Morley, eds., *New Space for Women.* Boulder, CO: Westview Press.

Steinberg, Lois Saxelby. 1981. "The Role of Women's Social Networks in the Adoption of Innovations at the Grassroots Level." In Catharine R. Stimpson, Elsa Dixler, Martha J. Nelson, and Kathryn Yatrakis, eds., *Women and the American City.* Chicago: University Chicago Press.

Stimpson, Catharine R. 1981. "Introduction." In Catharine R. Stimpson, Elsa Dixler, Martha J. Nelson, and Kathryn Yatrakis, eds., *Women and the American City.* Chicago: University of Chicago Press.

Stimpson, Catharine R., Elsa Dixler, Martha J. Nelson, and Kathryn Yatrakis, eds. 1981. *Women and the American City.* Chicago: University of Chicago Press.

Stowers, Genie N. L. 1994. "Providing Domestic Violence Services to Women in a Multicultural, Diverse Environment." Presented at the 1994 meetings of the Urban Affairs Association, New Orleans.

Thurston, Linda P. 1990. "Women Surviving: An Alternative Approach to 'Helping' Low-Income Urban Women." *Women and Therapy* 8, no. 4: 109–127.

Turner, Robyne S. 1995. "Concern for Gender in Central-City Development Policy." In Judith A. Garber and Robyne S. Turner, eds., *Gender in Urban Research.* Newbury Park, CA: Sage Publications.

Vaiou, Dina. 1992. "Gender Division in Urban Space: Beyond the Rigidity of Dualist Classifications." *Antipode* 24, no. 4: 247–262.

Wekerle, Gerda R. 1981. "Women in the Urban Environment." In Catharine R. Stimpson, Elsa Dixler, Martha J. Nelson, and Kathryn Yatrakis, eds., *Women and the American City.* Chicago: University of Chicago Press.

Wekerle, Gerda R., Rebecca Peterson, and David Morley, eds. 1980. *New Space for Women.* Boulder, CO: Westview Press.

Wolfe, Jeanne M., and Grace Strachan. 1988. "Practical Idealism: Women in Urban Reform, Julia Drummond and the Montreal Parks and Playground Association."

In Caroline Andrew and Beth Moore Milroy, eds., *Life Spaces: Gender, Household, Employment.* Vancouver, British Columbia: University of British Columbia Press.

Worobey, Jacqueline, and Ronald J. Angel, 1990. "Poverty and Health: Older Minority Women and the Rise of the Female-Headed Household." *Journal of Health and Social Behavior* 31 (December): 370–383.

Young, Alma H., and Jyaphia Christos-Rodgers. 1994. "Women's Resistance to Gendered Space in the Urban Environment: The Case of the St. Thomas Resident Council, New Orleans." Working Paper no. 24. College of Urban and Public Affairs, University of New Orleans.

Young, Alma H., and Kristine B. Miranne. 1995. "Women's Need for Child Care: The Stumbling Block in the Transition from Welfare to Work." In Judith A. Garber and Robyne S. Turner, eds., *Gender in Urban Research.* Newbury Park, CA: Sage Publications.

Part II

Governance and Politics

Chapter 9

Urban Government

Ann O'M. Bowman

Government is the heart of the urban political system. It is perennially maligned, subjected to constant tinkering, yet it is remarkably durable. Urban government is replete with dualities: monolithic and malleable, traditional, and innovative. This chapter explores urban government, highlighting key issues and questions.

OVERVIEW OF THE FIELD

Reform is one of the driving forces defining the field of urban government. It has proven to be a serviceable concept, useful beyond simply demarking a historical period or describing a set of structures. It is both a process and an end state, alternately idealized and demonized. For example, the number of American local governments exceeded 86,000 by 1992 (U.S. Department of Commerce 1993). To reformers from the classical school, the multiplicity of jurisdictions seems chaotic and counterproductive (Grodzins 1964). However, other observers of the metropolitan scene, the neoreformers, see multiple jurisdictions as providing "choices" for governmental consumers (Bish and Ostrom 1979; Parks and Oakerson 1989).

Those 86,000 units of local government can be classified into five types: counties, municipalities (or cities), towns and townships, special districts, and school districts.[1] Before proceeding further, some clarification is in order. State governments have subdivided their territory into 3,043 discrete subunits called counties.[2] Counties were created by states to function as their administrative appendages, managing activities of statewide concern at the local level. Among a county's traditional functions are property tax assessment and collection, law enforcement, elections, land transaction record keeping, and road maintenance. Over time, modernization and population growth placed additional demands on county governments; thus, their service offerings have expanded. Now health care and hospitals, pollution control, mass transit, industrial development, social services, and consumer protection may be county functions (U.S. Advisory Commission on Intergovernmental Relations [ACIR] 1982). Counties are increasingly regarded less as simple functionaries of state government and more as important policy-making units of local government.

A county may contain several cities; a city's territory may extend into more than one county. Cities are created through incorporation—the legal recognition of settlement patterns in an area. The rules for incorporation are created by the state, typically in the state constitution. The area slated for incorporation must meet certain criteria, such as population or density minimums. Residents of the settlement petition the state for a charter of incorporation. In most cases, a referendum is required. The final step is certification by the secretary of state that the legal requirements for incorporation have been met. New cities are created every year. For example, in 1991, 24 places incorporated and 5 cities disincorporated, or ceased to exist (U.S. Department of Commerce 1993).

Towns and townships are general-purpose units of local government, distinct from county and city governments. Only 20 states, primarily in the Northeast and Midwest, have official towns or townships. In some states these small jurisdictions have relatively broad powers; in others, they have a more circumscribed role. New England towns, along with those in New Jersey, Pennsylvania, and to some degree, Michigan, New York, and Wisconsin, enjoy fairly broad powers. In the remainder of the township states, the nature of township government is more rural, with service offerings limited to roads and law enforcement. The closer these rural townships are to large urban areas, the more likely they are to offer an expanded set of services to residents.

Special districts are created to meet service needs in a particular area. There are approximately 33,000 special districts around the country, and that number is increasing. Special districts overlay existing cities and counties, thus leading to a question posed by the U.S. Advisory Commission on Intergovernmental Relations (ACIR) (1982: 154): "If general-purpose local governments are set up to perform a broad spectrum of functions and if they collectively cover practically every square foot of territory in a state, why [are] special districts needed at all?" The answer is that special districts are useful structures for addressing some of the technical, financial, and political problems of cities and counties (J. Bollens 1957).

School districts are a special kind of special district and, as such, are considered one of the five types of local government.[3] Over the past half century, the number of school districts has dropped from 100,000 to less than 15,000. Financial considerations typically underlie the move to consolidate school districts.

Table 9.1 lists the types and numbers of local governments. On average, a state contains 60 counties, almost 400 cities, 300 school districts, 660 special districts, and, if it uses a township structure, another 830 of them. However, averaging the number of local governments masks the tremendous variation

Table 9.1
Number and Types of Local Government

Type of Local Government	Number
County	3,043
Municipality	19,296
Town/Township	16,666
School District	14,556
Special District	33,131
Total	86,692

Source: U.S. Bureau of the Census, 1993.

from one state to another. In a given metropolitan area, one finds a collection of autonomous, frequently overlapping, jurisdictional units. For example, the Pittsburgh metropolitan area contains 4 counties, 195 cities (55 of which have fewer than 1,000 residents), 117 townships, 331 special districts, and 92 school districts.

ISSUES IN THE FIELD

In his book *Governing Urban America*, Jones (1983: 8) identified five critical issues dominating the field: the issue of limited government, the choice between local autonomy and effective government, the issue of democratic accountability, the trade-off between efficient government and responsive government, and the issue of policy distribution. These issues remain important: How much government intervention is justifiable in contemporary urban society? What is the optimal size for a community? Is popular control of government being achieved? How can local governments balance the competing goals of efficiency and responsiveness? And finally, what are the distributional effects of urban public policies? These questions are woven through the discussion that follows.

Sorting Local Governments

A standard means of differentiating among governments at the local level is the breadth of their service delivery function. General-purpose local governments perform a wide range of governmental functions and include counties, municipalities, and towns and townships. Single-purpose local governments, such as school districts and special districts, have a specific purpose and perform one function.

An alternative means of classifying local governments is to use a more legalistic distinction: the existence of a charter that establishes the government as an artificial legal person and outlines its organization and powers. Municipal corporations have a charter; quasi-municipal corporations do not. Historically, cities and villages were chartered governments; counties, special districts, and townships were nonchartered governments. Zimmerman (1992: 164–165) identifies four primary differences between the two types:

1. The creation of a municipality is a bottom-up process; a majority of the voters residing in the area request the state legislature to create the municipality. The creation of a quasi-municipal corporation is top-down; the legislature may create the entity without the consent of the residents.

2. In addition to its governmental functions as an agent of the state, a municipal corporation may engage in proprietary, or business, functions. Quasi-municipal corporations are almost entirely agents of the state and therefore possess few proprietary functions.

3. The relatively broad sublegislative powers that municipal corporations enjoy means they can enact ordinances, while quasi-municipal corporations have limited ordinance-making power.

4. Although both types of governments may be sued, municipal corporations originally had greater protection from suit in the performance of traditional governmental functions such as public health and public safety. Quasi-municipal corporations possessed the same immunity from suit as the state. This distinction between the two types of local governments has diminished over time. In general, the trend has been for some quasi-municipal corporations, especially counties, to gain corporation status.

Counties and Cities. Most taxonomic schemes use a county's population size and its spatial relationship to the central city as classification tools. For example, Duncombe (1977) differentiated between core counties that contain large cities and fringe counties that abut the core county. The core county tends to serve as the work destination of the residents of the fringe counties. Fewer than 10 percent of the counties in the United States are core or fringe. Duncombe's other type of metropolitan county is the single-county metropolitan area. It differs from the core and fringe counties in that its largest cities do not attract commuters from nearby areas. Approximately 15 percent of American counties fall into this category. Marando and Baker (1993) adapted a classification to provide four categories of metropolitan counties: core counties; core contiguous counties; and two kinds of noncore contiguous counties, those with more than 250,000 residents and those with less than 250,000 inhabitants. Although most Americans live in metropolitan areas, most counties are nonmetropolitan, containing small cities and rural areas.

For municipalities, the issue of classification has to do with their charter. Charters vary in the mix of state-imposed uniformity and local self-determination involved. General charters grant the same powers and responsibilities to all cities, regardless of size. Special charters, on the other hand, are designed for a single municipality. An alternative to general and special charters is the classified charter, which establishes several population classes with a different charter for each grouping. Some states use a system of optional charters in which city voters select the charter they prefer. The kind of arrangement that grants the city the most autonomy is home rule. Under home rule, municipal corporations can draft, adopt, and amend their own charters. It provides the jurisdiction with the authority to handle matters of local concern. According to an ACIR report, 37 state constitutions contain provisions granting home rule to cities; in 24 states, constitutional home rule is extended to counties (U.S. ACIR 1993).

The Question of Special Districts. Special districts are defended because of their potential for efficient service provision and the likelihood that they will be responsive to constituents whose demands are not otherwise being met. For example, a problem may extend beyond jurisdictional lines; a special district can be created to fit the boundaries of the problem. Restrictive annexation laws and county governments with limited authority also encourage the use of special districts. And the creation of a special district does not affect the debt and tax ceilings imposed on general-purpose governments. Classical reformers tend to be skeptical of special districts, however. A common complaint is that special districts lack accountability. The public is often unaware of their existence; thus, they function free of much scrutiny. In addition, the proliferation of special districts complicates the development of comprehensive solutions to metropolitan problems (S. Bollens 1986).

Relationship to State Government

There is an inevitable strain in the relationship of states to their local governments. It results from a fundamental fact of governmental life: Local governments are creatures of the state.[4] In the words of the ACIR (1987: 54), "State legislatures are the trustees of the basic rules of local governance in America. The laws and constitutions of each state are the basic legal instruments of local governance." The ultra vires rule, or as it is more commonly known, Dillon's Rule, limits the powers of local government to those expressly granted by the state, those clearly implied by the expressed powers, and those indispensable to the stated objectives and purposes of the local government.[5]

Although the passage of time and the rewriting of state constitutions have softened the effect of Dillon's Rule, it remains the dominant doctrine in state-local relations. In practice, states have come to recognize that weak local units of government overburden the state; thus, many have undertaken efforts to assist and empower local government. Discretionary authority and mandates are two important areas.

Discretionary Authority. There is wide variation in how much and what kind of authority states give their local governments (ACIR 1993). Some states grant their localities wide-ranging powers to restructure themselves, to impose new taxes, and to take on additional functions. Others, much more conservative with their power, force local governments to turn to the legislature for approval to act. Oregon and Maine are examples of empowering states; Idaho and West Virginia, the opposite. Empowerment also depends on the type of local government. General-purpose governments typically have wider latitude than special-purpose entities like school districts. Even among general-purpose governments, there are different degrees of authority; counties tend to be more circumscribed in their ability to modify their form of government and expand their service offerings than cities are (Zimmerman 1983).

Local governments want their states to provide them with adequate funding and ample discretion. Local officials are supremely confident of their abilities to govern, given sufficient state support. But urban county officials express concern that neither their policy-making power nor their financial authority has kept pace with the increased administrative responsibilities placed on them by state government (Downing 1991). The recognition and correction of such conditions are the states' responsibility. Home rule was thought to be the answer; however, real home rule has been somewhat elusive. Constitutional reform may provide an avenue for relief. Berman and Martin (1988) found that the more recently a state has adopted its constitution, the more likely the document is to contain provisions that strengthen local governments.

State Mandates. Rather than let subgovernments devise their own solutions to problems, states frequently impose a remedy. From the perspective of state government, mandates are necessary to ensure that priorities are pursued and preferable goals are achieved. State mandates promote uniformity of policy from one jurisdiction to another, and they promote coordination, especially among adjacent jurisdictions.

Local governments see the issue quite differently. To them, state mandates (especially those that mandate a new service or impose a service quality standard) can be costly, they displace local priorities in favor of state priorities, and they limit the management flexibility of local governments. In response to local government pressure, approximately one third of the states have adopted mandate-reimbursement requirements. These measures require states either to reimburse local governments for the costs of state mandates or to give local governments adequate revenue-raising capacity to deal with them. Still, state officials defend mandates as a way to prod reluctant local governments into assuming their rightful responsibilities. The public seems to be more sympathetic to local governments' plight. In 1990, voters approved mandate-reimbursement measures appearing on the Florida and Wisconsin ballots (MacManus 1991). In Louisiana in 1991, voters approved a constitutional amendment that allows localities to ignore state mandates unless the state provides funding or authorizes local fund-raising mechanisms. The pressure for mandate-reimbursement requirements is likely to spread to other states.

Structural Arrangements

With the exception of special districts, local governments vest legislative authority in an elected governing body. County commissions, city councils, town selectmen, and school boards are the primary policy-making institutions in local government. The role of the governing board varies, depending on the presence of an elected executive, the number of other elected officials, and the use of professional administrators.[6]

About three quarters of U.S. counties operate without an elected executive, using a board of commissioners structure in which one member serves as presiding officer. Along with the board, a number of other county officials are elected, such as the sheriff, the county prosecutor, the clerk of the court, and the county tax assessor. The primary criticisms of the traditional structure are the lack of an elected central executive official and the absence of a professional administrator to manage county government. Reformers have advocated two alternative structures. In the county council–elected executive plan, voters elect an executive officer in addition to the governing board, thus resulting in a clearer separation between legislative and executive powers. The board sets policy, adopts the budget, and audits the financial performance of the county. The executive's role is to prepare the budget, supervise the implementation of board policy, and appoint department heads. In the other alternative structure, the council-administrator plan, the board hires a professional administrator to manage the daily operations of the county.

City governments operate with one of three structures: a mayor-council form, a city commission form, or a council-manager form. The three structures vary in the manner in which the executive branch is organized. In the mayor-council form of government, executive functions such as the appointment of department heads are performed by elected officials. This form of government can be subdivided into two types, depending on the formal powers held by the mayor. In a strong mayor-council structure, the mayor is the source of executive leadership and is responsible for daily administrative activities, the hiring and firing of top-level city officials, and budget preparation. Strong mayors can veto council actions. In a weak mayor-council structure, the mayor's role is more ceremonial. The council (of which the mayor may be a member) is the source of executive power. The council appoints city officials and develops the budget, and the mayor has no veto power.

Under the city commission form of government, legislative and executive functions are merged. Commissioners not only make policy as members of the city's governing body, but they also head the major departments of city government. The attraction of the commission form in the early 1900s as an alternative to the mayor-council structure was its ostensible lessening of politics in city government. But almost as fast as the commission form of government appeared on the scene, disillusionment set in. Commissioners became advocates of their own departments; elected officials were not necessarily good bureaucrats. One study showed that of the almost 200 cities reporting a commission structure in 1970, more than 42 percent had replaced it with another form by 1980 (Sanders 1982). By the 1990s, only a few cities were operating with a commission structure.

The third city government structure, the council-manager form, emphasizes the separation of politics from administration. Under this structure, the council hires a professional administrator to manage city government. The administrator (usually called a city manager) appoints and removes department heads, oversees service delivery, develops personnel policies, and prepares budget proposals for the council. The manager also makes policy recommendations to the city council; thus, the position can be an influential one. Svara's (1990) research on council-manager cities indicates that politicians and administrators typically have a working understanding about just how far the manager can venture into the policy-making realm of city government. As Morgan (1984) notes, managers who, with the acquiescence of their council, carve out an activist role for themselves may be able to dominate policy making in city government.

The "best" structure is a subject of disagreement (Blodgett 1994). Experts generally agree that structures lacking a strong executive officer are less preferable than others. Consequently, the weak mayor-council and the commission forms are less favorable. The strong mayor-council form of government is valuable for fixing accountability firmly in the mayor's office, and the council-manager system is credited with professionalizing city government by empowering skilled administrators.

As noted, local government structures are not immutable. Voters in St. Petersburg, Florida, approved a charter amendment that replaced their council-manager form with a strong mayor-council structure in 1993. Toledo, Ohio, having rejected such an action six years earlier, abandoned its council-manager plan in favor of a strong mayor in 1992. As the Toledo example shows, not all proposed switches win voter approval. The Kansas City, Missouri, electorate in 1989 voted down a plan to change from a weak-mayor to a strong-mayor structure. Throughout the country, interest remains high in designing a form of government that works. The early 1990s found cities as diverse as Dallas, Sacramento, and Dayton debating the utility of their governmental structures (Gurwitt 1993).

METHODOLOGICAL APPROACHES

Lawrence J. R. Herson's classic essay "The Lost World of Municipal Government" appeared in the *American Political Science Review* in 1957. In the piece, Herson criticized the literature on city government for, among other things, its naive and narrow reform bias. Work in the field suffered from several flaws including insularity and one-dimensional analysis. In other words, research in municipal government was not integrated with the larger literature in political science, and related to this, it erroneously pursued single-factor problem solving in what were actually multifactoral situations. Further, according to Herson, two serious breakdowns characterized the literature: Standards of proof were weak, and the logical imperative was not followed. As a result of these flaws, municipal government was judged "a stagnated area of political science" (330).

In the four decades since the appearance of the essay, the literature on municipal government has thrown off its reform cloak. Substantively, the work is broad and diverse, integrated not only with political science but with other fields such as economics, geography, and sociology (Judd and Swanstrom 1994). Methodologically, the research has become more sophisticated (Andranovich and Riposa 1993). Single-city case studies continue to prevail, but the best of that work is diachronic and multimethod.[7] The use of comparative case studies is increasing, as is the reliance on quantitative analytical techniques (Berry, Portney, and Thomson 1993). These days, municipal government is no lost world.

CURRENT STATE OF THE FIELD

In their work on public choice, Bish and Ostrom (1979) identified other orientations to urban government. Classical reform, of course, made their list, along with another: decentralization and community control. These orientations form the backdrop for a discussion of four contemporary items: representation, boundary change, interlocal cooperation, and governance.

Representation

Local governing boards tend to elect their members in one of two ways: either at large or by districts (or wards). In at-large elections, candidates compete jurisdiction-wide, and voters can vote in each council race. In district elections the competition is more localized; a voter can vote only in the council race in his or her district. Reformers advocated at-large elections as a means of weakening the geographic base of political machines because candidates running at large must appeal to a broad cross section of the population to be successful.[8]

There are significant consequences for the use of at-large electoral systems. Welch and Bledsoe's (1988) in-depth study of almost 1,000 city council members across the country revealed that at-large members tend to be wealthier and more highly educated than council members elected from districts. At-large council members devote less time to answering individual complaints and direct their attention to a citywide and business constituency.

Almost half of U.S. cities and most counties use an at-large method for electing their council members. The popularity of the method decreases as the jurisdiction's size increases, however. For example, only 15 percent of cities with populations above the half-million mark use at-large elections. At-large representation has been attacked for diminishing the likelihood that a member of a minority group can be elected. Heilig and Mundt's (1983) research on 313 cities indicated that when cities shifted from an at-large system to a district or mixed format (a combination of at-large and district seats), more blacks were elected to the council. Other research has shown this to be true, especially in cities where the black population is more than 20 percent (Renner 1988).

In general, studies have shown that changing the electoral system from at large to districts produces an overall increase in citizen participation, in terms of greater attendance at council meetings, higher voter turnout, and a larger number of candidates. It is not altogether clear that changing to districts will translate into policy benefits for the previously underrepresented sectors of the city, however. In terms of policy attitudes, Welch and Bledsoe (1988) found no significant difference between council members elected at large and those elected from districts.

There are ways of moderating the effects of an at-large system short of changing to districts. In a recent court case challenging at-large voting for a Maryland county commission, an alternative mechanism was imposed: cumulative voting (''New Voting System'' 1994). In the case at issue, no black candidate had ever been elected to the governing board of a county that was 21 percent black. The judge found that the at-large system diluted the black vote, thereby violating the Voting Rights Act of 1965. The judge imposed a cumulative voting solution in which candidates run countywide, and each voter has five votes to use as he or she wishes, either voted as a bloc for one candidate or spread among candidates. The intent is to make a systemic adjustment that will improve the electoral chances of, in this instance, black candidates.

Although the imposition of cumulative voting in Maryland became embroiled in legal challenges, other places have successfully implemented it. And in those communities, cumulative voting is producing different electoral outcomes for racial and ethnic minority candidates than would an at-large election. For example, in Alamogordo, New Mexico, a Latino candidate who would have finished fourth in a standard at-large election placed third in total votes cast through cumulative voting (Cole and Taebel 1992). With three seats to be filled, the difference between a third- and fourth-place finish meant the difference between winning and losing. As evidence mounts regarding the impact of cumulative voting, its use is likely to increase.

Boundary Change

Some of the country's most prominent cities have rather confined city limits. Almost half of the 50 most populated cities control less than 100 square miles of territory. Over time, many central cities have found themselves squeezed by the rapid growth and incorporation of territory just outside city limits and therefore beyond their control. To counteract the flight of people and jobs from the city and to assure themselves of adequate space for future expansion, some cities have sought to increase their territory through annexation. However, annexation is complicated by the existence of incorporated suburbs and the requirements of state law. In many older, established metropolitan areas the central city is hemmed in by incorporated suburbs, thus making annexation impossible (Fleischmann and Feagin 1987). And even in newer urban areas, defensive incorporation is on the rise. Rigos and Spindler (1991) found that the threat of annexation frequently stimulates the creation of new cities. The same state governments that determine the legal procedures for municipal incorporation design the annexation process. In states that make it difficult for cities to annex, cities may have to wait for landowners in an adjacent area to petition to be annexed. Even when a majority of the landowners request annexation, if the proportion is less than 75 percent, referendum elections must be held. State law may require a dual majority, that is, approval by both the existing city and the area to be annexed.

An alternative means of boundary change is city-county consolidation. This has remained one of the metropolitan reformers' major goals, yet fewer than 25 consolidations have occurred. The argument in favor of consolidation is straight-forward: Absorbing general-purpose jurisdictions into a single, countywide government unifies power and area. Areawide problem solving lends itself to economies of scale, thus producing, it is argued, more efficiency. Yet research comparing the taxing and spending policies of a consolidated jurisdiction with those of an unconsolidated counterpart did not demonstrate the expected efficiencies (Benton and Gamble 1984). Traditionally, opposition to consolidation has come from residents of unincorporated areas. More recently, resistance has grown among minorities who see it as diluting their political strength in the central city.

Boundary changes (or the lack thereof) profoundly affect the development of a metropolitan area (Orum 1995). The former mayor of Albuquerque, David Rusk (1993), uses the term ''elasticity'' to signify the ability of a city to expand its territory. Elastic cities have been able to keep pace with urban sprawl by adjusting their boundaries through mechanisms such as annexation; inelastic cities have not. These inelastic cities, confined to extant boundaries, have suffered population loss and tax base erosion, thereby producing higher levels of racial and class segregation in the metropolitan area.

Interlocal Cooperation

Short of formal mechanisms such as consolidation, central cities, their suburban governments, and counties are joining together in cooperative ventures. And local governments of all types are expanding their involvement with private firms and the third (i.e., nonprofit organizations) sector (Grell and Gappert 1993). This is not to say that concerns over turf or interjurisdictional jealousies are things of the past, but informal cooperation seems to provide a consensus ''half-a-loaf'' option.

The explanation for such cooperative behavior is in large part financial. Simply put, the cost of independently providing a service may exceed the public's preference for it.[9] Joint endeavors offer new resources, fresh ideas, and combined energies. ''Intercommunity partnerships'' involving private firms and third sector organizations, the academic community, and citizen leagues have proven valuable in some communities. An example is the Intergovernmental Cooperation Program (ICP) in the Pittsburgh area. The central purpose of the ICP is ''to identify emerging issues that offer timely opportunities for intergovernmental cooperation, to assemble resources for designing cooperative projects, and to monitor the implementation of cooperative projects'' (Dodge 1988: 7; see also Dodge 1992). Yet as Warren, Rosentraub, and Weschler (1992: 419) remind us with regard to volunteer activity, philanthropic organizations, and firms, ''the third and private sectors are resources to be incorporated into the urban governance systems rather than substituted for it.''

Portland, Oregon, has taken the concept of interlocal cooperation a step further with its 2040 Plan. The city, its suburbs, and outlying jurisdictions engaged their citizens in extensive debate to develop a regionwide vision for the future (Smith 1994). When the 2040 Plan has been approved by the relevant communities, it will be enforced by an elected, regionwide council that has the regulatory authority to force local government compliance. This is interlocal cooperation writ large.

Governance

Communities restructure their governments with the intent of improving governance. Candidates campaign for office, promising the same. However, there is no set of universally accepted criteria for evaluating the quality of governance. Even the definition of governance is subject to dispute. ''Effective governance will not be achieved until it is distinguished from the provision of a series of discrete urban goods and services and ad hoc responses to the urban crises of the day'' (Warren, Rosentraub, and Weschler 1992: 418–419). In other words, governance is more than service delivery and crisis management. It involves the building of institutions and processes that allow citizens to formulate and implement community policies in a collective and democratic manner.

The National Municipal League, a group that got its start during the reform movement, annually bestows its ''All-America City'' designation on a few select communities that display ''civic energy.'' In a related effort, Hatry (1986) settled on seven elements in his attempt to isolate characteristics that are plausibly related to governance. Well-governed communities exhibit tranquility among public officials, continuity in office of top-level managerial officials, use of analytical budgeting and planning processes, participative management, innovativeness, active public-private partnerships, and citizen input into government decisions. These seven elements offer some guidance for continued rumination about government structure and function.

FUTURE DIRECTIONS

Return to the dualities that opened the chapter. Although urban government is frequently perceived as monolithic and traditional, it is instead rather malleable and innovative. These days the concerns tend to be less philosophical than pragmatic. The future seems to be moving along two paths: redesign and reinvention.

Redesigning Urban Government

As urban populations spill beyond the suburbs into the unincorporated territory of counties, the pressure on local governments of all types grows. Fearful that these pressures have already overwhelmed county governments, the speaker of the California Assembly introduced legislation in 1991 to create a tier of regional governments in his state (''Counties out of Date'' 1991). Under the proposal, California would be divided into seven regions that would be governed by 13-member elected boards. These regional ''super'' governments would assume many of the development and infrastructure functions currently assigned to county governments. Although the bill did not pass, the larger point is that tinkering is no longer sufficient; fundamental restructuring of local governments is necessary. As a land use publication puts it: ''Local government boundaries are totally out of whack with the realities of economic geography or development patterns'' (Leinberger 1987: 7).

Interlocal cooperation, as discussed above, is the first step in the direction of more formal, multijurisdictional partnerships. One observer of the urban scene, newspaper columnist Neal R. Peirce (1994), has called for the creation of ''citistates,'' coherent urban entities formed from the central city and nearby communities. The justification is simple: Since economies are essentially regional in nature, governance can (and should) be, also. Ultimately, regional government may be necessary for effective competition in an increasingly global economy.

According to a new survey, the public may be receptive to structural innovation and redesign. Gerston and Haas (1993) found that public perception of trenchant urban problems has generated new support for regional government. As they note, ''With government boundaries and modern political problems increasingly not confluent, leaders and citizens alike must devise new schemes to overcome old jurisdictional lines'' (162–163). Yet on the heels of the Gerston and Haas work came evidence of contrary public sentiment. Surveys of residents of southern California report persistent negative attitudes toward regionalism (Baldassare 1994). Despite the enthusiasm of some scholars, pundits, and practitioners, redesigning urban government is likely to be a slow and uneven process.

Reform's New Clothes: Reinvention

Local government reform was a Progressive Era movement that sought to depose the corrupt and inefficient partisan political machines controlling many American cities. To the reformers, party government had led to the ''injection of political virus'' into municipal government, which had ''poisoned the system'' (Schiesl 1977: 7). Reformers preferred a government designed along the lines of a business corporation. They advocated fundamental structural changes in local government such as the abolition of partisan local elections, the use of at-large electoral systems, and the installation of a professionally trained city manager. The structures established during the Progressive Era—intended to make local government efficient and equitable—emphasized rules, standardization, and control. Osborne and Gaebler (1992), in their book, *Reinventing Government*, argue that these structures have outlived their usefulness. Bureaucracies have become cumbersome, the policy process a tangled maze. Critics contend that a governmental apparatus geared to solving the problems created by the partisan political machines of the early twentieth century is out of date. What is needed is a fresh vision complemented by new structures and new behaviors, so that local governments can lead the way into the twenty-first century. The new reformers, who eschew the label "reform," advocate an entrepreneurial government—one that is innovative and market oriented, that focuses on goals, and that empowers citizens.

NOTES

1. Readers interested in contemporary research on the various types of local governments should examine Berman's (1993) edited collection on county governments as well as the special 1993 issue of the journal *Publius* on "Counties in the Federal System," edited by Thomas; Burns's (1994) work on municipalities and special districts; Wikstrom's (1993) book on small-town politics; and the Meier, Stewart, and England (1989) volume on school districts.

2. There are no functional county governments in Connecticut and Rhode Island. In Louisiana, counties are called parishes; in Alaska, they are called boroughs.

3. The discussion in this chapter focuses on independent school districts. There are also more than 1,400 dependent school districts that operate as an extension of county, city, township, or state government.

4. Although the U.S. Constitution makes no mention of local governments, the federal government has become very involved with localities. National programs implemented at the local level, extensive federal financial assistance, and federal court decisions have enmeshed the two levels of government. See, for example, the essays on national urban policy in the May 1995 issue of *Urban Affairs Review* (vol. 30, no. 5) and the discussion of the evolution of the urban policy system in Kleinberg's (1995) book *Urban America in Transformation*. Another informative source on contemporary intergovernmental matters is the annual review issue of *Publius: The Journal of Federalism*, published every summer. For a broad overview of local governments in the federal system, see the 1990 report of the U.S. General Accounting Office, *Federal-State-Local Relations: Trends of the Past Decade and Emerging Issues*. The interests of local governments, especially cities and counties, are represented in Washington, D.C. by a multitude of groups. Prominent among them are the National League of Cities, the U.S. Conference of Mayors, the National Association of Counties, and the International City/County Management Association.

5. A ruling by Iowa Judge John F. Dillon in *City of Clinton* v. *Cedar Rapids and*

Missouri Railroad Company (1868), and his subsequent writing on the subject of municipal powers, yielded the phrase "Dillon's Rule."

6. An annual publication of the International City/County Management Association, *The Municipal Year Book*, contains material on governmental forms and structures. Summary data are provided every year; periodically, more detailed information is included for specific cities and counties.

7. For a discussion of case study methodology, see King, Keohane, and Verba (1995).

8. In 1994, the U.S. Supreme Court decided *Holder* v. *Hall*, a case challenging a Georgia county's single-commissioner form of government. Eleven Georgia counties use a structure in which one commissioner exercises all of the executive and legislative functions of county government. Black voters in Bleckley County challenged the single-commissioner system, charging that the arrangement violated the Voting Rights Act. Blacks make up nearly 20 percent of the county's population, but no black has ever run for, much less been elected to, the office of county commissioner. The petitioners sought the creation of a multimember commission, something that the Bleckley County electorate had previously rejected. The Court ruled that the size of a local governing board did not violate provisions of the Voting Rights Act.

9. Some of the renewed enthusiasm for interlocal cooperation is being fostered by the federal government. For example, when Congress passed the Intermodal Surface Transportation Efficiency Act (ISTEA) in 1991, it required the development of *regional* transportation plans for urban areas. See the discussion in Gage and McDowell (1995).

REFERENCES

Andranovich, Gregory D., and Gerry Riposa. 1993. *Doing Urban Research*. Newbury Park, CA: Sage Publications.

Baldassare, Mark. 1994. "Regional Variations in Support for Regional Governance." *Urban Affairs Quarterly* 30, no. 2: 275–284.

Benton, J. Edwin, and Darwin Gamble. 1984. "City/County Consolidation and Economies of Scale." *Social Science Quarterly* 65, no. 1: 190–198.

Berman, David R., ed. 1993. *County Governments in an Era of Change*. Westport, CT: Greenwood.

Berman, David R., and Lawrence L. Martin. 1988. "State-Local Relations: An Examination of Local Discretion." *Public Administration Review* 48, no. 2: 637–641.

Berry, Jeffrey M., Kent E. Portney, and Ken Thomson. 1993. *The Rebirth of Urban Democracy*. Washington, D.C.: Brookings.

Bish, Robert L., and Vincent Ostrom. 1979. *Understanding Urban Government*. Washington, D.C.: American Enterprise Institute.

Blodgett, Terrell. 1994. "Beware the Lure of the 'Strong' Mayor." *Public Management* 76, no. 1: 6–11.

Bollens, John C. 1957. *Special District Governments in the United States*. Berkeley: University of California Press.

Bollens, Scott. 1986. "Examining the Link between State Policy and the Creation of Local Special Districts." *State and Local Government Review* 18, no. 3: 117–124.

Burns, Nancy. 1994. *The Formation of American Local Governments*. New York: Oxford University Press.

Cole, Richard. L., and Delbert A. Taebel. 1992. "Cumulative Voting in Local Elections: Lessons from the Alamogordo Experience." *Social Science Quarterly* 73: 194–201. "Counties out of Date." 1991. *State Legislatures* 17, no. 3: 17.

Dodge, William R. 1988. "The Emergence of Intercommunity Partnerships in the 1980s." *Public Management* 70, no. 7: 2–7.

Dodge, William R. 1992. "Strategic Intercommunity Governance Networks." *National Civic Review* 82, no. 4: 411.

Downing, R. G. 1991. "Urban County Fiscal Stress." *Urban Affairs Quarterly* 27, no. 2: 314–325.

Duncombe, Herbert Sydney. 1977. *Modern County Government.* Washington, D.C.: National Association of Counties.

Fleischmann, Arnold, and Joe R. Feagin. 1987. "The Politics of Growth-Oriented Urban Alliances." *Urban Affairs Quarterly* 23, no. 2: 207–232.

Gage, Robert W., and Bruce D. McDowell. 1995. "ISTEA and the Role of MPOs in the New Transportation Environment." *Publius* 25, no. 3: 133–154.

Gerston, Larry N., and Peter J. Haas. 1993. "Political Support for Regional Government in the 1990s." *Urban Affairs Quarterly* 29, no. 1: 154–163.

Grell, Jan, and Gary Gappert. 1993. "The New Civic Infrastructure." *National Civic Review* 82, no. 2: 140–148.

Grodzins, Morton. 1964. "Centralization and Decentralization in the American Federal System." In Robert A. Goldwin, ed., *A Nation of States.* Chicago: Public Affairs Conference Center.

Gurwitt, Rob. 1993. "The Lure of the Strong Mayor." *Governing* 6, no. 10: 36–41.

Hatry, Harry P. 1986. "Would We Know a Well-Governed City If We Saw One?" *National Civic Review* 75, no. 3: 142–146.

Heilig, Peggy, and Robert J. Mundt. 1983. "The Effect of Adopting Districts on Representational Equity." *Social Science Quarterly* 64, no. 2: 393–397.

Herson, Lawrence J. R. 1957. "The Lost World of Municipal Government." *American Political Science Review* 51: 330–345.

Jones, Bryan D. 1983. *Governing Urban America.* Boston: Little, Brown.

Judd, Dennis R., and Todd Swanstrom. 1994. *City Politics: Private Power & Public Policy.* New York: HarperCollins.

King, Gary, Robert O. Keohane, and Sidney Verba. 1995. "Designing Social Inquiry: Scientific Inference in Qualitative Research." *American Political Science Review* 89, no. 2: 454–481.

Kleinberg, Benjamin. 1995. *Urban America in Transformation: Perspectives on Urban Policy and Development.* Thousand Oaks, CA: Sage Publications.

Leinberger, Christopher, as quoted in Libby Howland. 1987. "Back to Basics." *Urban Land* 46, no. 5: 7.

MacManus, Susan A. 1991. " 'Mad' about Mandates: The Issue of Who Should Pay Resurfaces in the 1990s." *Publius* 21, no. 3: 59–75.

Marando, Vincent L., and C. Douglas Baker. 1993. "Metropolitan Counties and Urbanization." In David R. Berman, ed., *County Governments in an Era of Change.* Westport, CT: Greenwood.

Meier, Kenneth J., Joseph Stewart, Jr., and Robert England. 1989. *Race, Class, and Education.* Madison: University of Wisconsin Press.

Morgan, David R. 1984. *Managing Urban America.* 2nd ed. Belmont, CA: Wadsworth.

"New Voting System Ordered to Help Blacks." 1994. *Christian Science Monitor*, April 7, 2.

Orum, Anthony M. 1995. *City-Building in America*. Boulder, CO: Westview.

Osborne, David, and Ted A. Gaebler. 1992. *Reinventing Government*. Reading, MA: Addison-Wesley.

Parks, Roger B., and Ronald J. Oakerson. 1989. "Metropolitan Organization and Governance: A Local Public Economy Approach." *Urban Affairs Quarterly* 25, no. 1: 18–29.

Peirce, Neal R. 1994. *Citistates*. Arlington, VA: Seven Locks Press.

Renner, Tari. 1988. "Municipal Election Processes." In *The Municipal Year Book 1988*. Washington, D.C.: International City Management Association.

Rigos, Platon N., and Charles J. Spindler. 1991. "Municipal Incorporations and State Statutes." *State and Local Government Review* 23, no. 2: 76–81.

Rusk, David. 1993. *Cities without Suburbs*. Washington, D.C.: Woodrow Wilson Center Press.

Sanders, Heywood T. 1982. "The Government of American Cities." In *The Municipal Year Book 1988*. Washington, D.C.: International City Management Association.

Schiesl, Martin J. 1977. *The Politics of Efficiency*. Berkeley: University of California Press.

Smith, Randolph P. 1994. "Region Idea Works, Oregon City Says." *Richmond Times-Dispatch*, October 30, A1, A18.

Svara, James H. 1990. *Official Leadership in the City*. New York: Oxford.

Thomas, Robert D., ed. 1993. "Counties in the Federal System." *Publius*, vol. 23, no. 1.

U.S. Advisory Commission on Intergovernmental Relations (ACIR). 1982. *State and Local Roles in the Federal System*. Washington, D.C.: ACIR.

U.S. Advisory Commission on Intergovernmental Relations (ACIR). 1987. *The Organization of Local Public Economies*. Washington, D.C.: ACIR.

U.S. Advisory Commission on Intergovernmental Relations (ACIR). 1993. *State Laws Governing Local Government Structure and Administration*. Washington, D.C.: ACIR.

U.S. Department of Commerce. Bureau of the Census. 1993. *1992 Census of Governments: Government Organization*. Vol. 1, no. 1. Washington, D.C.: Government Printing Office.

U.S. General Accounting Office. 1990. *Federal-State-Local Relations: Trends of the Past Decade and Emerging Issues*. Washington, D.C.: GAO.

Warren, Robert, Mark S. Rosentraub, and Louis F. Weschler. 1992. "Building Urban Governance: An Agenda for the 1990s." *Journal of Urban Affairs* 14, no. 3/4: 399–422.

Welch, Susan, and Timothy Bledsoe. 1988. *Urban Reform and Its Consequences*. Chicago: University of Chicago Press.

Wikstrom, Nelson. 1993. *The Political World of a Small Town*. Westport, CT: Greenwood.

Zimmerman, Joseph F. 1983. *State-Local Relations*. New York: Praeger.

Zimmerman, Joseph F. 1992. *Contemporary American Federalism*. New York: Praeger.

Chapter 10

Participation in Local Politics

Arnold Fleischmann

OVERVIEW OF THE FIELD

Political participation includes both individual and collective efforts to influence the choice of government personnel and policies. Studies at the local level cover the same forms of participation as research on state and national politics. Yet urban research differs from the wider body of literature on political behavior in the United States. Perhaps the most notable distinction is that participation occupies a less prominent role in urban scholarship. Research on American politics has been driven largely by studies of political behavior, especially voting. The same cannot be said of urban research: Between 1965 and 1987, just 14 percent of the articles published in *Urban Affairs Quarterly* dealt with political behavior (Schmandt and Wendel 1988).

Urban scholarship also has emphasized different types of participation. Like the American politics literature, elections have received a great deal of interest, but urban scholars have examined the electoral effects of the great structural diversity (form of government, procedures, etc.) not found at the state and national levels. Urban research has given less attention to interest groups and political parties but has produced more significant scholarship on contacting—citizen communications with public officials to obtain some benefit from government—and has been more attentive to social movements, grassroots mobilization, and protest.

These differences are due in part to the interdisciplinary nature of urban research, which includes political science, sociology, geography, public administration and policy, and planning. They also result from a pervasive, and often unstated, assumption that urban areas are continuously evolving. Within this context, participation is just one of the factors affecting, and affected by, urban development in the United States.

APPROACHES AND ISSUES

In many ways, research on local participation has been held captive by two debates: the urban reform movement of the early twentieth century and studies of community power beginning in the 1950s. Reformers promoted changes in government structure to eliminate political machines. Cities adopted them to varying degrees, and scholars have consistently included nonpartisan versus partisan ballots, at-large versus district representation, mayor-council versus council-manager systems, and other structural options in research on participation and policy.

Debates over community power raged for the better part of two decades, as scholars argued over whether economic elites dominated local politics. Much of the disagreement concerned methods for studying how local governments make decisions. The prolonged nature and prominence (and possibly tone) of these debates have meant that scholars studying the policy process are almost compelled to examine links between business and local government. This has been reinforced by public choice theory and the growing literature on economic development (see Stone 1980; Jones and Bachelor 1993: 3–20, 233–254).

In terms of methodology, urban research has relied heavily on case studies of specific cities and qualitative research techniques rather than the mathematical approaches typified by national election studies. Even though urban scholarship has relatively few nationwide studies, those with national samples have been able to analyze participation in terms of wide variation in cities' election procedures, form of government, economic base, population, and similar characteristics. Case studies have the advantage of in-depth analysis of a particular area and ready access to participants and public records, but scholars often quibble over comparisons among case studies.

CURRENT STATE OF THE FIELD

This section covers the major types of participation. Because of space constraints, the discussion highlights ''classic'' works and recent studies that both produce notable results and review a wide body of other research.

Campaigns and Elections

Research on elections has proliferated in the past two decades. It has emphasized the impact of structure (organization and procedures), especially on the composition of city councils, and the significance of race and ethnicity in voting patterns. The latter is particularly interesting since the vast majority of cities use nonpartisan elections, and voters therefore do not have party labels on ballots to use as a "cue" when choosing candidates.

Turnout. Scholars know surprisingly little about voter turnout in local elections. The difficulties of gathering data mean that there have been few national studies. Existing research indicates, though, that turnout in local races is low, usually well below levels in national and state elections.

In the last comprehensive survey of turnout, Karnig and Walter (1985) analyzed nearly 800 cities with at least 25,000 residents. They found that turnout in 1975 was lower in cities that had the council-manager form of government, nonpartisan ballots, and elections held on dates different from state and national races. Turnout was positively related to both the percentage of a city's population living in the same house as five years earlier and the share that was foreign born or of foreign parentage. Thus, neighborhood stability and the presence of ethnic politics may enhance turnout. Compared with similar data from earlier periods, average turnout in municipal elections dropped from 42.5 percent of the voting-age population during 1935–1937 to 35.2 percent in 1963 to 30.4 percent in 1975. Turnout in the two nearest presidential elections to these contests was 57.9 percent, 62.4 percent, and 54.9 percent, respectively.

Studies with a smaller sample also tell a story of low turnout. In their landmark research on 82 cities in the San Francisco Bay area, Eulau and Prewitt (1973: 228) found that average turnout in council elections during 1956–1966 was 46 percent of those registered (31 percent of voting-age adults). In another classic study, turnouts for mayoral elections in 18 large cities during 1948–1952 ranged from 30 percent to 52 percent of the voting-age population. These levels were more than 20 percent below the average for the two presidential elections during the period in 7 of the cities, and 15 to 20 percent lower in another 5 (Banfield and Wilson 1963: 224–225). More recently, turnout in heavily contested Democratic primaries in St. Louis during the 1980s generally was less than 25 percent of voting-age adults. Overall, there was little difference in black and white turnout, but it was much higher in more affluent black and white wards than their poorer counterparts (Stein and Kohfeld 1991: 238–239). Heilig and Mundt (1984: 76–81) did uncover a surge in turnout for the first election after the 10 cities in their study changed from at-large to district representation; it dropped subsequently, however.

Other research has considered the related questions of registration and roll-off. One study examined the effects of a black registration drive in Houston during 1976 (Vedlitz 1985). Turnout in the 1976 presidential election was lower among blacks registered during the drive than blacks who registered before or after the effort. Turnout dropped in 1980 for both blacks and whites who registered after the drive. Thus, voter registration drives may produce short-term gains in the size of the electorate but must be sustained to avoid the loss of new or previously infrequent voters. A reverse type of causation has occurred in New Orleans: The election of the first black mayor in 1979 had a positive effect on black registration but was unrelated to white registration (Parent and Shrum 1985).

Roll-off is the tendency of voters not to use all of their voting opportunities, usually by skipping offices or referenda below the major offices at the top of the ballot. A study of New Orleans elections during 1965–1986 found that roll-off is more extensive among black voters. Yet roll-off among black voters decreased as the number of black candidates competing for office increased; no such relationship existed between white roll-off and the racial composition of the candidate field (Vanderleeuw and Utter 1993). In the case of Detroit's at-large city council, roll-off dropped among blacks and increased for whites as the city shifted from a white to a black majority (Herring and Forbes 1994: 434–436).

Voting Patterns and Coalitions. Perhaps the most notable early work here was Banfield and Wilson's (1963: 224–242), which compared "public-regarding" and "private-regarding" voters. The former were largely middle- and upper-income Protestants, as well as blacks, who supported candidates and policies that increased services and taxes for a community. The latter were mainly working-class, ethnic homeowners, who were especially hostile to redistributive spending.

Much recent research has focused on polarized voting—coalitions in which white and black voters support opposing candidates. One of the landmark studies here examined the five largest southern cities during 1960–1977 (Murray and Vedlitz 1978). The authors found that racially polarized voting varied over time, among the cities, and by type of election. Polarization increased in all five places with the onset of the civil rights movement in the 1960s but dropped slightly by the 1970s in four of the cities. In Dallas, Houston, Memphis, and New Orleans, blacks and less affluent whites were most likely to forge coalitions in presidential and general elections, when better-off whites were likely to vote Republican. A similarly strong bond existed in Dallas and Houston for Democratic primaries. In contrast, blacks and more affluent whites in Atlanta voted together in municipal elections and Democratic primaries—where party labels did not separate candidates. The same coalition emerged in New Orleans Democratic primaries.

Bullock and Campbell (1984) used a survey covering the 1981 Atlanta mayoral election to sort out the effects of race and issues in a polarized contest that lacked racial appeals by candidates. Roughly three fourths of all voters favored a candidate of the same race, but they also agreed on issues or had neutral views of him. Just under 25 percent of both black and white voters preferred the issue stances of a candidate of the opposite race. Of such respondents, 77 percent of each group intended to "cross over" to vote for the candidate of the other race. The rest, who might be labeled "racist" voters for picking a candidate of the same race despite disagreeing with him on the issues, were a substantially small share of the electorate.

Race continues to be a salient factor in many local elections. In Washington,

D.C., black precincts vote alike, although black middle-income precincts could align with white middle- and upper-income areas (Henig 1993). In St. Louis, voting is polarized along racial lines but is complicated by factionalism, shifting alliances, and active ward politics (Stein and Kohfeld 1991). In Detroit, racial crossover voting has had an interesting history. As the city changed from a black to white majority, crossover voting increased among blacks and declined for whites. Crossover voting was lowest for both groups during the period when they reached parity in the population. Thus, crossover voting was more likely for a group when it comprised a dominant share of the electorate and may not have felt threatened by the other group. Moreover, blacks have become more likely to vote based on incumbency rather than race, while the opposite occurred for whites (Herring and Forbes 1994).

Coalitions may vary when communities are more diverse than narrow black-white splits. This may be particularly true in cities with concentrations of European ethnic groups, Latinos, and Asians. For instance, a study of the 1979 Democratic primary for city council in Philadelphia examined at-large candidates without party endorsements. These people did disproportionately well in precincts of their own ethnic background, with this advantage strongest for Poles, followed in order by Italian, Jewish, and Irish candidates (Featherman 1983). Similar ethnic cohesion occurred in Chicago, where Poles were given short shrift by the Irish-dominated machine and increasingly voted independently and for candidates of their own group during 1955–1977—the heyday of the Daley era (Inglot and Pelissero 1993).

In Los Angeles, candidates have attempted to pit ethnic groups against one another. This was especially true of Sam Yorty's efforts to keep Latino voters out of the liberal coalition of Jews and blacks that backed Tom Bradley for mayor in 1969. By appealing to Latinos, Yorty overcame a second-place finish in the primary to defeat Bradley in the general election. Bradley made inroads among Latino voters in 1973, however, when he won a rematch with Yorty. The future of coalition building in Los Angeles is clouded, though, by the lack of dominance by a single racial or ethnic group and the diversity within the Latino and Asian populations (Sonenshein 1993). In San Francisco, no single ethnic group constituted a majority of the city by 1990. During the 1970s and 1980s, a somewhat shaky progressive coalition was forged and elected two mayors but suffered several defeats to a so-called progrowth alliance. The progressives drew heavily from environmentalists, traditional liberals, populists, renters, gays and lesbians, blacks, and Hispanics—a series of groups who often did not see eye-to-eye. The other coalition was stronger among Asians and middle-income Anglos (DeLeon 1992).

Research has suggested that minority electoral gains are enhanced when blacks and Latinos mobilize politically and are incorporated into a coalition with liberal Anglos. Such alliances have a record of increased minority hiring and contracting by city governments, more diverse appointments to boards and commissions, and greater responsiveness regarding programs and service delivery.

These coalitions can unravel, however, over issues such as development and as particular minority groups splinter by class or factions aligned to particular candidates. Incorporation efforts also may have difficulty delivering long-term improvements in minority neighborhoods, especially in the face of diminishing federal resources (Browning, Marshall, and Tabb 1990; Peterson 1994).

In addition to the research on candidate-centered coalitions, other studies have looked at referendum voting. Hahn and Kamieniecki (1987) examined referenda in 40 cities between 1955 and 1970. They found that socioeconomic cleavages were more important predictors in referendum voting than in candidate elections. Social status, more than race or party, was the best predictor of voting patterns on nonexpenditure referenda. Support for referenda that would increase taxing and spending was positively related to the socioeconomic status of voters, although local differences proved more important than with nonexpenditure referenda. More recently, Button (1992) found that Florida seniors, who register and vote at significantly higher rates than younger citizens, emerged as an important force in opposition to school bond issues during the 1980s. They were not so highly mobilized against other tax issues, however.

Referenda can be especially volatile where the initiative exists—that is, citizens can use petitions to place policy questions on the ballot. In San Francisco, the progressive coalition used this process in its efforts to regulate the city's development. The slow-growth movement drew its strongest support from areas with high percentages of renters, middle-class residents, lesbians and gays, Hispanics, and blacks. Over time, the coalition increased its support among homeowners and blacks. It also mobilized on issues submitted to voters by the mayor and board of supervisors, helping to defeat a new stadium for the Giants baseball team (DeLeon 1992: 57–83, 107–122).

Campaigns and Outcomes. A substantial literature exists on the outcome of elections, but there is little on local campaign organizations, strategies, and activities. A study of campaign activities in the 1977 New Orleans primary found that incumbency and the degree of competition were better predictors of an election than were advertising, mass mobilization, research, elite mobilization, or personal contact—all of which suggest the difficulty in dislodging incumbents (Howell and Oiler 1981). There is also limited research on campaign financing. A recent study of Atlanta and St. Louis indicates that municipal elections attract substantial amounts of money from individuals and organizations. Incumbents did quite well in garnering contributions, and citywide candidates attracted sizable shares of their war chests from neighboring suburbs and other states. Similar to results from California and New York City, businesses, developers, and lawyers were the major sources of contributions (Stein and Fleischmann 1994).

Research on outcomes has been driven largely by concern for the effects of "the rules of the game," particularly the different methods of electing city councils. It is probably no coincidence that this topic is at the center of extensive litigation under the federal Voting Rights Act. Complaints of bias have been aimed at runoff and at-large elections, although a consensus is forming on both issues after years of heated debate. The bottom line on at-large elections is that blacks are underrepresented on councils relative to their share of a city's population when forced to run citywide as opposed to being elected from districts. There is no clear pattern for Hispanics, who tend to be less segregated than blacks and whose degree of representation varies by region (Welch 1990). Moreover, changing from at-large to district representation generally yields substantial gains in minority representation (Heilig and Mundt 1984: 58–63).

Under most runoff systems, if no candidate receives a majority, the top two finishers enter a second election so that there eventually is a winner with a majority. Critics have claimed that such procedures are biased against minority and female candidates. Research indicates otherwise, however. In an analysis of Dallas, Fort Worth, and San Antonio elections during 1951–1985, Fleischmann and Stein (1987) uncovered no systematic bias against black, Hispanic, or female candidates forced into runoffs. They did not consider, however, any disadvantage such candidates may have had in being able to make the runoff. Perhaps more startling was the fact that runoffs in Chicago during 1975–1991 advantaged minorities and women; they also helped the city's first black mayor, Harold Washington, replace backers of the former Daley machine with his supporters (Bullock and Gaddie 1994).

Critics also have assailed nonpartisan elections, claiming that they benefit Republicans (see Banfield and Wilson 1963: 155–164). Based on a 1982 national survey and other data, Welch and Bledsoe (1988) concluded that reality is more complex. If one considers the characteristics of a city, including the party composition of the electorate, Democrats were somewhat underrepresented in smaller cities with nonpartisan elections. In addition, higher-income people were overrepresented on councils with nonpartisan elections, as well as those with at-large representation. Yet the way council members performed their jobs had no relationship to being elected on a nonpartisan or partisan ballot. There were differences, though, between at-large and district council members in how they viewed constituent service and their obligation to the city as a whole.

Beyond questions of structure, there have been efforts to develop more elaborate statistical models of elections. The difficulty of gathering data typically limits such studies to a single jurisdiction. In an analysis of Cincinnati elections during 1969–1977, Lieske (1989) found that candidates' ability to generate votes was related most to their political following (support from previous campaigns), then to political resources (incumbency, campaign spending, and number of previous campaigns), endorsements (especially by newspapers), and personal achievements (education and occupation). Race and religion also had an effect. Lieske (1989: 169) saw his findings as part of "a growing body of thought that is reinterpreting American electoral politics within a framework of racial, ethnic, and cultural conflict."

Contacting

Contacting is an area where urban research has taken the lead compared with other fields in political science. That does not mean there is unanimous agreement, however, on research methods, findings, or interpretations. Studies have used two research strategies. One maps bureaucratic records of contacts to see how they vary among different types of neighborhoods. The other approach uses surveys of residents.

Who contacts, and why? Research on this question has focused on differences of class, race, and similar characteristics, as well as distinctions based on types of contacts with officials. One theory linked contacting to socioeconomic status, with the better educated and those with higher incomes more prone to use this form of participation. A competing model proposed an opposite pattern, namely, that less affluent neighborhoods contacted more often because of greater needs. A third view suggested that the middle class contacted more often because more affluent residents had fewer service needs and poor residents' attitudes or skills limited contacting. Some scholars also suggested that a central complaint or information office, rather than reliance on individual city departments, enabled different groups to contact at similar rates (see Sharp 1986).

Few contacting studies examine more than one city. Suffice it to say, the research findings often vary from place to place. The one overriding commonality is that contacting rates in many cities seem to be higher than voter turnout, approaching two thirds of all residents in at least one study. This is an interesting commentary about the rationality of making a demand of government officials as opposed to sending a rather vague and anonymous message with a vote. Results suggest that different patterns exist for contacting of a general nature compared with complaints about particular problems; contacting may even vary among agencies. While none of the models above provides a complete explanation, contacting may vary by individuals' race, socioeconomic status, age, political ties, perceived needs, and sense of political efficacy; it also may be affected by neighborhood organizations and characteristics of local governments (Sharp 1986; Hirlinger 1992). There is evidence that bureaucracies respond to contacts similarly whether cities have reformed or unreformed government structure (Mladenka 1981). Finally, contacting does not seem to be tilted as much toward higher-status individuals as are other forms of participation in the United States.

Political Parties

Research on political parties at the local level is sparse, in many ways because of cities' use of nonpartisan elections. Parties were, of course, an important— perhaps *the* important—method of participation in American cities for much of the nineteenth and early twentieth centuries. With links to immigrants, the working class, and business, political ''machines'' were party organizations that dominated many large cities in the Northeast and Midwest by delivering benefits to a variety of groups (Banfield and Wilson 1963; Bridges 1984; Jones 1981; Inglot and Pelissero 1993). Beginning during the Progressive Era, opponents attacked machines for corruption and undermined them with nonpartisan and at-large elections, civil service, council-manager government, and other "reforms" (Schiesl 1977).

Despite reform efforts, party organizations remain active and important at the local level (Crotty 1986). Their campaign activity may depend most on resources and the orientation of the local chairperson; their activity does not vary between partisan and nonpartisan cities, although parties in the latter may concentrate on other offices (Norrander 1986). Parties also can affect distributional politics, as with services, regulation, and government jobs (Jones 1981; Abney and Lauth 1986: 182–184; Stein and Kohfeld 1991). There may be renewed interest in local parties, though, as scholars look to counties, which overwhelmingly use partisan ballots and may reflect recent decades' changes in partisanship and suburban politics (see Bullock 1993).

Interest Groups

There seems little doubt that interest groups are key players in local politics. Scholars have devoted most of their attention to business groups, in part because of a widespread belief that business-led "regimes" (Stone 1989) or progrowth coalitions (Logan and Molotch 1987) shape the development of most cities and are in a powerful position due to local governments' need to encourage investment. The influence of business interests may be easy to see in the physical changes associated with urban development. Still, groups may be difficult to study at the local level because citizens can mobilize and gain access to government easily, which makes groups informal and fluid. In contrast, exerting pressure in Washington, D.C. or a state capital virtually requires formal, permanent organizations that should be easier to study.

In some communities, business-led coalitions have formed organizations that recruit and back a set of candidates in nonpartisan local elections. One study of such "slating groups" in three Texas cities found that their candidates lacked ethnic, racial, and class diversity. The organizations were able to use their middle-class, Anglo coalition to control city councils overwhelmingly for years and even decades (Fraga 1988).

One national survey during the 1980s found that 63 percent of municipal department heads believed that interest groups had "some" effect on policy, while 22 percent said that groups had "great" effect. Nonetheless, most thought the city council and chief executive had more influence. The department heads most frequently cited neighborhood groups as the most influential, followed by a range of business groups. Although none of these business interests individually was considered more influential than neighborhood groups, together they suggest the continued power of business in local politics (Abney and Lauth

1986: 195–212). Neighborhood groups have become quite common. Those in suburbs are more likely to have formed later and in response to development pressures; those in cities are more concerned with traffic, infrastructure, and safety. City groups are also more likely to cooperate with businesses and developers than their suburban counterparts (Logan and Rabrenovic 1990). As neighborhood groups have proliferated, often with recognition and authority from local governments, they may be reshaping methods of participating and the distribution of services at the local level (Thomas 1986; Berry, Portney, and Thomson 1993). In particular, cities that empower neighborhood associations as formal participants in local decision making may alter the balance between neighborhoods and business, are more responsive to neighborhood concerns, and enjoy decreased political conflict. Such associations also may enhance trust and knowledge regarding local government (Berry, Portney, and Thomson 1993).

Other Forms of Participation

Urban research also has examined other methods of participation. Public hearings, which often are required under state or federal law, may have little effect on cities' financial decisions (Cole and Caputo 1984). Citizen mobilization can have a substantial impact on officials' decisions over such matters as zoning, although such action occurs less frequently than is commonly thought (Fleischmann and Pierannunzi 1990). The use and effects of protest can be influenced by the openness of local political systems (Eisinger 1973) and stake of participants (Green and Cowden 1992), as well as the choice of strategies and attitudes of government officials (Schumaker 1975).

FUTURE RESEARCH

There are several interesting avenues of research that could enhance our understanding of participation in local politics. In terms of elections, there is a need to move beyond what may have become an excessive focus on relationships between structure and group representation. Important topics beginning to garner more attention include recruitment of candidates, campaign finances, and electoral strategies. An interesting, though still unexamined, direction in the contacting research is the "federalism" of such behavior. Namely, scholars have not compared the three levels of government in the same locations to explain variation in contacting patterns and responses.

In terms of collective forms of participation, there is promise in using counties, with their partisan elections, to expand research on the role of political parties in local politics. This could include important comparisons to state and national trends, as well as to cities in the same areas with nonpartisan elections. The study of interest groups is also being broadened to include seniors, gays and lesbians, and the growing diversity among Latinos and Asians.

There are several general questions that may deserve attention. One is the need to think about government structure broadly, not just in terms of issues raised in recent litigation or the traditional debates over urban reform and community power. The reason is straightforward: *Any* structure can have bias regarding participants or outcomes (see Stone 1980), but other factors also have consequences. It is also important to expand theoretical and empirical research to suburbs and Sunbelt metropolitan areas. Also worth considering is expanded public opinion research, particularly variation among cities in attitudes about trust in officials, provision of services, quality of life, and the like (see Baldassare 1985).

Finally, it might be worth asking, Does participation in local politics really matter? Scholars have demonstrated repeatedly that participation patterns are among the key factors shaping America's communities. This includes who gets elected, appointed, and hired to official public positions. Participation also affects the distribution of public services, the types of policies adopted by local governments, and important regulatory decisions.

REFERENCES

Abney, Glenn, and Thomas P. Lauth. 1986. *The Politics of State and City Administration.* Albany: State University of New York Press.

Baldassare, Mark. 1985. "Trust in Local Government." *Social Science Quarterly* 66, no. 3 (September): 704–712.

Banfield, Edward C., and James Q. Wilson. 1963. *City Politics.* New York: Vintage.

Berry, Jeffrey M., Kent E. Portney, and Ken Thomson. 1993. *The Rebirth of Urban Democracy.* Washington, D.C.: Brookings.

Bridges, Amy. 1984. *A City in the Republic: Antebellum New York and the Origins of Machine Politics.* Ithaca, NY: Cornell University Press.

Browning, Rufus P., Dale Rogers Marshall, and David H. Tabb, eds. 1990. *Racial Politics in American Cities.* New York: Longman.

Bullock, Charles S., III. 1993. "Republican Officeholding at the Local Level in Georgia." *Southeastern Political Review* 21, no. 1 (winter): 113–131.

Bullock, Charles S., III, and Bruce A. Campbell. 1984. "Racist or Racial Voting in the 1981 Atlanta Municipal Elections." *Urban Affairs Quarterly* 20, no. 2 (December): 149–164.

Bullock, Charles S., III, and Ronald Keith Gaddie. 1994. "Runoffs in Jesse Jackson's Backyard." *Social Science Quarterly* 75, no. 2 (June): 446–454.

Button, James W. 1992. "A Sign of Generational Conflict: The Impact of Florida's Aging Voters on Local School and Tax Referenda." *Social Science Quarterly* 73, no. 4 (December): 786–797.

Cole, Richard L., and David A. Caputo. 1984. "The Public Hearing as an Effective Citizen Participation Mechanism: A Case Study of the General Revenue Sharing Program." *American Political Science Review* 78, no. 2 (June): 404–416.

Crotty, William, ed. 1986. *Political Parties in Local Areas.* Knoxville: University of Tennessee Press.

DeLeon, Richard Edward. 1992. *Left Coast City: Progressive Politics in San Francisco, 1975–1991.* Lawrence: University Press of Kansas.

Eisinger, Peter K. 1973. "The Conditions of Protest Behavior in American Cities." *American Political Science Review* 67, no. 1 (March): 11–28.

Eulau, Heinz, and Kenneth Prewitt. 1973. *Labyrinths of Democracy: Adaptations, Linkages, Representation, and Policies in Urban Politics.* Indianapolis: Bobbs-Merrill.

Featherman, Sandra. 1983. "Ethnicity & Ethnic Candidates: Vote Advantages in Local Elections." *Polity* 15, no. 3 (spring): 397–415.

Fleischmann, Arnold, and Carol A. Pierannunzi. 1990. "Citizens, Development Interests, and Local Land-Use Regulation." *Journal of Politics* 52, no. 3 (August): 838–853.

Fleischmann, Arnold, and Lana Stein. 1987. "Minority and Female Success in Municipal Runoff Elections." *Social Science Quarterly* 68, no. 2 (June): 378–385.

Fraga, Luis R. 1988. "Domination through Democratic Means: Nonpartisan Slating Groups in City Electoral Politics." *Urban Affairs Quarterly* 23, no. 4 (June): 528–555.

Green, Donald Philip, and Jonathan A. Cowden. 1992. "Who Protests: Self-Interest and White Opposition to Busing." *Journal of Politics* 54, no. 2 (May): 471–496.

Hahn, Harlan, and Sheldon Kamieniecki. 1987. *Referendum Voting: Social Status and Policy Preferences.* New York: Greenwood Press.

Heilig, Peggy, and Robert J. Mundt. 1984. *Your Voice at City Hall: The Politics, Procedures and Policies of District Representation.* Albany: State University of New York Press.

Henig, Jeffrey R. 1993. "Race and Voting: Continuity and Change in the District of Columbia." *Urban Affairs Quarterly* 28, no. 4 (June): 544–570.

Herring, Mary, and John Forbes. 1994. "The Overrepresentation of a White Minority: Detroit's At-Large City Council, 1961–1989." *Social Science Quarterly* 75, no. 2 (June): 431–445.

Hirlinger, Michael W. 1992. "Citizen-Initiated Contacting of Local Government Officials: A Multivariate Explanation." *Journal of Politics* 54, no. 2 (May): 553–564.

Howell, Susan E., and William S. Oiler. 1981. "Campaign Activities and Local Election Outcomes." *Social Science Quarterly* 62, no. 1 (March): 151–160.

Inglot, Tomasz, and John P. Pelissero. 1993. "Ethnic Political Power in a Machine City: Chicago's Poles at Rainbow's End." *Urban Affairs Quarterly* 28, no. 4 (June): 526–543.

Jones, Bryan D. 1981. "Party and Bureaucracy: The Influence of Intermediary Groups on Urban Service Delivery." *American Political Science Review* 75, no. 3 (September): 688–700.

Jones, Bryan D., and Lynn W. Bachelor. 1993. *The Sustaining Hand: Community Leadership and Corporate Power.* 2nd ed. Lawrence: University Press of Kansas.

Karnig, Albert K., and B. Oliver Walter. 1985. "Municipal Voter Participation: Trends and Correlates." In Dennis R. Judd, ed., *Public Policy across States and Communities.* Greenwich, CT: JAI Press.

Lieske, Joel. 1989. "The Political Dynamics of Urban Voting Behavior." *American Journal of Political Science* 33, no. 1 (February): 150–174.

Logan, John R., and Harvey Molotch. 1987. *Urban Fortunes: The Political Economy of Place.* Berkeley: University of California Press.

Logan, John R., and Gordana Rabrenovic. 1990. "Neighborhood Associations: Their

Issues, Their Allies, and Their Opponents.'' *Urban Affairs Quarterly* 26, no. 1 (September): 68–94.

Mladenka, Kenneth R. 1981. ''Citizen Demands and Urban Services: The Distribution of Bureaucratic Response in Chicago and Houston.'' *American Journal of Political Science* 25, no. 4 (November): 693–714.

Murray, Richard, and Arnold Vedlitz. 1978. ''Racial Voting Patterns in the South: An Analysis of Major Elections from 1960 to 1977 in Five Cities.'' *Annals* 439 (September): 29–39.

Norrander, Barbara. 1986. ''Determinants of Local Party Campaign Activity.'' *Social Science Quarterly* 67, no. 3 (September): 562–571.

Parent, Wayne, and Wesley Shrum. 1985. ''Critical Electoral Success and Black Voter Registration: An Elaboration of the Voter Consent Model.'' *Social Science Quarterly* 66, no. 3 (September): 695–703.

Peterson, George E., ed. 1994. *Big City Politics, Governance, and Fiscal Constraints.* Washington, D.C.: Urban Institute Press.

Schiesl, Martin J. 1977. *The Politics of Efficiency: Municipal Administration and Reform in America, 1880–1920.* Berkeley: University of California Press.

Schmandt, Henry J., and George D. Wendel. 1988. ''Urban Research 1965–1987: A Content Analysis of *Urban Affairs Quarterly.*'' *Urban Affairs Quarterly* 24, no. 1 (September): 3–32.

Schumaker, Paul D. 1975. ''Policy Responsiveness to Protest-Group Demands.'' *Journal of Politics* 37, no. 2 (May): 488–521.

Sharp, Elaine B. 1986. *Citizen Demand-Making in the Urban Context.* Tuscaloosa: University of Alabama Press.

Sonenshein, Raphael J. 1993. *Politics in Black and White: Race and Power in Los Angeles.* Princeton: Princeton University Press.

Stein, Lana, and Arnold Fleischmann. 1994. ''Shaking the Money Tress: Assessing Local Campaign Contributions.'' Paper presented at the annual meeting of the Midwest Political Science Association, Chicago.

Stein, Lana, and Carol W. Kohfeld. 1991. ''St. Louis's Black-White Elections: Products of Machine Factionalism and Polarization.'' *Urban Affairs Quarterly* 27, no. 2 (December): 227–248.

Stone, Clarence N. 1980. ''Systemic Power in Community Decision Making: A Restatement of Stratification Theory.'' *American Political Science Review* 74, no. 4 (December): 978–990.

Stone, Clarence N. 1989. *Regime Politics: Governing Atlanta, 1946–1989.* Lawrence: University Press of Kansas.

Thomas, John Clayton. 1986. *Between Citizen and City: Neighborhood Organizations and Urban Politics in Cincinnati.* Lawrence: University Press of Kansas.

Vanderleeuw, James M., and Glenn H. Utter. 1993. ''Voter Roll-off and the Electoral Context: A Test of Two Theses.'' *Social Science Quarterly* 74, no. 3 (September): 664–673.

Vedlitz, Arnold. 1985. ''Voter Registration Drives and Black Voting in the South.'' *Journal of Politics* 47, no. 2 (May): 643–651.

Welch, Susan. 1990. ''The Impact of At-Large Elections on the Representation of Blacks and Hispanics.'' *Journal of Politics* 52, no. 4 (November): 1050–1076.

Welch, Susan, and Timothy Bledsoe. 1988. *Urban Reform and Its Consequences: A Study in Representation.* Chicago: University of Chicago Press.

Chapter 11

Neighborhoods

John Clayton Thomas

Neighborhood organizations, organizations of residents of communities within cities, are notorious for their volatility. Catalyzed by a particular issue or a strong leader, a neighborhood organization can assume a high profile in a city's politics, only to disappear from view almost overnight when the issue is resolved or the leader moves on to other pursuits.

Research on neighborhood politics and policies has followed a similar pattern over the last half of the twentieth century. After going virtually unnoticed by the scholarly community for most of the 1950s and 1960s, neighborhoods became a principal focus of urban research from the late 1960s through the middle 1980s. Since then, scholarly interest in neighborhoods has again fallen off such that by the mid-1990s relatively few scholars are focusing their research principally on neighborhoods.

This chapter has as its twin purposes to trace and to explain this mercurial history of research on neighborhoods. As part of that explanation, the chapter will also explore the principal theoretical issues that have arisen around neighborhoods and suggest possible directions for future research on neighborhoods. The concerns of this chapter, consistent with the focus of this book, are limited to research on politics and policies related to neighborhoods, excluding for the most part the extensive research on the geography, demography, and sociology of neighborhoods. *Neighborhood politics* refers to the role of neighborhood organizations, residents, and leaders in the political process. *Neighborhood policies,* in turn, refer to the various policies, federal and local policies in particular, addressed at reversing or preventing neighborhood decline.

OVERVIEW OF THE FIELD

An overview of research on neighborhoods might best begin at mid-twentieth century with, ironically, the presumed death of the American neighborhood. Critics of American society in the 1950s commonly depicted neighborhoods as dead or dying, victims of a transition to a mass society that was eroding all manner of personal relationships (Wellman and Leighton 1979: 368–371).

Neighborhood Politics

The rebirth or rediscovery of neighborhoods—and it is some of each—began in the late 1960s, catalyzed by the Great Society initiatives of the Johnson presidency. Those initiatives were directed principally at cities and often, as with the community action program (CAP) component of the War on Poverty, at low-income, predominantly minority neighborhoods. The intent was to reverse the decline of those neighborhoods, in part by organizing the communities themselves.

The federal initiatives combined with a growing civil rights militancy to stimulate extensive new political activity at the neighborhood level, what Bell and Held (1969) characterized as a "community revolution." According to a 1968–1969 survey of CAP neighborhoods, "something less than a third of [the] poor communities show marked political vitality, strong organizations, inventive leadership, active citizenry, and close attention to the coordination of efforts toward common goals," a level of activity presumably well above what would have been observed only a few years earlier (Lamb 1975: 5). Not all assessments were so positive (e.g., Ambrecht 1976; Gittell 1980), but few observers disputed the substantial rise in the level of neighborhood political activity.

What was first perceived as a revival limited to low-income minority neighborhoods was soon seen as reaching a broad range of urban neighborhoods. As early as 1969, Milton Kotler (1969: 9) was arguing that the "neighborhood is and always has been the basic unit of political life." A decade later, talk of a "national neighborhood movement" was common (Goering 1979).

The growth of this broader neighborhood movement was sparked by a number of factors. First, with African Americans from the South migrating to northern cities in unprecedented numbers during the 1950s and 1960s, many neighborhoods were experiencing rapid racial change. Although many whites sought simply to escape that racial change by exiting to suburbs, some chose to stay and fight for racial stability in their neighborhoods. Neighborhood organizations were one of the tools they used in this fight (see, for example, Thomas 1986: 28–33).

Second, federal and local policy changes in the 1970s encouraged more activity at the local level. Federal policies (see below for more detail) provided both direct funding and tax incentives to spur neighborhood political activity. At the local level, community planning experiments, efforts to plan for neighborhoods rather than only for the city as a whole, facilitated residents' involvement in shaping their communities (Needleman and Needleman 1974; Rohe and Gates 1985). A number of cities also revised their budgeting procedures to give prominent roles to neighborhoods in budget planning (Hallman 1984: 244–246).

As the level of neighborhood political activity increased, research on neighborhoods expanded. One body of research developed around questions of who participates in neighborhood organizations and where neighborhood organizations are likely to mobilize. Scholars were puzzled by the relatively high level of resident participation given the "public goods dilemma," wherein any resident stood to benefit from public goods gained through neighborhood activism regardless of whether the individual joined in that activism (e.g., O'Brien 1975: 24–25). A consensus gradually developed that neighborhood involvement could best be understood in the context of Hirschman's theory of "exit, voice and loyalty" (e.g., Hirschman 1970; Orbell and Uno 1972). Individual involvement could be seen in that context as (1) growing in part from factors common to other forms of political participation (e.g., socioeconomic status) but (2) also having some unique roots, such as homeownership and threats to neighborhood stability (see Cox and McCarthy 1980; Sharp 1980; Crenson 1983: 208–211; Thomas 1986: 58–60). Findings at the organizational level were similar (e.g., Rich 1980; Henig 1982).

Another body of research developed around questions of the roles and functions of neighborhood organizations. A first task was to identify the numerous types of neighborhood organizations, including at least (1) advocacy organizations based on community organizing, found principally in low-income areas; (2) social service organizations, which serve in effect as administrative arms of government, also found principally in low-income areas; (3) homeowner associations, formed in middle- to upper-income areas to protect neighborhood property values and quality of life; and (4) preservationist organizations, formed to assist in rebuilding property and property values in neighborhoods with deteriorated but historically unique architecture (on the various types, see Bell and Held 1969; Clay 1979; Gittell 1980; Hallman 1984; Fisher 1985; Thomas 1986).

Neighborhood Policies

The growing interest in neighborhood politics was paralleled by increased research attention to neighborhood policies. In a sense, neighborhood policies could include a broad range of social policies that affect neighborhoods (e.g., health care, welfare reform, substance abuse). For the most part, however, neighborhood policies have been defined more narrowly to include only those policies targeted at stabilizing or upgrading neighborhoods, including especially policies related to the racial integration, housing preservation and upgrading, economic development, and residential stability of neighborhoods.

The first efforts in these directions were the Great Society initiatives, especially the community action program and model cities, which were designed to mobilize residents of low-income neighborhoods and to reserve the economic and social decline of those areas. As a consequence of poor planning (Moynihan 1969) or other factors, these efforts were widely assessed as relatively ineffective in turning around neighborhoods.

The decade of the 1970s brought a variety of new policy initiatives targeted at neighborhoods (for an overview, see Downs 1981). The most notable of these was the federal Community Development Block Grant (CDBG) program, which, beginning in 1974, targeted substantial funding to developing and redeveloping low-income communities in U.S. cities (Dommel et al. 1982). The 1970s also brought the expanded use of historical preservation policies as a tool for redeveloping historical structures, including many residences, in U.S. cities (see, for example, Schill and Nathan 1983).

Although spending on neighborhood policies declined with federal cutbacks in the 1980s, the search for policy solutions for neighborhood problems continued. Some scholars argued from their research for targeting policy initiatives at homeowners or institutional actors, the actors whose efforts were supposedly crucial to neighborhood reinvestment (e.g., Taub, Taylor, and Dunham 1984; Galster 1987). Others pointed to a need to combat discriminatory real estate marketing practices that appeared to be perpetuating or increasing neighborhood segregation (Squires and Velez 1987). Many conservatives advocated the creation of "enterprise zones," that is, making available special incentives for economic investments in specific deteriorated neighborhoods (for an academic perspective, see Wolf 1990).

The Decline of Neighborhood Research

Scholarly interest in neighborhoods tailed off after the mid-1980s. The decline is especially pronounced for issues of neighborhood politics where only a few notable research products have surfaced in recent years (see, in particular, Berry, Portney, and Thomson 1993) but is also evident with neighborhood policy questions.

The reasons for the decline are not hard to find. When the tax revolt of the 1970s and 1980s forced governments at all levels to make do with less, neighborhood policies were among the principal targets of funding cutbacks. The climate for neighborhood policies also worsened at the local level when, in the face of federal cutbacks, municipal governments gave a higher priority to economic development due to its perceived potential for increasing local revenues. Although in theory neighborhoods could be viewed as a principal locus for economic development efforts, cities in practice usually gave first priority to their central business districts (CBDs), the high-visibility downtowns on which cities seem to think their economic fortunes depend. In a constant or declining sum game for municipal resources, more attention to downtowns meant less attention to neighborhoods. As funding for neighborhood policies diminished, the vitality of neighborhood organizations also suffered. With fewer resources to compete for, these inherently fragile organizations lost some of their incentive to remain organized.

Neighborhood organizations and policies did not disappear from U.S. cities in these years. To the contrary, as Berry, Thomson, and Portney (1993) document, where those organizations and policies became well entrenched in the 1970s, they usually survived or even flourished in the 1980s. New neighborhood initiatives, however, did not fare well.

Curiously, even as the clout of neighborhood organizations and the support for neighborhood policies waned, the place of neighborhoods in normative democratic theory was becoming more firmly established. A new "communitarian" school of thought called for "a renewal of commitment and community" (Bellah et al. 1985: 277). As Benjamin Barber (1984: 269) made clear, neighborhoods were essential to the communitarian vision of democracy: "[T]he first and most important reform in a strong democratic platform must be the introduction of a national system of *neighborhood assemblies* in every rural, suburban, and urban district in America."

THEORETICAL APPROACHES AND ISSUES

As research and scholarship on neighborhoods have accumulated, several theoretical issues have come into clear focus. In one way or another, almost all of these issues revolve around the political viability and utility of neighborhoods in urban political life and American democracy.

Neighborhood Political Power

A first issue concerns the potential political power of neighborhoods and neighborhood organizations. On the one hand, the potential for neighborhood clout is downplayed by the principal spokespersons for both sides in the recent debate over the influence of local politics in local affairs. Paul Peterson (1981) characterized local politics as essentially "groupless," with few local groups, such as neighborhood organizations, exerting much influence over municipal policies. Although taking issue with Peterson on the importance of politics at the local level, Clarence Stone (1989: 131–134) also concluded that neighborhoods are unlikely to prove important partners in the "urban regimes" that govern most American cities.

On the other hand, many scholars who have studied neighborhoods argue that their political power can be considerable. Research on Cincinnati, for example, reveals that (1) neighborhood organizations were able to open municipal decision-making processes to more neighborhood influence, and (2) stronger neighborhood organizations were able to use their strength to obtain more municipal funding (Thomas 1986: 90–94, 135–140). More recently, Berry, Portney, and Thomson, (1993: 157–158) report similar evidence of neighborhood political power from a study of five major U.S. cities.

This disagreement may derive in part from scholars looking at different cities or different areas. Stone may be correct that few U.S. cities featured neighborhoods as prominent regime partners during the 1980s, an era when the focus on economic development and on downtowns conflicted with the usual neighborhood priorities. Yet those who see neighborhoods as having clout may be accurate for many cities during the 1970s and early 1980s as well as for selected cities in more recent years (see, especially, Savitch and Thomas 1991; Berry, Portney, and Thomson 1993).

Neighborhoods may exert substantial influence in other areas, too, but in a manner not evident through the citywide approaches of Peterson and Stone. The diversity of neighborhood organizations nurtures a wide range of interests and demands, as illustrated by the many neighborhood "not in my backyard!" (NIMBY) protests against perceived locally undesirable land uses (LULUs). Even if a municipal government accedes to many NIMBY protests, the outcomes may be too diverse to be evident in any general patterns of city spending or policies.

Too Much Neighborhood Power?

Even as some scholars have doubted the power of neighborhoods, others have argued that they wield too much power. Douglas Yates (1977), for example, traced the roots of what he saw as an "ungovernable city" in part to a "bewildering array of street-level community organizations that seek to give voice to one neighborhood demand or another." Samuel Huntington (1975) has worried similarly that citizen participation initiatives, the initiatives that contributed to the rise of neighborhood organizations, have created an "excess of democracy," undermining the effective functioning of American government.

Research on neighborhood organizations suggests that these worries may be groundless. These organizations may have introduced some unwelcome complexity to the political process in their early years; change seldom comes without some discomfort. In more recent years, however, the evidence suggests that their effects are more likely to be salutary. According to a recent comparative study of a number of cities (Berry, Portney, and Thomson 1993: 158, 185, 201–202), neighborhood organizations tend to work cooperatively with businesses, provide a useful check against the domination of citywide interests, and are more likely to "defuse" than to spark conflict. Other studies have reached similar conclusions (see Henig 1982: 231–232; Thomas 1986).

Neighborhoods and Strong Democracy

If their effects can be salutary, could neighborhood organizations become the cornerstones of a revived or stronger American democracy? Communitarian theorists in recent times have envisioned such a potential (Barber 1984), and observers from virtually all points on the ideological spectrum have at other times voiced similar hopes. On the Left, Harry Boyte (1980: 4) has talked about a "backyard revolution" where "[m]yriad forms of protest, self help, community building, and insurgency grew and flourished at the grassroots, sending ripples through the entire culture." On the Right, conservatives have praised the organizing of neighborhoods as heralding a revival of "mediating institutions" that could help people help themselves, rather than relying on government (Berger and Neuhaus 1977). In the Center, the nonpartisan International City Management Association concluded that "government that is decentralized to the level of communities and neighborhoods may be the wave of the future" (Rutter 1980: 26).

Practitioners also envisioned more practical benefits from enhanced neighborhood democracy. In a time of governmental cutbacks, working with neighborhoods was viewed as a means to stretch limited governmental resources. Services that have been delivered by government alone could supposedly be "coproduced" by government and neighborhoods, reducing the cost of services and perhaps increasing their quality (Levine 1984).

Empirical research does not fully support this optimism. As perhaps the key finding of the literature on this point, Berry, Portney, and Thomson (1993: 284–285) found that political participation does not increase even in cities where there are both strong neighborhood organizations and effective structures for involving those organizations in local governance. Contrary to what communitarian theorists often argue, many citizens are intimidated, not attracted, by the opportunity for face-to-face communication that neighborhood meetings provide. Citizens may actually have a greater potential for identifying with a metropolitan government than with neighborhood organizations (Lyons, Lowery, and DeHoog 1992: 178–182).

At the same time, neighborhood organizations may hold the potential for strengthening democracy. If not attracting mobs of people, these organizations do attract some participants who might otherwise be uninvolved. They also provide a forum for addressing issues that cannot be adequately addressed by other means. Finally, as discussed below, these organizations may play an essential role in maintaining or reviving their neighborhoods.

Turning Neighborhoods Around

Perhaps the most difficult issue for students of neighborhood policies has been how to turn declining neighborhoods around. The issue consists of several interrelated issues: (1) how to achieve and stabilize residential integration, (2) how to persuade homeowners to invest and reinvest in homes in marginal areas, and (3) how to achieve commercial growth in these areas. With all of these issues, the problem may be less a disagreement between different perspectives than an inability to find policies that are both effective and affordable.

Anthony Downs (1981: 156–157) argued for a policy of targeting spending to areas that were needy but also capable of making good use of the funds.

In essence, that strategy was pursued with much of the federal CDBG spending during the 1970s and early 1980s (e.g., Dommel et al. 1982), but, as with the Great Society experiments, the results have been less than overwhelmingly successful.

Other scholars favor different or additional strategies, such as encouraging renovation of declining neighborhoods by middle-income populations (e.g., Clay 1979). Federal efforts to promote upgrading along these lines have yet to achieve much success, however (e.g., Varady 1986). Many analysts see neighborhood change as requiring simultaneous attacks on a number of fronts, some designed to remove destructive forces, others to build new positive structures (e.g., Marciniak 1981).

A consensus may be developing around this idea that only a multifaceted approach can succeed in turning around most declining neighborhoods. Illustrative of this approach, in one of the most insightful of the recent contributions to the neighborhood policy literature, Taub, Taylor, and Dunham (1984: 182–184) argue that avoiding decline in a transitional neighborhood requires the participation of committed corporate and institutional actors (''banks, universities, insurance companies, or manufacturing firms''), strong neighborhood organizations, and government.

This argument parallels one part of the recent literature on urban politics. The emphasis on the importance of both corporate actors and government echoes the importance accorded this combination in analyses of urban regimes in the urban politics literature. At the same time, the emphasis on the importance of neighborhood organizations departs from the consensus of the regimes literature. Yet Taub, Taylor, and Dunham (1984: 184–185) are able to document how neighborhood organizations have been effective in, for example, avoiding ''racial tipping'' of a neighborhood (i.e., tranformation from an integrated neighborhood, with 15 to 30 percent black residents, to an almost completely black neighborhood) by pursuing a three-part agenda to (1) ''maintain a stable real estate market,'' (2) ''maintain the quality of neighborhood schools,'' and (3) implement ''an anticrime package that includes establishing youth programs and promoting citizen crime-prevention activities.'' Their findings add to the mounting evidence of the importance of neighborhood organizations in maintaining and improving neighborhoods (e.g., Clay 1979; Schoenberg and Rosenbaum 1980: 150–151; Thomas 1986; Saltman 1990: 373–375). The importance of regimes in urban politics should not blind us to the potential importance of neighborhood actors in achieving positive neighborhood change.

FUTURE RESEARCH ISSUES

For all that has been learned about neighborhood politics and policies, many important questions remain unanswered. More research would be useful, for one thing, on this question of the political power of contemporary neighborhood organizations. How can we reconcile the considerable evidence of a significant neighborhood political presence with what appears to be the preeminent power of governing regimes in cities?

Questions also remain about the role neighborhoods can play in enhancing democracy. Should reform efforts focus on increasing the role of neighborhoods, or, as Lyons, Lowery, and DeHoog (1992) suggest, are we better advised to push for stronger metropolitan governments? A better understanding on the earlier issue of the place of neighborhoods in the context of urban regimes should also help here.

Future research should, however, recognize some facts often obscured in earlier research. First, neighborhoods as political actors are not a unitary force. It may be more appropriate to view neighborhoods not as a type of interest group but as a variety of interest groups, ranging from protective homeowner associations to community development authorities to service advocacy organizations. It is conceivable that the different types may play different roles in urban democracy and in the development of public policy.

Second, in a related manner, the focus on neighborhoods should broaden from central cities alone to encompass other municipalities, too. Suburban homeowner associations, sometimes known as ''residential community associations'' (RCAs), probably represent the largest growth area for neighborhood organizations (Dilger 1992). The failure to give much attention to these suburban neighborhood organizations severely limits the relevance of neighborhoods research.

Finally, more remains to be learned—and to be done—about turning around neighborhoods. The continuing decline of so many central city neighborhoods and now of many suburban areas underscores how we have failed to define effective means for rescuing neighborhoods and their residents from the forces of decline.

REFERENCES

Ambrecht, Biliana C. S. 1976. *Politicizing the Poor: The Legacy of the War on Poverty in a Mexican-American Community*. New York: Praeger.

Barber, Benjamin. 1984. *Strong Democracy: Participatory Politics for a New Age*. Berkeley: University of California Press.

Bell, Daniel, and Virginia Held. 1969. ''The Community Revolution.'' *Public Interest*, no. 16 (summer): 142–177.

Bellah, Robert N., Richard Madsen, William M. Sullivan, Ann Swidler, and Steven M. Tipton. 1985. *Habits of the Heart: Individualism and Commitment in American Life*. Berkeley and Los Angeles: University of California Press.

Berger, Peter L., and Richard John Neuhaus. 1977. *To Empower People: The Role of Mediating Structures in Public Policy*. Washington, D.C.: American Enterprise Institute.

Berry, Jeffrey M., Kent E. Portney, and Ken Thomson. 1993. *The Rebirth of Urban Democracy*. Washington, D.C.: Brookings Institution.

Boyte, Harry C. 1980. *The Backyard Revolution: Understanding the New Citizen Movement*. Philadelphia: Temple University Press.

Clay, Phillip L. 1979. *Neighborhood Renewal: Middle-Class Resettlement and Incumbent Upgrading in American Neighborhoods*. Lexington, MA: Lexington Books.

Cox, Kevin R., and Jeffrey McCarthy. 1980. ''Neighborhood Activism in the American City: Behavioral Relationships and Evaluation.'' *Urban Geography* 1: 22–38.

Crenson, Matthew A. 1983. *Neighborhood Politics*. Cambridge, MA: Harvard University Press.

Dilger, Robert Jay. 1992. *Neighborhood Politics: Residential Community Associations in American Governance*. New York: New York University Press.

Dommel, Paul R., John Stuart Hall, Victor E. Bach, Leonard Rubinowitz, Leon L. Haley, and John S. Jackson III. 1982. *Decentralizing Urban Policy: Case Studies in Community Development*. Washington, D.C.: Brookings Institution.

Downs, Anthony. 1981. *Neighborhoods and Urban Development*. Washington, D.C.: Brookings Institution.

Fisher, Robert. 1985. ''Neighborhood Organizing and Urban Revitalization: An Historical Perspective.'' *Journal of Urban Affairs* 7 (winter): 47–53.

Galster, George C. 1987. *Homeowners and Neighborhood Reinvestment*. Durham and London: Duke University Press.

Gittell, Marilyn, with Bruce Hoffacker, Eleanor Rollins, Samuel Foster, and Mark Hoffacker. 1980. *Limits to Citizen Participation: The Decline of Community Organizations*. Beverly Hills, CA: Sage.

Goering, John M. 1979. ''The National Neighborhood Movement: A Preliminary Analysis and Critique.'' *American Planning Association Journal* 45 (October): 506–514.

Hallman, Howard W. 1984. *Neighborhoods: Their Place in Urban Life*. Beverly Hills, CA: Sage.

Henig, Jeffrey R. 1982. *Neighborhood Mobilization: Redevelopment and Response*. New Brunswick, NJ: Rutgers University Press.

Hirschman, Albert. 1970. *Exit, Voice, and Loyalty*. Cambridge, MA: Harvard University Press.

Huntington, Samuel P. 1975. ''The Democratic Distemper.'' *Public Interest*, no. 41 (fall): 9–38.

Kotler, Milton. 1969. *Neighborhood Government: The Local Foundations of Political Life*. Indianapolis and New York: Bobbs-Merrill.

Lamb, Curt. 1975. *Political Power in Poor Neighborhoods*. Cambridge, MA: Schenkman.

Levine, Charles H. 1984. ''Citizenship and Service Delivery: The Promise of Coproduction.'' *Public Administration Review* 44: 178–187.

Lyons, W. E., David Lowery, and Ruth Hoogland DeHoog. 1992. *The Politics of Dissatisfaction: Citizens, Services, and Urban Institutions*. Armonk, NY: M. E. Sharpe.

Marciniak, Ed. 1981. *Reversing Urban Decline: The Winthrop-Kenmore Corridor in the Edgewater and Uptown Communities of Chicago*. Washington, D.C.: National Center for Urban Ethnic Affairs.

Moynihan, Daniel P. 1969. *Maximum Feasible Misunderstanding*. New York: Free Press.

Needleman, Martin L., and Carolyn Emerson Needleman. 1974. *Guerrillas in the Bu-*

reaucracy: The Community Planning Experiment in the United States. New York: John Wiley.

O'Brien, David J. 1975. *Neighborhood Organizations and Interest-Group Processes*. Princeton, NJ: Princeton University Press.

Orbell, John M., and Toru Uno. 1972. "A Theory of Neighborhood Problem Solving: Political Action vs. Residential Mobility." *American Political Science Review* 66 (June): 471–489.

Peterson, Paul. 1981. *City Limits*. Chicago: University of Chicago Press.

Rich, Richard C. 1980. "A Political-Economy Approach to the Study of Neighborhood Organizations." *American Journal of Political Science* 24 (November): 559–592.

Rohe, William M., and Laren B. Gates. 1985. *Planning with Neighborhoods*. Chapel Hill and London: University of North Carolina Press.

Rutter, Lawrence, ed. 1980. *The Essential Community: Local Government in the Year 2000*. Washington, D.C.: International City Management Association.

Saltman, Juliet. 1990. *A Fragile Movement: The Struggle for Neighborhood Stabilization*. New York: Greenwood Press.

Savitch, H. S., and John Clayton Thomas, eds. 1991. *Big City Politics in Transition*. Newbury Park, CA: Sage Publications.

Schill, Michael H., and Richard P. Nathan. 1983. *Revitalizing America's Cities: Neighborhood Reinvestment and Displacement*. Albany: State University of New York Press.

Schoenberg, Sandra Perlman, and Patricia L. Rosenbaum. 1980. *Neighborhoods that Work: Sources for Viability in the Inner City*. New Brunswick, NJ: Rutgers University Press.

Sharp, Elaine B. 1980. "Citizen Perception of Channels for Urban Service Advocacy." *Public Opinion Quarterly* 44 (fall): 362–376.

Squires, Gregory D., and William Velez. 1987. "Neighborhood Racial Composition and Mortgage Lending: City and Suburban Differences." *Journal of Urban Affairs* 9: 217–232.

Stone, Clarence. 1989. *Regime Politics: Governing Atlanta, 1946–1988*. Lawrence: University Press of Kansas.

Taub, Richard P., D. Garth Taylor, and Jan D. Dunham. 1984. *Paths of Neighborhood Change: Race and Crime in Urban America*. Chicago and London: University of Chicago Press.

Thomas, John Clayton. 1986. *Between Citizen and City: Neighborhood Organizations and Urban Politics in Cincinnati*. Lawrence: University Press of Kansas.

Varady, David P. 1986. *Neighborhood Upgrading: A Realistic Assessment*. Albany: State University of New York Press.

Wellman, Barry, and Barry Leighton. 1979. "Networks, Neighborhoods, and Communities." *Urban Affairs Quarterly* 14 (March): 363–390.

Wolf, Michael Allan. 1990. "Enterprise Zones: A Decade of Diversity." *Economic Development Quarterly* 4: 3–14.

Yates, Douglas. 1977. *The Ungovernable City: The Politics of Urban Problems and Policy Making*. Cambridge, MA: MIT Press.

Chapter 12

Central Cities and Suburbs

Douglas H. Adams and H. V. Savitch

While the issue is still debatable, much of the work on cities and suburbs points to the enduring and, in some cases, the growing interdependence between urban core and periphery. Pressures for economic development, globalization, environmental policies, and the sheer complexity of intergovernmental relations have in many ways brought cities and suburbs closer together. At the same time, social polarization, cultural differences, and the continuing crisis within central cores have driven cities and suburbs apart. The upshot of this ambivalence has produced a selective, incremental, and cautious cooperation between cities and suburbs. Increased attention to public-private partnerships is just one manifestation of this trend. The relationship is also mirrored through public benefit corporations that undertake special functions, special districts that cross local boundaries, and in some cases, an expanded authority for regional government.

There is also another dimension to the city-suburban tie, borne from the fact that suburbs are, in reality, outgrowths of central cores. Since World War II, there has been a dramatic resettlement of America's middle class from city neighborhoods into various forms of suburban enclaves. Demographic decentralization has affected virtually every locality. It has continued beyond the suburban rim and brought forth what has come to be known as exurbia, which is little more than more distant, dedensified suburbs. While Americans may have grown to take such changes in urban life for granted over the past five decades, from a global perspective, such decentralized, low-density settlements are unique in that they have made the United States the world's first suburban nation.

The most salient research in the field monitors, analyzes, and draws implications from these developments. Scholars have traced the evolution of cities and suburbs by examining whether city-suburban prosperity is interlinked, by investigating different modes of cooperation, and by examining the growth of new urban forms. In a somewhat more traditional vein, historians and sociologists have drawn upon the differences in urban or suburban lifestyles. Yet rarely do researchers conform to a single style, specific approach, or narrowly defined set of methods. Most findings rely on an assortment of modalities that overlap.

By looking at a variety of studies of cities and suburbs, we identify general research approaches and the way in which researchers identify and attack particular problems. Although it is not possible to construct an exhaustive list of examples within the limits of this chapter, we highlight that research that is distinguished by predominant characteristics and use it to sort through and categorize major research styles and findings. Accordingly, we divide our review into four areas: (1) historical narrative or ethnographic approach, (2) trend analysis, (3) analytical and/or statistical approaches, and (4) organizational approaches.

HISTORICAL NARRATIVE OR ETHNOGRAPHIC APPROACH

The historical narrative or ethnographic approaches are generally descriptive in style, with most relying on a chronological account of suburban development. Such studies portray the causes and effects of suburban growth by using archival and documentary research to lay out the dynamic of change.

The historical narrative and ethnographic approaches frequently seek to reveal recurrent patterns in different times and places, often within a comparative framework and typically within the parameters of a conceptual model or paradigm. Max Weber used the German term *verstehen*—"understanding"—in reference to an essential quality of social research, meaning that the researcher must be able to mentally take on the circumstances, views, and feelings of those being studied to interpret their actions appropriately (Babbie 1989). Hence, these forms of analysis proceed from a hefty collection of facts and the author's interpretation of this evidence. Ethnographic approaches follow a similar vein but are more inclined to use interviews, participant observation, and standard anthropological methods. Ethnographic accounts are also more prone to view suburban life from the standpoint of the participant and to embrace a more "subjective" analysis. Many historical narrative researchers detail the qualities unique to cities during a given time frame and comment on the changes that led to an altered form and the details unique to its very existence. A fine example of the ethnographic style is Herbert Gans's *The Levittowners* (1967).

The Levittowners is an ethnographic study of a single suburban area in New Jersey once known as Levittown, now known as Willingboro. Conducted in the late 1950s and early 1960s, Gans's contribution to the study of suburbs is valuable, due in part to both the time frame in which he writes and his adeptness at analyzing an evolving phenomenon from the participant observer perspective.

Having lived in the community for the first two years of its existence, Gans raises questions and addresses issues that delve into the very core of suburbanization as well as the resultant cultural and institutional changes. As a sociological study, it covers an array of issues in this bedroom community, ranging from class to politics, race to religion, and a variety of other elements that compose this social structure. In addition to attending meetings of different institutions (i.e., churches, school boards, etc.) and conducting interviews, Gans's research also employed a mail survey that was sent out to Levittowners *before* their exposure to this new type of lifestyle. Although Gans makes no claims regarding applicability of his findings to suburbs in different regions, the scope of his observations are broad enough for the reader to draw his own conclusions regarding the causes and effects of a suburban lifestyle on both the individual and society.

Another example of the historical narrative approach can be found in Kenneth Jackson's *Crabgrass Frontier* (1985). Jackson's rationale for studying the suburban phenomenon from the historical perspective is multifaceted. However, he makes a number of powerful arguments in explaining this approach, the strongest being that decisions made in the past impose powerful restraints on the future. Labeling suburbia as a concept defying definition, Jackson points out that individuals are likely to view it from particular perceptions.

Economists assign suburban status on the basis of functional relationships between the core and the surrounding region; demographers on the basis of residential density or commuting patterns; architects on the basis of building type; and sociologists on the basis of behavior or "way of life." The United States Bureau of the Census defines metropolitan areas as agglomerations with a central city of fifty thousand plus nearby areas with a "significant level" of commuting into the city and a specified amount of urban characteristics. (5)

In looking at the historical development of suburbs, Jackson focuses on some of America's oldest cities, particularly New York, Boston, Philadelphia, Cleveland, and St. Louis. Portions of his analysis use time series data to monitor changing conditions in select cities. Among the variables he uses to document the process of suburbanization are: central city population increases and decreases, commuting patterns and distance traveled to the workplace, population density per square mile, records of village incorporations, home values, degree of metropolitization (city population as a percentage of the metropolitan population), new housing starts, and a variety of other population demographic statistics.

A useful, though somewhat outdated, example of the narrative approach can be found in Downs's *Opening Up the Suburbs: An Urban Strategy for America* (1973). Among the primary concerns Downs addresses in this book are the economic divisions between cities and their suburbs. For Downs, "opening up the suburbs" translates into increasing the degree of economic diversity within the suburbs and giving economically disadvantaged individuals an opportunity to succeed. The findings of this book lead one to his conclusion that one of the fundamental goals of American society, true equality of opportunity, will not be attained within the framework of a divisive social system.

The arguments made by Downs build upon what he sees as injustices rooted not only in the economic divisions between cities and suburbs but in racial divisions accentuated by disproportionate suburban growth. The approaches advocated by Downs to better integrate metropolitan areas economically and racially are constructed with a recognition of potential political opposition to such efforts. Thus, Downs believes that for strategies to affect *both* city and suburban areas, middle-class dominance should be preserved in suburban areas targeted for integration while the inner-city quality of life is concurrently improved. Downs also recognizes the long-term value of accomplishing such ends through economic *incentives* rather than through varying forms of local mandates. Although the book is over 20 years old, the research approach taken by Downs reflects a movement toward recognizing the economic and social linkages between central cities and their surrounding suburbs.

Another important historical analysis to consider is Michael Danielson's "Differentiation, Segregation, and Political Fragmentation in the American Metropolis" (1972). In this carefully developed piece, Danielson historically traces the development of America's "differentiated metropolis." In using this term, Danielson is referring to the decentralization and fragmentation that have contributed to disparities and concentrations of poverty in center cities. Given that he points out the ways in which political fragmentation feeds the aforementioned process, through things such as land use policies, many important aspects of this work might also fall under the organizational approach. Danielson discusses ways of dealing with these problems, including taking more of the burden off of cities through intergovernmental assistance—a prescription that is covered in the section on organizational approaches.

Other historical narrative studies to consider are Robert Wood's *Suburbia* (1959) and *On the City's Rim* (1972) by Wirt et al.

TREND ANALYSIS

Some of the most creative research on cities and suburbs can be found in the analysis of major trends. Trend analysis explores the underlying dynamics of cities and suburbs in order to locate their future direction. The focus is often on what forces "push" or "pull" localities and how we can understand why some localities grow, while others do not. The answers often center on economic advantages or benefits in technology, business, or workforce training that accrue to particular localities. The most common form of trend studies uses U.S. census data to analyze changes within a population over a given period of time, comparing demographic, economic, and other variables.

Generally speaking, trend studies can have a dramatic impact on understanding shifts in important variables between cities and suburbs, while some studies appear to unlock "secrets" of local survival. The research orientation of these studies is more applied, and these types of studies are distinguished by a strong policy focus. More often than not, they are more apt to provide policy solutions to vexing questions—a factor that makes them popular with public officials, citizen groups, and journalists. Some of the best-known studies have been done by Joel Garreau (1991), Neil Peirce, Johnson, and Hall (1993), and David Rusk (1993). The multiauthored work by Peirce, Johnson, and Hall (1993) has attracted attention, as have studies published by the Advisory Commission on Intergovernmental Relations (ACIR) and the National League of Cities.

Joel Garreau's *Edge City* (1991) asks whether or not the city has recreated itself beyond the core by splitting into a miniaturized form he calls "edge cities." As a writer for the *Washington Post*, Garreau attempts to answer this question by pointing out that edge cities are distinctly different urban forms compared to conventional notions of cities. By examining factors that have generated edge cities, Garreau traces both their origins as well as the allure of their development. Combining his observations of human interaction and economic motivations, Garreau concentrates on the social and economic evolution of edge cities in large metropolitan areas. The areas focused on in *Edge City* are located on the outskirts of Boston, Detroit, Atlanta, Phoenix, San Francisco, and Washington, D.C., while a broader scope is taken for areas in New Jersey, Texas, and southern California.

At its core, Garreau's book attempts to discover the underlying motivations that have led to this revolutionary development and process of redefining urban space. Among the repercussions of this movement toward the "new frontier" are cities without distinct beginnings or endings to their boundaries—or as the author puts it, urban places with more jobs than bedrooms. Garreau also probes at questions as to whether contemporary American society has irreversibly altered its expectations of traditional cities and whether they will ultimately be made obsolete. The answer is not entirely dismal for older urban cores, however, and Garreau seeks to show how they can be utilized for arts, culture, government, and the like. Despite his effort to hold an olive branch out to traditional cities, the author's sympathies are clearly with newer, rather than older, urban forms, and so too does he believe that edge cities are at the cusp of the country's future.

Neil Peirce is a journalist who, like Garreau, has taken up the task of analyzing urban trends. Consistent with the majority of recent literature on city-suburb relationships, Peirce's research approach looks at the city in a regional context rather than as a distinct, separate entity. In *Citistates* (1993), Peirce, Johnson, and Hall postulate that in order for American citistates to survive and thrive in today's global economy, they must overcome three fundamental problems: the deep socioeconomic gulf between poor cities and affluent suburbs, physical sprawl and its environmental and social consequences, and the hesitation or unwillingness to create effective systems of coordinated governance for citistates.

Although most of the author's research is based on what he labels as "thorough and independent analysis'' of selected cities, Peirce's writing and research clearly take a more journalistic approach than other forms of trend analysis. Overall, it is highly qualitative in content and largely descriptive, though still quite useful because of its direct, policy-oriented approach.

In the preface to *Citistates*, Peirce outlines his research approach to each city as one that includes consultations with locally based people with university credentials; ''off-the-record'' interviews with the local power elite; helicopter, automobile, and walking tours of the city; and examination of press reports, academic research, budgets, plans, census reports, and interview notes from previous trips to the cities dating back approximately 30 years. In addition to two chapters devoted entirely to citistates, Peirce's book includes an overview of a half-dozen American cities: Phoenix, Seattle, Baltimore, Owensboro, Dallas, and St. Paul.

One of the more widely cited studies of late is David Rusk's *Cities without Suburbs*, which presents us with another example of the trend analysis approach. Like Kenneth Jackson, Rusk believes urban research is often overly fragmented along distinct disciplinary lines. Implicit in this view is Rusk's belief that however noteworthy, well written, or researched specific studies may be, they often do not probe at the root of the issue. The root of the issue, or ''urban problem,'' for Rusk is that many cities have not adapted to the significant shifts that have occurred from over five decades of mass suburbanization. Rusk follows the logic of his analysis by calling for metropolitan areas where there are no lines between cities and suburbs.

Because of Rusk's advocacy of metropolitan forms of government and his interest in institutional reform, his research can also be categorized under the organizational approach. Rusk's findings support the theory that cities capable of ''capturing'' suburban growth are economically more healthy, vibrant, and better able to bring about social justice by integrating schools and housing. To Rusk, cities and suburbs do not have mutually exclusive destinies. Instead, he sees them as complementary entities whose social and economic abilities are affected by the extent to which a naturally symbiotic relationship can be fostered.

In the trend analysis portion of his study, Rusk examines census data on 522 central cities in 320 metropolitan areas from 1950 to 1990. While Rusk's data are built upon a self-compiled data base, it is not included in the work. (In a section at the end of the book, Rusk provides an address where the data can be purchased.) Many of his findings stem from this very large, self-compiled data, all of which are pertinent to understanding the effects of over 50 years of suburbanization. Yet the unique aspect of Rusk's research may not be his methodology as much as the perspective he brings to the issue. Rusk's experience both as mayor of Albuquerque and as a New Mexico state representative provides him with a unique insight into the process and repercussions of suburbanization, the political factors at play, as well as the relative ability and willingness of cities to adjust to changing socioeconomic circumstances.

The Advisory Commission on Intergovernmental Relations has published a number of reports on issues of vital importance to cities and suburbs. Among the issues the ACIR has dealt with in the past are adequacy of local revenue bases, federal and state aid to localities, intergovernmental grants and their allocative formulas, ease or difficulty of annexation, political accountability, and the shifting assignment of functions among cities, counties, and independent and special districts (ACIR 1984).

Although some ACIR studies could conceivably be categorized under one or more of our four research approaches, *Fiscal Disparities: Central Cities and Suburbs* (1984) is based upon a trend analysis of key economic and demographic trends in standard metropolitan statistical areas (SMSAs). The report builds upon regional data showing which areas have experienced increases in population, as well as the changes in the racial proportions of SMSAs occurring from 1970 to 1980. Other standard variables, such as income, tax revenues, and educational and other expenditures, are also brought into the equation in an effort to better understand the ramifications of an increasing gap between cities and suburbs. In short, this report paints a picture showing an inverse relationship between population and income growth in the majority of suburban areas compared to that in central cities and poses a number of hypotheses as to how these and other trends affect one another.

ANALYTICAL AND/OR STATISTICAL APPROACHES

Strongly related to trend analysis are the analytical and/or statistical approaches. These approaches are distinguished by their inductive methods and almost exclusive reliance on data to draw conclusions.[1] This type of research builds its argumentation block by block and often has an applied policy component. Most of the research is done in the form of articles and monographs rather than books, and their succinct and empirical messages can be powerful. The difficulty of this approach is that data cannot always be separated.[2]

While the use of this approach is prevalent in recent studies, some of the best work using this approach has been done by two applied researchers, Larry Ledebur and William Barnes.[3] " 'All in It Together': Cities, Suburbs and Local Economic Regions'' (1993) is a study based on household income in 25 metropolitan areas. The study addresses two hypotheses with regard to the economic future of cities and suburbs:

- If cities and suburbs are economically independent, rather than interdependent, then changes in suburban incomes and central city incomes should not be related or move together.

- If there is some degree of interdependence, changes in suburban incomes would be related to changes in central incomes and vice versa (Ledebur and Barnes 1993).

Ledebur and Barnes's data suggest that an economic synergy exists between central cities and their suburbs. A regression analysis comparing median household income data from the 1980 and 1990 census implies a strong relationship (R^2 = .82) between central city income and suburban income.[4] With absolute income gains in the suburbs having been achieved in 24 of 25 metropolitan regions, Ledebur and Barnes pay particular attention to policy implications relevant to these data, concluding that policy makers should direct efforts at reducing growing differentials among different regions rather than on a city-to-city basis. In light of the current political environment, the authors further observe how policy makers are more likely to be responsive to "economic considerations" than to those involving social equity issues.

Other statistical studies using this methodological approach have been done by Hank Savitch and associates in "Ties that Bind" (1993). In studying the economic and social symbiosis between central cities and their respective suburbs, Savitch and his coauthors blend a variety of research techniques to test their proposition regarding this relationship.

Beginning with a literature review on the subject of city-suburban interdependence, the authors cite historical data to supplement their statistical analysis, which compares data taken from different editions of the *State and Metropolitan Data Book*. A series of statistical associations are undertaken on what they label as key indicators of metropolitan strength and interdependency. Among the associations made between cities and suburbs are per capita income, the stock and cost of office space, regional variations between prosperity and location, and the amount of metropolitan population contained within the borders of central cities or "inclusiveness." However, the various linkages and the conclusions drawn from these variables do not go unchallenged.

" 'Ties that Bind' Reexamined" by Blair and Zhang (1994) directly addresses the "Ties that Bind" article by arguing that the notion of suburban dependence on the economic performance of central cities is overstated, due in part to a lack of consideration of state-level variables. Along similar lines, another piece of work worth noting is a recently published article by Hill, Wolman, and Ford that also challenges aspects of "Ties that Bind," aspects of the work by Ledebur and Barnes, and other authors who have written on the dependency hypothesis. In the article "Can Suburbs Survive Without Cities? Examining the Suburban Dependence Hypothesis" (1995), the authors challenge elements of the dependency theory as presented by Ledebur and Barnes, Savitch, and others. In a well-constructed argument, Hill, Wolman, and Ford do not contest the notion of interdependency; rather, they elaborate on the causal direction of economic growth and believe that it is metropolitanwide growth that narrows economic disparities. In other words, strong central cities may not be as much of an influence on metropolitan growth as the other way around. Economic conditions of metropolitan areas have, perhaps, a greater effect on the conditions of central cities. The model they develop is consistent with the findings that link economic performance in central cities to outcomes of suburban residents, yet also ties divergence in metropolitan economics to overall performance (Hill, Wolman, and Ford 1994).

In a related article by Savitch and David Collins on the theme of city-suburb interdependence published in the *National Civic Review*, the authors look at this relationship from a different perspective. In "The Paradox of Diversity: Social Differences amid Common Regions" (1992), the authors highlight inner-city and suburban disparities, as well as factors of isolation between whites and nonwhites. By comparing demographic data from the 15 largest cities in the United States, using both the *County and City Data Book* and census data, the study looks at the percentages of blacks and Hispanics of each of the 15 cities and the respective degree of segregation within each MSA. Reiterating the findings of previous studies on how the fortunes of cities and suburbs are intertwined, the study uses data on city-suburban per capita income and other demographic data to demonstrate that less segregated cities are more prosperous. By illustrating this point, the case is again made for inclusionary relationships between cities and suburbs—ones where larger portions of metropolitan populations are retained within relative proximity to the city core.

ORGANIZATIONAL APPROACHES

The last type of research approach we have labeled organizational approaches. These approaches attempt to understand cities and suburbs by analyzing governmental and quasi-governmental institutions. The organizational approach bears a strong relationship to traditional legal and/or institutional studies typical of political science. To a certain extent, this type of analysis assumes that new organizational formats can shape socioeconomic dynamics through the interjection of public policy. An important subset of the organizational approach focuses on the processes as well as the forms of governmental reorganization.[5] In their book *Experiments in Metropolitan Government* (1977), James Horan and Thomas Taylor outline some of the basic techniques that have been used to address urban problems from the organizational approach and look at aspects involving both processes and form.

Among the options in government reorganization, Horan and Taylor discuss city consolidation, cooperative alternatives, and what they label as "two-level alternatives." The primary aims of the single-government alternative largely involve issues of efficiency and effectiveness of service delivery and are often focused on the older core cities. Government reorganization, according to the authors, is generally accomplished in three ways: annexation, municipal consolidation (i.e., merger of two or more incorporated cities), and city-county consolidation. As for the second approach, the cooperative alternative, Horan and Taylor outline what is essentially a voluntary technique often accomplished through informal agreements or formal interlocal agreements. Last, they discuss what they term the "two-level alternative," an approach based on the theory of federalism. In this latter approach, metropolitan governments are created within a two-tier framework through metrolocal governance. Although the authors distinguish between three separate two-tier forms, the essence of this approach is an areawide government where purely local functions remain with the existing local units.

Ten years after Horan and Taylor's book, David Walker breaks down some of Horan and Taylor's approaches in even greater detail in a 1987 article found in the *National Civic Review*. Walker's "Snow White and the 17 Dwarfs: From Metro Cooperation to Governance" is one of the quintessential organizational studies. Like Horan and Taylor's work, the contribution of Walker's study to understanding the way in which regional governance and service delivery are handled is valuable in that it recognizes city-suburb interaction from an organizational perspective. By looking at issues of governance and economic disparities between cities and suburbs, Walker analyzes 17 regional approaches to service delivery ranging from the simple to the complex.

The simplest, least controversial organizational approach laid out by Walker includes things such as interlocal cooperation, informal agreements, and other types of joint initiatives. On the other end of the spectrum, Walker acknowledges the most difficult approaches to metro regionalism as those involving complex consolidations and restructuring that create new areawide levels of government. A departure from traditional forms of urban governmental structure, the controversy in the latter approach comes with the reallocation of government resources, powers, and functions.

Like Rusk, Walker recognizes that the traditional conception of city and suburb as distinct entities is no longer valid; rather, the more effective governmental design is an amalgam of the traditional forms of city and suburban service delivery. By operationalizing each approach to urban service delivery, Walker's analysis not only defines the unique aspects of each governmental structure but outlines the key conditions (economic, geographic, etc.) that may make an approach more appropriate for a given region than another.

Another reference for this type of organizational research is a report done by the ACIR entitled *Metropolitan Organization: Comparison of the Allegheny and St. Louis Case Studies* (ACIR 1993). The study is an extension of an ACIR report published in 1988, *Metropolitan Organization: The St. Louis Case* (ACIR 1988). The 1993 study finds richness in the diversity of local governments. It argues that localities are best off when allowed to seek their own remedies, and found that fragmentation actually produced efficiencies. Where cooperation was desired, localities were quite capable of forming complex networks of cooperation.

An important piece of work on the processes of city-suburban governmental relations in the organizational context is Johnson and Harrigan's "Innovation by Increments: The Twin Cities as a Case Study in Metropolitan Reform" (1978). The authors argue that the Metropolitan Council in Minneapolis–St. Paul is an example of a nonincremental change, yet one where ongoing functioning involves incremental changes. They also discuss how it would be difficult to change other consolidated city-counties (i.e., Miami) through incremental changes due to differences in state government requirements for government reorganization, given that some states require referenda, while others do not.

Finally, an edited volume by Savitch and Vogel (1996) brings the experience of metropolitan reorganization up to date. The Savitch and Vogel work focuses on 10 metropolitan regions (New York, Los Angeles, St. Louis, Washington, D.C., Louisville, Pittsburgh, Miami, Minneapolis–St. Paul, Jacksonville, and Portland). One of the book's tenets is that regionalism is an outgrowth of conflicting pressures—some of which push toward building common institutions, while others pull away from comprehensive governance.

This book combines a socioeconomic profile of selected regions with their political components. The result is an analysis of regional political economies and their efforts to resolve metropolitan tensions. Using organizational models, Savitch and Vogel construct a continuum of regional cooperation. These range from efforts at single-tier governance (consolidation) to federated two-tier arrangements, and ultimately include incremental adjustment and public-private partnerships.

Savitch and Vogel conclude that no single pattern has evolved across the country, nor is any pattern likely to predominate. Instead, regions adopt multiple patterns of cooperation that reflect their history and makeup. In almost every metropolitan region, formal and informal forms of cooperation have taken root. These may be truncated and even stunted, but they endeavor to deal with problems that increasingly cross local boundaries.

DIRECTIONS FOR FUTURE RESEARCH: A PARADIGM SHIFT?

While there is evidence that cities and suburbs are interdependent, scholars continue to debate its causal nature, its interpretation, and its consequences. Do cities enhance suburban prosperity, or is it the reverse? Can suburbs that surround distressed cities do just as well as those that do not? More pointedly, are suburbs immune to the ills of central cities and must they care about what happens to central cities?

The issue of suburban reliance on vital central cities is critical to future research and to policy making. The 1994 Report from the National League of Cities (Barnes and Ledebur) argues that if suburban prosperity requires strong central cities, a strong *economic* justification can be made for addressing urban- and metropolitanwide assistance. On the other hand, if suburbs can get along just as well without vital central cities, the chances for urban assistance are likely to be diminished. In this era of suburban power, cities will not do well without help from the suburban seats in Congress and in the state legislatures, considering that realities are in many ways determined by political considerations.

The issue that underlies this question—indeed, haunts America—is whether central cities will soon be obsolete. Will they be the dinosaurs of a bygone era—replaced by suburbs and edge cities? Just 15 years prior to the publication of *Edge City*, Melvin Webber wrote an article entitled "Order in Diversity: Community without Propinquity." Webber predicted that spatial patterns would be more dispersed, regardless of efforts by urban planners and developers (Webber 1963). This form of development, claimed Webber, is due to a combination of currents—including technological advancement, the electronic age, and an increasingly diverse society. If suburbs, edge cities, and country hamlets are the sole future of America, the definition of a city will radically change, and so, too, will urban research.

NOTES

1. Examples of studies using the analytical and/or statistical approach not cited in this section include: J. Edwin Benton and Darwin Gamble, "City/County Consolidation and Economies of Scale: Evidence from a Time-Series Analysis in Jacksonville, Florida" (1984); Thomas Stanback and Richard Knight, *Suburbanization of the City* (1976); Thierry Noyelle and Thomas Stanback, "The Economic Transformation of American Cities" (1985); R. Nathan and C. Adams, "Understanding Central City Hardship" (1976).

2. When conducting this form of research, close attention should be paid to changes that have occurred in the U.S. census over the years, such as the redefinition of governmental units. These and other changes that have occurred are outlined in the *Census of Governments*. When longitudinal analysis of governmental units is done, for instance, not accounting for definitional changes may lead the researcher to serious errors. Since 1987, some governments have been reclassified on the basis of changes in the legal provisions governing their operation, new information, or the need to reflect the realities of existing fiscal arrangement in order to account for all governmental activities in statistical reporting (Census of Governments 1992: xv).

3. Recent National League of Cities reports include: Mark Alan Hughes, "Fighting Poverty in Cities: Transportation Programs as Bridges to Opportunity" (1989); Larry Ledebur, "City Fiscal Distress: Structural, Demographic and Institutional Causes" (1991); Michael Pagano, "City Fiscal Conditions in 1991" (1991); Larry Ledebur and William Barnes, "City Distress: Metropolitan Disparities and Economic Growth" (1992); Larry Ledebur and William Barnes, " 'All in It Together': Cities, Suburbs and Local Economic Regions" (1993); William Barnes and Larry Ledebur, "Local Economies: The U.S. Common Market of Local Economic Regions" (1994).

4. R^2 is the amount of explained variation, or the difference between the total variation and the unexplained variation. Thus, in a regression equation with an $R^2 = .82$, 82 percent of the variation in the dependent variable is explained by the independent variables in the equation.

5. For those interested in the organizational approach to studying cities and suburbs, other studies to examine include Larry Gerston and Peter Haas, "Political Support for

Regional Government in the 1990s: Growing in the Suburbs?'' (1993); Vincent Marando, ''City-County Consolidation: Reform, Regionalism, Referenda and Requiem'' (1979); Donald Phares, ''Bigger Is Better, Or Is It Smaller? Restructuring Local Government in the St. Louis Area'' (1989); Roger B. Parks and Ronald J. Oakerson, ''Metropolitan Organization and Governance: A Local Public Economy Approach'' (1989).

REFERENCES

Advisory Commission on Intergovernmental Relations (ACIR). 1984. *Fiscal Disparities: Central Cities and Suburbs, 1981: An Information Report.* Washington, D.C.: Government Printing Office.

Advisory Commission on Intergovernmental Relations (ACIR). 1988. *Metropolitan Organization: The St. Louis Case.* Washington, D.C.: ACIR.

Advisory Commission on Intergovernmental Relations (ACIR). 1993. *Metropolitan Organization: Comparison of the Allegheny and St. Louis Case Studies.* Washington, D.C.: ACIR.

Babbie, Earl R. 1989. *The Practice of Social Research.* Belmont: Wadsworth Publishing.

Barnes, William, and Kevin Eddins. 1993. *The State of America's Cities: The Ninth Annual Opinion Survey of Municipal Elected Officials.* Washington, D.C.: National League of Cities, Center for Research and Program Development.

Barnes, William, and Larry Ledebur. 1994. ''Local Economies. The U.S. Common Market of Local Economic Regions.'' A Research Report from the National League of Cities (August).

Benton, J. Edwin, and Darwin Gamble. 1984. ''City/County Consolidation and Economies of Scale: Evidence from a Time-Series Analysis in Jacksonville, Florida.'' *Social Science Quarterly* 65 (March): 190–198.

Blair J., and Z. Zhang. 1994. '' 'Ties that Bind' Reexamined.'' *Economic Development Quarterly* 8 no. 4 (November): 373–377.

Danielson, M. N. 1972. ''Differentiation, Segregation, and Political Fragmentation in the American Metropolis.'' In A. E. Keir Nash, ed., *Commission on Population Growth and the American Future, Research Reports,* Vol. IV, Governance and Population: The Governmental Implications of Population Change. Washington, D.C.: Government Printing Office.

Downs, Anthony. 1973. *Opening Up the Suburbs: An Urban Strategy for America.* New York: Oxford University Press.

Gans, Herbert J. 1967. *The Levittowners.* New York: Vintage Books.

Garreau, J. 1991. *Edge City: Life on the New Frontier.* New York: Anchor Books.

Gerston, Larry, and Peter Haas. 1993. ''Political Support for Regional Government in the 1990s: Growing in the Suburbs?'' *Urban Affairs Quarterly* 29, no. 1 (September): 154–163.

Hill, Edward, Harold Wolman, and Coit Cook Ford, III. 1994. ''Evaluating the Success of Urban Success Stories.'' *Urban Studies* 31, no. 6 (June): 835–850.

Hill, R. C. 1973. ''Urban Income Inequality.'' Ph.D dissertation, Department of Sociology, University of Wisconsin at Madison.

Horan, James F., and Thomas Taylor, Jr. 1977. *Experiments in Metropolitan Government.* New York: Praeger.

Hughes, M. A. 1989. ''Fighting Poverty in Cities. Transportation Programs as Bridges to Opportunity.'' A Research Report from the National League of Cities.

Hughes, M. A., with J. E. Sternberg. 1993. *The New Metropolitan Reality: Where the Rubber Meets the Road in Antipoverty Policy.* Washington, D.C.: Urban Institute.

Jackson, Kenneth T. 1985. *Crabgrass Frontier: The Suburbanization of the United States.* New York: Oxford University Press.

Johnson, W., and J. J. Harrigan. 1978. "Innovation by Increments: The Twin Cities as a Case Study in Metropolitan Reform." *Western Political Quarterly* 31, no. 2: 206–218.

Ledebur, L. C. 1991. "City Fiscal Distress: Structural, Demographic and Institutional Causes." A Research Report from the National League of Cities, March 1991.

Ledebur, L. C., and W. R. Barnes. 1992. "City Distress: Metropolitan Disparities and Economic Growth." A Research Report from the National League of Cities, September 1992.

Ledebur, L. C., and W. R. Barnes. 1993. " 'All in It Together': Cities, Suburbs and Local Economic Regions." A Research Report from the National League of Cities, February 1993.

Marando, Vincent L. 1979. "City-County Consolidation: Reform, Regionalism, Referenda and Requiem." *Western Political Quarterly* 32 (December): 409–421.

Nathan, R., and C. Adams. 1976. "Understanding Central City Hardship." *Political Science Quarterly* 91: 47–62.

Noyelle, Thierry, and Thomas Stanback. 1984. *The Economic Transformation of American Cities.* Totowa, NJ: Roman & Allenheld.

Pagano, Michael. 1991. "City Fiscal Conditions in 1991." A Research Report from the National League of Cities, July 1991.

Parks, Roger B., and Ronald J. Oakerson. 1989. "Metropolitan Organization and Governance: A Local Public Economy Approach." *Urban Affairs Quarterly* 25, no. 1 (September).

Peirce, Neal R., Curtis W. Johnson, and John Stuart Hall. 1993. *Citistates.* Washington, D.C.: Seven Locks Press.

Phares, Donald. 1989. "Bigger Is Better, Or Is it Smaller?" Restructuring Local Government in the St. Louis Area. *Urban Affairs Quarterly* 25, no. 1 (September): 5–17.

Rusk, D. 1993. *Cities without Suburbs.* Washington, D.C.: Woodrow Wilson Center Press.

Savitch, H. V., and D. Collins. 1992. "The Paradox of Diversity: Social Differences amid Common Regions." *National Civic Review* 9 (summer–fall): 326.

Savitch, H. V., D. Collins, D. Sanders, and J. P. Markham. 1993. "Ties that Bind: Central Cities, Suburbs, and the New Metropolitan Region." *Economic Development Quarterly* 7, no. 4: 341–357

Savitch, H. V., D. Sanders, and D. Collins. 1992. "The Regional City and Public Partnerships." In R. Berkman, J. F. Brown, B. Goldberg, and T. Mijanovich, eds., *In the National Interest: The 1990 Urban Summit.* New York: Twentieth Century Fund Press.

Savitch, H. V., and Ronald K. Vogel. 1996. *Regional Politics: America in a Post City Era.* Newbury Park, CA: Sage Publications.

Stanback, Thomas, and Richard Knight. 1976. *Suburbanization of the City.* Montclair, NJ: Allanheld, Osmun & Company.

United States Bureau of the Census. 1992. *Census of Governments.* Washington, D.C.: U.S. Government Printing Office.

Walker, D. B. 1987. "Snow White and the 17 Dwarfs: From Metro Cooperation to Governance." *National Civic Review* 76, no. 1: 14–28.

Webber, Melvin M. 1963. "Order in Diversity: Community without Propinquity." In Lowdon Wingo, ed., *Cities and Space: The Future Use of Urban Land*. Baltimore: Johns Hopkins Press.

Wirt, Frederick, Benjamin Walter, Francine F. Rabinovitz, and Deborah R. Hensler. 1972. *On the City's Rim: Politics & Policy in Suburbia*. Lexington, MA: Heath.

Wood, Robert Caldwell. 1959. *Suburbia, Its People and Urban Politics*. Boston: Houghton Mifflin.

Chapter 13

Metropolitan Government

Ronald K. Vogel

Over the last several decades, many central cities in the United States declined due to restructuring of the national economy from manufacturing to services. At the same time, decentralization of business and population extended urbanization into formerly rural areas. As a consequence, county governments were increasingly called upon to provide urban services while central city services tended to deteriorate. This led to greater fragmentation of the urban service delivery system and an increased level of conflict between cities and counties concerning the production, provision, and financing of urban services. Residents in unincorporated areas frequently still lack adequate basic services. And central cities often lack the tax base to sustain quality public services (Savitch and Thomas 1991).

Traditional reform solutions to the problem of metropolitan fragmentation and overlapping or duplicating services lean toward creating metropolitan government, often through city-county consolidation (Rusk 1993). However, the public choice school challenges the assumptions of the reformers that centralized services are necessarily more efficient or effective (Parks and Oakerson 1989). More recently, the "metropolitan governance without government" thesis has called into question the views of both these schools, pointing to the elaborate and complex set of metropolitan institutions that exist in most metropolitan areas but also raising questions as to whether this adds up to metropolitan governance (Barlow 1991; Rothblatt and Sancton 1993; Savitch and Vogel 1996).

THEORETICAL PERSPECTIVES ON METROPOLITAN GOVERNMENT

The Metropolitan Government School

Advocates of metropolitan government decry the problems of fragmented local government structure, which they believe leads to inefficient and ineffective services and inequalities in the financing and distribution of those services. They favor metropolitan government as a solution to these ills. In addition, they believe metropolitan government will allow the community to better compete in the global economy and plan the region's infrastructure and development (Barlow 1991; Keating 1995).

Metropolitan government may take the form of one-tier city-county consolidation, two-tier metropolitan government, or three-tier multicounty regional government. The National Association of Counties defines city-county consolidation or merger as the "unification of the governments of one or more cities with the surrounding county" (National Academy of Public Administration 1980: 74). Examples of one-tier metropolitan government established by city-county consolidation include Jacksonville–Duval County, Florida; Lexington–Fayette County, Kentucky; Nashville–Davidson County, Tennessee; and Indianapolis–Marion County, Indiana (Horan and Taylor 1977).

Other metropolitan government advocates favor a two-tier approach, wherein municipalities or neighborhood governments (the first tier) are maintained or created to provide local services such as neighborhood police patrols and parks, and the county or metropolitan government (the second tier) provides areawide or regional services such as sewage treatment and public transit. Examples of two-tier metropolitan governments include Miami–Dade County, Florida, and Toronto, Canada (League of Women Voters 1974; Committee for Economic Development 1970; Horan and Taylor 1977).

Both one- and two-tier approaches to metropolitan government occur within the boundaries of a single county. It is important to recognize that in many cases the metropolitan area covers a multicounty region. There are only two examples of multicounty regional government in the United States: the Greater Portland Metropolitan Service District (Oregon) and the Twin Cities Metropolitan Council (Minneapolis–St. Paul). Existing cities and counties are left in place with a third tier overlaying them. Among the services that might be provided by the regional government are comprehensive planning, land use planning, sewage treatment and disposal, water treatment and supply, water distribution, and public transportation (National Academy of Public Administration 1980: 86–87).

Evaluating Metropolitan Government. Scholars have identified a number of benefits associated with metropolitan government (Barlow 1991; Self 1982; Keating 1995). First, metropolitan governments reduce fiscal imbalances between central cities and suburbs through tax-sharing schemes. Second, they provide a capacity to engage in strategic planning for the region. Third, metropolitan governments have effectively carried out large-scale transportation planning. Initially focusing upon road building, metro governments later adopt more efficient transportation systems and a "balanced" transportation policy including the development of mass transit.

There are a number of criticisms of a metropolitan government. First, there is little evidence that greater efficiencies or economies of scale actually occur after city-county consolidation takes place (Condrey 1994; Benton and Gamble 1983; Horan and Taylor 1977). Second, minorities lose power with the creation of metropolitan government. Their power base is eliminated or weakened in the city, and the new metropolitan government ends up being dominated by the suburbanites (Swanson 1996; Jones 1991).

Third, where metropolitan governments exist they have a mixed record of performance, paying more attention to infrastructure development in the sub-urbanizing periphery, instead of concentrating on urban renewal and social needs of the central city. Fourth, existing metropolitan governments have been weak-ened by the failure to redraw boundaries to reflect population growth outside the metros' territory. In addition, metropolitan governments have been coopted, weakened, or dismantled when they challenged the central government's policies or threatened the local suburban interests through policies such as scattered site or fair-share housing (Barlow 1991; Self 1982). These problems are evident in examining prominent cases of metropolitan government in the United States (Savitch and Vogel 1996).

The few cases of metropolitan government in the United States do not provide reason to be overly optimistic about the performance of metropolitan govern-ment. Even if the record were better, the odds are against instituting any type of formal metropolitan government. This point cannot be emphasized enough: There have been *no new* metropolitan governments created in medium or large areas in the United States for nearly two decades.

The Public Choice School

The public choice or local public economy model opposes the metropolitan government school. Advocates of public choice believe that political fragmen-tation into many municipalities and special districts is good because it promotes competition among cities to provide good-quality services and low tax rates and allows residents to move to the city that best meets their needs. This process keeps officials accountable and ensures efficiency in services (U.S. Advisory Commission on Intergovernmental Relations [ACIR] 1987, 1993).

Public choice advocates do not worry about the existence of a large number of local governments (i.e., fragmentation). For proponents of public choice, the issue is whether the organization of local government is detrimental to the met-ropolitan community's ability to meet its needs. Cooperation between local gov-ernments and private actors can substitute for a single metropolitan government to provide services and address problems. Contrary to the metropolitan government school, public choice advocates argue that issues of regional concern can be addressed through special districts and public authorities. In fact, the multiple jurisdictions one finds in a metropolitan area are indicative that these concerns are being addressed and reflect a highly developed and complex form of organization. The public choice school challenges proponents of metropolitan government to provide evidence that a more centralized system produces more efficient or effective government.

Those who champion public choice believe that more efficient and effective public services at the local level will ultimately result from intercity competition for residences and businesses by promoting policies that keep tax rates low and provide good-quality basic services and a stable business climate. If governments become too inefficient in providing services or unresponsive to their citizenry, people will choose to "exit" the community. Out-migration and urban decline reflect such choices. As cities recognize these signs, they pursue policies that will provide more efficient and effective services to lure back lost residents and businesses (Bish and Ostrom 1979).

Evaluating Public Choice. The public choice approach to metropolitan government views local government fragmentation as a virtue instead of a vice. Lyons, Lowery, and DeHoog (1992) call into question the theoretical assumptions underlying public choice. After undertaking a study comparing citizen satisfaction with services in a consolidated metropolitan system with that of a fragmented one, they find citizens do not behave in the ways the Tiebout model suggests.

Other criticism of public choice is that it disregards the lack of equity in the financing and distribution of urban services in the metropolitan area, especially between the central city and suburbs (Warren, Rosentraub, and Weschler 1992). A second criticism is that cooperation among local governments within the metropolitan area has been assumed by public choice advocates more than it has been demonstrated (Warren, Rosentraub, and Weschler 1992). The public choice school has failed to investigate whether the complex system of local governance that they describe really adds up to a system of metropolitan governance. In addition, public choice researchers lack the data or evidence to bear out their conclusion that smaller is better (Keating 1995).

Metropolitan Governance without Government

According to I. M. Barlow, author of *Metropolitan Government* (1991), there has been a retreat from metropolitan government, not just in the United States but worldwide. "The retreat began in the USA in the 1960s when politicians and academics turned away from the idea of metropolitan government in the face of institutional obstacles and political opposition" (294). But even well-established metropolitan governments were dismantled or weakened in this period.

There are numerous obstacles in setting up metropolitan governments in the

United States. According to the Advisory Commission on Intergovernmental Relations, voters approved only 17 of the 83 referenda on city-county consolidation between 1921 and 1979 (ACIR 1993). In the 1980s, only 6 of the 27 consolidation efforts gained voter approval. The 4 efforts in counties with more than 200,000 people failed.[1] Some communities have voted city-county consolidation down as many as four times. This does not include the number of times city-county consolidation was considered but not presented to the voters.

Metropolitan government remains the exception rather than the rule.[2] For practical reasons, then, it is important to consider more carefully whether metropolitan governance may occur even in the absence of metropolitan government. According to Barlow (1991):

Metropolitan governance involves the governing of a metropolitan area without formal government at the metropolitan level. Instead, reliance is placed on special-purpose bodies, the joint efforts of local governments, and arrangements between levels of government. There is considerable fragmentation, both functional and territorial, and it is only by means of an array of institutional arrangements among the various agencies and governments that co-ordination and integration can be achieved. Metropolitan governance, therefore, is a system of governing in which intergovernmental relations—in the broadest sense—play a major role. (294)

A number of communities have taken steps to bring about greater coordination in the delivery of urban services. David Walker (1987) identifies several regional approaches to service delivery that range from easy to accomplish to difficult, including one-, two-, and three-tier government. The breadth and number of regional approaches to service delivery suggest that cooperation and coordination in urban service delivery do not depend upon the establishment of formal metropolitan or regional government.

The metropolitan governance without government thesis is distinguished from the public choice school in that it moves the focus from cooperation or coordination among local governments to provide urban services to a broader consideration of whether the metropolitan area or region can be said to be governed (i.e., act in purposive, goal-directed ways). Barlow (1991) provides a standard to measure whether these steps toward regional cooperation can effectively substitute for metropolitan government.

For an effective system, however, the relationships need to be such that they generate area-wide coordination and integration, and they need to be overseen by an ''umbrella'' body that has the capacity to view matters from a metropolitan perspective and to act in the metropolitan interest. (295)

Evaluating the Metropolitan Governance Thesis. There is some evidence that institutions are emerging in the public and private sectors in the United States to guide regional growth and development (Peirce, Johnson, and Hall 1993; Rothblatt and Sancton 1993; Savitch and Vogel 1996). Whether this new wave of regionalism will result in metropolitan governance is more open to question. The test of the "metropolitan governance without government" thesis is the existence of "area-wide coordination" among local governments and an "umbrella body" that can act on behalf of a metropolitan interest. Although metropolitan governance is a pragmatic response to the difficulties of establishing metropolitan government, there is much skepticism that it can serve as a replacement for metropolitan government.

If a successful system of metropolitan governance is not established, there will be renewed pressure to establish formal metropolitan government. These pressures stem from traditional arguments for metropolitan reform including the need to make government more "comprehensible" to the citizenry and to increase accountability and responsiveness of local government (Barlow 1991: 298–299). In addition to these, two old arguments on behalf of metropolitan government—"infrastructure-maintenance" and "economic competitiveness"—will be recycled and updated for the twenty-first century.

Additional pressures for metropolitan government will come from the need for massive investment in local infrastructure and "inter-city competition for economic growth" (299). The advent of an era of global economic competition will reinvigorate the traditional chamber of commerce argument that local government fragmentation hinders the ability to compete and that an increase in territory and population will enhance a community's ability to compete in the global marketplace.

Indeed, there has been some renewed interest in efforts to establish metropolitan government, spurred in large measure by David Rusk, a former mayor of Albuquerque, with the publication of his book *Cities without Suburbs* (1993). Rusk particularly favors city-county consolidation as a strategy to establish metropolitan government, arguing that cities that are inelastic—that is, cities that have been unable to extend their boundaries through annexation or by consolidation with the county—have done less well economically and suffer greater levels of fiscal stress, higher incidents of poverty, and more segregation than communities that have more elastic boundaries. He argues that even though consolidation is difficult to achieve politically, the associated economic and social benefits are enormous. But there is little reason to believe that metropolitan government will be more readily adopted now than in the past (see also Downs 1994).

METHODOLOGICAL ISSUES

In considering questions about metropolitan government and governance, one encounters three problems in the existing literature. The first concerns the normative or ideological foundation on which much of the analysis rests. The second concerns the specific way the metropolitan area or region is defined. The third concerns the actual way metropolitan government is operationalized both in the abstract and in specific cases.

Normative Bias of Research

In considering the field of metropolitan governance, one must recognize that much of the work is laced with normative biases. Each model of metropolitan governance has its own assumptions about the nature of the urban crisis and the appropriate remedies. Unfortunately, the line between analysis and advocacy has been very thin, and there is certainly reason to question researchers' objectivity (Rich 1980).

Advocates of metropolitan government, on the slimmest of evidence, continue unabashedly to assert metropolitan government as a panacea to solve urban problems. Rusk's (1993) study has increased awareness of inner-city distress, poverty, and inequality, bringing urban problems back into the national consciousness. Although well received, Rusk's study contributes to the myths about metropolitan government. The data presented illustrate his argument, but no statistical measures of association are offered to support his thesis concerning city elasticity and economic health. Serious questions must be raised about the direction of relationships he posits among variables, and many of the relationships are probably spurious. For example, economic health of cities probably has more to do with the region's economy than elasticity (Downs 1994). His recommended solution, metropolitan government, is unlikely to solve the problems he identifies.

Similarly, public choice advocates are ideologically disposed to favor decentralization but fail to acknowledge real inequalities in the financing and distribution of urban services associated with a fragmented local political system (e.g., ACIR 1993).

The normative bias associated with much of the research probably reflects real differences about the proper role of local government in society (Keating 1995). Nevertheless, it is troubling that social scientists seem to have contributed to the confusion in local debates about government reorganization (Savitch and Vogel 1996).

Defining the Region

The way the region is defined has great implications for the study of metropolitan government and governance. Is the appropriate way to define the region to focus on a political jurisdiction (e.g., the city or the county), a population enumeration unit (e.g., the metropolitan statistical area [MSA]), an economic unit (e.g., a labor or trade market), or a social unit (e.g., ethnic, racial, or cultural ties)?

Our view of the proper unit to correspond to the urban region has failed to keep up with the urban expansion. In the United States, the city corresponded fairly well with the urban region, for the most part, until the twentieth century. In the twentieth century, population shifted outside of the older central cities, particularly after World War II. However, a single political jurisdiction, the county, still encompassed most of the urban region. This led to a spate of efforts at city-county consolidation between the 1950s and the 1970s.

In the 1980s, however, continued suburbanization to outlying counties meant that no single overarching political jurisdiction existed that corresponded to the urban region. The most commonly used measure of urban regions is the MSA, which is a census designation that demarcates city regions based upon commuting and economic ties to a central city.

Self (1982) rejects census designations of metropolitan areas as a sufficient indicator of the metropolitan regions. He believes that they are problematic because they are expanded after new growth occurs. By definition, planning is not taking place within parts of the region until population expands into the areas sufficiently for them to be made part of a census-designated metropolis. Since planning is the key function that metropolitan governments are created for, the metropolitan area is an inadequate boundary for designating the region (Self 1982: 4).

Self proposes the "daily urban system" as the appropriate boundaries for a metropolitan region and the area over which a multipurpose metropolitan government or even a regional planning agency should oversee. This is the scope required for comprehensive planning purposes that link where people, jobs, and transportation locate with planning for resource conservation and the environment. Obviously, the planning powers that are provided to the government or organization are critical (5).

Rusk (1993) believes that city-county consolidation and aggressive annexation would result in de facto regional governments. However, even in cities where aggressive annexation or city-county consolidation has occurred, a large proportion of the region's population still lives outside of the central city or consolidated government's boundary. This does not disturb Rusk, who is willing to say a metropolitan government exists if 60 percent of the region's population are brought within a city or consolidated city-county's borders (89). Obviously, this fails Self's standard of planning effectiveness since much land and population are outside of the metropolitan government's reach.

Self's (1982) requirement that metropolitan or regional governments must have an adequate coverage to encompass the core and the periphery so as to be able to plan effectively for the region seems to be a necessary condition for metropolitan government (83). Rusk has redefined metropolitan government in such a way as to make it meaningless. However, there are obstacles to creating city regions, including the reluctance to eliminate "existing units such as counties" or to subordinate rural areas to city rule (Self 1982: 79–80).

Operationalizing Metropolitan Government

Metropolitan government is often left unoperationalized. The actual degree of fragmentation or centralization in local government structure may be unrelated to the existence of "metropolitan" government. City-county consolidation may or may not reduce local government fragmentation in the region. Complicating factors are the degree of functional fragmentation (e.g., special districts) and territorial or geographic fragmentation (e.g., presence of other small cities left out of the consolidation) (Vogel 1992: 24–25). For example, Swanson (1996) describes in Jacksonville how additional public authorities were created to carry out functions previously provided by city government prior to consolidation. These independent public authorities account for over 40 percent of all local spending in Jacksonville.

What at first appears highly centralized may actually be fragmented. The reverse is also true. Savitch and Vogel (1996) describe the case of Louisville–Jefferson County where a highly decentralized local governmental system (over 126 local governments in the county) on closer inspection has achieved a high level of political and administrative integration through adoption of a city-county compact that includes joint agency operation and tax sharing and the formation of a strong public-private partnership.

CURRENT STATE OF THE FIELD

Perspectives on metropolitan government have evolved from the unabashed advocacy of metropolitan government by progressive reformers as a panacea to solve urban ills to the revisionist public choice view that local government fragmentation is not the problem but the solution to urban problems (Rich 1980). Today, reformers may advocate either further centralization (Phares 1989) or decentralization (Oakerson and Parks 1991) or split the difference, calling for two-tier solutions (League of Women Voters 1974). Yet the evidence is inconclusive concerning the desirability and effectiveness of metropolitan government, on the one hand, or allowing such fragmented local political structures to remain in place (see Self 1982; Barlow 1991; ACIR 1993; Rothblatt and Sancton 1993).

In light of these difficulties, many academic scholars and practitioners have pragmatically substituted the goal of metropolitan governance for that of metropolitan government. But what does this actually mean in practice? Savitch and Vogel (1996) critique the normative bias associated with both the metropolitan government school and public choice school that does as much to constrain debate as elucidate it. In a new edited volume that brings together 10 new case studies of regional governance in the United States, they offer a more empirically grounded alternative to conceptualize metropolitan governance based upon how regions actually adapt and respond to competing pressures of centralization and decentralization.

According to Savitch and Vogel (1996), we must understand urban politics as regional politics, recognizing the political and economic interdependence of cities and suburbs in the metropolis. This interdependence fosters cooperation and coordination among local governmental and nongovernmental actors to finance and deliver urban services as well as to shape a regional urban and economic development strategy that can provide jobs and a reasonable quality of life for the citizenry. Yet social and economic disparities within regions, including racial and ethnic conflict, in combination with a fragmented local government structure that encourages intercity competition for revenue and jobs, result in higher levels of interlocal governmental conflict and hinder prospects for metropolitan or regional governance.

Savitch and Vogel offer a conceptualization of regional adaptations that more closely resembles the empirical reality classifying the institutional and behavioral adaptations of regions to the competing pressures toward centralization and decentralization. First, there are some regions that have established, at least on paper, formal *metropolitan governments* such as Miami–Dade, Minneapolis–St. Paul, Portland, and Jacksonville. These cases represent the most formal and institutional response to provide regional governance.

Then there are regions that have achieved a certain degree of coordination through a process of *mutual adjustment* that may take the form of *interlocal agreements* or *public-private partnerships*. Here, coordination results from formal and informal arrangements among and between the public and private actors in the region. Examples of mutual adjustment by interlocal government agreement include Washington, D.C.'s Council of Government and Louisville's Compact. Pittsburgh illustrates the case of mutual adjustment by public-private partnership.

A third set of cases demonstrates the third category, *avoidance and conflict*. New York, Los Angeles, and St. Louis have all failed to develop regularized coordination or cooperation within the region.

CONCLUSION

Metropolitan government remains an elusive goal in the United States. There is renewed interest in metropolitan governance in the United States amidst a general retreat from metropolitan government worldwide (Barlow 1991). While the scholars and ideologues have been debating the normative and empirical merits of public choice and metropolitan government, many communities in the United States have been pragmatically building a metropolitan system of governance. In doing so, they have chosen an incremental and pragmatic approach to metropolitan reform without regard to the ideal-type local government reorganization espoused by advocates of public choice or metropolitan government and ignorant of the experience of metropolitan government in the rest of the world.

What is needed are more case studies of the actual experience regions are having and consideration of whether metropolitan governance can effectively substitute for formal metropolitan government. The Intermodal Surface and Transportation Efficiency Act should be closely watched and offers a model of national action that may positively foster regional cooperation.

In addition, greater attention should be given to the way metropolitan government and regions are defined. To date, there is little direct evidence on the impact alternative regional governance patterns have on urban service delivery, economic and social disparities, or development in the metropolis. Future research should aim to provide policy makers and practitioners with more grounded and practical advice on building regionalism and to counter the level of disinformation prevalent in community dialogue about these issues.

NOTES

1. Louisville and Jefferson County, Kentucky, 1982 and 1983 (population: 684,648); Chattanooga and Hamilton County, Tennessee, 1984 (population: 287,740); Volusia and Halifax County, Florida, 1985 (population: 320,900); Sacramento and Sacramento County, California, 1990 (population: 914,700). (This information was compiled by Dan Durning of the Vinson Institute of Government, University of Georgia.)

2. The only metropolitan governments, other than consolidated city-counties, are Metro Miami–Dade, set up in 1958; Minneapolis–St. Paul, adopted in 1969; and Portland Metro, created in 1978. And there is some question as to whether these really satisfy the conditions of metropolitan or regional government (see edited volume by Savitch and Vogel [1996]).

REFERENCES

Barlow, I. M. 1991. *Metropolitan Government*. New York: Routledge.

Benton, Edwin J., and Darwin Gamble. 1983. "City/County Consolidation and Economics of Scale: Evidence from a Time-Series Analysis in Jacksonville, Florida." *Social Science Quarterly*, 190–198.

Bish, L. Robert, and Vincent Ostrom. 1979. *Understanding Urban Government: Metropolitan Reform Reconsidered*. Washington, D.C.: American Enterprise Institute for Policy Research.

Committee for Economic Development. 1970. *Reshaping Government in Metropolitan Areas: A Statement on National Policy by the Research and Policy Committee of the Committee for Economic Development*. New York: CED.

Condrey, Stephen. 1994. "Organizational and Personnel Impacts on Local Government Consolidation: Athens–Clarke County, Georgia." *Journal of Urban Affairs* 16, no. 4: 371–383.

Downs, Anthony. 1994. *New Vision for Metropolitan America*. Washington, D.C.: Brookings.

Horan, F. James, and G. Thomas Taylor. 1977. *Experiments in Metropolitan Government*. New York: Praeger.

Jones, Myra. 1991. Remarks in C. James Owen, ed., *Workshop in Metropolitan Government Strategies: Proceedings, 1990*. Fort Wayne: School of Public and Environmental Affairs, Indiana University–Purdue University at Fort Wayne.

Keating, Michael. 1995. "Size Efficiency and Democracy Consolidation, Fragmentation and Public Choice Theories of Urban Politics." In David Judge, Gerry Stoker, and Harold Wolman, eds., *Theories of Urban Politics*. Thousand Oaks, CA: Sage.

League of Women Voters Education Fund. 1974. *Prospects for Two Tier Government*. New York: Praeger.

Lyons, W. E., David Lowery, and Ruth Hoogland DeHoog. 1992. *The Politics of Dissatisfaction: Citizens, Services, and Urban Institutions*. Armonk, NY: M. E. Sharpe.

National Academy of Public Administration. 1980. *Metropolitan Governance: A Handbook for Local Government Study Commissions*. Washington, D.C.: U.S. Department of Housing and Urban Development.

Oakerson, Ronald, and Roger Parks. 1991. "Metropolitan Organization: St. Louis and Allegheny County." *Intergovernmental Perspectives* 17, no. 3: 27–34.

Parks, Roger, and Ronald Oakerson. 1989. "Metropolitan Organization and Governance—A Local Public Economy Approach." *Urban Affairs Quarterly* 25, no. 1: 18–29.

Peirce, Neal R., Curtis W. Johnson, and John Stuart Hall. 1993. *Citystates: How Urban America Can Prosper in a Competitive World*. Washington, D.C.: Seven Locks Press.

Phares, Donald. 1989. "Bigger Is Better or Is It Smaller? Restructuring Local Government in the St. Louis Area." *Urban Affairs Quarterly* 25, no. 1: 5–17.

Rich, Richard C. 1980. "The Complex Web of Urban Governance: Gossamer or Iron." *American Behavioral Scientist* 24: 277–298.

Robert, Warren, Mark Rosentraub, and Louis F. Wescheler. 1992. "Building Urban Governance: An Agenda for the 1990s." *Journal of Urban Affairs* 12, nos. 3–4: 399–421.

Rothblatt, Donald N., and Andrew Sancton, eds. 1993. *Metropolitan Governance: American/Canadian Intergovernmental Perspectives*. Berkeley: University of California, Institute of Governmental Studies Press.

Rusk, David. 1993. *Cities without Suburbs*. Washington, D.C: Woodrow Wilson Centre Press.

Savitch, H. V., and J. Clayton Thomas. 1991. *Big City Politics in Transition*. Newbury Park, CA: Sage.

Savitch, H. V., and Ronald K. Vogel, eds. 1996. *Regional Politics: America in a Post City Age*. Thousand Oaks, CA: Sage.

Self, Peter. 1982. *Planning the Urban Region—A Comparative Study of Policies and Organizations*. University: University of Alabama Press.

Swanson, Bert. 1996. "Jacksonville Consolidation and Regional Governance." In H. V. Savitch and Ronald K. Vogel, eds., *Regional Politics: America in a Post City Age*. Thousand Oaks, CA: Sage.

U.S. Advisory Commission on Intergovernmental Relations (ACIR). 1987. *The Organization of Local Public Economies*. Washington, D.C.: ACIR.

U.S. Advisory Commission on Intergovernmental Relations (ACIR). 1993. *State Laws Governing Local Government Structure and Administration*. Washington, D.C.: ACIR.

Vogel, Ronald K. 1992. *Urban Political Economy: Broward County, Florida*. Gainsville, FL: University Press of Florida.

Walker, David. 1987. "Snow White and the 17 Dwarfs: From Metro Cooperation to Governance." *National Civic Review* 76: 14–27.

Warren, Robert, Mark S. Rosentraub, and Louis F. Weschler. 1992. "Building Urban Governance: An Agenda for the 1990s." *Journal of Urban Affairs* 14, no. 3: 399–422.

Chapter 14

Urban Service Delivery

Ruth Hoogland DeHoog

Virtually all areas of urban politics and policy touch on public services and how they are delivered in city and county governments. Yet the study of urban service delivery is one that, on the face of it at least, is less entwined with the political questions than many other areas of study. In fact, economists and public administrationists have contributed to service delivery research as much as have political scientists. Public services are usually delivered by professional bureaucracies, and most service decisions are made outside the political limelight. Nonetheless, the degree to which political pressures affect such subjects as service distribution patterns or the methods of service delivery continues to be a key subtheme in this literature (Rich 1982). In fact, two now-classic works have argued that services "are the grist of urban politics" (Lineberry 1977: 12) and "service delivery lies at the heart of city government" (Yates 1977: 26). And the vigor of some of the scholarly debates in this literature indicates that there is more at stake than just how to pick up garbage, clean the streets, and structure police patrols.

OVERVIEW OF THE FIELD

Only a few of the works classified in the urban service delivery literature develop a broad approach to the subject. Certainly William Baer's "Just What Is an Urban Service, Anyway?" (1985) helps to identify some of the semantic and definitional issues. Two early works in the field have also been influential in linking urban services to broader issues in governance and politics. In *The Ungovernable City*, Douglas Yates (1977) argues that urban services are critical outputs of the fragmented and politicized urban policy-making system. Bryan Jones (1980) in *Service Delivery in the City* developed a more integrative study of citizen demands and bureaucratic decision making in several services in Detroit. More recently, Lyons, Lowery, and DeHoog (1992) in *The Politics of Dissatisfaction* have attempted to link the causes of citizen dissatisfaction to citizen responses within the government structural context. Others (e.g., Hero 1986) offer useful critiques of the field but fail to develop integrative or comprehensive approaches to the fragmented literature. In general, however, scholars examine one or two more narrowly defined areas within the urban services field.

Four general areas of inquiry can be discerned in the study of urban services and service delivery: (1) the organization of service delivery systems; (2) alternative methods of public service delivery; (3) the distribution patterns of public services; and (4) citizen satisfaction with public services. The first two areas are frequently linked by scholars, while the first and third topics of study are also logically and intellectually connected to each other.

This chapter will not review the substantive service delivery issues as they play out in the various urban service areas. Later chapters in this volume address several of the critical services. (Although local governments provide a wide range of public services, most of the scholarly attention has been focused on several visible public services common to all cities, especially police, streets, parks and recreation, and garbage collection.) In addition, some management topics such as technology and innovation in service delivery, street-level bureaucracy, and citizen participation in services are significant components of the literature, broadly defined, but the constraints of this chapter and volume do not permit adequate treatment of them. The aim of this chapter is to analyze, compare, and connect the four general areas of scholarly research about service delivery noted above.

THEORETICAL AND METHOLOGICAL APPROACHES

Probably the clearest theoretical orientation within the study of public service delivery is the public choice approach, which has been a major influence on political science and public administration more generally for at least two decades. Some scholars disagree over the two primary definitions of the approach: Is public choice (or rational choice, as in other areas of political science) research defined primarily by the methodology used (i.e., economic analysis to study public policy matters and institutional arrangements)? Or is it defined more by the ideological/structural prescriptions for generally more conservative, limited government, with a greater emphasis on citizen choice and a quasi-market model (Ostrom and Ostrom 1977; Ostrom, Bish, and Ostrom 1988)? Probably within urban politics at least, the latter definition of public choice is more commonly used, and it is the one used in this section.

A range of research questions, methods, and prescriptions might be considered part of the public choice approach, from studies of the alternative methods of service delivery (e.g., Savas 1987) to government size and structure (e.g., Ostrom, Tiebout, and Warren 1961) to citizen residential choice patterns (e.g., Schneider 1989). This approach, however, has been less concerned with equity or service distribution patterns than with economic efficiency and responsiveness to the preferences of the consumer/citizen. A basic concept of the field (Savas 1987) is understanding the characteristics of services or goods—that is, Can people who do not pay for them be excluded from their use, and are these services individually (rather than jointly) consumed? If the answer is no to both questions, the service is considered a public or collective good and, thus, quite likely a government responsibility. Other private, toll, or common-pool goods may also be provided by government, but they can be financed, produced, or regulated by government in a variety of methods. Use of market mechanisms is often recommended to maximize efficiency in service delivery.

Less visible in the literature over the last two decades has been the traditional reform approach that suggests that consolidation of services and units of government (e.g., city-county) may improve efficiency, equity, and responsiveness in service delivery, as well as allow local governments to address areawide problems more effectively (Advisory Commission on Intergovernmental Relations [ACIR] 1976). For example, large city-county consolidations have occurred in the metropolitan areas of Indianapolis–Marion County, Jacksonville–Duval County in Florida, and Lexington–Fayette County in Kentucky, among others. A recent work that addresses the debate between the public choice approach and the traditional reform model is Lyons, Lowery, and DeHoog (1992). It revives the debate by questioning some of the assumptions of the public choice approach (e.g., How informed and attentive are citizens to their governments and their service packages?) and offering some empirical evidence to suggest that the reform/metropolitan model might have some advantages over the public choice prescription for a fragmented metropolitan area. In particular, they found that the respondents in the consolidated Lexington system understood better who was responsible for providing their public services as compared with citizens in the fragmented Louisville area. The presumption is that informed citizens can be more effective in using complaint or demand mechanisms to improve their services.

Another method of distinguishing among the works in the service delivery literature is to point out that some have primarily an empirical or theoretical focus, while others have a more applied and prescriptive orientation. For example, the applied works might ask, How can services be improved to make them more efficient or more equitably distributed? This approach might examine some innovative practices or programs and suggest they be considered more broadly (e.g., Brudney 1990; Savas 1982, 1987). The many works by Savas (e.g., 1987) on municipal garbage collection have been fairly convincing about the advantages of using competitive suppliers (both public and private) to reduce costs of service. Certainly public administrationists and some economists tend to incorporate these more applied questions in their research. On the other hand, political scientists have often been more interested in empirical service questions about service patterns, citizen demand mechanisms, and bureaucratic-political interactions (e.g., Lineberry 1977; Sharp 1986; L. Stein, 1991). Obviously, we do not wish to make too clear a distinction here, since many empirical works have practical implications, and some applied works are based on key theoretical assumptions.

One of the perennial practical questions in this field that encounters key the-oretical assumptions is how to design and then evaluate service delivery systems. Four general types of criteria are most frequently chosen, and the dominant approaches in each of the four research areas examined below have their fa-vorites: (1) efficiency (public choice and reformers, alternative methods of serv-ice delivery), (2) effectiveness (public choice, citizen satisfaction), (3) equity (service distribution patterns), and (4) responsiveness (citizen satisfaction). Scholars in the service delivery literature tend to emphasize one or two of the criteria in evaluating services and may come to different conclusions or pre-scriptions as a result.

The study of urban services is marked by a mix of sophisticated research designs that are tailored to address the particular questions at hand. As with much of the urban research, truly comparative studies are often hampered by a multitude of political, structural, or community variables that may impact service delivery processes, outputs, and outcomes. Thus, several of the significant works in the literature focus on services within either a single city (e.g., Jones 1980), cities within a single state (e.g., Lyons, Lowery, and DeHoog 1992), or a com-parison of a small set of similar cities (e.g., Mladenka 1981). Relatively few of the studies examine urban counties, city-county consolidations, or special dis-tricts, although there are some exceptions (e.g., Lowery, Lyons, and DeHoog 1992; Schneider and Park 1989). Certainly the four specific research areas have prompted different research designs. It is these more focused literatures that we will examine next.

THE ORGANIZATION OF SERVICE DELIVERY SYSTEMS

The primary question of this long-standing literature is: How should urban governments be structured so as to provide efficient and effective services to meet residents' needs and preferences? Up until the 1970s, the almost-unanimous answer of reformers and political scientists (ACIR 1976; Zimmer-man 1970) had been to consolidate services and local units so as to improve accountability, develop economies of scale, and reduce waste, duplication, and political corruption. However, with the publication of Ostrom, Tiebout, and Warren's classic article (1961) "The Organization of Government in Metropol-itan Areas," and subsequent works by them, Elinor Ostrom (Ostrom and Os-trom 1977; E. Ostrom 1976), and Robert Bish (1971), the traditional wisdom was turned upside down. The public choice argument is that the fragmented, "polycentric" metropolitan area with many separate governments is efficient in that it offers consumer/citizens many residential choices and allows services to be provided in different-sized jurisdictions (with resulting economies of scale). Much of the work was based on applying economic principles and methods of analysis to the problem of urban jurisdictions and service delivery. An earlier, influential article by Tiebout (1956), "A Pure Theory of Local Expenditures," soon became part of urban politics, with its emphasis on residents "voting with their feet," by leaving a city offering an unsatisfactory service/tax package and moving to one that more accurately reflects their preferences. Thus, the rationale for keeping the more fragmented metropolitan system is efficiency of the quasi-market model that allows municipalities to compete for valued businesses and residents and consumer/citizens to move to more desirable communities. While other political scientists have questioned citizens' attentiveness to public services (Lyons, Lowery, and DeHoog 1992) and their mobility (Orbell and Uno 1972), as well as the economic inequality of the model (Hill 1974), Schneider's extensive research on suburbs in *The Competitive City* (1989) suggests that many municipalities do develop strategies that conform to this model. He and other scholars (e.g., Oakerson and Parks 1988; R. Stein 1990; Teske et al. 1993) have improved the model to account for citizen-government interactions and governments' strategic behavior within a competitive market for public services.

ALTERNATIVE METHODS OF PUBLIC SERVICE DELIVERY

Closely linked to the study of the structure of the metropolitan area is the examination of how public services should be delivered: through its own employees in house or in one of several alternative quasi-market mechanisms, such as contracting out, franchising, service shedding, volunteers, vouchers, coprovision, or coproduction. Of the four areas of urban service research, the study of service delivery methods is perhaps the least embedded in the urban politics literature. Public choice economist E. S. Savas has developed a summary of the various approaches and an argument for wider utilization of these techniques in *Privatization: The Key to Better Government* (1987). Other economists (e.g., Ferris 1984, 1986) and public administrationists (e.g., Kolderie 1986) have made major contributions to this literature, yet their work is more focused on administrative processes, service characteristics, and consequences of different service methods than on directly political questions. This is not to say, however, that certain institutional arrangements do not involve politics or produce political outcomes. (See, for example, L. Stein [1991] for a case on the consequences of privatization of St. Louis' City Hospital.)

A critical distinction in this literature is the difference between service production and provision (Savas 1982; Kolderie 1986). While cities may choose to *provide* (finance and arrange) certain services to their residents, they need not *produce* (deliver) the service with their own employees through traditional bureaucratic means. Instead, many cities may choose quasi-market or privatization approaches, usually for only a few services (R. Stein 1990). They frequently contract out for the services with other governments (Miller 1981) or with private for-profit or nonprofit agencies (Ferris 1986; Ferris and Graddy 1986; Osborne and Gaebler 1992), typically through a competitive bid or negotiation process. Research on contracting for garbage collection services is probably the most well developed of any service area, thanks to the works of Savas (1982, 1987). However, the discussion of alternative approaches also suggests that some methods also serve as citizen demand mechanisms to reveal real demand levels by, for example, allowing citizens to choose their delivery agents (for housing or education most often) through a voucher. To examine the relative efficiency and service quality issues of alternative service delivery methods, scholars have often used simple before/after research designs or some intracity comparisons where different methods are used.

Within this literature, the study of citizen involvement in service delivery has been an interesting subtheme (as well as a complex semantic quagmire), in that some urban services may lend themselves to the use of coprovision (Ferris 1984), that is, citizens volunteering their time or money in public services, whether through more formal volunteer programs (Brudney 1990) or through other forms of coproduction (Whitaker 1980; Brudney and England 1983) so as to reduce service costs. Increasingly, as cities have faced fiscal strain, they have had to consider how to trim their services. Some cities have gone so far as to engage in the more extreme form of privatization, load shedding (Savas 1987), in which a service is no longer provided by the public sector, although a private business may operate the service or facility instead (e.g., golf course, hospital).

While public choice scholars have promoted the use of alternative service delivery mechanisms, primarily on efficiency grounds, others have questioned whether the efficiency gains are real and whether other, negative consequences of privatization might occur. In particular, the role of citizens' voice and involvement in their communities (Morgan and England 1988) and related equity concerns have been raised (Sharp 1990) when extensive coprovision, contracting, and load shedding occur.

CITIZEN SATISFACTION WITH PUBLIC SERVICES

Early questions raised by cities and urban scholars were: How do citizens rate their public services? What factors affect their satisfaction levels? and What actions are they likely to take, should they be dissatisfied? The study of bureaucratic and political responses to citizen feedback and actions also became part of the literature on citizens and service delivery. In examining how citizens evaluate public services, a methodological debate has developed over the question of whether subjective citizen evaluations are related to objective measures of service quality (Stipak 1979; Brudney and England 1983; Percy 1986). This issue certainly is important when prescribing improvements in services or comparing cities' service performance but may be less important to those who are more interested in studying citizen perceptions apart from reality, as well as predicting their actions in response to negative perceptions.

The research on citizen evaluations of services indicates that sources of satisfaction/dissatisfaction are varied—from individual demographic characteristics (Hero and Durand 1980; McDougall and Bunce 1984), citizens' political efficacy (Sharp 1986; Stipak 1979), to their social investment (DeHoog, Lowery, and Lyons 1990) or stakeholding (Sharp 1986). Although the findings are somewhat mixed, the general pattern that emerges is that whites, residents with higher feelings of efficacy, and those who are attached to their communities tend to rate urban services as being better than do other citizens. Residents' social and governmental context has also provided another set of influences—that is, the socioeconomic type of neighborhood and the consolidated versus fragmented governmental structures (Sharp 1986; Lyons, Lowery, and DeHoog 1992). Though this literature again relates the type of institutional context to another area of service delivery (i.e., citizen attitudes), the relationships appear to be quite complex, and there is little consensus on the findings. The public choice scholars (Ostrom, Bish, and Ostrom 1988) suggest that citizens will be more informed and satisfied with service delivery if they reside in a municipality within the fragmented system. However, in *The Politics of Dissatisfaction* (1992), Lyons, Lowery, and DeHoog argue that their research does not support such a view. Their comparison research design, which surveyed residents in 10 communities within two metropolitan areas in Kentucky, indicated somewhat greater levels of satisfaction among citizens in the consolidated Lexington system. In addition, they find that citizens in fragmented systems were more confused about which services were provided by which jurisdiction, although how much this really matters to government strategic behavior has recently been challenged (Teske et al. 1993).

If residents are dissatisfied with their urban services, they may choose to respond in a variety of different ways, according to the literature. The integrative EVLN (exit, voice, loyalty, and neglect) model of Lyons and Lowery (1986) suggests that common behaviors run along both a constructive-destructive dimension and a passive-active dimension. (Exit and voice are active behaviors, while loyalty and neglect are passive. Voice and loyalty are the more constructive of these four options.) Others have focused on one or more of the citizen demand mechanisms, such as citizens contacting public officials, voting, or leaving a jurisdiction (e.g., Coulter 1988; Sharp 1986; Tiebout 1956), with a range of tests and results. Political and bureaucratic responses to these citizen behaviors also have been the subject of some study (Jones 1980; Schneider 1989), yet more research needs to be done on comparisons of these reactions, as well as modeling the complex interaction between citizens and government.

DISTRIBUTION OF URBAN SERVICES—PATTERNS AND CAUSES

One of the largest and most interesting bodies of research in urban services is the study of how urban services are distributed. The original questions were: Are city policies about service distribution discriminatory? Do certain neighborhoods or groups (e.g., the underclass) receive worse or fewer services than others? If there are inequalities, what factors create these patterns? The empirical answers to these questions have been somewhat mixed, but the early predominant view (Lineberry 1977; Mladenka 1980; Jones 1980) was that "unpatterned inequality" is the norm for most cities. Certainly few studies showed that all residents, groups, or geographic areas are treated equally in any given service; yet the racial or socioeconomic characteristics of the areas were not thought to make much difference. More often, administrative or bureaucratic rules or traditions have apparently influenced the service delivery patterns. More recent works have challenged this view, however, by questioning the methodology and definitions of the early works as well as offering new studies with different results.

The single city, comparative service design has been frequently found appropriate to these questions of service distribution patterns, with almost exclusive attention given to large central cities (for an exception, see Button 1982). An early and influential effort to examine this issue appeared in Levy, Meltsner, and Wildavsky's *Urban Outcomes* (1974), a study of the streets, schools, and libraries in Oakland, California. Lineberry's study of San Antonio in *Equality and Urban Policy* (1977) supported the early findings that service patterns in several municipal departments had more to do with bureaucratic decision rules than political influence. Later works on Detroit (Jones 1980), Chicago (Mladenka 1980), and Houston (Mladenka 1981) produced similar results.

Nonetheless, several scholars (Boyle and Jacobs 1982; Cingranelli 1981; Feiock 1986; Koehler and Wrightson 1987; McDougall and Bunce 1984; Miranda and Tunyavong 1994; L. Stein 1991) have found evidence of either discrimination against the underclass or political involvement in service delivery. They argue that the definitions of equity and the methodology of the earlier studies do not adequately reveal the socioeconomic or political variables. In their study of New York City, Boyle and Jacobs (1982) found patterns of service expenditures related to residents' tax contributions and their degree of dependence. Koehler and Wrightson (1987) reexamined the Chicago parks and uncovered some political evidence not seen by Mladenka (1980), which prompted him (1989) to reanalyze Chicago parks over time, with a new appreciation for both race and class factors. L. Stein (1991) determined that St. Louis politicians were often successful in controlling the city's service operations. More recently, Miranda and Tunyavong (1994) have found in yet another study of Chicago that political factors were especially influential in determining the more distributional policies of federal programs.

CURRENT STATE OF THE FIELD

Douglas Yates (1977) was convinced that one of the key problems with urban governance was that urban service delivery systems were too fragmented. Fragmentation also can be said to characterize the urban service delivery literature. Many scholars have limited their attention to just one question and fail to see how their research relates to the broader service literature as well as to urban politics. Linkages can be made, as some works (e.g., Lyons, Lowery, and DeHoog 1992) have shown, and we can, as a result, question assumptions and conclusions made in other related research areas.

A corresponding problem of the field is the lack of cumulativeness—that each succeeding wave of research does not often enough build on previous works, test conclusions, and refine methodologies. Rather, unresolved issues are left to dangle as new questions demand attention. Probably the most well-developed and cumulative area of research has been the service distribution literature. The debates about politics, race, and class versus administrative influences are quite lively and have developed some new twists in recent years. The apparently moribund study of how to organize the metropolitan area for more efficient, effective, and responsive services has also been reinvigorated with some recent citizen survey research comparing residents in fragmented and consolidated areas.

DIRECTIONS FOR FUTURE RESEARCH

Without a doubt, opportunities exist for much more additional research in any of the four areas we have examined in this chapter. Many unanswered questions remain, particularly about urban institutional forms, service delivery methods, and citizen attitudes toward services. New methods can be tried, such as more sophisticated longitudinal and comparative analyses of citizen attitudes. Additional cities and counties (small- and medium-sized, as well as the usual sites) might also be examined. Probably more important, we need to consider how the study of urban services might be improved and enriched by developing theoretical and methodological linkages among the four fields of inquiry. A more comprehensive and useful approach might well result if we can begin by questioning the compartmentalization and narrow treatment of urban services. If services are so essential to urban politics, how can we better explain the bureaucratic and political connections? What causal factors produce the various service patterns, levels, and mix that we find throughout the urban landscape? Do cities behave as rational actors by developing unique packages of services and taxes? Does it matter how urban jurisdictions are defined, as far as services and citizen attitudes about them are concerned? One way to explore the logical connections among these areas is to continue working with the relationships among institutional arrangements, characteristics of service delivery, and the citizen responses to services.

Institutional Arrangements	Service Delivery	Citizen Response
Fragmented	Quality	Satisfaction/dissatisfaction
Consolidated	Levels	Citizen contacting
Privatized	Mix	Political participation
Citizen demand mechanisms	Cost	Neglect/alienation
	Distribution	Exit
	Methods of delivery	

Obviously, service delivery issues also relate closely to other areas of urban politics and should not be seen as a separate topic. Although this chapter did not review it, the literature on the linkage between services and taxes should also continue to be explored, since an exclusive focus on services is unrealistic when understanding policy decisions and citizen responses. The literature on citizen demands (Coulter 1988; Jones 1980; Sharp 1986) and bureaucratic response is part of both the literature on citizen participation and service delivery and may continue to generate new approaches. In sum, the service delivery field offers a variety of methodological and theoretical approaches and addresses governmental structure, resource allocation, and citizen attitudes that will remain significant issues for the study of urban politics.

REFERENCES

Advisory Commission on Intergovernmental Relations (ACIR). 1976. *Improving Urban America: A Challenge to Federalism.* Washington, D.C.: ACIR.

Baer, William. 1985. "Just What Is an Urban Service, Anyway?" *Journal of Politics* 47:881–898.

Bish, Robert L. 1971. *The Public Economy of Metropolitan Areas.* Chicago: Markham.

Boyle, John, and David Jacobs. 1982. "The Intra-City Distribution of Services: A Multivariate Analysis." *American Political Science Review* 76:371–379.

Brudney, Jeffrey. 1990. *Fostering Volunteer Programs in the Public Sector.* San Francisco: Jossey-Bass.

Brudney, Jeffrey, and Robert England. 1983. "Toward a Definition of the Coproduction Concept." *Public Administration Review* 43 (January–February): 59–65.

Button, James. 1982. "Political Strategies and Public-Service Patterns: The Impact of the Civil Rights Movement on Municipal Service Distributions." In Richard Rich, ed., *The Politics of Urban Public Services.* Lexington, MA: Lexington Books.

Cingranelli, David L. 1981. "Race, Politics, and Elites: Testing Alternative Models of Service Distribution." *American Journal of Political Science* 25 (November): 664–692.

Coulter, Philip B. 1988. *Political Voice: Citizen Demand for Urban Public Services.* Tuscaloosa: University of Alabama Press.

DeHoog, Ruth Hoogland, David Lowery, and W. E. Lyons. 1990. "Citizen Satisfaction with Local Governance: A Test of Individual, Jurisdictional, and City Specific Explanations.'' *Journal of Politics* 52: 807–837.

Feiock, Richard C. 1986. ''The Political Economy of Urban Service Distribution: A Test of the Underclass Hypothesis.'' *Journal of Urban Affairs* 8, no. 3: 31–42.

Ferris, James M. 1984. ''Coprovision: Citizen Time and Money Donations in Public Service Provision.'' *Public Administration Review* 44 (July–August): 324–333.

Ferris, James M. 1986. ''The Decision to Contract Out.'' *Urban Affairs Quarterly* 22: 289–311.

Ferris, James M., and Elizabeth Graddy. 1986. ''Contracting Out: For What? With Whom?'' *Public Administration Review* 46: 332–344.

Hero, Rodney E. 1986. ''The Urban Service Delivery Literature: Some Questions and Considerations.'' *Polity* 18: 659–677.

Hero, Rodney E., and Roger Durand. 1980. ''Explaining Citizen Evaluations of Urban Services.'' *Urban Affairs Quarterly* 20: 344–354.

Hill, Richard C. 1974. ''Separate and Unequal: Government Inequality in the Metropolis.'' *American Political Science Review* 68: 1157–1168.

Jones, Bryan D., with Saadia Greenberg and Joseph Drew. 1980. *Service Delivery in the City.* New York: Longman.

Koehler, David H., and Margaret T. Wrightson. 1987. ''Inequality in the Delivery of Urban Services: A Reconsideration of the Chicago Parks.'' *Journal of Politics* 49 (February): 80–99.

Kolderie, Theodore. 1986. ''The Two Different Concepts of Privatization.'' *Public Administration Review* 43: 285–291.

Levy, Frank, Arnold Meltsner, and Aaron Wildavsky. 1974. *Urban Outcomes: Schools, Streets, and Libraries.* Berkeley: University of California Press.

Lineberry, Robert L. 1977. *Equality and Urban Policy: The Distribution of Municipal Public Services.* Beverly Hills, CA: Sage.

Lyons, W. E., and David Lowery. 1986. ''Citizen Responses to Dissatisfaction in Urban Communities.'' *Journal of Politics* 48: 321–346.

Lyons, W. E., David Lowery, and Ruth Hoogland DeHoog. 1992. *The Politics of Dissatisfaction: Citizens, Services, and Urban Institutions.* Armonk, NY: M. E. Sharp.

McDougall, Gerald S., and Harold Bunce. 1984. ''Urban Service Distributions: Some Answers to Neglected Issues.'' *Urban Affairs Quarterly* 19 (March): 355–371.

Miller, Gary. 1981. *Cities by Contract.* Cambridge: MIT Press.

Miller, Thomas I., and Michelle A. Miller. 1992. ''Assessing Excellence Poorly: The Bottom Line in Local Government.'' *Journal of Policy Analysis and Management* 11: 612–623.

Miranda, Rowan A., and Ittipone Tunyavong. 1994. ''Patterned Inequality? Reexamining the Role of Distributive Politics in Urban Service Delivery.'' *Urban Affairs Quarterly* 29 (June): 509–534.

Mladenka, Kenneth. 1980. ''The Urban Bureaucracy and the Chicago Political Machine: Who Gets What and the Limits of Political Control.'' *American Political Science Review* 74 (December): 991–998.

Mladenka, Kenneth. 1981. ''Citizen Demands and Urban Services: The Distribution of Bureaucratic Response in Chicago and Houston.'' *American Journal of Political Science* 25: 693–714.

Mladenka, Kenneth R. 1989. "The Distribution of an Urban Public Service: The Changing Role of Race and Politics." *Urban Affairs Quarterly* 24, no. 4: 556–583.

Morgan, David R., and Robert E. England. 1988. "The Two Faces of Privatization." *Public Administration Review* 48 (November–December): 979–987.

Oakerson, Ronald, and Roger Parks. 1988. "Citizen Voice and Public Entrepreneurship." *Publius* 19: 91–112.

Orbell, John, and Toru Uno. 1972. "A Theory of Neighborhood Problem-Solving: Political Action versus Residential Mobility." *American Political Science Review* 66: 471–486.

Osborne, David, and Ted Gaebler. 1992. *Reinventing Government.* Reading, MA: Addison-Wesley.

Ostrom, Elinor, ed. 1976. *The Delivery of Urban Services: Outcomes of Change.* Beverly Hills, CA: Sage.

Ostrom, Vincent, Robert L. Bish, and Elinor Ostrom. 1988. *Local Government in the United States.* San Francisco: Institute for Contemporary Studies.

Ostrom, Vincent, and Elinor Ostrom. 1977. "Public Goods and Public Choices." In E. S. Savas, ed., *Alternatives for Delivering Public Services: Toward Improved Performance.* Boulder, CO: Westview Press.

Ostrom, Vincent, Charles Tiebout, and Robert Warren. 1961. "The Organization of Government in Metropolitan Areas: A Theoretical Inquiry." *American Political Science Review* 55: 831–842.

Parks, Roger, and Elinor Ostrom. 1981. "Complex Models of Urban Service Delivery Systems." In Terry N. Clark, ed., *Urban Policy Analysis.* Beverly Hills, CA: Sage.

Percy, Stephen L. 1986. "In Defense of Citizen Evaluations as Performance Measures." *Urban Affairs Quarterly* 22: 66–83.

Rich, Richard, ed. 1982. *The Politics of Urban Public Services.* Lexington, MA: Lexington Books.

Savas, E. S. 1982. *Privatizing the Public Sector: How to Shrink Government.* Chatham, NJ: Chatham House.

Savas, E. S. 1987. *Privatization: The Key to Better Government.* Chatham, NJ: Chatham House.

Schneider, Mark. 1989. *The Competitive City: The Political Economy of Suburbia.* Pittsburgh: University of Pittsburgh Press.

Schneider, Mark, and Kee Ok Park. 1989. "Metropolitan Counties as Service Delivery Agents: The Still Forgotten Governments." *Public Administration Review* 49 (July–August): 345–352.

Sharp, Elaine B. 1986. *Citizen Demand-Making in the Urban Context.* Tuscaloosa: University of Alabama Press.

Sharp, Elaine B. 1990. *Urban Politics and Administration: From Service Delivery to Economic Development.* New York: Longman.

Stein, Lana. 1991. *Holding Bureaucrats Accountable: Politicians and Professionals in St. Louis.* Tuscaloosa: University of Alabama Press.

Stein, Robert M. 1990. *Urban Alternatives: Public and Private Markets in the Provision of Local Services.* Pittsburgh: University of Pittsburgh Press.

Stipak, Brian. 1979. "Citizen Satisfaction with Urban Services: Potential Misuse as a Performance Indicator." *Public Administration Review* 39 (January–February): 46–52.

Teske, Paul, Mark Schneider, Michael Mintrom, and Samuel Best. 1993. ''Establishing the Micro Foundations of a Macro Theory: Information, Movers, and the Competitive Local Market for Public Goods.'' *American Political Science Review* 87 (September): 702–713.

Tiebout, Charles M. 1956. ''A Pure Theory of Local Expenditures.'' *Journal of Political Economy* 64: 416–424.

Whitaker, Gordon. 1980. ''Coproduction: Citizen Participation in Service Delivery.'' *Public Administration Review* 40: 240–246.

Yates, Douglas. 1977. *The Ungovernable City*. Cambridge, MA: MIT Press.

Zimmerman, Joseph F. 1970. ''Metropolitan Reform in the U.S.: An Overview.'' *Public Administration Review* 30: 531–543.

Chapter 15

Urban Management

David R. Morgan and
David G. Carnevale

URBAN ADMINISTRATION AND MANAGEMENT

In recent times the growing competitiveness of the global economy has forced American business into major restructuring. Pressures of a different sort also compel American local governments to search for ways to control costs and improve workforce performance. More than any other reason, fiscal stress has forced municipal administrators to reconsider old ideas and abandon outmoded practices. Doing more with less has become the operative mantra. Cities responded by reconsidering the design and delivery of local services. Progressive managers sought to modify organizational cultures, missions, structures, and processes. Local agencies have become more customer focused and results oriented. They emphasize empowerment of employees by decentralizing authority and delegating responsibility. They exploit technological advancement and concentrate on continuously improving work processes. Obsolete concepts fade as management searches for innovative solutions to ever complex problems. The objectives: to lower costs, improve quality, and enhance performance. In this chapter, we review four principal management innovations used in local government: (1) quality improvement, (2) reinvention, (3) reengineering, and (4) performance measurement.

To provide a bit of background for this assessment of administrative innovations, we offer a brief comment on urban management as a field of study. Most public administration scholars probably would not consider urban management as a distinct or separate subfield. But under the dominant open systems theory, organizations are permeable, open to abundant outside forces. Context does matter, as we know from the continuing debate about the differences in private and public administration. Cities are special places with a history of governance and management that sheds light on administrative practice today. The early urban reform movement, for example, emphasized efficiency, professionalism, nonpartisanship, and city manager government. The tumultuous 1960s brought a new concern for "maximum feasible participation," community control, and service delivery responsive to traditionally forgotten groups. Still, scholars continued to stress the need to improve traditional management practices (Rapp and Patitucci 1977). Recent research also stresses service delivery, enhanced citizen responsiveness, and the powerful effects of private sector economic development (Sharp 1990; Morgan and England 1996). In short, there may be no separate subfield of urban management. But with its complex and distinctive environment, we should continue to see efforts to improve management practices that have special application to local governments.

Quality Improvement

Over the last decade, public and private organizations have implemented quality improvement innovations of all kinds to improve services, increase productivity, and cut costs. Out of this effort has evolved a set of strategies and techniques called total quality management (TQM). Its diffusion in local government is extensive and expanding. Although there is no single formula, TQM embraces a set of core assumptions. These draw prominently on the works of Crosby (1979), Deming (1986), Juran (1989), and the Japanese writer Ishikawa (1985).

A typical TQM system features the following elements:

1. The primary goal of the organization is customer or client satisfaction. "Customer" includes those internal to the organization such as employees in other departments as well as those external to the organization such as taxpayers, contractors, regulators, and suppliers.

2. Everyone in the organization must receive the tools and training needed to satisfy customer requirements.

3. Work processes are continuously improved as quality is "built in" rather than "inspected in."

4. There is a strong commitment to employee involvement, teamwork, and establishing a climate of mutual trust throughout the organization.

5. Senior elected or appointed officials ensure that a common vision prevails within the organization. They also are responsible for making the necessary system changes to guarantee quality.

Both external and internal pressures lead to quality improvement initiatives. West, Berman, and Milakovich (1993) identify the three most important external forces for introducing TQM in local government. They include citizen complaints, community planning activities, and voter demands. The three most important internal forces are city manager interest, the need to increase employee productivity, and budget pressures (West, Berman, and Milakovich 1994). The summary principle that accounts for interest in TQM at all levels of government is the enduring search for a management paradigm, one that is responsive to increasing taxpayer demands in an environment characterized by diminishing fiscal capacity.

Much of the evidence concerning the success of quality improvement applications in local government is anecdotal (e.g., Sensenbrenner 1991; Osborne and Gaebler 1992). However, West and Coauthors' (1994: 22) study of all U.S. cities with populations of 25,000 and more shows that

[l]arge majorities indicate positive results on . . . quality of product/service, productivity/ efficiency, customer satisfaction, amount of service to customers, timeliness of service . . . unit-wide communication, better group decision-making capabilities, improvements during a period of resource constraints, better informed decisionmaking, greater commitment to stakeholders, higher employee morale, and use of new performance measures.

The effects in local government are similar to those found at other governmental levels and in private industry. Where management is strongly committed to quality improvement, there is every prospect for more effective, efficient, and responsive government. The full impact of TQM initiatives must be evaluated over the long term, however. Experts caution that TQM is not a quick fix for systemic problems in government operations. The public landscape is littered with previously tried and mostly discarded schemes to improve government systems. In most of these cases (quality circles, for example), administrators simply expected too much too soon. Whether TQM will experience the same fate is an open question.

Historically, public administration has borrowed many of its innovative management practices from the business sector. An important issue is the extent to which public managers will have to modify TQM, the latest private sector import.

Swiss (1992) offers one of the earliest and still most influential statements on the suitability of TQM in government environments. He argues that ''orthodox TQM'' does not work well in the public sector:

1. Identification of customers in government is more difficult than in business. Moreover, there are conflicts and contradictions in customer expectations. Many of government's customers (the public-at-large) may not even be the recipients of the services they pay for.

2. The relationship of quality and cost is more complex for the government customer. In industry, the customer may be willing to pay more for quality because the buyer of the product is most often its user. In government, the person paying for the service may not be its user and will often sacrifice quality for lower cost.

3. In the public arena the product is often a service. This opens the door to difficult issues of customer evaluation. The consumer, for example, may judge the service not

only on the result but also on the appearance and behavior of the person delivering it.

4. Government focuses on inputs and processes, which can lead to goal displacement if agencies neglect outcomes. This natural inclination subverts initiatives to improve quality.

5. The culture of government fosters fairly rapid turnover of executive leadership, creating formidable problems for major system change. In Deming's (1986) terms, "constancy of purpose" becomes difficult to achieve.

Milakovich (1990) adds to the list of challenges facing government leaders in implementing TQM. He observes, for example, that contemporary performance appraisal methods, dependence on Theory X management, fear of change, and annual budgeting practices make improving quality in the government context more demanding. Hyde (1992: 36) acknowledges such obstacles but argues that public organizations should give TQM "an objective test and a full evaluation." Rago (1994) agrees. The problems are real, but he urges public managers not to overemphasize their significance. He thinks TQM can be successfully integrated into government operations.

Like other managerial innovations, TQM holds considerable promise. If officials are willing to make the investment in time and resources, quality management can lead to a more responsive and accountable local government.

Reinventing Government

Now seems the time for "re-ing" local government—restructuring, revitalizing, reinventing, and reengineering (see Marlow et al. 1994). Of these new approaches, the most widely discussed is "reinventing," the currently popular phrase from Osborne and Gaebler's (1992) book of the same name. One review even suggests that *Reinventing Government* has become a "bible for practitioners and policymakers" (Lynch and Markusen 1994). The book has prompted substantial response, pro and con, in a very short time. And its influence can be seen in various ways. For example, while not using the reinventing term, the Report of the National Performance Review (1993), chaired by Vice President Al Gore, relies heavily on some of Osborne and Gaebler's ideas.

This is not the place for a detailed review of *Reinventing Government*. Suffice it here to say that Osborne and Gaebler above all declare the need for a fundamental rethinking about how governments operate. They call for entrepreneurial government, one that promotes competition, empowers employees, treats service recipients as customers, decentralizes authority, and relies on market mechanisms to fulfill public purposes. They also want public managers to emphasize outcomes, not inputs, and focus on the mission rather than rules and procedures. The authors insist that these are not idealistic concepts; they are practical ideas that state and local governments are implementing with growing success around the country. In fact, one of the criticisms of the book is that it really offers few new ideas. One reviewer asks, "Reinvent Government or Re-discover It?" (Goodsell 1993). Such ideas as competition, contracting out, par-ticipatory management, and performance measurement have been around for a long time. Yet the book offers more than a repackaging of old ideas. Otherwise, state and local practitioners would not have responded so positively to Osborne and Gaebler's 10 principles.

Another of Osborne and Gaebler's favorite solutions has found considerable favor: entrepreneurial government. The authors treat the concept broadly; it cer-tainly goes far beyond running government like a business (Osborne and Gaebler 1992: 20). Many local officials sign on when entrepreneurialism refers to an experimental and innovative approach and not just making a profit (Walters 1992: 24). The place of competition in local government is still debated, of course. But *Reinventing Government* expresses no doubt. The various business-like practices that Osborne and Gaebler discuss flow consistently from the core belief in the need to inject government at all levels with more competition (Felts 1993: 316). According to Lynch and Markusen (1994: 128), "Ultimately, the book's entire architecture rests upon the construct of public sector as monop-oly." But these critics contend that the authors overstate the case for market solutions to public problems. Above all, they worry about the lack of account-ability and responsiveness to democratic controls that accompany a heavy reli-ance on privatization and contracting out.

Some critics point to little new in *Reinventing Government*. Others insist that many of the authors' solutions are unrealistic, that few of their ideas will really work (Vocino 1993). Yet much of what Osborne and Gaebler advocate is indeed becoming more and more common among progressive private firms—stressing quality, flattening hierarchies, satisfying customers, and involving employees in decision making. Maybe they have oversold their perspective and relied on too many catchphrases. Perhaps their evidence is "transparently thin" (DiIulio 1993: 52), or the book contains "less than meets the eye" (Vocino 1993). These charges are leveled at most popularizers. Two related criticisms are compelling, however. Some state and local practitioners have asked, "How do you really *do* it?" In short, the book is "long on suggestions but short on steps for actual implementation" (Walters 1992: 40). And as Vocino (1993) argues, the authors virtually ignore politics and the need for coalition building. Even if some of their solutions are technically correct, he states, they may not be politically feasible.

Reengineering

The latest hot management trend in local government is reengineering, another approach that recently diffused from the private sector. Michael Hammer's 1990 article in the *Harvard Business Review* first introduced the concept to the busi-ness world. Unlike the more comprehensive reinventing approach, reengineering concentrates almost exclusively on changing the work process within an organization. This doesn't mean that reengineering has modest goals. To the contrary. In Hammer's words, "At the heart of reengineering is the notion of discontinuous thinking—of recognizing and breaking away from the outdated rules and fundamental assumptions that underlie operations" (107). Reengineering strives to break away from these procedures and force the organization to find imaginative new ways to accomplish work.

According to Stewart (1993: 42), reengineering calls for the radical redesign of organizational processes. The key question is, "If we could start from scratch, how would we do this?" Then, "Do it that way." The literature reflects some cases of dramatic improvement using this approach. Hammer (1990) tells the story of Ford Motor Company's plans to revamp its accounts payable operation. Initially, management thought it could cut the payroll about 20 percent, reducing the workforce from 500 to 400. Installing a new computer system was presumably the solution. Then they discovered that Mazda employed only 5 people in accounts payable. This prompted a total rethinking of the process. Management identified a whole sequence of steps with accompanying paperwork that Mazda apparently had eliminated. Ford then decided to follow suit. It implemented "invoiceless processing," which abolished the labor-intensive task of matching purchase orders with invoices. The changes were radical, the results striking. Ford achieved a 75 percent reduction in head count—not the 20 percent originally envisioned.

The literature does contain a few brief descriptions of local sector applications of reengineering (see the symposium, Hale and Hyde 1994). Most involve a work process that was heavily dependent on handling and storing of paper. For example, Napa County, California, streamlined its public assistance application process. It integrated various social service programs, computerized its myriad forms, and instituted an "interactive" interview conducted by specially trained case workers. The county reduced the waiting time for applicants from eight hours to a few minutes (Linden 1993). The Department of Probation in New York City reengineered its $24 million system for supervising 80,000 probationers. It computerized voluminous paper files, capitalized on automated interconnections with other databases to track probationers, and established an interactive system of self-reporting by 20,000 low-risk probationers. Such changes enabled the agency to maintain its workload while absorbing a 33 percent reduction in probation officers. It also saved $3.3 million a year (Mechling 1994: 44).

The creative use of technology characterizes most reengineering success stories. Yet Hammer (1990) insists that it is not an information technology issue but rather a work design and organizational change issue. It requires people to think about the *process* involved rather than along departmental or functional lines. Mechling (1994) identifies three areas that hold the greatest promise for reengineering in the public sector: customer service, program integration, and overhead. Most applications today emphasize *customer service*. Private corporations have made giant strides in using information technology to provide 24-

hour service to and from virtually any location. The use of ATM (automatic teller machine) machines in supermarkets and 1–800 numbers for credit card purchases are but two examples. Public sector applications also stress customer service, for example, by streamlining an application process and the self-service convenience of probation reporting. *Program integration* has considerable potential as well. So many local services require multiple forms and visits to various offices. The result is often "death by handoff." Someone drops the ball when a case or application is passed along from one person or program to another. "Information technology can bridge the gaps that make these hand-offs less risky," says Harvard University's Mechling (1994: 48). Finally, reengineering can reduce *overhead*. By reducing handoffs and eliminating whole organizational levels, information networks permit a flattened organizational structure. The agency ends up with fewer paper pushers, coordinators, and supervisors.

It all sounds promising. But a recent *Informationweek* article suggests that at least two thirds of reengineering projects fail (Caldwell 1994). What are the obstacles that local managers should know about? In a survey of 400 U.S. and Canadian firms, the number-one reason—cited by 60 percent—was, not surprisingly, "resistance to change." Next were "limitations of existing systems" and lack of top executive support (52). According to Stewart (1993), organizations can increase the odds for success in several ways. Strategy is the first concern. Reengineering is about operations; only strategy can tell you whether the operation matters. In the words of one consultant, "Don't pave cow paths" (Linden 1993: 12). Second, lead from the top. The person in charge must have enough clout to force sometimes balky departments to work together. Third, Stewart says, "create a sense of urgency." Fear, resistance, cynicism, and political pressure can derail the most ambitious plans. Major restructuring also may be costly and time-consuming. But some executives indicate that experience more than the particular approach or methodology is the key to a reengineering triumph (Caldwell 1994: 52).

Hammer worries that the term is being devalued. "People take last year's project that didn't make it . . . put on a reengineering label and try to sneak it through this year" (cited in Martin 1993: 30). Still, most observers of private sector applications believe that reengineering is not a mere fad. Done properly, Stewart (1993: 41) believes it "delivers gains in speed, productivity, and profitability." It requires consultants, of course. And such efforts may work only in the proper organizational culture. An environment amenable to continuous improvement and with an emphasis on quality management may be a critical prerequisite.

Performance Measurement

Many proposed reforms should bring an increase in operational flexibility. With decentralization, the removal of nonessential layers of supervision, contracting out, and reorganizing around process rather than function, local managers also need to reexamine old methods of accountability. The Report of the National Performance Review (1993: 68), for example, addresses the issue of performance accountability. One of its six steps to a more responsive federal government is holding "every organization and individual accountable for clearly understood, feasible outcomes." The national government is an easy target for its failure to justify the results of so many far-flung and complex programs. But local governments over the years also must plead guilty. Too often they fail to provide enough information to allow elected officials and the public to evaluate agency performance. In 1979, Fox (1979: 1) quotes a Flint, Michigan, official who complains, "As a councilman, I do not receive a single report that tells me how our city government is doing." Perhaps matters have improved since then. Again, maybe not. A 1992 review article in *Public Administration Review* bears the title "Get Ready: The Time for Performance Measurement Is Finally Coming" (Epstein and Fass Associates 1992). And *Reinventing Government* devotes an entire appendix to the "Art of Performance Measurement."

Even before the recent flurry of reform proposals, enlightened local managers had begun to recognize the need to concentrate on the results or outcomes of public programs. Planning, Programming, Budgeting System (PPBS) and various versions of program budgeting highlighted the need to measure outcomes. The advantages of such an emphasis are several (Fountain and Roob 1994: 7). First, the use of performance measures can help assess the efficiency and effectiveness of the process of converting resources into outputs. Second, they can help managers understand the link between outputs and desired objectives. And finally, performance indicators can show both elected officials and the larger citizenry what the city is accomplishing.

An abundance of literature old and new discusses how to measure and report on municipal achievements. In 1992, the Governmental Accounting Standards Board issued seven research reports on the subject, titled *Service Efforts and Accomplishments Reporting*. The volumes include 12 state and local services, from police protection, road maintenance, and water supply to sanitation collection and disposal (see Epstein 1992). The Urban Institute and the International City Management Association also have sponsored a comprehensive applied volume with the title *How Effective Are Your Community Services?* (Hatry et al. 1992). A recent issue of *Public Productivity and Management Review* contains a symposium on performance measurement as well (Bouckaert 1993). So a wealth of ideas along with an abundance of specific measures are readily available to city officials.

One special case of performance monitoring is worth brief discussion. Regardless of how one views the book *Reinventing Government*, there is no doubt that competition at the local level is increasing, especially contracting out. Space limitations preclude a review of the myriad issues related to privatization. But we must mention that contracting out and other forms of private service delivery require special attention to monitoring and measuring results. As Rehfuss (1990: 45) points out, alleged failure to monitor effectively is almost a routine criticism of contracting out. He concedes that it may often be the Achilles heel of the process. Effective monitoring virtually requires specific performance standards. Otherwise, how does a municipality know if the contractor has met the prescribed standards? Citizen complaints and contractor reports are essential, of course. But cities also should adopt clearly written specifications and develop understandable, significant, attainable, and measurable objectives.

As suggested above, performance measurement has been around a long time. That fact alone may suggest, regardless of any reform momentum, that measuring outcomes is far from easy. Cost is always a concern. Performance measurement, especially monitoring, is labor intensive. Yet cities don't need to reinvent the wheel; some indicators have become widely accepted (e.g., crime rates, certain indicators of air and water quality). With so many reports on the subject, a city may not need a consultant to develop a good program. A second barrier to the process is fear; both program managers and elected officials fear that interest groups and the media may use service measures against them (Wholey and Hatry 1992: 609). What if we don't achieve our objectives? Won't there be hell to pay? A third problem: Agency heads and managers may push for measures that will make them look good or objectives that are easy to attain. Or conversely, a preoccupation with measurement might lead to program distortions, such as creaming—searching for those clients most likely to succeed (Lipsky 1980: 48–51). Finally, Walters (1994) names politics as the most serious and basic problem. As with budgeting, you cannot take the politics out of something that so directly impacts the public. As Dearborn comments: "If the public and political leaders like a certain program, it will get funded. We actually have some ideas of what works and what doesn't in crime and drugs, but a lot of politicians and a lot of the population don't like the solutions. As long as those people are paying taxes, that's how the system will respond" (quoted in Walters 1994: 35).

But the public also wants assurances that government programs work well. With the whole thrust toward improving quality, flattening the hierarchy, and using market mechanisms to deliver services, local agencies will be under growing pressure to measure their performance and account for their results.

CONCLUSION

Local government in the future must still get by modestly (Rutter 1980: 93–94). Revenue constraints will continue to dominate municipal decision making. So the search persists for organizational design and innovations in service delivery that can hold down costs without sacrificing quality. Privatization is no fad; local managers will continue the pursuit of competition as a pivotal strategy in the quest to do more with less. Economic development holds similar appeal. Growing the local economy has multiple benefits, not the least of which is to augment the local tax base. The use of public-private partnerships may increase as policy makers search for ways of enlarging the participation of the business community. All of these areas should afford ample opportunity for future urban research. But above all, practitioners remain focused on improving the capacity to deal with change (see Manion 1993: 81–82). Managing organizational change represents the largest challenge for urban practitioners and researchers alike.

Despite evidence that innovative management practices are possible and necessary, successful change is never easy in local government. Obstacles abound. Public organizations are sometimes unwilling to make the up-front contributions in both money and time. A second potential problem: Organizational leadership may be reluctant to empower employees. Third, adversarial labor-management relations may preclude the cooperation essential to achieve desired results. A fourth impediment is: Public leaders often have very short time horizons compared to their private sector counterparts. Local officials may pursue short-term projects with immediate political payoffs at the expense of long-term objectives. Fifth, innovations don't just happen. They must be carefully planned and tailored to fit the particular organizational culture. Across-the-board strategies imported wholesale from the business community may not be suitable for city government. Finally, transforming public organizations requires overcoming the presence of multiple interest groups with sometimes profound policy differences (Swiss 1992; Carnevale 1995).

We must recognize, too, that bold new management practices can sometimes create more problems than they solve or deliver less than they promise (Gabris 1986). Critics of rational-comprehensive approaches (Lindblom 1959; Cohen, March, and Olsen 1972) have long complained about unrealistic proposals for sweeping organizational change. They cite such obstacles as the limitations of human problem-solving capacities, time constraints, unforeseen costs, and the pervasiveness of political influences. Yet muddling through may not suffice in today's climate of unending crisis. No doubt, the barriers to imaginative problem solving are formidable, but the magnitude of the problems facing urban America demands action. Creative and courageous managers can make municipal government work better. And the public now demands nothing less.

REFERENCES

Bouckaert, Geert, ed. 1993. "Performance Measurement and Public Management." *Public Productivity and Management Review* 17 (fall): 29–68.

Caldwell, Bruce. 1994. "Missteps, Miscues." *Informationweek*, June 20, 50–61.

Carnevale, David G. 1995. *The Trustworthy Organization*. San Francisco: Jossey-Bass.

Cohen, Michael, James March, and Johan Olsen. 1972. "Garbage Can Model of Organizational Choice." *Administrative Science Quarterly* 17 (March): 1–25.

Crosby, Philip B. 1979. *Quality Is Free*. New York: McGraw Hill.

Deming, W. Edwards. 1986. *Out of Crisis*. Cambridge, MA: MIT Center for Engineering Study.

DiIulio, John J., Jr. 1993. "Thinking in Moderation." *Washington Monthly* (March).

Epstein, Paul D., and Fass Associates. 1992. "Get Ready: The Time for Performance Measurement Is Finally Coming!" *Public Administration Review* 52 (September–October): 513–519.

Felts, Arthur A. 1993. "Entrepreneurial Government." *Public Productivity and Management Review* 16 (spring): 315–320.

Fountain, James, Jr., and Mitchell Roob. 1994. "Service Efforts and Accomplishment Measures." *Public Management* 76 (March): 6–12.

Fox, Douglas M. 1979. *Managing the Public's Interest.* New York: Holt, Rinehart and Winston.

Gabris, Gerald T. 1986. "Recognizing Management Technique Dysfunctions." *Public Productivity Review*, no. 40: 3–19.

Goodsell, Charles T. 1993. "Reinvent Government or Rediscover It?" *Public Administration Review* 53 (January–February): 85–87.

Hale, Sandra, and A. C. Hyde, eds. 1994. "Reengineering in the Public Sector" [symposium]. *Public Productivity and Management Review* 18 (winter): 127–197.

Hammer, Michael. 1990. "Reengineering Work: Don't Automate, Obliterate." *Harvard Business Review* 68 (July–August): 104–112.

Hatry, Harry, Louis Blair, Donald Fisk, John Greiner, John Hall, Jr., and Philip Schaenman. 1992. *How Effective Are Your Community Services?* 2nd ed. Washington, D.C.: Urban Institute and International City Management Association.

Hyde, Albert C. 1992. "The Proverbs of Total Quality Management: Recharting the Path to Quality Improvement in the Public Sector." *Public Productivity and Management Review* 16 (fall): 25–37.

Ishikawa, K. 1985. *What Is Total Quality Control? The Japanese Way.* Englewood Cliffs, NJ: Prentice-Hall.

Juran, Joseph. 1989. *Juran on Leadership for Quality.* New York: McGraw-Hill.

Lindblom, Charles E. 1959. "The Science of 'Muddling Through.' " *Public Administration Review* 19 (spring): 79–88.

Linden, Russ. 1993. "Business Process Reengineering: Newest Fad, or Revolution in Government?" *Public Management* 75 (November): 9–12.

Lipsky, Michael. 1980. *Street-Level Bureaucracy.* New York: Russell Sage Foundation.

Lynch, Roberta, and Ann Markusen. 1994. "Can Markets Govern?" *The American Prospect* 16 (winter): 125–134.

Manion, Patrick. 1993. "Promoting Excellence in Management." In Charldean Newell, ed., *The Effective Local Government Manager.* 2nd ed. Washington, D.C.: International City/County Management Association.

Marlow, Herbert, Jr., Ronald Nyhan, Lawrence Arrington, and William Pammer, Jr. 1994. "The *Re-ing* of Local Government: Understanding and Shaping Governmental Change." *Public Productivity and Management Review* 17 (spring): 299–311.

Martin, John. 1993. "Reengineering Government" *Governing* (March).

Mechling, Jerry. 1994. "Reengineering: Part of Your Game Plan?" *Governing* (February).

Milakovich, M. E. 1990. "Total Quality Management for Public Productivity Improvement." *Public Productivity and Management Review* 14 (fall): 19–32.

Morgan, David R., and Robert E. England. 1996. *Managing Urban America.* 4th ed. Chatham, NJ: Chatham House.

Osborne, David, and Ted Gaebler. 1992. *Reinventing Government*. Reading, MA: Addison-Wesley.

Rago, William V. 1994. "Adapting Total Quality Management (TQM) to Government: Another Point of View." *Public Administration Review* 54 (January–February): 61–64.

Rapp, Brian W., and Frank M. Patitucci. 1977. *Managing Local Government for Improved Performance*. Boulder, CO: Westview.

Rehfuss, John. 1990. "Contracting Out and Accountability in State and Local Governments: The Importance of Contract Monitoring." *State and Local Government Review* 22 (winter): 44–48.

Report of the National Performance Review. 1993. *Creating a Government that Works Better and Costs Less*. Washington, D.C.

Rutter, Laurence. 1980. *The Essential Community: Local Government in the Year 2000*. Washington, D.C.: International City Management Association.

Sensenbrenner, Joseph. 1991. "Quality Comes to City Hall." *Harvard Business Review* 69 (March–April): 64–75.

Sharp, Elaine B. 1990. *Urban Politics and Administration*. New York: Longman.

Stewart, Thomas A. 1993. "Reengineering: The Hot New Managing Tool." *Fortune*, August 23, 41–48.

Swiss, James E. 1992. "Adapting Total Quality Management (TQM) to Government." *Public Administration Review* 52 (July–August): 356–362.

U.S. General Accounting Office. 1994. *Management Reforms: Examples of Public and Private Innovations to Improve Service Delivery*. Washington, D.C.

Vocino, Thomas. 1993. "Is 'Reinventing Government' the Answer?" *Public Administration Times*, May 1.

Walters, Jonathan. 1992. "Reinventing Government: Managing the Politics of Change." *Governing* (December).

Walters, Jonathan. 1994. "The Benchmarking Craze." *Governing* 7 (April): 33–37.

West, Jonathan, Evan Berman, and Michael Milakovich. 1993. "Implementing TQM in Local Government: The Leadership Challenge." *Public Productivity and Management Review* 17 (winter): 175–189.

West, Jonathan, Evan Berman, and Michael Milakovich. 1994. "Total Quality Management in Local Government." In *Municipal Year Book*. Washington, D.C.: International City and County Management Association.

Wholey, Joseph, and Harry Hatry. 1992. "The Case for Performance Monitoring." *Public Administration Review* 52 (November–December): 604–610.

Chapter 16

Budgeting in the City

Irene Rubin

OVERVIEW

Public budgeting deals with the allocation of public resources. Much of the best-known literature on public budgeting deals with the national level because of the scope of public spending and its impact on people's lives and on the economy (e.g., Schick 1980, 1990, 1995; Cogan, Muris, and Schick 1994; Wildavsky 1964; Fisher 1975). Another large chunk of the literature deals with public budgeting broadly, making little distinction between levels of government (e.g., Hyde 1992; Schick 1987; Rubin 1988). Municipal budgeting addresses many of the same issues as the literature on state and federal budgeting, such as budget process reform and the contestation of power between branches of government. But at the local level there is less focus on the deficit, on the effect of the budget on the economy, and on entitlements and more on accountability, participation, and democracy.

This chapter summarizes 120 years of municipal budgeting in terms of three main themes.[1] The first theme is that budgeting power has shifted among the mayor (and later the city manager), the council, and the citizens in an attempt to control spending, break the backs of political machines, and reduce or increase the power of blacks, ethnic minorities, and the poor. The underlying issues include representativeness, accountability, effectiveness, and efficiency.

The second theme is that taxpayers have sometimes accepted and sometimes rejected taxes, depending on their economic circumstances, the level and fairness of taxes, and whether they were getting the services they wanted. An underlying set of questions is whether those who pay the taxes control the composition and level of spending, whether there is a public interest represented by government that is broader than the interests of specific groups of taxpayers, and whether government has become an unyielding force wrenching taxes from an unwilling and unconsulted public. These issues concern the nature of democracy as it changes over time.

The third theme is that the relationships between the mayor or manager, the budget office, and the departments have changed, as financial conditions have changed and as the power of the chief executive has increased. The old model of adding up departments' requests to make the budget has largely disappeared; political machines, dependent on patronage and highly decentralized departments, are generally dead; mayors and managers now generally control the bureaucracy and the budget process. These issues address the controllability of the bureaucracy and the desirable level of centralization.

The Shifting Balance between the Legislature, the Executive, and the Public

Early budget reformers gave explicit attention to how European-style efficiency could be combined with American-style democracy (Fairlie 1923: 1–44; Cleveland 1909, 1915; Ford 1915: 1–14; Buck 1929: 453–458; Goodnow 1913: 68–77). They interpreted the democracy-efficiency tensions in terms of controlling waste and reducing spending (efficiency) and thwarting political machines (democracy). The reformers tried to achieve these ends by shifting the location of budget-making power.

The Civil War was followed by rapid urbanization, competition for railroad connections, and a frenzy of boosterism. When a recession began in 1873, many cities found themselves with heavy debt burdens and failed railroad investments. Taxpayers did not have the resources to keep paying for city services and debt repayment and, in some cases, just stopped paying taxes (Platt 1983). The pressure to reduce spending was tremendous.

One of the early steps taken to keep expenditures down was to disempower city councils with respect to the budget because councils would push up expenditures. At the same time, there was no desire to strengthen the chief executive, because a strong mayor might become a boss. One result was the creation of Boards of Estimate and Apportionment, first seen in New York City in 1873 (Viteritti 1989). These boards typically combined the mayor, an elected controller, the president of the board of aldermen, and other officials and sometimes citizens in one budgeting board. Governmental spending was virtually impossible unless there was widespread consensus that it occur.

As municipal problems grew worse and remained unaddressed, and as the memory of the 1873 recession began to fade, pressure for more activist and efficient forms of budgeting grew. In cities that had adopted Boards of Estimate, the mayors were gradually given control over a majority of the board through appointment power. For example, in 1893 in New York City, the mayor gained control of the Board of Estimate through the appointment of a majority of the board. In cities that had no Board of Estimates, the mayor's budgeting power was gradually strengthened, while the councils were generally kept weak in an effort to control patronage and the spending demands of the poor (Rochester Bureau of Municipal Research 1923: 11; Griffith 1974: 181; Schiesl 1977: 105).

By the beginning of the Progressive Era, around the turn of the century, the role of the public in budgeting became more directly relevant. Efforts to disempower the councils and keep out the poor were accompanied by efforts to allow the *real* public to express its will. For example, Baltimore stripped the council of budget power (Rea 1929; Hollander 1899) in an effort to keep out machines and the poor and, in doing so, allow the real public to directly influence and control government (Crooks 1968). A number of reforms were passed, including direct primaries, Australian ballots, and laws against corrupt election judges and payments for votes. Underlying this model was a belief that the dominant force necessary to achieve good government was an "enlightened and organized public sentiment" (85).

The budget reformers of the New York Bureau of Municipal Research, a business-funded research and reform group who were trying to improve budgeting in New York City from 1907 to about 1915, emphasized this antimachine, direct role of the public. The public was to be educated to budgetary issues, they were to inform public officials of what they wanted the government to provide in the way of services, and they were to act as a backstop if government officials did not do as they were supposed to. Public accounting was to be improved so that reporting to the public would be interpretable and comprehensive; these reports would allow the public to see what was right and what was wrong and how their money had been spent. Budget exhibits, not unlike fairs, were put on to show the public what kinds of services were being performed and at what costs, to get the public involved in the issues (Allen 1950: 165).

These New York Bureau reformers also emphasized New England town meeting–type public participation and control and insisted that budget hearings take place early enough in the decision making to influence outcomes (Cleveland 1898, 1913; Allen 1908, 1917). Machines were seen as distorting the true citizen input (Cleveland 1909); direct, unmediated citizen input was seen as a way of keeping government honest (Cleveland 1913). But it required active government effort to educate the public and make them interested (Allen 1950).

Recommendations for more public participation earlier in the budget process did not catch on. Many cities did hold pro forma hearings later in the budget process but reported that citizens were generally uninterested in them (Buck 1929: 393). In a few cities, however, the mayor or manager attempted to stir up interest by holding public meetings on the budget in different parts of the community while the council was considering the budget. The mayor would explain the budgetary proposals and invite questions and criticisms. The pattern of holding pro forma hearings relatively late in the budget process and then complaining that the citizens were uninterested has persisted until the present.

Some of the public participation reforms, such as requirements for referenda for bond or tax increases, remain in place. They result in the possibility of voicing disapproval but not much opportunity for the citizens to steer government budgeting in a positive direction. The combination of efficiency and democracy that was worked out allowed the general voting public to say no.

Tax Resistance: The Exercise of the "No" Option

While everyone grumbles about taxes, most of the time, they pay them. Sometimes, however, the democratic consensus about taxes disintegrates. Breakdowns often occur during or just after a lengthy period of rapid increase in government spending. The expansion may be accompanied by large amounts of borrowing. Tax burdens that were carried comfortably during a period of general prosperity become intolerable when recession reduces citizens' ability to pay for the greatly enlarged taxes. The pattern of expenditure growth followed by recession contributing to tax protests characterized the 1870s and the 1930s.

Assessment practices have also contributed to tax resistance. Assessment practices have often been political and irregular. Citizens were buffered by the political process and infrequent assessments from increases in assessed valuation. The improvement of assessment practices in the early years of this century created pressure on taxpayers. For example, personal property was supposed to be taxed in many states at the same rate as real estate; but most personal property had escaped reporting. Since real estate taxes had to be higher to compensate for the lower personal property tax rolls, the threat of applying the same rate to personal property and forcing it on the roll suggested near confiscation of profits, motivating frantic efforts to limit taxes. Also, efforts to bring assessments up to 100 percent of sales value created fear that property tax rates would not be reduced to compensate for the increased assessed valuation, creating pressure to mandate property tax rate limits as a condition of reforming assessment practices.

The reform of assessments was often done clumsily. In Chicago in the late 1920s, assessment was challenged by taxpayers, resulting in the suspension of collections for several years, followed by efforts to speed up payments thereafter, threatening taxpayers severely, and contributing to a widespread tax revolt (Beito 1989; Simpson 1930). Rapid growth in population and rapidly increased assessed valuations contributed to the Proposition 13 tax limitation movement in California in the 1970s.

While periods of tax resistance have often looked similar despite the passage of time, there have also been some long-term changes that have influenced successive waves of tax resistance. Over time, more people in the country could afford to buy homes, increasing the popular base for a tax revolt. Partly in response to this massive pressure, cities have reduced their dependence on property taxes, increasing their reliance on sales taxes and fees, shifting the burden of taxes more onto consumers and the poor, and shifting the political configuration of tax resistance.

Episodes of Tax Resistance. The first wave of tax resistance related to municipal budgeting occurred in the 1870s and 1880s. Taxpayers, strapped by the recession in 1873, were unable to pay for the burdens of increased expenditures. A second period of major property tax protest occurred in response to both the spending increases of the Progressive Era and the improvements in assessment processes that marked the early decades of this century. A third major antitax period occurred during the early years of the Great Depression. More recently, the 1970s marked a renewal of tax protests (Merriman 1987).[2] A few examples of tax resistance illustrate their political dynamics.

In Houston, the civic elite paid taxes and controlled expenditures. They demanded projects they wanted and were willing to pay for. The recession that began in 1873 ruptured this relationship; not only were the elite unwilling and unable to continue to pay for bonds they had supported in the past, but when they withdrew support, the council and mayor realized that services had to continue, that city hall served some other purpose than the developmental goals of the city's business elite, namely, to serve a broader public. The tension between service delivery, taxpayer pressure, and bondholder pressure made it clear that there were at least three distinct groups pressuring for different public policies where before there had been only one (Platt 1983).

Ohio's 1 percent law was an example of the second wave of tax limits, just after the Progressive Era. The cause this time was the expansion of spending during the Progressive period combined with efforts to reform property tax assessments (Atkinson 1923; Wilcox 1922). Many other states besides Ohio reacted in a similar way. Nine states had adopted statutory or constitutional limits on property taxation between 1871 and 1880, and the 6 new states admitted shortly thereafter followed the pattern of putting property tax restrictions in their constitutions, but by 1924, 40 states had maximum property tax levies and others had restrictions on the rate of growth in levies and maximum per capita spending (Merriman 1987: 17).

A whole wave of property tax limitations occurred during the Great Depression, in response to declining assessments and property owners' fears of losing their property because of their inability to pay taxes. At least 13 states imposed new or tightened restrictions on local governments' ability to levy property taxes. Large taxpayers and realty companies lobbied heavily to reduce property taxes substantially (21). The effect was often major cuts in operating expenditures and shifts to other sources of revenue, which often fell more heavily on the poor (Merriman 1987: 21; Atkinson, in Leet and Paige 1936: 74). In some cases (as in Indiana), these new limitations were adopted directly by the state legislature. In other cases, popular agitation played a larger role. In Iowa, at least 50,000 people signed petitions urging adoption of a 10–mill property tax limit being considered by the legislature (Merriman 1987: 21).

The fourth major period of tax limitation occurred during the 1970s. Between 1970 and 1976, nine states adopted levy limits, and one state adopted an expenditure lid. In 1978, six states passed tax limits including California's Proposition 13 (27). In 1980, Massachusetts passed Proposition 2½, and voters in

Missouri approved the Hancock amendment, which required that local citizens must approve any local tax, license, or fee increase (28).

Not all the tax limits resulted from tax protests. Some authors have argued that the increase in state aid to local governments that characterized the period justified tighter state administrative control over local taxing and spending to prevent squandering of the new state aid (25–26). In some states, such as New Jersey, the state legislature sought to win voter approval of alternate taxes by holding down the property tax burden. In New Jersey, in 1973, a court mandated equalization of education, requiring state funding. To fund the schools the state had to enact a state income tax, but to gain enough support for it, proponents agreed to limit increases in county property tax levies to 5 percent, municipal appropriations to 5 percent, and increases in state government spending to the percentage increase in per capita income. The purpose of the county and municipal caps was to prevent these government units from interfering with the property tax relief that the state legislature wished to generate through new school aids. The cap on state spending reportedly was motivated by a sense of fairness.

But in a number of states it was the citizens who demanded an end to accelerating assessments and property tax bills. Economic stagnation combined with inflation pushed up housing prices more quickly than incomes, creating taxpayer pressure to control property tax rates and assessments. Reassessment practices exaggerated these problems (Peters and Rose 1980: 33–51; Peters 1980: 23–48; Sears and Citrin 1985). Equally important, homeownership was more widespread among the population than in earlier years, helping to create broader political coalitions looking for property tax relief. Smaller homeowners did not benefit proportionally from the tax limitations in California, however (Lo 1990).

Summary. Each cycle of tax resistance has been a little different from the others. In some periods, it has been aimed at holding back growth in property tax levels; at other times, it has been aimed at massive reduction in levies and rates. At times the tax resistance was led by a narrow group of elite taxpayers who controlled city hall; at other times, realtors and large property owners led the resistance. In more recent times, the coalitions have continued to broaden as homeownership expanded, increasing the number of those affected by property taxation.

As property taxes have been curtailed, states have generally allowed local governments new sources of revenue, and cities have of necessity diversified their revenue sources. This diversification has created the possibility of new coalitions, broader than property owners and more inclusive of the poor. Missouri's 1980 tax limitation measure required a vote on any tax or fee increase, not just property taxes. The politics of taxation in St. Louis suggests that the poorer part of the population is reluctant to vote more taxes on itself for a spending policy that benefits primarily large corporations and economic developers. They have had little control over spending and have refused to pay additional taxes. As the poor pay a larger proportion of the tax burden, it seems only reasonable that they should increase their power over spending and taxing decisions.

The changing nature of the burden of local taxes and tax resistance has outlined a concept of spending by and for whom. In the early years, there was often a congruence between elite property tax payers and the deciders of how public money would be spent; their definition of what the public sector should spend on was what would benefit them, including the construction of wharves, roads, and public markets. That congruence gradually eroded as a dependent population came to need public services that they were not paying for directly.

The well-to-do became increasingly unwilling to pay property taxes to the extent that they felt they could no longer control spending and that the tax revenue was being spent on the poor. The property tax shrank as a proportion of total taxation, and a broader group of public service consumers paid a larger share of municipal taxes. Elites who managed to retain control over spending taxed the general populace, including the poor, to benefit themselves, controlling spending policies. But that broader group, now paying taxes through the purchase of goods and services, seems to have said, at least in St. Louis, ''We don't have to approve increased spending that ignores our goals.'' Ironically, at least in Missouri, successful property tax protest has given the poor a voice, even if just to say no.

Internal Restructuring: Mayors, Budget Offices, and Departments

A third theme in the budget literature is the relationship between the chief executive, the budget office, and the departments, and how and why these relationships have changed.

Mayors (and later, managers) gradually took increased control over budgeting. The Progressive Era emphasis on efficient spending shifted to the post-Progressive effort to hold down spending levels. The executives began to wonder how to control the departments' budget requests.

Arthur Buck reported in 1929 that only a few large cities, such as New York, Detroit, and Boston, had established budget offices (290). These offices did not generally set out limits for the departments, so the budget process began with a request for estimates from the departments (301–302). But as early as 1922, with the advent of the city manager government in Berkeley, California, the budget office and the city manager began to set targets for the departments (307). This innovation in Berkeley is what is now called target-based budgeting (Rubin 1991).

Changes in the budgetary relationship between the executive and the departments came more slowly to strong mayor cities and cities with Boards of Estimate than to city manager cities. But even in these cities, the relationship with the departments has changed. Two examples, from St. Louis and Boston, illustrate these changes.

St. Louis still uses the Board of Estimate from that was first adopted in New York City in 1873. The Board of Estimate exercises almost complete control over the budget. Yet within this structure, the mayor has been able to negotiate a leadership position and has gradually taken control over the budget office, which formally reports to the whole Board of Estimate but in fact reports to the mayor, and has increased the mayor's control over the departments.

The shift to having the budget office report to the mayor began in the early 1970s and was completed in the early 1980s. In the early 1980s, the departments still formulated their own budgets, but Mayor Vincent Schoemehl, elected in 1981, changed the pattern by picking his own department heads and weakening the commissioner system. He transferred some of the commissioners and per-suaded others to be more amenable (Rubin and Stein 1990: 423; Rubin 1992: 462). By 1987, the budget director had created a program and performance budget. This format helped make policy goals in the budget more visible and more achievable within the constraints of very tight budgets. Strengthening the budget office with respect to the departments was a central part of Schoemehl's strategy.

Boston has a strong mayor form. Mayor Ray Flynn's budget office introduced a program and performance format in 1986. Flynn was reacting both to a string of deficits that had plagued the city for years and to the business community's charge that he was uninterested in management. He convened a private sector task force shortly after his election in 1985; they recommended a series of changes in financial management, most of which the mayor adopted. The re-forms were implemented from the top down. The formerly decentralized de-partments were just told to do it (Rubin 1992: 461).

Making the departments responsive to the mayor's policy objectives was part of the intent of Boston's budget reforms. "The idea was to help the departments improve their management simultaneously with making them more accountable to the strategic goals of the mayor" (461).

This combination of trying to hold costs down and service levels up through improved budgetary management and at the same time make departments more responsive to the mayor's policy initiatives within a highly constrained budget has been a powerful incentive for centralization of budgetary power in the may-or's hands and the consequent empowerment of the budget office with respect to the departments.

In recent years, combinations of tax revolts, more volatile revenue sources, and deep and long recessions have impacted many cities, not only in the North-east and Midwest but also in the Southwest. Budgeting has had to be able to help prioritize cutbacks and minimize damage to operations. Over the past de-cade and a half, there has been increased emphasis on zero-based budgeting and particularly on target-based budgeting, which has become quite widespread.

Target-based budgeting strengthens the budget office's ability to set totals and keep request levels down but strengthens the departments' ability to make man-agerial choices within those overall limits. This division of responsibility impresses upon the department the need to keep service levels up within limited resources, without the budget office trying to second-guess managers and without forcing the managers to play games with the budget office to get needed expenses. The explicit focus of target-based budgeting is to hold down expenses and to create some flexibility during tight times by creating a system of rank-ordered unfunded priorities that can be supported by slight overcutting and by underestimates of revenue. But the implicit focus of target-based budgeting has been to realign the power of the budget office and the department heads and to keep each doing what they do best. As a result, this budget procedure has been welcomed both in overcentralized city manager cities, as a relief to departments who gain badly needed autonomy, and in less reformed cities, where game playing between departments and the budget office has made budgeting look like an irrational (not nonrational) process.

DIRECTIONS FOR FUTURE RESEARCH

Since the 1970s, there has been a marked effort to increase the influence on budgeting of ethnic groups who were intentionally blocked from such influence in earlier periods. Councils have been changed from completely at-large elections to partly at-large, partly district in a number of cities to make minority representation easier. But these efforts come on top of years of structuring budget processes to keep the poor out. The budgetary powers of the councils have not necessarily increased to accommodate the new council members, and the recent periods of acute fiscal stress in many central cities have further limited the potential impact of these changes. Carolyn Adams has described how limited and symbolic the impact of the council members has been in Philadelphia over capital spending, because the money is just not there (Adams 1988). Nevertheless, the direction of recent change has been to add back the council as a budget actor in some capacity in cities that have disempowered the councils. How widespread have these efforts been, and how successful? Have the councils added staff or hired consultants or municipal research bureaus to give them more sophistication in understanding the budget? In more reformed cities, such as Phoenix, how has the partly at-large, partly district election system worked, especially in budgeting? Has it helped represent neighborhoods and ethnic and racial groups in the budget? How do these structural changes compare with the direct involvement and education of citizens to play a decision-making role in budgeting, such as occurs in Dayton? Has the demise of political machines made the representation of the poor in city decision making less threatening? Have any of these efforts improved budgeting or made it worse?

Has there been a change in the political power exerted by the relatively less well-to-do to the extent that they pay a larger share of the local tax burden? How common is the St. Louis model, in which a white mayor cut services and increased spending on major economic development projects, opposed by a black population that felt squeezed out of city benefits? How has budgeting changed with a shift to a black mayor?

To what extent is the so-called tax revolt a reflection of the shifting tax burden, where more people and new people are feeling increased burdens relative to their income? Or are citizens less likely to feel the gap between income and taxation in sales taxes than in property taxes? Are more taxes being hidden, as, for example, new housing prices reflect developer fees, which citizens probably do not see as taxation? Has the public sector response to tax revolt been more an increase in accountability and citizen involvement in decision making or more an effort to make taxes less visible and more comfortable, paid a little at a time, so citizens don't see the total anywhere? What determines the balance of the response? How much is constrained by state laws? Are we solving the tax revolt? Was the tax revolt the result of inability to pay taxes that were rising more quickly than income, or anger at government, to the extent that these are separable attitudes? To what extent is the answer to tax revolt to limit the functions of government and to what extent it is to make government more accountable and more responsive? Will tax revolt be dampened if government solves problems that citizens want addressed, like fixing potholes, clean and safe drinking water, low crime rates, and convenient transportation? Is target-based budgeting successfully addressing both these models, by keeping overall spending down and simultaneously creating flexibility to pursue a limited number of policy advertised mayoral policy priorities?

Policy making through the budget process has become common. What has been the impact of that policy-making process? Have mayors been able to make a difference? Or is the scope of their authority so limited that their policy initiatives are mostly symbolic? What has been the content of the mayor's policies, as reflected in the budget? How has this policy content been presented in the budget? How has it varied from city to city, and from one administration to another within the same city? Are mayors simply trying to carry out campaign promises, or are they doing "policy analysis" in an effort to solve problems, or both? If there is policy analysis, is it done in the budget office, or elsewhere; and if elsewhere, how is it integrated into the budget?

Overall, we need better understanding of what has been happening to municipal budgeting, how cities have been responding to widespread problems such as tax resistance, and what responses seem to have been working. Fear of political machines has ebbed; that may make it an appropriate time to restore power to councils and to citizens. Such a restoration should not only regenerate local democracy; it may also renew citizen willingness to pay for highly desirable public services such as bridges, highways, and schools.

NOTES

1. These themes are not inclusive. In particular, the struggles over state supervision and control of local budgeting have been omitted, but they are presented elsewhere (Rubin 1994).

2. Merriman's periods of tax and expenditure limitation play down the importance of the postprogressive reaction, while my own periodization emphasizes this period. The

difference in approach is based on the severity of the constraints; Merriman found the constraints during this period to be milder than during earlier and later periods. My periodization is based on the number of tax limits passed rather than their severity.

REFERENCES

Adams, Carolyn Teich. 1988. *The Politics of Capital Investment: The Case of Philadelphia.* 202. Albany, NY: SUNY Press.

Allen, William H. 1908. *Efficient Democracy.* New York: Dodd, Mead.

Allen, William H. 1917. " 'The Budget Amendment of the Maryland Constitution.' " *National Municipal Review* 6, no. 4: 485–491.

Allen, William H. 1950. *Reminiscences.* Oral History Collection, Housed at Columbia University. Microfiche.

Atkinson, Raymond C. 1923. "The Effects of Tax Limitation upon Local Finance in Ohio 1911–1922." Ph.D. dissertation, Columbia University, Cleveland. Offset.

Beito, David. 1989. *Taxpayers in Revolt: Tax Resistance during the Great Depression.* Chapel Hill: University of North Carolina Press.

Buck, Arthur E. 1929. *Public Budgeting.* New York: Harper.

Cleveland, Frederick A. 1898. *The Growth of Democracy in the United States or the Evolution of Popular Cooperation in Government and Its Results.* Chicago: Quadrangle Press.

Cleveland, Frederick A. 1909. Dimensions of Accounting Theory and Practice. New York: Longmans, Green. (Arno Reprint: 1980: *Chapters on Municipal Administration and Accounting*)

Cleveland, Frederick A. 1913. *Organized Democracy: An Introduction to the Study of American Politics.* New York: Longmans, Green, and Co.

Cleveland, Frederick A. 1915. "Evolution of the Budget Idea in the United States." *The Annals of the American Academy of Political and Social Science* 62 (November): 15–35.

Cogan, John E., Timothy J. Muris, and Allen Schick. 1994. *The Budget Puzzle: Understanding Federal Spending.* Stanford, CA: Stanford University Press.

Crooks, James B. 1968. *Politics and Progress: The Rise of Urban Progressivism in Baltimore, 1895–1911.* Baton Rouge: Louisiana State University Press.

Fairlie, John. 1923. "The Separation of Powers." *Michigan Law Review* 21 (February): 1–44.

Fisher, Louis. 1975. *Presidential Spending Power.* Princeton: Princeton University Press.

Ford, Henry Jones. 1915. "Budget Making and the Work of Government." *The Annals of the American Academy of Political and Social Science* 62 (November): 1–14.

Goodnow, Frank J. 1913. "The Limit of Budgetary Control." *American Political Science Review, Supplement* 7 (February): 68–77.

Griffith, Ernest Stacey. 1994. *History of American City Government: The Progressive Years and Their Aftermath, 1900–1920.* New York: Praeger.

Hollander, J. H. 1899. *The Financial History of Baltimore.* Johns Hopkins University Studies in Historical and Political Science. Baltimore: Johns Hopkins Press.

Hyde, Albert C., ed. 1992. *Governmental Budgeting.* 2nd ed. Pacific Grove, CA: Brooks/Cole.

Leet, Glen, and Robert Paige, eds. 1936. *Property Tax Limitation Laws.* Statements by

24 Authorities. Public Administration Service, no. 36. Chicago: Public Administration Service.

Lo, Clarence Y. H. 1990. *Small Property versus Big Government: Social Origins of the Property Tax Revolt*. Berkeley: University of California Press.

Merriman, David. 1987. *The Control of Municipal Budgets*. New York: Quorum.

Peters, B. Guy. 1980. "Fiscal Strains on the Welfare State: Causes and Consequences." In Charles H. Levine and Irene S. Rubin, eds., *Fiscal Stress and Public Policy*. Beverly Hills: Sage. 23–48.

Peters, B. Guy, and Rose Richard. 1980. "The Growth of Government and the Political Consequences of Economic Overload." In Charles H. Levine, ed., *Managing Fiscal Stress*. Chatham, NJ: Chatham House. 33–51.

Platt, Harold. 1983. *City Building in the New South: The Growth of Public Services in the Houston, Texas, 1830–1910*. Philadelphia: Temple University Press.

Rea, Leonard Owens. 1929. *The Financial History of Baltimore 1900–1926*. Johns Hopkins University Studies in Historical and Political Science. Baltimore: Johns Hopkins Press.

Rochester Bureau of Municipal Research. 1923. *Report of the Study of the Financial Condition and Practices of the City of Rochester*. Rochester, NY: Rochester Bureau.

Rubin, Irene S. 1991. "Budgeting for Our Times: Target Based Budgeting." *Public Budgeting and Finance* 11 (fall): 5–14.

Rubin, Irene. 1992. "Budget Reform and Political Reform: Conclusions from Six Cities." *Public Administration Review* 52 (September–October): 454–466.

Rubin, Irene. 1994. "State Controls over Local Budgeting." Paper presented at the Urban Affairs Meeting at New Orleans, March 3, 1994.

Rubin, Irene S., ed. 1988. *New Directions in Budget Theory*. Albany: State University of New York Press.

Rubin, Irene S., and Lana Stein. 1990. "Budget Reform in St. Louis: Why Does Budgeting Change?" *Public Administration Review* 50 (July–August): 420–426.

Schick, Allen. 1980. *Congress and Money*. Washington, D.C.: Urban Institute.

Schick, Allen. 1990. *The Capacity to Budget*. Washington D.C.: Urban Institute Press.

Schick, Allen. 1995. *The Federal Budget: Politics, Policy, and Process*. Washington, D.C.: Brookings.

Schick, Allen, ed. 1987. *Perspectives on Budgeting*. 2nd ed. Washington, D.C.: American Society for Public Administration.

Schiesl, Martin. 1977. *The Politics of Efficiency: Municipal Administration and Reform in America 1800–1920*. Berkeley: University of California Press.

Sears, David O., and Jack Citrin. 1985. *Tax Revolt: Something for Nothing in California*. 2nd ed. Cambridge: Harvard University Press.

Simpson, Herbert D. 1930. *Tax Racket and Tax Reform in Chicago*. Chicago: Institute of Economic Research.

Viteritti, Joseph P. 1989. "The Tradition of Municipal Reform: Charter Revision in Historical Context." In Frank Mauro and Gerald Benjamin, eds., *Restructuring the New York City Government*. New York: Academy of Political Science.

Wilcox, Clair. 1922. "Rate Limitation and the General Property Tax in Ohio." Master's thesis, Ohio State University.

Wildavsky, Aaron. 1964. *The Politics of the Budgetary Process*. Boston: Little, Brown.

Part III

Development

Chapter 17

Urban Economy

Cynthia Negrey

OVERVIEW

As urban economies in the United States have grown, been transformed, declined, and diversified over the course of the twentieth century, urban scholars have documented those processes and addressed their theoretical significance. Topical issues such as the relationship between industrialization and urbanization and metropolitan growth have received considerable attention in the past, and today the most pressing economic issues facing urban scholars have to do with the consequences for urban areas of structural economic changes, such as the shift from manufacturing to services, the microelectronic revolution, and the globalization of production.

Structural economic changes have affected the nature and types of jobs available to workers in the United States. Today manufacturing jobs make up a smaller portion of overall employment than just a few decades ago; and jobs in the service sector have grown dramatically, constituting the vast majority of all employment. Although some professionals who provide services (for example, physicians and attorneys) have reasonably secure jobs that pay high salaries, many jobs in the service sector are unstable, low wage, and part-time (for example, retail clerks in stores). The microelectronic revolution has affected how Americans work. Computer-driven technologies have increased productivity in manufacturing facilities, permitting the production of more goods with fewer workers. Microcomputers are widespread in offices and retail outlets as well, enhancing the productivity of clerical workers, clerks, and managers. With the globalization of production, increasing numbers of unskilled jobs that used to be performed in the United States are now done in developing countries where labor costs are substantially lower (see Hodson and Sullivan [1995] for a comprehensive overview of changes in employment and occupations).

Scholars interested in the consequences of such structural economic changes for urban areas have worked from within two major theoretical perspectives—human ecology and urban political economy.[1] As will be discussed in more detail below, urban political economy is the dominant theoretical framework today. A social conflict–oriented approach, it emerged in the 1960s in reaction to the ecological approach. That approach had favored an interpretation of competitive markets as the driving force behind urban development with little attention given to class conflict.

THEORETICAL APPROACHES

Human Ecology

Frisbie and Kasarda (1988) have provided an excellent comprehensive overview of the vast literature generated by human ecologists. Here I will review only that subset that bears most directly on the subject of urban economy.

The Chicago School of human ecology originated early in the twentieth century at a time of tremendous urban and economic growth in the United States. Industrialization accelerated near the end of the nineteenth century when the nation's resources were mobilized for manufacturing production and urban centers exploded with rapid population growth and the influx of immigrants (Reich 1983: 23–43). At that time, factory districts and population centers were concentrated near one another in the dense urban core, as modes of transportation of the day did not permit regular distant passenger travel. At the turn of the century 60 percent of the American population was rural, but by 1920 slightly more than half of the population resided in urban areas (Frisbie and Kasarda 1988: 630). Population and commercial activity began to disperse as less expensive land became available beyond the urban core, infrastructure developed, and transportation improved.

Sociologists Robert Park (1936), Ernest Burgess (1925), Louis Wirth (1928), and others posited community models designed to describe and explain urban growth and the composition of subareas within cities. Those early human ecologists conceived of the city as in part analogous to a biological organism. They believed that cities evolved in space in response to competitive forces in the urban land market in a process similar to that by which organisms evolve in response to natural selection. Thus, urban areas were dynamic adaptive systems in which competition served as the principal organizing force (Frisbie and Kasarda 1988: 632). In an era during which the ideology of laissez-faire predominated, industries and commercial institutions competed for strategic locations that provided them with economic advantages. The result was spatial differentiation and segregation of various industries, social classes, and activity patterns into relatively homogeneous "natural areas" that evolved not through planning or design but primarily through competition in the marketplace (Frisbie and Kasarda 1988: 632).

The classical models of urban growth—concentric zone theory (Burgess 1925), sector theory (Hoyt 1939), and multiple nuclei theory (Harris and Ullman 1945; Ullman and Harris 1970)—were precursors to numerous studies of metropolitan growth (especially Duncan et al. 1960) that sought to understand the nature of the national system of metropolitan areas (Wanner 1977; South and Poston 1980, 1982), the functions each area serves for the social system overall (Bean, Poston, and Winsborough 1972), and the interrelationships among the various metropolitan areas (Eberstein and Frisbie 1982; Meyer 1984, 1986; Marshall and Stahura 1986). Drawing on structural-functionalist (Durkheim 1933; Parsons 1951) concepts of functional specialty and social stability, human ecologists conceived of metropolitan areas as performing differentiated specialized economic functions, derived from each locale's neoclassical economic ''comparative advantage,'' which contributed to the perpetuation of the national system as a whole.

In addition to exploring a national system of metropolitan areas, human ecologists have studied continuing population deconcentration and the polycentric metropolitan form (Hall and Hays 1980; Van den Berg et al. 1982; Edmonston and Guterbock 1984) and the revival of nonmetropolitan areas (Beale 1975; Frisbie and Poston 1975, 1978; Kasarda 1980; Wilson 1984), particularly as those population patterns are coterminous with the dispersal of economic activity from the urban core and the information flows associated with electronic communication (Calhoun 1986; Kasarda 1980).

Urban Political Economy

In the late 1960s the second and more critical of the two prominent theoretical approaches emerged, that of urban political economy. Walton (1993) provides an excellent comprehensive overview of this perspective. As he notes, urban crises—such as racial segregation and conflict, poverty, and riots—that could not be explained by the ecological approach fostered an intellectual crisis among urban scholars and spawned a paradigm shift. The old ecological theory emerged from and ''was designed for an era of migrant adaptation, urban growth and differentiation, social mobility, and community'' (302). But the urban crises of the 1960s demanded a theoretical perspective to explain social inequality and unrest. The new approach was informed by the writings of Karl Marx ([1867] 1977) and, particularly in the United States, C. Wright Mills (1956). Marx's work especially gave urban scholars a perspective from which to understand the social relations of production under capitalism and from which to analyze those relations as the economic base from which much social inequality and conflict arise. Sociologist Manuel Castells (1975, 1977, 1983, 1989) and geographer David Harvey (1973, 1985a, 1985b) were among the first and most influential writers in this tradition who sought to develop a structural explanation of urbanization and to understand "urban form and process in the workings of capital accumulation" (Walton 1993: 302). Such a structural approach locates urbanization within the context of "the quest for profit and domination, and the state's attempts to moderate domestic conflict between social classes" (Zukin 1980: 579).[2] Castells argued that "there was a unity to urban phenomena that lay in the connection between spatial relations and the process of collective consumption" (Walton 1993: 305), and Harvey conceived of urbanization as "the uniquely modern mechanism of capitalist accumulation" (305). As Walton summarizes Harvey:

The urban process under capitalism arises from the interplay of accumulation and class struggle. Thus, the "built environment" is produced to serve production, circulation, and consumption. It changes in response to periodic and inherent crises which invigorate class struggles nascent in a continuous process of uneven development. What we see and reify as the city is a physical network of factories, stores, offices, schools, and roads, all hitched to the primary function of accumulating capital and all vulnerable to decay understood as devaluation (e.g., abandoned plants or railroads) stemming from failing [*sic*] profits and the obligation of capital to plow new circuits. Change results from crises which are costly in terms of devaluation and the resistance of those left behind by the next cycle. (308)

David Gordon applied the urban political economy perspective to the history of American cities and examined the "historical links between capitalism and urban development" (1978: 27). He argued that the United States has passed through three stages of capital accumulation, and urban development has passed through three corresponding stages. Thus, he identified the commercial city, which dated from the colonial era to the midnineteenth century; the industrial city, which dated from the middle to late twentieth century; and the corporate city, from about 1920. Transitions from one stage to the next were characterized by problems in the capital accumulation process itself, especially the ability of the capitalist class to retain control of production. As such, capital accumulation and class struggle are major factors in urban development.

CURRENT STATE OF THE FIELD

Today urban political economy is the dominant theoretical perspective in the scholarly study of urban economy, and its adherents have generated numerous insightful case studies of major U.S. and international cities. In the 1970s and early 1980s much energy was directed toward analysis of the growth of "Sunbelt" cities (Feagin 1985; Perry and Watkins 1977; Sawers and Tabb 1984). More recently, many case studies have focused on the consequences of economic restructuring for particular urban areas. Fainstein et al. (1986), for example, provide comparative historical case studies of New Haven, Detroit, New Orleans, Denver, and San Francisco. All five were local industrial economies attempting in the late twentieth century to reorient to a service economy. All five also have substantial minority and lower-income populations. They differ, however, in political histories and government efforts to restructure the local economy in the face of structural economic change. Logan and Swanstrom (1990) extend that theme in a volume that examines economic restructuring as a diverse, global process. They argue there are "many species of restructuring" because urban regions have different regimes of governance and labor relations, they are tied to different sorts of multinational firms, and they have different relations to national governments whose principal institutions are dissimilar (5).

Several authors (Hill and Indergaard 1987; Hill and Negrey 1987, 1989, 1991; Koritz 1991; Moore and Laramore 1990; Negrey and Zickel 1994; Peterson and Vroman 1992; Stanback 1985; Wallace and Rothschild 1988) have examined the consequences for urban areas of deindustrialization—defined by Bluestone and Harrison (1982: 6) as "widespread, systematic disinvestment in the nation's basic productive capacity"—noting patterns of overall employment change as related to decreases in manufacturing employment, uneven development, and skill composition of the available labor pool. Contributors to a volume edited by Smith and Feagin (1987) examine Buffalo, New York City, Detroit, Houston, and Los Angeles in the context of a changing global economy and shifting international division of labor.

The intellectual struggle to make sense of a diverse network of urban areas, linked together in the organizational web of transnational corporations (Smith and Feagin 1987: 4) and transnational market spaces (Sassen 1994: xiv), has spawned a number of typologies that seek to capture the essence of U.S. urban economies undergoing fundamental structural transformation. These typologies differ from the national system of metropolitan areas identified by human ecologists in that urban political economists see economic differences across locales as products of uneven development, not necessary functional specialty. Uneven development is understood as a process endemic to capitalism, which concentrates and centralizes capital in some areas and creates social and economic crisis in areas where disinvestment occurs (Marx [1867] 1977; Walton 1987: 93–94).

In Mollenkopf's (1983) typology, there are three broad types of urban economies in the postwar United States: old cities, which were historically major industrial centers that never became administrative and service nodes; new cities, concentrated largely in the American Southwest with no industrial legacy, that grew during and after World War II as a result of expanding high-technology industries in the region; and mixed cities, with characteristics of both the old and new, representing historically significant production centers that developed strong corporate, banking, and health and human services activities. Stanback (1985) developed a more complex typology by examining employment change from 1976 to 1983 and classifying metropolitan areas into six major categories: (1) nodal cities, having diverse services economies; (2) functional-nodal centers, areas combining manufacturing and specialized services; (3) government-education centers, which are state capitals, major university communities, or both; (4) education-manufacturing centers, which are traditional manufacturing centers with important local universities; (5) production centers, specializing in routine manufacturing processes or mining with administrative functions; and (6) resort-residential centers, which are retirement-vacation areas. Negrey and Zickel (1994), who analyze population and employment trends from the early 1970s to late 1980s for 140 metropolitan areas, distinguish classic deindustrializing centers, stable centers in transition, innovation centers, new services centers, and new manufacturing centers.

Much of the literature in the urban political economy tradition has been synthesized into a new theoretical treatment by Logan and Molotch (1987), dubbed the "growth-conflict" perspective (Feagin 1987: 517). They argue that the city is a commodity where exchange values and use values compete. As such, "place entrepreneurs" seek to sell the city, or at least strategic locations within it, for private gain—an objective often at odds with the more modest desires of residents who use the city to satisfy essential needs of life. That conflict determines the shape of the city, the distribution of people, and the way they live together. There is social conflict around the issue of growth because the advantages and disadvantages of growth are distributed unevenly.

With increased capital mobility and the lower capacity of government to enforce development conformity among localities, Logan and Molotch (1987: 258–277) foresee diverse urban conditions resulting from the uneven capacity of localities to attract growth. These diverse urban conditions are represented in the following types: headquarters cities, innovation centers, production modules, Third World entrepôts, and retirement centers.

DIRECTIONS FOR FUTURE RESEARCH

A conceptual gap rooted in different fundamental assumptions about economic and social relationships precludes much intellectual dialogue between human ecologists and urban political economists. Human ecologists draw their understanding of urban economies from the structural-functionalist notion that as societies industrialize, they become more differentiated; threats of fragmentation are counterbalanced by functional specialization and interdependence. Urban political economists, on the other hand, understand urban economies as products of profit seeking and class conflict. While human ecologists adopt the neoclassical assumption of self-regulating markets, urban political economists see markets as objects and subjects of class domination and resistance.

Although human ecologists continue to study economic processes, particularly as they affect population patterns, for the foreseeable future urban political economy will likely continue to be the most influential of the two theories. The latter's foundation in an understanding of capitalist relations of production and social conflict renders the theory most fitting in an era of economic volatility associated with structural economic change, corporate restructuring, technological innovation, and labor displacement and contingency. Yet the urban political economy tradition would be strengthened by the addition of more systematic examination of industries, occupations, labor markets, and ethgender (Geschwender 1992) groups. Much of the literature in that tradition is qualitative and theoretical in scope, and a strong theoretical foundation has been laid indeed. The many typologies are useful heuristic devices, but the underlying structure of urban economies remains vague and the subject of considerable conjecture. More concrete, systematic, comparative analysis of industries, occupations, labor markets, and ethgender groups across locales and across time is necessary for a thorough and far-reaching understanding of the consequences of structural economic change for urban areas.[3] While that research strategy renders theoretical issues of urbanism subordinate to theoretical issues of structural economic change, urban areas remain important as the particular contexts within which structural economic change occurs and because such change is manifest differently across locales (Negrey and Zickel 1994).

A study by Snow (1983) is a pertinent example. He analyzed the electronics industry in San Jose, California, particularly as offshore sourcing has affected employment opportunities and occupational distribution among ethgender groups there. In comparing electronics employment in the United States and San Jose, Snow found that overall employment growth in the industry in the United States masked declines among production workers and women. Snow's careful scrutiny of electronics employment in San Jose revealed shifting employment patterns among different occupational and ethgender groups despite overall employment growth in that metropolitan area.

A recent study by Mollenkopf and Castells (1991) presents a similar kind of analysis. To uncover the causes and consequences of emerging patterns of inequality in New York City, the authors examine class, race, ethnic, and gender divisions as they intersect with the city's economic transformation. They provide detailed analyses of employment and earnings trends among various ethgender groups within particular industries. They find that economic restructuring in New York City has produced an organizational nucleus of professionals and managers in the corporate, nonprofit, and public sectors composed disproportionately of white males who have benefited directly from the city's corporate economy. The remaining social strata are placed in increasingly diverse positions with a multiplicity of interests divided by race, ethnicity, nativity, and gender. Increasing fragmentation hinders political alliances between and among the organized core of professionals and managers and the disorganized periphery of varied ethgender groups (Mollenkopf and Castells 1991: 16–17).

More systematic, concrete, comparative studies would not only further the interests of accumulated knowledge, but they also could be useful to practitioners struggling to formulate meaningful urban policy (and labor policy) in a volatile economic climate. Theory development is, of course, an important and necessary academic exercise, but in an era of tight budgets, academicians are increasingly asked to justify their existence with "useful" research. Concrete, systematic, comparative examination of structural economic change takes urban scholars in that very direction.

NOTES

1. Urban economists, as distinct from urban political economists, reflect the ideology of their home discipline (economics) in that they tend to favor market solutions to urban problems and they generally accept uncritically the values of private profit and economic growth. In the 1960s the author of the first major urban economics text claimed that "economics is the last of the social sciences to recognize the city as an important unit for classification and analysis" (Thompson 1965: 431; see also Lineberry 1980: 301). In the very same edited collection, a prominent urban sociologist (Sjoberg 1965: 157) complimented his own discipline by suggesting that most urbanists would consider it the most theoretically fertile (Lineberry 1980: 301). Urban economics matured in the 1970s as an outgrowth of regional economics. As such, urban economists have shared the concerns of their forebears, particularly land use, location theory, housing, interregional movement of factors of production, transportation, and urban and regional growth. In addition, they have studied intrametropolitan development and the structure of urban areas, especially but not exclusively as those relate to race. Public finance and municipal service provision have also been rich areas of study for urban economists. Goldstein (1980) provides an excellent review of the accumulated body of work by urban economists. Recently, urban economists have begun to explore the consequences for economic growth of increased inequality between rich and poor, noting slower job and income growth in cities with wide wage inequities (Bernstein 1994). Relatedly, the economic ties between central cities and their suburbs (Savitch 1993) has become an important research topic as central cities struggle to find effective redevelopment strategies and seek to determine the extent to which their economic interests are distinct from or tied to those of the larger metropolitan area that envelopes them.

It also should be noted that urban economists differ from urban political economists not only in terms of ideological orientations underlying theoretical approaches to research problems. They also differ methodologically, with urban economists preferring highly quantitative econometric models and urban political economists favoring more qualitative interpretations. There is somewhat more compatibility between urban economists and human ecologists in that they tend to share an uncritical acceptance of self-regulating markets, and both groups tend to favor quantitative approaches. Because the human ecologists have sociology as their home discipline rather than economics, however, the human ecologists work from within a tradition of sociological theory rather than economic theory, and they place considerably more emphasis on population patterns.

Urban political economists whose principal theoretical concerns are community decision making and urban governance and not economic structure and process per se, such as Kantor (1988) and Peterson (1981), are also excluded from discussion in this chapter. Kantor and Peterson are both concerned with the relative (lesser) power of local government vis-à-vis corporate activity. While this author agrees with that analysis, the focus of this chapter is economic structure and process, not governance. Such analytic separation of economy and polity may be falsely dichotomous (Smith 1988), but I believe it is necessary in this brief treatment of urban economy.

2. Gottdiener (1985) criticizes both approaches: the human ecologists for being overly

technologically determinist and the political economists for being prone to seeing capitalist conspirators around every urban corner. Frisbie and Kasarda (1988) provide a useful discussion of Gottdiener's work in this regard. Swanstrom (1993) has also criticized urban political economists for being economic determinists.

3. Fainstein et al. (1986: v) have noted the difficulties associated with gaining funding for large projects when working from a critical theoretical paradigm.

REFERENCES

Beale, Calvin L. 1975. "The Revival of Population Growth in Nonmetropolitan America." Economic Development Division, Economic Research Service, U.S. Department of Agriculture (ERS605). Washington, D.C.: Government Printing Office.

Bean, Frank D., Dudley L. Poston, Jr., and Halliman H. Winsborough. 1972. "Size, Functional Specialization, and the Classification of Cities." *Social Science Quarterly* 53: 20–32.

Bernstein, Aaron. 1994. "Inequality: How the Gap between Rich and Poor Hurts the Economy." *Business Week*, August 14, 78–83.

Bluestone, Barry, and Bennett Harrison. 1982. *The Deindustrialization of America.* New York: Basic Books.

Burgess, Ernest W. 1925. "The Growth of the City." In Robert Park, Ernest Burgess, and Roderick D. McKenzie, eds., *The City*. Chicago: University of Chicago Press.

Calhoun, Craig J. 1986. "Computer Technology, Large Scale Social Integration and the Local Community." *Urban Affairs Quarterly* 8: 204–228.

Castells, Manuel. 1975. "Is There an Urban Sociology?" In C. Pickvance, ed., *Urban Sociology: Critical Essays*. New York: St. Martin's Press.

Castells, Manuel. 1977. *The Urban Question*. Cambridge, MA: MIT Press.

Castells, Manuel. 1983. *The City and the Grassroots: A Cross-cultural Theory of Urban Social Movements*. Berkeley: University of California Press.

Castells, Manuel. 1989. *The Informational City: Economic Restructuring and Urban Development*. London: Blackwell.

Duncan, Otis Dudley, W. Richard Scott, Stanley Lieberson, Beverly Duncan, and Hal H. Winsborough. 1960. *Metropolis and Region*. Baltimore: Johns Hopkins Press.

Durkheim, Emile. 1933. *The Division of Labor in Society*. Glencoe, IL: Free Press.

Eberstein, Isaac W., and W. Parker Frisbie. 1982. "Metropolitan Function and Interdependence in the U.S. Urban System." *Social Forces* 60: 676–700.

Edmonston, Barry, and Thomas M. Guterbock. 1984. "Is Suburbanization Slowing Down? Recent Trends in Population Deconcentration in U.S. Metropolitan Areas." *Social Forces* 62: 905–925.

Fainstein, Susan S., Norman I. Fainstein, Richard Child Hill, Dennis Judd, and Michael Peter Smith, eds. 1986. *Restructuring the City*. New York: Longman.

Feagin, Joe R. 1985. "The Socioeconomic Base of Urban Growth: The Case of Houston and the Oil Industry." *American Journal of Sociology* 90, no. 6: 1204–1230.

Feagin, Joe R. 1987. "Urban Political Economy: The New Paradigm Matures." *Contemporary Sociology* 16, no. 4: 517–519.

Frisbie, W. Parker, and John D. Kasarda. 1988. "Spatial Processes." In Neil J. Smelser, ed., *Handbook of Sociology*. Newbury Park, CA: Sage.

Frisbie, W. Parker, and Dudley L. Poston, Jr. 1975. "Components of Sustenance Organization and Nonmetropolitan Population Change." *American Sociological Review* 40: 773–784.

Frisbie, W. Parker, and Dudley L. Poston. 1978. *Sustenance Organization and Migration in Nonmetropolitan America.* Iowa City: Urban Community Resource Center.

Geschwender, James A. 1992. "Ethgender, Women's Waged Labor, and Economic Mobility." *Social Problems* 39, no. 1: 1–16.

Goldstein, Gerald S. 1980. "Recent Developments in Urban Economics." *American Behavioral Scientist* 24, no. 2: 228–276.

Gordon, David M. 1978. "Capitalist Development and the History of American Cities." In William K. Tabb and Larry Sawers, eds., *Marxism and the Metropolis.* 1st ed. New York: Oxford University Press.

Gottdiener, Mark. 1985. *The Social Production of Urban Space.* Austin: University of Texas Press.

Hall, Peter, and Dennis Hays. 1980. *Growth Centers in the European Urban System.* Berkeley: University of California Press.

Harris, Chauncey, and Edward Ullman. 1945. "The Nature of Cities." *Annals of the American Academy of Political and Social Science* 242: 7–17.

Harvey, David. 1973. *Social Justice and the City.* Baltimore: Johns Hopkins University Press.

Harvey, David. 1985a. *Consciousness and the Urban Experience.* Baltimore: Johns Hopkins University Press.

Harvey, David. 1985b. *The Urbanization of Capital.* Baltimore: Johns Hopkins University Press.

Hill, Richard C., and Michael Indergaard. 1987. "Downriver: Deindustrialization in Southwest Detroit." In Scott Cummings, ed., *Business Elites and Urban Development: Case Studies and Critical Perspectives.* Albany: State University of New York Press.

Hill, Richard C., and Cynthia Negrey. 1987. "Deindustrialization in the Great Lakes." *Urban Affairs Quarterly* 22, no. 4: 580–597.

Hill, Richard C., and Cynthia Negrey. 1989. "Deindustrialization and Racial Minorities in the Great Lakes Region." In D. Stanley Eitzen and Maxine Baca Zinn, eds., *The Reshaping of America: Social Consequences of the Changing Economy.* Englewood Cliffs, NJ: Prentice-Hall.

Hill, Richard C., and Cynthia Negrey. 1991. "Deindustrialization and Uneven Development in the Great Lakes Region." In Marvel Lang, ed., *Contemporary Urban America: Problems, Issues, and Alternatives.* Lanham, MD: University Press of America.

Hodson, Randy, and Teresa A. Sullivan. 1995. *The Social Organization of Work.* 2nd ed. Belmont, CA: Wadsworth Publishing Company.

Hoyt, Homer. 1939. *The Structure and Growth of Residential Neighborhoods in American Cities.* Washington, D.C.: Government Printing Office.

Kantor, Paul, with Stephen David. 1988. *The Dependent City.* Glenview, IL: Scott, Foresman and Company.

Kasarda, John D. 1980. "The Implications of Contemporary Redistribution Trends for National Urban Policy." *Social Science Quarterly* 61: 373–400.

Koritz, Douglas. 1991. "Restructuring or Destructuring: Deindustrialization in Two Industrial Heartland Cities." *Urban Affairs Quarterly* 26, no. 4: 497–511.

Lineberry, Robert L. 1980. "From Political Sociology to Political Economy." *American Behavioral Scientist* 24, no. 2: 299–317.

Logan, John R., and Harvey L. Molotch. 1987. *Urban Fortunes: The Political Economy of Place*. Berkeley: University of California Press.

Logan, John R., and Todd Swanstrom. 1990. *Beyond the City Limits: Urban Policy and Economic Restructuring in Comparative Perspective*. Philadelphia: Temple University Press.

Marshall, H., and J. Stahura. 1986. "The Theory of Ecological Expansion: The Relation between Dominance and Suburban Differentiation." *Social Forces* 65: 352–369.

Marx, Karl. 1977. *Capital*. Vol. 1. New York: Vintage. (Originally published 1867)

Meyer, D. R. 1984. "Control and Coordination Links in the Metropolitan System of Cities: The South as Case Study." *Social Forces* 63: 349–362.

Meyer, D. R. 1986. "The World System of Cities: Relations between International Financial Metropolises and South American Cities." *Social Forces* 64: 553–581.

Mills, C. Wright. 1956. *The Power Elite*. New York: Oxford University Press.

Mollenkopf, John H. 1983. *The Contested City*. Princeton: Princeton University Press.

Mollenkopf, John H., and Manuel Castells, eds. 1991. *Dual City: Restructuring New York*. New York: Russell Sage Foundation.

Moore, Thomas S., and Aaron Laramore. 1990. "Industrial Change and Urban Joblessness: An Assessment of the Mismatch Hypothesis." *Urban Affairs Quarterly* 25, no. 4: 640–658.

Negrey, Cynthia, and Mary Beth Zickel. 1994. "Industrial Shifts and Uneven Development: Patterns of Growth and Decline in U.S. Metropolitan Areas." *Urban Affairs Quarterly* 30, no. 1: 27–47.

Park, Robert. 1936. "Human Ecology." *American Journal of Sociology* 42: 1–15.

Parsons, Talcott. 1951. *The Social System*. New York: Free Press.

Perry, David, and Alfred Watkins, eds. 1977. *The Rise of the Sunbelt*. Beverly Hills, CA: Sage.

Peterson, George E., and Wayne Vroman. 1992. *Urban Labor Markets and Job Opportunities*. Washington, D.C.: Urban Institute Press.

Peterson, Paul E. 1981. *City Limits*. Chicago: University of Chicago Press.

Reich, Robert B. 1983. *The Next American Frontier*. New York: Times Books.

Sassen, Saskia. 1994. *Cities in a World Economy*. Thousand Oaks, CA: Pine Forge Press.

Savitch, H. V., David Collins, Daniel Sanders, and John Markham. 1993. "Ties that Bind: Central Cities, Suburbs, and the New Metropolitan Region." *Economic Development Quarterly* 7, no. 4, 341–357.

Sawers, Larry, and William K. Tabb, eds. 1984. *Sunbelt/Snowbelt: Urban Development and Regional Restructuring*. New York: Oxford University Press.

Sjoberg, Gideon. 1965. "Theory and Research in Urban Sociology." In P. M. Hauser and L. Schnore, eds., *The Study of Urbanization*. New York: John Wiley.

Smith, Michael Peter. 1988. *City, State, and Market: The Political Economy of Urban Society*. New York: Basil Blackwell.

Smith, Michael Peter, and Joe R. Feagin, eds. 1987. *The Capitalist City*. Oxford and New York: Basil Blackwell.

Snow, Robert T. 1983. "The New International Division of Labor and the U.S. Work Force: The Case of the Electronics Industry." In June Nash and Patricia Fernandez-Kelly, eds., *Women, Men, and the International Division of Labor*. Albany: State University of New York Press.

South, Scott J., and Dudley L. Poston, Jr. 1980. "A Note on Stability in the U.S. Metropolitan System, 1950–1970." *Demography* 17: 445–450.

South, Scott J., and Dudley L. Poston, Jr. 1982. "The U.S. Metropolitan System: Regional Change, 1950–1970." *Urban Affairs Quarterly* 18: 187–206.

Stanback, Thomas M., Jr. 1985. "The Changing Fortunes of Metropolitan Economies." In Manuel Castells, ed., *High Technology, Space, and Society*. Beverly Hills, CA: Sage.

Swanstrom, Todd. 1993. "Beyond Economism: Urban Political Economy and the Postmodern Challenge." *Journal of Urban Affairs* 15, no. 1: 55–78.

Thompson, W. R. 1965. "Urban Economic Development and Growth in a National System of Cities." In P. M. Hauser and L. Schnore, eds., *The Study of Urbanization*. New York: John Wiley.

Ullman, Edward, and Chauncey Harris. 1970. "The Nature of Cities." In Albert N. Cousins and Hans Nagpaul, eds., *Urban Man and Society: A Reader in Urban Ecology*. New York: Knopf.

Van den Berg, Leo, Roy Drewett, Leo H. Klaasen, Angelo Rossi, and Cornelius H. T. Vijverberg. 1982. *Urban Europe: A Study of Growth and Decline*. New York: Pergamon Press.

Wallace, Michael, and Joyce Rothschild, eds. 1988. *Deindustrialization and the Restructuring of American Industry*. Vol. 3 of Research in Politics and Society. Greenwich, CT: JAI Press.

Walton, John. 1987. "Theory and Research on Industrialization." *Annual Review of Sociology* 13: 89–108.

Walton, John. 1993. "Urban Sociology: The Contribution and Limits of Political Economy." *Annual Review of Sociology* 19: 301–320.

Wanner, R. A. 1977. "The Dimensionality of the Urban Functional System." *Demography* 14: 519–537.

Wilson, Franklin D. 1984. "Urban Ecology: Urbanization and Systems of Cities." *Annual Review of Sociology* 10: 283–307.

Wirth, Louis. 1928. *The Ghetto*. Chicago: University of Chicago Press.

Zukin, Sharon. 1980. "A Decade of the New Urban Research." *Theory and Society* 9: 575–601.

Chapter 18

Urban Planning and Development

Robyne S. Turner and Jerry Kolo

The Industrial Revolution and the technological advancements of the nineteenth century have shaped our views of urban places and their development. Sociologists such as Emile Durkheim suggest that cities are organic places, meaning that their social linkages are complex and exploitive (see Tönnies 1983). Spates and Macionis (1987) note that the city cannot be understood using any single point of view. Instead, the development of cities is an interdisciplinary exploration, exposing social, political, economic, and geographical linkages between people and space. This chapter examines those linkages in the context of how the planning process has changed over time and how that has affected planning policy and development. Planning practitioners and scholars have responded to the challenges of urban development and growth by adapting planning phases as a response to the changing dynamics and issues of information and technology.

OVERVIEW OF URBAN DEVELOPMENT AND PLANNING

Planning seeks to use information to address urban issues and problems, often through a rational and systematic process. After the Industrial Revolution, planners sought to resolve the problem of cities filled with people in search of jobs and other opportunities for personal advancement (Hall 1989; Ravetz 1986). Planning focused narrowly on the physical or spatial aspects of cities with little regard to social, political, and economic concerns. Planning had little effect on the problems of cities, resulting in criticisms of, and challenges to, the tenets of the profession. Since these formative years, planning has undergone what Brooks (1988) termed *critical junctures* that result in discernible planning phases. These phases have had major determining effects on the changing roles of urban planners and the context for planning policy.

The challenge of urban development as a means to manage cities is to find common ground among governments at the local, state, and federal levels, neighborhoods and communities, and the private sector. Planning encompasses development, changes, and conflict over land use. Planning, politics, and the economy are linked by the need to develop land and build viable, livable cities (Stone 1989; Logan and Molotch 1987; Jacobs 1961, 1984; Castells 1977).

PHASES IN PLANNING THOUGHT AND PRACTICE

Cities evolved from simple agrarian communities where social relationships were tightly knit to complex and socially loose urban communities where people related to each other impersonally and as a means to personal ends. Worldwide, people increasingly live in large and crowded cities. Changes in urban development have been accompanied by changes in how planners are expected to approach their profession and how planning information is to be related to problems and issues. The context of urban development changed from simple commerce and trade centers to complex operations concentrated in urban regions during the Industrial Revolution. In the Post–World War II years, the explosion of transportation and construction technology altered the spatial configuration of cities through suburban and, eventually, exurban development patterns.

The nature of urban planning evolved in both its theoretical and practical dimensions. The complex problems that accompanied America's sudden and rapid urban development required a strategic, institutional approach (Judd 1984). Planning became a key strategy to address urban problems, particularly on the heels of the 1893 Chicago Exposition, when Daniel Burnham, John Root, and Frederick Law Olmstead, among others, announced the birth of planning (Levy 1991). Their "city beautiful" was the first theme of the American planning movement.

From those early years, the scope of planning has progressively broadened. Planning scholars created development guidance systems exemplified by the leading paradigms in the field, viz: synoptic, disjointed incremental, maieutic, advocacy, mixed scanning, communicative, social learning, and transactive theories. Though these theories are widely applied to planning practice today, they are criticized for being inadequate, lacking imagination, limited by convention, and failing to integrate the totality of the various elements of community decision making (Weiss and Woodhouse 1992; Verger and Kadelan 1994).

We identify four modern phases of urban planning as the profession copes with the changing nature of urban development. These phases are accompanied by distinct planning philosophies and roles for planners (Table 18.1). The transdisciplinary nature of the planning profession cuts across the specific boundaries of academic disciplines and proposes solutions that acknowledge the multifaceted dimensions of urban development.

Table 18.1
Four Phases in Urban Planning

Phase	Philosophy	Focus/Context	Planner's Role
Urban design	Physical determinism	Space/ structures	Technician
Politico-behavioral	Environmental possibilism/ democratic participation	Politics	Policy analyst/ bureaucrat
Quantitative/ technological	Physical determinism/survey-analysis-plan	Technology/ data	Technician/ researcher
Social welfare/ community development	Environmental possibilism/capacity building/empowerment	People/ community	Advocate/ catalyst

Phase 1: Physical Planning/Urban Design

The first phase of urban planning was an effort to address the problems of cities by reorganizing urban space and land use. Physical determinism guided the placement of structures and use of land in order to affect social space and the behavioral use of space (Spates and Macionis 1987; Ravetz 1986). Several models of good cities emerged, most notably urban utopias such as Ebenezer Howard's garden city; Paolo Soleri's Acology; Doxiadis's Ecumenopolis; Frank Lloyd Wright's Broadacre City; Le Corbusier's Radiant City; and Tony Garnier's Cite Industrielle (see Spates and Macionis 1987; van der Ryn and Calthorpe 1986). A common weakness of these utopias is their single-purpose model, which contradicts the diverse purpose that a city must serve.

Urban design and the evolution of planning after the Industrial Revolution were based on the premise that good design would necessarily result in better social conditions. The philosophy of physical determinism guided planning thought and practice long into the 1950s. Design focused on the physical aspect of cities to the neglect or detriment of the social/human dimension. Some of the greatest cities ever designed around the world exemplify the urban design tradition, such as William Penn's Philadelphia, Pennsylvania; James Oglethorpe's Savannah, Georgia; and Major Pierre L'Enfant's Washington, D.C. (So and Getzels 1988; Levy 1991).

The design tradition notwithstanding, business needs and landowner demands sometimes exceeded the capacity for planning. City forms tend to follow city functions by adapting design to the needs of residents. Technology, particularly transportation and communications, allowed development to fan out from city centers to the suburbs, draining wealth from the city. Segregation by income, class, race, and ethnicity increased as opportunities expanded to develop urban and suburban land. Political oversight of central cities increased, and additional political entities emerged in newly incorporated suburbs.

Today, urban design and form are of two divergent patterns: fragmented sprawl and neotraditional planned development. Fragmented sprawl is a contiguous development pattern that is inefficient in terms of service and infrastructure cost and unattractive aesthetically. However, its pattern appeases the desire for low-density housing. Suburban governments downplay the cost of sprawl because suburbs remain a popular choice of homebuyers (Audirac, Shermyen, and Smith 1990). Population growth produces a temporary economic prosperity through construction and development-related jobs. Residents soon become plagued by problems of traffic congestion and overcrowded services. Politicians often respond to these problems by enacting zoning, planning, and growth management policies and practices (DeGrove 1984), albeit long after development patterns are established (Vogel and Swanson 1989).

Sprawl may be reaching its peak as a development pattern, as distances between suburbs and the urban core become longer. The emerging edge cities are the result of the desire of residents and businesses to escape the problems of central cities, yet these edge places are taking on the classic functions and patterns of central cities (Garreau 1991).

The principles of neotraditional development have been practically applied to award-winning designs by town planners such as Peter Calthorpe and the team of Andres Duany and Elizabeth Plater-Zyberk. The appeal of their and other neotraditional designs is that they offer the amenities of planned suburbs and reduce the problems and inefficiencies of sprawl. This design trend advocates the modern application of traditional physical design to reintroduce pedestrian-friendly cities based on higher (but controlled) densities, multiuse designations, an emphasis on transit, and social familiarity (Christoforidis 1994). Design and functional aesthetics are central to this development pattern through public art, pedestrian-friendly public spaces, streetscaping, and other approaches that make urbanites comfortable, safe, and active users of public spaces (Whyte 1988). Applying neotraditional design to larger developments such as new subdivisions requires government approval by meeting criteria specified in zoning ordinances, planned unit development regulations, land use codes, and comprehensive or growth management plans (Goodman and Freund 1967).

Role of Planners. The urban design phase required planners to play the role of technicians. As technicians, planners developed trademark tools that helped them shape physical space. These tools centered on the ability to lay out specific designs, relying on mapping and land use as the means by which they would address urban problems. The result is that planners were nonpolitical technocrats that could be used as a design tool themselves by the political interests who sorted out the costs and benefits of urban development (Altshuler 1965). Over time, however, these design tools resulted in specific policies that are considered the foundations of government efforts to organize cities.

Planning Policy Tools: Zoning and Growth Management. First used coherently by Edward Bassett in New York in 1917, the constitutionality of zoning was established in 1926 (*Euclid* v. *Ambler*) as a local power to regulate the use of land. In the 1970s, planning made a leap from traditional Euclidian zoning to comprehensive planning, incorporating unprecedented uses of intergovernmental rules and regulations (Popper 1988). The "quiet revolution" expanded the jurisdiction for land development decisions from local agencies to county, regional, state, and national levels with requirements for citizen participation.

Despite the creation of vast public policy mechanisms as a response to public participation, the results of zoning have become parochial and exclusionary (Merriam, Brower, and Tegeler 1985). For instance, the "not in my backyard" (NIMBY) syndrome conveys the public's backlash to uncontrolled development and growth. Demands for participation and a hearing for the collective good have collapsed into demands for individual protection from perceived noxious uses by using development tools to control physical design. The body of law that addresses the issue of "taking" (the use of regulations such as growth management and environmental protection to direct the use of land) has evolved from the local to national level to address the public, government, and private developer conflicts (Wise 1992).

State governments have responded to the divergence of opinions on local development by requiring local governments to prepare comprehensive plans and growth management policies. These regulations address a broad range of concerns but primarily emphasize physical aspects of development such as placement and provision of infrastructure, utility management, protection of natural resources, traffic management, and availability of open space (Gale 1992; DeGrove 1984; Bollens 1992). Debate continues on the issue of the benefit of growth management planning and who receives those benefits (Brower, Godshalk, and Porter 1989).

Phase 2: Politicobehavioral Planning

The inadequacy of urban design to deal effectively with urban social and economic problems soon convinced planners that they needed to inject their views into municipal-level political and economic processes in order to get the requisite backing to implement their technical plans. The underlying philosophy of the politicobehavioral phase was aptly described as planners being the power behind the throne and, in general, as a phase of executive dominance in planning (Catanese 1984; Brooks 1988). This phase required planners to have skills that enabled them to play the roles of policy architects and analysts, lobbyists, advocates, community organizers, and public educators about planning issues (Rabinovitz 1969).

The Role of Planners. Planners took on the role of policy advocates for urban design through political and economic forums for the implementation of such programs as Model Cities and Urban Renewal. Planners and other local officials became the core of the public sector response to and oversight of planning and urban development outcomes. Over time, this view of development has bifurcated into alternative growth patterns that planning departments may advocate for, using traditional urban design expertise. Planning departments articulate alternative growth patterns by including issues of equity and aesthetics in their plan recommendations (Krumholz and Forester 1990; Davidoff 1965; Albrechts 1991).

Policy Tools. One of the more controversial planning options is to put development issues to a public vote through referendum. California cities have used referendums to allow voters to determine the direction and scope of growth (Caves 1992; Donovan and Neiman 1992). Voters, however, may not have a consensus on the specific elements of growth management and development as they have passed conflicting resolutions in the same election. Another option is to use democratic forums such as the American Assembly, charrettes, and town meetings to plan and resolve disputes over issues of development competition (Vogel and Swanson 1989). There is valuable support, however, for incorporating citizens' views into the public planning process (Gans 1991).

A more controlled process for planning removes decision making from the major public forums and out of the political process by using quasi-governmental bodies such as downtown and community development agencies. Financing and planning can be combined with land development powers and taxing authority to allow development decisions to be made by employing public/private partnerships secured with private funding (Frieden and Sagalyn 1989; Keating 1986). The degree to which public authority is enmeshed with narrowly prescribed private interests is the subject of much debate. Private interests may subsume public interests, making the public sector foils for development interests (Dreier and Ehrlich 1991; Turner 1992).

Phase 3: Quantitative/Technological Planning Trend

The exponential increase and availability of information have guided this phase of planning. The ability to synthesize and manipulate this information to guide planning decisions altered the planning tasks as well as affected the relationship between planning decision processes and those interests seeking to affect those planning decisions. This phase seeks to place planning within the constraints of rational analysis where decisions are guided by the assessment and interpretation of data.

The underlying philosophy of this planning phase is that through detailed surveys and data manipulation, planners can produce plans to address an infinite variety of urban problems. It allows planners to explore the reaches of physical determinism using technological applications while producing a variety of options to meet the political demands of many interests. This trend can be seen most clearly as a complement to the other planning phases, rather than as a distinctly isolated phase (Brooks 1988).

Role of Planners. Planners are expected to be researchers and technicians in this phase. Transportation, land use, housing, and the environment are issues that have been profoundly affected by the use of new data analysis techniques that not only guide the complex analysis of conditions but direct the regulatory process as well. Computer technology is a critical tool for planners and has enabled the development of sophisticated software to map, plot, and dissect space from both ground and aerial perspectives. It allows planners to go beyond professional design preferences and political demands, to plot out specific applications in future scenarios based on a wide variety of potential changes in population, resource use, car trips, density, and other variables.

Policy Tools. Geographic information systems (GIS) is an important application of technology in many urban planning departments. It allows planners not only to plot land uses and other activities but to measure the impact of those activities on the land, infrastructure, and other land uses. For instance, trips generated by developments can be plotted on existing roadways to measure the level of congestion now and in the future, helping planners to identify the potential costs of such development (Onsrud and Rushton 1995). Impact fees must be set by law according to the actual impact of any development subject to the fee and can be determined using these sophisticated methods (Nelson 1988). Frequently, this technology is applied to transportation management in order to make decisions about public policy and expenditures for mass transportation, highway construction, and new development. In addition, technology is playing an increasingly important role in environmental management, focusing on the impact of development on habitats, water supplies, and resource availability and degradation.

Phase 4: Social Welfare/Community Development

American cities have been undergoing serious changes as they grow. The most profound changes are social and affect the most politically and economically vulnerable populations of low-income and minority persons. Hall (1989: 281) characterizes this decay as "city pathological revisited," implying that conditions in modern cities are again showing the pathological conditions of cities in the preplanning era. This planning phase addresses the responsibility of government to manage the uneven impact of development across class, gender, and race (Mier 1993). Women in cities are particularly vulnerable to the economic impacts of urban land use changes (Garber and Turner 1994). Minorities, particularly African Americans, have struggled with ghettoization resulting in social and economic isolation as inner cities undergo commercial revitalization (Wilson 1987). The planning process has been called into question for its prejudice against consideration of economic and social impacts as new developments are approved (Davis 1992).

Role of Planners. The role of planners in this phase is to be advocates of the issues and concerns of those people who are affected by dramatic social and economic forces that are changing their environment (Checkoway 1994). Planners act to facilitate and advocate for community organizing, education, and enabling participation and control by residents and neighborhood groups. Advocates of this position have loudly challenged planners to continue these roles and to develop the knowledge and skill base for effective social planning (Krumholz and Forester 1990).

Policy Tools. A final frontier for representing alternative points of view is through neighborhood-based organizations (Fisher and Kling 1993). Organizations that rely on grassroots momentum leverage the public sector by participating in the government arena as a means to change the plans of private sector developers (Jezierski 1990). Nonprofit organizations have been successful in housing and community development (Goetz 1993; Vidal 1992). Grassroots movements may stimulate the adoption of progressive policies designed to protect neighborhood interests from development encroachment, particularly where it concerns minorities and low-income areas (Clavel 1983).

THE NEED FOR NEW PLANNING TRENDS/FUTURE RESEARCH PROSPECTS

We contend that planning is at a crossroads. Brooks (1988) argues that planners have lost sight of the visionary and humanistic purpose of their profession. These debates buttress the notion that there is a crisis of identity and focus in planning. Fortunately, this crisis does not diminish or negate the importance or relevance of planning in our problem-ridden cities. In light of this, planning research must be aware of, and responsive to, the dynamics, process, and challenges of urban development in cities.

We suggest that there is a need for a new planning model that has broader scopes and more integrative approaches to community elements than the four major phases discussed here. Part of the future research prospects for planners is the articulation of the tenets and principles of this emerging planning model (Hall 1989). The suggestions that follow draw on key elements of past trends, exemplifying what new planning can be—most important, inclusive and comprehensive, in order to deal with the complexities of urban places. The challenges of urban development are currently manifested by the physical structure, sociocultural makeup, economic status, and political astuteness of the various neighborhoods in a city, highlighting differences in socioeconomic status. Cities are witnessing an increasing withdrawal of residents from the collective effort of urban development, and consequently, people are quick to support initiatives, programs, and taxes that benefit only their respective interests and/or neighborhoods. This posture suggests that residents do not acknowledge, nor are they aware of, the synergistic relationship between the various issues that face the entire city that constitute the city development agenda.

Connective Planning and Integrative Community Development

Connective planning (Verger and Kadelan 1994) and integrative community development (ICD) are emerging variations of earlier planning trends and suggest that planning is integral to the development of urban places where intricate relationships within community life demand a "connectedness" of approaches and institutional arrangements. Urban development and planning research must explore strategies that deal with the integrative nature of urban issues and explore the synergy between urban issues that address people's values within the context of their resources.

Verger and Kadelan (1994: 1) use the term "connective planning" to describe the kind of goal-driven planning that goes beyond conventional practice, stating that "connective planning is a value-driven planning discipline to help realize a goal whose achievement requires more than conventional wisdom or practice." The principal tenet is that culture should be the foundation for planning as implied in the work by Freire (1979). Friedman (1973) definitively argues that progressive planning can be achieved only if planners relate their expert or "processed" knowledge to the "experiential" knowledge of the people whose problems are being addressed by planning. Efforts by planners to effect this connection requires vision, passion, and commitment (Verger and Kadelan 1994). This complements Brooks's (1988: 246) contention that planning should "visualize the ideal future community and . . . work toward its realization." Connective planning, then, allows planners and the community to discover and create connections between thoughts (values) and action (plans).

Integrative community development is an emerging planning model that seeks to develop a mechanism for defining and understanding the relationship between people and their values, in terms of their views of important issues, their priorities, and resources and capacity to address the issues (Roberts 1979; Esman 1969; Korter 1980; Rondinelli and Ingle 1981; Rubin 1994). ICD blends the technical aspect of planning (survey, research, analysis, and design) with the political, economic, and social aspects of cities. ICD is the outgrowth of community planning experiences of the authors in the urban metropolitan region of south Florida (CURE 1994) and follows the lead of other community development experts, paralleling some of the examples in the community planning literature (see Faludi 1973; Etzioni 1995).

In ICD, planners facilitate a blended practice to mutually determine urban futures through community-based action plans based on a mutual determination of the urban environment using the praxis of technology, design, and culture. The final component of ICD is to institutionalize the arrangements as procedure to move the community to its desired status, integrating community knowledge with public process.

While ICD has great potential as a successful means of urban planning, it is necessary to make definitive links to the existing body of literature and theories of urban development. We suggest that research paths include an examination of the connections between underlying philosophies of planning and skill requirements for successful implementation; an understanding of the unique contexts of urban planning trends that affect the output and the ability to effectively practice planning that allows the transfer of knowledge and skills from unique spatial settings to more generalizable settings; and an exploration of the normative expectations that planning models can link knowledge to action across the disciplines to build our understanding of urban development.

REFERENCES

Albrechts, Louis. 1991. "Changing Roles and Positions of Planners." *Urban Studies* 28, no. 1: 123–137.

Altshuler, Alan. 1965. *The City Planning Process*. Ithaca, NY: Cornell University Press.

Audirac, Ivonne, Ann Shermyen, and Marc Smith. 1990. "Ideal Urban Form and Visions of the Good Life." *Journal of the American Planning Association* 56, no. 3: 470–482.

Bollens, Scott. 1992. "State Growth Management." *Journal of the American Planning Association* 58, no. 4: 454–466.

Brooks, Michael P. 1988. "Four Critical Junctures in the History of the Urban Planning Profession." *Journal of the American Planning Association* 54, no. 2: 241–248.

Brower, David, David Godshalk, and Douglas Porter, eds. 1989. *Understanding Growth Management*. Washington, D.C.: Urban Land Institute.

Castells, Manuel. 1977. *The Urban Question*. Translated by Alan Sheridan. Cambridge: MIT Press.

Catanese, Anthony. 1984. *The Politics of Planning and Development*. Beverly Hills, CA: Sage.

Caves, Roger. 1992. *Land Use Planning: The Ballot Box Revolution*. Newbury Park, CA: Sage.

Center for Urban Redevelopment and Empowerment (CURE). 1994. "*Final Report: I-95. Assembly.*" Ft. Lauderdale, FL: CURE.

Checkoway, Barry, ed. 1994. "Symposium: Paul Davidoff and Advocacy Planning in Retrospect." *Journal of the American Planning Association* 60, no. 2: 139–234.

Christoforidis, Alexander. 1994. "New Alternatives to the Suburb: Neo-traditional Developments." *Journal of Planning Literature* 8, no. 4: 429–440.

Clavel, Pierre. 1983. *The Progressive City*. New Brunswick, NJ: Rutgers University Press.

Davidoff, Paul. 1965. "Advocacy and Pluralism in Planning." *Journal of the American Planning Association* 31: 331–338.

Davis, Mike. 1992. *City of Quartz*. New York: Vintage Books.

DeGrove, John. 1984. *Land Growth & Politics*. Chicago, IL: American Planners Press.

Donovan, Todd, and Max Neiman. 1992. "Citizen Mobilization and the Adoption of Suburban Growth Controls." *Western Political Quarterly* 45, no. 3: 651–676.

Dreier, Peter, and Bruce Ehrlich. 1991. "Downtown Development and Urban Reform." *Urban Affairs Quarterly* 26, no. 3: 354–376.

Esman, Milton J. 1969. *Institution-Building as a Guide to Action*. Monograph. Washington, D.C.: U.S. Agency for International Development.

Etzioni, Amatai, ed. 1995. *New Communitarian Thinking*. Charlottesville: University of Virginia Press.

Faludi, Andreas, ed. 1973. *A Reader in Planning Theory*. New York: Pergamon Press.

Fisher, Robert, and Joseph Kling. 1993. *Mobilizing the Community*. Newbury Park, CA: Sage.

Freire, Paolo. 1979. *Pedagogy of the Oppressed*. New York: Seabury.

Frieden, Bernard, and Lynn Sagalyn. 1989. *Downtown, Inc.* Cambridge: MIT Press.

Friedman, John. 1973. *Retracking America: Theory of Transactive Planning*. Garden City, NY: Anchor Press.

Gale, Dennis. 1992. "Eight State-Sponsored Growth Management Programs." *Journal of the American Planning Association* 58, no. 4: 425–439.

Gans, Herbert. 1991. *People, Plans, and Policies*. New York: Columbia University Press.

Garber, Judith, and Robyne Turner. 1994. *Gender in Urban Research*. Newbury Park, CA: Sage.

Garreau, Joel. 1991. *Edge City*. New York: Anchor Books.

Goetz, Edward. 1993. *Shelter Burden*. Philadelphia, PA: Temple University Press.

Goodman, William, and Eric Freund, eds. 1967. *Principles and Practice of Urban Planning*. Washington, D.C.: International City Managers' Association.

Hall, Peter. 1989. "The Turbulent Eighth Decade: Challenges to American City Planning." *Journal of the American Planning Association* 54, no. 3: 275–282.

Jacobs, Jane. 1961. *The Death and Life of Great American Cities*. New York: Random House.

Jacobs, Jane. 1984. *Cities and the Wealth of Nations*. New York: Random House.

Jezierski, Louise. 1990. "Neighborhoods and Public-Private Partnerships in Pittsburgh." *Urban Affairs Quarterly* 26, no. 2: 217–250.

Judd, Dennis. 1984. *The Politics of American Cities*. New York: Little, Brown.

Keating, Dennis. 1986. "Linking Downtown Development to Broader Community Goals." *Journal of the American Planning Association* 52, no. 1: 133–141.

Korter, David C. 1980. "Community Organization and Rural Development." *Journal of Planning Education and Research* 11, no. 1: 51–65.

Krumholz, Norman, and John Forester. 1990. *Making Equity Planning Work*. Philadelphia, PA: Temple University Press.

Levy, John. 1991. *Contemporary Urban Planning*. Englewood Cliffs, NJ: Prentice-Hall.

Logan, John, and Harvey Malotch. 1987. *Urban Fortunes*. Berkeley: University of California Press.

Merriam, Dwight, David Brower, and Philip Tegeler, eds. 1985. *Inclusionary Zoning Moves Downtown*. Washington, D.C.: Planners Press APA.

Mier, Robert. 1993. *Social Justice and Local Development Policy*. Newbury Park, CA: Sage.

Nelson, Arthur. 1988. "Symposium: Development Impact Fees." *Journal of the American Planning Association* 54, no. 1: 3–78.

Onsrud, Harlan J., and Gerard Rushton. 1995. *Sharing Geographic Information*. Piscataway, NJ: CUPR/Rutgers University.

Popper, Frank. 1988. "Understanding American Land Use Regulation since 1970." *Journal of the American Planning Association* 54, no. 3: 291–301.

Rabinovitz, Francine. 1969. *City Politics and Planning*. New York: Atherton.

Ravetz, Alison. 1986. *The Government of Space: Town Planning in Modern Society*. Boston, MA: Faber and Faber.

Roberts, Hayden. 1979. *Community Development: Learning and Action*. Toronto: University of Toronto Press.

Rondinelli, Dennis A., and M. D. Ingle. 1981. "Improving the Implementation of Development Programs." In G. S. Cheema, ed., *Institutional Dimensions of Regional*

Development. Singapore: Maruzen Asia (for the United Nations Center for Regional Development).

Rubin, Herbert J. 1994. "There Aren't Going to Be Any Bakeries Here If There Is No Money to Afford Jellyrolls: The Organic Theory of Community Based Development." *Social Problems* 41, no. 3: 401–424.

So, Frank, and J. Getzels, eds. 1988. *The Practice of Local Government Planning.* 2nd ed. Washington, D.C.: International City Management Association.

Spates, James L., and John J. Macionis. 1987. *The Sociology of Cities.* 2nd ed. Belmont, CA: Wadsworth.

Stone, Clarence. 1989. *Regime Politics.* Lawrence: University Press of Kansas.

Tönnies, Ferdinand. 1983. "Gemeinschaft and Gesselshaft." In Roland Warren and Larry Lyon, eds., *New Perspectives on the American Community.* Homewood, IL: Dorsey Press.

Turner, Robyne. 1992. "Growth Politics and Downtown Development." *Urban Affairs Quarterly* 28, no. 1: 3–21.

van der Ryn, Sym, and Peter Calthorpe. 1986. *Sustainable Communities.* San Francisco, CA: Sierra Club Books.

Verger, Morris D., and Norman Kadelan. 1994. *Connective Planning.* New York: McGraw-Hill.

Vidal, Avis. 1992. *Rebuilding Communities.* New York: CDRC, New School for Social Research.

Vogel, Ronald, and Bert Swanson. 1989. "The Growth Machine versus the Antigrowth Coalition." *Urban Affairs Quarterly* 25, no. 1: 63–85.

Weiss, Andrew, and Edward Woodhouse. 1992. "Reframing Incrementalism: A Constructive Response to the Critics." *Policy Sciences* 25, no. 3: 255–273.

Whyte, William. 1988. *City.* New York: Anchor Books.

Wilson, William J. 1987. *The Truly Disadvantaged.* Chicago, IL: University of Chicago Press.

Wise, Charles. 1992. "The Changing Doctrine of Regulatory Taking and the Executive Branch." *Administrative Law Review* 44, no. 2: 403–427.

Chapter 19

Economic Development

David L. Imbroscio

OVERVIEW OF THE FIELD

Economic development has been described, without hyperbole, as an "obsession" among urban public officials (Brintnall 1989: 4). In response to the massive restructuring of urban economies in the postwar era, for more than three decades these officials have pursued with great zeal a number of public policies designed to increase the level of economic development in their communities (see Sharp 1990). No other policy area has commanded the "high, often unique, place" on local political agendas (Eisinger 1988: 19–20). In fact, in a comprehensive survey of over 300 cities, mayors listed economic development as one of their top priorities more often than any other policy activity (Bowman 1987: 8).

As the proliferation of economic development activities transformed the content of urban policy agendas, urban scholarship, too, was transformed. This transformation is best represented by the emergence of urban political economy "as a central [if not *the* central] paradigm in urban research today" (Vogel 1992: 1). Following the seminal work of Molotch (1976) and Peterson (1981), many urban political economists have provided compelling explanations of urban phenomena by placing economic development matters at the heart of their analyses of cities (see, for example, Stone 1989; Elkin 1987; Swanstrom 1985; Judd 1984).

In definitional terms, Bingham, Hill, and White (1990: 7) point out that "[e]ssentially," economic development "is the creation of jobs and wealth." At some level this conception is no doubt accurate; wealth and employment creation are clearly central to the process of economic development. Nonetheless, precisely specifying the concept is more problematic than this terse phrase suggests. Complications stem, most notably, from the commonly recognized fact that the process of economic "development" should be distinguished from simple economic "growth" (Eisinger 1988: 36–41; Gunn and Gunn 1991: 124; Sharp 1990: 218; Bowman 1987: 6). Therefore, many scholars see economic development as a broader notion, where the creation of wealth and jobs should enhance "social well-being" (Bowman 1987: 6), that is, should serve "the short- and long-run interests of the broad population" (Bingham and Mier 1993: vii).

APPROACHES TO THE FIELD

The study of economic development is a multidisciplinary endeavor marked by an unusually high degree of heterogeneity. For example, the authors of the 12 core chapters in a recent edited volume on the subject—Bingham and Mier's *Theories of Local Economic Development*—managed to discuss and analyze "more than 50 theories drawn from the various social sciences that pertain directly to economic development" (Bingham and Mier 1993: xv). Unquestionably, there are many different ways to approach the field.

Amidst this disarray, one clear and useful way to gain an understanding of the field is to focus on various *approaches or strategies* for achieving urban economic development.[1] In particular, conceiving a dichotomy between two broad approaches or strategies is especially appropriate. These strategies are what might be called the *traditional* approach and the *alternative* approach (or what Clavel and Kleniewski [1990] label the "mainstream" approach and "progressive" approach).[2]

The traditional (or mainstream) approach often includes, but is not limited to, a "corporate-centered" urban economic development strategy, where downtowns are restructured "into modern 'corporate centers' of offices, up-scale commercial establishments and residences, hotels, and other tourism and convention facilities" (Levine 1988: 119; also see Elkin 1987: 96–97; Hill 1983: 102–106). More generally, traditional strategies emphasize (1) bricks and mortar approaches to economic development, usually involving large-scale changes in land use patterns and/or (2) the public provision of financial incentives to attract investment into the city. In philosophical terms, the roots of these strategies are traceable to what Barnekov and Rich (1989: 213) following Warner (1968) call the "cultural tradition of privatism—a tradition that historically has tied the fortunes of cities to the vitality of their private sectors and encouraged a reliance on private institutions [rather than public control and planning] for urban development" (cf. Robinson 1989: 285; Leitner and Garner 1993: 59–60).

While the traditional (or mainstream) approach to urban economic development is empirically pervasive in cities, the alternative (or progressive) approach remains conspicuously less developed. Alternative (or progressive) strategies also contrast with traditional (or mainstream) strategies because, as Clavel and Kleniewski (1990: 202) point out, the former are "pro-labor and community," while the latter are "pro-business." The alternative approach is composed of a diverse collection of urban economic development options; hence, characterizing it in specific terms is more difficult. Nevertheless, as will be sketched below, five relatively distinct conceptual models are clearly emerging from current economic development theory and practice.

CURRENT STATE OF THE FIELD

Much of the recent urban economic development literature purports to demonstrate that the commonly employed traditional (or mainstream) strategies are—as Mier and Fitzgerald (1991: 270) succinctly note—"not working." Critics of the mainstream approach charge that, taken together, these efforts exacerbate the uneven development of cities (Fainstein and Fainstein 1983; Levine 1987); leave cities continually dependent on attracting and/or retaining footloose capital (Olson 1987; Imbroscio 1995); create an asymmetry between the public and private sector, as the latter reaps most of the benefits, while the former bears most of the costs (Squires 1989; Barnekov and Rich 1989); fail to improve the plight of disadvantaged city residents (Krumholz 1991; Hill 1983; Leitner and Garner 1993); focus too heavily on physical approaches to redevelopment (Elkin 1987; Stone, Orr, and Imbroscio 1991); and produce benefits that are captured largely by surrounding suburbs or that escape the local area altogether (Riposa and Andranovich 1988; Friedland 1983).

This research has logically led the field of urban economic development on a search for more suitable strategies. Currently, this search is beginning to yield fruitful results, as recent scholarship is providing a rudimentary knowledge of local economic development efforts not fitting the traditional model. As alluded to above, such alternative economic development efforts remain largely experimental and embryonic. Yet by drawing upon both the theoretical literature and the disparate practices undertaken in a variety of cities, five conceptual models for alternative local economic development can be delineated (see Table 19.1).

The Neomercantilist Strategy

The first alternative strategy can be best labeled a modern "mercantilist" approach to urban economic development. This label is appropriate because this strategy emphasizes maximizing the benefits accruing to the *local* economy from the economic development process. Its key goals include promoting indigenous development generated from within the local economy itself, as opposed to a reliance on development attracted from the outside (see Eisinger 1988); increasing interindustry dependence, so that the purchasing and procurement activities of local industries provide substantial economic stimulation to other local industries (see Meehan 1987; Luria and Russell 1981); and slowing the leakage of economic resources from the local economy (see Morris 1982).

To realize these goals, several specific economic development efforts can be

Table 19.1
Alternative Strategies for Urban Economic Development

Strategy	Description	Goals	Components
Neomercantilist	Maximizing the benefits accruing to the local economy	Indigenous development Interindustry dependence Slowing resource leakage	Enterprise development Local ownership Import substitution Local finance
Municipal Enterprise	Increasing nontraditional local public ownership	Reducing capital mobility Additional public revenue Public control of assets	Direct ownership Retained ownership Equity holdings
Community-Based	Creating community-owned and -controlled economic institutions	Community economic autonomy Growth for marginalized Lessening uneven development	Community land trusts Worker-owned firms Community finance Community development corporations
Progressive Regulatory	Innovative use of local regulatory powers	Reducing capital mobility Lessening uneven development Balancing benefits/costs	"Linkage" policies Eminent domain Plant closing laws "Clawbacks"
Human Capital	Building job-related skills and knowledge	More opportunities for poor Improved investment climate Widening self-sufficiency	School system reform School compacts Early childhood education Training/retraining

derived from the neomercantilist strategy. Policies to stimulate *enterprise development*—that is, the rapid formation and expansion of small businesses in the city—would be prominent here. This development harnesses existing entrepreneurial initiative and talent and, generally, contributes to the dynamism and resilience of the local economy, creating a development process that is both self-sustaining and self-renewing (see Shapero 1985). Other major efforts include promoting *local ownership* of business enterprises, as—compared to nonlocal businesses—they purchase more supplies locally, are less mobile, and provide for a greater recirculation of profits in the local economy (Gunn and Gunn 1991; Alperovitz and Faux 1984); increasing *import substitution* in the local economy, which creates "a greater degree of local self-sufficiency" (Watkins 1980: 133) and "mobilizes local resources in a fashion that greatly enhances their productivity" (Persky, Ranney, and Wiewel 1993: 21); and tapping *innovative local finance sources* (such as municipal pension funds or linked deposits), which allow locally generated finances to provide the local economy with additional stimulation (see Rifkin and Barber 1978; Rosen 1988).

The Municipal Enterprise Strategy

A second alternative strategy for local economic development involves decentralized public ownership of economic enterprises and other productive assets. Cities traditionally have owned airports, convention centers, sports stadia, hospitals, and public utilities. In contrast, this strategy involves "nontraditional" local public enterprises such as hotels, retail establishments, manufacturing facilities, and sports teams. The key goals of this strategy include reducing the degree of capital mobility in the urban economy, as publicly owned investment is anchored locally (see Lynd 1989); providing additional revenues to local government via public profits (see Osborne and Gaebler 1992); and augmenting the degree of public control over how economic assets are used (see Sagalyn 1990).

Specific economic development efforts fall into three major groupings: *direct public ownership (of economic enterprises)*, the most straightforward way this strategy is pursued (see Frug 1980); *retained public ownership (of productive assets)*, where accumulated public properties, such as land or capital facilities, are leased to private entrepreneurs—but with a provision for the retention of public ownership (see Clavel 1986); and *public equity holdings (in private enterprises)*, in which cities gain partial ownership in development projects or local businesses, usually through the provision of public financing (see Cummings, Koebel, and Whitt 1988).

The Community-Based Strategy

A "community-based" approach to urban economic development represents a third alternative strategy. This strategy involves the creation of new, community-owned and -controlled economic institutions, governed by democratic procedures, and usually based in neighborhoods suffering from prior disinvestment. Being neither privately nor publicly owned, these "collective" institutions fall into the "third sector," often operating on a nonprofit basis. The key goals of the community-based strategy include increasing community autonomy over local economic resources (see Bruyn 1987); bringing those citizens marginalized by traditional economic institutions into the urban growth process (see Boyte 1980); and lessening the uneven development of cities (see Levine 1989).

The comprehensive model for this alternative urban economic development strategy involves building institutions that base all three key factors of production—land, labor, and capital—in the local community (Bruyn 1987; Gunn and Gunn 1991): *Community land trusts* acquire and hold real estate in the community interest (see White and Matthei 1987); *worker-owned firms* give employees (labor) ownership and managerial control of business enterprise (see Dahl 1985); and *community finance institutions* (such as community development credit unions and community development banks) provide investment capital for community-based economic development (see Swack 1987; Parzen and Kieschnick 1992). Moreover, *consumer cooperatives* extend the community-based strategy from the production side of local economic development to the consumption side (see Hammond 1987), while *community development corporations*—the core institution of this strategy (Perry 1987)—ideally serve as the "crucial coordination agent" for the overall process of community-based economic development (Bruyn 1987: 16).

The Progressive Regulatory Strategy

A fourth alternative strategy involves the innovative use of local regulatory powers to accomplish progressive economic development ends. Many key goals of the progressive regulatory strategy parallel those of the other alternative strategies. These goals include lessening the degree of capital mobility in the local economy (see Portz 1990); reducing the uneven development of cities (see Goetz 1990); and balancing better the benefits and costs of economic development between the private and public/community sectors (Stone 1987).

In specific terms, the progressive regulatory strategy includes, most prominently, *"linkage" policies*—a type of exaction imposed on private developers of the city's prime real estate obligating them "to contribute to special funds to meet community needs in such areas as housing, job training, public transportation, and child care" (Levine 1989: 30; Garber 1990; Smith 1989). Among other economic development efforts are *eminent domain takings*, where the city uses its powers to condemn an exiting business firm, preventing its departure (Imbroscio 1993); *plant closing laws*, which require, for example, the advance notice of a plant shutdown (Portz 1990);[3] and the imposition of *clawbacks*—that is, financial sanctions or penalties levied on firms receiving public subsidies (such as tax abatements) but failing to achieve agreed-upon economic performance goals, usually measured in job creation or retention (Peters 1993).

The Human Capital Strategy

A final alternative local economic development strategy focuses on building increased job-related skills and knowledge among the urban citizenry. Its key goals include providing more opportunities for the economically disadvantaged to reap the benefits of local economic development (see Stone, Orr, and Imbroscio 1991); improving the local investment climate by creating a more productive workforce (see Krumholz 1991); and making economic self-sufficiency as widely based as possible in the face of rapid technological change (see Imbroscio et al. 1995).

Among the specific efforts of this strategy are measures designed to *reform urban school systems* in ways improving both basic and vocational education (Meyer 1991); the creation of *school compacts* with the local business community, guaranteeing jobs and financial resources for higher education to public school students meeting performance criteria (Orr 1992); improved efforts for *early childhood education*, increasing the school ''readiness'' of children (Stone, Orr, and Imbroscio 1991); and innovative *job training and retraining* programs (Fitzgerald 1993).

DIRECTIONS FOR FUTURE RESEARCH

The focus of this chapter points to two crucial directions for future research in the field of urban economic development. First, scholarship must provide a more thorough understanding of the constraints—political, legal, institutional, fiscal, ideological, and economic—currently inhibiting the fuller development of the alternative strategies sketched above (see Imbroscio 1997). Only through this understanding can we begin to identify the processes that must be altered in order to ensure that these constraints are overcome.[4]

Second, if the alternative strategies are in fact implemented more fully in cities, future research must attempt to evaluate these efforts. Most important, research must determine whether the intended goals of each strategy are being obtained. Likewise, any additional impacts (positive or negative) that the alternative strategies have on the local economic development process must be examined carefully.

By pursuing this twofold research agenda, urban scholarship potentially can make a considerable contribution to the improvement of current political practice in the realm of urban economic development.

NOTES

1. Another way to understand the field is to specify numerous explanations of why and how economic development occurs, for example, economy base theory, location

theory, central place theory, and product cycle theory. See Gittell (1992: 19–25), Sharp (1990: 219–233), Blakely (1989: 60–67), Malizia (1985: 34–44), and Watkins (1980). Practical treatments of urban economic development are offered by Blakely (1989), Malizia (1985), Levy (1990), and McLean and Voytek (1992). These works provide guidance to practitioners attempting to design and implement an economic development program on the local level.

2. Others making a similar distinction between what is essentially a "traditional" approach and an "alternative" approach to local economic development include Robinson (1989), Goetz (1990), Eisinger (1988), and Krumholz and Forester (1990).

3. Although most of this legislation has come from the federal and state levels, such laws also have been enacted in various cities (Eisinger 1988: 312; Portz 1990: 165).

4. A literature is now emerging that begins to address this question. See, for example, Imbroscio (1995) on neomercantilism; Stone, Orr, and Imbroscio (1991) on human capital; Garber (1990) on progressive regulation; Cummings, Koebel, and Whitt (1988) on municipal enterprise; and Vidal (1992) on community-based development.

REFERENCES

Alperovitz, Gar, and Jeff Faux. 1984. *Rebuilding America*. New York: Pantheon.
Barnekov, Timothy, and Daniel Rich. 1989. "Privatism and the Limits of Local Economic Development Policy." *Urban Affairs Quarterly* 25: 212–238.
Bingham, Richard D., Edward W. Hill, and Sammis B. White, eds. 1990. *Financing Economic Development: An Institutional Response*. Newbury Park, CA: Sage Publications.
Bingham, Richard D., and Robert Mier. 1993. *Theories of Local Economic Development*. Newbury Park, CA: Sage Publications.
Blakely, Edward J. 1989. *Local Economic Development: Theory and Practice*. Newbury Park, CA: Sage Publications.
Bowman, Ann O'M. 1987. *The Visible Hand*. Washington, D.C.: National League of Cities.
Boyte, Harry. 1980. *The Backyard Revolution*. Philadelphia: Temple University Press.
Brintnall, Michael. 1989. "Future Directions for Federal Urban Policy." *Journal of Urban Affairs* 11: 1–19.
Bruyn, Severyn T. 1987. "Beyond the Market and the State." In Severyn T. Bruyn and James Meehan, eds., *Beyond the Market and the State: New Directions in Community Economic Development*. Philadelphia: Temple University Press. 3–27.
Clavel, Pierre. 1986. *The Progressive City: Planning and Participation, 1969–1984*. New Brunswick, NJ: Rutgers University Press.
Clavel, Pierre, and Carol Kleniewski. 1990. "Space for Progressive Local Policy: Examples from the U.S. and U.K." In John Logan and Todd Swanstrom, eds., *Beyond the City Limits*. Philadelphia: Temple University Press. 199–236.
Cummings, S. B., C. T. Koebel, and J. A. Whitt. 1988. "Public-Private Partnerships and Public Enterprise." *Urban Resources* 5: 35–36, 47–48.
Dahl, Robert A. 1985. *A Preface to Economic Democracy*. Berkeley: University of California Press.
Eisinger, Peter K. 1988. *The Rise of the Entrepreneurial State*. Madison: University of Wisconsin Press.

Elkin, Stephen L. 1987. *City and Regime in the American Republic*. Chicago: University of Chicago Press.

Fainstein, Susan S., and Norman I. Fainstein. 1983. "Regime Strategies, Communal Resistance, and Economic Forces." In Susan S. Fainstein, Norman I. Fainstein, Richard Child Hill, Dennis R. Judd, and Michael Peter Smith, eds., *Restructuring the City*. New York: Longman. 245–282.

Fitzgerald, Joan. 1993. "Labor Force, Education, and Work." In Richard D. Bingham and Robert Mier, eds., *Theories of Local Economic Development*. Newbury Park, CA: Sage Publications. 125–146.

Friedland, Roger. 1983. *Power and Crisis in the City*. New York: Macmillan.

Frug, Gerald E. 1980. "The City as a Legal Concept." *Harvard Law Review* 93: 1059–1154.

Garber, Judith A. 1990. "Law and the Possibilities for a Just Political Economy." *Journal of Urban Affairs* 12: 1–15.

Gittell, Ross J. 1992. *Renewing Cities*. Princeton, NJ: Princeton University Press.

Goetz, Edward G. 1990. "*Type II Policy* and Mandated Benefits in Economic Development." *Urban Affairs Quarterly* 25: 170–190.

Gunn, Christopher, and Hazel Dayton Gunn. 1991. *Reclaiming Capital: Democratic Initiatives and Community Development*. Ithaca: Cornell University Press.

Hammond, Jean. 1987. "Consumer Cooperatives." In Severyn T. Bruyn and James Meehan, eds., *Beyond the Market and the State: New Directions in Community Economic Development*. Philadelphia: Temple University Press. 97–112.

Hill, Richard Child. 1983. "Crisis in the Motor City." In Susan Fainstein, Norman I. Fainstein, Richard Child Hill, Dennis R. Judd, and Michael Peter Smith, eds., *Restructuring the City*. New York: Longman. 80–125.

Imbroscio, David L. 1995. "An Alternative Approach to Urban Economic Development: Exploring the Dimensions and Prospects of a 'Self-Reliance' Strategy." *Urban Affairs Review* 30, no. 6, 840–867.

Imbroscio, David L. 1995. "Baltimore and the Human-Investment Challenge." In F. Wagner, eds., *Central City Revitalization*. Newbury Park, CA: Sage Publications. 38–68.

Imbroscio, David L. 1997. *Reconstructing City Politics: Alternative Economic Development and Urban Regimes*. Newbury Park, CA: Sage Publications.

Imbroscio, David L., Marion Orr, Tim Ross, and Clarence Stone. 1993. "Overcoming the Economic Dependence of Urban America." *Journal of Urban Affairs* 15: 173–190.

Judd, Dennis R. 1984. *The Politics of American Cities*. Boston: Little, Brown.

Krumholz, Norman. 1991. "Equity and Local Economic Development." *Economic Development Quarterly* 5: 291–300.

Krumholz, Norman, and John Forester. 1990. *Making Equity Planning Work*. Philadelphia, PA: Temple University Press.

Leitner, Helga, and Mark Garner. 1993. "The Limits of Local Initiatives: A Reassessment of Urban Entrepreneurialism for Urban Development." *Urban Geography* 14: 57–77.

Levine, Marc V. 1987. "Downtown Redevelopment as an Urban Growth Strategy: A Critical Appraisal of the Baltimore Renaissance." *Journal of Urban Affairs* 9: 103–123.

Levine, Marc V. 1988. "Economic Development in States and Cities: Toward Democratic and Strategic Planning in State and Local Government." In Marc V. Levine,

Carol MacLennan, John J. Kushma, and Charles Nobels, eds., *The State and Democracy*. New York: Routledge. 111–146.

Levine, Marc V. 1989. "The Politics of Partnership: Urban Redevelopment since 1945." In Gregory D. Squires, ed., *Unequal Partnerships: The Political Economy of Urban Redevelopment in Postwar America*. New Brunswick, NJ: Rutgers University Press. 12–34.

Levy, John M. 1990. *Economic Development Programs for Cities, Counties, and Towns*. New York: Praeger.

Luria, Dan, and Jack Russell. 1981. *Rational Reindustrialization*. Detroit: Widgetripper Press.

Lynd, Staughton. 1989. "The Genesis of the Idea of a Community Right to Industrial Property in Youngstown and Pittsburgh, 1977–1987." *Changing Work* (spring): 14–19.

McLean, Mary L., and Kenneth P. Voytek. 1992. *Understanding Your Economy: Using Analysis to Guide Local Strategic Planning*. Chicago: Planners Press.

Malizia, Emil E. 1985. *Local Economic Development: A Guide to Practice*. New York: Praeger.

Meehan, James. 1987. "Working toward Local Self-Reliance." In Severyn T. Bruyn and James Meehan, eds., *Beyond the Market and the State: New Directions in Community Economic Development*. Philadelphia: Temple University Press. 131–151.

Meyer, Peter B. 1991. "Local Economic Development: What Is Proposed, What Is Done, and What Difference Does It Make?" *Policy Studies Review* 10: 172–180.

Mier, Robert, and Joan Fitzgerald. 1991. "Managing Economic Development." *Economic Development Quarterly* 5: 268–279.

Molotch, Harvey. 1976. "The City as a Growth Machine." *American Journal of Sociology* 82: 309–332.

Morris, David. 1982. *The New City-States*. Washington, D.C.: Institute for Local Self-Reliance.

Olson, Deborah Groban. 1987. "Employee Ownership: An Economic Development Tool for Anchoring Capital in Local Communities." *Review of Law and Social Change* 15: 239–267.

Orr, Marion. 1992. "Urban Regimes and Human Capital Policies: A Study of Baltimore." *Journal of Urban Affairs* 14: 173–187.

Osborne, David, and Ted Gaebler. 1992. *Reinventing Government*. Reading, MA: Addison-Wesley.

Parzen, Julia Ann, and Michael Hall Kieschnick. 1992. *Credit Where It's Due: Development Banking for Communities*. Philadelphia: Temple University Press.

Persky, Joseph, David Ranney, and Wim Wiewel. 1993. "Import Substitution and Local Economic Development." *Economic Development Quarterly* 7: 18–29.

Perry, Stewart E. 1987. *Communities on the Way: Rebuilding Local Economies in the United States and Canada*. Albany: State University of New York Press.

Peters, Alan H. 1993. "Clawbacks and the Administration of Economic Development Policy in the Midwest." *Economic Development Quarterly* 7: 328–340.

Peterson, Paul. 1981. *City Limits*. Chicago: Chicago University Press.

Portz, John. 1990. *The Politics of Plant Closings*. Lawrence: University Press of Kansas.

Rifkin, Jeremy, and Randy Barber. 1978. *The North Will Rise Again: Pension, Politics, and Power in the 1980s*. Boston: Beacon Press.

Riposa, Gerry, and Greg Andranovich. 1988. "Economic Development Policy: Whose Interests Are Being Served?" *Urban Resources* 5: 25–34, 42.

Robinson, Carla Jean. 1989. "Municipal Approaches to Economic Development: Growth and Distribution Policy." *Journal of the American Planning Association* 55: 283–294.

Rosen, David Paul. 1988. *Public Capital*. Washington, D.C.: National Center for Policy Alternatives.

Sagalyn, Lynne B. 1990. "Public Profit Sharing: Symbol or Substance." In Terry Lassar, ed., *City Deal Making*. Washington, D.C.: Urban Land Institute. 139–153.

Shapero, Albert. 1985. "Entrepreneurship: Key to Self-Renewing Economies." Reprinted in Malizia, E. E. 1985. *Local Economic Development: A Guide to Practice*. New York: Praeger. 209–218.

Sharp, Elaine. 1990. *Urban Politics and Administration*. New York: Longman.

Smith, Michael Peter. 1989. "The Uses of Linked-Development Policies in U.S. Cities." In Michael Parkinson, Bernard Foley, and Dennis R. Judd, eds., *Regenerating the Cities: The UK Crisis and the US Experience*. Glenview, IL: Scott Foresman. 85–99.

Squires, Gregory D. 1989. "Public-Private Partnerships: Who Gets What and Why." In Gregory D. Squires, ed., *Unequal Partnerships: The Political Economy of Urban Redevelopment in Postwar America*. New Brunswick, NJ: Rutgers University Press. 1–11.

Stone, Clarence N. 1987. "Summing Up: Urban Regimes, Development Policy, and Political Arrangements." In C. Stone and H. Sanders, eds., *The Politics of Urban Development*. Lawrence: University Press of Kansas. 269–290.

Stone, Clarence N. 1989. *Regime Politics: Governing Atlanta, 1946–1988*. Lawrence: University Press of Kansas.

Stone, Clarence N., Marion Orr, and David Imbroscio. 1991. "The Reshaping of Urban Leadership in U.S. Cities: A Regime Analysis." In M. Gottdiener and C. Pickvance, eds., *Urban Life in Transition*. Newbury Park, CA: Sage Publications. 222–239.

Swack, Michael. 1987. "Community Finance Institutions." In Severyn T. Bruyn and James Meehan, eds., *Beyond the Market and the State: New Directions in Community Economic Development*. Philadelphia: Temple University Press. 79–97.

Swanstrom, Todd. 1985. *The Crisis of Growth Politics*. Philadelphia: Temple University Press.

Vidal, Avis C. 1992. *Rebuilding Communities: A National Study of Urban Community Development Corporations*. New York: Community Development Research Center, Graduate School of Management and Urban Policy, New School for Social Research.

Vogel, Ronald K. 1992. *Urban Political Economy*. Gainsville: University Press of Florida.

Warner, Sam Bass. 1968. *The Private City*. Philadelphia: University of Pennsylvania Press.

Watkins, Alfred. 1980. *The Practice of Urban Economics*. Beverly Hills, CA: Sage Publications.

White, Kirby, and Charles Matthei. 1987. "Community Land Trusts." In Severyn T. Bruyn and James Meehan, eds., *Beyond the Market and the State: New Directions in Community Economic Development*. Philadelphia: Temple University Press. 41–64.

Part IV
Problems and Policy

Chapter 20

Policy Process

Elaine B. Sharp

OVERVIEW OF THE FIELD: A POLICY SPHERES PARADIGM

Scholarship on the urban policy process has sometimes been embedded in analyses of community power (Wirt 1974; Dahl 1961), sometimes treated as a manifestation of political culture (Banfield and Wilson 1963; Wolfinger and Field 1966), frequently approached from an institutionalist perspective (Lineberry and Fowler 1967; Lyons 1978; Mladenka 1980), and synthesized in explicit process models (Waste 1989). But for over a decade, study of the urban policy process has perhaps been most strongly influenced by the organizing framework of policy spheres, or domain theory. That policy framework, set forth in Paul Peterson's classic *City Limits* (1981), suggests that the character of politics and policy-making dynamics depend upon the type of urban policy that is at issue. When developmental matters are at stake, policy making tends to be elite dominated and consensual; when allocational matters are at issue, policy making tends to be high profile, pluralistic, and conflictual; redistributional matters occupy a distinctly minor place in local policy making because of the threat that they pose to the city's position in the competition for economic investment. Furthermore, domain theory offers a contingent perspective on the importance of particular variables in the policy-making process. Fiscal capacity, for example, is stipulated to be an important determinant of redistributive policy, a less important predictor of allocational policy, and largely irrelevant for developmental policy. This and other contingencies concerning policy determinants are logically derived from the premise that intercity competition for private investment makes developmental policy nondiscretionary for all cities, in contrast with the other two spheres of policy.

While the initial controversy over Peterson's work has abated, the framework remains indirectly influential. For example, the avalanche of scholarship on urban economic development that occurred in the 1980s was largely conducted without an eye to the politics surrounding traditional urban service delivery, or allocational politics. It is as though the two forms of urban policy making are fully established as different and disconnected spheres, and separate subfields of inquiry have developed to pursue each.

THEORETICAL ISSUES

As this chapter will show, there is much of value in a conceptualization that emphasizes the distinctiveness of the different spheres of urban policy making. However, a survey of the literature on urban policy making suggests several problems with this paradigmatic, organizing framework as well. First, the framework does not outline a truly comprehensive set of policy spheres. That is, important types of urban policy are omitted. Second, while important features of policy making in the three spheres are outlined, the many variables that have been the focus of urban policy research are only in a fragmentary way treated in the contingent terms that the policy spheres paradigm suggests and the interactions among the policy spheres are inadequately addressed. This chapter outlines these limitations and moves toward an elaboration of the policy spheres paradigm.

Omitted Spheres

The categories of developmental, allocational, and redistributional policy surely encompass a great deal of urban policy. For each sphere, we have research both on the political dynamics surrounding policy making and on the analytics of policy effectiveness; and each sphere incorporates research in the quantitative, hypothesis-testing mode, case study research, and prescriptive research. The study of development policy, for example, includes attention to the various policy tools or strategies that subnational governments use to attract economic investment (Eisinger 1988; Bingham, Hill, and White 1990; Green 1991; McGowan and Ottensmeyer 1993), the dynamics surrounding public-private partnerships for economic development (Cummings 1988; Squires 1989; Stephenson 1991), the emergence of and politics surrounding the use of policy tools for growth limitation (Schneider and Teske 1993; Bollens 1990; Baldassare and Protash 1982), and much more. Scholarship focused on the allocational sphere of policy making includes attention to the importance of metropolitan organization in structuring service delivery patterns (Schneider 1989; Lyons, Lowery, and DeHoog 1992); on the key role that bureaucratic discretion plays in the distribution of city services within jurisdictions (Meier, Stewart, and England 1991; Jones 1980); on the impact that citizen-initiated contacting (Sharp, 1986; Coulter, 1988), neighborhood organization activity (Berry, Portney, and

Thomson 1993), and others forms of local political participation can have on the responsiveness of city service delivery to citizen preferences; on the role of class, race, and ethnicity in the distribution of city jobs (Eisinger 1982; Mladenka 1991) and basic city services (Lineberry 1977; Cingranelli 1981; Mladenka 1989); and much more. And scholarship on the redistributional sphere includes attention to whether the political incorporation of minorities in governing coalitions affects the responsiveness of policy to the needs of minority populations (Browning, Marshall, and Tabb 1984; Wong 1990), the intergovernmentalization of local redistributional policy (Kantor 1988), the scope and consequences of particular problems of poverty, such as homelessness (Dear and Wolch 1987), the causes and consequences of concentrated urban poverty (Galster and Hill 1992; Jencks and Peterson 1991), and the importance of social disruption as well as fiscal capacity in driving local redistributional efforts (Sharp and Maynard-Moody 1991).

Government Organization. But it is also quite clear that attention to these three spheres of policy making omits attention to at least two additional types of policy. One of these omitted spheres concerns decision making about the institutional arrangements of governance itself, or something akin to Lowi's (1972: 300) added category of constituent policy. As outlined by Parks and Oakerson (1989: 24–25), policy making of this type is distinct from decision making about the production of city services; it involves higher-level governance issues, such as which institutions will make decisions about service provision and the choice of rules for making decisions about metropolitan governance. In particular, this sphere of policy making involves those occasions in which annexation, interlocal service agreements, and related policies either are used or are the objects of possible reform and restructuring.

There is, of course, a substantial literature on service delivery within the metropolitan context, derived from the powerful insights of the Tiebout model. But most of this research focuses on policy making and citizen choice within the constraints of existing metropolitan structures, with the very best of this research investigating whether the implications of Tiebout's model can be seen in the differing policy outcomes of more and less fragmented metropolitan areas (Schneider 1989; Dolan 1990; Lyons, Lowery, and DeHoog 1992). Apart from some vintage literature on metropolitan consolidation efforts (Marando 1979; Rosenbaum 1974), there is much less attention to the development and use of policies that structure the metropolitan system in the first place.

Recently, however, attention has begun to turn more heavily to these issues. Rusk (1993), for example, suggests that differences in annexation laws are an important factor in the prosperity and well-being of cities and provides a contemporary look at the metropolitan consolidation question. Stein (1989) shows that variation in the functional responsibility of cities and their consequent taxing and spending policies are a function of metropolitan age and annexation authority. Fuchs (1992) investigates the decision-making processes that led to the creation of special districts and the assignment of functional responsibilities in

Chicago and argues that these helped relieve it from the fiscal strains that beset New York City. And Burns (1994) investigates the political dynamics surrounding the formation of subnational governments. Yet another stream of research relevant to this omitted policy sphere is that body of work focusing on the strategic uses of quasi-governmental "authorities." Muniak (1990), for example, shows how airport development in the metropolitan Washington area was affected by strategic policy making surrounding the creation of the Metropolitan Washington Airports Authority, which resolved the conflicting interests of two states, the District of Columbia, and three existing airports. And Brierly (1990: 999) investigates policy making surrounding the creation of state development authorities, showing that creation of such authorities is a reaction to "declining economic performance."

Social Regulatory Policy. A second sphere of policy activity that is omitted from the theory of policy spheres is that involving conflicts over rights, or the local equivalent of what Tatalovich and Daynes (1988) call "social regulatory" policy. To some extent, this policy arena has been subsumed under one or another of the traditional policy spheres. Peterson (1981:158–162), for example, treated the issues of residential integration, equality of educational opportunity, affirmative action in local government hiring, and the like, as involving a tension between redistributional politics and allocational politics. From this perspective, minority politics involves the politics of demand making by African Americans for a fair share of divisible benefits, even if it means redistribution of shares toward the minority community, and the tendency for whites to view all black demands as redistributional and "beyond the capacity of local officials to grant" (159). But some issues involving racial and ethnic minorities, such as the treatment of African American citizens by law enforcement officers, are not as readily understood in terms of conflict over shares of divisible benefit, because they involve rights claims and justice issues rather than traditional "service delivery" issues, and urban governments face a variety of policy conflicts other than traditional issues of minority politics that have to do with justice and rights. A number of cities have faced conflicts over the addition of gay rights language to human relations ordinances, for example (Cicchino, Deming, and Nicholson 1991), and Wichita became the center of national attention as local authorities grappled with the issues involved in the handling of abortion protesters.

Theoretical perspectives and assumptions that have guided research on the allocational politics surrounding conflict over traditional city service delivery are likely to be inadequate for understanding of the policy-making process involving these rights and justice issues, for several reasons. First, allocational politics typically involves geographically based local interest groups, such as neighborhood associations, because the city services at issue are allocated areally. By contrast, the conflicts swirling around rights issues may frequently involve social movements and local interests that are not territorially based. Laura Woliver (1993), for example, explores several cases of local conflict over rights issues. These efforts for grassroots-initiated reform involved ad hoc interest groups, such as the Coalition for Justice in Milwaukee and the Committee to Recall Judge Archie Simonson in Madison, whose genesis, dynamics, and likely impact on policy outcomes are substantially different from that of neighborhood organizations.

Second, the study of distributional issues that fit neatly into the allocational sphere has focused primarily upon bureaucratic, mayoral, and to a lesser extent, local legislative venues for policy making. The role of the judiciary and the link between judicial policy making and other aspects of local policy making have been understudied (Feiock 1989). In the sphere of rights-based issues, however, the courts are much more likely to be key decision-making venues, and the actions of judges, prosecutors, and others in the criminal justice system are frequently the target of movements for reform. Recent research on the New Jersey Supreme Court's role in prompting local legislative responses with respect to fair housing exemplifies the interesting work that can and should be pursued in this regard (Anglin 1994).

UNFINISHED AGENDA AND DIRECTIONS FOR FUTURE RESEARCH

The other limitation of the policy spheres approach is that it has not yet been developed to its full potential as a contingency theory of policy making for at least three reasons. First, with rare exceptions, research has not explicitly focused on the way in which the type of policy making at issue shapes the dynamics of policy making. Second, new developments are transforming the character of urban phenomena, thereby undermining the meanings that have traditionally been attached to some concepts and exacerbating the problem of defining truly distinctive policy spheres. Third, while the distinctive character of politics and policy making within each sphere is important, the interconnections between the policy domains are also important. While there are fragments of useful work already available in this regard, much work needs to be done on the implications of policy making in one sphere for policy making in the others. The following sections take up these three problems in turn.

Lack of Attention to the Contingencies of Policy Type

Like Lowi's (1972) classic work, Peterson's delineation of a domain theory of urban policy making was notable and galvanizing because it suggested explicit and logically compelling ways in which the character of urban politics and policy making would be affected by the type of issue at stake. But this theoretical perspective has not been as fully elaborated and empirically supported as might have been hoped. There are several notable exceptions. One is Peterson's (1986) own follow-up work on the intergovernmental dynamics of policy making, a study that suggests that intergovernmental cooperation is easiest when developmental policy is at issue, while conflict is relatively more likely when it is redistributional policy that is being implemented. Another exception is Kenneth Wong's (1990) assessment of education and housing programs in Milwaukee and Baltimore, which suggests that redistributional policy is enhanced by professionalism in local institutions and by black representation in local politics; that developmental policy becomes much less consensual under conditions of neighborhood activism; and that the decentralized, pluralistic portrait of allocational policy making must be tempered by acknowledgment of the centralizing effects of bureaucratic decision rules and the elite-dominated nature of allocational policy making in a time of budgetary retrenchment. Schneider (1989) systematically uses domain theory in his investigation of the impact of competition on suburban city spending—an investigation that finds that competition among local governments diminishes allocational spending, increases developmental spending, and has mixed effects on redistributional spending. Finally, Stein (1990) has explicitly used policy domain as a theoretical contingency in his examinations of municipal functional scope and service arrangements.

While these works show important efforts to incorporate domain theory in empirical analyses, the enterprise has a long way to go. More typically, factors of interest in the study of urban policy making are investigated in the context of only one sphere of policy making; or disparate islands of research will explore the impact of one or more variables in different spheres of policy making without developing an overarching assessment showing comparisons and contrasts across policy spheres and linkages to domain theory itself. For example, "fiscal stress" and "economic need" have been used as predictor variables in studies of both developmental policy making and allocational policy making. In the former case, fiscal stress has been found to be a very important determinant of the extent to which cities make use of various developmental policy tools (Rubin and Rubin 1987; Sharp 1989a, 1989b); with respect to the latter, fiscal stress or economic need has not been consistently found to motivate important service delivery innovations such as privatization or intergovernmental service contracting (Benton and Menzel 1992; Morgan and Hirlinger 1991). These outcomes are theoretically "odd" from the perspective of domain theory. Yet these discrepancies between the empirical findings and domain theory typically are not commented upon.

Yet another example of the failure to explore the comparative domain significance of a variable found to be important in a particular policy sphere involves the concept of "policy tools." Researchers interested in accounting for variation in the extent to which different cities engage in economic development activity have considered, among other factors, important features of different economic development policy tools. Consistent with Salamon's (1989: 44) work, for example, developmental policy tools have been differentiated according to the degree to which they are visible to taxpayers (Sharp and Elkins 1991; Rubin and Rubin 1987; Feiock and Clingermayer 1986), and these differences in visibility have been linked, theoretically and empirically, to cities' patterns of uptake of various development policy tools. There is also a substantial body of work evaluating the relative effectiveness of particular policy tools (Dewar 1990; Green 1991) or broad categories of development policy tools, such as Eisinger's (1988) distinction between "supply-side" and "demand-side" policies for development. But, with one major exception, a policy tools approach has not been as characteristic of research on allocational or redistributional policy. That major exception is the body of work on the privatization of city services (Savas 1987; Berenyi and Stevens 1988; Stein 1990; Smith and Lipsky 1993), a research cluster that includes explicit research on the comparative effectiveness of traditional government service delivery and services provided through contracting with private firms. Even here, a policy tools approach is underdeveloped. Other policy tools of the privatization type, such as franchises and vouchers, have not come in for the attention that contracting has. Hence, there are fewer empirical building blocks for a comparative assessment of the effectiveness of various policy tools used in the allocational and redistributional spheres. Much more also needs to be done to learn whether the factors that enhance the uptake of particular policy tools in the developmental arena have the same impact vis-à-vis the uptake of those policy tools in the allocational or redistributional arenas and whether the effectiveness of a particular policy tool is contingent on the policy sphere in which it is used.

Transformations in the Character of Urban Phenomena

Research on policy making in the various policy spheres confronts yet another kind of challenge as well. This challenge stems from the changing character of urban phenomena. As a result of these changes, variables that have been the traditional stock in trade of empirical analysis in the urban area may no longer tap what we once thought they did; and reconceptualization becomes as important as data collection.

Consider, for example, the concept of reform. There is a long tradition in urban research that examines the possible policy consequences of reform structures such as the city manager plan, at-large districts, and nonpartisanship, relative to nonreform structures such as strong mayors, district elections, and partisan elections (Lineberry and Fowler 1967; Liebert 1974; Morgan and Pelissero 1980; Welch and Bledsoe 1988). Although reform structures clearly have an impact on descriptive representation and certain features of governance processes, empirical research has not shown a link between reform versus nonreform structures and policy views of elected officials (Welch and Bledsoe 1988), and when aggregate policy outcomes, such as overall taxing and spending, are at issue, there is little empirical support for the notion that reform institutions make any difference (Morgan and Pelissero 1980). However, reform structures have been empirically linked with policy outcomes within particular policy spheres. For example, Morgan and Hirlinger (1991) find that the existence of council-manager government is a very modest but positive predictor of intergovernmental contracting for public works and support services. In the realm of developmental policy making, Feiock and Clingermayer (1986) have found that the presence of unreformed political institutions enhances the likelihood that a city will use various economic development policies.

But the problem with assessment of the impact of reformism on urban policy is that change in reform institutions has undercut the clarity of meaning of the reform concept. A large number of cities have hybrid arrangements, rather than purely "reformed" or purely "nonreformed" structures. Representational systems that combine some at-large with some district council seats are becoming increasingly common, and a number of cities with strong mayor systems have added chief administrative officers (CAOs) with all the professionalism of the city manager (Sharp 1989a). These sorts of institutional adaptations and hybrids can, of course, be partly captured through indexes of reform that count the proportion of seats that are at-large or weight a CAO arrangement as the near-equivalent of the council-manager plan. But what may really be in question is the basic conceptualization of reform. Categorization based upon formal structures may be less useful than clear conceptualization of the dimensions of reformism, as in Wong's (1990: 100) treatment of professional autonomy from political influence.

Similarly, the impact of neighborhood organizations in the urban policy process has long been of interest. Traditionally, however, neighborhood organizations have been conceptualized as voluntary, nongovernmental organizations, mobilizing to fight for the neighborhood's fair share of allocational services, to resist the siting of facilities such as homeless shelters, mental health clinics, and drug treatment centers that are crucial to the delivery of redistributional service, and to press for developmental policies that reflect the inclusion of residential interests, not just the downtown interests. Recently, however, newer forms of neighborhood organization have emerged. These residential community associations (Dilger 1992) are more like private governments than voluntary organizations. They can assess dues and fees from residents, they provide a variety of allocational services that city governments have traditionally provided, they manage commons areas, and they have control over the development of entire subdivisions.

The emergence of such organizations means that our conceptualization of neighborhood organization, like our conceptualization of urban reform, must change. And that reconceptualization will have important implications for our understanding of policy making in the various spheres. The politics of allocation, for example, may not be nearly as participatory, pluralistic, and conflictual in areas under the control of residential community associations as Peterson (1981) posited them to be. And a new conceptualization of reform may offer new insights into the circumstances under which developmental decision making can be as consensual and elite dominated as Peterson (1981) claimed it to be.

Interconnections among Policy Domains

Finally, much more needs to be done by way of theoretical development and empirical investigation of the interconnections between and among policy spheres. While domain theory rightly points up the distinctive political dynamics within each policy-making sphere, there are good reasons to consider the implications that decision making in any sphere has for the others.

One example of the need for comparison across spheres is in the area of research on the distribution of policy outcomes. Much of the initial research on this topic focused on allocational services, such as residential streets, libraries, policing, fire protection, refuse collection, and parks (Lineberry 1977; Levy, Meltsner, and Wildavsky 1974; Mladenka 1980). These studies generally concluded that distribution is the result of rational-technocratic decision rules rather than class or racial preferences, political rewards, and the like. But as Baer (1985) has argued, the results might have been quite different had the studies focused on regulatory staff functions or capital-intensive services. And the developmental domain is characterized by just such services, with its amalgam of land use regulatory decisions, airport and harbor development, downtown renewal projects, and other site-specific, long-term projects. And while the method of research has typically been the case study rather than the sort of quantitative analysis represented in early studies of urban service distribution, research on economic development policy making has indeed emphasized the ways in which race, business power, and the imperatives of electoral coalition building and regime maintenance are essential to understanding the policy decisions that are made (Feagin 1988; Stone 1989). In short, conclusions about the dynamics of service distribution have been too narrowly based within the allocational domain, particularly since scholars have "extrapolated the findings to urban *resource allocation* more generally" (Miranda and Tunyavong 1994: 510). Application of a comparative policy spheres approach to this research question could clarify important differences in distributional dynamics by policy sphere. And it could highlight important similarities that might otherwise be overlooked. For example, Bachelor's (1994) discussion of the "solution sets" that can dominate economic development policy making can perhaps be viewed as the developmental sphere equivalent of the bureaucratic decision rules that play such an important role in service distribution within the allocational sphere.

The study of fiscal policy is another key place in which the interactions among policy spheres can be observed. Existing research suggests a number of such interactions. For example, excessive responsiveness to redistributional, or even allocational, demands is one of the key explanations for fiscal stress (Rubin 1982; Shefter 1985), which in turn can threaten the economic competitiveness of the city, or at the very least push the city toward a more centralized, developmentally oriented mode of budgeting (Kantor 1988) as a way out of fiscal crisis. Note that the opposite point of view is rarely considered. Excessive responsiveness in the developmental sphere is not treated as a possible explanation of fiscal crisis, despite the fact that a number of developmental policies involve substantial risk taking by government as it moves into public-private partnerships and despite the fact that excessive tax abatements, sports stadium subsidies, and other developmental subsidies can add to a city's financial burdens.

While these various theories and bodies of empirical work suggest some interaction among the policy spheres, that interaction is typically not the focus of the work, and the dynamics of the interaction are not well developed. Instead, the separateness of the different spheres of policy is emphasized. Indeed, at least one theorist, Stephen Elkin (1987), suggests that those involved in growth politics have little reason to be involved in other policy arenas. He argues that while land interests care about "the delivery of the kind of services that are thought to make investment more attractive," about competitive tax rates, and about the avoidance of racial turmoil and the proper allocation of police services, such "prodevelopment forces" are "unlikely to dominate across the full range of policy arenas" (50). This is partly because most of the preferences that prodevelopment forces have in policy arenas other than development are already institutionalized and partly because "most day-to-day actions of city governments have little direct bearing on land use and investment matters" (50). Hence, local politicians can be left to manage such affairs in ways that are helpful in their need to build political alliances.

Nevertheless, Elkin and others writing in the tradition of regime theory provide one of the most promising avenues for consideration of the interactions among various policy spheres. Because of its concern with the ways in which informal arrangements are used to build bridges between political power and economic power, studies in the regime theory tradition tend to focus primarily upon the handling of developmental issues. Nevertheless, the rapidly developing research on regimes offers substantial insights into the ways in which redistributional and allocational policies are handled in distinctive types of regimes. For example, in stark contrast with Peterson's (1981) thesis that redistributional issues are marginalized in local politics, we now have research on a nationwide sample of cities showing widespread use of *developmental policies that incorporate redistributive policy* by mandating that developers provide social services, hire or train local residents, provide contributions for affordable housing, designate a set percentage of involvement by minority business enterprises, or in other ways target the benefits of development toward otherwise disadvantaged groups (Goetz 1990).

We also have case studies of several urban regimes in which redistributional issues were central (DeLeon 1992; Mier 1993). Both in the case of Harold Washington's administration in Chicago and in the case of San Francisco's progressive politics, redistributional and allocational issues were intertwined with development issues in a way that makes the distinctiveness of the spheres less important than the relationships among them. For example, Proposition M, the centerpiece of San Francisco's emergent antigrowth regime, included specific attention to affordable housing, preservation of "neighborhood-serving retail uses,'' and priorities for resident employment and ownership of businesses (DeLeon 1992: 70). While the sphere of developmental policy in San Francisco still included the usual decisions over downtown office development, sports facilities, and the like, the extent to which the "use values" of existing residents are affected by development and the need to redistribute some of the gains of development toward the less advantaged had become part of the same policy sphere. In the case of Chicago under Harold Washington, the developmental sphere took on distinctly allocational and redistributional aspects as the Washington regime introduced policies emphasizing affirmative action hiring, local purchasing, employment training, and housing rehabilitation (Mier 1993: 58).

In sum, progressive regimes exemplify a resurgence of allocational and even redistributional policy making, even within the rubric of the developmental sphere. This contrasts sharply with the autonomy of the developmental sphere in a "corporate" regime such as Atlanta's (Stone 1989). Other types of regimes involve still different types of interaction among the policy spheres.

In some ways, regime theory may seem the antithesis of domain theory. In particular, its emphasis on differences in governing coalitions rather than differences in policy spheres would seem to take research in a distinctly different direction from the contingencies that are at the heart of domain theory. Viewed from a broader perspective, however, regime theory offers the potential to elaborate upon domain theory and, in the process, to enrich understanding of policy-making processes. Domain theory suggests that the factors that influence policy will differ based upon the type of policy that is at issue; regime theory suggests that a given policy issue will not be handled in the same way in different settings, because of different imperatives for coalition formation. What this suggests is a matrix model of the urban policy process. That is, the nature of the policy process, and the role of any particular explanatory variable in that process, is doubly contingent—it is a function of both the character of the local regime and the nature of the policy at issue; and the interpretation of the latter is affected by the former.

REFERENCES

Anglin, Roland. 1994. "Searching for Justice: Court-Inspired Housing Policy as a Mechanism for Social and Economic Mobility." *Urban Affairs Quarterly* 29 (March): 432–453.

Bachelor, Lynn. 1994. "Regime Maintenance, Solution Sets, and Urban Economic Development." *Urban Affairs Quarterly* 29: 596–616.

Baer, William C. 1985. "Just What Is an Urban Service Anyway?" *Journal of Politics* 47 (August): 880–895.

Baldassare, M., and W. Protash. 1982. "Growth Controls, Population Growth, and Community Satisfaction." *American Sociological Review* 47 (3): 339–346.

Banfield, Edward, and James Q. Wilson. 1963. *City Politics.* Cambridge: Harvard and MIT Press.

Benton, J. Edwin, and Donald C. Menzel. 1992. "Contracting and Franchising County Services in Florida." *Urban Affairs Quarterly* 27: 436–456.

Berenyi, Eileen B., and Barbara J. Stevens. 1988. "Does Privatization Work: A Study of the Delivery of Eight Local Services." *State and Local Government Review* (winter): 11–20.

Berry, Jeffrey, M. Ken Portney, and Ken Thompson. 1993. *The Rebirth of Urban Democracy.* Washington, D.C.: Brookings.

Bingham, Richard D., Edward W. Hill, and Sammis B. White, eds. 1990. *Financing Economic Development.* Newbury Park, CA: Sage.

Bollens, Scott A. 1990. "Constituencies for Limitation and Regionalism: Approaches to Growth Management." *Urban Affairs Quarterly* 26: 46–67.

Brierly, Allen B. 1990. "Economic Development Authorities in the American States: The Organizational Response to Economic Decline." *Policy Studies Journal* 18: 999–1014.

Browning, Rufus, Dale Rogers Marshall, and David Tabb. 1984. *Protest Is Not Enough.* Berkeley: University of California Press.

Burns, Nancy. 1994. *The Formation of American Local Governments: Private Values in Public Institutions.* New York: Oxford University Press.

Cicchino, Peter M., Bruce R. Deming, and Katherine M. Nicholson. 1991. "Sex, Lies and Civil Rights: A Critical History of the Massachusetts Gay Civil Rights Bill." *Harvard Civil Rights/Civil Liberties Law Review*, vol 26, no. 2 (summer).

Cingranelli, D. 1981. "Race, Politics, and Elites: Testing Alternative Models of Municipal Service Distribution." *American Journal of Political Science* 25: 664–692.

Coulter, Philip B. 1988. *Political Voice: Citizen Demand for Urban Public Services.* Tuscaloosa: University of Alabama Press.

Cummings, Scott, ed. 1988. *Business Elites & Urban Development.* Albany: State University of New York Press.

Dahl, Robert. 1961. *Who Governs?* New Haven: Yale University Press.

Dear, Michael, and Jennifer Wolch. 1987. *Landscapes of Despair.* Princeton: Princeton University Press.

DeLeon, Richard. 1992. *Left Coast City.* Lawrence: University Press of Kansas.

Dewar, Margaret E. 1990. "Tax Incentives, Public Loans, and Subsidies: What Difference Do They Make in Nonmetropolitan Economic Development." In Richard Bingham, Edward Hill, and Sammis White, eds., *Financing Economic Development: An Institutional Response.* Newbury Park: Sage, 40–54.

Dilger, Robert. 1992. *Neighborhood Politics: Residential Community Associations in American Governance.* New York: New York University Press.

Dolan, Drew. 1990. "Local Government Fragmentation: Does It Drive Up the Cost of Government?" *Urban Affairs Quarterly* 26, no. 1 (September): 28–45.

Eisinger, Peter. 1982. "Black Employment in Municipal Jobs: The Impact of Black Political Power." *American Political Science Review* 76: 380–392.

Eisinger, Peter. 1988. *The Rise of the Entrepreneurial State.* Madison: University of Wisconsin Press.

Elkin, Stephen. 1987. *City and Regime in the American Republic.* Chicago: University of Chicago Press.

Feagin, Joe R. 1988. *Free Enterprise City.* New Brunswick, NJ: Rutgers University Press.

Feiock, Richard. 1989. "Support for Business in the Federal District Courts: The Impact of State Political Environment.'' *American Politics Quarterly* 17 (January): 96–104.

Feiock, Richard, and James Clingermayer. 1986. ''Municipal Representation, Executive Power, and Economic Development Policy Activity.'' *Policy Studies Journal* 15, no. 2: 211–229.

Fuchs, Ester. 1992. *Mayors and Money*. Chicago: University of Chicago Press.

Galster, George C., and Edward W. Hill. 1992. *The Metropolis in Black and White*. New Brunswick, NJ: Rutgers University Press.

Goetz, Edward. 1990. ''Type II Policy and Mandated Benefits in Economic Development.'' *Urban Affairs Quarterly* 26: 170–190.

Green, Roy E., ed. 1991. *Enterprise Zones: New Directions in Economic Development*. Newbury Park: Sage.

Jencks, Christopher, and Paul E. Peterson. 1991. *The Urban Underclass*. Washington, D.C.: Brookings.

Jones, Bryan D. 1980. *Service Delivery in the City: Citizen Demand and Bureaucratic Rules*. New York: Longman.

Kantor, Paul. 1988. *The Dependent City*. Glenview, IL: Scott Foresman.

Levy, Frank, Arnold J. Melsner, and Aaron B. Wildavsky. 1974. *Urban Outcomes*. Berkeley: University of California Press.

Liebert, Roland. 1974. ''Municipal Functions, Structure, and Expenditures: A Reanalysis of Recent Research.'' *Social Science Quarterly* 54 (March): 765–783.

Lineberry, Robert. 1977. *Equality and Urban Policy*. Beverly Hills: Sage.

Lineberry, Robert, and Edmund Fowler. 1967. ''Reformism and Public Policies in American Cities.'' *American Political Science Review* 61 (September): 701–716.

Lowi, Theodore. 1972. ''Four Systems of Policy, Politics, and Choice.'' *Public Administration Review* 33, no. 4 (July–August): 298–310.

Lyons, William. 1978. ''Reform and Response in American Cities: Structure and Policy Reconsidered.'' *Social Science Quarterly* 59 (June): 118–132.

Lyons, W. E., David Lowery, and Ruth Hoogland DeHoog. 1992. *The Politics of Dissatisfaction: Citizens, Services, and Urban Institutions*. Armonk. NY: M. E. Sharpe, Inc.

McGowan, Robert P., and Edward J. Ottensmeyer, eds. 1993. *Economic Development Strategies for State and Local Governments*. Chicago: Nelson-Hall.

Marando, Vincent. 1979. ''City-County Consolidation: Reform, Regionalism, Referenda and Requiem.'' *Western Political Quarterly* 32 (December): 409–421.

Meier, Kenneth, Joseph Stewart, Jr., and Robert E. England. 1991. ''The Politics of Bureaucratic Discretion: Educational Access as an Urban Service.'' *American Journal of Political Science* 35: 155–177.

Mier, Robert. 1993. *Social Justice and Local Development Policy*. Newbury Park, CA: Sage.

Miranda, Rowan A., and Ittipone Tunyavong. 1994. ''Patterned Inequality? Reexamining the Role of Distributive Politics in Urban Service Delivery.'' *Urban Affairs Quarterly* 29 (June): 509–534.

Mladenka, Kenneth. 1980. ''The Urban Bureaucracy and the Chicago Political Machine: Who Gets What and the Limits to Political Control.'' *American Political Science Review* 74 (December): 991–998.

Mladenka, Kenneth. 1989. ''The Distribution of an Urban Public Service: The Changing Role of Race and Politics.'' *Urban Affairs Quarterly* 24: 556–583.

Mladenka, Kenneth. 1991. "Public Employee Unions, Reformism, and Black Employment in 1,200 American Cities." *Urban Affairs Quarterly* 26: 532–548.

Morgan, David R., and Michael W. Hirlinger. 1991. "Intergovernmental Service Contracts: A Multivariate Explanation." *Urban Affairs Quarterly* 27 (September): 128–144.

Morgan, David, and John Pelissero. 1980. "Urban Policy: Does Political Structure Matter?" *American Political Science Review* 74 (December): 999–1006.

Muniak, Dennis. 1990. "Federal Divestiture, Regional Growth, and the Political Economy of Public Authority Creation: The Emergence of the Metropolitan Washington Airports Authority." *Policy Studies Journal* 18: 943–960.

Parks, Roger B., and Ronald J. Oakerson. 1989. "Metropolitan Organization and Governance: A Local Public Economy Approach." *Urban Affairs Quarterly* 25: 18–29.

Peterson, Paul. 1981. *City Limits*. Chicago: University of Chicago Press.

Peterson, Paul. 1986. *When Federalism Works*. Washington, D.C.: Brookings.

Rosenbaum, Walter. 1974. *Against Long Odds: The Theory and Practice of Successful Governmental Consolidation*. Beverly Hills: Sage.

Rubin, Irene. 1982. *Running in the Red*. Albany: State University of New York Press.

Rubin, Irene S., and Herbert J. Rubin. 1987. "Economic Development Incentives: The Poor (Cities) Pay More." *Urban Affairs Quarterly* 23: 37–62.

Rusk, David. 1993. *Cities without Suburbs*. Washington, D.C.: Woodrow Wilson International Center for Scholars.

Salamon, Lester M. 1989. "The Tools Approach: Basic Analytics." In L. Salamon, ed., *Beyond Privatization: The Tools of Government Action*. Washington, D.C.: Urban Institute Press. 23–49.

Savas, Emanuel S. 1987. *Privatization: The Key to Better Government*. Chatham, NJ: Chatham House.

Schneider, Mark. 1989. *The Competitive City*. Pittsburgh: University of Pittsburgh Press.

Schneider, Mark, and Paul Teske. 1993. "The Anti-Growth Entrepreneur: Challenging the 'Equilibrium' of the Growth Machine." *Journal of Politics* 55, no. 3: 720–736.

Sharp, Elaine B. 1986. *Citizen Demand-Making in the Urban Context*. Tuscaloosa: University of Alabama Press.

Sharp, Elaine B. 1989a. "City Management in an Era of Blurred Boundaries." In H. George Frederickson, ed., *Ideal & Practice in Council-Manager Government*. Washington, D.C.: ICMA.

Sharp, Elaine B. 1989b. "Institutional Manifestations of Accessibility and Urban Economic Development Policy." *Western Political Quarterly* 44, no. 1 (March): 129–147.

Sharp, Elaine B. 1990. *Urban Politics and Administration*. New York: Longman's.

Sharp, Elaine B., and David R. Elkins. 1991. "The Politics of Economic Development Policy." *Economic Development Quarterly* 5, no. 2 (May): 126–139.

Sharp, Elaine B., and Steven Maynard-Moody. 1991. "Theories of the Local Welfare Role." *American Journal of Political Science* 35, no. 4 (November): 934–950.

Shefter, Martin. 1985. *Political Crisis, Fiscal Crisis: The Collapse and Revival of New York City*. New York: Basic Books.

Smith, Steven R., and Michael Lipsky. 1993. *Nonprofits for Hire: The Welfare State in the Age of Contracting*. Cambridge: Harvard University Press.

Squires, Gregory, ed. 1989. *Unequal Partnerships: The Political Economy of Urban Redevelopment in Postwar America.* New Brunswick, NJ: Rutgers University Press.

Stein, Robert. 1989. ''Market Maximization of Individual Preferences and Metropolitan Municipal Service Responsibility.'' *Urban Affairs Quarterly* 25: 86–116.

Stein, Robert. 1990. *Urban Alternatives: Public and Private Markets in the Provision of Local Services.* Pittsburgh: University of Pittsburgh Press.

Stephenson, Max. 1991. ''Whither the Public-Private Partnership? A Critical Overview.'' *Urban Affairs Quarterly* 27: 109–127.

Stone, Clarence. 1989. *Regime Politics.* Lawrence: University Press of Kansas.

Tatalovich, Raymond, and Byron W. Dayness. 1988. *Social Regulatory Policy: Moral Controversies in American Politics.* Boulder: Westview Press.

Waste, Robert J. 1989. *The Ecology of City Policymaking.* New York: Oxford University Press.

Welch, Susan, and Timothy Bledsoe. 1988. *Urban Reform and Its Consequences.* Chicago: University of Chicago Press.

Wirt, Fred. 1974. *Power in the City: Decisionmaking in San Francisco.* Berkeley: University of California Press.

Wolfinger, Raymond E., and John Osgood Field. 1966. ''Political Ethos and the Structure of Government.'' *American Political Science Review* 60 (June): 306–326.

Woliver, Laura. 1993. *From Outrage to Action: The Politics of Grass-Roots Dissent.* Urbana: University of Illinois Press.

Wong, Kenneth. 1990. *City Choices.* Albany: State University of New York Press.

Chapter 21

Housing

R. Allen Hays

The study of housing, in the context of urban affairs, is a multidisciplinary endeavor. From political science come studies of the housing policy process at the national and the local levels (Dommel 1980; Bratt 1989; Goetz and Sidney 1994; Hays 1995). From sociology comes the analysis of neighborhood interactions, of the dynamics of racial and ethnic strife, and of the impact of homelessness (Fried 1966; Hoch and Slayton 1989; Monti 1989; 1993; Burt 1992). From geography and planning come studies of the spatial impacts of social, political, and economic forces (Varady and Raffel 1993; Stegman 1979; Rohe and Stegman 1993). And, from economics comes the analysis of housing markets, housing costs, and the impact of various strategies for government intervention (Downs 1973; Solomon 1974; Struyk and Bendick 1981; Hughes and Sternlieb 1987).

Housing is of central importance in the study of urban affairs for several reasons. First, shelter is on almost anyone's list of the most basic human needs. The quality of housing in a city, thus, is a reflection of that community's ability to provide its citizens with their basic needs. Second, housing occupies a great deal of the physical space in the city, and it, therefore, shapes, and is shaped by, land use decisions, as well as determining much of the city's physical appearance. Third, housing is distributed as a commodity within the capitalist market economy. It reveals clearly the workings of the market system and its impact, for good or ill, on social and political relationships, as well as on the distribution of goods and services. Finally, housing has been the object of frequent governmental interventions in social and economic processes, since, left to themselves, these processes often fail to produce positive outcomes for many members of society. The study of housing policy reveals, therefore, both the strengths and the limitations of the role of the state in supplementing or altering market outcomes.

In this chapter, each of these four facets of the housing issue will be briefly reviewed, with careful attention given to theoretical and methodological issues, as well as the relevant literature. The final section will discuss issues for future research and policy development.

HOUSING AS A BASIC NEED

Much of the literature on urban housing simply takes for granted the importance of shelter as a basic need and then moves on to discuss broader social, economic, or political issues. However, it is useful to consider why shelter is fundamental to human existence and what kinds of needs it serves. Such considerations are essential to a proper theoretical understanding of the housing issue.

The most direct answer to the question of why housing is important is that shelter has a direct impact on the physical health and safety of its occupants. If it is heated, lighted, or ventilated inadequately or unsafely, or if it is unclean or allows access by vermin, the potential negative consequences for physical well-being are not difficult to measure. The health problems faced by those without any secure habitation whatever brought this physical impact into sharp relief (Burt 1992). However, beyond the most basic elements of shelter, there is room for disagreement as to what level of shelter is ''necessary.'' At one time, housing with two to four persons per room and no indoor plumbing was the norm in American society, but as standards and expectations have risen, such housing would almost universally be considered unsafe and inadequate today. Some housing analysts never tire of telling us how much better our housing has become (Hughes and Sternlieb 1987). Moreover, some have questioned the necessity of the extensive regulations enforced in the name of health and safety. Are these regulations vital to the well-being of households, or do they unreasonably force up the price of housing, thus contributing to the affordability problems for the poor (Welfeld 1988)?

Despite the importance of physical health and safety, few would argue that shelter derives its importance solely from this first level of Abraham Maslow's hierarchy of needs (Maslow 1970). Our physical surroundings also satisfy, or fail to satisfy, our second most basic psychological needs for safety and security, and they structure our interactions with those to whom we are most closely attached emotionally, thus affecting what Maslow called our third-level need for ''belonging.'' Homeless people are often afflicted with a chronic sense of insecurity and find it difficult to maintain family and friendship ties with those who are housed. For this reason, many of them measure high on psychological tests for depression and anxiety, even if they are not clinically mentally ill (Burt 1992).

Moving higher on Maslow's scale, we find that being able to choose where we live and to control its interior and exterior appearance provides a mode of self-expression that enhances both self-esteem and self-actualization. Rachel Bratt (1989) laments the lack of attention to this dimension of housing in the policy literature and is able to cite mainly studies from other countries that have given it detailed attention. Moving from the status of renter to that of home-owner has often been linked with important boosts to self-esteem and self-confidence.

Moreover, housing places human beings in a larger neighborhood and community context that may leave them feeling powerless and alienated or make them feel an important part of a functioning community. This, in turn, has an impact on the whole range of what Maslow calls our higher-level functioning. This relationship is strongly demonstrated in the literature on neighborhood organizations that are working to improve their shared environment (Peterman 1993; Monti 1989; Bratt 1989).

It should be stressed, of course, that all of these psychological variables exist in a *mutually* causal relationship with shelter. At times, an individual's inability to meet basic needs in other aspects of her or his life fosters a destructive relationship with the housing she or he occupies. Thus, while adequate housing is important, it has sometimes unreasonably been expected to bear all the burden of eliminating social pathologies. Observers are dismayed when the problems of life in poverty invade federally assisted housing and tend to blame the programs themselves, rather than the limited impact that even the best housing can have on deep social problems. And proponents of programs to foster home-ownership have often made exaggerated claims as to the psychological transformations that can result from a change in housing tenure (Hays 1993; Kemeny 1981).

HOUSING AND PHYSICAL SPACE

Each type of housing unit competes with other housing types, and with non-housing uses, for the limited useful space in any city. Topography and technology initially shape the accessibility and desirability of land for various uses. Then the structures built on that land, and the uses to which they are put, affect its desirability for subsequent uses, as well as the desirability of neighboring parcels. Molotch has argued that much of urban politics and economics is shaped by this basic struggle over physical space (Molotch 1976). Neighborhoods are designed for a certain type of housing, and their residents fight desperately to keep out other uses that might negatively affect their property values or their quality of life. Investors seek maximum return from each parcel of land and often try to evade responsibility for the externalities they generate for those occupying adjacent properties.

An important theoretical perspective on this process is provided by Davis and Whinston (1966), who argue that investment decisions by adjacent property owners are governed by a "Prisoners' Dilemma" game, in which each player's outcome is affected by the others' decisions and yet each has imperfect knowledge with which to predict those decisions. In a deteriorating neighborhood, the interdependence of property values means that an outcome in which all owners invest simultaneously in property improvements would maximize everyone's benefit by mutual reinforcement of values. However, since each owner's worst outcome is to invest when others do not (thereby losing the value of the investment due to surrounding deterioration), and since each is unsure of whether the neighbors will invest, the actual outcome is often mutual noninvestment, an outcome that minimizes potential losses.

Another dimension of space usage is its relationship to social stratification. One of the strongest forces affecting the use of urban space is the tendency for persons to group themselves according to economic, cultural, or ethnic stratification. There are three basic motivations for this sociospacial structuring: (1) to structure social relations by limiting interactions to neighbors who share "desirable" traits according to the individual's value structure; (2) to create a neighborhood that, by its location and aesthetics, is a visible symbol of one's social standing; and (3) to preserve the investment value of one's property, which is viewed as a direct result of (1) and (2).

Although this socioeconomic "sorting" of neighborhoods is a normal product of a society in which material status is highly valued, its impact on those on the bottom rungs is profoundly negative. Left undisturbed, this process allows those with the most political and economic clout to choose their space first, while those of lower socioeconomic status must settle for whatever is left over. The space allocated to the least advantaged by this status system leaves them physically isolated from the opportunities and services that might enhance their upward mobility, thereby contributing to the self-perpetuating nature of poverty (Wilson 1987; Case and Katz 1991). The efforts of almost all federal housing programs to improve the lives of the poor have been compromised by the intense hostility engendered by attempts to house them in proximity to persons of higher incomes.

HOUSING AND THE MARKET ECONOMY

The production and distribution of housing as a commodity through the private market has, on a macroeconomic scale, proved much more efficient than state-based attempts to decommodify housing and allocate it according to central planners' definitions of need. Before their demise in the late 1980s, the centrally planned economies of Eastern Europe and the Soviet Union deliberately neglected housing production in favor of development of basic industries, with the result that shortages and overcrowding were the norm in those countries. The decoupling of the price of housing from its actual cost contributed not only to these shortages but to poor construction and maintenance. Moreover, while previous housing inequalities were initially reduced in these systems, new and glaring inequalities emerged from the abuse of bureaucratic power and privilege to obtain scarce units (Szelenyi 1983; Morton 1987; Telgarsky and Struyk 1991). During the same period of time, in almost all market economies, the quantity and quality of housing available to most citizens steadily improved.

Nevertheless, in spite of clear advantages on the macrolevel, market economies, in the total absence of state intervention, produce or reinforce serious problems in the distribution of housing services to large groups within the population. One of the central tasks of housing policy analysts is to understand these fundamental problems as a basis for recommending and evaluating policy responses to them.

The first problem is that labor markets drive the wages of millions of full-time workers below the level where they can purchase minimum, decent housing without sacrificing other basic needs. (Of course, part-time or zero participation in the labor force reduces even further the resources available.) This is especially true in the intensely competitive global economy that has emerged in the last 30 years, in which the earnings of persons without advanced education or training have steadily declined. As a result, in virtually all market economies, there is a chronic gap between the cost of building and operating housing at a profit and the level of housing expenditures that are affordable, by any reasonable standard, to those at the bottom of the income scale. As long as this gap exists, the market system will not produce decent housing for the poor without state intervention.

The second problem is that the market responds all too well to consumer preferences for spatial segregation by class and race generated by the social forces discussed previously. Since consumers seek to purchase social status and social homogeneity, along with a physical structure, as part of the housing commodity, this element figures heavily into its price. Therefore, each consumer has a financial as well as a social stake in maintaining the social character of the neighborhood. To counteract this element of the market system requires state interventions of the greatest sophistication, involving substantial political risk. Even well-intended state interventions often reinforce, rather than counteract, market outcomes with regard to social stratification (Goetz and Sidney 1994).

Third, the housing supply is extremely vulnerable to fluctuations in credit markets, due to the large role that consumer and investor debt plays in the cost of housing. When credit becomes tight, and interest rates rise, the availability and affordability of housing are threatened, even for households well above the poverty level. Adjustments in the availability of credit are a part of the normal workings of the market system, yet citizens and governments often believe that their housing is on the front line in absorbing such adjustments. This has led to numerous state interventions designed to stabilize the cost and availability of credit for housing investment (Semer et al. 1976).

Finally, housing markets are often slow to adjust to shifting demographic trends, due to the scope and duration of the process of producing housing units. As family size and composition change, different housing needs rapidly emerge, often more quickly than producers can respond (Hughes and Sternlieb 1987). While temporary in the structural sense, these gaps can produce housing shortages for particular groups. In addition, the market tends to standardize the housing product and, thus, may not respond adequately to smaller groups of consumers with specialized needs. Large families, families whose members have physical disabilities, and individuals who require group or supported housing are households frequently ill-served in the housing market, absent state intervention.

GOVERNMENT INTERVENTION

Since most persons living in mixed economies eschew total government takeover of housing production, and yet are frequently dissatisfied with market outcomes, such economic systems are characterized by a myriad of state interventions to correct real, or perceived, market failures. Thus, another major challenge for housing policy analysts is to arrive at an analytical framework for classifying and evaluating such government interventions.

Government interventions can be most usefully classified according to the strategic choices implicit in their designs. (The classification presented here was first developed in Hays 1994b.) The first is the choice of a *target population*. While it is common to think of housing assistance as aimed primarily at the poor, in fact the middle class and above have been the beneficiaries of some of the most generous government assistance in many countries. Assistance has aimed at correcting societywide housing shortages created by economic crises or war, at counteracting the fluctuations in credit mentioned above, or at promoting homeownership.

The second fundamental choice is the *tenure* to be favored by government intervention. While in some mixed economies rental housing is considered an acceptable tenure for all classes of people, others view homeownership as a socially desirable goal, because of the traits of frugality, responsibility, and civic-mindedness it is believed to produce (Kemeny 1981; Choko 1993). Thus, government interventions promote a higher level of ownership than the market would normally produce.

A third choice is the *mode of production*. Programs may rely on new construction, on rehabilitation, on improved utilization of the existing standard housing stock, or on some mixture of these strategies. In some cases, these choices are based on philosophical, or ideological, predispositions, yet they also respond to the nature of the current housing supply. For example if there are widespread shortages of units, new construction will be pursued, whereas if large numbers of deteriorated but structurally sound units are available, rehabilitation will recommend itself.

The final choice relates to the *mechanism* of intervention, a choice greatly influenced by the other three choices just described. The tax system has been a frequent mechanism for intervention (Aaron 1972; Slitor 1976; Dolbeare 1986).

Selective tax breaks are offered, either to stimulate private investor involvement in low-income housing or to support homeownership for the middle class or above. Another mechanism has been government involvement in the housing credit system, either directly through public lending institutions or indirectly through insurance or subsidies to private lenders.

The above mechanisms are frequently insufficient to lower costs to levels affordable by the very poor. Public ownership and operation of housing has commonly been used to provide such extremely low-cost housing, although it has also been used to relieve chronic housing shortages for all classes, as in Great Britain after World War II. However, due to the many problems encountered by publicly owned housing and to increases in the overall supply and quality of privately produced housing, direct housing allowances to low-income families to enable them to obtain housing on the private market are now the strategy of choice in most capitalist countries (Struyk and Bendick 1981; Hays 1994). In cases where the state supports new housing construction, many countries rely on "third sector" nonprofit entities, such as cooperatives or community development corporations (CDCs) to deliver and manage an increasing share of this construction (Bratt 1989; Rasey 1993).

A serious methodological problem in examining these strategies is the determination of their true costs. The full extent of subsidies for a particular kind of housing may be hidden by their sheer complexity and by the length of time over which subsidies are paid out. Some obfuscation is deliberate, as policy makers often have an incentive to hide the full costs of what they are doing. For example, tax incentives were an important part of government-subsidized private sector production programs for low-income housing in the 1960s and 1970s, yet they were seldom presented up front as a part of the cost of the program (U.S. GAO 1980).

However, the most profound questions in the evaluation of government policies deal with assessing their impact on individuals and on society. In another article, I have argued that the most important criteria in evaluating any housing policy are quality, equity, efficiency, choice, and community (Hays 1994a). Here I will briefly discuss these criteria in relation to the issues raised above.

The criterion of *quality* may be linked with the earlier discussion of the need for housing to meet minimum standards of health, safety, and comfort. Most government interventions have improving quality as a fundamental goal, because of the central role of housing in meeting basic physical human needs and because of the cost obstacles to market production of housing that meets these needs for low-income persons. Most programs improve the quality of housing relative to that provided by the market, but the literature shows that they fall far short of expectations in many respects.

Eugene Meehan (1979) provides one of the most thorough demonstrations that public housing quality is vulnerable to the vagaries of funding availability and to the inefficiency of public bureaucracies. Yet the quality of low-income units built by the private sector with public subsidies often falls victim to the profit-maximizing strategies of investors, ranging from shoddy construction to management with an eye to tax write-offs rather than long-term provision of good, low-rent housing. Providing a sound housing stock requires a long-term investment in maintenance and management, as well as an initial investment in construction. Meehan's analysis, plus many other public and private program evaluations, reveals that both public and semipublic programs have much more difficulty in meeting these long-term commitments than in erecting the housing to begin with (Bratt 1989).

The criterion of *equity* relates, in its broadest sense, to providing a fairer distribution of housing services. Considerable disagreement exists on what constitutes a "fair" distribution. Capitalist economies depend on a certain degree of inequality in order to function, yet extreme inequality generates serious social costs and violates social and ethical norms of human compassion. What constitutes a reasonable level of government intervention is one of the pivotal ideological issues defining contemporary politics. While policy analysts often attempt to be neutral as regards these broader value questions, such questions, in fact, color every aspect of policy evaluation. The underlying (and I believe valid) assumption implicit in designing and evaluating government interventions on behalf of the poor is that serious housing deprivation is morally repugnant, as well as practically self-destructive for any society.

Within this broader context, more specific questions of equity arise. Housing programs are frequently criticized when their assistance targets a "better-off" group, when the needs of a "worse-off" group are not being met. This would seem an obvious principle of vertical equity, and yet it sometimes conflicts with the need to avoid isolation and stigmatization of poor recipients by providing their assistance in conjunction with aid to a broader range of incomes. Such a broadening of the subsidy base may also be necessary to ensure adequate political support to keep the program alive. Of course, equity questions are not as severe in comprehensive systems that provide graduated levels of aid up to the point on the income scale where self-provision of housing is clearly feasible. Choices become difficult when resources are allocated to meet only a portion of the legitimate needs.

The *efficiency* criterion relates to minimizing expenditures of scarce public resources for housing while producing the maximum benefit to recipients. The evaluation of efficiency depends very much on the actual, as well as the stated, goals of the program and on the political and economic context in which the program is being implemented. In the 1930s, when the supply of private market housing for the poor was grossly inadequate, public construction of housing seemed the best strategy, particularly as it met an additional goal of putting construction workers back to work. It filled a gap in the housing supply that the market was not close to filling at that time.

However, the private construction industry never accepted competition from the public sector as legitimate. In order to coopt them into supporting housing for the poor, and under the rubric of the greater "efficiency" of the for-profit sector, public housing was supplemented, and later supplanted, by construction subsidies to the private sector. In the end, this type of housing did not prove any more efficient to construct than publicly owned housing, when the total of direct and indirect subsidies was added in (U.S. GAO 1980), and some of the social problems associated with public housing also plagued privately owned developments. In addition, the market was producing quality housing units that could be made to "filter" down to lower-income persons through modest, direct-income subsidies, such as housing vouchers. Therefore, it came to be regarded as very inefficient to produce additional *new* units of housing for the poor, whether they were publicly or privately owned.

The criterion of *choice* relates to the degree of control that individuals have over their physical and social environment. Control can be exercised through the initial choice of where to live or through the household's ongoing relationship with their surroundings while they occupy a housing unit. The assistance provided through both publicly owned housing and government-subsidized privately owned housing was initially project based; that is, a household had to live in a designated low-income housing development in order to receive the reduced-cost housing. This limitation on choice proved to be stigmatizing for low-income families, in that their place of residence clearly identified them as disadvantaged. Moreover, by concentrating large numbers of low-income persons in one place, the social pathologies associated with poverty were intensified, creating negative, destructive social environments in many public and private projects.

In addition, the relationship between the tenants and their public or public-assisted landlords was frequently adversarial. Since tenants had no individual or collective stake in the project, there was nothing to restrain destructive behavior by some of them. Moreover, neglect of the physical and social environment by the managing entity was common. In the case of public housing, this was due both to lack of federal funds for maintenance and renovation and to bureaucratic ineptitude at the local level. In private developments, neglect often reflected the lack of concern with project income as a source of return on investment, since short-term fees or tax incentives were the main motivation for investors.

Housing vouchers are widely viewed as the best vehicle for the restoration of household choice, as well as the most efficient subsidy mechanism. Households can scatter themselves among "ordinary" housing developments, thus avoiding isolation and stigmatization. However, the reality is that, even with vouchers, low-income households' choices are still limited, by the overall supply and cost of housing and, in the case of racial and ethnic minorities, by ongoing housing discrimination and neighborhood exclusion. Therefore, they must be supplemented by the creation or renovation of housing in neighborhoods likely to be occupied by lower-income households. Some of the negative effects of this concentration can be counteracted by community-based and community-organized housing development, in which the neighborhood itself assumes responsibility for developing the housing and, equally important, for ongoing maintenance of the physical and social quality of the area.

This suggests that the criterion of choice is strongly related to the final criterion—*community*. In order for an individual household to enjoy the full benefits of its housing unit, it must be part of an active, vital community, existing within the surrounding physical space. As noted earlier, this not only secures the ongoing physical quality of the unit and guards against pathologies that threaten safety but provides individuals with opportunities to express and empower themselves creatively.

All too often, the private market solution to community is the intensification of social homogeneity in the ''better'' neighborhoods, coupled with disinvestment, or exploitative investment, in lower-income areas. The market merely reflects social preferences, but in the process, it intensifies their impact. As an example, consider the redlining of a neighborhood by credit institutions. It reflects declining preferences for the area on the part of those with the resources to maintain its values, but it also cuts off resources from those investors ''foolish'' enough to retain faith in the area, that is, the very people who might rescue it from the spiral of decline.

Therefore, government intervention is a necessary tool in the pursuit of community, although poorly planned interventions have certainly contributed to its destruction in the past. Two strategies commonly advocated for increasing community in disadvantaged neighborhoods are homeownership and community-based housing.

Homeownership, while increasing the household's control over its own dwelling, is also frequently seen as the key to increasing the household's stake in the community, both financially and psychologically. However, most of the current subsidies for homeownership in the United States operate through the tax system and concentrate their benefits on upper-middle-class households who would almost certainly choose ownership without the subsidy (Dolbeare 1986; Center on Budget and Policy Priorities 1991). Federal homeownership subsidies for the poor have frequently been poorly designed or executed, as in the Section 235 program, or extremely limited in scope, as in public housing sales (Hays 1995; McClaughry 1975; Rohe and Stegman 1992). However, numerous local and nonprofit initiatives show that this can be a successful strategy if carefully planned and targeted at appropriate households (Bratt 1989).

The strategy of community-based housing development has been used to empower low-income households, for whom homeownership may not be feasible or appropriate. Nonprofit developers encountered many difficulties in the 1960s and 1970s, but recent decades have seen the development of tough, sophisticated community development corporations, with greater expertise and greater support by national networks (Rasey 1993). These corporations are both the vehicle and the result of careful neighborhood organization and leadership capacity building (Gittell 1992; Fisher 1994).

FUTURE ISSUES FOR RESEARCH AND ACTION

The provision of housing, especially for those to whom the market does not respond, has never been simple or easy. Ongoing housing policy analysis provides a vehicle through which evaluative information can be accumulated and exchanged, with the goal of constant improvement in the quality of policy making. An overview of the housing literature over the last 30 years reveals a gradual increase in the realism and sophistication with which these difficult problems are addressed.

However, housing policy does not exist in a political and social vacuum. The most serious threat to its continued evolution exists not within the housing policy community but in the surrounding milieu. Over the last 15 years, there has been an escalating ideological attack on the legitimacy and efficacy of public, collective action, particularly directed at actions by the federal government and at efforts to assist the disadvantaged. This attack is justified by the myth of the total inefficacy of government, in which the very real failures of past government efforts are exaggerated and woven together into a seemingly impenetrable, foregone conclusion that nothing government does can ever work. While the stated aim of such criticism is to "improve" or "streamline" public policies, its underlying goal is the disengagement of the public sector from such efforts, so that resources will not have to be redistributed from the more privileged elements in society to pay for them (Congressional Quarterly 1994).

At the root of this attack is a rejection of society's moral obligation to assist the poor in any but the most limited and punitive ways. The disadvantaged are viewed as totally responsible for their own condition, through their moral inferiority. Elements of overt nativism and racism are also increasingly surfacing in this brew. Government programs are seen as encouraging or rewarding the immorality of their recipients and therefore as exacerbating, rather than ameliorating, their problems (Murray 1984; Mead 1986). Accompanying this rejection of the poor is an extreme faith in the market or marketlike solutions for the problems of the poor. Privatization of public housing is pushed as a radically new concept, as if public housing were ever anything more than a marginal solution for an extremely disadvantaged population within a housing system that is already overwhelmingly private. And these "free marketers" conveniently ignore the vast subsidies provided to the nonpoor by the tax system and other subsidized goods and services (National Center for Neighborhood Enterprise 1984).

The term *liberal* became associated, in the 1960s, with a naive faith in the ability of "quick-fix" federal programs, utilizing limited resources, to solve complex social problems. Conservative critics rightly pointed out the unjustified optimism and potential for unkept promises inherent in this approach, and they took the lead in suggesting some modes of intervention, such as housing vouchers, that would prove more efficient and less stigmatizing than earlier approaches. However, the mode of attack described above can best be characterized as reactionary, not conservative, since it indiscriminately dismantles collective efforts while leaving no viable alternatives in their place.

The most serious problem for those who study housing policy is, therefore, to restore the fundamental legitimacy of the policy process in the eyes of the public and of decision makers. A progressive position must be developed that is realistic about the difficulty and expense of solving housing and other problems and yet resolute in its conviction that collective solutions are not only possible but essential. The current critique of government programs is popular because it resonates with central values held by most Americans—suspicion of government and suspicion of the poor (Kusnet 1992; Ladd 1993). However, public opinion surveys also repeatedly show strong elements of compassion for the less fortunate and a belief in the value and necessity of specific government efforts to help them. These beliefs provide a basis of support for collective action.

New appeals for collective action must, however, be couched in terms of the values that the public holds dear, and new programs must genuinely support and foster those values. First, housing programs, and other social programs, must actively and visibly encourage individual responsibility and independence on the part of their beneficiaries. To say this is not to sweep aside the importance of social and economic structural factors in creating poverty and other social problems. Programs that do not also attack these underlying factors will never succeed. However, beneficiaries must be encouraged to exert whatever positive control over their circumstances is possible in order that they may gain self-respect as well as the respect of the citizens who pay for such programs.

Second, programs must involve the community, or neighborhood, in taking responsibility for its own future. Both progressives and reactionaries express this principle, but in the latter case, it means abandonment of poor neighborhoods to their own fate, while in the former, it means providing resources in empowering rather than controlling ways. While the federal government cannot abandon its commitment to overarching societal values, such as equal opportunity, nor can it fail to insist on honest, efficient administration of its resources, it can continue to move toward a primary role of providing funds, while local organizations provide the leadership and administration. Just because reactionaries use block grants and decentralization as a smokescreen for withdrawal of support does not mean these approaches lack merit.

Third, housing programs must utilize market mechanisms effectively to achieve their goals while ensuring that social goals remain central. Ironically, the failures of past government policies have as much to do with the intrusion of the private goals of the privileged into their execution as to the inherent limitations of action for the collective good. The failures of public housing occurred, in large part, because a profit-motivated private housing industry joined with middle-class neighborhoods seeking to preserve or enhance property values to create a marginalized program designed only to cheaply warehouse the poor. Nevertheless, it is difficult to imagine any nonmarket mechanism for the overall distribution of housing that could equal the market's efficiency or productivity. The Eastern European experience shows that total decommodification of housing leads to imbalances in supply and demand, inefficient subsidies to those who can afford to pay more for their housing, and politicization of access to the best-quality housing.

In the end, the intrusion of private goals into the public policy process is a political problem more than an economic problem. As Lowi's (1979) analysis suggests, those already privileged by the market seek additional advantages through government action, including the manipulation of programs that are justified in terms of assisting the disadvantaged. The key to operating public programs that successfully meet social goals is the political mobilization and will of those who are genuinely committed to those goals. It is only this mobilization that keeps assistance to those at the bottom of the income distribution at adequate levels and accurately targeted, whether the assistance is delivered through cash vouchers, through neighborhood-based housing development, or any combination of mechanisms.

The above analysis is certainly not "value neutral," yet it is impossible to do policy analysis without making fundamental value choices about the nature of the public enterprise. If one genuinely believes in a Social Darwinist, laissez-faire view of society, then the only honest policy analysis is to figure out how quickly public efforts can be dismantled. However, if one believes in the importance of collective action to solve the many unsolved problems left by the workings of an unfettered capitalist system, then to discuss technical policy problems while the whole effort is being challenged is like redecorating the state dining room while the ship is sinking. Urban housing policy may not have a future if these fundamental struggles are not joined and won.

REFERENCES

Aaron, Henry J. 1972. *Shelter and Subsidies: Who Benefits from Federal Housing Policies?* Washington, D.C.: Brookings Institute.

Bratt, Rachel G. 1989. *Rebuilding a Low-Income Housing Policy*. Philadelphia, PA: Temple University Press.

Burt, Martha R. 1992. *Over the Edge: The Growth of Homelessness in the 1980s*. New York and Washington, D.C.: Russell Sage Foundation and the Urban Institute Press.

Case, Anne C., and Lawrence Katz. 1991. *The Company You Keep: The Effects of Family and Neighborhood on Disadvantaged Youths*. Cambridge, MA: National Bureau of Economic Research.

Center on Budget and Policy Priorities and National Low Income Housing Information Service. 1991. *A Place to Call Home: The Crisis in Housing for the Poor*. Washington, D.C.: Center on Budget and Policy Priorities and National Low Income Housing Information Service.

Choko, Marc H. 1993. "Homeownership: From Dream to Materiality." In R. Allen Hays, ed., *Ownership, Control, and the Future of Housing Policy.* Westport, CT: Greenwood Press. 3–38.

Congressional Quarterly, Inc. 1994. "Detours Ahead as GOP Drives to Reshape Government." *Weekly Reports,* November 19, 3331–3346.

Davis, Otto A., and Andrew B. Whinston. 1966. "The Economics of Urban Renewal." In James Q. Wilson, ed., *Urban Renewal: The Record and the Controversy.* Cambridge, MA: MIT Press. 50–67.

Dolbeare, Cushing N. 1986. "How the Income Tax System Subsidizes Housing for the Affluent." In Rachel Bratt, ed., *Critical Perspectives on Housing.* Philadelphia, PA: Temple University Press. 264–271.

Dommel, Paul R. 1980. "Social Targeting in Community Development." *Political Science Quarterly* 95 (fall): 465–478.

Downs, Anthony. 1973. *Federal Housing Subsidies: How Are They Working?* Lexington, MA: D. C. Heath, Lexington Books.

Fisher, Robert. 1994. *Let the People Decide: Neighborhood Organizing in America.* New York: Twayne Publishers.

Fried, Marc. 1966. "Grieving for a Lost Home: Psychological Costs of Relocation." In James Q. Wilson, ed., *Urban Renewal: The Record and the Controversy.* Cambridge, MA: MIT Press. 359–379.

Gittell, Ross J. 1992. *Renewing Cities.* Princeton, NJ: Princeton University Press.

Goetz, Edward G., and Mara Sidney. 1994. "Revenge of the Property Owners: Community Development and the Politics of Property." *Journal of Urban Affairs* 16, no. 4: 319–334.

Hays, R. Allen. 1993. "Ownership and Autonomy in Capitalist Societies." Introduction to *Ownership, Control, and the Future of Housing Policy.* Westport, CT: Greenwood Press. viii–xxiii.

Hays, R. Allen. 1994a. "Housing Privatization: Social Goals and Policy Strategies." *Journal of Urban Affairs* 16, no. 4: 295–318.

Hays, R. Allen. 1994b. "Housing Subsidy Strategies." In Willem Van Vliet, ed., *Encyclopedia of Housing.* Westport, CT: Greenwood Press.

Hays, R. Allen. 1995. *The Federal Government and Urban Housing: Ideology and Change in Public Policy.* 2nd ed. Albany: State University of New York Press.

Hoch, Charles, and Robert A. Slayton. 1989. *New Homeless and Old: Community and the Skid Row Hotel.* Philadelphia: Temple University Press.

Hughes, James W., and George Sternlieb. 1987. *The Dynamics of America's Housing.* New Brunswick, NJ: Center for Urban Policy Research.

Kemeny, James. 1981. *The Myth of Home-Ownership.* London: Routledge and Kegan Paul.

Kusnet, David. 1992. *Speaking American: How the Democrats Can Win in the Nineties.* New York: Thunder's Mouth Press.

Ladd, Everett C. 1993. "The 1992 Vote for President Clinton: Another Brittle Mandate?" *Political Science Quarterly* 108, no. 1: 1–28.

Lowi, Theodore. 1979. *The End of Liberalism: The Second Republic of the United States.* 2nd ed. New York: W. W. Norton.

McLaughry, John. 1975. "The Troubled Dream: The Life and Times of Section 235 of the National Housing Act." *Loyola University Law Journal* 6 (winter): 1–45.

Maslow, Abraham H. 1970. *Motivation and Personality.* New York: Harper & Row.

Mead, Lawrence M. 1986. *Beyond Entitlement: The Social Obligations of Citizenship.* New York: Free Press.

Meehan, Eugene. 1979. *The Quality of Federal Policymaking: Programmed Failure in Public Housing.* Columbia: University of Missouri Press.

Molotch, Harvey. 1976. "The City as a Growth Machine." *American Journal of Sociology* 82 (September): 390–431.

Monti, Daniel J. 1989. "The Organizational Strengths and Weaknesses of Resident Managed Public Housing Sites in the United States." *Journal of Urban Affairs* 11: 39–52.

Monti, Daniel J. 1993. "People in Control: A Comparison of Residents in Two U.S. Housing Developments." In R. Allen Hays, ed., *Ownership, Control, and the Future of Housing Policy.* Westport, CT: Greenwood Press. 162–176.

Morton, Henry W. 1987. "Housing Quality and Housing Classes in the Soviet Union." In Horst Herlemann, ed., *Quality of Life in the Soviet Union.* Boulder, CO: Westview Press. 95–115.

Murray, Charles. 1984. *Losing Ground: American Social Policy, 1950–1980.* New York: Basic Books.

National Center for Neighborhood Enterprise. 1984. *The Grass Is Greener in Public Housing: From Tenant to Resident to Homeowner.* Washington, D.C.

Peterman, William. 1993. "Resident Management and Other Approaches to Tenant Control of Public Housing." In R. Allen Hays, ed., *Ownership, Control, and the Future of Housing Policy.* Westport, CT: Greenwood Press. 161–176.

Rasey, Keith P. 1993. "The Role of Neighborhood-Based Housing Nonprofits in the Ownership and Control of Housing in U.S. Cities." In R. Allen Hays, ed., *Ownership, Control, and the Future of Housing Policy.* Westport, CT: Greenwood Press. 195–224.

Rohe, William M., and Michael A. Stegman. 1992. "Public Housing Homeownership: Will It Work and for Whom?" *Journal of the American Planning Association* 58 (spring): 144–157.

Rohe, William M., and Michael A. Stegman. 1993. "Converting Multifamily Housing to Cooperatives: A Tale of Two Cities." In R. Allen Hays, ed., *Ownership, Control, and the Future of Housing Policy.* Westport, CT: Greenwood Press. 139–158.

Semer, Milton P., Julian H. Zimmerman, Ashley Foard, and John M. Frantz. 1976. "A Review of Federal Subsidized Housing Programs." In U.S. Department of Housing and Urban Development, *Housing in the Seventies. Working Papers: National Housing Policy Review.* Vol. 1. Washington, D.C.: GPO.

Sliltor, Richard E. 1976. "Rationale of the Present Tax Benefits for Home-Ownership." In U.S. Department of Housing and Urban Development. *Housing in the Seventies. Working Papers: National Housing Policy Review.* Vol. 1. Washington, D.C.: GPO.

Solomon, Arthur P. 1974. *Housing the Urban Poor: A Critical Evaluation of Federal Housing Policy.* Cambridge, MA: Joint Center for Urban Studies of MIT and Harvard University.

Stegman, Michael A., 1979. *Housing Investment in the Inner City: The Dynamics of Decline.* Cambridge, MA: MIT Press.

Struyk, Raymond J., and Marc Bendick, Jr. 1981. *Housing Vouchers for the Poor: Lessons from a National Experiment.* Washington, D.C.: Urban Institute Press.

Szelenyi, Ivan. 1983. *Urban Inequalities under State Socialism*. New York: Oxford University Press.

Telgarsky, Jeffrey P., and Raymond Struyk. 1991. *Toward a Market Oriented Housing Sector in Eastern Europe*. Washington, D.C.: Urban Institute Press.

Twentieth Century Fund. 1991. *More Housing More Fairly: Report of the Twentieth Century Fund Task Force on Affordable Housing*. New York: Twentieth Century Fund Press.

U.S. Department of Housing and Urban Development (HUD). 1976. *Housing in the Seventies Working Papers: National Housing Policy Review*. 2 vols. Washington, D.C.: GPO.

U.S. General Accounting Office (GAO). 1980. *Evaluation of Alternatives for Financing Low and Moderate Income Rental Housing*. Report to Congress by the Comptroller General. Washington, D.C.: GPO.

Varady, David P., and Jeffrey A. Raffel. 1993. "Two Approaches to School Desegregation and Their Impacts on City-Suburban Choice." *Journal of Urban Affairs* 15, no. 6: 259–274.

Welfeld, Irving. 1988. *Where We Live: A Social History of American Housing*. New York: Simon and Schuster.

Wilson, William J. 1987. *The Truly Disadvantaged*. Chicago: University of Chicago Press.

Chapter 22

Urban Poverty, Public Policy, and the Underclass

Scott Cummings and Margaret Killmer

This chapter examines how the term *underclass* is used in current research about urban poverty. The theoretical and methodological applications of the term are summarized and critically evaluated. Use of underclass theory and research in current policy debates about urban poverty are explained. Special attention is given to the policy controversies emanating from the application of underclass theory and research to racial and ethnic inequality in American cities.

COLLAPSE OF THE LIBERAL POLICY AGENDA

By 1980, it was widely assumed by the general public that governmental efforts to reduce urban poverty could be counted among the numerous policy failures of the 1960s. While some of the federal initiatives originating in the War on Poverty era earned a fair amount of praise (Levitan and Taggart 1987), by the end of the Carter presidency many public officials and policy analysts had grown increasingly skeptical about the liberal programs of the 1960s (Abramowitz 1992).

Most policy analysts agree that the Reagan presidency assigned very low priority to federally sponsored programs to aid the urban poor and to revitalize cities. Reagan's critical attitude toward the welfare state and subsidized urban development projects was increasingly shared by the general public and by many intellectuals and university-based policy researchers. Murray (1984) denounced welfare programs because they perpetuated rather than reduced poverty, and recommended a complete reappraisal of established poverty and community development policy.

Murray's opinions gained widespread credibility within Washington policy circles. The idea that federal urban development programs were capable of revitalizing cities was increasingly defined as inflationary and fiscally irresponsible. By the mid-1980s, the liberal policy initiatives of the 1960s were widely repudiated, even among those who once championed earlier efforts to reduce urban poverty through federal interventions (Strickland and Judd 1982). A growing conservative trend in the intellectual community galvanized around the idea that federal urban policy had consistently lagged far behind the demographic and development trends shaping the nation's metropolitan areas. Critics contended that federal initiatives were sporadic and uncoordinated, too expensive, ineptly managed, and accomplished very little (Gorham and Glazer 1976; Kaplan and James 1990; Loewenstein 1971).

Urban problems were treated in isolation from their demographic, political, and economic causes. Urban renewal, critics maintained, was implemented without regard to a growing historic preservation movement. Important historic structures were frequently demolished by urban renewal programs, the architectural integrity of many cities being undermined in the process (J. Wilson 1966). Urban renewal was allegedly pursued in isolation from an overall downtown redevelopment plan and without adequate attention to the housing needs of those displaced by the "federal bulldozer" (M. Anderson 1964).

Federal housing programs were formulated in isolation from school desegregation policy and other important initiatives in the civil rights arena. Forced busing fragmented the connection between school and community. While Housing and Urban Development (HUD) sought to provide more shelter for low- and moderate-income families, housing officials and community activists paid little or no attention to the fact that most federal programs actually reinforced existing patterns of racial segregation. Efforts to provide equality of educational opportunity and desegregate the nation's schools were actually undermined by HUD programs designed to expand housing choices among the urban poor (Orfield 1978). It was not until the latter years of the Carter administration that efforts were made to bring a moderate degree of coordination among urban policies in housing, education, and civil rights (Falk and Franklin 1976). By that time, public enthusiasm for any type of federal intervention had seriously eroded.

Community development programs, others contended, were also implemented in an uncoordinated and sporadic manner. In the face of long-term urban development trends, neither the Community Development Block Program nor Urban Action Grant funds could alter the growing polarization between city and suburb. Nor could they reverse the outward migration of people and capital to the suburbs. Federal revitalization programs were poorly conceived in Washington, badly coordinated among various governmental jurisdictions, and inadequately monitored at the local level (Pressman and Wildavsky 1980). Funds were spent too often on questionable projects or maneuvered into programs not initially authorized by federal legislation.

Social welfare policies, critics maintained, were implemented without adequate attention to the erosion of jobs beginning to occur in the manufacturing sector. While many welfare programs designed during the War on Poverty era made important contributions to the lives of the urban poor, they did little to bring the marginal classes of urban society closer to the economic mainstream. And programs to enfranchise the urban poor in city politics were not coordinated with established party processes. As a result, community action programs conflicted with local party machinery in many cities and produced what Daniel Moynihan (1975) called a "maximum feasible misunderstanding" over how to manage the War on Poverty.

By 1980, it was no surprise that the federal government began a systematic disengagement from efforts to revitalize cities and reduce poverty among its inhabitants. In December 1980, one of the last acts of the Carter administration was to publish the final report of the U.S. President's Commission for a National Agenda for the Eighties (1980). The report opened with the declaration: "A unified and coherent national urban policy designed to solve the problems of the nation's communities and those that live in them is not possible" (6).

Between 1981 and 1983, expenditures allocated to nondefense programs steadily dropped both as a percentage of the gross national product and in absolute dollar figures (Aaron and Associates 1983). The major targets for budget reductions included social security, Medicare and Medicaid, higher education and student loans, aid to disadvantaged school districts, unemployment insurance, housing assistance and grants for urban development, grants for job training and creation, financial aid to the poor and elderly, grants for urban social services, and legal assistance for the poor.

The federal budget cuts directed toward social program expenditures continued throughout the Reagan presidency. Reagan's budget for 1986 targeted the Department of Housing and Urban Development, the Small Business Administration, the Community Development Block Grant Program, the Urban Development Action Grant program, Aid to Families with Dependent Children (AFDC), and other social welfare services and benefits for additional cuts in federal assistance (Bourne 1991).

The policies initiated during the Reagan years continued unabated during the presidency of his successor, George Bush. By 1988, federal urban policies and social programs for the urban poor had become so unpopular that the Democratic candidate for president, Michael Dukakis, steadfastly avoided defining himself as a "liberal" and attempted to distance his campaign and political image from the social programs of the 1960s. And it is unlikely that Bill Clinton will be able to rekindle public support for the liberal agenda of the 1960s.

THE EMERGENCE OF UNDERCLASS THEORY AND RESEARCH

It is within the shifting political context of the 1980s that the term *underclass* made its conceptual debut into the public policy arena. While there is some debate over the precise origins of the term, most recent treatises on the topic identify Kenneth Auletta's *The Underclass* (1982) as the first fully developed exposition of underclass theory. While Gunner Myrdal (1963) briefly described the emergence of an "underclass" in an earlier work, it was Auletta who described what appeared to be a relatively permanent group of individuals who were marginal to the economic mainstream. This group, the urban underclass, was characterized by high rates of poverty, crime, and related social pathologies. The group appeared to be growing in numbers and was capable of perpetuating itself from one generation to the next.

The term *underclass* has since developed as a synonym for a category of individuals and families that are permanently poor. As explained by Peterson (1991), the underclass refers to groups that fall outside the normal categories of class analysis, including the lowly lumpen proletariat described by Marx. The underclass is not only marginal to and separate from middle- and working-class America; it is even peripheral to the lower class. The term denotes a group of individuals that is literally below or "under" the working and lower classes. Peterson maintains that underclass theory emerged in response to the continuing "poverty paradox," the fact that rates of poverty appeared to increase in the face of escalating federal efforts to lower them.

Research efforts to explain the causes behind rising rates of poverty prior to the full exposition of underclass theory reveal considerable variation among policy analysts. Some researchers maintain that the fiscal crisis accompanying the collapse of the liberal welfare state is responsible for producing more poor people. In 1983, an Urban Institute report examining the American economy predicted that the annual deficit was on a course that would ultimately exceed $200 billion by 1984 and $300 billion by the end of the decade (Mills and Palmer 1983).

Citing spiraling federal deficits and the cuts in federal programs that accompanied it, a special House Subcommittee on Public Assistance and Unemployment Compensation reported in 1984 that the number of families living in poverty had steadily increased since 1980. The 39 million people living in poverty in 1983 was the highest number reported since 1964 and the highest rate of poverty since 1965. The committee reported that approximately 868,000 people joined the ranks of the poor in 1983. Most significant was the committee's observation that "cuts in Federal Welfare spending are largely responsible" for increasing rates of poverty (4).

Other researchers offer similar interpretations. Bartelt (1993) maintains that rising rates of homelessness are directly associated with the collapse of federal housing programs. Stern (1993) suggests that changing regulations and recent cutbacks in the AFDC program increased the number of families living in poverty. Anglin and Holcomb (1992) maintain that sweeping cuts in all areas of family support programs have swelled the ranks of the poor, especially among female-headed households.

More consistent with the skepticism accompanying the dismantling of the liberal welfare state, however, a number of policy researchers claim that the poor continue to perpetuate themselves from one generation to the next due to their dysfunctional culture and maladaptive personal values and habits. While sharp controversy continues to surround the idea of a "culture of poverty," it remains a popular explanation for the persistence of urban poverty. According to this view, the lifeways, institutions, and values of the poor are maladaptive and pathological, resulting in intergenerational poverty and dysfunctional and self-destructive behavior.

Perhaps the most widely debated recent explanation of the poverty paradox is that offered by Charles Murray (1984). He contends that the culture of the poor is neither pathological nor maladaptive. On the contrary, the poor have made rational and strategic adaptations to the unique and unusual provisions of the welfare state itself. In fact, welfare benefits provide a destructive set of incentives to the poor, resulting in higher rates of broken families, spiraling rates of fertility among the poor, and reduction in the motivation to find work in the mainstream economy. Welfare eligibility requirements encourage fathers to be absent from the home, encourage more out-of-wedlock births, and increase the number of female-headed households and children now living in poverty.

Underclass theory provided a sharp counterpoint to these popular interpretations. The most fully articulated theory of the underclass was provided by William Wilson. His work most clearly explains the relationship between changes in the larger society and the persistence of urban poverty. It also addresses why the underclass emerged at this particular juncture of American urban history. Contrary to those who identified the demise of the welfare state and the fiscal crisis itself as the primary causes of increasing rates of poverty, and those like Murray who held the perverse incentives of the welfare system responsible for the emergence of the underclass, Wilson maintained that structural changes in the American economy caused rates of poverty to rise in cities.

In *The Declining Significance of Race*, Wilson (1978) suggested that traditional forms of prejudice and discrimination were becoming less persuasive as explanations of continued poverty among racial minorities. In order to reduce racial inequality in American cities, he concluded that more attention should be given to issues of economic development, training, and job creation. In *The Truly Disadvantaged*, Wilson (1987) fully elaborated his ideas about the relationship among the changing urban economy, racial inequality, and public policy. It is from this watershed book that most of our current thinking about underclass theory and research is drawn.

Wilson argued that structural shifts in the U.S. economy toward greater reliance on service industries had a major influence on employment opportunities within the center city. Far more than a shift in employment, however, these changes foreshadowed the abandonment of much of the industrial and urban landscape. The term *deindustrialization* is now used to describe the twin processes of an employment shift from manufacturing and the simultaneous disinvestment in its physical plant. According to policy analysts like Bluestone and Harrison (1982), certain kinds of private investment decisions, in tandem with sweeping demographic shifts, have undermined the economic vitality of U.S. cities.

In pursuit of higher profits and lower investments in the cost of labor, many corporations have abandoned cities altogether and relocated to rural regions or, in some cases, to other parts of the world. Downtown facilities and buildings, fully depreciated and costly to renovate, have been abandoned without serious financial losses. During the 1970s, plant closings and shutdowns devastated the employment base of many cities and undermined the structure of neighborhood life and culture (Alperovitz and Faux 1984). While capital is mobile, U.S. downtowns and their residents are not.

Northern and midwestern cities were affected most severely by the reorganization of basic industry. The restructuring of the economy and the suburbanization of business and industry accelerated the demographic and political changes occurring within the older, industrial cities. Bluestone and Harrison (1982) report that between 32 and 38 million jobs were lost during the 1970s. The personal and social costs of deindustrialization were immense. In addition to lost wages and productivity, many workers and their families suffered physical and emotional disorders after losing their jobs. Cities lost revenues and became unable to sustain the provision of services to residents. Businesses closed in response to a drop in disposable income and consumer spending. Higher levels of unemployment strained the demand on federal programs providing benefits to individuals and families.

Because of these changes in the U.S. economy, Wilson contended that a growing group of people were increasingly victimized by and rendered marginal to the social and cultural mainstream. He observed that the plight of racial minorities was becoming worse at the very time in which civil rights gains were at their greatest. During a period when levels of racial discrimination appeared to be at their lowest levels, the economic position of African Americans and other peoples of color was deteriorating. He concluded, therefore, that the growth of the urban underclass was more a product of changing economic conditions rather than traditional forms of overt discrimination.

Directly challenging the idea that welfare benefits and eligibility requirements created incentives undermining the vitality of the African American family, he presented evidence and argument showing that declining job opportunities available to minority males rendered them incapable of supporting a family. One of the more deleterious results of declining job opportunities in the central city, he contends, were sharp increases in the number of families with children living in poverty. He suggested that policies designed to guarantee civil rights and reduce levels of discrimination would probably have minimal effects in reducing poverty. He concluded, therefore, that policies designed to stimulate economic development, job training, and job creation will be more effective antidotes to urban poverty. He also suggests that policy interventions will probably be more politically appealing if they are universal in nature and not designed to benefit one group or category of individuals.

Wilson's analysis was simultaneously clever and controversial. By focusing upon the larger economy and the structural changes occurring within it, he was able to explain why the fiscal crisis undermined the liberal policy agenda and simultaneously increased rates of urban poverty. By targeting larger economic changes and the process of deindustrialization, he was able to provide a powerful counterpoint to those who argued that the welfare state itself was defective and the culture of the poor was largely responsible for their miserable conditions. By targeting the fiscal crisis, deindustrialization, and disinvestment, he was able to alter significantly the intellectual debate over public policy and the poor. His analysis shifted attention from the personal qualities of the poor and their culture, the welfare state, and its deficiencies to economic development policy, full employment, and job training.

His argument was controversial, however, in that it tended to draw attention away from racial discrimination and prejudice. By reducing the importance of racial discrimination as a major cause of rising rates of poverty, he undermined part of the political rationale for particularistic forms of policy intervention in which racial and cultural minorities were the intended beneficiaries. This issue will be addressed in more detail in the concluding section of this chapter. At this point, it is important to trace the pervasive influence of the term *underclass* in policy research and show how the debate over the causes of urban poverty has been influenced by it.

THE PROLIFERATION OF UNDERCLASS RESEARCH

Since Wilson's watershed exposition of underclass theory, an impressive volume of findings has been produced by the social science and policy research community. Similar to the introduction of new scientific paradigms, the term *underclass* has stimulated innovative thinking about the urban poor and rekindled debate over urban development policy. Several important recent volumes devoted to underclass theory and research have been produced. Jencks and Peterson (1991) have compiled a comprehensive overview of research findings dealing with the growth of the underclass. Katz (1993) has assembled a historical overview of underclass theory and research. Marks (1991) has critically summarized and reviewed recent sociological research dealing with the urban underclass. And W. Wilson (1993) himself has published an edited volume addressing various aspects of his earlier work. All of these books and articles constitute excellent sources of information for students of underclass theory and research.

Over the past decade, underclass theory has made its way into such diverse fields as urban development and economics, criminal justice and corrections, comparative urban studies, urban and regional planning, law and public administration, sociology, and social work. The variety and volume of research findings have been extraordinary.

In the field of criminal justice, underclass theory has been used to explain the recent rise of gangs in cities experiencing deindustrialization and disinvestment (Hagedorn 1987; Cummings and Monti 1993). Gangs offer access to illegal enterprise and, consequently, employment opportunities within deteriorating urban economies (Curtis 1984). Many criminologists also contend that rising crime rates, especially among minority youth, are a direct result of the structural changes identified by Wilson as responsible for the growth of the underclass (e.g., DiIulio 1989; Sampson and Laub 1993; Hagan 1993; Turk 1993; Liska 1993; Duster 1987). In the field of corrections, underclass theory is frequently used to examine and analyze the increasingly crowded conditions found in the urban judicial system and the increasingly complex problems associated with the juvenile justice system (Myers 1993; Backstrand, Gibbons, and Jones 1992; Farnworth, Thornberry, and Kronhn 1994; Duster 1987).

Underclass theory has helped focus more attention on the increasing number of women and children living in poverty. It has also renewed debate on Daniel Moynihan's (1965) controversial interpretation of family breakdown among African Americans. Social workers and sociologists argue that increasing structural strains upon poor families will likely place greater demands upon the social welfare system in the future (Gottschalk 1990; Reischauer 1987a, b; Osterman 1991; Tienda 1990; Edin 1991). Research also indicates that the absence of labor market opportunities for minority males negatively affects their ability to provide family support (Sullivan 1989; Testa et al. 1989; Mead 1991; Standing 1990). The growth of the urban underclass has also been called upon to explain rising rates of illegitimacy among the poor (McLanahan and Garfinkel 1989; Olsen and Farkas 1990; Vinovskis 1988).

Urban planners, public administrators, and specialists in urban law and poverty have felt compelled to address the political and legal implications of underclass theory. In 1993, *Law and Society Review* published a special issue dealing with crime, public policy, and the underclass. Earlier, the journal *Social Problems* (1991) published a special issue covering numerous facets of the underclass in the United States and attempted to address the policy implications of its growth. Even earlier, the journal *Public Management* published a special issue examining how city administrators could address the increasing infrastructure and service needs created by the growth of the urban underclass (see Mendonsa 1990). And one year earlier (1989), the *Annals of the American Academy of Political and Social Science* published a symposium on the ghetto underclass. Over the past five years, the official journal of the American Planning Association, the *Journal of the American Planning Association*, featured important discussions addressing public policy and the urban underclass (e.g., Gans 1990).

Urban economists have been greatly influenced by Wilson's argument that structural changes in the larger economy shape the job opportunities available to members of the underclass and negatively influence wages and neighborhood economies (Handy 1993; Petersen 1992; Corcoran, Gordon, and Laren 1990). Because of underclass theory, urban development specialists have reexamined ideas about public policy interventions dealing with income transfers, business relocation, and the spatial concentration of the poor (Carson 1986; Danziger and Gottschalk 1987).

Underclass theory and research have found their way into comparative urban studies (Galbraith 1992). Numerous studies have appeared attempting to apply the term to poverty in British and other European cities (e.g., Heisler 1994). Underclass research has become popular in Britain (e.g., Murray 1990; Sivanandan 1990; Macnicol 1987; Pinch 1993) due to the apparent growth of its urban poverty classes and the gradual dismantling of its welfare state under Thatcher (Westergaard 1992; Morris and Irwin 1992; Payne and Payne 1994).

Nearly every facet of recent research dealing with contemporary urban poverty has been touched in some manner by underclass theory. Research dealing with housing and the homeless has been executed from an underclass perspective (Bartelt 1993; Kasarda 1989; Rossi and Wright 1989; Wagner and Cohen 1991). Research examining changing rates of substance abuse reflects an underclass viewpoint (Barr, Farrell, and Barnes 1993). Recent trends in urban demography, especially those related to racial and ethnic segregation, have incorporated underclass theory into published research findings (Santiago and Wilder 1991; Rosenbaum, Popkin, and Kaufman 1991; Massey, Gross, and Eggers 1991; Massey 1990). Students of American minority relations have debated whether underclass theory applies more to African Americans and Hispanics in comparison to other groups (Moore 1989; Flores 1989). Even psychiatry has dabbled in underclass theory in an effort to explain the pressing problems facing minority males in a changing urban economy (Long and Vaillant 1984).

Not only has underclass theory stimulated research on the causes of urban poverty in numerous social science disciplines; the term has also prompted methodological innovations and debate. By the late 1980s, many social scientists were beginning to raise important questions about use of the term in public policy circles. Kornblum (1984) had earlier contended that the concept of an underclass combined too many disparate types of people and behaviors. As a result, the term was conceptually ambiguous and potentially biased. Other critics tended to agree.

Ethnographers noted that the behavioral characteristics of the underclass were not always consistent with established notions about them (Anderson 1989). Hughes (1989) and Muzzio (1989) criticized use of the term *underclass* in poverty research because the concept was too broad. They noted that the term had not been used in an empirically rigorous manner and resisted valid and reliable operationalization. Consequently, serious research on its growth and development had been impeded.

Other researchers reported that measurement of underclass growth and expansion, as well as sound operational definitions of its membership, relied too heavily upon census data (Sherraden 1984; Littman 1991; Jargowsky 1994). Some argued that geographic indices measuring the spatial concentration of the poor had not been adequately incorporated into operational discussions of the underclass (Greene 1991).

Ricketts and Sawhill (1988) published an important summary of the methodological criticisms of underclass research. In their article, they developed a summary of underclass measures and indices derived from census information and other data sources. They conclude that the term *underclass* is not useful "unless it is conceptually distinguishable from poverty" (324). They also conceded that their own operational measures suffered from numerous limitations and called for students of the term to develop a new conceptual approach in order to understand the causes of urban poverty better.

Gans (1990) took a much harsher stand against the conceptual and methodological deficiencies of the term *underclass*. Because of the ambiguous nature of the term, he warned that it posed political dangers preventing an informed debate over public policy and the urban poor. Because of this, he recommended the term be dropped altogether.

In his presidential address before the American Sociological Association, W. Wilson (1991) himself raised important critical questions about the term his research helped to popularize. Largely in agreement with the critical comments of Gans, Wilson warned that underclass research had been deficient in many important ways. He conceded that it might be more appropriate to simply talk about urban poverty rather than be sidetracked by debate over whether or not an underclass exists. Whatever deficiencies the term might have, he observed, they should not detract from resolving the pressing needs of the urban poor.

Despite the enduring controversy over use of the term, we have accumulated an impressive volume of research findings about the urban underclass. From this growing body of research, it is possible to draw several important conclusions about the nature and magnitude of urban poverty. Some of the recent empirical findings support initial thinking about the underclass. Some do not.

First, while some indices of poverty have increased over the past decade, there appears to be no consistent overall pattern. Jencks (1991) provides an excellent empirical summary of what we currently know about the underclass. While rates of male joblessness and unwed parenthood have increased since 1970, welfare dependency has remained stable. While greater public attention to urban violence has occurred, actual rates of violent crime have remained consistent. Dropout rates have declined, while reading and mathematical skills have increased. Teenage parenthood increased during the 1970s but has remained fairly constant throughout the 1980s. More important, poverty itself, while falling steadily between 1940 and 1970, has not exhibited significant change since that time. The empirical findings, therefore, do not support the idea of a rapidly growing urban underclass. Rather, the more accurate picture is that while urban poverty remains a persistent and complex problem, its magnitude has remained fairly consistent.

Second, it is not clear that larger transformations in the American economy have produced declining job opportunities in selected urban labor markets. Bluestone and Harrison (1982) identified the nature and magnitude of these changes in the 1980s. More recently, Freeman (1991) has shown that the employment situation of minority youth is particularly sensitive to state and local labor markets. Cities with vital urban economies have lower rates of poverty and a smaller proportion of individuals classified as members of the underclass (Osterman 1991). Local labor market variables, especially those measuring economic stability, appear associated with desire to work and lower levels of job shiftlessness (Tienda and Stier 1991), delayed childbirths (Duncan and Hoffman 1991), school dropout rates, and lower rates of marriage (Mare and Winship 1991).

Third, the relationship between urban poverty and rates of residential segregation is not as clear as underclass theory might contend. While Wilson contended that middle-class blacks were leaving urban ghettos, the evidence shows that rates of social class segregation have remained stable over the past three decades (Farley 1991; Massey and Eggers 1990). While black out-migration to the suburbs has occurred over the past two decades, only modest changes in the overall rate of racial segregation have been registered. At the same time, data do support the idea that in many cities blacks live in increasingly more impoverished neighborhoods (Farley 1991). Levels of neighborhood impoverishment, however, do not appear related to changing rates of black out-migration or degree of racial segregation.

In summary, it is clear that the term *urban underclass* has had an important and pervasive influence upon social science research. Perhaps more important, it has renewed public policy debate over the most effective way to reduce levels of urban poverty. We can explain its influence on public policy debate by returning to the political issues raised at the outset of this chapter.

UNDERCLASS THEORY AND PUBLIC POLICY

In *The Truly Disadvantaged* (1987), W. Wilson chastised the liberal policy and intellectual communities for failure to face squarely the increasingly serious problem of urban poverty. He identified four major failures in the liberal viewpoint. First, they failed to address any behavior among the poor that might be interpreted as unflattering or pejorative in order to avoid being labeled racist. Second, they failed to use the term *underclass* because some conservatives found it appealing. Third, they romanticized selected aspects of ghetto culture and by so doing drew attention away from the poor's dreadful economic conditions. Fourth, they relied too heavily upon racial discrimination and prejudice as the primary explanations for the growth of urban poverty. As a result, they prevented development of a more comprehensive and informed national urban policy.

Wilson argued that the condition of the underclass was caused primarily by economic dislocations in the larger economy. As a result, public policy should be oriented toward economic development, the creation of jobs, and educational training rather than sponsoring a new round of civil rights laws. While conceding that the racial division of labor had been created by prior decades of discrimination, he did not agree that current discrimination was responsible for the appearance of the underclass. Accordingly, public policy to benefit the urban poor, especially minority families and individuals, should not be premised upon remedies to reduce discrimination. Rather, public policy should be oriented toward urban economic development. He did not recommend that public policy be designed to benefit one particular group but that it should be universal in nature. Liberal programs, according to Wilson, had failed to understand the nature and causes of urban poverty. It was no surprise, therefore, that liberal programs had failed.

At the center of Wilson's position is found the reason why underclass theory and research have proven to be so controversial in the public policy arena. Underclass theory informed public policy debate in three controversial ways. First, it questioned the role of prejudice and discrimination as causes of contemporary urban poverty and consequently helped delegitimate racism as a political justification for certain kinds of policy interventions. Second, it shifted the debate over policy intervention from the individual and cultural characteristics of the poor to discussion over the best way to treat the structural causes of economic dislocation. Third, it stressed the need for universal policy interventions, not ones that targeted special groups and populations.

Public policies designed to benefit particular groups have come under increasing criticism over the past decade. Affirmative action policies have been challenged both intellectually and in the legal system. Critics argued that by downplaying the role of discrimination as a major cause of urban poverty, Wilson's use of underclass theory played into conservative hands, segregationists, and those committed to dismantling the liberal welfare state.

Some contend that Wilson's formulation of underclass theory has helped draw attention away from racial discrimination and its continued presence in American society (Fainstein 1986–1987). A related set of concerns deals with Wilson's position that public policy will be more effective if directed toward the structural causes of poverty.

Skocpol (1991) summarizes the nub of this political debate by examining social policies that target particular groups versus those that are more universalistic in nature. While Wilson advocates universal policies to alleviate urban poverty, Skocpol observes that these policies are too expensive and typically do not reach the intended beneficiaries. Furthermore, the American public has made it clear that it will no longer pay for these types of programs. Skocpol observes, however, that public opposition to targeted programs is as strong as opposition against universalistic efforts. Many policy analysts still support targeted policies and complain that underclass research has helped undermine them (Greenstein 1991).

In summary, underclass theory and research continue to generate spirited debate in public policy circles. Conservatives find the term *underclass* useful in their efforts to dismantle racially targeted social programs and reform the welfare system. Many liberals find the term politically incorrect because of its blunt characterization of the poor and thus fear that the idea might feed notions that the poor are "undeserving." Despite debate and persistent disagreement over utility of the term, it has clearly stimulated widespread reexamination over how we think about the urban poor. In *The Structure of Scientific Revolutions*, Kuhn (1962: 6) observed that when a "profession can no longer evade anomalies that subvert the existing tradition of scientific practice," the stage is set for a revolution in the way in which we think about the world. While the notion of an urban underclass may not qualify as a "scientific revolution," it has deeply influenced social science thinking about the urban poor and the public policies directed toward them.

REFERENCES

Aaron and Associates. 1983. "Non-Defense Programs." In J. A. Pechman, ed., *Setting National Priorities*. Washington, D.C.: Brookings Institution.

Abramowitz, M. 1992. "The Urban Boom: Who Benefits?" *Washington Post*, May 10, H1.

Alperovitz, G., and G. P. Faux. 1984. *Rebuilding America*. New York: Pantheon Books.

Anderson, E. 1990. *Streetwise: Race, Class, and Change in an Urban Community*. Chicago: University of Chicago Press.

Anderson, M. 1964. *The Federal Bulldozer: A Critical Analysis of Urban Renewal, 1949–1962*. Cambridge: MIT Press.

Anglin, R., and B. Holcomb. 1992. "Poverty in Urban America: Policy Options." *Journal of Urban Affairs* 14: 447–468.

Auletta, K. 1982. *The Underclass*. New York: Random House.

Backstrand, J. A., D. C. Gibbons, and J. F. Jones. 1992. "Who Is in Jail? An Examination of the Rabble Hypothesis [Views of John Irwin]." *Crime & Delinquency* 38 (April): 219–229.

Barr, K. E. M. 1993. "Races, Class, and Gender Differences in Substance Abuse: Evidence of Middle-class/Underclass Polarization among Black Males." *Social Problems* 40 (August): 314–327.

Bartelt, D. W. 1993. "Housing the 'Underclass.' " In M. B. Katz, ed., *The "Underclass" Debate: Views from History*. Princeton, NJ: Princeton University Press.

Bluestone, B., and B. Harrison. 1982. *The Deindustrialization of America*. New York: Basic Books.

Bourne, L. S. 1991. "Recycling Urban Systems and Metropolitan Areas: A Geographical Agenda for the 1990s and Beyond." *Economic Geography* 67, no. 3: 188.

Carson, E. D. 1986. "The Black Underclass Concept: Self-Help vs. Government Intervention." *American Economic Review* 76 (May): 347–350.

Corcoran, M., R. Gordon, and D. Laren. 1990. "Effects of Family and Community Background on Economic Status." *American Economic Review* 80 (May): 362–366.

Cummings, S. B., and D. J. Monti. 1993. *Gangs*. Albany: State University of New York Press.

Curtis, L. A. 1984. "Underclass, Structural Unemployment & Labor Markets . . . Legal and Illegal." *Corrections Today* 46 (June): 94–95+.

Danziger, S., and P. Gottschalk. 1987. "Earnings Inequality, the Spatial Concentration of Poverty, and the Underclass.'' *American Economic Review* 77 (May): 211–215.

DiIulio, J. J. 1989. ''The Impact of Inner-city Crime.'' *Public Interest* 96 (Summer): 28–46.

Duncan, G. J., and S. D. Hoffman. 1991. ''Teenage Underclass Behavior and Subsequent Poverty: Have the Rules Changed?'' In C. Jencks and P. E. Peterson, eds., *The Urban Underclass*. Washington, D.C.: Brookings Institution. 155–174.

Duster, T. 1987. ''Crime, Youth Unemployment, and the Black Urban Underclass.'' *Crime & Delinquency* 33 (April): 300–316.

Edin, K. 1991. ''Surviving the Welfare System: How AFDC Recipients Make Ends Meet in Chicago.'' [Part of a Special issue on the underclass in the United States] *Social Problems* 38 (November): 462–474.

Fainstein, N. I. 1986–1987. ''The Underclass/Mismatch Hypothesis as an Explanation for Black Economic Deprivation.'' *Politics & Society* 15, no. 4: 403–451.

Falk, D., and H. M. Franklin. 1976. *Equal Housing Opportunity: The Unfinished Agenda*. Washington, D.C.: Potomac Institute.

Farley, R. 1991. ''Residential Segregation of Social and Economic Groups among Blacks, 1970–80.'' In C. Jencks and P. E. Peterson, eds., *The Urban Underclass*. Washington, D.C.: Brookings Institution.

Farnworth, M., T. P. Thornberry, and M. D. Kronhn. 1994. ''Measurement in the Study of Class and Delinquency: Integrating Theory and Research.'' *Journal of Research in Crime and Delinquency* 31 (February): 32–61.

Flores, H. 1989. ''The Selectivity of the Capitalist State: Chicanos and Economic Development.'' *Western Political Quarterly* 42 (June): 377–395.

Freeman, R. B. 1991. ''Employment and Earnings of Disadvantaged Young Men in a Labor Shortage Economy.'' In C. Jencks and P. E. Peterson, eds., *The Urban Underclass*. Washington, D.C.: Brookings Institution. 103–121.

Galbraith, J. K. 1992. ''Culture of Contentment.'' *New Statesman & Society* 5 (May 8): 14–16.

Gans, H. J. 1990. ''Deconstructing the Underclass: The Term's Dangers as Planning Concept.'' *Journal of the American Planning Association* 56 (Summer): 271–277.

Gorham, W., and N. Glazer, eds. 1976. *The Urban Predicament*. Washington, D.C.: Urban Institute.

Gottschalk, P. 1990. ''AFDC Participation across Generations.'' *American Economic Review* 80 (May): 367–371.

Greene, R. 1991. ''Poverty Concentration Measures and the Urban Underclass.'' *Economic Geography* 67 (July): 240–252.

Greenstein, R. 1991. ''Universal and Targeted Approaches to Relieving Poverty: An Alternative View.'' In C. Jencks and P. E. Peterson, eds., *The Urban Underclass*. Washington, D.C.: Brookings Institution. 437–459.

Hagan, J. 1993. ''Introduction: Crime in Social and Legal Context.'' [Part of a symposium: ''Crime, Class, and Community—An Emerging Paradigm''] *Law & Society Review* 27, no. 2: 255–262.

Hagedorn, J. M. 1987. *People and Folks*. Chicago: Lakeview Press.

Hagedorn, J. M. 1991. ''Gangs, Neighborhoods, and Public Policy.'' [Part of a special issue on the underclass in the United States] *Social Problems* 38 (November): 529–542.

Handy, J. W. 1993. "Community Economic Development: Some Critical Issues." [Part of a special issue in honor of Robert S. Browne] *Review of Black Political Economy* 21 (Winter): 41–64.

Heisler, B. S. 1994. "Housing Policy and the Underclass: The United Kingdom, Germany, and the Netherlands." *Journal of Urban Affairs* 16: 203–220.

Hughes, M. A. 1989. "Misspeaking Truth to Power: A Geographical Perspective on the 'Underclass' Fallacy." *Economic Geography* 65 (July): 187–207.

Jargowsky, P. A. 1994. "Ghetto Poverty among Blacks in the 1980s." *Journal of Policy Analysis and Management* 13 (Spring): 288–310.

Jencks, C. 1991. "Is the American Underclass Growing?" In C. Jencks and P. E. Peterson, eds., *The Urban Underclass*. Washington, D.C.: Brookings Institution. 28–100.

Jencks, C., and P. E. Peterson, eds. 1991. *The Urban Underclass*. Washington, D.C.: Brookings Institution.

Kaplan, M., and F. J. James, eds. 1990. *The Future of National Urban Policy*. Durham: Duke University Press.

Kasarda, J. D. 1989. "Urban Industrial Transition and the Underclass." *Annals of the American Academy of Political and Social Science* 501: 26–47.

Katz, M. B., ed. 1993. *The "Underclass" Debate: Views from the History*. Princeton, NJ: Princeton University Press.

Kornblum, W. 1984. "Lumping the Poor: What Is the 'Underclass'?" *Dissent* 31 (Summer): 295–302.

Kuhn, T. S. 1962. *The Structure of Scientific Revolutions*. Chicago: University of Chicago Press.

Levitan, S. A., and R. Taggart. 1987. *The Promise of Greatness*. Cambridge: Harvard University Press.

Liska, A. E. 1993. "Social Structure and Social Control: Building Theory." [Part of a symposium: "Crime, Class, and Community—An Emerging Paradigm"] *Law & Society Review* 27, no. 2: 345–353.

Littman, M. S. 1991. "Poverty Areas and the 'Underclass': Untangling the Web." *Monthly Labor Review* 114 (March): 19–32.

Loewenstein, L. K., ed. 1971. *Urban Studies: An Introductory Reader*. New York: Free Press.

Long, J. V. F., and G. E. Vaillant. 1984. "Natural History of Male Psychological Health: Escape from the Underclass." *American Journal of Psychiatry* 141 (March): 341–346.

McLanahan, S., and I. Garfinkel. 1989. "Single Mothers, the Underclass and Social Policy." *Annals of the American Academy of Political and Social Science* 501: 92–104.

Macnicol, J. 1987. "In Pursuit of the Underclass [Great Britain]." *Journal of Social Policy* 16 (July): 293–318.

Mare, R. D., and C. Winship. 1991. "Socioeconomic Change and the Decline of Marriage for Blacks and Whites." In C. Jencks and P. E. Peterson, eds., *The Urban Underclass*. Washington, D.C.: Brookings Institution. 175–202.

Marks, C. 1991. "The Urban Underclass." *Annual Review of Sociology* 17: 445–466.

Massey, D. S. 1990. "American Apartheid: Segregation and the Making of the Underclass." *American Journal of Sociology* 96 (September): 329–357.

Massey, D. S., and M. L. Eggers. 1990. "The Ecology of Inequality: Minorities and the

Concentration of Poverty, 1970–1980.'' *American Journal of Sociology* 95: 1153–1188.

Massey, D. S., A. B., Gross, and M. L. Eggers. 1991. ''Segregation, the Concentration of Poverty, and the Life Chances of Individuals.'' *Social Science Research* 20 (December): 397–420.

Mead, L. M. 1991. ''The New Politics of the New Poverty.'' *Public Interest* 13 (Spring): 3–20.

Mendonsa, A. A. 1990. ''Underclass Families: The Challenge We Must Meet.'' [Part of a symposium: ''Managing Our Human Infrastructure Needs''] *Public Management* 72 (May): 4–7.

Mills, G., and G. Palmer. 1983. *The Deficit Dilemma.* Washington, D.C.: Urban Institute Press.

Moore, J. 1989. ''Is There a Hispanic Underclass?'' [Review of the literature] *Social Science Quarterly* 70 (June): 265–284.

Morris, L., and S. Irwin. 1992. ''Employment Histories and the Concept of the Underclass.'' *Sociology* 26 (August): 401–420.

Moynihan, D. P. 1965. *The Negro Family: The Case for National Action.* Washington, D.C.: Office of Planning and Research, Department of Labor.

Moynihan, D. P. 1975. *Maximum Feasible Misunderstanding: Community Action in the War on Poverty.* New York: Free Press.

Murray, C. 1984. *Losing Ground: American Social Policy, 1950–1980.* New York: Basic Books.

Murray, C. 1990. ''The British Underclass.'' *Public Interest* 99 (Spring): 4–28.

Muzzio, D. 1989. ''The Urban Basement Revisited.'' [Review article] *Urban Affairs Quarterly* 25 (December): 352–365.

Myers, M. A. 1993. ''Inequality and the Punishment of Minor Offenders in the Early 20th Century.'' [Part of a symposium: ''Crime, Class, and Community—An Emerging Paradigm''] *Law & Society Review* 27: 313–343.

Myrdal, G. 1963. *The Challenge of Affluence.* New York: Pantheon Books.

National Urban League. 1990. *The State of Black America.* New York: National Urban League.

Olsen, R. J., and G. Farkas. 1990. ''The Effect of Economic Opportunity and Family Background on Adolescent Cohabitation and Childbearing among Low-Income blacks.'' *Journal of Labor Economics* 8 (July): 341–362.

Orfield, G. 1978. *Must We Bus?* Washington, D.C.: Brookings Institution.

Osterman, P. 1991. ''Welfare Participation in a Full Employment Economy: The Impact of Neighborhood.'' [Part of a special issue on the underclass in the United States] *Social Problems* 38, (November): 475–491.

Payne, J., and C. Payne. 1994. ''Recession, Restructuring and the Fate of the Unemployed: Evidence in the Underclass Debate.'' *Sociology* 28: 1–19.

Petersen, C. D. 1992. ''Can JOBS Help the Underclass Break the Cycle of Poverty?'' *Journal of Economic Issues* 26 (March): 243–254.

Peterson, P. E. 1991. ''The Urban Underclass and the Poverty Paradox.'' In C. Jencks and P. E. Peterson, eds., *The Urban Underclass.* Washington, D.C.: Brookings Institution. 3–27.

Pinch, S. 1993. ''Social Polarization: A Comparison of Evidence from Britain and the United States.'' *Environment and Planning* 25 (June): 779–795.

Pressman, J. L., and A. Wildavsky. 1980. *Implementation.* Berkeley: University of California Press.

Reischauer, R. D. 1987a. "The Underclass [United States]." *Public Management* 69 (May): 6–7.

Reischauer, R. D. 1987b. "America's Underclass." *Public Welfare* 45 (Fall): 26–31.

Ricketts, E. R., and I. V. Sawhill. 1988. "Defining and Measuring the Underclass [United States]." *Journal of Policy Analysis and Management* 7 (Winter): 316–325.

Rosenbaum, J. E., S. J. Popkin, and J. E. Kaufman. 1991. "Social Integration of Low-Income Black Adults in Middle-class White Suburbs [Gautreaux Program]." *Social Problems* 38 (November): 448–461.

Rossi, P. H., and J. D. Wright. 1989. "The Urban Homeless: A Portrait of Urban Dislocation." *Annals of the American Academy of Political and Social Science* 501: 132–142.

Sampson, R. J., and J. H. Laub. 1993. "Structural Variations in Juvenile Court Processing: Inequality, the Underclass, and Social Control." [Part of a symposium: "Crime, Class, and Community—An Emerging Paradigm"] *Law & Society Review* 27, no. 2: 285–311.

Santiago, A. M., and M. G. Wilder. 1991. "Residential Segregation and Links to Minority Poverty: The Case of Latinos in the United States." [Part of a special issue on the underclass in the United States] *Social Problems* 38 (November): 492–515.

Sherraden, M. W. 1984. "Working Over the 'Underclass.' " *Social Work* 29 (July–August): 391–392.

Sivanandan, A. 1990. "The Common Hurt of the Underclass." [Marxism today's New Times] *New Statesman & Society* 3 (February 16): 28–30.

Skocpol, T. 1991. "Targeting within Universalism: Politically Viable Policies to Combat Poverty in the United States." In C. Jencks and P. E. Peterson, eds., *The Urban Underclass.* Washington, D.C.: Brookings Institution. 411–436.

Standing, G. 1990. "The Road to Workfare: Alternative to Welfare or Threat to Occupation?" *International Labour Review* 129, no. 6: 677–691.

Stern, M. J. 1993. "Poverty and Family Composition since 1940." In M. B. Katz, ed., *The "Underclass" Debate: Views from History.* Princeton, NJ: Princeton University Press.

Stickland, D., and D. Judd. 1982. "Capital Investment in Neighborhoods." *Population Research and Policy Review* 2, 68–79.

Subcommittee on Public Assistance and Unemployment Compensation. Committee on Ways and Means. U.S. House of Representatives. 1984. *Families in Poverty: Changes in the "Safety Net."* Washington, D.C.: U.S. Government Printing Office.

Sullivan, M. L. 1989. "Absent Fathers in the Inner City." *Annals of the American Academy of Political and Social Science* 501: 48–58.

Testa, M., M. Astone, M. Krogh, and N. K. Neckerman. 1989. "Employment and Marriage among Inner-City Fathers." *Annals of the American Academy of Political and Social Science* 501: 79–91.

Tienda, M. 1990. "Welfare and Work in Chicago's Inner City." *American Economic Review* 80 (May): 372–376.

Tienda, M., and H. Stier. 1991. "Joblessness and Shiftlessness: Labor Force Activity in

Chicago's Inner City.'' In C. Jencks and P. E. Peterson, eds., *The Urban Underclass*. Washington, D.C.: Brookings Institution. 135–154.

Turk, A. T. 1993. "Back on Track: Asking and Answering the Right Questions." [Part of a symposium: "Crime, Class, and Community—An Emerging Paradigm"] *Law & Society Review* 27, no. 2: 355–359.

U.S. President's Commission for a National Agenda for the Eighties. 1980. *Urban America in the Eighties: Perspectives and Prospects*. Washington, D.C.: Government Printing Office.

Vinovskis, M. A. 1988. "Teenage Pregnancy and the Underclass." *Public Interest* 93 (Fall): 87–96.

Wagner D., and M. B. Cohen. 1991. "The Power of the People: Homeless Protestors in the Aftermath of Social Movement Participation. [Part of a special issue on the underclass in the United States] *Social Problems* 38, 543–561.

Westergaard, J. 1992. "About and Beyond the 'Underclass': Some Notes on Influences of Social Climate on British Sociology Today; BSA Presidential Address, 1992." *Sociology* 26 (November): 575–587.

Wilson, J. Q. 1966. *Urban Renewal: The Record and the Controversy*. Cambridge: MIT Press.

Wilson, W. J. 1978. *The Declining Significance of Race: Blacks and Changing American Institutions*. Chicago: University of Chicago Press.

Wilson, W. J. 1987. *The Truly Disadvantaged: The Inner City, the Underclass, and Public Policy*. Chicago: University of Chicago Press.

Wilson, W. J. 1991. "Studying Inner-city Social Dislocations: The Challenge of Public Agenda Research." *American Sociological Review* 56 (February): 1–14.

Wilson, W. J. 1993. *Sociology and the Public Agenda*. Newbury Park, CA: Sage Publications.

Chapter 23

Urban Education, Politics, and Policy

Kenneth K. Wong

OVERVIEW: FROM CENTRALIZED AUTHORITY TO FRAGMENTATION

Big-city school systems in the 1990s differ substantially from those of the early 1960s. Three decades ago, schools in central cities were governed by a strong central bureaucracy that functioned primarily to provide basic instructional services to the city's growing school-age population. School politics at that time clearly fit the "bureaucratic insulation" model (Bidwell 1965; Peterson 1976; Weick 1976; Weber 1947). It resembled a complex hierarchical structure with centralized authority. The organization's insiders enjoyed autonomy from outsiders' influence because the former possessed expertise and information on how the system operated. External pressures from state and federal government were largely absent. Within districts, teachers' unions were still in their formative years, and parent and community groups were generally not well organized. When allocating resources, the lay school board largely followed the suggestions made by professional administrators. School politics, in short, were largely embedded in the organizational milieu of the district.

Today, the central city school system is no longer governed by a strong central authority, and its leadership lacks control over crucial policy matters. Court rulings, state laws, and federal mandates have played a significant role in defining the organizational life of students and teachers. Yielding to political demands, many districts have adopted shared decision making between the central office and the school site. In addition to basic instruction, urban schools now offer a wide range of social services to their clients, many of whom come from low-income, minority, single-parent family backgrounds. Urban schools now rely heavily on intergovernmental revenues.

Table 23.1
A Synthesized Framework on the Four Patterns of Urban School Politics

Mechanisms of Institutional Change	Unit of Analysis	
	District as a Unitary Actor	Multilevel within District
"Voice" (Political)	Managing Interest Groups (A)	Shared Governance (B)
"Choice" (Marketlike)	Competition from Suburban and Nonpublic Schools (C)	Choice within Public Schools (D)

Taken together, these changes have transformed the politics of education in the nation's big cities. This chapter examines the political and socioeconomic changes that have reshaped big-city school systems in recent decades, arguing that the top leadership of the central city school system has lost much of its autonomy in making educational policy. Instead of a top-down authority structure, urban districts now maintain characteristics of both central authority and fragmentary politics. While the central bureaucracy continues to grow, multiple centers of power from both within and outside the school system become increasingly prominent. The big-city school system of the 1990s must confront the problems of producing a coherent system of governance.

A SYNTHESIZED FRAMEWORK ON SCHOOL POLITICS

At the risk of oversimplifying, we propose an analytical framework that captures the politics of both centralization and fragmentation in urban education. More specifically, as Table 23.1 suggests, the top leadership of the school system is no longer autonomous from powerful sources of policy influence. Major corporate actors (e.g., unions and state agencies), organized interests (e.g., racial groups), and individual clients shape urban school policy through two different mechanisms—"voice" and "choice" (Hirschman 1971). *Voice* refers to the political process through which parents, other clients, and corporate actors select candidates, lobby government officials, influence legislation, and gain representation; *choice* designates the marketlike decisions made by parent-consumers to choose schooling services for their children.

Furthermore, voice and choice can be differentiated by shifting our unit of analysis on the school system. From the "unitary" perspective, the school system can be seen as a unitary actor making policy choices in a constrained environment. In this regard, competition from other educational providers (e.g., nonpublic schools) poses a challenge to the public school system as a whole.

Likewise, from this perspective, competing interest groups (such as businesses and unions) can be seen as external constraints imposed on the local school autonomy. Viewing the school system as a single entity yields valuable insight, but it is equally important to take into consideration various components and multiple layers within the school system. Layers in the educational enterprise include federal and state agencies, district office, schools, and classrooms. Using this "organizational" perspective, division of responsibilities among various layers of the district policy-making organization is also relevant in understanding the weakening of central authority. Further, at the neighborhood level, school politics can be seen as a function of competition among different curricular options within the public sector.

As Figure 23.1 suggests, the interplay of the two policy mechanisms—choice and voice—and the two modes of analysis—unitary and organizational—is likely to produce four sets of politics. These can be distinguished as (1) the politics of managing competing interests (cell A in Figure 23.1), (2) the politics of shared decision making (cell B), (3) the politics of competition from suburban and nonpublic schools (cell C), and (4) the politics of choice within the public sector (cell D). Our understanding of each kind of politics comes from the literature in the field of educational politics. The politics of organizational adaptation draws on the literature on the school board and its relationship with the school superintendent, the development of the school bureaucracy, interest group politics, and political representation. The politics of shared governance can be illuminated by the scholarship in site-based management, parental empowerment, and other decentralization experiments in big-city districts. The politics of exiting to suburban and nonpublic schools is closely related to studies of the political economy of urban schools, school closing in the context of enrollment decline, and the politics of school finance. Finally, the discussion of the politics of choice within the public sector will be based on studies on schooling choice, magnet programs in public schools, educational vouchers, and the private versus public school debate.

Although it does not cover the entire field, the framework serves two important purposes. First, it captures the current intellectual movement in the field of urban education politics. Currently, our analytical shift has taken two directions that are clearly reflective of the new reality in school governance. The first tendency is to move away from the top of the school system (i.e., central authority) and focus on school sites. The "traditional" bureaucratic structure that preserves insiders' autonomy is gradually transformed into a more decentralized configuration with greater accountability at the neighborhood level. It has shifted some authority to school sites and parent councils. The central bureaucracy is expected to give fewer commands and to provide more technical support for the local staff and parents. The second trend suggests that researchers not only examine the political role that parents and other clients have played in influencing school policy but also recognize that parents can act as consumers in the educational marketplace. The notion of bureaucratic control is clearly weakened as urban schools introduce marketlike mechanisms such as schooling choice. Consequently, in the 1990s, the urban district may be seen as consisting of diverse governing structures that are bound together by a less "dictatorial" central bureaucracy.

Second, the analytical framework offers a balanced understanding of school politics—identifying both unity and disagreement in the research. In this regard, the variety in governing arrangements within the urban school system represents a critical development in the politics of education. We can no longer fully understand school politics by focusing our research efforts at the top of the system (i.e., the school board, the central office, and the superintendency). Nor can we gain an accurate view of the complexity of city schools by just looking at the school and its immediate neighborhood. In order to understand changing school politics, we need to examine in a more systematic manner the variety of governing structures—with their differing degrees of centralization and different forms of client participation—within the school policy organization. Let us now turn to each of the four political patterns.

POLITICS OF MANAGING COMPETING INTERESTS

The "traditional" politics of organizational adaptation—the bureaucracy responds incrementally to competing demands from interest groups—is most likely to be found where the district's central office enjoys substantial authority and where parents and other clients use political channels to exercise their influence. The best evidence on this kind of politics comes from two bodies of literature: (1) multiple centers of power and (2) race relations.

How Central Authority Manages Interest Groups

The district's central authority has to deal with well-organized competing interests. The literature suggests at least two understandings. On the one hand, researchers find the school system can benefit from interest group activities as it incorporates the latter's demands. On the other hand, studies show that urban schools are increasingly threatened by organized interests, such as the taxpayers' revolt and the teachers' unions.

Incorporating Competing Interests. School responsiveness to its diverse clients is seen in the development of an increasingly professionalized system. In his study of three central city districts from 1870 to 1940, Paul Peterson (1985) talked about the "politics of institutionalization," where clients who had previously been excluded from school services gradually gained admissions to the system. Competition among various interests and diverse actors shaped the organizational development of schools. Conflicts were generated by competition among status groups due to ethnic, racial, and religious cleavages, as in the nineteenth century and the midtwentieth century. Class conflict, however, dominated school politics in the first decades of the twentieth century. Given the diverse sources of political conflict, no single interest group was found to prevail in all school issues. Thus, the three case studies suggested that the business elites prevailed in taxation issues, while the working-class organizations exercised substantial influence over compulsory education. In vocational education, compromise was found.

While diverse actors and interests contributed to an expanding school system in the three cities, the real winners were the school system and its changing clientele. To be sure, there was self-interest involved in the process. After all, the system did gain in prestige, political support, and organizational capacity. But, as Peterson argued, "this self-interest was disciplined by a concomitant concern for the public interest and, in any case, was readily distinguishable from the class interests of corporate elites" (207). These middle-class school professionals were just as likely to cooperate with trade union leaders and working-class groups as well as big businesses in the popularization of the educational system during this period. The urban public school system practiced the politics of nonexclusion, gradually expanding services from the middle-class to the low-income populations and from the native stocks to various immigrant and racial groups. In his study of the Chicago Teachers Union, Grimshaw (1979) also found that school administrators and school programs benefited more during the period of reform governance than in the years of machine dominance. Indeed, in central city school systems, the central bureaucracy has adopted objective, universalistic criteria in distributing resources to neighborhood schools (Levy, Meltsner, and Wildavsky 1974; Burkhead 1967; Katzman 1971; James, Kelly, and Garms 1966; Peterson 1981).

Autonomous Centers of Power. One set of studies is concerned about the emergence of seemingly autonomous power centers in shaping school policy. One contending interest is an increasingly skeptical property taxpayer population. In many cities, a substantial number of middle-class families no longer enroll their children in public schools (Wong 1995; Kirst and Garms 1980). The aging of the city's taxpaying population has placed public education in competition with transportation and hospital and community development over local tax revenues.

Another center of power is the teachers' union. Grimshaw's (1979) historical study of Chicago's Teachers Union suggests that the union has gone through two phases in its relationship with the city's political machine and school administration. During the formative years, the union largely cooperated with the political machine in return for a legitimate role in the policy-making process. In the second phase, which Grimshaw characterized as "union rule," the union became independent of either the local political machine or the reform factions. Instead, it looked to the national union leadership for guidance and engaged in tough bargaining with the administration over better compensation and working conditions. Consequently, Grimshaw argued that policy makers "no longer are able to set policy unless the policy is consistent with the union's objectives" (150). In the current reform climate, greater attention has been given to rethinking the role of the union. The Chicago Teachers' Union has established the Quest Center to strengthen professional development (see Ayers 1993). Drawing on lessons from various districts where unions have become change agents, Kerchner and Caufman (1993) proposed a framework for "professional unionism." This new organizing system has three characteristics. First, traditional separation between management and labor will be replaced by a mode of shared operation (e.g., team teaching, site decision making). Second, adversarial relationships will give way to a strong sense of professional commitment and dedication. Third, unions will incorporate "the larger interests of teaching as an occupation and education as an institution" (19). These emerging concepts are likely to revise our seemingly dated understanding of labor union politics, which to a large extent is based on the industrial relations model developed during the New Deal of the 1930s and the 1940s.

Managing Race Relations

In the post-*Brown* and post–civil rights movement era, big-city districts began to respond to demands from minority groups by decentralizing certain decision-making powers to the community. By the 1980s, parent empowerment at school sites had gained support from reform interest groups, businesses, and elected officials. Minority groups have also gained representation at the district level of leadership. In the 1980s, many major urban districts were governed by a school board dominated by minority representatives, who, in turn, selected a minority individual to the position of school superintendent (Jackson and Cibulka 1992).

Minority representation has improved educational equity for minority students in at least two ways. First, minority groups can put pressure on the school bureaucracy to allocate resources in an equitable manner (Ravitch 1974; Rogers 1968). In 1986, a coalition of black and Hispanic groups filed suit against the Los Angeles school district for failing to provide equal resources and experienced teachers to predominantly minority schools in the inner-city neighborhoods (*Rodriguez* v. *Los Angeles Unified School District*). Five years later, the litigation was brought to an end when the state superior court approved a consent decree requiring the district to equalize the distribution of experienced teachers among schools and to allocate basic resources and supplies on an equal, per pupil basis (Schmidt 1992). Similar organized actions are found in other cities where the school population has undergone major demographic changes.

Further, minority representation affects personnel policy, which in turn may have instructional consequences for disadvantaged pupils. Using data from the Office of Civil Rights in districts with at least 15,000 students and 1 percent black, Meier, Stewart, and England (1989) examined the practice of second-generation discrimination in the classroom following the implementation of school desegregation plans. They found that black representation on the school board has contributed to the recruitment of black administrators, who in turn have hired more black teachers. Black teachers, according to this study, are crucial in reducing the assignment of black students to classes for the educable mentally retarded. Black representation in the instructional staff also reduces the number of disciplinary actions against black students and increases the latter's participation in classes for the gifted. Another study found that increases in the number of Hispanic teachers tend to reduce dropout rates and increase college attendance for Hispanic students (Fraga, Meier, and England 1986). In other words, minority representation tends to reduce discriminatory practices and facilitate equal opportunities in the classroom.

POLITICS OF SHARED GOVERNANCE

Shared governance differs from district to district in terms of the degree of power sharing between the central administration and the school sites, the locus of discretionary authority (i.e., subdistrict or school), and the relative role of the professional staff and the lay (parent) representatives. This section examines the process of decision making in the decentralized context. In particular, we will discuss the extent to which parents enjoy substantive power in making major decisions at the school site.

When School Professionals Dominate

School professionals often exercise a great deal of control even in decentralized governance. The process of decentralization does not necessarily lead to parent empowerment. When given the opportunity, parents (particularly from low-income minority groups) do not always exercise their political rights. As demonstrated by the low level of citizen participation in local elections, citizens' choices are often not readily discernible (Verba and Nie 1972; Dahl 1961). Substantial variation in the quality of political involvement also exists among different occupational and socioeconomic groups. The electoral strength of minority groups, for example, is often tempered by their low level of registration and turnout. Katznelson (1981) observed a continuation of an uneven distribution of electoral strength among various ethnic communities in the decentralized New York school system even after the black protest movement. In each of the five school board elections in North Manhattan during the 1970s, the "old" neighborhood groups, predominantly Jewish and Irish population, continued to dominate the electoral outcomes, thereby maintaining a substantial majority over the "new" groups in the black and Hispanic neighborhoods. In recent years, school election in the 31 decentralized districts in New York has continued to attract very low turnouts.

Even when the community and parents are included in school governance, their authority in personnel issues is seriously challenged by the teachers' union. This was most evident in the intense conflict between the union and the community governing board in the Ocean Hill–Brownsville experimental district in New York City during the late 1960s. When the locally elected board fired 10 teachers, the union responded with what came to be the first of a series of major strikes. After several strikes and numerous incidents that escalated racial conflict in the community, a state supervisory board was created to protect teachers' union rights from any community board decisions (Meranto 1970; Ravitch 1974). Personnel matters that were related to collective bargaining were taken outside of the local governing body under a revised notion of community governance in New York. The Ocean Hill–Brownsville district was incorporated as part of a larger community district, which constituted 1 of the 31 districts in the decentralized school system. Another controversial decentralization experiment was Detroit, where the central board shared powers with eight regional boards between 1969 and 1982. Early on, the public rejected attempts to use decentralization to improve racial desegregation. Over their tenure, the decentralized boards were charged with corruption and inefficiency (Campbell et al. 1985; Grant 1971). Finally, the system was recentralized in 1982.

Union rights and electoral barrier notwithstanding, parental participation can be further constrained by institutional arrangements. The best example on parents' limited influence in school site decisions is provided by Malen and Ogawa (1988). Based on an in-depth analysis of eight schools in Salt Lake City, the two researchers concluded that decentralized governance did not "substantially alter the relative power" relationship between the school principal and the parents. Their study suggested several constraints on parental power. First, the site-level partnership consisted of two structures: one for the principal and staff and the other for both professionals and parents. Naturally, the professionals dominated decision making because they controlled the agenda, maintained privileged access to information on school operation, and possessed expertise knowledge. Second, parents were not given the discretionary power over the bulk of the school expenditures. They were not involved in the hiring (and firing) of the principal, and only occasionally were they asked to evaluate the performance of the school staff. Third, parents were not elected but received "invitations" from the principal to participate (on cooptation, see Jennings 1980). Consequently, parent members shared similar values with the principal and acted primarily as supporters of "system maintenance" (see also Mann 1974). Similar findings of limited parental impact are suggested in an earlier review by Boyd and Crowson (1981). In federally funded compensatory education, parent advisory councils also have modest impact on program design and implementation (McLaughlin and Shields 1986; Wong 1990).

When Parents Are Empowered

The best recent effort to make sure that parents are indeed the key decision makers is found in the local school council in the Chicago Public Schools. Following a long legislative process, the 1988 Chicago School Reform Act (P.A. 85–1418) mandates comprehensive reforms in school governance (Wong and Rollow 1990). The current school reform in Chicago represents an opportunity for parents, school staff, and community groups to work together on educational improvement. The reform is designed to restore public confidence by granting parents substantial "ownership" over schools. To enhance accountability, the central office has decentralized policy making to locally elected parent councils and the principal at the school site. The 11-member council consists of 6 parents (i.e., the majority), 2 community representatives, 2 teachers, and the principal. There is also one student member at the high school level. The first council election in 1989 seems to have provided for a fair representation of various minority groups in the school system.

Members of the local council are given substantial authority: They can hire and fire the principal, allocate school funds, and develop school improvement plans. With training and support from business and public interest groups, local councils have written their bylaws, approved current school budgets, and successfully reviewed the principals' contract. The first major exercise of parental power was demonstrated in the decision on the principalship, a leadership position that would advance educational improvement. Of the 276 principals (representing half of the schools in the system) who were up for review in March 1990, 82 percent were retained in a new four-year contract (see Designs for Change 1990; Wong 1994). Councils that were dominated by racial minorities retained their white principals at a high rate of 78 percent. However, principals who failed to get contract renewal were more likely to hold "interim" positions in predominantly Hispanic schools. In these neighborhoods, community groups seemed particularly active in pushing for the selection of candidates that promised to be more responsive to their needs, such as solving the problem of overcrowding in the classroom.

POLITICS OF MARKET COMPETITION

City schools are adversely affected by the politics of exiting—where schooling choice made by individual families has accumulated a pattern of middle-class migration from central city schools (Hirschman 1971; Tiebout 1956; Chubb and Moe 1990; Coleman, Kelly, and Moore 1975; Coleman and Hoffer 1987). Clearly, suburbanization has contributed to the sociodemographic disadvantages of the urban district. This is especially evident in major metropolitan areas, where schools in outlying suburban communities are predominantly white and those in central cities primarily serve minority, low-income pupils (Orfield 1988). These demographic changes have political consequences. Exiting politics has put central city schools at an increasingly disadvantageous position in competing for state funding.

Exiting decisions of middle-class families and businesses not only weaken the tax base for city schools, but they also reduce the political influence of the urban district in the state legislature. The latter is illustrated in the city-suburban contention over aid to the disadvantaged in the state legislature (Cronin 1973; Berke, Goertz, and Coley 1984). Coalition building for targeted funding for the urban disadvantaged pupils is difficult when the state lawmakers have to deal with powerful constituencies in suburban middle-class communities. In Illinois, for example, the 1978 legislature reduced the weights assigned to poor students, which in effect, decreased state aid to inner-city schools. Of the 86 lawmakers who voted for the bill, 85 represented districts outside the city of Chicago. In contrast, 47 of the 64 legislators who voted against the measure came from both major parties in Chicago. Regional cleavages tend to undermine funding support for central city schools (Wong 1989). The trend has worsened over time. During the 1980s, Chicago held 30 percent of the seats in the state house. Now it maintains only 24 percent of the seats. Chicago's influence was further eroded in 1992 when the legislative remap gave Republicans control over the Senate. With control over both the governorship and the Senate, Republicans in Illinois have taken several initiatives to constrain the influence of the Chicago Teachers Union and to introduce alternative ways (such as vouchers) in school service delivery. The Democratic majority in the state house, though heavily reliant on union support in elections, finds it increasingly difficult to defend union demands in the climate of fiscal retrenchment.

POLITICS OF COMPETITION WITHIN THE PUBLIC SECTOR

As governmental institutions, urban schools are facing several key policy challenges—retention of middle-class families, racial integration, service provision for children of poverty, and improvement in student performance, among others. To meet these challenges, urban school districts have developed a set of "mediated choice programs"—student schooling choice mediated by a complex selection process. They are often referred to as magnet programs. According to a major study conducted in 1983, there were over 1,100 magnet schools in 130 urban districts of more than 20,000 students (Blank et al. 1983). By 1989, there were over 2,500 magnet schools, of which 60 percent operate at the elementary level (U.S. Secretary of Education 1989). Among the big-city districts with prominent magnet programs are Milwaukee, Houston, Los Angeles, Chicago, San Diego, and Cincinnati. New York's District 4, which includes Spanish Harlem, has made choice mandatory for its 23 junior high schools since 1983.

The most important feature of choice in public schools is that it combines marketlike mechanisms for parents with a decentralized authority system. Magnet schools or programs within a school are distinguished by academic specialties, such as the fine arts, math and science, and foreign languages. Enrollment in these programs is not restricted by the regular attendance boundaries. Instead, admissions are governed by racial requirements and other selective criteria and by the fact that nonpublic schools are not part of the arrangement. In many districts, schools enjoy discretion in pupil selection, using criteria that include entry test results, parental agreements, teacher recommendations, and other measures of a student's fitness to enroll in a particular program.

Choice programs are controversial. Magnet programs tend to "cream off" better students and other resources out of their neighborhood schools (Downs 1970). Local residents may perceive that the conversion of their neighborhood school to a choice program deprives them of direct access to their community-based service institution (Metz 1986). Questions have been raised on the implementation of a systemwide choice plan—distribution of school information to all parents, transportation cost, and compliance with civil rights provisions. In short, choice programs may come into conflict with other restructuring efforts in public schools (Cibulka 1990) and may destabilize school governance (Weeres 1988).

Concerns over inequity notwithstanding, choice programs have become quite effective in addressing the institutional and political needs of the urban district. First, magnet schools and a voluntary student transfer policy serve an important role in bringing about racial integration without aggravating racial conflict (Rossell 1990). Second, choice programs are often established to retain a middle-class presence in city schools. While Hirschman and other policy analysts argue that reform in public schools, like other "monopolized" public services, is not likely to be driven by the exit of their clientele, the emergence of choice programs seems to offer a counterexample. In Buffalo, for example, choice programs were used to retain white pupils as well as to attract students from nonpublic schools. Between 1977 and 1986, over 2,800 pupils left the nonpublic sector to enroll in Buffalo's choice programs. Whites comprised 4 out of 5 of the new enrollees (Rossell 1987). In Chicago, the opening of Whitney Young Magnet High School in 1975 was clearly designed to complement the city's urban renewal efforts (Campbell and Levine 1977; Wong 1992). The specialized curriculum in magnet schools can match the needs of the local labor market (Borman and Spring 1984).

Third, choice programs are innovative efforts to improve educational quality. It should be noted that the early voucher experiment in Alum Rock produced no discernible difference in students' academic outcomes between choice and nonchoice programs (Capell and Doscher 1981). Evaluation of recent choice programs, however, offers some evidence that connects choice (i.e., student self-selection and site-level governance) to educational improvement. As a 1982 report observed, magnet schools have expanded their initial focus on racial balance to include "an emphasis on providing quality education or educational options for the district" (Fleming et al. 1982; also see Raywid 1985). Using a longitudinal data set on Buffalo's 10 early childhood magnet programs, two analysts concluded that beginning in the third project year students in these programs "systematically perform at a statistically significant and higher level in both reading and mathematics than do the control-group comparisons" (Haskins and Alessi 1989). Better student performance was said to be linked to better curricular planning, greater parental involvement, higher level of racial integration, and more effective instructional practices. The real challenge is whether similar student gains can be accomplished when the small-scale choice programs become systemwide policy.

DIRECTIONS FOR FUTURE RESEARCH

What is particularly striking in this partial review of the politics of education is the fact that diverse governing structures coexist within the urban school system. As suggested in the synthesized framework, one finds choice programs in the midst of a powerful central bureaucracy in the urban district. One also sees dedicated parents vigorously involved in site-level governing councils, while others continue to exit to the nearby district or the nonpublic sector. Thus, the urban school organization consists of diverse structures that are distinguishable by their particular kind of politics. To understand the totality of the politics of urban education, one clearly needs to differentiate both the balance of power between layers within the school policy organization as well as the ways parents and other clients exercise their influence in school affairs.

Institutional diversity challenges policy makers and researchers to address two sets of questions: What are the major functions that the public school system serves? and What kind of institutional and political arrangements would best serve those functions? As a growing field of study, scholarship in the politics of urban education will continue to provide a useful groundwork for formulating solutions to these critical policy issues. Let me conclude by raising a broader challenge for researchers who approach public school systems as an institution.

The current round of rethinking about the central authority and shared governance should be expanded to include all major governing institutions at the districtwide level, namely, the mayor's office, the central office bureaucracy, the superintendency, the teachers' union, the media, and other organized interests. Specifically, we have not seen many systematic studies on the role of the mayor in the appointment of school board members since Paul Peterson's (1976) analysis of how Mayor Daley balanced the interests between his political machine and the reform faction in the Chicago board during the 1960s and early 1970s. Peterson's frameworks of pluralist versus ideological bargaining remain an original contribution to the literature. Very few empirical studies have produced the kind of detailed account on the way the school bureaucracy operates as did the works of David Rogers (1968) and Robert Havighurst (1964). Likewise, we have not conducted a thorough examination of the superintendency in the tradition of Larry Cuban's research on the three urban school chiefs (1976). Finally, much empirical research is needed on the changing power relations between the teachers' union and the school board (Kerchner and Koppich 1993), the media, business, local colleges and teacher training institutions, foundations (see McKersie 1993), and other organized interests in the current context of school reform. In short, we need to reconceptualize the role and the connection of key institutions in urban school governance.

REFERENCES

Ayers, William. 1993. "Chicago: A Restless Sea of Social Forces." In Charles Kerchner and Julia Koppich, eds., *A Union of Professionals*. New York: Teachers College Press.

Berke, Joel, Margaret Goertz, and R. Coley. 1984. *Politicians, Judges, and City Schools: Reforming School Finance in New York*. New York: Russell Sage Foundation.

Bidwell, Charles 1965. "The School as a Formal Organization." In James March, ed., *Handbook of Organizations*. Skokie: Rand McNally.

Blank, Rolf K., et al. 1983. *Survey of Magnet Schools: Analyzing a Model for Quality Integrated Education*. Washington, D.C.: James H. Lowry and Associates and Abt Associates.

Borman, Kathryn, and Joel Spring. 1984. *Schools in Central Cities*. White Plains, NY: Longman.

Boyd, William L., and Robert Crowson. 1981. "The Changing Conception and Practice of Public School Administration." In David C. Berliner, ed., *Review of Research in Education*. Vol. 9. Washington, D.C.: American Educational Research Association.

Burkhead, Jesse. 1967. *Input and Output in Large-City High Schools*. Syracuse: Syracuse University Press.

Campbell, Connie, and Daniel Levine. 1977. "Whitney Young Magnet High School of Chicago and Urban Renewal." In Daniel Levine and Robert Havighurst, eds., *The Future of Big-City Schools*. Berkeley: McCutchan Publishing.

Campbell, Roald, Luvern Cunningham, Raphael Nystrand, and Michael Usdan. 1985. *The Organization and Control of American Schools*. 5th ed. Columbus, OH: Charles E. Merrill Publishing.

Capell, F., and L. Doscher. 1981. *A Study of Alternatives in American Education, Vol. VI: Student Outcomes at Alum Rock 1974–1976*. Santa Monica: Rand Corporation.

Chubb, John, and Terry Moe. 1990. *Politics, Markets, and America's Schools*. Washington, D.C.: Brookings Institution.

Cibulka, James. 1990. "Choice and the Restructuring of American Education." In William Boyd and Herbert Walberg, eds., *Choice in Education: Potential and Problems*. Berkeley: McCutchan.

Coleman, James S., and Thomas Hoffer. 1987. *Public and Private High Schools*. New York: Basic Books.

Coleman, James S., Sara Kelly, and John Moore. 1975. *Trends in School Desegregation, 1968–73*. Washington, D.C.: Urban Institute.

Cronin, James. 1973. *The Control of Urban Schools*. New York: Free Press.

Cuban, Larry. 1976. *Urban School Chiefs under Fire*. Chicago: University of Chicago Press.

Dahl, Robert. 1961. *Who Governs?* New Haven: Yale University Press.

Designs for Change. 1990. *Chicago Principals: Changing of the Guard*. Chicago: Author.

Downs, Anthony. 1970. "Competition and Community Schools." In Henry Levin, ed., *Community Control of Schools*. New York: Clarion Books.

Fleming, P., et al. 1982. *Survey of Magnet Schools: Interim Report*. Washington, D.C.: James H. Lowry & Associates.

Fraga, Luis, Kenneth Meier, and Robert England. 1986. "Hispanic Americans and Educational Policy: Limits to Equal Access." *Journal of Politics* 48: 850–876.

Grant, W. 1971. "Community Control vs. Integration: The Case of Detroit." *Public Interest* 24 (summer): 62–79.

Grimshaw, William. 1979. *Union Rule in the Schools*. Lexington: D.C. Heath.

Haskins, Guy, and Samuel Alessi. 1989. "An Early Childhood Center Developmental Model for Public School Settings." *Teachers College Record* 90, no. 3: 415–433.

Havighurst, Robert. 1964. *The Public Schools of Chicago*. Chicago: Board of Education.

Hirschman, Albert. 1971. *Exit, Voice, and Loyalty*. Cambridge: Harvard University Press.

Jackson, Barbara, and James Cibulka. 1992. "Leadership Turnover and Business Mobilization: The Changing Political Ecology of Urban School Systems." In James Cibulka, Rodney Reed, and Kenneth Wong, eds., *The Politics of Urban Education in the United States*. London: Falmer Press.

James, H. Thomas, James A. Kelly, and Walter Garms. 1966. *Determinants of Educational Expenditures in Large Cities of the United States*. Palo Alto, CA: School of Education, Stanford University.

Jennings, Richard. 1980. "School Advisory Councils in America: Frustration and Failure." In G. Baron, ed., *The Politics of School Government*. New York: Pergamon Press.

Katzman, Martin. 1971. *The Political Economy of Urban Schools*. Cambridge, MA: Harvard University Press.

Katznelson, Ira. 1981. *City Trenches*. New York: Pantheon.

Kerchner, Charles, and Krista Caufman. 1993. "Guiding the Airplane While It's Rolling Down the Runway." In Charles Kerchner and Julia Koppich, eds., *A Union of Professionals*. New York: Teachers College Press.

Kerchner, Charles, and Julia Koppich, eds. 1993. *A Union of Professionals*. New York: Teachers College Press.

Kirst, Michael, and Walter Garms. 1980. "The Political Environment of School Finance Policy in the 1980s." In James Guthrie, ed., *School Finance Politics and Practices—The 1980s: A Decade of Conflict*. Cambridge: Ballinger.

Levy, Frank, Arnold Meitsner, and Aaron Wildavsky. 1974. *Urban Outcomes*. Berkeley: University of California Press.

McKersie, William. 1993. "Philanthropy's Paradox: Chicago School Reform." *Educational Evaluation and Policy Analysis* 15, no. 2: 109–128.

McLaughlin, Milbrey, and Patrick Shields. 1986. "Involving Parents in Schools: Lessons for Policy." Paper prepared for the Conference on Effects of Alternative Designs in Compensatory Education, June, Washington, D.C.

Malen, Betty, and Rodney Ogawa. 1988. "Professional-Patron Influence on Site-Based Governance Councils: A Confounding Case Study." *Educational Evaluation and Policy Analysis* 10, no. 4: 251–270.

Mann, Dean. 1974. "Political Representation and Urban School Advisory Councils." *Teachers College Record* 75, no. 3: 279–307.

Meier, Kenneth, Joseph Stewart, and Robert England. 1989. *Race, Class, and Education*. Madison: University of Wisconsin Press.

Meranto, Philip. 1970. *School Politics in the Metropolis*. Columbus, OH: Charles E. Merrill Publishing Co.

Metz, Mary. 1986. *Different by Design: The Context and Character of Three Magnet Schools*. New York: Routledge and Kegan Paul.

Orfield, Gary. 1988. "Race, Income and Educational Inequality: Students and Schools at Risk in the 1980s." In Council of Chief State School Officers, *School Success for Students at Risk.* Orlando: Harcourt, Brace & Jovanovich.

Peterson, Paul E. 1976. *School Politics Chicago Style.* Chicago: University of Chicago Press.

Peterson, Paul E. 1981. *City Limits.* Chicago: University of Chicago Press.

Peterson, Paul E. 1985. *The Politics of School Reform 1870–1940.* Chicago: University of Chicago Press.

Ravitch, Diane. 1974. *The Great School Wars.* New York: Basic Books.

Raywid, Mary Anne. 1985. "Family Choice Arrangements in Public Schools: A Review of Literature." *Review of Educational Research* 55, no. 4: 435–467.

Rogers, David. 1968. *110 Livingston Street.* New York: Random House.

Rossell, Christine. 1987. "The Buffalo Controlled Choice Plan." *Urban Education* 22, no. 3: 328–354.

Rossell, Christine. 1990. *The Carrot or the Stick for School Desegregation Policy.* Philadelphia: Temple University Press.

Schmidt, Peter. 1992. "Decree to Reallocate Resources in L.A. Schools Approved." *Education Week* (September 9): 12.

Tiebout, Charles. 1956. "A Pure Theory of Local Expenditures." *Journal of Political Economy* 64 (October): 416–424.

U.S. Secretary of Education. 1989. *Educating Our Children: Parents & Schools Together.* Washington, D.C.: Department of Education.

Verba, Sidney, and Norman Nie. 1972. *Participation in America.* New York: Harper and Row.

Weber, Max. 1947. *The Theory of Social and Economic Organization.* New York: Free Press.

Weeres, Joseph. 1988. "Economic Choice and the Dissolution of Community." In William Boyd and Charles Kerchner, eds., *The Politics of Excellence and Choice in Education.* London: Falmer.

Weick, Karl. 1976. "Educational Organizations as Loosely Coupled Systems." *Administrative Science Quarterly* 21: 1–9.

Wong, Kenneth K. 1989. "Fiscal Support for Education in American States: The 'Parity-to-Dominance' View Examined." *American Journal of Education* 97, no. 4: 329–357.

Wong, Kenneth K. 1990. *City Choices: Education and Housing.* Albany: State University of New York Press.

Wong, Kenneth K. 1992. "Choice in Public Schools: Their Institutional Functions and Distributive Consequences." In Kenneth K. Wong, ed., *Politics of Policy Innovation in Chicago.* Vol. 4 *Research in Urban Policy.* Greenwich, CT: JAI Press.

Wong, Kenneth K. 1994. "Linking Governance Reform to Schooling Opportunities for the Disadvantaged." *Educational Administration Quarterly* 30, no. 2: 153–177.

Wong, Kenneth K. 1995. "Transforming Schools." In Peter Cookson and Barbara Schneider, eds., *Creating School Policy: Trends, Dilemmas, and Prospects.* New York: Garland.

Wong, Kenneth K., and Sharon Rollow. 1990. "A Case Study of the Recent Chicago School Reform." *Administrator's Notebook* 34, no 5: 5–6.

Chapter 24

Police, Crime, and Crime Prevention

Susan Bennett

During the 1994 congressional elections, many candidates worked to portray themselves as tough on crime. Their focus reflects many citizens' concerns: In 1994, 56 percent of respondents identified crime and violence as one of the country's two most serious problems. No other problem generated so much consensus. Although many factors contribute to this concern, a rising crime rate is certainly one (Flanagan and Maguire 1994: 152). From 1982 to 1992, the violent crime rate rose from 571.1 per 100,000 to 757.7 per 100,000, while the property crime rate remained virtually stable (352). Americans are more concerned, however, about changes in the kind of violence we are experiencing. Popular wisdom combines the crack explosion, youth gangs, assault weapons, and drive-by shootings in an image of urban violence. Although not all these assumptions are true (Klein, Maxson, and Cunningham 1991), both offenders and victims of violence are getting younger, and the availability of more lethal weapons is a contributing factor (National Research Council 1993). At the same time, Americans doubt police capacity to protect them: 54 percent of respondents in a 1993 poll had either "not very much" confidence or no confidence in the police's ability to protect them from violent crime (Flanagan and Mcguire 1994: 165).

Historically, the role of police has been crime prevention—acting to prevent crime *before* it happens. In establishing Great Britain's first police force, Sir Robert Peel wrote: "It should be understood . . . that the principal object to be attained is the prevention of crime. . . . The absence of crime will be considered the best proof of the complete efficiency of the Police" (National Crime Prevention Institute 1986: 13). With the advent of professional policing, however, police focused more on crime control—responding to crime *after* it has happened. Community policing emphasizes crime prevention again; it advocates a proactive approach to crime and encourages police-community partnerships.

This chapter reviews what we know about police capacity to prevent and control crime and considers some policy issues. It discusses theoretical issues in the field, some methodological problems, and the current state of knowledge. It excludes broader considerations about the police, such as the police as a form of social control used by dominant groups (see Jackson 1989). Nor does it discuss the effect of other criminal justice agencies (e.g., courts), though that cannot realistically be separated from attempts to make the police more effective. Finally, the chapter focuses on Part I crimes (such as robbery and burglary), with no consideration for white-collar crimes, corporate crimes, and the like. This focus represents the bias of policy discussions and research, rather than a conviction that these are the most important crimes in our society.

THEORETICAL ISSUES

Three theoretical issues in the debate over police capacity to prevent crime include the division between individual and structural explanations for crime, the identification of fear of crime as a social problem, and the role of social and physical incivilities in generating crime.

Individual and Structural Explanations for Crime

To prevent crime, it may seem logical to start with the causes of crime. James Q. Wilson (1985:6) asserted, however, that "a free society can do so little about attacking these causes [of crime] that a concern for their elimination becomes little more than an excuse for doing nothing" (cf. Currie 1985). Nonetheless, one's perspective on the causes of crime influences the policies that one recommends. Very broadly, perspectives on the causes of crime can be divided into individual and structural approaches.

The dominant criminological research since World War II has focused on offenders' motivations. Researchers and policy makers who ask why certain individuals commit crimes also tend to propose policies to influence individual decisions and behaviors. Often this individual-level approach relies on deterrence theory: If the cost of a crime sufficiently exceeds its benefits, individuals will not commit the crime. Policy can influence the cost of offending by increasing the certainty of being caught, the severity of the punishment, or the swiftness of the punishment. This approach is seen in the longer mandatory sentences for drug-related offenses and the increase in crimes punishable by death in Clinton's 1994 crime bill. Although researchers have seriously questioned the efficacy of deterrence (Currie 1985; Lab 1988; Walker 1989), it appeals strongly to common sense and is supported by numerous researchers and policy makers (Wilson 1985; Wilson and Herrnstein 1985). Another often-cited individual approach is social control theory, especially as delineated by Travis

Hirschi (Vold and Bernard 1986). It argues that social bonds to family, school, and peers decrease the likelihood that individuals will engage in delinquent behaviors. Although individual-level theories vary, they all suggest policies that focus on changing individuals and their immediate environment (e.g., families) to prevent crime.

Related approaches focus on available opportunities for crime. First, routine activity theory examines spatial configurations of communities and their crimogenic effect (Cohen and Felson 1979; Cohen 1981). Its focus is the effect of routine activities on the distribution of targets, offenders, and guardians across geographic areas and the resulting crime patterns. Second, defensible space or crime prevention through environmental design (CPTED) looks to reduce crime by physical changes in the environment. CPTED practitioners assume that we cannot change offenders' motivations, but we can decrease their *opportunities* for crime (Newman 1972). Physical environments that increase the ability to see suspicious behaviors, "harden" targets with locks and other equipment, and encourage people to take on the role of "guardians" for the area decrease the opportunities. In part, the physical changes reduce crime indirectly, by leading to more "territorial functioning" by legitimate users of the area and changing the local social climate (Lab 1988; Taylor, Gottfredson, and Brower 1984; Taylor and Gottfredson 1986).

In contrast, individuals who focus on structural causes of crime generally propose social and economic policies to reduce crime. One such approach argues that poverty, unemployment, and underemployment are positively related to the crime rate (Currie 1985). Judith and Peter Blau (1982), however, found that *inequality* is a more important determinant of violent crimes than poverty or unemployment (cf. Bursik and Grasmick 1993a; Golden and Messner 1987; Hagan and Peterson 1995; Sampson and Laub 1993). A second approach based on social ecology asserts that some communities experience more social disorganization because of their functional position within the city, resulting in more crime and a higher concentration of offenders (Bursik and Grasmick 1993b; Byrne and Sampson 1986; Kornhauser 1978). Previously dormant, the social ecology approach generated a growing body of research in the 1980s; and it can be informative for community policing. Structural approaches vary in several aspects: the emphasis on social or spatial differentiation; the importance of poverty, inequality, or social stratification; the role of subcultures in transmitting deviant values and behaviors; and the importance of local communities as a locus of social control. These approaches suggest policies aimed at reducing poverty, inequality, unemployment and underemployment, social disorganization in communities, and the like, to prevent crime.

More recently, researchers attempted to integrate the individual and structural perspectives. Although integration seems necessary for better explanations of criminal behavior, its feasibility and success are still uncertain (Byrne and Sampson 1986; Bursik 1988; Bursik and Grasmick 1993b; Hagan and Peterson 1995).

Clearly, the potential role of the police in crime prevention varies with the factors believed to cause crime. Deterrence theories posit a much stronger police role than do structural theories. Some researchers think an emphasis on the structural causes has, in fact, reduced efforts to use the police for crime prevention (Sherman 1992).

Fear of Crime as a Social Problem

As crime concerns grew, researchers and policy makers realized that fear of crime was also a problem (Skogan and Maxfield 1981). Afraid of becoming a victim, city residents withdrew from the community—staying home at night and avoiding certain places. Such withdrawal decreases the quality of life for individuals and the community. From the opportunity reduction approach, residents' withdrawal even meant that crime was likely to increase, as fewer people served as guardians for the area.

Despite considerable research, there is still debate about the conceptualization of fear of crime. Ferraro and LaGrange (1987) criticize the lack of specification in the usual measures: the failure to distinguish between fear, risk, and vulnerability; between general and personal assessments; between judgments, values, and emotions. They assert that fear of crime is only the emotional component. Other researchers argue that its conceptualization depends in part on the purpose of the research: For instance, measurements that confound dimensions may work well for program evaluations (Baumer and Rosenbaum 1980). Researchers have also questioned whether the current measures of fear of crime reflect a fear of strangers or whites' racism (Skogan 1994).

As research documented residents' fear of crime, policy makers included its reduction in prevention programs. It has been criticized as a ''softer'' goal, more easily achieved than reducing crime (Curtis 1988) and based on an unproven causal model that posits that fear of crime increases crime (Currie 1988).

Physical and Social Incivilities

Fear of crime studies found, surprisingly, only a modest relationship between an individual's victimization experiences and his/her fear of crime (Skogan and Maxfield 1981). Follow-up research suggested that fear of crime was also influenced by one's vulnerability and the prevalence of physical and social incivilities (e.g., trash and panhandlers) in the community (Baba and Austin 1991; Hunter 1978; Skogan and Maxfield 1981). Incivilities occur more often than crime and serve as cues about the community. Individuals expect communities with more incivilities to be more tolerant of disorder and crime, and they experience higher fear as a result.

Incivilities are also expected to increase crime. Wilson and Kelling's (1982) influential model hypothesizes that incivilities are interpreted by potential offenders as indicating a community that is more tolerant of, or less likely to take action against, criminal incidents. Seeing better opportunities in these communities, offenders commit more crimes there and cause further community deterioration. If incivilities are a cause of crime and fear of crime (cf. Greene and Taylor 1988; Skogan 1990), then police may prevent crime through order maintenance, an aspect of police work deemphasized by the professional model.

METHODOLOGICAL ISSUES

Of the many methodological issues in criminological research, three problems are discussed: studying rare events, measurement difficulties for many major concepts, and analytical problems in testing causal models.

Studying Rare Events

Although the common perception is that crime is ubiquitous, crimes are relatively rare. Their infrequency becomes obvious in attempts to study particular crimes, communities, or groups of offenders or victims (Sherman 1986: 362). The low numbers make it difficult to estimate trends or program effects reliably. Gabor (1981) could not assess the displacement effects of an Operation Identification program because of the low number of burglaries. Similarly, attempts to look at police responses often flounder over insufficient cases. Bayley and Garofalo (1989) could not assess the efficacy of police responses to potentially violent situations because of the very few incidents that threatened violence and still fewer incidents in which it occurred.

Measurement of Major Concepts

The major problem is the measurement of crime, raising both reliability and validity issues (National Research Council 1993; Seidman and Couzens 1974; Skogan 1975). The most common source of crime statistics is the Uniform Crime Report (UCR) produced by the Federal Bureau of Investigation (FBI) from local jurisdictions' reports. Some of the many problems with UCR statistics include the level of unreported crime (which varies by offense), changing definitions of crime, variations across officers and departments in the classification of crime incidents, failure to record multiple victimizations, changes in recording systems, and political motivations to downgrade and underreport crime. Furthermore, officers' behavior varies across neighborhoods: Their level of activity, arrest decisions, and willingness to comply with complainants' requests depend in part on community characteristics. These variations reduce the ability to make neighborhood comparisons (Bursik 1988; Smith 1986).

UCR statistics also limit the types of crimes counted. They focus primarily on "street crimes" like burglary and robbery but provide little information on white-collar crimes or corporate crimes. Nor do the classifications allow researchers to identify easily incidents of drug trafficking or domestic violence, despite the current salience of these crimes.

Victimization surveys address some of these concerns, especially unreported crime. Though useful, the surveys have limitations (Skogan 1981). They require large samples for reliable estimates, which increases their costs and makes them impractical for smaller areas or populations. They are subject to respondents' memory bias, interpretation of events as criminal, and willingness to discuss their victimizations. The surveys are also generally limited to residents in the area, excluding visitors and people who work there as potential victims.

When focusing on the efficacy of crime prevention, researchers face difficulties of measuring nonevents (i.e., crimes that did not occur) and the displacement of crime. In response to crime prevention efforts, an offender can change the place, time, method, target, or type of crime, besides deciding not to commit a crime. All but the last are examples of displacement. Because offenders can change their crime in so many ways, it is difficult to detect the displacement effect in crime reports. Generally, displacement is considered a failure and is often used to argue against some tactics (especially those aimed at "opportunity reduction"; Repetto 1976). Barr and Pease (1990) suggest that displacement need not be viewed as failure. Assuming crime is unavoidable, it is possible (though not perhaps politically feasible) to use displacements to create a more equitable distribution of crime.

Several major concepts remain the focus of measurement disputes, and many are only indirectly measured (Sampson 1986). Bursik and Grasmick (1993b: xi) state that "the measurement of the central concepts underlying all theories of neighborhoods and crime . . . is still a fairly crude and indirect procedure." Unfortunately, obtaining direct measures for many concepts is both costly and difficult.

Testing Deterrence Theory

Obviously, possible deterrent effects are crucial to decisions about policing strategies. The substantial research on this question, however, is plagued with methodological problems. Like much criminological research, deterrence research has measurement problems, primarily in measuring police activity (Decker and Kohfeld 1985; Sampson and Cohen 1988). The major problems in deterrence research, however, are analytical: the simultaneous relationship between arrest rates and crime rates, the use of common terms on both sides of the equation, and unrealistic assumptions in models designed to deal with the simultaneity issue. These issues have been reviewed elsewhere (Blumstein, Cohen, and Nagin 1978).

Testing Community Theories

The reemerging social ecology research faces several analytical difficulties. In part, it is these problems that have limited its acceptance.

Establishing that group or compositional effects operate separately from individual effects is problematic. Do we have more (or less) crime when poverty is concentrated in certain communities than we would have if the poor were randomly distributed throughout the city? Is the variation across communities explained solely by variation between individuals in those communities? Unfortunately, many ecological studies have not controlled for individual-level effects (Byrne and Sampson 1986). Although contextual analyses can separate compositional and individual effects, the data collection costs are often prohibitive, as one needs community- and individual-level data for numerous locations.

Much ecological research is cross-sectional, yet the theory is based on a *process* of community development. When Shaw and McKay did the initial research, urban community structure was stable. Research, however, has demonstrated that community structures have changed significantly since then and are influenced by more than the "natural market forces" originally posited by the theory (Bursik 1988). Testing the model requires longitudinal data—also increasing data collection costs. Despite an increase in longitudinal data sets, they are still rare (Bursik 1988; Bursik and Grasmick 1993b; Byrne and Sampson 1986).

Often variables of interest are highly collinear, making multivariate analyses problematic. For example, the racial composition and poverty levels of U.S. communities are strongly correlated: "the disentanglement of the effects of racial composition and poverty/inequality seems to be the major focus of current research on the social ecology of crime" (Byrne and Sampson 1986: 6).

Finally, the social processes that mediate between community characteristics and crime patterns are rarely measured. Although numerous studies have found a relationship between poverty and crime, the nature of that relationship has been variously explained—through individual motivations and decisions, subculture theories (subcultures of violence and of poverty), and community contextual factors.

CURRENT KNOWLEDGE OF POLICE WORK AND CRIME PREVENTION

Citizens are most familiar with professional policing, which focuses on providing rapid response to 911 calls. Although departments also have units to solve reported crimes or deal with victimless crimes, the allocation of police resources is determined largely by citizens calling the 911 reporting system. Generally, the emphasis has been on the equity and efficiency of this policing style, rather than its effectiveness (Eck and Rosenbaum 1994). The first two parts of this section review the effectiveness of strategies within this policing style. The third section discusses community policing and its possible effectiveness.

Patrol Strategies

Deterrence studies assess the effects of the certainty, severity, and celerity of punishment on crime rates. They suggest that improving certainty of apprehension is the best way to increase deterrence, as that is the weakest point (Currie 1985; Walker 1989). Traditionally, we have relied on uniformed patrol to provide deterrence through their visibility.

Preventive Patrol. Pessimism about preventive patrol undoubtedly started with the Kansas City patrol experiment. The experiment compared districts that received no patrol, normal patrol, or increased patrol (Kelling et al. 1974). The lack of significant differences in crime, arrests, or victimizations between the districts led many to agree with the police chief "that routine preventive patrol in marked police cars has little value in preventing crime" (Sherman 1986: 359). Although some methodological problems weaken that conclusion, the Kansas City experiment raised significant questions about patrol as a deterrent.

Arrests. Other studies have examined the possible effects of arrests. As noted, this research has numerous methodological problems, and the findings are mixed. Although these mixed results might be due to variations in research design, a series of experimental studies on the effects of arrest on domestic violence also had mixed findings. Four studies concluded that arrests reduced domestic violence, but the other three found that arresting the offender *increased* future violence. One study found that arrests were more likely to deter those who were employed and to escalate the violence of those who were unemployed (Sherman 1992). In short, arrests may either decrease or increase an offender's criminal activity, and we know little about the different effects across offenders or crimes.

Rapid Response. The professional model also emphasizes responding quickly to calls for service. It seems logical that a quicker response will mean more success in making arrests. Yet research shows that about two thirds of 911 calls report crimes that occurred some time before they were discovered (Walker 1989: 134). Even when victims or witnesses can report the crime in a more timely fashion, they delay in calling. A Kansas City study found that victims delay an average of 41 minutes (Sherman 1986: 360). When the biggest delay is between the time of occurrence and reporting, faster police response is unlikely to make much difference.

Proactive Patrol. Despite the limited deterrence of preventive patrol, some researchers have argued that proactive patrol, in which officers vigorously enforce even minor ordinances, has a deterrent effect. A San Diego study found that extensive use of field interrogations decreased target crimes by 20 percent; nor did community attitudes toward the police worsen (Boydstun 1975). Two studies using aggregate data for about 150 cities confirmed its effectiveness: Proactive policing (arrests for disorderly conduct and driving under the influence) increased arrest certainty and decreased burglary and robbery (Sampson and Cohen 1988; Sampson 1986). On the negative side, the Newark Fear Reduction Program included an "intensive enforcement program" similar to proactive patrol. Afterward, residents were more satisfied with their community, but they were also more fearful and more likely to identify neighborhood incivility problems (Skogan 1990: 118–119). Proactive policing may reduce some crime but may also have negative side effects.

Despite the apparent effectiveness of proactive patrol, many people are reluctant to advocate it, given its association with police brutality and riots. Commissions of both the 1930s and 1960s that investigated urban riots concluded that aggressive policing in minority communities contributed to the riots (Skolnick and Fyfe 1993: 78).

Foot Patrols. If proactive patrol raises images of overly aggressive, even brutal police officers, foot patrol raises images of Officer Friendly. It is expected to prevent crime by strengthening relationships between officers and residents and increasing officers' knowledge of the community. It is also assumed that officers on foot are more likely to take action against minor offenses and incivilities; in this sense, foot patrol is similar to proactive policing. Numerous anecdotes illustrate its effectiveness, but evaluations are mixed. A Newark study (Pate 1986) found that introducing foot patrols reduced residents' concern about disorder and crime but not reported crimes or victimizations. More recent evaluations concluded that when implemented alone, foot patrols do little to decrease crime, calls for service, or residents' fear of crime (Bowers and Hirsch 1987; Cordner 1994). In contrast, foot patrol as part of community policing in Flint, Missouri, substantially decreased both crimes and calls for service after three years (Trojanowicz 1986). These conclusions are weakened by the lack of a comparison group. Though few studies have demonstrated such clear-cut gains, foot patrol seems more effective when combined with community policing.

Focused Interventions

Most police strategies are assumed to work for all crimes and offenders. Some strategies focus, however, on particular crimes, offenders, or locations. This section reviews stings, saturated patrols (patrols of hot spots), career criminal units, and crackdowns.

Stings. In sting operations, undercover officers offer criminal opportunities, usually to suspected criminals. A common sting operation has officers pose as fences to purchase stolen property. Generally, evaluations concluded that stings are effective in recovering stolen property and developing prosecutable cases. For crime prevention, however, the conclusions are negative. Pennell (1979) found that despite efficient sting operations in San Diego, property crimes continued to increase, as did the value of stolen property. Other studies found that stings had no effect on crime (Raub 1984; Weiner, Cheist, and Hart 1984) or caused a short-term increase during the sting (Langworthy 1989).

In addition, many are concerned about the ethics and legality of stings. These concerns include undercover work's contribution to police corruption, use of excessive trickery or coercion, covering up offenses committed by informers, political misuse of stings, and a reduction of protected freedoms. ''Some of the new police undercover work has lost sight of the profound difference between carrying out an investigation to determine whether a suspect is, in fact, breaking the law, and carrying it out to determine whether an individual *can be induced* to break the law'' (Marx 1982: 173).

Career Criminal Units. Numerous studies have found that a small proportion of offenders commit the majority of crimes. A modest increase in their incarceration would reduce crime substantially. Numerous programs target career criminals based on that rationale. Few programs have been evaluated, but two evaluations provide mixed results. In a Kansas City program, officers made only six arrests for the targeted crimes/offenders and had only a 31 percent conviction rate (Walker 1989: 139–140). A Washington, D.C. program had more success: Officers arrested 58 percent of the targeted group (140). Those arrested had more prior arrests than other arrestees, and the cases were more likely to result in a conviction and longer sentences (Martin and Sherman 1986). This success must be weighed against the substantial costs of approximately $25,000 per conviction (Walker 1989: 140). There is disagreement whether these results constitute modest success or an expensive strategy that accomplishes little.

Crackdowns. Crackdowns are an ''attempt to communicate a far more powerful threat of apprehension and punishment than does 'normal' policing'' (Sherman 1990: 2). Generally, crackdowns include increased sanctions, a stronger police presence, or both, and heavy publicity to ensure public awareness. A familiar form of crackdown is increased sanctions and arrests for drunk driving. Sherman (1990) found that 15 of 18 crackdown studies showed an initial deterrent effect. The effect decayed in longer-term crackdowns, though not in short-term crackdowns. In fact, in some short-term crackdowns there was a residual deterrent effect, that sometimes lasted longer than the crackdown. The residual effects of short-term crackdowns suggest that shorter crackdowns, with changing targets, might be an effective way to increase deterrent effects of policing (Repetto 1976; Sherman 1990).

Despite these successes, using crackdowns has at least two potential problems. First, crackdowns may cause displacement. For instance, studies of drug crackdowns found that one increased street robberies and another increased homicides substantially (Sherman 1990: 19–23). Second, short-term crackdowns may harm relations with the community. Crackdowns are often used in community policing to help a community ''reclaim'' a high-crime area and make residents feel safer. Evaluators, however, found that they did not enhance residents' feelings of safety.

When a high level of enforcement is provided and then withdrawn suddenly, the general response of most residents in anger. In such instances the police lose credibility and the project legitimacy in the eyes of the community.

Although intensive enforcement efforts . . . may make clear and immediate impacts on the levels of crime in any given community, their long-term impacts are highly suspect. (Sadd and Grinc 1994: 47)

Saturation Patrols. Saturation patrols concentrate a large number of officers in a location that has a high crime rate, often referred to as a "hot spot." Similar to crackdowns in the concentration of resources, they lack the publicity of crackdowns. Available evaluations indicate that saturation patrols significantly decrease crime. New York City subway crime declined when the number of officers increased by 158 percent, although crime increased after two years. The cost is prohibitive, however. Sherman estimates the subway patrol deterred crime at about $35,000 per felony (1990: 30). More recently, Minneapolis increased patrol presence at hot spots by 250 percent and decreased calls for service in those locations by 13 percent, at a cost of $1,000 per prevented crime (Sherman 1992: 202). The effectiveness of saturation patrols may warrant their use in high-crime locations for a limited time, but their cost prohibits wider or more regular use.

Community Policing

Community policing grew out of concerns about the professional model of policing. Responding reactively to 911 calls does little to prevent crimes. A domestic violence call gets the same response whether it was the first reported incident or the twenty-fifth. Officers' isolation from the community is also problematic. Police rely heavily on information from citizens; but officers receive less information on motor patrol and are less able to assess it. In response, three policies developed under the community policing umbrella: developing a partnership with communities and other agencies to handle problems; reestablishing the order maintenance role of police; and developing a proactive, problem-solving approach to crime and quality-of-life problems. The expected benefits are extensive: improved job satisfaction among police officers, more effective use of police resources, improved police-community relations, empowerment of local communities, increased neighborhood viability, and reduction in fear of crime and crime.

Implementation Problems. Although many departments claim to have switched to community policing, the programs are so varied that it is difficult to know what such a statement means. The variations make it difficult for departments to learn from each other's experiences and to determine effectiveness in achieving goals. In departments that seriously attempted community policing, several implementation difficulties undermined its possible effectiveness. First, many police officers, including middle managers, resist the change. Many officers see community policing as "soft," as "social work." For middle managers, it means less control over officers and increased difficulty in supervising. Second, community policing requires extensive training of police officers and of residents (Sadd and Grinc 1994). Prior experience suggests that multiple training sessions are needed to upgrade officers' skills as they acquire experience. Third, community policing requires that officers have time to work with the community, without answering calls for service. Numerous departments have found it difficult to free officers' time for community policing and still respond adequately to 911 calls (Skogan 1994). Fourth, forming partnerships with the community is difficult for police, especially in high-crime or minority communities where residents tend to be distrustful of police. Unfortunately, police often choose to work with those residents who are already organized, which gives a class and race bias to community policing (Skogan 1990). Finally, the broad focus on quality-of-life issues means the police need to work collaboratively with other city agencies. It is rare for a police department to have working relationships with other agencies, and this aspect of the program often fails. Community policing requires a substantial change in the organization and functioning of police departments. It cannot be quickly implemented, nor is it likely to succeed without serious commitment from upper echelons in the department and city government.

Effects on Communities. A good overview of community policing's effects is provided in Skogan's (1994) analysis of the components of six programs. All programs most consistently influenced residents' attitudes about police services. Half reduced residents' fear of crime, and slightly less than half reduced their perceptions of community incivilities. They had little effect on either victimization or drug availability. Three intensive enforcement efforts were less successful than community policing in improving the community. These findings are similar to other evaluations, which often find that residents' perceptions improve, but crime does not decline. More problematically, evaluations often find that the positive changes occur among white residents and homeowners but not minority residents or renters (Skogan 1990, 1994). If police work with dominant community groups, then community policing will continue to disadvantage marginalized groups. Particularly in heterogeneous communities, one should consider whose ''order'' is being maintained and who is identified as the problem. Although numerous problems remain, early evaluations suggest that community policing can reduce residents' fear of crime and may reduce crime by improving police-community relations and strengthening communities.

FUTURE DIRECTIONS

For both theoretical and practical reasons, further research in both the social ecology of crime and the integration of the individual and structural explanations of crime seems the most fruitful. Attempts to explain crime solely through structural or individual factors go against both common sense and our current knowledge. More important, attempts to curb crime through deterrence in the last 12 to 15 years have resulted in substantial social costs with relatively few benefits. The United States currently imprisons a larger proportion of its population than any other country. In a time of fiscal constraint, states are spending increasing proportions of their budgets to build and maintain prisons, yet most also have serious overcrowding problems. In turn, fewer monies are available for other social programs, such as education and health care. Minority communities bear much of this burden: As many as one in three black males is imprisoned or on probation or parole. At the same time, the violent crime rate has continued to rise. The difficulties and infeasibility of further increasing deterrent effects suggest that we need to explore other policies to reduce crime, especially violent crime. Focusing on both the structural and individual factors leading to crime does not necessitate a deemphasis on the role of police in crime prevention. Community policing is well suited to such a "multiprong" approach.

Our current emphasis on a punitive, deterrent approach to crime prevention has another serious cost: the weakening of many civil rights and liberties through policies to strengthen the criminal justice system by removing some checks previously placed on its actions (e.g., protection against unreasonable search and seizure). Certainly we have a serious crime problem; but in considering how to alleviate that problem, we must also remember to assess the costs of many of the proposed policies.

Crime prevention efforts, perhaps more so than other forms of applied social science, have the potential for abuse. In the words of Wolfgang and Ferracuti (1967: 284), we must ask, "To what extent are we willing to change the traditional democratic constraints that normally function to restrict society's manipulative control over behavior, even the conduct of criminals, in order to reduce crimes of violence?" (Hawkins 1985: 100)

REFERENCES

Baba, Yoko, and D. Mark Austin. 1991. "Neighborhood Environmental Satisfaction, Victimization, and Social Participation as Determinants of Neighborhood Safety." *Environment and Behavior* 21: 763–780.

Barr, Robert, and Ken Pease. 1990. "Crime Placement, Displacement, and Deflection." In M. Tonry and N. Morris, eds., *Crime and Justice: A Review of Research*. Vol. 12. Chicago: University of Chicago Press.

Baumer Terry L., and Dennis P. Rosenbaum. 1980. "Measuring 'Fear of Crime.' " Paper presented at the Special National Workshop on Research Methodology and Criminal Justice Program Evaluation, Baltimore, Maryland.

Bayley, David H., and James Garofalo. 1989. "The Management of Violence by Police Patrol Officers." *Criminology* 27, no. 1: 1–23.

Blau, Peter, and Judith Blau. 1982. "The Cost of Inequality: Metropolitan Structure and Violent Crime." *American Sociological Review* 47: 121.

Blumstein, Alfred, Jacqueline Cohen, and Daniel Nagin. 1978. *Deterrence and Incapacitation: Estimating the Effects of Sanctions on Crime Rates*. Washington, D.C.: National Academy Press.

Bowers, William J., and John H. Hirsch. 1987. "The Impact of Foot Patrol Staffing on Crime and Disorder in Boston: The Unmet Promise." *American Journal of Police* 6, no. 1: 17–44.

Boydstun, John. 1975. "San Diego Field Interrogation: Final Report." Washington, D.C.: Police Foundation.

Bursik, Robert J., Jr. 1988. "Social Disorganization and Theories of Crime and Delinquency: Problems and Prospects." *Criminology* 26, no. 4: 519–551.

Bursik, Robert J., Jr., and Harold G. Grasmick. 1993a. "Economic Deprivation and Neighborhood Crime Rates, 1960–1980." *Law and Society Review* 27, no. 2: 263–283.

Bursik, Robert J., Jr., and Harold G. Grasmick. 1993b. *Neighborhoods and Crime: The Dimensions of Effective Community Control.* New York: Lexington Books.

Byrne, James M., and Robert J. Sampson. 1986. "Key Issues in the Social Ecology of Crime." In J. M. Byrne and R. J. Sampson, eds., *Social Ecology of Crime.* New York: Springer-Verlag.

Cohen, Lawrence. 1981. "Modeling Crime Trends: A Criminal Opportunity Perspective." *Journal of Research in Crime and Delinquency* 18: 138–164.

Cohen, Lawrence, and Marcus Felson. 1979. "Social Change and Crime Rate Trends: A Routine Activities Approach." *American Sociological Review* 44: 588–608.

Cordner, Gary W. 1994. "Foot Patrol without Community Policing: Law and Order in Public Housing." In D. P. Rosenbaum, ed., *The Challenge of Community Policing.* Thousand Oaks, CA: Sage.

Currie, Elliott. 1985. *Confronting Crime.* New York: Pantheon Books.

Currie, Elliott. 1988. "Two Visions of Community Crime Prevention." In Tim Hope and Margaret Shaw, eds., *Communities and Crime Reduction.* London: Her Majesty's Stationery Office.

Curtis, Lynn. 1988. "The March of Folly: Crime and the Underclass." In Tim Hope and Margaret Shaw, eds., *Communities and Crime Reduction.* London: Her Majesty's Stationery Office.

Decker, Scott H., and Carol W. Kohfeld. 1985. "Crimes, Crime Rates, Arrests, and Arrest Ratios: Implications for Deterrence Theory." *Criminology* 23, no. 3: 437–450.

Eck, John E., and Dennis P. Rosenbaum. 1994. "The New Police Order: Effectiveness, Equity, and Efficiency in Community Policing." In D. P. Rosenbaum, ed., *The Challenge of Community Policing.* Thousand Oaks, CA: Sage.

Ferraro, Kenneth F., and Randy LaGrange. 1987. "The Measurement of Fear of Crime." *Sociological Inquiry* 57: 70–101.

Flanagan, Timothy J., and Kathleen Maguire. 1994. *Sourcebook of Criminal Justice Statistics—1993.* Washington, D.C.: U.S. Government Printing Office.

Gabor, Thomas. 1981. "The Crime Displacement Hypothesis: An Empirical Examination." *Crime and Delinquency* 27: 390–404.

Golden, Reid M., and Steven F. Messner. 1987. "Dimensions of Racial Inequality and Rates of Violent Crime." *Criminology* 25, no. 3: 525–541.

Greene, Jack R., and Ralph Taylor. 1988. "Community Based Policing and Foot Patrol: Issues of Theory and Evaluation." In J. R. Greene and S. D. Mastrofski, eds., *Community Policing: Rhetoric or Reality.* New York: Praeger.

Hagan, John, and Ruth D. Peterson, eds. 1995. *Crime and Inequality.* Stanford: Stanford University Press.

Hawkins, Darnell R. 1985. "Black Homicide: The Adequacy of Existing Research for Devising Prevention Strategies." *Crime and Delinquency* 31 (January): 83–103.

Hayeslip, David, and Gary Cordner. 1987. "The Effects of Community Oriented Patrol of Police Officer Attitudes." *American Journal of Police* 1: 95–119.

Hunter, Albert. 1978. "Symbols of Incivility: Social Disorder and Fear of Crime in Urban

Neighborhoods.'' Presented at the annual meeting of the American Society of Criminology, Dallas, Texas.

Jackson, Pamela Irving. 1989. *Minority Group Threat, Crime, and Policing: Social Context and Social Control*. New York: Praeger.

Kelling, George L., Tony Pate, Duane Dickman, and Charles Brown. 1974. *The Kansas City Preventive Patrol Experiment*. Washington, D.C.: Police Foundation.

Klein, Malcolm, Charyl Maxson, and Lea Cunningham. 1991. '' 'Crack,' Street Gangs, and Violence.'' *Criminology* 29, no. 4: 623–650.

Kornhauser, Ruth R. 1978. *Social Sources of Delinquency*. Chicago: University of Chicago Press.

Lab, Steven P. 1988. *Crime Prevention: Approaches, Practices and Evaluations*. Cincinnati, OH: Anderson Publishing Co.

Langworthy, Robert H. 1989. ''Do Stings Control Crime? An Evaluation of a Police Fencing Operation.'' *Justice Quarterly* 6, no. 1: 27–45.

Lurigio, Arthur J., and Dennis P. Rosebaum. 1994. ''The Impact of Community Policing on Police Personnel: A Review of the Literature.'' In D. P. Rosenbaum, ed., *The Challenge of Community Policing*. Thousand Oaks, CA: Sage.

Martin, Susan E., and Lawrence W. Sherman. 1986. ''Selective Apprehension: A Police Strategy for Repeat Offenders.'' *Criminology* 24, no. 1: 155–173.

Marx, Gary T. 1982. ''Who Really Gets Stung? Some Issues Raised by the New Police Undercover Work.'' *Crime and Delinquency* 28, no. 2: 165–193.

National Crime Prevention Institute. 1986. *Understanding Crime Prevention*. Stoneham, MA: Butterworth Publishers.

National Research Council. 1993. *Understanding and Preventing Violence*. Edited by Albert J. Reiss, Jr., and Jeffrey A. Roth. Washington, D.C.: National Academy Press.

Newman, Oscar. 1972. *Defensible Space*. New York: Macmillan Publishing.

Pate, Anthony M. 1986. ''Experimenting with Foot Patrol: The Newark Experience.'' In D. P. Rosenbaum, ed., *Community Crime Prevention*. Beverly Hills, CA: Sage.

Pennell, Susan. 1979. ''Fencing Activity and Police Strategy.'' *Police Chief* 46, no. 9: 71–75.

Raub, Robert. 1984. ''Effects of Antifencing Operations on Encouraging Crime.'' *Criminal Justice Review* 9, no. 2: 78–83.

Repetto, Thomas A. 1976. ''Crime Prevention and the Displacement Phenomenon.'' *Crime and Delinquency* 22: 166–177.

Sadd, Susan, and Randolph Grinc. 1994. ''Innovative Neighborhood Oriented Policing: An Evaluation of Community Policing Programs in Eight Cities.'' In D. P. Rosenbaum, ed., *The Challenge of Community Policing*. Thousand Oaks, CA: Sage.

Sampson, Robert J. 1986. ''Crime in Cities: The Effects of Formal and Informal Social Control.'' In A. J. Reiss, Jr., and M. Tonry, eds., *Communities and Crime*. Chicago: University of Chicago Press.

Sampson, Robert J., and Jacqueline Cohen. 1988. ''Deterrent Effects of the Police on Crime: A Replication and Theoretical Extension.'' *Law and Society Review* 22, no. 1: 163–189.

Sampson, Robert J., and John H. Laub. 1993. ''Structural Variations in Juvenile Court Processing: Inequality, the Underclass, and Social Control.'' *Law and Society Review* 27, no. 2: 285–311.

Seidman, David, and Michael Couzens. 1974. "Getting the Crime Rate Down: Political Pressures and Crime Reporting." *Law and Society Review* 8: 456–493.

Sherman, Lawrence. 1986. "Policing Communities: What Works?" In A. J. Reiss, Jr., and M. Tonry, eds., *Communities and Crime*. Chicago: University of Chicago Press.

Sherman, Lawrence. 1990. "Police Crackdowns: Initial and Residual Deterrence." In M. Tonry and N. Morris, eds., *Crime and Justice: A Review of Research*. Vol. 12. Chicago: University of Chicago Press.

Sherman, Lawrence. 1992. "Attacking Crime: Police and Crime Control." In M. Tonry and N. Morris, eds., *Modern Policing*. Chicago: University of Chicago Press.

Skogan, Wesley G. 1975. "Measurement Problems in Official and Survey Crime Rates." *Journal of Criminal Justice* 3: 17–32.

Skogan, Wesley G. 1981. *Issues in the Measurement of Victimization*. Washington, D.C.: U.S. Government Printing Office.

Skogan, Wesley G. 1990. *Disorder and Decline: Crime and the Spiral of Decay in American Neighborhoods*. New York: Free Press.

Skogan, Wesley G. 1994. "The Impact of Community Policing on Neighborhood Residents: A Cross-Site Analysis." In D. P. Rosenbaum, ed., *The Challenge of Community Policing*. Thousand Oaks, CA: Sage.

Skogan, Wesley G., and Michael Maxfield. 1981. *Coping with Crime: Individual and Neighborhood Reactions*. Beverly Hills, CA: Sage.

Skolnick, Jerome H., and James J. Fyfe. 1993. *Above the Law: Police and the Excessive Use of Force*. New York: Free Press.

Smith, Douglas A. 1986. "The Neighborhood Context of Police Behavior." In A. J. Reiss, Jr., and M. Tonry, eds., *Communities and Crime*. Chicago: University of Chicago Press.

Smith, Douglas A., and Patrick R. Gartin. 1989. "Specifying Specific Deterrence: The Influence of Arrest on Future Criminal Activity." *American Sociological Review* 54: 94–105.

Taylor, Ralph B., and Stephen D. Gottfredson. 1986. "Environmental Design, Crime, and Prevention." In A. J. Reiss, Jr., and M. Tonry, eds., *Communities and Crime*. Chicago: University of Chicago Press.

Taylor, Ralph B., Stephen D. Gottfredson, and Sidney Brower. 1984. "Block Crime and Fear: Defensible Space, Local Social Ties, and Territorial Functioning." *Journal of Research in Crime and Delinquency* 21, no. 4: 303–331.

Trojanowicz, Robert C. 1986. "Evaluating a Neighborhood Foot Patrol Program: The Flint, Michigan, Project." In D. P. Rosenbaum, ed., *Community Crime Prevention*. Beverly Hills, CA: Sage.

Vold, George B., and Thomas J. Bernard. 1986. *Theoretical Criminology*. New York: Oxford University Press.

Walker, Samuel. 1989. *Sense and Nonsense about Crime: A Policy Guide*. 2nd ed. Pacific Grove, CA: Brooks/Cole Publishing Company.

Weiner, K., C. Cheist, and W. Hart. 1984. "Stinging the Detroit Criminal: A Total System Perspective." *Journal of Criminal Justice* 12, no. 3: 289–302.

Wilson, Deborah G., and Susan F. Bennett. 1994. "Officers' Response to Community Policing: Variations on a Theme." *Crime and Delinquency* 40, no. 3: 354–370.

Wilson, James Q. 1985. *Thinking about Crime*. Rev. ed. New York: Vintage Books.

Wilson, James Q., and Richard Herrnstein. 1985. *Crime and Human Nature*. New York: Simon and Schuster.

Wilson, James Q., and George L. Kelling. 1982. "Broken Windows." *Atlantic Monthly* (March): 29–38.

Wycoff, Mary Ann, and Wesley G. Skogan. 1992. *Quality Policing in Madison: An Evaluation of Its Implementation and Impact* (Grant no. 87–IJ-CX-0062). Washington, D.C.: National Institute of Justice.

Chapter 25

Urban Health, Politics, and Policy

Ann Lennarson Greer

OVERVIEW

Urban health politics and policies attempt to define and fulfill the responsibilities of cities for the health of their populations, especially in regard to the hazards and dangers of urban life and the uneven concentration of disease in cities. Curiously, it is the very neighborhoods of greatest hazard and misery that are typically also the sites of the preeminent teaching hospitals from which miraculous treatments are diffused to the world. Scott Greer has said of the city: "As the place of possible cures, it creates illness; as the last hope of the hopeless, it is a citadel of death. The richer the society and the more dominant the city within it, the more these truths hold'' (Greer 1983: 7). In addition to this paradox, there are three additional conundrums facing the researcher into urban health politics and policies.

The first concerns urban health care as a topic of research. While responsibility for health and health care is fundamentally local, it is rarely the focus of "urban" research and almost never reflects urban social or governmental theory. If urban research ignores health, equally health research ignores localities. Research from the vantage point of medicine and health services focuses on diseases, treatments, and health care resources (facilities, personnel) as if these were not embedded in local realities, as if their existence and functioning were not intrinsically a reflection of local history and local decisions. As researchers demur, cities and counties struggle with both escalating costs of existing programs (often the biggest item in the city or county budget), unmet health care needs that seemingly require additional resources, and a whole array of associated issues such as the role of health services in providing jobs and stimulating economic growth.

A second puzzle concerns the scant attention of urban scholars to the politics, control, and accountability of nonprofit organizations. In no area of activity have nonprofit organizations, the so-called third sector, been more dominant than in caring for the urban ill and disabled. The predominant form of organization in health care is the nonprofit organization. Most hospitals, community clinics, counseling centers, rehabilitation programs, and halfway houses are nonprofit entities. They are governed by private citizen boards that generally decide where they will locate and who they will serve. These nonprofit organizations consume vast public health dollars through receipt of entitlement program payments, categorical grants, and service contracts. Unlike private business and government, the nonprofit sector remains essentially local. This prompted Peter Drucker to suggest recently that the third sector could be the vehicle by which society might address problems of community integration and citizen action to which global economic enterprises and current governments are ill-suited. But the "social sector," as Drucker dubs it, is no better conceptualized or understood than the human services for which it takes so much responsibility (Drucker 1994).

A third conundrum surrounds the organization of medical work and the authority and accountability of the doctor and other health professionals. Health services are distinguished from most other types of work by the lack of a legitimate hierarchy of control. Doctors generally consider themselves accountable to their patients and to their peers, or to their patients as evaluated by their peers, and not to organizations or employers. In respect of this position and given the historic power of medical professionals, structures and means of accountability have evolved as primarily professional activities (peer committees in hospitals, for example) rather than activities of management or government. This makes accountability a thorny problem.

The lack of hierarchical control further reflects the organization of work in the health services, which is more horizontal than vertical and very fluid in nature. For the most part, the care that patients receive is arranged by front-line health professionals such as doctors who refer patients among themselves and to health care organizations with which they are affiliated. The professional's assessment of the patient's problem guides the selection of health care resources to be invoked. Connections are achieved, and work monitored, through networks of consultation and referral. This "medical model of organization," and the attitudes that go with it (that each patient is unique and only local peers can evaluate the quality or efficiency of care), is a major frustration to planners, regulators, administrators of health care organizations, and the government and corporate payers of health care costs.

The stakes for government are high. In 1990, states and localities devoted 11 percent of their budgets to health, up from 9 percent in 1980. Health expenditures represented 15 percent of the federal budget (up from 12 percent). Public budgets together comprised 42 percent of total health spending (De Lew, Greenberg, and Kinchen 1992: 154).

Scope and Definitions

There are four areas of inquiry that have tended to organize scholarship on urban health. The first is *public health* concerned with the protection and improvement of population health by organized community effort. Typical programs address infectious disease and its control through immunization and quarantine; air, water, and food safety; sanitation and occupational health and safety; preventive medicine; and health education. Important to public health is study of the epidemiology. Concerned with the incidence and distribution of disease in time and space, epidemiology raises problems for study and action by highlighting factors associated with disease, for example, socioeconomic differences (Palen and Johnson 1983; Mechanic 1989: chap. 5; Greer 1978; Feinstein 1993). Public health activities are conducted by the public sector with the activities of cities and counties predominant. The study of public health tends to stand alone as a field of inquiry.

More frequently in the public eye and much more controversial are *clinical services*. Clinical medicine focuses on the medical problems and health of individual persons and provides services to one person at a time. The activities of doctors and hospitals are the most visible manifestations of clinical medicine. Clinical services are provided by both the private and public sectors, but the typical organizational provider is a nonprofit organization. In discussing the clinical health services, providers are the professionals and organizations that provide health care services to patients or consumers of health care. These services include primary care, which is basic or general health care. Primary care services are the point where patients enter or should enter the system, where illness prevention is a focus, and where, ideally, the total care a patient may receive is managed. The "acute" episode of illness is its flare-up or dramatic moment, for example, a heart attack, a high fever, or a gunshot wound. Acute episodes of illness may entail hospitalization, specialist consultation, and advanced technology. It is cheaper to treat problems at earlier stages through preventive or public health steps (proper diet, removal of environmental hazards) than at the acute stage. Chronic disease exists when cure is not possible, and efforts are directed to sustaining the patient at a maximal level of function using drug regimes, exercise, supervision, and the like.

Mental health services can be classified as either public health or clinical medicine but have tended to follow a separate policy history and constitute a distinct area of inquiry. Treatment approaches may emphasize pharmacology, physiology, family function, or social adjustment. Medical strategies such as involuntary hospitalization face difficult issues of civil rights. Social strategies such as group homes must cope with social stigma attaching to mental illness. The incapacity of mental patients has meant that their cause has been usually advanced by advocates rather than by members of the group (Greer and Greer 1984).

In the area of *physical disabilities*, definitions have been in flux (Behney,

Burns, and Banta 1983) and efforts to change them a major focus of activism. Landmark civil rights legislation, the Americans with Disabilities Act (ADA) of 1990 required accommodation of the physical world to make it accessible to persons with impairments (Percy 1992). This expanded attention from patient-focused treatments (e.g., physical therapy) and aids (e.g., wheelchairs) to environmental change. The dramatic effects of this legislation on access to buildings and elevators, public transportation, and the like, are obvious to even the most casual observer.

THEORETICAL APPROACHES

Many of the problems that shape contemporary health politics and policies stem from the need to deliver services that are (1) complex and diffusely organized; (2) imbued with considerations of compassion and beneficence; and (3) local and idiosyncratic in provision and governance. Dominant policy themes are thus (1) the means to achieve service integration and (2) the locus of responsibility for care, quality assurance, and payment. Service integration is obstructed by important tensions between the public and the private sectors, among self-governing professionals committed to different theoretical approaches, and between professionals and public groups including governmental bodies. With respect to responsibility, we see recurring tensions between individual interest and common interest, between stability and change, and between the smaller and larger community (Minar and Greer 1969).

Historical Studies

Among the disciplines that have contributed to our understanding of these tensions and the political and policy problems that they generate, the most illuminating work comes from the historians. Historical effort is essential for anyone baffled by the structural complexity of the health care system, the strange array of professional and organizational actors who play roles in it, and the passions that drive its politics.

Public Health and Social Reform. Public health as a concern was closely associated with the growth of cities. The sanitation and health practices that sustained rural villages were inadequate or impossible in industrial cities. As waves of immigrant groups poured into congested neighborhoods in the late nineteenth century, garbage and animal waste remained in the streets, infiltrated the water supply, or was recycled to feed farm animals. Malnutrition among desperately poor immigrants was commonplace. Infectious disease spread rapidly through overcrowded tenements (Duffy 1978; Palen and Johnson 1983).

Urban public health movements preceded their scientific basis by about a half century. The germ theory of disease was established only toward the end of the nineteenth century, following highly significant gains in public health. The nineteenth-century Sanitation Movement based its fruitful campaign against urban filth on a vague theory of "miasma" or noxious air (Rosenberg and Smith-Rosenberg 1978; S. Greer 1978). Only later did the germ theory of disease explain why its urban cleanup was so effective against infectious disease. Antidisease campaigns were often closely associated with antipoverty campaigns. Leaders of many social reform movements arose from the middle- and upper-class volunteers, especially women, who entered shudderingly bad urban neighborhoods to aid the victims of pestilence. The first efforts to calculate the economic cost of disease in terms of lost worker productivity date from the late nineteenth century (Duffy 1978).

Public health reform was often highly controversial. Reformers were generally drawn from upper-class and better-educated elements of the population but filth and germs were citywide. Leavitt (1982) and Fox (1978) recount the resistance that crusading citizens and public health professionals encountered as they fought to report and quarantine the contagiously ill (which might cost detainees their jobs), to remove garbage (which was otherwise collected by housewives and children who resold it for petty cash), and to close unsanitary dairies (especially the cow-in-the-backyard variety, which provided some poor people with income and others with affordable milk). Similarly, local doctors resisted requirements to report disease, which they saw as an attack on medical autonomy and patient confidentiality. Fox cautions that post hoc explanations of public health reform should avoid the temptation to overstate the persuasiveness of science and idealism in achieving reforms. Public health activities reflected the social and political structures of their cities. The Commissioner of Health in New York City used Tammany Hall politics and patronage to get tuberculosis cases reported (Fox 1978).

Henrik Ibsen's play *An Enemy of the People*, first performed in 1882, offers a literary version of the dynamics these historians report. In it, a local doctor identifies a bacteriological cause of illness in the community's water, which is the basis of its economy. The doctor fails to persuade his fellow citizens of the health danger and is shunned for his efforts. To today's audience, the city fathers who rise against him are uncaring capitalists. With the germ theory of disease promulgated about 1880 and not generally accepted until later, most viewers in 1882 would have shared the city fathers' skepticism of the radical new science advanced by the doctor.

Cities as Repositories of Medical Resources. If nineteenth-century cities offered unprecedented opportunity for the spread of disease, so also these cities were fertile ground for the advancement of empirical medicine and the emergence of new knowledge and medical roles. The latter decades of the nineteenth century saw broad advances in the biological and physical sciences that were critical to the development of scientific medicine. Advocates of the scientific approach established educational programs in the urban public hospitals where varieties of disease could be most fully observed. Thus, from the beginning, the teaching hospital was an urban institution where doctors provided free care in exchange for the opportunity to learn. Many leaders of the nineteenth-century health and welfare campaigns arose from the ranks of the young doctors who trained in these first teaching hospitals (Duffy 1978). At the same time, the stage was set for conflict about health care priorities between those who viewed the public hospital as a charitable community service (including public officials representing medically needy neighborhoods) and the medical school officials who saw it as a temple of medical science and education (Davis et al. 1983; Shonick 1980).

The rise of medicine oriented to disease pathogenesis and treatment also marked a shift in the attention of medical leaders from the environmental causes of poor health to providing access to care. The first campaign for community clinics to improve the access of the poor to health services began in 1910 (Rosen 1978). The ensuing neglect of environmental and behavioral aspects of health has been brilliantly criticized (McKeown 1979) but with minimal effect.

State mental hospitals were established widely in the years after 1850. The establishment of the mental "asylums" away from the pressures of the city was a hard-fought victory for reformers who argued that the mentally ill should be removed from the jails and almshouses of stress-ridden cities to therapeutic country sites (Greer and Greer 1984). Like the urban public hospitals, these institutions proved critical to the empirical observation of mental illness. Psychiatry as a medical specialty arose in the state hospitals. Unlike the urban public hospitals that during this period shed almshouse clients and strengthened their medical image, the asylums quickly became dumping grounds for all manner of problem persons, of whom there were many among disoriented immigrants far from home and family (Grob 1980).

The federal Community Mental Health Centers (CMHCs) program in the 1960s was the reaction. The campaign for community care was propelled by midtwentieth century breakthroughs in pharmacology (which enabled doctors to stabilize formerly intractable patients) and by sociological findings that showed institutionalization to have its own adverse consequences (Greer, Greer, and Anderson 1983). Like the earlier battle for asylums, community care was a victory for passionate reformers. The federal program provided CMHCs with direct grants to last eight years, after which it was expected that the money saved on state hospitals could be redirected to the community centers.

It should be noted that urban public hospitals did not entirely escape the problem of the poor whose hospitalization reflected inability to cope. According to Rosenberg (1982), it took the Philadelphia General Hospital about a century to make the transition from almshouse to hospital. A full transition may be impossible. To this day, police and others continue to deliver problems to the door of the public hospital. At any given moment, the country's large public hospitals contain hundreds or thousands of tiny babies and helpless elderly whose families cannot be found for discharge. Deinstitutionalization of the state mental hospitals has exacerbated this problem in many locales.

Beneficence and the Nonprofits. As a sense of treatable illness took form and hospitals emerged as places of cure, both public and private hospitals grew rapidly in number. The late nineteenth and early twentieth centuries saw an expansion of nonprofit institutions that established themselves as charitably motivated tax-exempt institutions serving the medical needs of local "community" or an ethnic group within it (Vogel 1978; Rosen 1963; Rosner 1988; Seay and Vladeck 1988). Care of the poor was central to the missions of these early institutions. They accomplished it by philanthropic donation and by what we now call "cost shifting," that is, charging the costs of free or discounted care to the wealthier patients who used the same facility. Institutions founded with benevolent purpose to provide fairly simple medical care have faced a number of twentieth-century challenges arising from the great expansion in the complexity and effectiveness of medical treatments, on the one hand, and the fragmentation of the caring community, on the other. Not the least of these problems is that of self-definition.

Government and Politics

Governmental Responsibility. At the local level, public responsibility for the provision of various health services varies from state to state, county to county, and city to city. Services may be provided by a municipality, a county, a township, a hospital district, or any other entity having taxing powers. Many further complexities reflect diverse local histories and local solutions to local problems. Davis et al. (1983) provide several examples of the typically complicated organizational structures that characterize the public provision of health care. The public hospital in Cincinnati is a former municipal hospital that is now officially a state institution. It serves the population of the city and surrounding county. Its doctors work for the medical school. It is linked to clinics run by its former sponsor, the city. In Santa Clara, California, the hospital is under control of a county executive. Its medical services are provided by a private medical group under contract with the county. County-sponsored primary care is provided by contract with clinics run by community groups (Davis et al. 1983: 56–57). With so many stakeholders, great complexity surrounds attempts to modify or alter the pattern of services. As each entity has its own constituencies, there is also the potential for contentiousness as that which erupted in St. Louis over the closure of one of the city's two public hospitals. This became a major city political issue when black activists rallied to oppose closure of the institution, which had historically served the black community (Davis et al. 1983; Schmandt and Wendel 1983). The St. Louis example is reminiscent of Elling's account (1963) of competition among voluntary community hospitals in the 1950s for philanthropic funding. Elling's case study showed how self-consciously hospitals of that era understood and appealed to their class and ethnic group constituencies. The competition for money and patients on the part of public and private institutions is not less today and cries out for similar description.

Funding. Federal funds flow into the community through two primary routes. The first is the federal health insurance programs: Medicare, a national program for the elderly, and Medicaid, a federal-state partnership for welfare recipients. Medicare and Medicaid are entitlement programs directed to individuals. Existing local providers such as doctors and hospitals are paid for services provided to beneficiaries. Medicare policies are set nationally, although quality review is delegated to state-level organizations. Within broad federal guidelines, Medicaid programs are controlled by states, which determine benefits, eligibility, and level of provider payment. States also decide how enrollees may obtain care, whether, for example, they will have free choice of doctor or get care through health maintenance organizations (HMOs). When states set generous Medicaid policies, the burden on localities is reduced. Nationwide 68 percent of Medicaid recipients are women and children who qualify as recipients of Aid to Families with Dependent Children (AFDC). Except for this group, recipients must be poor and disabled. Forty percent of individuals below the poverty level are excluded from Medicaid coverage (De Lew, Greenberg, and Kinchen 1992).

Other federal funds reach the local community through categorical grants. Federal categorical health grants date from 1912 when Congress targeted certain needs of children. Since that time, the needs of women and children have remained the most constant interest of the federal government, although categorical programs proliferated until the early 1980s when 25 direct grant programs (i.e., grants from the federal government to local organizations) were collapsed into five block grants to be administered by the states. Federal categorical grants generate conflict between the federal level with its interest in knowing that grant monies reach target populations and the local level, which wishes to maximize discretion in the use of money (Davis et al. 1983). Localities complain of inefficiencies arising from overlapping programs serving the same group, individuals in marginal categories "falling through the cracks," inability to coordinate services, and excessive overlay of federal and state bureaucracy. Today's withdrawal of federal involvement leaves states to struggle with program development and resource allocation. AIDS (acquired immune deficiency syndrome) grants in California illustrate how complex this can be. The state initially awarded AIDs grants to local departments of health. Subsequently, in response to political pressure in San Francisco, it made grants through the city's department of public health to community groups representing differentiated segments of the population at risk of AIDs. With over 750 such groups in San Francisco, the applicant pool was large. A consolidation is now under way with the state seeking applications from provider consortia.

Service Organization. Concern to simplify the flow of money has been matched by concern to rationalize delivery. Several comparative case studies describe the difficulties encountered when localities attempt to reorganize services for greater efficiency. One well-documented case is the Municipal Health Services Program, which was funded by the Robert Wood Johnson Foundation (RWJF) to demonstrate the potential for cities to save money by moving primary care from expensive public hospital emergency rooms (ERs) to lower-cost community sites (Davis et al. 1983; Ginzberg et al. 1985). General ignorance about the organization of local services permitted the foundation to begin with a major false assumption, namely, that the health departments and public hospitals of large cities fell under the executive authority of the mayor. In only 2 of the 5 cities that received RWJF grants were the hospital and the health department under the same governmental auspices, and in none was the mayor a strong figure who was ''willing and able to shift resources from a long-standing governmental unit, the city hospital, in order to increase those of . . . the neighborhood health center'' (Ginzberg et al. 1985: 114). The refusal of mayors to reallocate resources recalled the failure of the federally funded CMHCs program to attract state resources away from state mental hospitals (Greer, Greer, and Anderson 1983). Domain conflict similarly obstructed merger implementation in 12 cities that merged their public health departments and public hospitals (Shonick 1980).

All of these studies describe tensions among professionals and organizations having different missions (hospital versus community services, clinical versus public health services, public versus nonprofit services, teaching and research versus clinical care, academic versus community medicine). In all cases, reorganization problems were stickier if medical schools were involved or the number of differing agencies increased, as, for example, when city consolidations included mental health agencies. To the extent that professionals fail to cooperate, reformers have also been disappointed by the inability of professional managers to achieve reorganization. According to Shonick (1980), the resistance of professionals to organizational changes was exacerbated when they were initiated by higher managers who emphasized economic goals over service goals.

Shonick's findings may speak to the contemporary reorganization of health services that is driven by economic objectives. Few studies address problems of reorganization or the functioning of privatized services, although Goldner's sketch (1983) of conflict in New York over the city's ambulance service contracts suggests there will be considerable room for new controversy. Dependent upon ambulances for hospital admissions, both public and private hospitals accused the ambulances of partiality in choice of hospital destination and fought the awarding of contracts to ambulances affiliated with competitors.

New York ambulance services highlight the complex relations between public and private agencies that share the same geography and must cooperate with each other in innumerable ways but also compete for patients, funds, and government approvals, which all affect their ability to survive. There are other underlying, and more long-standing, public-private hostilities reported in studies of local coordination. The public sector accuses the private of ''creaming'' or selecting out financially advantaged patients who might otherwise stabilize the budgets of public providers. Private sector institutions accuse the public sector of being inefficient and uncompetitive while at the same time complaining when it competes for the (paying) patients that they consider to be rightly ''theirs.''

Mandates and Regulation. Perhaps because of the strong commitments of independent health professionals and organizations to their own goals and approaches, most health policy does not entail reorganization but attempts to use regulation, mandates, and funding incentives to motivate change. The National Health Planning Act of 1974 created regional planning agencies to coordinate health services on an areawide basis, intending that the agencies' planning recommendations would be backed by state-level financial penalties. Goldner (1983) describes the resentment of nonprofit hospital boards in New York City to this public sector challenge to private governance and to the behind-the-scenes "quiet politics" of the third sector. Although voluntary hospitals were very successful in appealing restrictive decisions at higher levels of review, their dissatisfaction no doubt contributed to the demise of the planning effort in the early 1980s.

Urban Studies

Many funding and coordination problems among hospitals and other health services are linked to the fragmentation of communities that accompanied suburban expansion after World War II (Greer 1978). For decades, hospitals and doctors have been following their patients to the suburbs with two important results. The first is the lack of available providers in inner-city neighborhoods. As early as the 1960s, two programs of the Great Society addressed the declining availability of urban health providers: the Neighborhood Health Centers (NHCs) program and the National Health Service Corps (NHSC). These funded community clinics in underserved areas and gave scholarships to medical trainees who would subsequently practice for a period in underserved communities. They emphasized neighborhood primary care and sought to provide culturally sensitive care, in contrast to that other prominent urban provider, the teaching hospital. Community clinics from this period survive today in communities across the country. Although they provide a relatively small portion of the total care received by the urban poor (the amount differing greatly by city), they embody cherished ideals that perennially recur in urban health politics.

The differentiation of communities by economic class also undermined the tradition of benevolent "cost shifting" as a means to pay for the care of the poor. As the clienteles of inner-city doctors and hospitals came increasingly to include only one economic class, inner-city providers found themselves with few customers to whom costs could be shifted (Wolfe 1993). Consequences included the need to raise the rates of insured patients far above the cost of the care those patients received, skewing services to attract suburban patients with good insurance, or increasing volume ("Medicaid mills"). Unfavorable patient mixes were a central dynamic in the closure of urban hospitals between World War II and 1990. During this period, nearly half of inner-city hospitals closed or relocated. Especially likely to disappear were hospitals that served racial minorities (Sager 1983; Whiteis 1992).

After 1965, hospital closures also included a number of public hospitals whose viability was undermined in part by the loss to private institutions of those Medicare and Medicaid patients who were successfully mainstreamed. Faced with rising medical costs and declining hospital censes, a number of local governments closed their public hospitals or turned them over in whole or part to other sponsors, as illustrated by the examples of Cincinnati and St. Clara County above. Neighborhood citizens and their professional and governmental allies argued that local government could discharge its obligation as "provider-of-last-resort" more cheaply through contract with private sector providers whose costs did not incorporate the costs of medical education. In a number of inner cities, however, the only hospital remaining in 1990 was the teaching hospital, suggesting that the only ally powerful enough to save them was in fact the medical school. As medical training rather than population need becomes the basis for public hospital survival, issues of governance and accountability become entangled with issues of care availability (Ginzberg et al. 1985: 85–87).

Economic Models

The health services in the United States are undergoing a major transformation that began in the 1980s. It entails a fundamental redefinition of the purpose, ideology, organization, and accountability of health care. Driven by economic theories and the management models of private industry, it challenges the historic mission of health care professionals and nonprofit organizations.

The conceptualizations that drive health care reform assume rational economic buyers, rather than altruists, philanthropic organizations, and professionals guided by ideals of service. Advocates hold that if a competitive market is brought into existence, the cumulative actions of rational buyers will produce acceptable services at acceptable prices. In discussing the changes, Burns (1990) distinguishes *organizations*, which are instrumentalities for achieving a goal such as profit, from *institutions*, which embody many values and serve many constituencies. Hospitals, along with other health care providers, have historically functioned as community institutions. The new health care models treat them as competitive business organizations.

The redefinition of the health care enterprise arose from concern over the rising costs of health care and the perception that these can be controlled by price competition. Since the mid-1980s, large payers of clinical health care (government and employers) have attempted to use fixed price payments (prospective payment systems, or PPSs) and prepaid service plans (HMOs) to create profit-loss incentives and businesslike corporate structures. The presumption of rational economic motivation on the part of patients and providers contrasts with earlier assumptions that held that neither patients nor providers of health care behaved as rational economic persons.

The new health care industry projects health care to be purchased from business entities capable of offering a comprehensive range of services. These may be called HMOs, *integrated systems*, or *accountable health plans*. Fearful of exclusion, community health providers (hospitals, home care services, doctors

offices, laboratories, nursing homes) are rapidly combining by merger or purchase under corporate umbrellas. Such corporate arrangements are felt to be the
only means of assuring access to patients and protecting income against the
leverage of volume purchasers.

The definition of employers as buyers who purchase services in volume from
providers who compete economically for their business marks the end of cost
shifting as a way of funding the care of the poor. It is increasingly difficult to
pass unpaid care on to cost-conscious corporate buyers. As the care of increasing
numbers of patients comes under competitive bid, all health care organizations,
public as well as private, are compelled to participate. They market themselves
by their low price, unique technology, or sophisticated medical staff, focusing
on the high revenues associated with the health needs of well-insured patients.
The most conspicuous example is the competition among hospitals to provide
services to the victims of heart attacks who are disproportionately white middle-
aged males, the best-insured group in the population. There is far less interest
in providing prenatal care to pregnant teenagers. To the extent that the scholars
and the public accept the competitive business model, the benevolent ethos of
the health professions and the nonprofit, tax-exempt, ''social'' sector is turned
on its head. Pollitt (1993) has described the demoralization of public service
professionals when accountability is measured by commercial success rather
than by service or good works. Many in the public are dismayed when economic
pressures force closure of institutions without review of the contextual effects
of closure. In addition to access, there are consequences of losing a facility for
both jobs and street safety, the latter enhanced by a hospital's 24-hour activity.

Public accountability is severely strained in this model. Indeed, the competitive market was specifically advanced as a means of avoiding public discussion
and associated controversy. Alain Enthoven, the principal architect of ''managed
competition,'' argued that market competition was preferable to planning and
regulation precisely because its results (hospital closures, etc.) appeared as the
result of ''impersonal forces'' rather than political decisions (Enthoven 1979;
see also Greer and Greer 1990).

Except for a few economists recently concerned with local ''market areas''
(Luft et al. 1986), there is no conceptual room in prevailing models for local
areas. Topics such as community need, resource planning, and accountability
that should be of interest to urbanists are absent from the literature. In prevailing
models, the individual is not a member of a community but of a buyer group,
is not a citizen but a consumer. As Enthoven advised, the model provides no
significant forums for discussion of community priorities.

Data Problems

Most of what we know about urban health derives from a limited number of
case studies. Severe data problems limit opportunities for quantitative analysis
beyond the achievements of epidemiological research in highlighting the con-

centration of problems in population categories. We lack national data for sub-areas of cities (Mechanic 1989: chap. 9) and indicators of the relative success of a city in coping with health issues (Palen and Johnson 1983; Greer 1986). Efforts to compare state and local health spending require several databases and heroic assumptions (Davis et al. 1983).

DIRECTIONS FOR FUTURE RESEARCH

The major themes identified in this chapter—service organization and community responsibility—continue to be important and to generate new conflicts as novel structures of integration and accountability replace the traditional ones. The implementation of radical new forms presents grounds for conflict at every point including ideology, goals, organization, methods, and accountability. Every health care organization is currently considering its position, its potential partners, and its strategy for survival. There will be inevitable conflict as health care professionals, who have had difficulty in cooperating among themselves, struggle to maintain their professional goals, identities, and work preferences in the face of attempts to manage them hierarchically for economic efficiency.

In the new environment, poor neighborhoods that afford little opportunity for profit will likely be neglected, as may the quality of care (Relman 1994). As local hospitals continue to close or fail to meet the expectations of citizens for service and perhaps compassion, public officials will face pressure to address problems. There will be renewed calls for regulation, for insurance for the uninsured, for services to categorical groups, and for services to underserved communities. Citizens who question the direction of activity will be disappointed at the lack of local public forums for their concerns. How the new business interests will interact with those representing geographic communities or their special needs is a topic for urgent study.

The major dispute in the field today is the unstated one between those who assume that social and political design is necessary to an equitable, high-quality, accountable health system and those who adopt a strict market approach, turning all issues into matters of payment. The reform ''debate'' lopsidedly reflects only the latter. Urbanists and the social sciences, excepting economics, have contributed little. Our understanding of the dramatic events now transforming urban health care will be severely limited if community dynamics and needs are not included. Again, a comment of Scott Greer (1978) is to the point: ''The major dialectic in human history is not . . . the purely ideational conflict and resolution posited by the Hegelians . . . [nor] the conflict between haves and have nots which Marx and his followers assumed. . . . The dialectic is between action and its results, on the one hand, and our interpretation of those results on the other'' (45).

In the case of health politics and policy, the raw social material is complex, dynamic, and laden with significant conflict. The limited interest of urbanists in conceptualizing and studying these topics is stunning.

REFERENCES

Behney, Clyde J., Ann Kesselman Burns, and H. David Banta. 1983. "The City and Disability." In Ann Lennarson Greer and Scott Greer, eds., *Cities and Sickness: Health Care in Urban America*. Urban Affairs Annual Reviews, vol. 25. Beverly Hills, CA: Sage Publications.

Burns, Lawton R. 1990. "The Transformation of the American Hospital: From Community Institution toward Business Enterprise." In C. Calhoun, ed., *Comparative Social Research*. Vol. 12. Greenwich, CT: JAI Press. 77–112.

Davis, Edith M., Michael L. Millman, Patricia Alt Maloney, Albert A. Bocklet, Ann Lennarson Greer, David E. Hayes-Bautista, Ann Akridge Jones, and George Dorian Wendel. 1983. *Health Care for the Urban Poor: Directions for Policy*. Landmark Studies. Totowa, NJ: Rowman and Allanheld.

De Lew, Nancy, George Greenberg, and Kraig Kinchen. 1992. "A Layman's Guide to the U.S. Health Care System." *Health Care Financing Review* 14: 151–169.

Drucker, Peter F. 1994. "The Age of Social Transformation." *Atlantic Monthly* 274: 53–92.

Duffy, John. 1978. "Social Impact of Disease in the Late 19th Century." In Judith Walzer Leavitt and Ronald L. Numbers, eds., *Sickness and Health in America*. Madison: University of Wisconsin Press. 395–402.

Elling, Ray H. 1963. "The Hospital Support Game in Urban Center Institution." In Eliot Freidson, ed., *The Hospital in Modern Society*. New York: Free Press. 73–111.

Enthoven, Alain C. 1979. "Consumer-Centered vs. Job-Centered Health Insurance." *Harvard Business Review* 57: 141–152.

Feinstein, Jonathan. 1993. "The Relationship between Socioeconomic Status and Health: A Review of the Literature." *Milbank Quarterly* 71: 279–322.

Fox, Daniel M. 1978. "Social Policy and City Politics: Tuberculosis Reporting in New York, 1889–1900." In Judith Walzer Leavitt and Ronald L. Numbers, eds., *Sickness and Health in America*, Madison: University of Wisconsin Press. 415–431.

Ginzberg, Eli, Miriam Ostow, Edith M. Davis, Patrician Maloney Alt, Albert Bocklet, Ann Lennarson Greer, David E. Hayes-Bautista, and George Dorian Wendel. 1985. *Local Health Policy in Action*. Landmark Studies Conservation of Human Resources Series. Totowa, NJ: Rowman and Allanheld.

Goldner, Fred H. 1983. "Politics as Accusation: New York's Public and Voluntary Hospitals." In Ann Lennarson Greer and Scott Greer, eds., *Cities and Sickness: Health Care in Urban America*. Urban Affairs Annual Reviews, vol. 25. Beverly Hills, CA: Sage Publications.

Greer, Ann Lennarson. 1986. "The Measurement of Health in Urban Communities." *Journal of Urban Affairs* 8: 9–22.

Greer, Ann Lennarson, and Scott Greer. 1990. "Some Consequences of Market Forces in U.S. Hospitals: Lessons for the New Look NHS?" *Health Services Management* 86: 180–182.

Greer, Ann Lennarson, Scott Greer, and Tom Anderson. 1983. "The City's Weakest Dependents: The Mentally Ill and the Elderly." In Ann Lennarson Greer and Scott Greer, eds., *Cities and Sickness: Health Care in Urban America*. Urban Affairs Annual Reviews, vol. 25. Beverly Hills, CA: Sage Publications.

Greer, Scott. 1978. "Professional Self-Regulation in the Public Interest: The Intellectual

Politics of PSRO.'' In Scott Greer, Ronald D. Hedlund, and James L. Gibson, eds., *Accountability in Urban Society: Public Agencies under Fire*. Urban Affairs Annual Reviews, vol. 15. Beverly Hills, CA: Sage Publications.

Greer, Scott. 1983. ''Health Care in American Cities: Dedicated Workers in an Undedicated System.'' In Ann Lennarson Greer and Scott Greer, eds., *Cities and Sickness: Health Care in Urban America*. Urban Affairs Annual Reviews, vol. 25. Beverly Hills, CA: Sage Publications.

Greer, Scott, and Ann Lennarson Greer. 1984. ''The Continuity of Moral Reform: Community Mental Health Centers.'' *Social Science and Medicine* 19: 397–404.

Grob, Gerald N. 1980. ''Institutional Origins and Early Transformation: 1830–1855.'' In Joseph P. Morrissey, Howard H. Goldman, and Lorraine V. Klerman, eds., *The Enduring Asylum: Cycles of Institutional Reform at Worcester State Hospital*. New York: Grune and Stratton.

Leavitt, Judith Walzer. 1982 *The Healthiest City: Milwaukee and the Politics of Health Reform*. Princeton: Princeton University Press.

Luft, Harold S., J. C. Robinson, D. W. Garnick, R. G. Hughes, S. J. McPhee, S. S. Hunt, and J. Showstack. 1986. ''Hospital Behavior in a Local Market Context.'' *Medical Care Review* 43: 217–252.

McKeown, Thomas. 1979. *The Role of Medicine: Dream, Mirage, or Nemesis?* Princeton: Princeton University Press.

Mechanic, David, ed. 1989. *Painful Choices: Research and Essays on Health Care*. New Brunswick: Transaction Publishers.

Minar, David W., and Scott Greer. 1969. ''The Concept of Community.'' In David W. Minar and Scott Greer, eds., *The Concept of Community*. Chicago: Aldine. ix–xii.

Palen, J. John, and Daniel M. Johnson. 1983. ''Urbanization and Health Status.'' In Ann Lennarson Greer and Scott Greer, eds., *Cities and Sickness: Health Care in Urban America*. Beverly Hills, CA: Sage Publications.

Percy, Stephen L. 1992. *Disability, Civil Rights, and Public Policy: The Politics of Implementation*. Tuscaloosa: University of Alabama Press.

Pollitt, Christopher. 1993. *Managerialism and the Public Services*. 2nd ed. Oxford: Blackwell Publishers.

Relman, Arnold S. 1994. ''The New Medical-Industrial Complex.'' In Howard D. Schwartz, ed. *Dominant Issues in Medical Sociology*. 3rd ed. New York: McGraw-Hill.

Rosen, George. 1963. ''The Hospital: Historical Sociology of a Community Institution.'' In Eliot Freidson, ed., *The Hospital in Modern Society*. New York: Free Press. 1–36.

Rosen, George. 1978. ''The First Neighborhood Health Center Movement—Its Rise and Fall.'' In Judith Walzer Leavitt and Ronald L. Numbers, eds., *Sickness and Health in America: Readings in the History of Medicine and Public Health*. Madison: University of Wisconsin Press.

Rosenberg, Charles E. 1982. ''From Almshouse to Hospital: The Shaping of Philadelphia General Hospital.'' *Milbank Quarterly* 60: 108–154.

Rosenberg, Charles E., and Carroll Smith-Rosenberg. 1978. ''Pietism and the Origins of the Public Health Movement: A Note on John H. Griscom and Robert M. Hartley.'' In Judith Walzer Leavitt and Ronald L. Numbers, eds., *Sickness and Health in America: Readings in the History of Medicine and Public Health*. Madison: University of Wisconsin Press.

Rosner, David. 1988. "Heterogeneity and Uniformity: Historical Perspectives on the Voluntary Hospital." In J. David Seay and Bruce C. Vladeck, eds., *Sickness and in Health: The Mission of Voluntary Health Care Institutions*. New York: Mc-Graw-Hill.

Sager, Alan. 1983. "The Reconfiguration of Urban Hospital Care: 1937–1980." In Ann Lennarson Greer and Scott Greer, eds., *Cities and Sickness: Health Care in Urban America*. Urban Affairs Annual Reviews, vol. 25. Beverly Hills, CA: Sage Publications.

Schmandt, Henry J., and George D. Wendel. 1983. "Health Care in America: A Political Perspective." In Ann Lennarson Greer and Scott Greer, eds., *Cities and Sickness: Health Care in Urban America*. Urban Affairs Annual Reviews, vol. 25. Beverly Hills, CA: Sage Publications.

Seay, J. David, and Bruce C. Vladeck, eds. 1988. *Sickness and in Health: The Mission of Voluntary Health Care Institutions*. New York: McGraw-Hill.

Shonick, William. 1980. "Mergers of Public Health Departments with Public Hospitals in Urban Areas: Findings of 12 Field Studies." *Medical Care*, vol. 18, no. 8 (supp.).

Vogel, Morris J. 1978. "Patrons, Practitioners, and Patients: The Voluntary Hospital in Mid-Victorian Boston." In Judith Walzer Leavitt and Ronald L. Numbers, eds., *Sickness and Health in America: Readings in the History of Medicine and Public Health*. Madison: University of Wisconsin Press.

Whiteis, David G. 1992. "Hospital and Community Characteristics in Closures of Urban Hospitals, 1980–87." *Public Health Reports* 107: 409–416.

Wolfe, Marie. 1993. " 'No Margin, No Mission': Challenge to Institutional Ethics." *Business and Professional Ethics Journal* 12: 39–49.

Chapter 26

Equal Opportunity
in the City

Lana Stein

Over the past two decades and more, America's cities have dealt with a number of civil rights issues concerning participation, employment, housing, and public education (see Darden, Dunlop, and Galster 1992 for an overview). This chapter will examine who serves in government and who gets what from government and the interrelationship between them. Paul Peterson (1981) felt that local government could address the needs of minority residents through the allocation of municipal jobs and services. Eisinger (1982a, 1982b) and Browning, Marshall, and Tabb (1984) were among the first to look at conditions under which such consideration might take place. Here, we will look at both electoral rules and allocation of jobs, appointments, and contracts to both minorities and women. In addition, municipal action regarding sexual preference also will be discussed.

ELECTORAL RULES

The Voting Rights Act of 1965 broke down the traditional barriers preventing exercise of the franchise by African Americans in southern states. In time, the focus went beyond barriers to registration and turned instead to whether electoral rules or the drawing of district boundaries effectively disenfranchised African Americans and other groups by diminishing the likelihood of electing minorities to office.

The debate regarding the effect of electoral rules—namely, district versus at-large elections—on the selection of blacks to city councils has become a heated one in the federal courts and in academic journals as well. Many scholars feel that the institution of at-large council elections in the early twentieth century was designed to replace immigrant officeholders with native-born experts (e.g., Hofstadter 1955: 142–145; Hays 1984: 65; Schiesl 1977: 149–152). In the 1970s and after, suits charged that such elections now prevented the election of the city's new minority groups because of generally polarized voting patterns.

Among scholars, Karnig and Welch (1980) and Engstrom and McDonald (1981) presented data demonstrating that blacks were underrepresented in cities using at-large elections and that increased representation occurred when selection by districts was introduced. Bullock and MacManus (1987) and Bullock (1989) took issue with this research and its conclusion regarding the greater equity of the district system. In the at-large system, they found that minority voters frequently supported winning candidates. By creating principally black districts, there would be little need for whites to reach out to black voters, or vice versa. However, these arguments do not take into account the symbolic importance underlying the election of African Americans or other minorities for members of their own group. The emphasis on district elections and on drawing district boundaries to maximize minority concentration is at least in part predicated on the notion that white voters do not cast ballots for nonwhite candidates. Current literature documents that cross-racial voting does occur, but its extent depends on the context of the election and the nature of the city. Sonenshein (1993) describes an active biracial election coalition in Los Angeles that made possible the election of Tom Bradley as mayor in a city less than 20 percent black. Such election coalitions are quite rare in the more polarized cities of the Midwest and Northeast with their large minority populations. Yet recent studies utilizing geomapping techniques that link either survey results or precinct returns with census block unit data show that some whites will vote for blacks in certain elections (Stein and Kohfeld 1991; DeLorenzo, Kohfeld, and Stein 1994). Whites who are better educated and homeowners and who live in integrated neighborhoods (DeLorenzo, Kohfeld, and Stein 1994; Carsey 1995) are more likely to cast ballots for African Americans in citywide races.

The debate over district elections and the nature of the districts that are drawn will remain at the forefront of both judicial action and scholarly study. Supreme Court rulings involving congressional districts in North Carolina, Georgia, Louisiana, and other states cannot help but affect the selection of municipal legislators. Representation has considerable symbolic importance for urban residents and, as will be shown below, some substantive impact as well.

EMPLOYMENT

Paul Peterson (1981: 154–162) describes municipal employment as an allocative function. While holding the number of jobs—and hence the budget—constant, a mayor can target those jobs to certain groups. Historically, a place on the public payroll has been linked to political victory. Many European immigrant groups used city jobs as a means to social and economic mobility. Machine politics facilitated this process. The introduction of civil service by reformers intent on eradicating the machines retarded ethnic workforce participation for a time in many cities. In cities where reformers had less influence, the Irish, then the Italians, Jews, and Eastern Europeans dominated both local politics and city jobs. Although Erie (1989) maintains that reliance on patronage jobs actually retarded Irish attainment of middle-class status, the conventional wisdom still regards municipal patronage as an opening door for urban newcomers.

In keeping with the traditional mind-set, African Americans have preferred governmental employment to a more uncertain private sector (Eisinger 1986). Ironically, city jobs were not made as available to the growing black urban population as they had been to previous immigrant groups. The U.S. Commission on Civil Rights (1969) found that blacks made up only a small proportion of municipal workers in certain large cities in the late 1960s. This conclusion echoes the *Report of the National Advisory Commission on Civil Disorders* (1968: 7), which said that "the proportion of Negroes in local government was substantially smaller than the Negro proportion of the population." Rodgers and Bullock (1972: 123) maintain that cities discriminated in hiring as much as any private employer. Underrepresentation of African Americans and other minority groups was most pronounced in the protective services, police and fire. The National Advisory Commission on Civil Disorders (*Report* 1968: 17) found that in cities experiencing riots "the abrasive relationship between the police and the minority communities has been a major—and explosive—source of grievance, tension and disorder." William G. Lewis's (1989) study of black employment in city police departments described resistance to the hiring of blacks by police unions. Similarly, the white firefighters' union actively opposed the stationing of black and white staff members at the same firehouse in St. Louis (Stein 1991).

The Congress did not originally include local or state government in the Title VII provisions of the Civil Rights Act of 1964. Title VII equal employment provisions, and subsequent federal affirmative action orders, applied to cities only after the enactment of the Equal Employment Opportunity (EEO) Act of 1972. Following the passage of this act, cities had to begin to furnish data on their workforce composition (EEO-4 form) yearly. As recipients of federal funding, they were required to assess the representativeness of their workforce by function, level, and in toto. If underrepresentation existed in their cities, they had to develop goals and timetables designed to increase the minority presence. Cities' progress—or the lack thereof—was reviewed when general revenue sharing and other federal grants were allocated. Threatened cutoffs were tools to stimulate compliance and worked in Columbia, South Carolina, and other locations (Stein and Condrey 1987).

Soon, scholars began to examine models of minority and female workforce participation in order to identify the factors that make certain cities more equitable employers. Works by Dye and Renick (1981) and Mladenka (1989a, 1989b) found a significant relationship between black and Hispanic representation on city councils and their workforce representation. From their study of 10 California cities, Browning, Marshall, and Tabb (1984: 245–250) concluded that it is not enough to have minority council members to bring about change; these council members have to be part of a dominant liberal coalition.

A number of studies demonstrate the importance of a minority mayor in relation to minority hiring. Eisinger's (1982a, 1982b) and Stein's (1986) models show a significant positive effect, although Mladenka's (1989a, 1989b) do not. (Mladenka included the largest number of cities in his model—over 1,100, including many without minority residents.) Case studies by Nelson and Meranto (1977), Eisinger (1980), and Levine (1974) describe the changes in hiring practice made by mayors Richard Hatcher, Carl Stokes, Maynard Jackson, and Coleman Young in Gary, Cleveland, Atlanta, and Detroit, respectively. In addition, Stone's (1989) look at regime politics in Atlanta further details the changes in employment policy fostered by Jackson in his first two terms. A comparative look at six southern cities (Stein and Condrey 1987) documents the influence of black mayors in Augusta and Birmingham, as well as Atlanta, on municipal workforce composition.

The ability of a mayor to affect who is hired is best illustrated by examining Jackson's mayoralty in Atlanta from 1974 to 1981. In order to increase the number of African Americans in nontraditional positions in Atlanta's workforce, Maynard Jackson eliminated testing for most public jobs. He continually monitored each department's progress and queried the department head about his or her hiring efforts on a regular basis (Stein and Condrey 1987). Atlanta also had to change its methods of recruitment, particularly for the police department. Under Jackson's white predecessor, Ivan Allen, Jr., special advertising was directed at the black community featuring a black officer, and mobile recruitment vans visited black neighborhoods in Atlanta and other southern cities. The purpose was to show reluctant African Americans that the department really wanted people like them to apply (Stein and Condrey 1987).

In addition to the positive effects engendered by minority elected officials, Stein (1986) found that governmental structure affected minority workforce participation. All other things being equal, the mayor-council form was related to increased minority workforce participation. The presence of a formal civil service commission, on the other hand, had a deleterious effect on such participation.

Yet another element that affects municipal workforce composition in a number of cities is the consent decree. Federal judicial action occurs after discrimination complaints have been filed with state equal opportunity offices, are found to have merit, and are not resolved at that level. Federal district judges have ordered consent decrees affecting hiring practices in a number of cities. Frequently, police and fire departments are involved. The consent decree is a spur to change recruitment and promotion patterns, and in some cities, such as St. Louis, the decree stipulated that one black firefighter be hired for every white. Atlanta, Macon, Birmingham, San Francisco, and numerous other cities have had to comply with the terms of such decrees affecting all or part of their workforce (see Stein and Condrey 1987). W. Lewis (1989) found the consent decree, along with the emergence of black police chiefs, to have had significant effects on the hiring of black police officers. White police and fire unions, however, often fought these decrees in court, and during the Reagan and Bush years, the U.S. Department of Justice frequently intervened on the side of plaintiffs who sought to overturn these consent decrees, meeting with some success in the 1990s.

Economic conditions also affect minority hiring. While good times and full city coffers mean new positions (and the opportunity to hire more minorities), the reverse is also true. The fiscal difficulties experienced by many large cities in the 1980s and 1990s have led to hiring freezes, layoffs, and in some bailiwicks, contracting out, and privatization. A case study of employment patterns in St. Louis (Stein 1994) shows a reduction in both raw numbers and the percentage of black city employees following layoffs and the privatization of the city's public hospital and clinics. In addition, the U.S. Supreme Court ruled in 1984 in *Memphis* v. *Stotts* that seniority—not representativeness—remains the most important criterion governing layoffs. Naturally, layoffs first affect the most recently hired in a particular category, and recent hires are more likely to be nonwhite and/or female than are workers with greater seniority.

In the last few years, the high court has cut around the edges of affirmative action, although it has not outlawed the fundamental policy. In fact, the Civil Rights Restoration Act of 1991 brought back practices to measure adverse impact that were found in the 1971 *Griggs* v. *Duke Power* decision (Player 1992: 90; Graham 1990: 183, 185). In the last half of the 1980s, the Supreme Court had abrogated major sections of *Griggs*, including the use of statistical documentation to establish hiring bias.

Observers of Washington politics speculated that the Reagan administration would backpedal affirmative action in order to conform with its negative rhetoric on the subject and its well-publicized role in judicial cases. However, few instances of a federal go-slow attitude were discovered in a 1985 survey of local personnel administrators in large cities (Stein 1987: 270). Only 6.8 percent of the respondents reported that federal officials were "desirous of softening city affirmative action agreements or consent decrees." (In fact, representation of women and minorities at the federal level increased during the Reagan years [G. Lewis 1988].)

The thrust for equal employment in local government has resulted in a thorough reexamination of traditional hiring methods. Administrators began to validate tests for job relatedness and expanded recruitment considerably. Elected officials began to appreciate the desirability of a workforce resembling the city's population. The allocation of jobs became to many a strategy of providing municipal goods to an increasing segment of the population without incurring sizable monetary costs, at least in central cities with appreciable minority populations.

A new direction in research regarding cities' employment patterns is to ascertain whether one minority may benefit at the expense of another. McClain

(1993) tested this concept in cities with sizable Hispanic and African American populations. Her data did not demonstrate that either African Americans or Hispanics disadvantaged the other group, but she called for further research to test this theory in a larger number of cities.

Women also have been underrepresented in city workforces. Part of the reason stems from the traditional stereotypes of male and female jobs. Many city employees perform unskilled or skilled manual labor in departments such as streets, public utilities, and parks, traditionally seen as male jobs. In addition, the protective services were overwhelmingly male until the 1970s. Historically, executive positions in finance or planning had few female occupants either. Thus, greater female representation would depend both on increased hiring opportunities made available to women in nontraditional areas and on women choosing those occupations.

Grace Hall Saltzstein (1986) looked at the factors associated with greater female representation in municipal work forces. Saltzstein (1986: 157) found that the presence of a woman mayor had a significant effect on women's workforce presence. In a similar vein, housing affirmative action in the office of the mayor or city manager was a boon to female hiring (156). She also found that an expanding public sector aided changes to the workforce composition (156). In years to come, scholars should ascertain whether women and minorities are to be found at the top ranks of city employment in a meaningful fashion.

MAYORAL APPOINTMENTS

Municipal employment is one mechanism a minority or female mayor may use to transfer public benefits. Another is appointments to executive positions, boards, and commissions. Many of the latter may carry policy-making capacity, such as those dealing with airports, port authorities, housing, or economic development. A cross-national examination of such municipal appointees that looks at ascriptive characteristics and economic background is still needed.

Case studies indicate that white mayors may use the appointment process to reach out to different sections of the community and confer legitimacy. Minority mayors are most likely to increase these efforts at diversity. For example, Perry and Stokes (1987: 245) found that New Orleans' first black mayor, Ernest Morial, followed his white predecessor's example and continued to increase the number of black department heads. Morial also appointed the first black police chief and sanitation department head. Wilson Goode took similar action in Philadelphia (Adams 1994: 22). Morial and Goode are not alone among black mayors in making such changes because appointments at this level, as Perry and Stokes (1987: 244) note, affect policy making and are a source of "symbolic or group pride." As indicated earlier, this area deserves further cross-national study and also more case study examination.

MUNICIPAL CONTRACTING

Another important way in which a city can affect the well-being of segments of its citizenry is in the dispersal of contracts for supplies, services, and construction. Historically, minority and female contractors have been few, particularly in construction. Through alterations to city purchasing practices and in targeting contracts and subcontracts to firms owned by minorities and women, cities may enable such firms to grow and prosper. In particular, issuance of contracts or subcontracts may enable minority or female-headed firms to develop bonding capacity that many have not been able to obtain. When such capacity is attained, firms can compete for much larger contracts in the public or private sphere.

From the 1960s on, the federal government encouraged a minority set-aside program, and mayors, including many minority mayors, employed it. However, in *City of Richmond* v. *Croson*, the U.S. Supreme Court ruled that such set-asides were not constitutional unless a clear history of discriminatory behavior in contracting by a city could be documented (see Eisinger 1994: 141; Rice 1991). This ruling created a certain apprehension among city administrators. Documentation could be difficult and costly to assemble. In addition, there have been numerous charges by politicians and others that contracts are given to firms headed by minorities or women but actually controlled by white males.

Despite the legal and other difficulties inherent in the set-aside process, some minority and nonminority mayors (male and female) have continued to try to target their city's purchasing power. Ernest Morial set up such a program in New Orleans, and Atlanta, Philadelphia, San Francisco, Chicago, and Washington, D.C., among others, used set-asides to assist minority businesses (Perry and Stokes 1987: 246). A survey by the National Institute of Purchasing (MacManus 1990: 455–473) found that 24 percent of cities had modified their purchasing policies to target minority businesses. Bowman (1987) found that a quarter of the cities she surveyed also said that they had taken steps to address minority business development.

The mayor most identified with influencing his business community to hire African Americans and in directing city contracts to black-owned firms is Maynard Jackson of Atlanta. During his first two terms, Jackson reordered "relationships in Atlanta. Airport construction provided especially strong leverage, and Jackson claimed that its contracts created twenty-one black millionaires" (Stone 1989: 145). However, Stone cautions that such set-asides may only "enlarge the 'club' " a bit but not fundamentally change economic relationships (145–146).

Although minority set-asides are mentioned in several case studies such as Eisinger's 1994 work, to date there has been no comprehensive examination of the practice and its effects in a sizable sample of cities. The purchasing dimension has barely been touched. A further aspect deserving study is the selection of legal and accounting firms. With over $300 million in bonds for a new airport as a wedge, Maynard Jackson facilitated the hiring of blacks for the first time in bond firms wishing Atlanta's business. Eisinger (1994) points out certain limitations to the use of contracting to promote minority business development. In Milwaukee, most minority firms engaged in retail trade and did not serve as commodity suppliers. In addition, he notes that there is no linkage established between the minority contracts awarded and any minority hires generated.

THE ISSUE OF SEXUAL PREFERENCE

A new civil rights struggle is being waged today by homosexuals and lesbians to put an end to discrimination in employment and other areas. Gay municipal workers also have tried to secure domestic partnership agreements. These agreements provide that an employee's partner be covered by health insurance and other benefits. Legislation banning discrimination against gays has been passed in a number of cities, including New York City, Cincinnati, and St. Louis. Sometimes this new manifestation of the equal rights agenda has provoked strong opposition, particularly from the religious Right, including petition drives to overturn ordinances prohibiting discrimination based on sexual preference. Riccucci and Gossett (1995) provide the first systematic analysis of municipal laws and agreements affecting homosexuals and lesbians.

IMPLICATIONS

Overall, the expansion of opportunities to members of minority groups and women has increased middle-class membership and assisted some firms. However, Nelson points out that black mayors, for example,

have been modestly successful in increasing access to public resources by members of the black middle class [, but] they have been unsuccessful in significantly altering the social and economic positions of the black community as a whole. Public employment and public contracts are not the solution to chronic poverty in central cities, especially when they are not coupled with development policies designed to assist the low income. (1987: 174)

In a later work, Nelson (1990: 191) admits that many of the most critical problems facing the cities, such as chronic poverty, are beyond the reach of local officials. Hence, allocative actions remain a principal tool for local government to secure inclusion of those previously not part of policy making or implementation.

It is clear that municipal employment, appointments, and procurement are quite different than they were in 1950 when municipal government truly was a white male club. Progress in these areas has been both substantive and symbolic. Urban ills remain, but those who attempt to address these ills in many city governments now more resemble the population they serve. Allocation of normally authorized benefits has been used to redistribute to new groups, in much the way cities have behaved for over 100 years.

THE NATURE OF FUTURE RESEARCH

In the preceding sections, certain areas needing the attention of urban scholars have been mentioned. However, the real research challenge of the next decade or so will be to document the changes brought about by fundamental shifts in civil rights policies that were forged in the 1960s. A more conservative U.S. Supreme Court appears to be narrowing the terms of the Voting Rights Act, and major changes to federally directed affirmative action seem likely. If such changes do take place, there may be impacts on who is elected to office, who the public sector employs, and which company benefits from governmental business. If the United States and its cities have become more evenhanded in the last two and one half decades, there will be no abrupt break with past trends. However, many feel that there will be ample opportunity to measure changed outcomes.

It has always seemed obvious that the rules of the game, which are never neutral, certainly affect outcomes. That has been documented in the policy areas addressed in this chapter. Certainly a major deviation from the rules now in place will keep many urban scholars occupied over the decades ahead.

REFERENCES

Adams, Carolyn T. 1994. "Race and Class in Philadelphia Mayoral Elections." In George E. Peterson, ed., *Big-City Politics, Governance, and Fiscal Constraints.* Washington, D.C.: Urban Institute Press.

Bowman, Ann. 1987. *Tools and Targets: The Mechanics of City Economic Development.* Washington, D.C.: National League of Cities.

Browning, Rufus P., Dale Rogers Marshall, and David Tabb. 1984. *Protest Is Not Enough.* Berkeley: University of California Press.

Bullock, Charles S., III. 1989. "Symbolics or Substance? A Critique of the At-Large Election Controversy." *State and Local Government Review* 21 (fall): 91–99.

Bullock, Charles S., III, and Susan A. MacManus. 1987. "Structural Features of Municipal Elections and Black Descriptive Representation." Paper presented at the annual meeting of the Southern Political Science Association, November 5–7, Charlotte, North Carolina.

Carsey, Thomas M. 1995. "The Contextual Effects of Race on White Voter Behavior: The 1989 New York City Mayoral Election." *Journal of Politics* 57: 221–228.

Darden, Joe T., Harriet Orcutt Dunlop, and George C. Galster. 1992. "Civil Rights in Metropolitan America." *Journal of Urban Affairs* 14: 469–496.

DeLorenzo, Lisa, Carol Kohfeld, and Lana Stein. 1994. "Racial Voting Patterns in Recent St. Louis Elections: Emerging Biracial Coalitions." Paper presented at the annual meeting of the Midwest Political Science Association, April 8–10, Chicago, Illinois.

Dye, Thomas R., and James Renick. 1981. "Political Power and City Jobs: Determinants of Minority Employment." *Social Science Quarterly* 62: 457–486.

Eisinger, Peter K. 1980. *The Politics of Displacement*. New York: Academic Press.

Eisinger, Peter K. 1982a. "Black Employment in Municipal Jobs: The Impact of Black Political Power." *American Political Science Review* 76: 380–390.

Eisinger, Peter K. 1982b. "The Economic Conditions of Black Employment in Bureaucracies." *American Journal of Political Science* 26: 864–871.

Eisinger, Peter K. 1986. "Local Civil Service Employment and Black Socioeconomic Mobility." *Social Science Quarterly* 67: 169–175.

Eisinger, Peter K. 1994. "City Government and Minority Economic Opportunity." In George E. Peterson, ed., *Big-City Politics, Governance, and Fiscal Constraints*. Washington, D.C.: Urban Institute Press.

Engstrom, Ronald, and M. D. McDonald. 1981. "The Election of Blacks to City Councils." *American Political Science Review* 75 (June): 344–354.

Erie, Stephen. 1989. *Rainbow's End*. Berkeley: University of California Press.

Graham, Cole Blease, Jr. 1990. "Equal Employment Opportunity and Affirmative Action." In Steven W. Hays and Richard C. Kearney, eds., *Public Personnel Administration, Problems and Prospects*. 2nd ed. Englewood Cliffs, NJ: Prentice-Hall.

Hays, Samuel P. 1984. "The Politics of Reform in the Progressive Era." In Harlan Hahn and Charles H. Levine, eds., *Readings in Urban Politics*. 2nd ed. New York: Longman.

Hofstadter, Richard. 1955. *The Age of Reform*. New York: Random House.

Karnig, Albert K., and Susan Welch. 1980. *Black Representation and Urban Policy*. Chicago: University of Chicago Press.

Levine, Charles H. 1974. *Racial Conflict and the American Mayor*. Lexington, MA: Lexington Books.

Lewis, Gregory B. 1988. "Progress toward Racial and Sexual Equality in the Federal Civil Service." *Public Administration Review* 52: 700–707.

Lewis, William G. 1989. "Toward Representative Bureaucracy: Blacks in City Police Organizations." *Public Administration Review* 52: 257–267.

McClain, P. D. 1993. "Urban Violence: Agendas, Politics, and Problem Redefinition." In P. D. McClain, ed., *Minority Group Influences: Agenda Setting, Formulation, and Public Policy*. Westport, CT: Greenwood.

MacManus, Susan. 1990. "Minority Business Contracting with Local Government." *Urban Affairs Quarterly* 25: 455–473.

Mladenka, Kenneth R. 1989a. "Barriers to Hispanic Employment Success in 1,200 Cities." *Social Science Quarterly* 70: 391–407.

Mladenka, Kenneth R. 1989b. "Blacks and Hispanics in Urban Politics." *American Political Science Review* 83: 165–191.

Nelson, William E., Jr. 1987. "Cleveland: The Evolution of Black Political Power." In Michael B. Preston, Lenneal J. Henderson, Jr., and Paul L. Puryear, eds., *The New Black Politics*. 2nd ed. New York: Longman.

Nelson, William E., Jr. 1990. "Black Mayoral Leadership: A Twenty-Year Perspective." *National Political Science Review* 2: 188–195.

Nelson, William E., and Philip J. Meranto. 1977. *Electing Black Mayors*. Columbus: Ohio State University Press.

Perry, Huey L., and Alfred Stokes. 1987. "Politics and Power in the Sunbelt: Mayor

Morial of New Orleans.'' In Michael B. Preston, Lenneal J. Henderson, Jr., and Paul L. Puryear, eds., *The New Black Politics.* 2nd ed. New York: Longman. 222–255.

Peterson, Paul E. 1981. *City Limits.* Chicago: University of Chicago Press.

Player, Mack A. 1992. *Federal Law of Employment Discrimination* St. Paul, MN: West Publishing.

Report of the National Advisory Commission on Civil Disorders. 1968. New York: Bantam Books.

Riccucci, Norma M., and Charles W. Gossett. 1995. ''Employment Discrimination in State and Local Government: The Lesbian and Gay Male Experience.'' Unpublished paper.

Rice, Mitchell F. 1991. ''Government Set-Asides, Minority Business Enterprises, and the Supreme Court.'' *Public Administration Review* (March–April): 114–121.

Rodgers, Harrell R., Jr., and Charles S. Bullock III. 1972. *Law and Social Change.* New York: McGraw-Hill.

Saltzstein, Grace Hall. 1986. ''Female Mayors and Women in Municipal Jobs.'' *American Journal of Political Science* 30: 140–164.

Schiesl, Martin J. 1977. *The Politics of Efficiency.* Berkeley: University of California Press.

Sonenshein, Raphael. 1993. *Politics in Black and White: Race and Power in Los Angeles.* Princeton: Princeton University Press.

Stein, Lana. 1986. ''Representative Local Government: Minorities in the Municipal Work Force.'' *Journal of Politics* 48: 694–713.

Stein, Lana. 1987. ''Merit Systems and Political Influence: The Case of Local Government.'' *Public Administration Review* 47: 263–271.

Stein, Lana. 1991. *Holding Bureaucrats Accountable: Professionals and Politicians in St. Louis.* Tuscaloosa: University of Alabama Press.

Stein, Lana. 1994. ''Privatization, Work Force Cutbacks, and African-American Municipal Employment.'' *American Review of Public Administration* 24: 181–192.

Stein, Lana, and Stephen E. Condrey. 1987. ''Integrating Municipal Work Forces: A Study of Six Southern Cities.'' *Publius* 17: 93–104.

Stein, Lana, and Carol W. Kohfeld. 1991. ''St. Louis's Black-White Elections: Products of Machine Factionalism and Polarization.'' *Urban Affairs Quarterly* 27: 227–248.

Stone, Clarence N. 1989. *Regime Politics: Governing Atlanta.* Lawrence: University Press of Kansas.

U.S. Commission on Civil Rights. 1969. *For All the People . . . A Report on Equal Opportunity in State and Local Government.* Washington, D.C.: Government Printing Office.

Chapter 27

Urban Transportation

Edward Weiner

OVERVIEW

Transportation is a significant and pervasive activity in the economy and has major impacts on the environment and quality of life. Consumer spending on transportation approximates 13 percent of total personal expenditures, exceeded only by spending on housing and food. Total spending on transportation is estimated to be about 17 percent of the gross national product (GNP).

The nature of the current transportation system has evolved over the almost five decades since the end of World War II and is largely dominated by the automobile. Of the more than 3.7 trillion annual passenger miles traveled in the United States, the automobile sector accounted for 89 percent, with aviation accounting for 10 percent and all other modes approximately 1 percent (U.S. Department of Transportation 1992b).

Urban areas have been seeking new ways to provide transportation service in a cost-effective manner that is consistent with their economic, environmental, and social goals. They have sought alternatives to the use of automobiles, especially transit, and to manage the use of automobiles to make the most efficient use of the capacity that is available, by measures such as carpooling and vanpooling. But there is still widespread and growing congestion and air quality problems.

Two recent pieces of legislation, the Clean Air Act Amendments of 1990 and the Intermodal Surface Transportation Efficiency Act (ISTEA) of 1991, are expected to have a major impact on the provision of transportation facilities and services and on environmental quality, particularly air quality. The Clean Air Act Amendments of 1990 require urban areas to meet specific national ambient air quality standards (NAAQSs). The act details the timetable for meeting these standards, the steps that need to be taken if these standards are not met, and the sanctions for not meeting the standards.

The ISTEA of 1991 offers greater flexibility for state and local agencies to fashion transportation solutions to best suit their particular needs and objectives. ISTEA authorizes $151 billion over six years for highways, mass transit, and safety programs. In a major breakthrough, the act created a Surface Transportation Program (STP) with flexible funding that opened the door to new opportunities to address transportation problems. The STP makes funds available for a broad range of highway, mass transit, safety, and environmental purposes. It was authorized at $23.9 billion over six years at an 80 percent federal matching share.

These two acts require integrated land use–transportation planning with the goal of reducing congestion and air pollution while meeting the economic requirements of the region for mobility.

ISSUES IN TRANSPORTATION POLICY

Travel Patterns

In 1990, 62 percent of the nation's 242 million daily passenger trips were made in urban areas. Of these, 87 percent were made by automobiles or trucks, 2 percent by public transportation, and the remaining 11 percent by other means, primarily walking and school bus (Reed, Vincent, and Keyes 1994). For a handful of the larger metropolitan areas with dense employment and residential cores, however, travel by mass transportation constitutes a significant proportion of daily work trips. For example, the percentage using transit for the journey to work in 1990 was 28 percent in New York, 14 percent in Chicago, 11 percent in Philadelphia, 9 percent in San Francisco, 14 percent in Washington, D.C., and 11 percent in Boston (Rosetti and Eversole 1993).

In a study of national commuting patterns, Pisarski (1987) identified three major national trends. These trends clearly indicate that major changes have occurred in work travel and that these changes would continue for the foreseeable future. First was "the worker boom," which was a dramatic increase in the number of workers, and therefore in the number of commuters, in excess of population growth. From 1950 to 1980, the employed civilian workforce grew by more than 40 million persons, an increase of 65 percent, while population grew only 50 percent. This was the result of the post–World War II "baby boomer" generation reaching working age and a sharp increase in women participating in the workforce.

Second was "the suburban commuting boom," which was due to the large number of jobs that located in the suburbs. Since 1950, 86 percent of metropolitan growth has occurred in the suburbs. Between 1960 and 1980, two thirds of metropolitan job growth went to the suburbs. Consequently, 58 percent of all commuter trips are now suburb to suburb, making it the dominant commuting pattern and replacing suburb to central city travel.

Third was "the private vehicle boom," in which private vehicles per capita almost doubled between 1960 and 1980. The number of households with zero and one vehicle actually decreased, whereas those with two or more increased. Work travel by private vehicles increased from 70 to 85 percent of all work travel. Transit's share of the work travel market halved from 12.6 percent to 6.2 percent.

Data from the 1990 Nationwide Personal Transportation Study paint an even more overwhelming picture of the dominance of the automobile in American society (Hu and Young 1992). Nationwide, the percentage of households with no automobile dropped to 9 percent, while households with two or more automobiles reached 58 percent, and even more astonishing, the percentage of households with three or more automobiles reached almost 20 percent. The average number of miles driven annually reached almost 16,000 (25,744 vehicle kilometers) for men. However, women are quickly catching up, with an increase to 9,400 vehicle miles (15,125 vehicle kilometers) driven in 1990 compared to 5,300 (8,528 vehicle kilometers) in 1969.

In addition, work trips are continuing to decline as a proportion of all travel. Work trips have dropped to 26 percent of trips from 32 percent in 1969. This has been more than offset by the increase in family and personal business trips.

It has been theorized that many of the recent changes in travel patterns are the result of the increasing number of two-worker and single-adult households. These households, especially those with children, make many more family and personal business trips often as part of the trip to or from work. These include dropping off and picking up children at school or day care, shopping, and other errands that need to be fit into a very time-constrained lifestyle.

Two-worker households also have a more difficult decision process to determine where to locate. In the past, one-worker households could select a residential location to minimize the journey to work along with the other location factors. This is less possible when there are two work destinations to consider and where there is a need to have travel flexibility to allow personal and family business trips during the day.

The housing market significantly affects residential choice along with transportation costs. Households choose a residential location with the amenities they value while minimizing their costs. Generally, households can trade higher transportation costs for lower housing costs by moving further away from the city center. And many have been moving considerable distances in order to find affordable housing. However, as long as the full costs of their decision are not felt in terms of congestion costs, travel time cost, energy use, and environmental damage, the basic economics continues to encourage a suburban sprawl pattern of development.

Congestion, Environmental, and Energy Implications

This reliance on the automobile has produced a number of undesirable effects, particularly with regard to traffic congestion, air pollution, and energy consumption. Alan Altshuler provides an extensive review of the major issues and problems associated with the expanded use of automobiles in urban areas (Altshuler, Womak, and Pucher 1979).

Increased use of automobiles has expanded urban congestion into the suburban portion of many urban areas. The Texas Transportation Institute estimates that congestion costs in the largest 39 urbanized areas were $34 billion in 1989 (Hanks and Lomax 1992). The 1991 Highway Performance Report produced by the U.S. Federal Highway Administration shows that in 1989, 70 percent of urban interstate highways and 43 percent of major arterials in urban areas were congested or highly congested (U.S. Department of Transportation 1993a).

In the years after the passage of the Clean Air Act Amendments of 1970, considerable progress was made in reducing air pollution in the nation's urban areas. Average automobile emissions dropped from 85 grams per mile of carbon monoxide (CO) in 1970 to 25 grams per mile in 1988. Lead usage in gasoline dropped by 99 percent between 1975 and 1988. From 1978 to 1988, transportation-related emissions decreased 38 percent for CO, 36 percent for hydrocarbons, and 15 percent for NOX (nitrogen oxide). The reduction occurred despite a 24 percent increase in vehicle miles of travel during the same period (U.S. Department of Transportation 1990).

Nevertheless, by 1990, 95 urban areas failed to meet the national ambient air quality standard for ozone, and 41 areas failed to meet the NAAQS for CO. More than half of the population now live in nonattainment areas.

With regard to energy, transportation directly and indirectly consumes more than one quarter of all energy and over 60 percent of all petroleum in the United States. In 1989, transportation consumed almost 4 billion barrels of petroleum. Highway vehicles consumed 78 percent of the energy in the transportation sector. Automobiles have, however, become more energy efficient. New car fuel efficiency has more than doubled in 15 years, from 13.8 miles per gallon (5.9 kilometers per liter) in 1974 to 28.3 miles per gallon (12.0 kilometers per liter) in 1989. Nevertheless, the average automobile still consumed about 690 gallons (2,612 liters) annually (Davis and Hu 1991).

Automobile use has made us more dependent on foreign petroleum sources. In recent years, petroleum imports reached a low in 1985, when imports were 32 percent of consumption. But imports have been growing since then and now represent over 45 percent of consumption.

CURRENT STATE OF THE FIELD

Federal Transportation Legislation

With the completion of the National Interstate and Defense Highway System provided for in the Surface Transportation Assistance Act of 1982, the legislative focus shifted to the nature and size of the postinterstate program. The ISTEA of 1991 authorized $155 billion over six years for highways, mass transit, and safety programs. In a major breakthrough, the act created a surface transportation program with flexible funding that opened the door to new opportunities to address statewide and urban transportation problems (Weiner 1992).

The purpose of the act was set forth in its statement of policy:

It is the policy of the United States to develop a National Intermodal Transportation System that is economically efficient and environmentally sound, provides the foundation for the Nation to compete in the global economy, and will move people and goods in an energy efficient manner.

The act established a National Highway System (NHS) consisting of 155,000 miles of interstate highways, urban and rural principal arterials, and other strategic highways. The NHS was funded at $21 billion over six years at an 80 percent federal matching share. ISTEA created a new block grant program, the Surface Transportation Program, which makes funds available for a broad range of highway, mass transit, safety, and environmental purposes. The STP was authorized at $23.9 billion over six years at an 80 percent federal matching share. Each state was required to set aside 10 percent of the funds for safety construction activities and another 10 percent for transportation enhancements. The remaining 80 percent was to be allocated statewide. A new Congestion Mitigation and Air Quality Improvement Program was authorized for transportation projects in ozone and carbon monoxide nonattainment areas.

Transit programs were authorized at $31.5 billion for the six-year period. The Section 3 Discretionary and Formula Capital Grant program was reauthorized with minor changes. The federal matching share was increased from 75 percent to 80 percent. The Section 9 Formula program was authorized at $16.1 billion for the six-year period with few changes in the program structure.

Clean Air Act Amendments of 1990

The Clean Air Act Amendments were passed after extensive debate in the Congress. The transportation sections of the act address the attainment and maintenance of NAAQSs that set the maximum allowable levels of various pollutants in the air. Nonattainment areas are classified for ozone, CO, and particulate matter in accordance with the severity of the air pollution problem. Depending on the degree to which an area exceeds the NAAQSs, that area is required to implement various control programs and to achieve attainment of the NAAQSs within a specified period of time. The areas that are furthest out of compliance were given the longest length of time to achieve the standards (U.S. Environmental Protection Agency 1990).

States were required to develop state implementation plans (SIPs) detailing their plans to meet the NAAQSs within the legislated deadlines. As part of the SIPs, states were required to reduce volatile organic compound (VOC) emissions by 15 percent from 1990 baseline emissions over the six years following enactment. In addition to the 15 percent reduction, emissions arising from growth in vehicle miles of travel had to be offset with other reductions in emissions. In more severe nonattainment areas, transportation control measures (TCMs) needed to be implemented to reduce the use of vehicles by shifting travel to alternate modes such as transit and ridesharing, or shortening the trip length, or using other approaches including telecommuting (Hawthorn 1991).

The "conformity" provisions in the 1990 act were expanded from the Clean Air Act Amendments of 1977. A conformity determination is made to assure that federally assisted projects or actions conform to an SIP. No project could cause or contribute to new NAAQS violations nor increase the frequency or severity of any existing violations of any standard nor delay the timely attainment of any required NAAQS. The process recognizes that transportation-related air quality issues have to be analyzed on a systemwide basis and controlled through regional strategies to be effective. The Clean Air Act Amendments of 1990 expand the "sanctions" where states fail to carry out requirements of the act, including withholding of federal funding for highway projects.

The Clean Air Act Amendments of 1990 create a major challenge to transportation planners to continue to provide urban mobility while meeting the requirements to improve air quality under tight time deadlines.

Nature of the Urban Transportation Problem

Throughout most of this century, transportation planning in urban areas has focused on improving access to central cities and especially to downtowns. Downtowns were the heart of the cities; they contained most of the residences, employment, shopping, and cultural and recreational activities. As the downtowns went, so went the metropolitan areas.

Even in the aftermath of World War II as returning servicemen established families and located in the suburbs, the orientation was toward downtown. Even though suburbs were growing, they were bedroom communities for the employment that was still predominantly located in downtowns and on the periphery of downtowns. The planning of the National System of Interstate and Defense Highways connected downtowns, with the new beltways intended to divert bypass traffic around downtowns so as not to interfere with the downtown-oriented traffic. Few planners guessed that these beltways would soon be overwhelmed by so-called local traffic.

Through the 1970s and 1980s, evidence mounted of the huge shift in first residences and then jobs to the suburbs and beyond. Yet planners still focused on the suburbs as support communities for downtowns and central cities. Much effort in urban transportation was concentrated on better access to and within downtowns while suburban roads overflowed with traffic, which generally had neither the origin nor destination in the downtown.

With these shifts in development patterns, suburbs flourished with new homes and jobs while central cities suffered the loss of their most affluent and educated citizens. Urban areas have now reached the point where many downtowns have seriously declined and are badly deteriorated. With this decentralization of activities has come a decline in public transportation, particularly in the small and medium urban areas. Gray and Hoel (1992) review the issues, options, and challenges related to public transportation.

The suburban areas have "evolved" into full-service communities that now contain residences, jobs, shopping, entertainment, and education. Most suburban residents never go into their downtowns except on rare occasions. Yet these suburbs were not planned as separate entities for transportation purposes, and the issue here is how to retrofit transportation services and facilities into these former bedroom communities.

It is unlikely that much progress will be made in reducing congestion and air pollution without facing the land development element of the picture. It is the dispersed pattern of residences, businesses, and other activities that makes the automobile so essential for travel. To make group modes of transportation, such as bus and rail transit, more workable, densities would need to be higher and developments designed more efficiently. This would require a degree of land use planning and control that has not been widely practiced to date, as well as changes in those policies that have supported dispersed, low-density development. The Transportation Research Board (1991) explored many of these issues in a Conference on Transportation, Urban Form, and the Environment.

Furthermore, the development of exurban communities is now occurring with the same reckless abandon that characterized the growth of many suburban communities 20 years ago. It seems that little has been learned from the experiences of the last 30 years.

Many forces have acted to bring about these development patterns including changes in the demographic diversity, including rising immigration; in the economic base of the nation and the shift to a service-based economy; in technology, especially communications technology; in lifestyles, such as the increase of two-worker and single-parent households; and in the trend to more flexible and flatter organizational arrangements that is reflected in the restructuring of many businesses in recent years. There needs to be a better understanding of these forces and those that will affect development patterns in the future. There also needs to be an understanding of the economic, social, and environmental implications of these forces.

From a transportation point of view, urban areas are faced with three problems: What will be the future role of the downtown and central city, and how can transportation be used to support that evolving role? How can transportation be retrofit into existing suburbs that were originally built as bedroom communities and are now full-service communities? and, What role should transportation play in the development of the exurbs so that there will not have to be a need to retrofit them with efficient transportation systems 10 to 20 years into the future?

Institutional and Planning Issues

The institutional arrangements in most urban areas do not lend themselves to the coordination and integration of the various elements needed to bring about more efficient travel and land use patterns. The institutional arrangement is fragmented vertically between various levels of government; horizontally among the large number of local units of government; and functionally among transportation, land use, air quality, and other service areas. There is little effort aimed at merging these institutions in most urban regions. In short, governmental boundaries do not encompass the problem areas. It is only at the state level of government that the jurisdiction is broad enough to address the problems of urban regions.

The federal government has promoted a regional approach to addressing transportation problems for several decades. The Federal-Aid Highway Act of 1962 was the first piece of federal legislation to mandate urban transportation planning as a condition for receiving federal funds in urbanized areas. It asserted that urban transportation was to be addressed on a cooperative basis among governmental jurisdictions, encompass all modes of transportation, and be integrated with land development activities. Weiner (1987, 1992) traces the evolution of urban transportation planning.

The requirements for urban transportation planning have been extended and broadened in succeeding pieces of legislation. Currently, all urbanized areas with a population of 50,000 or more must have a metropolitan planning process to be eligible for federal highway and mass transit funds. In each urbanized area, a single organization is to be designated jointly by the governor and general-purpose units of government in the region. Membership on this Metropolitan Planning Organization (MPO) is to be by principal elected officials of general-purpose units of government. The metropolitan planning process is to be carried out jointly by the MPO, the state, and publicly owned operators of mass transportation service.

Every metropolitan planning process must develop a long-range transportation plan describing policies, strategies, and changes in facilities that are proposed for the next 20-year period, including analysis of transportation system management (TSM) strategies to make more efficient use of the existing transportation system. In addition, a transportation improvement program (TIP) is required, which is a staged, multiyear (three- to five-year) program of transportation improvement projects that are consistent with the transportation plan. Only transportation projects on the TIP can be implemented. The transportation plan, the TIP, and individual transportation projects must be in conformance with the state implementation plan under the Clean Air Act.

The metropolitan planning process provides a framework and rational process for setting goals for the areas, identifying problems, analyzing options for addressing these problems, and coming to agreement on strategies and policies to implement. It also provides a basis for the federal government to make metropolitan transportation funding decisions.

FUTURE DIRECTIONS FOR TRANSPORTATION POLICY

The Options

From a transportation perspective, there are a wide array of options for the future. A conference sponsored by the Transportation Research Board focused on the issues and factors affecting future highway and transit policy and requirements (Transportation Research Board 1988).

With the wide domination of the automobile in urban transportation, transportation policy and planning in the future need to focus on providing mobility without major expansion of highway facilities and capacity and to contribute to meeting air quality objectives, energy conservation, and overall sustainable urban development. Options to achieve these goals can be divided into three categories: those that improve the technology of the automobile; those to better manage the use of the automobile; and those that provide alternatives to the automobile.

In the first instance, much has been done to increase energy efficiency and reduce the pollutant emissions from vehicles through more efficient engine designs, air pollution control devices, and elimination of leaded gas. The biggest payoff to improving energy efficiency and air quality from a transportation perspective will continue to come from reductions in emissions in the vehicle itself. This is particularly true in addressing the problem of cold starts, which account for 50 percent of vehicle emissions. Further improvements can come from wider use of alternative cleaner fuels, more efficient combustion brought about by new microelectronic technology, and alternately electric cars. Reformulated gasoline, with increased oxygen content, low sulfur, and other significant adjustments, is also receiving substantial attention as a contributor to lower emissions.

Second, the *use* of the automobile can be more efficient. For example, the use of high-occupancy lanes can improve the effectiveness of the highway system and reduce drive-alone trips, but only if trip-makers will change their travel behavior (Institute of Transportation Engineers 1993). This can be reinforced with more aggressive parking policies, which increase the price and reduce the supply of spaces. In Boston, for example, restrictions on downtown parking led to a 70 percent increase in transit ridership. But this increase was only possible because they had an extensive, mature transit system and relatively high development densities. More efficient use of automobiles can also be accomplished by increasing automobile user fees through tolls, electronic pricing, or peak-period licensing schemes.

Road pricing is now a widely discussed option to reduce congestion (National Research Council 1994). Road pricing is not the panacea for congestion but one option that is available along with many other approaches. The full range of consequences from such a program are still not known, especially on low-income households and downtown businesses. Nevertheless, it is time that a serious road-pricing program be tried. The program needs to be carefully designed in setting the pricing structure, dealing with the revenue raised, and mitigating potential negative consequences on any group of the population. It is important that there be a sound evaluation of the results of this program so that we can all better understand the potentials and limitations of this option.

In addition, advanced traffic management systems under development can smooth traffic flow, increase highway capacity, and reduce pollutant emissions (U.S. Department of Transportation 1992a). Proposals for advanced driver information systems and eventually advanced vehicle control systems will assist drivers in making more efficient use of highway capacity as well as improve air quality and safety.

Third, much more will need to be done to develop viable alternatives to the private automobile. Of particular concern is the growing numbers of elderly persons who will continue to reside in suburban areas and who will increasingly need automobile substitutes. Innovative, market-oriented approaches will be needed to provide public transportation services. This will require the involvement of the private sector more directly and encouraging competition in service provision. Careful land use and site planning have been used to facilitate and promote transit ridership. Some new office parks have done this successfully.

The use of advanced communication technology will assist in providing information to the public and in improving the efficiency of public transportation services. Considerable research and development are under way on automated guideway systems, magnetically levitated trains, and even personalized rapid transit systems, all of which may play a role in serving this market.

New strategies are being developed to mitigate suburban congestion under the general category of transportation demand management (Higgens 1990). Transportation demand management is a process designed to change transportation demand. Transportation demand management is aimed at reducing peak period automobile trips by either eliminating the trip, shifting it to a less congested destination or route, diverting it to a higher-occupancy mode, or time shifting it to a less congested period of the day. Transportation demand management strategies often work in conjunction with transportation system management measures.

Transportation demand management is most often focused on a suburban activity center but is also used for central business districts and radial corridors. Transportation demand management strategies require the cooperation of many agencies and organizations including developers, landowners, employers, business associations, and state and local governments.

In some instances, legal support is provided in the form of a trip reduction ordinance to strengthen compliance with the transportation demand management measures. The first areawide trip reduction ordinance in the United States was adopted in Pleasanton, California, in 1984. A trip reduction ordinance provides some assurance that consistent standards and requirements would be applied to all businesses in the area and gives these businesses the legal backing to implement automobile reduction strategies. Although the main goal of most trip reduction ordinances is to mitigate traffic congestion, improvement in air quality is an important goal as well. Trip reduction ordinances require businesses and employers to establish a transportation demand management plan, implement a transportation demand management program, monitor progress, update the plan periodically, have a professionally trained coordinator, and in some instances, achieve a specified level of trip reduction with fines and penalties for violations.

Transportation demand management measures include improved alternatives to driving alone, such as pooling; incentives to shift modes, such as subsidizing transit fares and vanpooling costs; disincentives to driving, such as higher parking fees and reduced parking supply; and work hours management, such as flexible work hours and compressed workweeks. Employer-sponsored ride-sharing programs are encouraging more commuters to pool rather than use their vehicle alone. Private businesses are grouping into transportation management associations that are launching areawide vanpooling programs and free shuttle bus service financed through annual membership fees.

Transportation demand management strategies are becoming more important in addressing suburban traffic problems as urban areas are finding increasing difficulties in expanding highway capacity and meeting air pollution standards. A number of companies, as well as several state and local agencies, are experimenting with telecommuting for their employees. Telecommuting has the potential to reduce peak-hour vehicle commuting and the resulting air pollution (U.S. Department of Transportation 1993b).

In recent years there has been a huge upsurge of interest in building new urban rail transit systems and extensions to existing ones. Many of the urban areas planning and constructing new rail systems have lower densities of development, more dispersed travel patterns, and smaller central cores than older areas that have long had rail transit. As a result, it is more difficult for rail systems in these areas to provide a competitive advantage over the automobile. Ridership levels are often lower than for rail systems of comparable size in denser areas. In many of these instances, high-quality express bus service, high-occupancy lanes, ride sharing, and other transportation system management strategies may be more cost-effective in serving these travel needs.

NOTE

Publications by the U.S. Department of Transportation can be obtained from: Technology Sharing Program, U.S. Department of Transportation, 400 Seventh Street, SW, Washington, D.C. 20590.

REFERENCES

Altshuler, Alan, James P. Womak, and John R. Pucher. 1979. *The Urban Transportation System: Politics and Policy Innovation*. Cambridge, MA: MIT Press.

Cevero, Robert. 1986. *Suburban Gridlock*. New Brunswick, NJ: Center for Urban Policy Research.

Davis, Stacy C., and Patricia S. Hu. 1991. *Transportation Energy Data Book—Edition 11*. Oak Ridge, TN: Oak Ridge National Laboratory. January.

Gray, George E., and Lester A. Hoel, eds. 1992. *Public Transportation*. 2nd ed. Englewood Cliffs, NJ: Prentice-Hall.

Hanks, James W., and Timothy J. Lomax. 1992. *1989 Roadway Congestion Estimates and Trends*. College Station, TX: Texas Transportation Institute. July.

Hawthorn, Gary. 1991. "Transportation Provisions in the 1990 Clean Air Act Amendments of 1990." *ITE Journal* (April): 17–24.

Higgens, Thomas J. 1990. "Demand Management in Suburban Settings." *Transportation* 17: 93–116.

Hu, Patricia S., and Jennifer Young. 1992. *National Personal Transportation Survey—Summary of Travel Trends*. Washington, D.C. U.S. Department of Transportation, Federal Highway Administration. March.

Institute of Transportation Engineers. 1993. *Implementing Effective Travel Demand Management Measures*. Washington, D.C.: ITE. June.

Meyer, Michael D., and Eric J. Miller. 1984. *Urban Transportation Planning: A Decision-Oriented Approach*. New York: McGraw-Hill.

National Research Council. 1994. *Curbing Gridlock: Peak-Period Fees to Relieve Traffic Congestion*. Vols. 1–2. Washington, D.C.: National Academy Press.

Pisarski, Alan E. 1987. *Commuting in America—A National Report on Commuting Patterns and Trends*. Westport, CT: Eno Foundation for Transportation, Inc.

Reed, Marshall, Mary Jane Vincent, and Mary Ann Keyes. 1994. *Urban Travel Patterns—1990 National Personal Transportation Survey*. Washington, D.C.: U.S. Department of Transportation, Federal Highway Administration. April.

Rosetti, Michael, and Barbara Eversole. 1993. *Journey to Work Trends in the United States and Its Major Metropolitan Areas, 1960–1990*. Washington, D.C.: U.S. Department of Transportation Federal Highway Administration. November.

Smerk, George M. 1991. *The Federal Role in Urban Mass Transportation*. Indianapolis, IN: Indiana University Press.

Transportation Research Board. 1988. *A Look Ahead—Year 2020*. Special Report 220. Washington, D.C.: TRB.

Transportation Research Board. 1991. *Transportation, Urban Form, and the Environment*. Special Report 231. Washington, D.C.: TRB.

U.S. Department of Transportation. 1990. *National Transportation Strategic Planning Study*. Washington, D.C.: DOT. March.

U.S. Department of Transportation. 1992a. *IVHS Strategic Plan—Report to Congress.* Washington, D.C.: DOT. December 18.

U.S. Department of Transportation. 1992b. *National Transportation Statistics.* Washington, D.C.: DOT. June.

U.S. Department of Transportation. 1993a. *The Status of the Nation's Highways, Bridges, and Transit Conditions and Performance.* 103rd Cong. 1st sess. H. Doc. 103–2.

U.S. Department of Transportation. 1993b. *Transportation Implications of Telecommuting.* Washington, D.C.: DOT. April.

U.S. Environmental Protection Agency. 1990. *Clean Air Act Amendments of 1990— Detailed Summary of Titles.* Washington, D.C.: EPA. November 30.

Weiner, Edward. 1987. *Urban Transportation Planning in the U.S.—An Historical Overview.* New York; Praeger Publishers.

Weiner, Edward. 1992. *Urban Transportation Planning in the U.S.—An Historical Overview.* Rev. ed. Washington, D.C.: U.S. Department of Transportation. November.

Chapter 28

Cities and the Environment

Dennis R. Judd

THE EVOLUTION OF THE FIELD

The environmental crisis is certain to be the among the leading issues of the twenty-first century.[1] The vast literature on the environment is composed, for the most part, of studies of climatic change; the interrelationships that compose ecological systems; the global impact of pollution, energy, and resource consumption; and the policy alternatives available to nations and the world community. Only recently has a literature emerged linking cities to environmental issues, and for the most part, this literature is focused specifically upon policies of "sustainable development" or upon conservation measures such as recycling and the use of energy (e.g., Gordon 1990). Rarely has the overall role of cities in environmental issues been considered. This is odd because, historically, not only have cities been the locus for most concerns about the environmental impacts of human activities; they have also given rise to the institutions mediating the relationship between human beings and the natural environment.

Cities evolved to assert human mastery over nature. The oft-noted tendency in Western culture to regard nature as hostile and savage, a beast to be tamed, has often been traced to the Judeo-Christian religious tradition that placed the human soul at the center of all creation (Oelschlaeger 1991: 65–67). As an alternative to this interpretation, a hostile attitude toward nature might just as persuasively be traced to the rise of cities. As urban people retreated from nature, they increasingly regarded it as something to fear and subdue. These attitudes have only very recently begun to give way, among affluent populations in Western nations, to an idealization of nature and wilderness as places of tranquillity, solitude, and refuge from the pressures of urban life (281–319).

Lewis Mumford noted that from their earliest beginnings to the present, cities have been fundamental shapers of the natural environment (Mumford 1938). Cities originally emerged to protect and organize agricultural endeavors, which involved the clearance of forest, grasslands, and other native habitats. Likewise, from the eleventh to the thirteenth centuries an immense expansion of arable land occurred in Europe. The massive clearing of forests to increase agricultural production was a direct outcome of the building of walled cities that could be defended from attack. The existence of such cities facilitated both rapid population growth and merchant economies that promoted and demanded increasing agricultural output (Mumford 1938). After the seventeenth century the rise of industrial cities brought about environmental destruction on a grand scale. The concentration of populations in industrial cities set off an unprecedented population explosion, an enormous increase in the demand for food and other resources, and—commensurate with the inflow of population and goods to urban centers—an exponential increase in urban effluents in the form of industrial toxins and human wastes.

The Italian theorist Karl Polanyi called the rise of capitalism and the explosion of urban population that accompanied it the "Great Transformation" (Polanyi 1944). In A.D. 1500 the world's population numbered an estimated 500 million people, and it took until 1830 for this population to double. In another 100 years it doubled again. By 1960—only 30 years later—the world's population reached 3 billion people, and by 1975 it had reached 4 billion. Another billion people were added by 1986. Present projections place the world's population at over 8 billion by 2025 and, assuming 1990 fertility levels, 21 billion by 2050. More than 90 percent of the increase in the world's population will occur in the less-developed countries, mostly in urbanized areas (Dogan and Kasarda 1988: 13–19).

The number of large cities is also expected to climb rapidly. In 1950 there were just 5 metropolises of more than 4 million people in the developing nations. By 1985 there were 28, which is expected to increase to 50 by the turn of the century and to 114 by 2025. One third of the population of the developing nations will live in these giant cities. By 2025, the average population of these urban agglomerations will reach 9 million in Africa and 9.4 million in Latin America and South America (Dogan and Kasarda 1988: 13–19).

Urbanization on this scale is impacting both urban and natural environments.[2] The physical (built) environment of rapidly growing megacities is characterized by overcrowding and infrastructure overloading, as well as by a host of environmental problems that substantially define the quality of urban life. The urban environment is likely to follow the trends of recent decades and continue to deteriorate, characterized by extremes of wealth and poverty, high unemployment rates, intensified ethnic and racial conflict, inadequate housing, health and nutrition problems, inadequate water supplies and waste disposal systems, overloaded transportation systems, air and water pollution, and increasing levels of crime and social disorder.[3]

The natural environment beyond urbanized areas is also being impacted by rapid urbanization. We can conceive of these impacts, basically, as fitting into two categories: the production of effluents (solid wastes and toxins spewed into air and water) and the consumption of resources. Cities have access to huge hinterlands; indeed, today every region on earth is subjected to the effects of urban production and consumption imperatives. Abel Wolman (1965) has used the phrase "the metabolism of cities" to express the idea that, like living organisms, cities transport, consume, and excrete energy and matter. Through these processes, cities influence environments far beyond areas of population concentration.

Urbanized areas are composed of, and are linked to one another by, intricate systems of transport; without these, their metabolic processes would quickly cease. Urban populations consume immense quantities of food, water, wood, petroleum, minerals, and other materials. Urbanization is sustained by a complex web of infrastructure; indeed, it may be said that the planet has slowly been covered by a veneer of infrastructure reaching to the remotest parts of the globe. This infrastructure exists to supply energy (electric transmission, oil and slurry pipelines); transport people and goods (roads and highways, bridges, trains, ships, systems of mass transit, airports); supply water (dams, reservoirs, aqueducts, canals, and pipes); and carry effluents and wastes from the cities (sewer systems, landfills). Recently, electronic highways and the airways constitute critical infrastructure grids. The degree to which people are tied into these infrastructure grids is made obvious when natural disasters disrupt and destroy infrastructure networks. The Florida hurricane of 1992, the floods in the American Midwest and in Europe in 1993, and the Los Angeles earthquake of 1994 all revealed the immediate importance and the vulnerability of infrastructure both within and beyond urban areas.

Cities impact the natural environment by releasing pollutants and wastes into the air, water, and ground. Many of these by-products of urban life are toxic, and in an effort to disperse them away from urban populations, they are typically dumped into landfills, spewed into the air, released into bodies of water, or shipped to distant locations. The environmental consequences of urban effluents are far-reaching. Air pollution is carried by winds far from cities, resulting in the acidification of water and soil all along the eastern seaboard of the United States and throughout Europe. Acid snow even shows up in one of the most remote mountain ranges in the United States, the Wind River Range in Wyoming (Rawlins 1993). Acid precipitation is killing forests and destroying fish and wildlife over large areas of Eastern Europe (Silvan 1992: 90). Some biologists have cited acidification as the most likely cause of a worldwide plunge in amphibian populations and many other life forms (Wilson 1992).

Since the mid-1980s, media coverage of global warming and the erosion of the ozone layer has provoked renewed public interest in environmental issues. Most of the carbon dioxide, methane, nitrous oxide, and chlorofluorocarbons that are spewed into the air are produced in urban areas. Despite well-publicized environmental regulations and agreements among the advanced industrialized nations, the worldwide emission of these gases continues to rise (White and Whitney 1992: 27–28). Even a modest change in the world's mean annual temperature over the next century is likely to induce large-scale environmental changes. For example, if some of the ice locked up in polar glaciers and ice caps were to melt, rising sea levels would immediately threaten to inundate the large number of cities situated close to estuaries, rivers, and seacoasts (31–32).

HOW CITIES MEDIATE BETWEEN HUMAN POPULATIONS AND THE ENVIRONMENT

The impact of human beings on their environments cannot be expressed as a straightforward correlation between population density and the environment. Obviously, human beings possess the capacity to mold their immediate social and physical environments and to mediate their relationship with the natural environment. Indeed (as noted earlier), this capacity is the defining characteristic and reason-for-being of cities. Cities can be viewed as *mechanisms of human intentionality*.[4] The social relationships, spatial forms, patterns of resource consumption, and other characteristics of cities are outcomes of human agency and do not arise by accident. The environmental impacts of cities may be mediated by urban land use policies and planning, by the quality and type of urban infrastructure, and by changes in the behavior of urban populations. Some of the most important policies administered by governments can be listed as follows:

1. Land use and planning. Cities may be either relatively compact, vertical, and densely populated, as in Hong Kong, Singapore, and Tokyo, or spread out and horizontal, as in Houston, Texas, and Phoenix, Arizona. Sprawled cities invade land that might be allocated for other uses. In addition, the transportation systems associated with urban sprawl are energy inefficient and polluting.

Urban planning and land use policies differ sharply among nations. Land use policies in some European countries have preserved greenbelts and other open spaces and reduced the conversion of agricultural land to urban uses. In Europe, central governments exert direct influence over city development and planning (Heidenheimer, Heclo, and Adams 1983: 237–273), and cities also have broad land use and planning authority. For example, Stockholm owns much of the land within its borders, and it is also able to bank land throughout its metropolitan region. Dutch municipalities also engage in extensive land banking (97, 240–243). In contrast, in the United States, sprawl is generally unregulated. Because of this, year by year suburban development swallows up open space at a rate far exceeding suburban population growth. For example, though the New York region's population grew by only 5 percent between 1964 and 1989, the amount of developed land increased by 61 percent. In this 25-year period, urban sprawl consumed 23 percent of the undeveloped land in the metropolitan area (Regional Plan Association 1990: 3).

2. Construction and design of the built environment. Cities may be composed of a built environment that is relatively energy efficient or inefficient or that

uses materials that minimize or maximize the use of renewal resources. Ver-
nacular architectural styles in desert regions utilize shading plants, breezeways,
ramadas, high ceilings, and thick insulating walls to keep buildings cool (an
example of the use of such strategies in modern architecture is the Arizona
Center in Phoenix). However, in the American Sunbelt, buildings rarely employ
these techniques. Instead, architects employ massive doses of air conditioning,
which allows them to build without regard to energy efficiency.

   3. Transportation. Urban populations may rely upon systems of mass transit,
as in Moscow, Russia, or on the automobile, as in most urban areas in the United
States. In Europe, governments heavily subsidize mass transit and make it expensive to drive automobiles (Heidenheimer, Heclo, and Adams 1983: 254–
259). In the United States, a combination of public subsidies for highways and
disinvestment in mass transit has resulted in a heavy reliance on the automobile.
In most metropolitan areas, less than 10 percent of commuters use public transportation, and in most Sunbelt cities, the proportion is 5 percent or less (Judd
and Swanstrom 1994: 209). As a result, in the United States there were 61 yards
of roadway per vehicle in 1970, but only 39 yards by 1986. Between 1970 and
1987, the distance Americans commuted by automobile within urban areas rose
by 50 percent (Wald 1990).

   There is a direct relationship between urban sprawl and gasoline consumption.
In sprawled-out Houston, residents use 567 gallons per capita per year, compared to 335 gallons per capita in the New York region (in Manhattan, gasoline
consumption is still less, 90 gallons per capita) (Newman and Kenworthy 1989:
26–27). Per capita gasoline use in the United States is 4 times as high as Europe's and almost 10 times as high as Japan's (van Vliet— 1992: 181). Even
so, autos dominate the physical structure of most cities in Europe (Deelstra 1992:
71). Autos account for a high percentage of all ozone-destroying and greenhouse
gases in Europe as well as in the United States (71). As a consequence, on both
continents automobile exhausts are a chief cause of acid precipitation.

   4. Use of water. Water use in cities continues to rise rapidly. The construction
of modern sewage systems late in the nineteenth century sharply increased water
consumption in European and U.S. cities, and consumption has steadily risen
since. The huge quantities of water expelled by cities is a major source of
pollution of groundwater, rivers, bays, and oceans.

   In the United States, a disproportionate share of the nation's population
growth since World War II has occurred in the Sunbelt. Typically, cities in the
Southwest use prodigious amounts of waters to maintain lawns, swimming
pools, fountains, and artificial ponds and lakes. In 1994 the nation's fastest-
growing city, Las Vegas, threatened to tap into underwater basins and aquifers
supplying water to a large part of the West if changes weren't made to allow it
to pipe more water from the Colorado River. This action was only the most
recent chapter in an increasingly desperate search for water by cities in the arid
Southwest.

   5. Disposal of solid wastes. Many cities in Europe and the United States are running out of space to dispose of their solid wastes and have, as a consequence, begun to search farther and farther afield for disposal sites. The problem of solid waste disposal is especially acute in the United States, where households produce more than twice the per capita volume of waste than households anywhere else in the world (van Vliet— 1992: 184). Solid waste dumps are a significant source of groundwater contamination. Some cities, such as New York City, dump large quantities of waste at sea.

6. *Sewage and toxic waste disposal.* Municipal sewage is a primary source of environmental pollution. Even in the advanced industrial nations with the most sophisticated sewer systems, large quantities of untreated sewage continue to be dumped into rivers and harbors. In Canada, for example, one third of the total volume of municipal sewage produced in the mid-1980s was discharged untreated (Richardson 1992: 153).

7. *Air pollution regulations.* Around the world, air pollution in urban areas is a significant, sometimes dangerous, problem. In 1988, 48 percent of Americans lived in areas that exceeded the national ambient air quality standards (van Vliet 1992: 188). In 1993, Mexico City was forced to order some industries to close temporarily because of dangerous air pollution levels. In 1988 Los Angeles violated air quality standards 176 days of the year. As a result of such extraordinary levels of pollution, the Los Angeles metropolitan area has been forced to adopt strict regulations requiring that all cars be converted to electricity or other "clean" fuels by the year 2007 ((Reinhold 1989). Government action does make a difference; in 1990 the Environmental Protection Agency reported that 10 million fewer Americans were breathing unhealthful air than a decade before (Stammer 1991).

As noted previously, there are far-reaching regional and global consequences of air pollution. Acid rain, the shrinking of the ozone layer, and the greenhouse effect are all interrelated, and all are linked to urban air pollution.

The impact of human populations on the environment cannot sensibly be discussed without considering how cities mediate that impact. Cities may be constructed and administered to use more or less land and to minimize or maximize the use of energy and other resources. They may build infrastructure and pursue policies that increase or reduce effluents and pollutants. These are policy choices presided over by governments.

CITIES, GOVERNMENTS, AND ENVIRONMENTAL POLICIES

National, subnational, and local governments interact in complex ways to implement environmental policies. To understand how pivotal cities are to the environmental policy agenda, it is necessary to (1) place cities within their national political contexts; (2) describe the governmental structures and relationships within urban areas; (3) describe the degree to which cities possess the autonomy to implement environmental policies; and (4) discuss the degree to which cities represent their citizens and can mobilize support for such environmental policies as recycling and energy conservation.

There is a broad popular impression that national governments preside over the most important environmental policies. This impression derives, no doubt, from the fact that most environmental policy emerged in an era in which the media made pollution a national issue and in which citizens expected national governmental leadership. In the United States, the federal government enacted a series of laws in the 1960s to clean up air and water. After a massive oil spill off the coast of Santa Barbara, California, in 1969, public concern about the environment peaked. Congress subsequently passed the National Environmental Protection Act of 1969, and President Richard Nixon created the Environmental Protection Agency, by executive order. Congress continued to refine legislation all through the 1970s and 1980s. Similarly, during the same period European nations have enacted a complex mix of environmental legislation.

National legislation in all Western countries is administered by some combination of national, subnational, and local governments. The decentralization of the policy process is particularly accentuated in the United States. Its exceptionally fragmented federal system dictates complicated enforcement procedures wherein federal agencies attempt to set standards for air pollution abatement, water quality control, and other matters, but state and local governments remain as the principal enforcers of many environmental laws (Robertson and Judd 1989: 321–353). More than half the environmental programs funded by governments in the United States are actually implemented by cities (Nicholson-Lord 1987). In addition, there are a wide variety of policies funded and administered either by state and local governments or solely at the local level, and these have significant impacts on the environment. Included in this category of policies would be landfill regulation, energy conservation and recycling, and the preservation of open space in and near urban areas.

Governmental structures and relationships within urban areas may facilitate or hinder the implementation of policies that impact the environment. In the United States, for example, national and state governments exercise no meaningful oversight over land use policies, and the multitude of local governments that make up most urban areas use zoning controls for their own often parochial purposes (Judd and Swanstrom 1994: 223–241). As a result, comprehensive regional planning simply cannot take place. Without planning, urban sprawl occurs mainly according to the logic of the property market.

The American pattern reflects the high degree of autonomy granted to municipalities in the United States' federal system (Judd 1995: 212–230). This autonomy makes regional environmental policies within urban areas difficult or impossible to achieve. Even so, for a long time individual cities have used their authority to build infrastructure and enact policies to manage urban environmental impacts.

Compared to cities, national governments are latecomers to the field of environmental policy. In the latter third of the nineteenth century, deteriorating conditions in the industrial cities forced them into an unprecedented round of infrastructure investments. Because of rising standards of public health and the availability of new technologies, cities in Europe and the United States undertook huge investments in water and sanitary sewer systems, transportation improvements (bridges, paved streets, streetcars), and parks. In the United States, the number of miles of sewer pipe laid increased fourfold from 1890 to 1909 (Teaford 1990). The consumption of water soared because the new sewer systems required huge volumes of water to flush wastes from the cities. The construction of integrated sewer systems and the adoption of new water filtration technologies, when combined with new building regulations and public health measures, quickly and dramatically reduced disease rates in cities in the first years of the twentieth century (Schultz 1989: 174).

Cities also invested in a variety of urban amenities. The Parks and City Beautiful movements, both supported by urban elites and a growing middle class, spawned demands for improved parks with ponds, formal gardens, bandstands, ball fields, broad tree-lined avenues, ornate public buildings, and other amenities. Urban dwellers began to expect a level of city services and amenities that was unthinkable only a few years earlier. The squalor of the nineteenth-century city began to yield to the relative safety, cleanliness, and health of the twentieth-century city. The rising expectations about what urban life could offer were also reflected in new ideas of town planning. In England, Ebenezer Howard and his disciples spread the gospel of garden cities (Creese 1966), while in the United States the suburbs became the object of Arcadian fantasies about the blending of countryside and city (Stilgoe 1988).

In response to the new wave of middle-class demands and also to accommodate the automobile and truck, in the 1920s another round of urban investment was initiated. Cities invested heavily in street paving, automated street lights, curbing, improved lighting, and airports. Though this constant process of urban infrastructure investment was slowed by the Great Depression and, subsequently, by World War II, it resumed at a furious pace after the war. An extraordinary period of central city urban renewal, highway building, and suburban construction was initiated in the 1950s, and in many ways, it has not run its course. An expensive, constantly expanding infrastructure network sustains the low-density urban patterns that have been given such exaggerated expression in the United States.

Though preoccupied with infrastructure development, the cities also took action to clean up some forms of environmental contamination. In England and the United States, chronic air pollution and some serious pollution episodes in the 1940s and 1950s brought, initially, local smoke ordinances aimed at reducing the use of coal (C. Jones 1975: 23). Smoke pollution abated, but it was soon replaced by factory and auto-related air pollution. Water pollution became a noxious problem as cities continued to pour their untreated sewage into rivers and harbors. Rachel Carson's book *Silent Spring* (1972) provoked concerns that environmental problems were truly global in nature, a point driven home by subsequent research showing that the residues of pesticides and poisons could be found in the tissues of animals and humans even in the Arctic. Only then did national governments become involved in environmental issues in a consequential way.

The phrase "think globally, act locally" expresses the idea that environmental problems are global, but the most effective political actions and policies are local. It is clear that contemporary environmental problems are closely linked to urbanization and therefore to the authority of governments within urban areas. Cities are the locus for democratic political expression. As David Harvey has observed, "Any political movement that does not imbed itself in the urban process is doomed to failure in advanced capitalist society" (Harvey 1989). Cities posses the ability to mobilize citizens on behalf of energy conservation, recycling, the preservation of open space, and other efforts (Gordon 1990).

CURRENT ISSUES INVOLVING CITIES AND THE ENVIRONMENT

In the advanced industrial nations, though governments preside over a complex mix of antipollution and conservation policies, few serious attempts have been made to reduce environmental impacts by changing consumption behaviors. This is no mere oversight; the contradiction between environmentalism and high resource consumption is embedded within environmental movements themselves. In the West, environmental consciousness and political action have evolved in step with prosperity. Young, educated, more prosperous urban dwellers are more environmentally minded than any other population sectors (Hays 1987: 40–52). As in the past, affluent urban dwellers have demanded relatively high levels of "aesthetic" urban amenities. In recent decades, the middle classes have broadened their scope to embrace concerns about the effects of pollutants and toxins and, since the 1970s, have become concerned about global issues such as rainforest destruction and the loss of wilderness and natural habitats (Hays 1987). In response, governments have adopted relatively strict pollution controls and have set aside wilderness and recreation areas. In general, policies to mitigate the effects of high consumption have been limited to some relatively minor conservation actions, such as recycling—embraced because it is practical but also relatively painless.

Because consumption is the defining cultural characteristic of life in the affluent Western nations, one must be skeptical that the kinds of environmental impacts that high consumption sustains—monocultural agricultural regimes, the proliferation of new toxic chemicals, destructive forestry practices, the production of new chemicals—will easily be curbed. Some environmental activists in the West have come to recognize the importance of changing patterns of consumption in the richer nations. The term *sustainable development* became popularized in 1987 when the World Commission on Environment and Development (WCED) used it to describe a process of economic growth with "the ability to ensure the needs of the present without compromising the ability of future generations to meet their own needs" (WCED 1987: 43; also see Kreimer 1993). It should be emphasized that although the idea of sustainable development has gained intellectual currency, no countries in the West currently engage in sustainable development, nor is it plausible to think their governments intend to pursue such policies.

In the developing nations, environmental concerns have been almost completely subordinated to the imperative of economic growth. These countries are urbanizing at a rapid rate, and their cities typically contain or are surrounded by festering slums often lacking even rudimentary infrastructure and services. In Latin American and South American cities, approximately 25 percent of urban residents lack direct access to drinking water, and they are therefore forced to rely on unfiltered and contaminated water (Di Pace et al. 1992: 213). A large number of sprawling slums are not served by sewage systems of any kind. Possibly as much as half of all solid wastes generated in the sprawling slums of Latin America are not picked up by public authorities (215). Crime and social disorder are pandemic and are not confined to the slums. Cities in Asia and Africa are also growing so rapidly that urban infrastructure is at the breakdown point (Pernia 1992; Wekwete 1992).

Urbanization in the Third World reveals that the quality of urban and natural environments is intimately linked. The governments of developing nations quite naturally regard "poverty and its consequences for the quality of life of the population [as] a more pressing need than are global climate change and macro environmental issues of world concern" (Di Pace et al. 1992: 209). As long as these conditions exist, the national governments of those countries will pursue policies to promote either rural resettlement (of the Amazon, for example) or the large-scale, even reckless, utilization of natural resources. Even the relatively modest antipollution and conservation policies pursued in the advanced nations will appear to be unaffordable luxuries.

The leaders of underdeveloped nations respond to their problems by promoting industrialization, rural resettlement, and the exploitation of their natural resources. The leaders of developing nations frequently express the suspicion that conservation is a gimmick being foisted on them to deny them the same level of prosperity as is available in the West. Those aspects of environmentalism tied to upper-middle lifestyles give weight to their suspicions. In 1987 two sociologists in the United States proposed the creation of the "Buffalo Commons," a vast national park to be created by enclosing all of the contiguous counties in the high plains containing two persons per square mile or less. Such a park would stretch from the northern border of North Dakota to parts of Texas and would be hundreds of miles wide in some places (Matthews 1993). From the perspective of the developing nations, it must sometimes seem that Western environmentalists regard the underdeveloped world as a Buffalo Commons, to be exploited for its natural resources in part but the rest to be preserved for biological diversity, the production of oxygen, and ecotourism.

The Third World is not alone in coping with intractable urban problems. The people of Eastern Europe live in a landscape that is extraordinarily polluted, a legacy of a forced industrialization initiated by the central planners of Communist governments (Silvan 1992). Upon taking power after World War II, the Communists dismantled local governments in most of the countries of Eastern Europe. Industrial development was promoted with no regard for its social or ecological effects. Urban infrastructure was ignored or badly built. The high-sulfur brown coal used in factories and power plants polluted soil and air, killing forests and drastically reducing ecological diversity (Silvan 1992: 90–93).

Without local governments, the citizens of Communist countries found it difficult or impossible to influence the policies that were bringing about these ecological disasters. Indeed, it is interesting that the authoritarian nature of the Communist states was expressed by the destruction of local governments. Cities are key components of governmental authority and primary implementors of a variety of public policies. In the twentieth century, as in the past, they will be central players in devising and implementing effective environmental policies.

The United States may well be entering a period in which the role of states and cities in environmental regulation will be enhanced and the powers of the national government reduced. Since the election of Republican majorities in the House and Senate in 1994, the political atmosphere has decidedly favored decentralizing policies to states and local governments. Environmental problems, however, do not respect governmental boundaries. It is probable that a sorting-out process will occur in which some environmental responsibilities will become (or remain) primarily local, while others will remain firmly in the hands of national governments or will become subject to international agreements. Cities will always play pivotal roles as mediators between people and the environment, but they will never again hold a monopoly over environmental policies.

NOTES

1. Research on cities and the environment is much more developed in Europe than in the United States; indeed, it is accurate to say that research in the United States is at a formative stage, at best. The most comprehensive treatment available is Willem van Vliet— (1992).

2. Though the distinction between the urban and the environmental is necessarily artificial, I employ it here for analytical purposes. Actually, there are few, if any, "natural" environments that are not impacted by urban infrastructure or institutions. Likewise, within urban areas, parks and other open spaces may logically be considered natural environments.

3. See Dogan and Kasarda (1988: 19) and Stren, White, and Whitney (1992: 2) for similar lists of the environmental impacts of urbanization.

4. This definition was inspired by Richard Knight's term "the intentional city" (Knight 1989: 225–226). Knight refers to the fact that cities are able to adopt policies that influence their economic destinies.

REFERENCES

Carson, Rachel. 1972. *Silent Spring*. New York: Houghton Mifflin.

Creese, Walter L. 1966. *The Search for Environment: The Garden City: Before and After*. New Haven: Yale University Press.

Cushman, John H. 1994. "Clinton Seeks Ban on Export of Hazardous Waste." *New York Times*, March 1, B2.

Davis, Mike. 1992. *City of Quartz*. New York: Vintage Books.

Deelstra, Tjeerd. 1992. "Western Europe." In Richard Stren, Rodney White, and Joseph Whitney, eds., *Sustainable Cities: Urbanization and the Environment in International Perspective*. Boulder, CO: Westview Press. 61–82.

Di Pace, Maria, Sergio Federovisky, Jorge E. Hardoy, Jorge H. Morello, and Alfredo Stein. 1992. "Latin America." In Richard Stren, Rodney White, and Joseph Whitney, eds., *Sustainable Cities: Urbanization and the Environment in International Perspective*. Boulder, CO: Westview Press. 205–228.

Dogan, Mattei, and John D. Kasarda, eds. 1988. *The Metropolis Era: A World of Giant Cities*. Vol. 1. Newbury Park, CA: Sage Publications.

Fischer, Claude S. 1984. *The Urban Experience*. New York: Harcourt Brace Jovanovich.

Gallion, Arthur B., and Simon Fraser. 1983. *The Urban Pattern: City Planning and Design*. 4th ed. New York: Van Nostrand Reinold Company.

Gordon, David, ed. 1990. *Green Cities: Ecologically Sound Approaches to Urban Space*. New York: Black Rose Books.

Harvey, David. 1989. *The Urban Experience*. Baltimore: Johns Hopkins University Press.

Hays, Samuel P., in collaboration with Barbara D. Hays. 1987. *Beauty, Health, and Permanence: Environmental Politics in the United States, 1955–1985*. Cambridge, MA: Cambridge University Press.

Heidenheimer, Arnold J., Hugh Heclo, and Carolyn Teich Adams. 1983. *Comparative Public Policy: The Politics of Social Choice in Europe and America*. New York: St. Martin's.

Jones, Charles O. 1975. *Clean Air: The Policies and Politics of Pollution Control*. Pittsburgh: University of Pittsburgh Press.

Jones, Emrys. 1976. *Towns and Cities*. London: Oxford University Press.

Jones, Emrys. 1990. *Metropolis: The World's Great Cities*. London: Oxford University Press.

Judd, Dennis R. 1995. "Cities, Political Representation, and the Dynamics of American Federalism." In Bryan D. Jones, ed., *The New American Politics: Reflections on Political Change and the Clinton Administration*. Boulder, CO: Westview Press. 212–230.

Judd, Dennis R., and Todd Swanstrom. 1994. *City Politics: Private Power and Public Policy*. New York: HarperCollins.

Knight, Richard V. 1989. "City Development and Urbanization: Building the Knowledge-Based City." In Richard V. Knight and Gary Gappert, eds., *Cities in a Global Society*. Urban Affairs Annual Reviews, vol. 35. Newbury Park, CA: Sage Publications. 223–244.

Kreimer, Alcira, et al., eds. 1993. *Towards a Sustainable Urban Environment: The Rio de Janeiro Study*. New York: World Bank.

Matthews, Anne. 1993. *Where the Buffalo Roam*. New York: Grove Press.

Mumford, Lewis. 1938. *The Culture of Cities*. New York: Harcourt Brace Jovanovich.

Newman, Peter G., and Jeffrey R. Kenworthy. 1989. "Gasoline Consumption and Cities." *Journal of the American Planning Association* 55 (winter): 24–30.

Nicholson-Lord, David. 1987. *The Greening of the Cities*. London: Routledge & Kegan Paul.

Oelschlaeger, Max. 1991. *The Idea of Wilderness*. New Haven, CT: Yale University Press.

Palen, John J. 1975. *The Urban World*. New York: McGraw-Hill.

Pernia, Ernesto M. 1992. "Southeast Asia." In Richard Stren, Rodney White, and Joseph Whitney, eds., *Sustainable Cities: Urbanization and the Environment in International Perspective*. Boulder, CO: Westview Press. 233–259.

Polanyi, Karl. 1944. *The Great Transformation*. Boston: Beacon Press.

Rawlins, C. L. 1993. *Sky's Witness: A Year in the Wind River Range*. New York: Henry Holt.

Regional Plan Association. 1990. *Annual Report, 1990*. New York: Regional Plan Association.

Reinhold, Robert. 1989. "Southern California Takes Steps to Curb Its Clean Air Pollution." *New York Times*, March 18.

Richardson, Nigel H. 1992. "Canada." In Richard Stren, Rodney White, and Joseph Whitney, eds., *Sustainable Cities: Urbanization and the Environment in International Perspective*. Boulder, CO: Westview Press. 145–168.

Robertson, David B., and Dennis R. Judd. 1989. *The Development of American Public Policy: The Structure of Policy Restraint*. New York: HarperCollins.

Sassen, Saskia. 1994. *Cities in a World Economy*. Thousand Oaks, CA: Pine Forge Press.

Schultz, Stanley K. 1989. *Constructing Urban Culture: American Cities and American Planning, 1800–1920*. Philadelphia: Temple University Press.

Shrybman, Steven. 1990. "International Trade and the Environment." *Alternatives* 17, no. 2: 20–29.

Silvan, Jurai. 1992. "Eastern Europe." In Richard Stren, Rodney White, and Joseph Whitney, eds., *Sustainable Cities: Urbanization and the Environment in International Perspective*. Boulder, CO: Westview Press. 83–104.

Stammer, Larry. 1991. "Smoggiest Cities See Dip in Pollution." *Los Angeles Times*, November 11, A1.

Stilgoe, John R. 1988. *Borderland: Origins of the American Suburb, 1820–1939*. New Haven: Yale University Press.

Stren, Richard, Rodney White, and Joseph Whitney, eds. 1992. *Sustainable Cities: Urbanization and the Environment in International Perspective*. Boulder, CO: Westview Press.

Teaford, Jon. 1990. *The Unheralded Triumph: City Government in America, 1870–1900*. Baltimore, MD: Johns Hopkins University Press.

van Vliet—, Willem. 1992. "The United States." In Richard Stren, Rodney White, and Joseph Whitney, eds., *Sustainable Cities: Urbanization and the Environment in International Perspective*. Boulder, CO: Westview Press. 169–204.

Wald, Matthew L. 1990. "How Dreams of Clean Air Get Stuck in Traffic." *New York Times*, March 11.

Ward, Barbara. 1976. *The Home of Man*. New York: W. W. Norton & Co.

Wekwete, K. H. 1992. "Africa." In Richard Stren, Rodney White, and Joseph Whitney, eds., *Sustainable Cities: Urbanization and the Environment in International Perspective*. Boulder, CO: Westview Press. 105–140.

White, Rodney, and Joseph Whitney. 1992. "Cities and the Environment: An Overview." In Richard Stren, Rodney White, and Joseph Whitney, eds., *Sustainable Cities: Urbanization and the Environment in International Perspective*. Boulder, CO: Westview Press. 8–52.

Wilson, Edward O. 1992. *The Diversity of Life* New York: W. W. Norton & Co.

Wolman, Abel. 1965. "The Metabolism of Cities." *Scientific American* (September): 179–188.

World Commission on Environment and Development (WCED). 1987. *Our Common Future*. London: Oxford University Press.

Chapter 29

National Urban Policy

Ronald K. Vogel

OVERVIEW OF THE FIELD

Since the New Deal, the government of the United States has been involved in urban affairs. The usual mechanism of federal involvement was the grants-in-aid system whereby the central government would establish grant programs embodying national priorities. State and local governments would apply for these grants, providing matching funds and meeting federal program requirements, thus implementing national policy (Kleinberg 1995; Mollenkopf 1983). By 1990, there were more than 500 categorical grants distributing more than $150 billion in federal aid to state and local governments (Rich 1993: 23).

Yet national urban policy has rarely been the result of deliberate, comprehensive, or strategic thinking about development policy for urban areas or the proper role of cities in the intergovernmental system (Kaplan 1990). Instead, urban policy has usually been a by-product of other national policy goals with respect to the economy, defense, transportation, health, education, welfare, or civil rights (Mohl 1993b). Thus, nonurban policy may be more important for cities than formal urban policy (Cuciti 1990; Kaplan 1995).

The ambivalence of Americans toward cities (Elazar 1967) is reflected in the lack of an integrated national urban policy. Federal neglect of cities changed to outright hostility during the Reagan and Bush administrations when the federal government drastically reduced urban aid while urban problems were worsening (Symposium 1995; Symposium 1992; Barnes 1990; Fainstein and Fainstein 1989).

The need for a coherent national urban policy has been vigorously debated through the years (Kaplan and James 1990). Urbanists, politicians, and policy experts differ on whether there is an urban crisis, whether a sustainable political coalition can be built to support an integrated urban policy, and what that policy would entail. In this chapter, I review the nature of the present urban crisis, the evolution of national policy affecting urban areas, and the current debate over whether to pursue a place-based strategy to aid cities or to focus on universal programs to aid individuals.

THE NATURE OF THE URBAN CRISIS?

Although there has been much talk of an urban crisis, there is no agreement that there is an urban crisis or what form that crisis takes (Goldwin 1968; Sommer 1993). Instead, the crisis has been redefined as one set of urban issues replaces another on the "national agenda" in response to changing federal priorities, shifting electoral fortunes, or media attention to urban problems (Weiher 1989).

Urban has become synonymous with the *central city*—places of population loss, economic decline, crime, fiscal crisis, high taxes, poor services, deteriorated housing, concentrated poverty, and minorities. "The central city was where urban problems were isolated and contained" (Ames et al. 1992: 199). This is contrasted with the suburbs, which were associated with growth, new housing, jobs, good schools, and an overall good quality of life. It is this disparity between central cities and suburbs that has come to define the urban crisis today. A snapshot of trends associated with the urban crisis is provided in Table 29.1.

With respect to the economy, the urban crisis is manifested in higher unemployment rates and poverty rates and lower median family income compared to the suburbs (Wolman et al. 1992; Anglin and Holcomb 1992). Crime has also reached crisis proportions, especially violent crime and homicide in central cities (Gordon et al. 1992; McClain 1995). The inner city is experiencing a crisis of housing affordability that leaves homeownership out of the reach of most low-income inner-city residents (Schwartz et al. 1992). Public education has stopped functioning in many central cities with dropout rates as high as 50 percent (Raffel et al. 1992: 264). The cities' problems are exacerbated by a fiscal crisis (Ladd 1994; Bowman, MacManus, and Mikesell 1992), which leaves cities struggling to provide even basic services (Bahl, Duncombe, and Schulman 1990) or invest in infrastructure (Pagano 1990).

Racial segregation in the American metropolis is closely related to the myriad of urban problems (Darden, Duleep, and Galster 1992). Problems associated with economic restructuring, poverty, crime, housing, education, and fiscal stress all unduly impact minorities concentrated in the central cities, limiting their economic and educational opportunities. A major factor in the concentration of minorities in central cities is racial discrimination, including practices such as steering and redlining (Darden, Duleep, and Galster 1992). However, the social isolation of minorities in central cities and growing central city–suburban disparities also are related to economic restructuring (i.e., the transformation from

Table 29.1
Selected Statistics for 94 Large U.S. Cities[a]

	1960	1970	1980	1990
Population as percent of U.S.	26.1%	22.5%	20.9%	20.1%
Percent minority population	18.9	24.1	37.1	40.1
Unemployment rate	5.5	4.7	7.3	8.1
Percent employed in manufacturing	25.3	22.1	17.4	14.0
Median family income as a percent of U.S. median family income	106.7	100.4	92.6	87.5
Family poverty rate	17.2	11.0	13.6	15.1
Percent population in census tracts with more than 40% poverty	8.0	5.1	8.1	10.8
Female headed families with own chldren as percent of all families	7.9[b]	10.4	13.8	14.5

[a]Based on the 10 largest metropolitan statistical area (MSA) central cities in 1980 with the exception of Anchorage, Fort Lauderdale, Jackson (MS), Jersey City, Newark, and Amarillo, for which tract-level data were not available in 1960.
[b]Estimated.

Source: U.S. Census data for 1960, 1970, and 1980, as compiled by John D. Kasarda, *Urban Underclass Database Machine Readable Files* (NY: Social Science Research Council, 1992, 1993) (except as noted). Calculations by U.S. Department of Housing and Urban Development. Reproduced from: U.S. Congress, Office of Technology Assessment (1995), *The Technological Reshaping of Metropolitan America*, OTA-ETI-643 (Washington, DC: U.S. Government Printing Office), September, p. 88.

a manufacturing-based economy to a service-based economy), which has led to the development of an inner-city underclass (W. Wilson 1987).

HISTORICAL DEVELOPMENT OF NATIONAL URBAN POLICY

Although it took the riots of the 1960s to make us notice the urban crisis, it was actually many years in the making. Kleinberg (1995) traces the evolution of federal programs and activity shaping local development to explain the existing fragmented metropolis and associated central city–suburban disparities. More often than not, national urban policy has been a product of disjointed incrementalism, the by-product of other national priorities or action. Deliberate efforts to craft a national urban policy are rare.

The New Deal Era

Under the New Deal, the federal government instituted a number of programs to help stimulate the economy and provide work relief for millions of unemployed Americans. These programs had dramatic impacts upon the urban land-scape, providing major public infrastructure and housing in the central cities but also providing mortgage subsidies and insurance that would lead to massive suburbanization (Kleinberg 1995: 97). In addition, they stabilized the city-based industrial economy and led to the development of a fairly large and stable middle class.

"Decentralized administration" or "localization" became the model form of federal-state-local relations in redistributive programs such as public housing and urban renewal. This has proved to be an obstacle in implementing these programs, as middle-class constituencies at the local level have been able to dominate the local administration of these programs, preventing public housing from being placed in suburban areas, for instance, or altering the purposes of urban renewal from neighborhood revitalization to "slum removal."

A segregated metropolis was a foregone conclusion not only because of the difficulty of placing public housing in the suburbs but by the Federal Housing Administration's refusal to insure mortgages in central city neighborhoods or to provide loan assistance to African Americans. This led to continued decline of the inner city, spurring more middle-class and white flight, and to the concentration of African Americans in the cities (115).

Post–World War II—Suburbanization and Urban Renewal

Following World War II, central cities were greatly affected by dual migration involving middle-class out-migration to new jobs and housing in the suburbs and in-migration of minorities and poorer groups from rural areas (Kleinberg: 1995: 121). Kleinberg traces these trends to New Deal housing policies and the interstate highway system that encouraged middle-class suburbanization while New Deal agricultural policies to limit agricultural production and World War II policies that led to "mechanization of Southern agriculture" displaced "millions of farm laborers and tenants" from rural areas (121). The interstate highway system inevitably led to the multicentered metropolis, disrupting established minority and working-class neighborhoods in the inner city (Kleinberg 1995; Angotti 1993; Mohl 1993a).

Dual migration, interstate highways, and economic decline placed tremendous pressures on cities, leading to the deterioration of inner-city neighborhoods and decline in the central business districts. The federal response was to propose a national program of urban redevelopment in the Housing Act of 1949. Initially, the focus was to remove slums and replace them with public housing. But within a short time, the act was amended, shifting the emphasis in urban renewal from housing to urban redevelopment (Kleinberg 1995: 122, 145).

The War on Poverty

President Lyndon Johnson's War on Poverty heralded a new day in intergovernmental relations with the advent of creative federalism. Under creative federalism, the federal government's aid to communities would bypass not only states but even city government as the federal government funded community action agencies that were in many cases independent of local government. There was tremendous proliferation in the number of categorical grants, which served as the primary vehicle for Johnson's Great Society programs.

Johnson's antipoverty effort was intended to empower the poor and provide them the means to take more direct control over the social welfare system by increasing and improving social services to the poor (e.g., Head Start), coordinating local public and private assistance to the poor, and increasing participation of the poor in poverty programs through "maximum feasible participation" (Kleinberg 1995: 158). However, mayors objected to the introduction of the poor with their new power base and resources thrust into the local decision-making arena. Business elites were dismayed by the power of the poor to upset urban renewal focused on slum removal or commercial development. Social service agencies resented the criticism and intrusion of the poor into their decision making and the establishment of rival services (163).

By 1968, the federal government changed the thrust of national urban policy away from maximum feasible participation. The new Department of Housing and Urban Development (HUD) was created in 1965 (Mayer 1995) and launched the Model Cities program. Model Cities was designed to "be a new start, aimed at combining more sensitive physical renewal with expanded social services and improved service coordination while avoiding the turbulence of the Community Action Program" (Kleinberg 1995: 176).

Model Cities was originally conceived as a pilot program with a small number of cities to be identified and offered major federal aid to combat the problems of poverty and inner-city decline. To build a congressional support, the program eventually was expanded to include 66 cities (177). The initial thrust of Model Cities involved prospective cities engaging in intensive comprehensive planning to renew slum neighborhoods. Selected cities would then receive annual grants over five years to implement the plans. Cities would be provided wide discretion in the use of federal money and could use the action grants as the local matching share for other federal categorical grants (178).

The Model Cities program clearly put the mayors back in charge of the urban revitalization. The City Demonstration Agency, under the mayor's control, would develop plans and receive federal aid to implement the plans. The aim of antipoverty programs was no longer to empower the poor or overturn the prevailing community power structure.

Nixon's New Federalism

Early in the Nixon administration, some efforts were made to fashion a national urban policy that tied central city decline and growth policy. In the early 1970s, there was concern that there would be a surge in population, perhaps as many as 100 million people, most concentrated in a few giant megalopolises

(Orlebeke 1990). This led to calls for new towns and the appending of growth policy to urban policy. Growth policy would eventually fall by the wayside as migration trends reversed and birthrates declined. Urban policy was soon replaced with New Federalism and central city concerns relegated to the back burner as Richard Nixon declared the national urban crisis over (Orlebeke 1990).

New Federalism involved a reorientation of the role of the central government in policy making. Between 1963 and 1968, 400 new categorical grants had been created (Kaplan 1995: 663). Under New Federalism, categorical grants were to be scaled back. In their place, the national government would provide broad direction for urban policy through block grants and revenue sharing, leaving localities to use the money as they saw fit. Urban problems were to be tackled from below, with the federal government providing the fiscal resources to allow the local government to solve its own problems. Thus, New Federalism is also sometimes referred to as Fiscal Federalism.

Over a five-year period, more than $30 billion was transferred to states and local governments under revenue sharing with no strings attached to the money. Revenue sharing entailed a major shift in national urban policy away from targeting aid to places based upon need or distress. Many of the cities receiving aid were in the suburbs, and central cities did not have to direct the aid to poorer neighborhoods or antipoverty programs. Many large cities spent the money on basic services such as police and fire instead of antipoverty programs (Kleinberg 1995: 191–192).

The Nixon administration also proposed the consolidation of a number of categorical grants to block grants (Rich 1993). While not entirely successful in this effort, partially because of fear that the real intention was to reduce programs and aid to urban areas, two new block grants were created that became important elements of national urban policy: the Comprehensive Employment and Training Act (CETA) in 1973 and the Community Development Block Grant (CDBG) in 1975 (Kleinberg 1995: 195; Rich 1993: 30).

As a block grant, CDBG provided local governments with more discretion, flexibility, and certainty in planning local development. However, it also reduced the targeting of federal urban aid to larger and older central cities. CDBG involved a regional redistribution of urban aid from the Northeast and Midwest to the Sunbelt and from larger, older (and often more distressed) central cities to suburban and nonmetropolitan cities (Kleinberg 1995: 199; Rich 1993: 89, 103). Within cities, CDBGs meant that federal urban aid was no longer targeted to distressed or poor neighborhoods or even antipoverty programs. Cities were free to identify their own priorities (Rich 1993: chaps. 2–3).

Carter's New Partnership

New Federalism, and its associated decentralization and defunding, marked a great retreat from the federal government's commitment to antipoverty programs and efforts to empower and target aid to the poor. Ironically, although President

Jimmy Carter was more sympathetic to the plight of the nation's cities, growing federal budget deficits, a severe national recession, and high inflation limited his ability to propose major new initiatives. It was in the Carter administration that urban policy programs were faced with real budgetary cuts and greater reliance placed on a market strategy to revitalize urban areas (Kleinberg 1995: 210).

Carter set in place an antirecessionary stimulus package and proposed a "New Partnership" with cities, states, and private industry by leveraging investment in inner cities through various incentives offered to the private sector. Although a proposed national development bank was never created, a new grant program, the Urban Development Action Grant (UDAGs), was to be a major legacy of his national urban policy. Carter retargeted urban aid to central cities facing severe economic decline. It was hoped that a combination of antirecessionary stimulus programs (fiscal and public works), UDAGs (economic development targeted to large economically depressed cities), alongside the existing CDBG program (broader community development but retargeted to cities in severe economic decline), and a revamped CETA program focusing on job training and public employment for the hard-core unemployed would lead to greater local revenue and job growth addressing the fiscal incapacity of cities and the great unemployment problems (Kleinberg 1995: 210–213; Rich 1993: 37–43).

Carter also empaneled a national commission to chart an agenda for the 1980s, including solutions to the urban crisis (United States 1980a, 1980b). Carter was forced to repudiate his own commission's recommendation that urban aid should be targeted to individuals as opposed to places, including providing inner-city unemployed residents with assistance in relocating to areas with greater job prospects (Orlebeke 1990: 198).

Urban policy, however, took a back burner to the growing federal budget deficits and problems in the international arena. Carter's fiscal conservatism led him to favor a more restrained intervention in urban problems than traditional liberal democratic policies, ultimately leading to Senator Ted Kennedy's challenge in the Democratic primaries in 1980. CDBGs and UDAGs produced a lot of development in urban areas but had a poor record of actually producing jobs or increasing local tax revenues, and the aid was still not targeted on poor neighborhoods within those cities, and the shift away from social services to physical development remained. In addition, UDAGs heralded a shift from economic development targeted to the unemployed to economic development targeted to business. UDAGs set the foundation for the local public-private partnerships for economic and community development that was to become the cornerstone of the Reagan urban policy (Kleinberg 1995: 211, 224). Carter found it easier to talk of a comprehensive national urban policy than to craft one (Kaplan 1990; Schambra 1990).

Retrenchment—Reagan and the Aftermath

Carter had attempted to fashion an integrated national urban policy. The Reagan approach was to substitute national economic policy for urban policy and to restore dual federalism embodied in his own version of New Federalism that entailed program turnbacks and elimination or consolidation of categorical grants into block grants. Budget and economic policy would lead to healthy cities. If the nation's economy was strong, its cities, and the people who lived in them, would be strong. This led to greatly reduced federal involvement in urban affairs and major cutbacks in federal aid to state and local government (Cuciti 1990; Warren 1990).

If there was an urban crisis, it was the result of misguided governmental policy that interfered with the proper workings of the marketplace. National intervention in urban areas eclipsed local sovereignty, which would only be restored if the federal government stopped fostering local dependence on Washington through grants-in-aid, mandates, and intrusive regulations. This dual sovereignty philosophy nicely reinforced the Reagan economic program of large tax cuts and budget cuts (Kaplan and James 1990).

Urban programs were specifically targeted for large cuts. Between 1980 and 1990, Caraley (1992) reports a 46 percent cut "or some $26 billion in constant 1990 dollars" from "grant programs that benefited city governments" (8) (see also Ladd 1994). Budget cuts of 57 percent gutted and decimated HUD, which was also embroiled in several scandals and corruption. Urban interests or concerns were effectively barred from influencing national policy making during the Reagan years (Berkman 1990; Wood and Klimkowsky 1990: 256).

Whether by design or accident, the structural deficits ensured that there would not be money available for large domestic policies or urban revitalization programs. Further, by withdrawing existing financial support from the local level, the Reagan administration ensured that many programs "turned back" to the states and localities would be discontinued, which corresponded with his conservative ideology that government should provide only the most basic services that the market would not provide. Urban problems were moral failures on the part of individuals and not a result of an economy that did not provide sufficient jobs or a political structure that segregated people in the metropolis by race and class. Distinctions were made between the "truly needy" and thus "deserving" and those "welfare cheats." Few cities or states were in a position to take on added service responsibilities when faced with their own fiscal crises (Orlebeke 1990: 200; Palmer and Sawhill 1984).

The one new urban policy initiative advocated by Kemp and endorsed by George Bush was the Enterprise Zone program, which would provide incentives and tax breaks to businesses that relocated or expanded in designated areas that had concentrated poverty or high unemployment (Barnes 1990). Ironically, the Enterprise program was finally enacted after the Los Angeles riots but vetoed by Bush because it included some tax increases in the bill; he had campaigned on a platform of no new taxes.

Rediscovering the Cities—Clinton and Empowerment

During the 1992 presidential elections, Bill Clinton called for greater attention to the plight of cities and received much support from cities in the Northeast and Midwest. Clinton's election brought a change in federal posture toward cities. Mayors were once again invited to the White House, and cities and urban problems were once again placed on the national agenda. An immediate move that demonstrated Clinton's commitment to tackle urban problems was the appointment of two popular mayors to cabinet-level positions—Henry Cisneros at HUD and Federico Peña at Transportation (Shafroth 1993: 2).

For the first few months of Clinton's presidency, it looked as if the cities would get what they wanted out of the administration. Clinton proposed an antirecessionary package to assist cities in economic recovery. The antirecessionary package called for Congress to pass a $30 billion economic stimulus program; $10 billion was to be spent by the summer of 1993 to get out of the recession by funding summer youth employment and public infrastructure projects already waiting to go in cities across America.

Clinton's proposal was based upon a U.S. Conference of Mayor's proposal (Shafroth 1993: 1; Zuckerman 1992: 2905). Much of the money was to come from the peace dividend that never materialized. Clinton initially pushed for the antirecession package, but he was distracted by other issues and it was never passed amid concerns over deficit reduction. This was not a sign that boded well for the nation's mayors.

The cornerstone of Clinton's national urban policy was the Empowerment Zone program offered as a way to revitalize distressed inner-city neighborhoods (U.S. Department of Housing and Urban Development 1995; Hambleton 1995). About $3.5 billion is to be spent in the Empowerment Zone demonstration program. Although sharing similarities with the Enterprise Zones advocated by Reagan and Bush, there are important differences. Clinton's Empowerment Zones emphasize "the coordination of government aid to distressed areas, rather than tax breaks for business that locate there" (Katz 1993: 1880). Community building, including infrastructure investment and human capital development, is emphasized as much as tax credits and business incentives to create jobs.

The Empowerment Zone program ties the conservative appeal of Enterprise Zones that emphasize private investment, business development, and an entrepreneurial spirit as the way to create jobs with a return to the 1960s liberal orientation of government intervention to remake people and communities. Community plans under the Empowerment Zone program were to be targeted specifically to poor neighborhoods in central cities. In addition, reminiscent of the 1960s antipoverty programs, the community plans were to be a grassroots product where poor people in the targeted areas decided upon programmatic emphasis and priorities. The role of the city was to coordinate and support grassroots planning.

The program was set up as a demonstration program. Originally there were to be nine Empowerment Zones, six urban and three rural. The urban zones were targeted to large and distressed cities. HUD received over 500 applications from communities to be designated Empowerment or Enterprise cities. Atlanta, Baltimore, Chicago, Detroit, New York, and Philadelphia/Camden were chosen as the original six Empowerment cities, later supplemented with the addition of Los Angeles and Cleveland (U.S. Congress, OTA 1995: 36). Although ostensibly the cities were to be chosen competitively, it was almost a foregone conclusion which cities would be selected. The Empowerment cities receive up to $100 million to spend over a 10-year period.

An additional 60 Enterprise communities were designated. These cities qualified for about $3 million in federal aid. Although not a lot of additional money will come to these Enterprise communities, the federal government would "take a more active role in coordinating economic development and federal aid in all of the designated zones" (Katz 1993: 1880). Communities designated Empowerment or Enterprise communities were required to have a strategic plan to use the resources, and this plan was to be the result of a grassroots effort. Additionally, HUD has set aside other grants to draw upon in support of Empowerment and Enterprise community programs, and the Treasury Department will provide tax credits to businesses.

Aside from the Empowerment Zone program, there are no other specifically urban policies on the horizon. There has been little in the way of specific targeted urban policy, but when added together, there are quite a few national policies that can help urban areas. Clinton administration priorities in health care, welfare reform, and crime legislation all would have consequences for urban areas. But the Republican sweep of the House and Senate in 1994 ended any real chance for specific urban aid programs. Some argue that given the weak position of cities, it makes more sense tactically to try to accomplish urban concerns through universal programs rather than place-based (targeted to cities) programs, which cannot generate sufficient political support (W. Wilson 1987).

Although there is a desperate need for a national urban policy that is focused and well funded, there is little reason to expect one to be created, given the budgetary and political constraints. The Empowerment Zones are at best a demonstration program and will probably have limited impact. Lemann (1994) believes that the Empowerment Zone program is based on a faulty model of urban revitalization that is premised on making ghetto neighborhoods attractive for business investment and job creation. According to Lemann, this antipoverty strategy failed in the 1960s and will have no more success in the 1990s.

420   *Problems and Policy*

ISSUES IN NATIONAL URBAN POLICY MAKING

Should There Be a National Urban Policy?

Many observers believe that a comprehensive national urban policy is both politically infeasible and unwise. The *President's Commission for a National Agenda for the Eighties* (United States 1980a, 1980b) claimed that urban problems were local problems and that there was no need for a comprehensive national urban policy. If there was a need for federal aid, it was to assist individuals (rather than places) to leave declining cities and pursue opportunities elsewhere. Although the Carter administration repudiated the commission's findings, these ideas formed the basis for the Reagan era urban policy of a nonurban policy and hostility to cities (Wood 1991).

Some urbanists advocate a nonurban policy approach for pragmatic reasons (Kaplan 1995; Kaplan and James 1990). They argue that domestic programs targeted to people, rather than urban policies targeted to places, have greater support among the public and ultimately benefit cities more than place-specific programs. Programs targeted at individuals (e.g., income support and job training) will reach inner-city residents without the programs being labeled urban policy. The argument is that the way to bring cities back into the mainstream is to promote policies that are aimed at individuals and universal.

Others argue that a formal integrated and comprehensive national urban policy is necessary. Wood (1995) criticizes Kaplan's abandonment of a national urban policy focused on places (i.e., cities). He argues that people live in places, and national urban policy must take this directly into account. Kantor (1991) calls for a greater federal role in regulating urban development to liberate cities from economic dependency on private business and allow for greater local initiative to undertake progressive social policy.

President Clinton's *National Urban Policy Report* calls for a continued strong federal presence to assist urban areas and residents (U.S. Department of Housing and Urban Development 1995). This is consistent with the Office of Technology Assessment (OTA) position that national urban policy should embrace the best of both people and place policies to "address the problems of distressed urban places and their residents" (U.S. Congress, OTA 1995: 29). This could take the form of assisting some poorer residents to move to places with greater economic opportunities, improving urban mass transit to ensure that poorer inner-city residents can physically get to job sites in the suburbs, and reinvesting in depressed inner-city neighborhoods (e.g., Enterprise and Empowerment Zones).

However, the reality of federal budget deficits and the Republican sweep of the Congress in 1994 suggest that both people and place urban policies are likely to be reduced or eliminated in the future. Recognizing these constraints, the Clinton administration has made efforts to shift urban policy from an exclusive focus on central cities—for which it is difficult to fashion an electoral or congressional coalition—to a focus on metropolitan regions tying the fortunes of central cities and suburbs (U.S. Department of Housing and Urban Development 1995; Cisneros 1995a, b). The Empowerment Zone and Enterprise Zone programs would target places—distressed inner-city neighborhoods. At the same time, nonurban people policies that would benefit cities include education and job training, welfare reform, crime policy, and universal health insurance. But the thrust of Clinton's proposed urban policy bears as much or more resemblance to conservative recommendations (Heritage Foundation 1992) than big-city mayors' or liberal democrats' (Berkman 1990). The Clinton administration offers empathy, access, and voiced concern. Even before the Republican sweep of Congress in 1994, the Clinton administration did not offer a comprehensive urban policy, money, or follow-through.

Obstacles to National Urban Policy Making

Few presidents have sought to establish a clear and comprehensive national urban policy and make it a centerpiece of their domestic policy (Nenno 1995). That is not to say that all presidents have been unconcerned with the problems of cities. Instead, nonurban policy has substituted for urban policy (e.g., health policy, welfare policy, transportation policy) (Cuciti 1990). Domestic policies, other than urban policy, have proven more amenable to electoral politics and coalition building in the Congress (Barnes 1990). Now urban issues only come into the national consciousness after outbreaks of civil disturbance and riots or dramatic incidents of inner-city violence that receive media coverage.

There are many obstacles to national urban policy making including limited knowledge concerning urban problems (their causes, consequences, and solutions), institutional barriers (budget deficits, federalism, limited local autonomy, weakness of HUD), and political obstacles (Kaplan and James 1990). Many factors account for the reticence of actors in the American political system to design and implement a strong national urban policy. First is the American ambivalence toward cities, which means that national institutions will be reluctant to pursue urban policy aggressively (Elazar 1967).

Second, suburban interests are stronger than central city interests, brought on by three decades of suburbanization (Schneider 1992). This makes it difficult to find enough "urban" votes in the Congress. Cities are less important in candidate selection and national electoral coalitions. Suburban residents feel few ties to the central city. Further complicating the ability to forge an urban coalition is the nonrepresentative character of the U.S. Senate (Caraley 1992).

Third, economic restructuring has divided urban interests as cities compete for business (Kantor 1991). Sunbelt cities have different problems than old industrial cities. It is harder to fashion a united front.

Fourth, the large deficits preclude ambitious national urban initiatives (i.e., a Marshall Plan for cities) (Reischauer 1990).

Fifth, the American political system is more suited to incrementalism than rational comprehensive policy making. Efforts to construct a comprehensive urban policy end up being laundry lists of programs rather than an integrated urban policy. Comprehensive urban policy making suggests targeting on the basis of need, but targeting a set of programs for central cities leads to programs without a constituency for adoption (Mollenkopf 1983, 1995).

Sixth, urban problems are complex. There is some doubt as to whether social scientists can comprehend causes of urban problems, let alone devise appropriate solutions. In addition, successfully implementing urban programs is a challenge because it requires coordinating the actions of several different agencies and levels of government (Kaplan and James 1990).

Finally, a major problem in forging a national urban policy is the weak institutional capacity of HUD (Wood and Klimkowsky 1990). It suffers from low prestige (257), competes with several other federal departments over programs and budgets (258), suffers a weak clientele base with conflicting interests (259), is responsible for implementing complex, infeasible, or underfunded programs that often conflict (261), has limited jurisdiction over programs affecting urban development (262), does not have a "monopoly" of expertise in housing or urban development, and lacks an institutional basis of support in the federal government, leaving it victim to shifting priorities and ideologies of the president (266). Wood and Klimkowsky (1990) believe that "the symbolic implications of the abolition of HUD probably would be stronger than the functional implications" (275). The Clinton administration did consider eliminating HUD in December 1994 (Cisneros 1995a).

To succeed, national urban policy must be attentive to problems of coordination and the problem of congressional logrolling that makes it difficult to target urban programs. Given the obstacles to effective urban policy making at the national level, there is considerable debate, then, about whether it is even wise to try to create a comprehensive national urban policy.

DIRECTIONS FOR FUTURE RESEARCH

Several conclusions can be drawn from this review of the literature on national urban policy. First, urbanists must devote renewed attention to the actual conditions that prevail in urban areas. Discussion of the nature of urban problems and whether this constitutes an urban crisis necessarily entails value judgments. However, much of the debate concerning urban problems is based more upon myths, misconceptions, or outright falsehoods than on empirical reality.

Second, urbanists need to engage in more careful thought about what "urban" and "urban policy" actually entail. When we live in an urban society, it may no longer be productive to talk of urban problems. By an *urban policy*, do we mean a policy to cherish and revitalize the physical city, a policy to enhance individual quality of life, whether by universal or targeted policies, or a policy to address the "underclass" problem concentrated in cities? The recent movement toward relabeling *urban* as *metropolitan* is a step in this direction (Mollenkopf 1995). But cities need a substantive urban policy more than a change in rhetoric.

Third, more awareness and understanding of how the interorganizational network of urban policy making operates and what policies it can effectively pursue would help to clarify what role is left for Washington in an era of fiscal constraint, the prevalence of market ideology, and the inability to fashion a national urban coalition. Urbanists have tended to decry national policy priorities and actions over the years. There can be no doubt that cities have been greatly shaped by national activity over the last 70 years and that the central government has been abrogating its responsibility to cities and the citizens who live in them. Yet urban policy also is a function of state, local, private, and nonprofit initiatives.

In spite of the "crises" that ravage the cities, they have proved remarkably resilient and show signs of renewed vigor as we enter the twenty-first century. Yet this must be tempered by the evidence that the actual quality of life experienced by inner-city residents has been declining over the last several decades. No doubt, state and local initiative is important, but without direct federal aid and intervention in the form of a national urban policy, it is unlikely that cities can effectively address the myriad of problems they face.

REFERENCES

Ames, C. David, Nevin C. Borwn, Mary Helen Callahan, Scott B. Cummings, Sue Marx Smock, and Jerome M. Ziegler. 1992. "Rethinking of American Urban Policy." *Journal of Urban Affairs* 14, nos. 3–4: 197–216.

Anglin, Roland, and Briavel Holcomb. 1992. "Poverty in Urban America Policy Options." *Journal of Urban Affairs* 14, nos. 3–4: 447–468.

Angotti, Thomas. 1993. *Metropolis 2000: Planning, Poverty and Politics*. New York: Routledge.

Bahl, Roy, William Duncombe, and Wanda Schulman. 1990. "The New Anatomy of Urban Fiscal Problems." In Marshall Kaplan and Franklin James, eds., *The Future of National Urban Policy*. Durham, NC: Duke University Press.

Barnes, William R. 1990. "Urban Policies and Urban Impacts after Reagan." *Urban Affairs Quarterly* 25, no. 4: 562–573.

Berkman, Ronald. 1990. *In the National Interest: The 1990 Urban Summit*. New York: Twentieth Century Fund Press.

Bowman, H. John, Susan MacManus, and John L. Mikesell. 1992. "Mobilizing Resources for Public Services: Financing Urban Governments." *Journal of Urban Affairs* 14, nos. 3–4: 311–335.

Caraley, Demetrios. 1992. "Washington Abandons the Cities." *Political Science Quarterly* 107: 1–30.

Cisneros, G. Henry. 1995a. "Legacy for a Reinvented HUD Charting a New Course in Changing and Demanding Times." *City Scape: A Journal of Policy Development and Research* 1, no. 3: 145–152.

Cisneros, G. Henry. 1995b. "Regionalism: The New Geography of Opportunity." Washington, D.C.: U.S. Department of Housing and Urban Development.

Cuciti, L. Peggy. 1990. "A Non Urban Policy: Recent Policy Shifts Affecting Cities."
    In Marshall Kaplan and Franklin James, eds., *The Future of National Urban
    Policy.* Durham, NC: Duke University Press.

Darden, T. Joe, Harriet Orcutt Duleep, and George C. Galster. 1992. "Civil Rights in
    Metropolitan America." *Journal of Urban Affairs* 14, nos. 3–4: 469–496.

Elazar, J. Daniel. 1967. "Are We a Nation of Cities?" In Robert A. Goldwin, ed., *A
    Nation of Cities.* Chicago: Rand McNally.

Fainstein, Susan, and Norman Fainstein. 1989. "The Ambivalent State: Economic De-
    velopment Policy in the U.S. Federal System under the Reagan Administration."
    Urban Affairs Quarterly, 25, no. 1: 41–62.

Goldwin, Robert A. 1968. *A Nation of Cities.* Chicago: Rand McNally and Company.

Gordon, Diana R., Jack R. Greene, Diane Steelman, and Samuel Walker. 1992. "Urban
    Crime Policy." *Journal of Urban Affairs* 14, nos. 3–4: 359–375.

Hambleton, Robin. 1995. "The Clinton Policy for Cities: A Transatlantic Assessment."
    Planning Practice and Research 10, nos. 3–4: 359–377.

Kantor, Paul. 1991. "A Case for a National Urban Policy: The Governmentalization of
    Economic Dependency." *Urban Affairs Quarterly* 26, no. 3: 394–415.

Kaplan, Marshall. 1990. "National Urban Policy: Where Are We Now? Where Are We
    Going?" In Marshall Kaplan and Franklin James, eds., *The Future of National
    Urban Policy.* Durham, NC: Duke University Press.

Kaplan, Marshall. 1995. "Urban Policy, an Uneven Past, an Uncertain Future." *Urban
    Affairs Review* 30, no. 5: 662–680.

Kaplan, Marshall, and Franklin James, eds. 1990. *The Future of National Urban Policy.*
    Durham, NC: Duke University Press.

Katz, Jeffrey. 1993. "Enterprise Zones Struggle to Make Their Mark." *Congressional
    Quarterly* (July 17), 1880–1881.

Kleinberg, Benjamin. 1995. *Urban America in Transformation: Perspectives on Urban
    Policy and Development.* Thousand Oaks, CA: Sage Publications.

Ladd, Helen. 1994. "Big City Finances." In George E. Peterson, ed., *Big-City Politics,
    Governance, and Fiscal Constraints.* Washington, D.C.: Urban Institute Press.
    201–269.

Lemann, Nicholas. 1994. "The Myth of Community Development." *New York Times
    Magazine,* January 9, 26–31.

McClain, D. Paula. 1995. "Thirty Years of Urban Policies: Frankly, My Dears, We Don't
    Give a Damn!" *Urban Affairs Review* 30, no. 5: 641–644.

Mayer, S. Neil. 1995. "HUD's First 30 Years: Big Steps down a Longer Road."
    City Scape: A Journal of Policy Development and Research (HUD) 1, no. 3:
    1–29.

Mieczkowski, Tom, M. Douglas Anglin, Shirley Coletti, Bruce D. Johnson, Ethan A.
    Nadelmann, and Eric D. Wish. 1992. "Responding to America's Drug Problems:
    Strategies for the 1990s." *Journal of Urban Affairs* 14, nos. 3–4: 337–357.

Mohl, A Raymond. 1993a. "Race and Space in the Modern City: Interstate-95 and the
    Black Community in Miami." In R. Arnold Hirsch and Raymond A. Mohl, eds.,
    Urban Policy in Twentieth Century America. New Brunswick, NJ: Rutgers Uni-
    versity Press.

Mohl, A Raymond. 1993b. "Shifting Patterns of American Urban Policy since 1900."
    In R. Arnold Hirsch and Raymond A. Mohl, eds., *Urban Policy in Twentieth
    Century America.* New Brunswick, NJ: Rutgers University Press.

Mollenkopf, John. 1983. *The Contested City.* Princeton, NJ: Princeton University Press.

Mollenkopf, John. 1995. "What Future for Federal Urban Policy?" *Urban Affairs Review* 30, no. 5: 657–660.

Nenno, K. Mary. 1995. "Urban Policy Revisited: Issues Resurface with a New Urgency." In Roger W. Caves, ed., *Exploring Urban America*. Thousand Oaks, CA: Sage Publications.

Orlebeke, J. Charles. 1990. "Chasing Urban Policy: A Critical Retrospect." In Marshall Kaplan and Franklin James, eds., *The Future of National Urban Policy*. Durham, NC: Duke University Press.

Pagano, A. Michael. 1990. "Urban Infrastructure and City Budgeting: Elements of a National Urban Policy." In Marshall Kaplan and Franklin James, eds., *The Future of National Urban Policy*. Durham, NC: Duke University Press.

Palmer L. John, and Isabel V. Sawhill. 1984. *The Regan Record: An Assessment of America's Changing Domestic Priorities*. Cambridge, MA: Ballinger Publishing Company.

Raffel, A. Jeffry, William Lowe Boyd, Vernon M. Briggs, Eugene E. Eubanks, and Roberto Fernandez. 1992. "Policy Dilemmas in Urban Education Addressing the Needs of Poor, at Risk Children." *Journal of Urban Affairs* 14, nos. 3–4: 263–289.

Reischauer, D. Robert. 1990. "The Rise and Fall of National Urban Policy: The Fiscal Dimension." In Marshall Kaplan and Franklin James, eds., *The Future of National Urban Policy*. Durham, NC: Duke University Press.

Rich, J. Michael. 1993. *Federal Policymaking and the Poor*. Princeton, NJ: Princeton University Press.

Schambra, A. William. 1990. "Policy Liberalism: National Community Liberalism and the Prospect for National Urban Policy." In Marshall Kaplan and Franklin James, eds., *The Future of National Urban Policy*. Durham, NC: Duke University Press.

Schwartz, C. David, David W. Bartelt, Richard Ferlauto, Daniel N. Hoffman, and David Listokin. 1992. "A New Urban Housing Policy for the 1990s." *Journal of Urban Affairs* 14, nos. 3–4: 239–262.

Shafroth, Frank. 1993a. "Cisneros Plans Increased Role for Cities." *Nation's Cities Weekly* 16, no. 7 (February 15): 1–2.

Shafroth, Frank. 1993b. "President Challenges America with Plan: Cities Have Big Role to Play." *Nation's Cities Weekly* 16, no. 8 (February 22): 1–2.

Sommer, Jack. 1993. "Renewing a Dialogue on Urban America." In Jack Sommer and Donald A. Hicks, eds., *Rediscovering Urban America*. Washington, D.C.: U.S. Department of Housing and Urban Development.

Symposium. 1992. "Toward an Urban Policy Agenda for the 1990's." *Journal of Urban Affairs*, vol. 14, nos. 3–4.

Symposium. 1995. "Special Essays." *Urban Affairs Review*, vol. 30, no. 5.

United States. 1980a. *President's Commission for a National Agenda for the Eighties*. Englewood Cliffs, NJ: Prentice-Hall.

United States. 1980b. *President's Commission for a National Agenda for the Eighties, Urban America in the Eighties: Perspectives and Prospects*. Englewood Cliffs, NJ: Prentice-Hall.

U.S. Congress. Office of Technology Assessment (OTA). 1995. *The Technological Reshaping of Metropolitan America* (OTA-ETI-643). Washington, D.C.: Government Printing Office. September.

U.S. Department of Housing and Urban Development. 1995. *Empowerment: A New Covenant with America's Communities—President Clinton's National Urban Policy*

Report. Washington, D.C.: Department of Housing and Urban Development, Office of Policy Development and Research.

Warren, Robert. 1990. "National Urban Policy and the Local State: Paradoxes of Meaning, Action and Consequences." *Urban Affairs Quarterly* 25: 541–561.

Weiher, R. Gregory. 1989. "Rumors of the Demise of the Urban Crisis Are Greatly Exaggerated." *Journal of Urban Affairs* 11, no. 3: 225–242.

Wilson, Q. James. 1967. "The War on Cities." In Robert A. Goldwin, ed., *A Nation of Cities*. Chicago: Rand McNally.

Wilson, William Julius. 1987. *The Truly Disadvantaged—The Innercity, the Underclass and Public Policy*. Chicago: University of Chicago Press.

Wolman, Harold, Royce Hanson, Edward Hill, Marie Howland, and Larry Ledebur. 1992. "National Urban Economic Development Policy." *Journal of Urban Affairs* 14, nos. 3–4: 217–238.

Wood, Robert. 1991. "Lessons from the Paleozoic Age of Urban Affairs." *Journal of Urban Affairs* 13, no. 1: 111–117.

Wood, Robert. 1995. "A Personal Commentary on the Perils of Multiple Authorship Even Among Friends." *Urban Affairs Review* 30, no. 5: 687–689.

Wood, Robert, and Beverly M. Klimkowsky. 1990. "HUD in the Nineties: Doubt-Ability and Do-Ability." In Marshall Kaplan and Franklin James, eds., *The Future of National Urban Policy*. Durham, NC: Duke University Press.

Zuckerman, Jill. 1992 "Austere Times Offer Few Urban Solutions." *Congressional Quarterly* (September 26): 2904–2905.

Appendix: Data Sources and Secondary Information Found in Urban Document Centers and State and Local Archives

Gary Cornwell and Bert E. Swanson

The American community has been a rich setting for academic research because of its convenience, manageability, and importance. Long (1986) urged scholars and practitioners to seriously keep social and economic books if their policies are to be subject to evaluation. The Chicago School began the pursuit for empirical evidence on the ecological patterns of ethnic and class cleavages of urban places, and political behavior continues to fascinate scholars and practitioners alike as they try to understand the social, economic, and political dynamics of communities big and small (Swanson and Swanson 1977). Students of the quality of life have prepared extensive sets of conditions to be considered by policy makers (Rossi and Gilmartin 1980). Similar reports have been made available for individuals to consider when contemplating a move from one community to another, some of which are available on computer disk (Boyer and Savageau 1989).

Readily available urban data involve primary and secondary sources. Primary data require field investigations involving face-to-face interviews with questionnaires and other information-collecting formats. Researchers collect primary information through direct contact with public officials (elected, top administrators, or street-level bureaucrats) and informal participants (voters, economic elites, community leaders, and challengers to the powers that be).

Secondary data, the focus of this chapter, refer to information that has already been compiled for legal, monitoring, and analytic purposes. These materials are collected by governments, some of which are legally required, and by social service agencies and commercial firms that need to know what decisions and actions have been taken. Some agencies attempt to identify community problems and consequences that may have resulted from prevailing socioeconomic and political conditions.

Here we assume the urban investigator has a clear research design. Before one proceeds, a thorough review of existing materials should be undertaken to determine what information is readily available. This recognizance effort should determine what information is readily available from a central depository source, what may be located in some local archival source, and what must be collected by a direct field research operation. If significant data are not available then the investigator should reformulate the research design and/or seek substitute indicators.

These preliminary steps should provide an opportunity to explore the reliability, timeliness, and meaning of data. Simple population counts, for example, have for decades been challenged by local officials as having been undercounted. U.S. Census officials tend to dismiss these challenges as insignificant. However, for researchers these challenges, if valid, reveal a potential flaw for the subcommunity analysis, especially of low-income and minority families. While most transactional data are dynamic and occur momentarily, the 10-year intervals of most census materials, and samples at that, require caution. The cash flow through financial institutions at the end of the year, normally thought to be an indicator of fiscal health, may or may not take into account the movement of assets to minimize one's tax burden.

This chapter identifies those information sources that can be readily and quickly retrieved from a modern library. It includes "raw" unanalyzed data held in central depositories and local archival centers. The best available sources will be identified and discussed in general terms, especially local archives, since there is such wide variation in local record keeping.

GENERAL RESEARCH REPORTS

Any research endeavor must begin with a formalized search strategy as well as a review of the existing literature. Sage's Applied Social Research Methods Series contains a number of valuable sources designed to assist the urban researcher. In addition, there are a number of subject-specific guides available that will assist the researcher to design and implement a search strategy. It is important to realize, however, that the information infrastructure is in a state of accelerated evolution. Internet access to virtually thousands of databases is revolutionizing data availability and retrieval. It is imperative for researchers not only to be familiar with online information; they must also be adept at the technology necessary to locate and capture this information. The following publications, arranged by broad subject area, provide the foundation upon which the urban researcher should build.

General Guides

Most major libraries will have a variety of sources that will guide the researcher through the development of his or her search strategy. The following guides have been reviewed and offer excellent starting points:

Doing Urban Research. This volume offers a deeper understanding of how urban research is conducted, as well as the obligations associated with doing urban research.

Integrating Research: A Systematic Approach. Assuming the researcher has some familiarity with research methods and statistics, this volume provides an alternative approach for conducting the integrative research review.

Political Science: Illustrated Search Strategy and Sources. While specifically relating to political science, this volume easily crosses over into the realm of urban research and offers an up-to-date and comprehensive approach to basic social science research strategy and sources.

The Whole Internet User's Guide & Catalog. An excellent introduction to navigating the internet that, despite its age, remains one of the best internet guides available.

Indexes

Once the search strategy has been determined, there are a number of available indexes and finding aids. Not surprisingly, many of the best indexes are those that have been around the longest. The following indexes are suggested as essential; however, as the information industry evolves, new finding aids are appearing at an astonishing rate. The well-informed librarian remains the most valuable intermediary for any search.

American Statistics Index (ASI) and *Statistical Reference Index (SRI).* Prepared by the Congressional Information Service, these indexes are also available as part of the *Statistical Masterfile* CD-ROM (compact disk read-only memory). *ASI* and *SRI* provide table-level indexing of federal and state/nongovernment statistics, respectively. They are also available on microfiche.

Index to Current Urban Documents. Primarily an index to local government publications, some state documents that deal specifically with eligible cities or counties are also included. Publications are available through the Urban Documents Microfiche Collection.

Contemporary Subject Headings for Urban Affairs. This is the subject authority list for the *Index to Current Urban Documents.* It provides the researcher with a checklist of terms that may be used when conducting a reference search.

Lycos and WebCrawler. These are representative of the search engines that provide access to information on the internet. There are also such programs as Mosaic and Netscape that allow the researcher "point and choose" access to internet sites.

NewsBank. This CD-ROM index provides subject access to hundreds of local newspapers clippings. A corresponding collection of all the indexed articles is available on either microfiche or CD-ROM.

Social Science Citations Index. Among the many uses of this comprehensive index is the ability to locate articles on a particular subject or author by searching citations to published books and articles.

PAIS International in Print. Excellent index to scholarly journals and magazines.

Urban Affairs Abstracts. Monthly index and abstracting service to journal, newsletter, and periodical articles dealing with urban information. Typical subjects covered include aging, business and industry, community development, employment and labor, energy, land use, public policy, transportation, and many more.

Sage Urban Studies Abstracts. Each issue contains abstracts of important recent literature relating to urban studies. Scope is international in coverage.

Solutions for Technology-Sharing Networks. Includes briefs on innovative projects and programs prepared by local governments.

General

The following publications are national in coverage but will, at a minimum, include general information for most large metropolitan areas.

Statistical Abstract of the United States. Issued annually since 1878, it is the primary source for statistical information. Primarily national in scope, some information is provided at the region, state, and municipal level. All tables list source material that, in many cases, can be consulted for additional information. Most recently available in CD-ROM format.

County and City Data Book. Contains general statistical information for the United States, states, countries, and metropolitan areas over 25,000. Also available in CD-ROM format.

Municipal Year Book. Prepared by the Association of City Managers, it is an excellent source for local government information for counties. Information is provided on the type of government, local officials, and municipal phone numbers. In addition, each issue of this annual publication contains articles and bibliographic citations of general interest.

American Cost of Living Survey. Compilation of reported prices for products, services, and comparative cost of living in 443 cities.

Election Data Book. Election data are often very difficult to obtain for small metropolitan areas. It reports on voter registration, turnout, and votes cast in presidential, senatorial, and congressional races at the state, county, and congressional district levels. Local newspapers remain the best source and many are indexed by *News-Bank* and *Lexis/Nexis.*

Crime in the United States. Provides data on a variety of crimes, including the number of offenses known to police for cities above 10,000.

Census Reports

The number, range, and format of reports produced by the United States Bureau of the Census are too numerous to list here. The Census Bureau does, however, publish an annual guide that lists and abstracts census publications. Publications such as *ASI* identify and index census documents. With regard to "decennial censuses," an abundant amount of information does exist in print format. However, prior to the 1990 census, researchers seeking "detailed" information for small geographic areas used magnetic tape. Beginning with the 1990 census, detailed social and economic information is available at the "block group" level for the entire United States on CD-ROM. Similarly, general population information at the block level is also available for the entire United States. Before beginning any research using census data, it is highly recommended that the researcher contact a knowledgeable librarian for information regarding availability and comparability of data and for assistance with census terminology and geography. The following census CD-ROM products are offered as representative of sources widely available to the urban researcher:

1990 Census of Population and Housing—Public Law 94–171 Data. Contains a count of all persons and housing units by geographic area. It also includes a breakdown by race, Hispanic origin, and persons 18 years old and over. It also presents data at the "block" level.

1990 Census of Population and Housing—Summary Tape File 1A. Contains 100 percent data from the 1990 census. Population items include age, race, sex, marital status, Hispanic origin, household type, and household relationship; cross tabulations are also available. Housing items include occupancy/vacancy status, tenure, units in structure, contract rent, meals included in rent, value, and number of rooms in housing unit. Housing data are cross-tabulated by race or Hispanic origin of householder or by tenure.

1990 Census of Population and Housing—Summary Tape File 3A. Contains sample data weighted to represent the total population. The file also contains 100 percent counts and unweighted sample counts for total persons and total housing units. Population items include age, ancestry, educational attainment, income in 1989, marital status, occupation, poverty status in 1989, travel time to work, and so on. Housing items include age of householder, heating fuel, kitchen facilities, mortgage status, selected monthly owner costs, utilities in rent, year structure built, and so on. It provides data for states, counties, and cities down to the block group level.

1990 Census of Population and Housing—Equal Employment Opportunity File. Is based on civilian labor force data from the 1990 decennial census, containing two sample-based sets of tabulations. The first set is a cross tabulation of a detailed census occupation distribution by sex, race, and Hispanic origin. The second set shows educational attainment for selected age groupings, by sex, race, and Hispanic origin.

1990 Census of Population and Housing—Special Tabulation on Aging. Contains data for all persons and housing units. It has sample data weighted to represent the total population, as well as 100 percent counts and unweighted sample counts for total persons and total housing units.

1990 Census Transportation Planning Package—Statewide and Urban CTPP. Prepared jointly by the U.S. Departments of Transportation and Commerce (1994) it provides special tabulations of 1990 census data tailored to meet the data needs of transportation planners. These tabulations also contain a wealth of general-interest information on the workforce by place of work.

The Complete Economic and Demographic Data Source. Summarizes the results of the

Woods & Poole Economics forecasting model and provides statistical projections for every state, county, and metropolitan area in the United States on subjects such as population, employment, income, and retail sales. It is available in print and CD-ROM format.

Source Book of Zip Code Demographics. Presents age, housing, demographic, and income profiles for every zip code in the United States.

Online Sources

An increasing number of valuable sources are available via the internet. For example, the search "urban and research" resulted in over 1,000 "hits" including an online version of the *International Journal of Urban and Regional Research* and numerous articles on "Doing Research in Urban and Regional Planning." There are also many federal agency "bulletin boards" available that contain information on demographics, housing, and the economy. In addition to the internet, a number of online sources are available from private vendors. Since access and availability of these services are in constant flux, the researcher should consult the local library for assistance.

Lexis/Nexis. Full-text online database of approximately 4,000 "files" containing about 200 million documents ranging from general news (including newspapers and periodicals) to federal and state laws and administrative codes. Lexis/Nexis is available to researchers on a subscription basis. Periodically, this source provides Hot Line, a daily political report on elections.

URBAN-L. List serves available through the internet. Users may subscribe free of charge to this discussion group through LISTSER@TREARN, a group established for the exchange of information and ideas on the science of urban planning.

CENDATA. Available as File 580 through the DIALOG Information Retrieval Service. It contains selected statistical data from censuses, surveys, press releases, and product information. Subjects include agriculture, business, industry, construction, population, and industry as well as information from the 1990 decennial census.

LOGIN (Local Government Information Network). Provides a series of databases containing information on practical approaches and solutions to problems and issues facing local governments. Information regarding subscriptions to this bibliographic database is available from LOGIN at 1–800–328–1921.

Geographic Information Systems (GIS)

An exciting new development for the urban researcher is the emergence of Geographic Information Systems (GIS). This powerful tool displays spatial data allowing the researcher to view information as if it were layers (e.g., transportation, rivers, topography, population, census tracts, and economic values) and then integrate the parts as desired (Swanbeck and Hernon 1993). In other words, through the use of GIS-based software the researcher could layer "block group" economic data from the Census Bureau's STF3A file with map information derived from the TIGER (Topologically Integrated Geographic Encoding and Reference Service) database and create a customized map for any area in the country. Many local governments have already used GIS technology to produce a vast array of geographically displayed data for their communities. Examples include (1) detailed land use information; (2) crime locator systems for specific neighborhoods; (3) structural characteristics of buildings and locations of hazardous materials; (4) code enforcement actions; (5) data on student achievements; and (6) customer usage data for various utilities.

State Depository of Local Materials

Most states acquire and distribute documents from their depository program. Researchers should consult the reference librarian for information regarding the comprehensiveness and indexing of such materials. While there is a certain amount of consistency in federal and privately produced publications, there is tremendous variance among publications at the state and local level. For example, many states produce annual statistical abstracts equivalent to the one produced by the federal government, while others produce only brief summaries every 10 years. *SRI* remains the best tool available for locating statistical information in state documents.

State Publications and Depository Library: A Reference Handbook. Provides a state-by-state analysis of existing depository library programs. Although dated, it gives researchers an insight into the type and variety of documents likely to be distributed through a particular state depository program.

Local Government Financial Reports. Under the auspices of a lead agency such as the Department of Banking or Finance, the researcher can expect to find local government financial reports containing such information as revenues and expenditures for local governments.

Official Tabulation of Votes. Most states produce tabulations of voting returns for major elections. It should be stressed that there is considerable variation from state to state regarding comprehensiveness. The researcher should be prepared to contact local election boards or review newspapers for complete local election results.

Municipal Government Reference Sources: Publications and Collections. Produced by the Government Documents Round Table of the American Library Association, it is a state-of-the-art listing of municipal documents. While there has been some discussion about updating this publication, at the time of this writing, there were no firm plans to do so. Despite its publication date, the comprehensiveness of this volume warrants its review.

Federal Depository Library Program (FDLP)

The FDLP is a national resource network designed to ensure free public access to government-produced and published information. Consisting of over 1,400 libraries throughout the country, it is predicated on the notion that all U.S. federal documents, regardless of content or format, should be readily available to the American people. In addition, the Depository Library Program provides an effective, low-cost mechanism for federal agencies to disseminate government information to virtually every congressional district in the country.

There are two basic types of libraries in the FDLP, regional depositories and selective depositories. Regional depositories automatically receive all publications distributed through the program and retain them permanently. Selective depositories, on the other hand, may choose which publications they receive and are only required to retain them for five years. Virtually all academic, state, and large public libraries are depositories for federal publications. Nearly all of these libraries select the basic sources listed in the references section of this appendix. In addition, most depositories also select census material for their state or region.

All depositories, regardless of whether or not they select a particular document, should have the basic indexes available for identifying government information. In addition, most areas have networks in place for the rapid sharing of depository information.

LOCAL ARCHIVAL AND OTHER MATERIALS

When one has exhausted the materials found in central depositories, federal and state, but additional information is needed, the researcher should explore what is available in the community. There is a near-infinite variety of local information sources. From experience, one soon learns that each community has its own approach to data retention, and each organization, public and private, has its own files and rules of access. This section suggests ways to effectively maximize local data collection. Certain patterns emerge, dependent on official requirements and organizational policies.

State government mandates, which vary from state to state, require which records must be sent to the state such as detailed local budgets, gross property assessment data, election returns of state officers, crime reports, and so forth. In addition, each local government must retain all local ordinances, election returns, budget materials, complete property ownership and valuations, crime statistics, and comprehensive land use plans, as well as choose to retain various special study reports. Some big cities have official historical archives, with extensive historical and current records. Some even include "oral" histories of prominent residents; for example, New York has an official archivist, while Houston has its special collection in the library.

Larger communities have local organizations that collect information that they consider important for their purposes. The chamber of commerce focuses on economic data, while social service agencies focus on health, welfare, education, and housing information. Each private agency has established its own sense on what information it retains and what rules and procedures govern access. Local newspapers can be used as the "chronicle of record," inasmuch as they monitor and report on many aspects of life in the community. They no longer allow researchers access to their "morgue" clipping files; for a fee, they search and provide copies of specific items. Very large newspapers provide a detailed index of news reports; some provide full text in computer data sources such as NewsBank and Lexis/Nexus systems.

Most communities do not have a systematic, comprehensive, and central depository of local records. Seldom are local agencies required to file their data, records, or even special studies with any central archive or library. Therefore, the researcher should approach the community as a mosaic of data sources. Nor should one expect that all records will continue to exist. Historical records are periodically "purged"—their files occasionally lost or destroyed by fires, floods, vandalism, or just plain neglect. Perhaps the single most important factor for a well-kept record retention program is the integrity of some librarian or clerk; so the quality of the program can and does vary over time with changes in personnel. More recently, some local governments have begun the arduous task of formulating data retention policies.

Some local governments make copies of their publications available to the local public library or a city-maintained municipal collection. The researcher should check with either the city manager's office or the local public library to determine where municipal documents are archived.

One should expect access to local archives to be constrained by several conditions. First is the often-frustrating process of learning which local office has what materials. Second, access may be limited by office hours and whether officials are busy attending to some official deadline such as preparations for an election, budget presentation, or a hearing on some aspect of a comprehensive land use plan. Third, the cost of duplication of documents can range from a nominal amount to several dollars a page. Fourth, most agencies retain their materials in storage facilities in an adjoining building, and access may take hours or a day.

Some officials are more willing than others to provide access to public information. Federal and state government offices, which retain information about local governments, can require that the researcher give adequate advanced notice, and they sometimes insist on a formal written request under the Freedom of Information Act. Some local officials view researchers with suspicion and use their rules of access to inhibit, if not frustrate, those they consider capable of stirring up "bad" publicity. Their procedures can cause costly delays in fieldwork if not anticipated; therefore, advanced planning should be undertaken.

Local data sources are scattered throughout the community. Some are located at the city hall or the county court house or at some annex building blocks away. Other materials are located at the central public library, which may also collect from private economic and social agencies.

Governmental Structures, Functions, and Operations

Some county and city planning agencies also provide a table of organization of each departmental unit in their annual budgets plans. Some governmental departments have written a mission statement that includes a staffing of each department. Lists of community organizations are occasionally compiled by a social service agency or a governmental agency that wishes to refer those in need of assistance. Each list generally identifies officers or key contact persons of the organization. The best comprehensive overview of local governmental structure, functions, and agencies has been complied by the League of Women Voters who periodically publish "Know Your Local Government." Occasionally, an academic or student has written such a piece if reporting on local politics.

Public Officials (Present and Past)

A list of present public officials can be obtained from the clerk or secretary of the respective local government or agency. That is, each unit of government has a list of those who currently serve. Seldom has any single agency compiled a comprehensive list of all public officials. An exception would be large cities that have directories of public officials sometimes referred to as the "green" or "red" book. For a list of past public officials, one should try the same source or seek the help of a diligent public librarian or historian who may have kept such a record.

Biographical information on public officials is best gleamed from newspaper sketches when the officials run for office. The public library generally has created, if not systematically, "vertical" files with such information. These files often contain announcements of important events in the lives of prominent residents and obituary sketches from the newspaper. In addition, NewsBank's "Names in the News" has compiled an index of the more prominent names in the country.

Election Returns

The location of voter registration is generally found in the county election office. It keeps detailed registration records by precinct. Some states are under the Federal Civil Rights Act and must keep records by race. In addition, some counties record data by gender. This is also the best source for historical records. Many places have relied on handwritten reports, but more recently, registration information has been computerized.

The retention of election results for long-term trends is more problematic. While the county election office may have some recent records, city election results are sometimes kept by the city clerk and school board. A detailed description of these measures—for example, a bond election—can generally be found in the office that retains the election results.

The political rhetoric of election campaigns is best recorded by the local media. Newspaper coverage of the campaign, often sketchy and sometimes biased, is often the main source to learn about community issues. Selective local observers (insiders) may be available to provide the views of local politics. Some newspapers endorse their preferred candidates on the editorial page just prior to election.

Budgets and Public Finance

Each government retains its own historic budget information. This bulky published budget is an annual "plan" to begin the new fiscal year. The comptroller or revenue office produces an annual finance report of selected items for all city and county governments in the state. The State Education Office may prepare a similar report. If long-term budget information, earlier copies may be available in the local public library. Some cities have put budget information on computer storage disks, often inaccessible to researchers.

The most reliable budget source is the comprehensive annual financial report (CAFR). This document has been prepared by an independent auditor and attests to the fact that budget items have been received and spent as reported by the budget officer. Some CAFRs provide historical economic trends that affect public finance. A number of cities have implemented the "Fiscal Trend Monitoring System" developed by International City Management Association (ICMA), which has identified some 35 relevant fiscal indicators.

Another source providing a comprehensive view of a community can be found in bond disclosures. Capital-lending institutions generally require local governments to provide ample information concerning socioeconomic conditions of the community as well as specific materials on political and management conditions that might affect the safety of investment.

Local Ordinances and Resolutions

The researcher will find that local ordinances and resolutions are historically retained by the clerk or recorder. Occasionally, they are not in order or well kept. They are generally indexed by very large governments but are kept in chronological order rather than subject order. Seldom are there any elaborate notes pertaining to the discussions associated with the decisions—only the recorded text and vote. To go beyond these bare records, one should resort to the local newspaper reports or ask a well-informed person in or out of city hall.

Community Plans

Most communities have prepared a number of plans. The most common are land use plans, referred to as the Master, Comprehensive, or Land Development

Regulations. Typically, these contain city and/or county information regarding future land use plans, housing, recreation, open space, traffic, environment, drainage, and capital improvements. The plans are generally found in the planning agency that is primarily responsible for development. Some communities have prepared strategic plans that guide long-range thinking and action. The local chamber of commerce generally initiates these exercises. These plans attempt to be an integrative approach to community development and seek consensus among the prime movers, public and private.

Some states require localities to prepare development of regional impact (DRI) reports on larger-sized projects. These are designed to report the nature and environmental impact of planned developments. Included in these reports are the potential impact of a development on the economy, public facilities, transportation, housing, natural resources, and the environment.

Property Ownership and Value

The full record of all property in the community can be found in the county property assessor's office. There is found a detailed listing of all property ownership, record of improvements, and assessed value. There are several problems with assessment data. First, ownership may be obscured in complex corporate and trust arrangements. Second, actual value is often considerably greater than assessed value. While most state constitutions require assessments to be at full or market value (what a willing buyer and seller settle upon), most local assessments are much lower. The range may vary from 10 to 90 percent of true value.

Business and Economic Activities

The local chamber of commerce is a good source on business trade activities. It monitors real estate transactions and conducts selective surveys on what it believes to be important local business developments. The chamber of commerce generally has a file on the total number of business firms. Some list them by size, at least the largest employers—either number of employees or payroll. Some government building departments systematically collect information on building permits issued by the building department of local government.

Performance Evaluation

City and county managers generally submit an annual report with the proposed budget plan that discusses past achievements and proposals for the future. Some provide a citizens' report to inform the public about public service programs. Some cities engage in detailed departmental evaluations of goals and achievements. In larger communities a local university or newspaper may conduct public opinion polls to assess the performance of government.

Perhaps the best evaluation evolves during election campaigns, the time when opponents are most likely to discuss the performance of incumbents in critical detail. Some candidates for the mayoralty prepare position papers that articulate how they propose to resolve specific problems. One can review their proposals to determine how well campaign promises have been implemented. Candidate debates and forums are another source where protagonists discuss the incumbent's performance. Occasionally, newspapers commission public opinion polls to report on the performance of public officials. Some top administrators are evaluated by elected officials, and local newspapers sometimes report these ''grades.'' Publicized low grades have been taken as a sign by administrators to consider looking for their next position.

Quality-of-Life Indicators

A growing number of national organizations and communities have compiled a variety of socioeconomic and political indicators of community life (Barrett and Greene 1993; Marlin 1992; Boyer and Savageau 1989; Consumer Guide Editors 1988; Jacksonville Community Council 1985–).

Community Agenda Setting

Some mayors follow the format of the president and governors and make a State of the City Address that not only lists past achievements but identifies important problems the mayor expects the city to resolve. Some local governments submit a list of legislative priorities concerning public projects, regulations, and finance to the state legislative delegation.

Less formal, but potentially more important, are the community agenda items adopted by the local chamber of commerce. These chambers have a committee on public affairs that studies and recommends a series of very specific policies, programs, and projects for local government to adopt and implement. Metropolitan newspapers often prepare an extensive report on the highlights of the past year at year's end. Some papers editorially offer a list of agenda items at about the same time.

REFERENCES

Andranovich, Gregory D., and Gerry Riposa. 1993. *Doing Urban Research*. Vol. 33 of Applied Social Research Methods Series. Newbury Park: Sage Publications.

Barrett, Katherine, and Richard Greene. 1993. ''Focus on the Best.'' *Financial World*, 36–37.

Boyer, Richard, and David Savageau. 1989. *Places Rated Almanac*. New York: Prentice-Hall.

Congressional Information Service. 1974–. *American Statistics Index*. Washington, D.C.: CIS.

Consumer Guide Editors. 1988. *Best-Rated Retirement Cities.* New York: Sig Classics.

Contemporary Subject Headings for Urban Affairs: Compiled by Greenwood Press for the Urban Documents Program. 1983. Westport, CT: Greenwood Press.

Cooper, Harris M. 1984. *Integrating Research: A Systematic Approach.* Vol. 2 of Applied Social Research Methods Series. Beverly Hills: Sage Publications.

Darnay, Arsen J., and Helen S. Fisher. 1994. *American Cost of Living Survey.* Detroit: Gale Research Inc.

Election Data Book: A Statistical Portrait of Voting in America. 1992–. Lanham: Bernan Press.

Financial World. 1993. *Rating America's Large Cities,* 162, no. 5. March 2, 36–37.

Hernon, Peter, ed. 1978. *Municipal Government Reference Sources: Publications and Collections.* Prepared by the Government Documents Roundtable of the American Library Association. New York: R. R. Bowker Company.

Index to Current Urban Documents. 1972–. Westport, CT: Greenwood Press.

International City Management Association. 1934–. *Municipal Year Book.* Washington, D.C.: ICMA.

Jacksonville Community Council, Inc. 1985–. *Life in Jacksonville.* Jacksonville, FL: JCC.

Krol, Ed. 1992. *The Whole Internet User's Guide & Catalog.* Sebastopol: O'Reilly & Associates.

Lane, Margaret T. 1981. *State Publications and Depository Library: A Reference Handbook.* Westport, CT: Greenwood Press.

Lexis/Nexis. 1973–. Dayton: Mead Data Central, Inc. (Online full-text database)

Long, Norton E. 1986. ''Symposium on Municipal Social and Economic Accounting.'' *Journal of Urban Affairs* 8, no. 2: 1–98.

Lowery, Roger C., and Sue A. Cody. 1993. *Political Science: Illustrated Search Strategy and Sources.* Ann Arbor: Pierian Press.

Marlin, John T. 1992. *Livable Cities Almanac.* New York: Harper Perennial.

National League of Cities. 1971–. *Urban Affairs Abstracts.* Washington, D.C.: NLC.

NewsBank Index. 1981–. New Canaan: NewsBank.

PAIS International in Print. 1991–. New York: Public Affairs Information Service. (Continues *PAIS Bulletin,* 1915–1990, and *PAIS Foreign Language Index,* 1976–)

Rossi, Robert J., and Kevin J. Gilmartin. 1980. *The Handbook of Social Indicators.* Garland: STMP Press.

Sage Urban Studies Abstracts. 1973–. Beverly Hills, CA: Sage Publications.

Social Sciences Citations Index. 1972–. Philadelphia, PA: Institute for Scientific Information.

Solutions for Technology–Sharing Networks. 1989–1990. Washington, D.C.: Public Technology, Inc.

Sourcebook of Zip Code Demographics. 1984–. Fairfax: CACI Marketing Systems.

Statistical Reference Index. 1980–. Washington, D.C.: Congressional Information Service.

Swanbeck, Jan, and Peter, Hernon, eds. 1993. *Depository Library Use of Technology: A Practitioner's Perspective.* Norwood, NJ: Ablex Publishing.

Swanson, Bert E., and Edith P. Swanson. 1977. *Discovering the Community.* New York: Irvington Publishers, Inc.

U.S. Department of Commerce. Bureau of the Census. 1878–. *Statistical Abstract of the United States.* Washington, D.C.: Government Printing Office.

U.S. Department of Commerce. Bureau of the Census. 1949–. *County and City Data Book*. Washington, D.C.: Government Printing Office.

U.S. Department of Commerce. Bureau of the Census. 1985–. *Census Catalog and Guide*. Washington, D.C.: Government Printing Office. (Continues *Bureau of Census Catalog*, 1964–1984, *Catalog of United States Census Publications*, 1952–1963, and *Census Publications Catalog and Subject Guide*, 1946–1951)

U.S. Department of Commerce. Bureau of the Census. 1991a. *1990 Census of Population and Housing—Public Law 94–171 Data*. Washington, D.C. (CD-ROM)

U.S. Department of Commerce. Bureau of the Census. 1991b. *1990 Census of Population and Housing—Summary Tape File 1A*. Washington, D.C. (CD-ROM)

U.S. Department of Commerce. Bureau of the Census. 1992. *1990 Census of Population and Housing—Summary Tape File 3A*. Washington, D.C. (CD-ROM)

U.S. Department of Commerce. Bureau of the Census. 1993. *1990 Census of Population and Housing—Equal Employment Opportunity File*. Washington, D.C. (CD-ROM)

U.S. Department of Commerce. Bureau of the Census. 1994. *1990 Census of Population and Housing—Special Tabulation on Aging*. Washington, D.C. (CD-ROM)

U.S. Department of Justice. Federal Bureau of Investigation. 1958–. *Crime in the United States*. Washington, D.C.: Government Printing Office.

U.S. Department of Transportation. Bureau of Transportation Statistics. 1994. *1990 Census Transportation Planning Package—Statewide and Urban CTPP*. Washington, D.C. (CD-ROM)

Woods & Poole Economics. 1984–. *The Complete Economic and Demographic Data Source*. Washington, D.C.: WPE.

World Resources Institute. 1992. *Environmental Almanac*. Boston: Houghton Mifflin.

Index

About the Contributors

DOUGLAS H. ADAMS earned his Ph.D. in Urban and Public Affairs at the University of Louisville.

SUSAN BENNETT is an associate professor in the Public Services Program at DePaul University.

ANN O'M. BOWMAN is a professor of political science at the University of South Carolina.

DAVID G. CARNEVALE is director of Programs in Public Administration in the Department of Political Science at the University of Oklahoma.

GARY CORNWELL is a university librarian and federal document librarian at the University of Florida.

SCOTT CUMMINGS is a professor of urban policy at the University of Louisville and editor of the *Journal of Urban Affairs*.

RUTH HOOGLAND DeHOOG is an associate professor of political science and director of the Master of Public Affairs (MPA) Program at the University of North Carolina at Greensboro.

RICHARD E. DeLEON is chair of the Political Science Department at San Francisco State University.

PETER EISINGER is a professor of political science and public policy and director of the La Follette Institute of Public Affairs at the University of Wisconsin.

ARNOLD FLEISCHMANN is an associate professor of political science at the University of Georgia.

ANN LENNARSON GREER is a professor of sociology and urban studies at the University of Wisconsin at Milwaukee.

R. ALLEN HAYS is director of the Graduate Program in Public Policy and professor of political science at the University of Northern Iowa.

DAVID L. IMBROSCIO is an assistant professor of political science at the University of Louisville.

LOUISE JEZIERSKI is an assistant professor of sociology and the Urban Studies Program at Brown University.

DENNIS R. JUDD is a professor of political science at the University of Missouri at St. Louis and editor of the *Urban Affairs Review*.

MARGARET KILLMER is a doctoral student in urban and public affairs at the University of Louisville.

JERRY KOLO is an associate professor of urban and regional planning at Florida Atlantic University and director of the Center for Urban Redevelopment and Empowerment.

LARRY LYON is a professor of sociology and director of the Center for Community Research and Development at Baylor.

JASON MILLER is a research associate with the Center for Community Research and Development at Baylor.

DAVID R. MORGAN is a professor of political science at the University of Oklahoma.

CYNTHIA NEGREY is an associate professor of sociology at the University of Louisville.

J. JOHN PALEN is a professor of sociology at Virginia Commonwealth University.

DIANNE M. PINDERHUGHES is a professor of political science and Afro-American studies and director of the Afro-American Studies and Research Program at the University of Illinois at Urbana-Champaign.

IRENE RUBIN is a professor in the Public Administration Division at Northern Illinois University and editor of *Public Administration Review*.

H. V. SAVITCH is a professor of urban policy and director of the MPA Program at the College of Business and Public Administration at the University of Louisville and coeditor of the *Journal of Urban Affairs*.

ELAINE B. SHARP is a professor and chair of political science at the University of Kansas.

LANA STEIN is an associate professor of political science at the University of Missouri at St. Louis.

GENIE N. L. STOWERS is an associate professor of public administration at San Francisco State University.

BERT E. SWANSON is a professor of political science and urban studies at the University of Florida.

JOHN CLAYTON THOMAS is professor and director of the School of Public Administration and Urban Studies at Georgia State University.

ROBYNE S. TURNER is associate professor of political science at Florida Atlantic University and book review editor of the *Urban Affairs Review.*

RONALD K. VOGEL is an associate professor of political science at the University of Louisville.

EDWARD WEINER is a senior policy analyst in the Office of the Secretary of the U.S. Department of Transportation.

KENNETH K. WONG is an associate professor in the Department of Education at the University of Chicago.

ISBN 0-313-29166-7

90000>

EAN

9 780313 291661

HARDCOVER BAR CODE